THE HISTOR

GENERAL

GLANMOR W

THE FOUNDATIONS OF MODERN WALES

WALES
1642–1780

BY

GERAINT H. JENKINS

Professor of Welsh History,
University of Wales,
Aberystwyth

Oxford   New York

OXFORD UNIVERSITY PRESS

1993

Oxford University Press, Walton Street, Oxford OX2 6DP

Oxford New York Toronto
Delhi Bombay Calcutta Madras Karachi
Kuala Lumpur Singapore Hong Kong Tokyo
Nairobi Dar es Salaam Cape Town
Melbourne Auckland Madrid
and associated companies in
Berlin Ibadan

Oxford is a trade mark of Oxford University Press

First published 1987
First issued as an Oxford University Press Paperback 1993

British Library Cataloguing in Publication Data
Data available

Library of Congress Cataloging in Publication Data
Jenkins, Geraint H.
The foundations of modern Wales : Wales 1642–1780 / by Geraint H.
Jenkins.
p. cm.—(History of Wales; v. 4)
Originally published: Oxford: Clarendon Press. 1987.
Includes bibliographical references and index.
1. Wales—History. I. Title. II. Series.
942.9 s—dc20 [942.9] DA714.H58 1993 vol. 4 [DA720] 92-25830
ISBN 0-19-285278-7

1 3 5 7 9 10 8 6 4 2

Printed and bound in Great Britain by
Biddles Ltd, Guildford and King's Lynn

For Ann

Gwir a chelwydd sydd mewn pliscyn
fel mewn wy mae gwyn a melyn
hola'r gwir: daioni derbyn
heded gwalch dros fin yr ellyn

Morgan Llwyd

The [Welsh] people in general are so different from the English,
one is amazed to think they are subjects to the same Monarchy.

Elizabeth Baker, July 1772

PREFACE

In the following pages I have tried to present as rounded a portrait as possible of the experiences of the people of Wales in a seminal period in their history. In the course of reading for, and writing this book, my respect for the achievements of the age has grown appreciably, and I have come to believe that the foundations of modern Wales were laid during the period between the troubled years of the Civil War and the beginnings of the Industrial Revolution around 1780. These years witnessed a marked growth in population, agrarian improvements, the development of heavy industries, fresh market opportunities, improved communications, swelling trade, significant urban growth, striking advances in the provision of educational facilities and the growth of literacy, the emergence of Methodism, the rejuvenation of Dissent, and a revival of Welsh culture. All these were formative forces in the making of modern Wales.

This book has been nearly six years in the making, and I must confess that preparing a work of synthesis such as this has brought its share of frustration as well as satisfaction. The most frustrating obstacle has been the unsatisfactory and sometimes woeful state of our knowledge about a whole range of important subjects. In view of the lack of either primary sources or extensive secondary material on topics such as demography, the size of households, social structure, local government, urban growth, crime, foreign trade, and much else, it is not hard to understand why this period has often been neglected and misunderstood by historians. There is much spade work still to be done and no one is more aware than I of the limitations of the chapters which follow. Even so, I have tried not to shirk my duty to offer generalizations, make judgements, and occasionally chance my arm in assessing matters which hitherto have been only partially explored. The lack of basic ground-work in key areas, however, has not spoiled my enjoyment of the undertaking. I have derived great pleasure and satisfaction from reading the work of other scholars in this field, and it has been a particularly delightful privilege to rub shoulders (from afar) with such gifted and colourful individuals as Vavasor Powell, Lewis Morris, Howel Harris, Sir Humphrey Mackworth, Richard Price, and Iolo Morganwg.

In researching and writing a book of this length, I have contracted a number of obligations and debts of gratitude. The degree to which I have drawn on the researches of others will be apparent to anyone familiar with the historical literature of this period, but I should like in particular to express my admiration for the work of A. H. Dodd, David W. Howell, R. T. Jenkins, J. Frederick Rees, William Rees, Thomas Richards, Gomer M. Roberts, P. D. G. Thomas, and J. Gwynn Williams. I owe a heavy debt also to young and enthusiastic scholars whose research theses have made it possible to examine aspects of this period more fully than ever before. I should especially like to thank Gareth Evans, Melvin Humphreys, David Jenkins, Philip Jenkins, Joanna Martin, Glyn Parry, Adrian Teale, and Gareth Haulfryn Williams for placing their knowledge at my disposal.

I have been fortunate to receive generous assistance from many friends and colleagues. I am deeply grateful to David Howell, Brian Howells, Brynley F. Roberts, and Peter Thomas for reading drafts of chapters and for offering helpful criticism and words of encouragement. Professor Ralph A. Griffiths sacrificed part of his summer vacation in order to read the whole typescript, and I am indebted to him for ironing out faulty logic and cumbersome prose. My chief obligation is to Professor Emeritus Glanmor Williams, the general editor of this series. My early research as a post-graduate was launched under his direction, and the inspiration of his scholarship and friendship has guided my work ever since. He has read and corrected the typescript with meticulous care, and no one could have given more generously of his time, wisdom, and experience. I acknowledge my debt to him with great respect and warm affection. To all who have helped to improve this book I tender my sincere thanks. It hardly needs to be said that the errors which remain are my own responsibility.

I have visited many libraries, museums, and record offices and I am grateful to the staff of those repositories listed in the bibliography for welcoming a reader who made a heavy claim on their time and patience. In particular, the readiness of the staff of the National Library of Wales to make available hundreds of manuscripts and printed books, and to assist me in innumerable ways, eased my task enormously. My research in various archives was generously supported by awards from the Sir David Hughes-Parry Fund of the University College of Wales, Aberystwyth, and from the Twenty-Seven Foundation. I am extremely grateful to Gwyn Jenkins and Glyn Parry for helping me locate manuscripts, and to Philip Henry Jones and Eiluned Rees for giving me the benefit of their expertise in bibliographical matters. Dr W. T. R. Pryce kindly permitted me to borrow and use his splendid map on Welsh language zones, and I should like to thank C. Roy Lewis and Michael G. Jones for preparing each map with great care and attention. My colleagues in the Department of Welsh History have provided a congenial atmosphere in which to work, and I should like to praise my students for enduring my curious enthusiasm for this period and for patiently listening to my ideas and prejudices. I owe special thanks to Carys Briddon and Delyth Fletcher for coping ably and cheerfully with the task of typing the manuscript. It is also a pleasure to thank Mr Ivon Asquith of the Oxford University Press and Mr John Rhys of the University of Wales Press for their courteous assistance at every stage of publication.

My principal debt is to my long-suffering family. Although I suspect that several of them have silently cursed this book, they have made many sacrifices which have helped to ensure its completion. I should like to record my gratitude to my parents for their selfless help and encouragement over the years. I never cease to be astonished by the ability of Gwenno, Angharad, and Rhiannon, my three young daughters, to cope with a father who spends much more of his time living in the past than in the present. My greatest obligation is to my wife, Ann Ffrancon, and I dedicate the book to her with my deepest love and affection.

GERAINT H. JENKINS

The Department of Welsh History,
University College of Wales, Aberystwyth
Calan Gaeaf, 1986

A NOTE ON DATING
AND PUNCTUATION

In the text all dates prior to 1752 are given according to the Old Style of the Julian Calendar, but the year is taken as beginning on 1 January rather than on 25 March.

I have modernized the spelling and punctuation of passages quoted from manuscripts or printed documents. Quotations in Welsh have been translated into English.

CONTENTS

LIST OF MAPS

ABBREVIATIONS

Add. Letters	Hugh Owen (eds.), *Additional Letters of the Morrises of Anglesey (1735–1786)* (Parts 1–2, London, 1947–9)
Arch. Camb.	*Archaeologia Cambrensis*
BBCS	*The Bulletin of the Board of Celtic Studies*
BL	The British Library, London
Y Bywg.	*Y Bywgraffiadur Cymreig hyd 1940* (London, 1953)
DNB	*The Dictionary of National Biography*
DWB	*The Dictionary of Welsh Biography* (London, 1959)
Gweithiau	J. H. Davies and T. E. Ellis (eds.), *Gweithiau Morgan Llwyd o Wynedd* (2 vols., Bangor, 1899; London, 1908)
HMC	*Historical Manuscripts Commission Reports*
JWBS	*The Journal of the Welsh Bibliographical Society*
Morris Letters	J. H. Davies (ed.), *The Letters of Lewis, Richard, William and John Morris of Anglesey (Morrisiaid Môn) 1728–1765* (2 vols., Aberystwyth, 1907–9)
NLW	The National Library of Wales, Aberystwyth
NLWJ	*The National Library of Wales Journal*
PRO	The Public Record Office, London
THSC	*The Transactions of the Honourable Society of Cymmrodorion*
TRHS	*The Transactions of the Royal Historical Society*
WHR	*The Welsh History Review*

PART I

STRIFE AND UPHEAVAL
1642–1660

CHAPTER I

THE CIVIL WARS AND THE INTERREGNUM

In the summer of 1642 an impoverished, downtrodden, and sleepy nation on the outer fringes of Europe was drawn into a civil war which few of its people had sought. Before the outbreak of civil strife there was a widespread air of foreboding in Wales: 'the end of the world is not far off',[1] cried John Griffith of Cefnamwlch in Caernarfonshire, as his fellow gentry besought King Charles I and his Parliament to settle their differences amicably. But as the misunderstanding and distrust between both parties deepened, hopes of avoiding bloodshed faded. On 6 August 1642 Samuel Wood, steward to Sir John Trevor of Trefalun, declared: 'I see the whole nation is almost every man furiously bent for war and bloodshed and do express themselves very boldly'.[2] Had Welshmen at the time known what the future held they would have been horrified. For many old, familiar landmarks were destroyed after 1642: following the bitter strife of civil war, Parliament was purged by the army, the king was executed, the monarchy and the House of Lords were temporarily abolished, and a republican government ruled for eleven years. The mass of the Welsh people, remote from London and preoccupied chiefly with the task of making ends meet, was bewildered to find that political crisis at Westminster had led to civil war and republican rule. But there were also well-informed observers who were mindful of the political and ideological issues at stake and who interpreted them in different ways. James Howell, a fervent royalist, believed that he was living in 'a topsy-turvy world'[3] in which the very foundations of the traditional order were being undermined. Conversely, the revolutionary period kindled great expectations in the mind of Morgan Llwyd, the Puritan saint. He, too, believed that 'the pillars of the world'[4] were shaking, but he was convinced that these convulsive years heralded a new millennium in the course of which the saints would rule with justice and magnanimity.

Most Welshmen regarded the coming of war with deep apprehension, for the threat to order, stability, and common decency was a very real one.

---

[1] A. H. Dodd, *A History of Caernarvonshire 1284–1900* (Caerns. Hist. Soc., 1968), p. 106.
[2] Anthony Fletcher, *The Outbreak of the English Civil War* (paperback edn., London, 1985), p. 265.
[3] James Howell, *Epistolae Ho-Elianae* (2nd edn., London, 1650), p. 254.
[4] *Gweithiau*, i. 128.

The mere thought of civil strife sent shivers of fear down the spine of landed Titans. In a speech to the House of Lords in December 1642, the earl of Pembroke voiced the unthinkable: 'we hear every base fellow say in the street as we pass by in our coaches, that they hope to see us a foot shortly and to be as good men as the Lords; and I think they will be as good as their words, if we take this course'.[5] Sir Thomas Salusbury of Lleweni, fearful of a 'perpetual war', warned of the example of Holland, which had been 'the stage of war' and 'the cockpit of all Christendom' ever since its subjects had challenged the authority of its sovereign.[6] Brooding long over the indescribable horrors which had befallen Germany and central Europe during the Thirty Years' War, men were convinced that untold misery would engulf the kingdom in the form of famine, pestilence, fire, and economic dislocation. Not surprisingly, in view of the likely economic consequences of civil strife, landed proprietors fervently hoped that a single major battle would bring men to their senses and the war to a speedy conclusion.

The line-up at the outbreak of hostilities was neither clear cut nor tidy. On balance, however, the more populous and economically advanced areas of England and Wales, including London and many ports, were for Parliament, whilst the more sparsely populated and underdeveloped areas of the north and west of England, and Wales, supported the Crown. From the outset it was vitally important for the king to control the borderlands, for Wales could not only provide him with wealth, victuals, and armies, but might also afford an avenue to Ireland should foreign relief be required. Conversely, Parliament was determined to drive a wedge through the royalist barricade on the Welsh Marches. Sea power, too, was a crucial strategic factor. No waterway was more important to both parties than the Irish Sea. Royalist authority over north Wales would depend heavily on the ability of the king's vessels to maintain control of the seas, whilst parliamentary ships would be obliged to patrol the Irish Sea in order to repel potential invaders from Ireland and capture strategic landing-places like Milford Haven and the Menai Straits.

In spite of his many personal defects, Charles I was able to induce awe and evoke respect among Welshmen simply by virtue of his kingship. Ever since Henry Tudor's dazzling victory at Bosworth Field in 1485, the Welsh had nursed a warm affection and respect for the Crown. This fondness had persisted throughout the Tudor age and had been transferred, virtually undiluted, to the Stuarts. Those well-versed in politics were not, of course, so ingenuous as to see Charles as a paragon of virtue, but his call to arms nevertheless struck a deep responsive chord in their hearts. Welsh gentlemen, in particular, were deeply conscious of the extent to which their

---

[5] J. S. Morrill, *The Revolt of the Provinces* (paperback edn., London, 1980), p. 36.
[6] Norman Tucker, *Denbighshire Officers in the Civil War* (Denbigh, n.d.), pp. 96–8.

political and personal fortunes were bound up with the monarchy. Many of them had obtained status, offices, and sinecures at the Stuart court by picking their way skilfully amid various factions and alliances. Linked to the monarchy by sentiment and interest alike, they were men who believed in maintaining the traditional canons of legitimate authority and the established social order. The very thought of revolution filled them with dread: Charles stood for order, security, and prosperity, and they feared that a rebel victory might unleash violent and anarchic forces which would endanger the lives and property of all men of wealth and good breeding. In the event of a parliamentary victory, they would be likely to forfeit their positions as Members of Parliament, local administrators, and civil magistrates. The prospect of 'base men' snatching these exclusive privileges from their hands filled them with unease and horror.

There were other equally potent rallying cries in the king's hour of need in the summer of 1642. To devout gentlemen and clergymen, rebellion against the king was a heinous sin. The biblical verse, 'for who can stretch forth his hand against the Lord's anointed, and be guiltless?' (1 Sam. 26:9), was never far from their lips. Sir Thomas Salusbury vowed passionately that he and his household would serve the Lord and the Lord's anointed. Clergymen simply could not bring themselves to take up arms against God's servant and pledged their unswerving devotion to the royalist cause by shunning the 'fanatic party' and, in some cases, enlisting as soldiers or offering their services as chaplains to the king's armies. In many different ways, Welsh royalists expressed their loyalty to Charles. Some, like the fabulously wealthy marquis of Worcester, spent lavishly in the king's cause. William Price of Rhiwlas in Merioneth bought uniforms and distributed them among his tenants for the coming fray. Defiant gestures were legion. Sir Nicholas Kemeys of Cefnmabli boasted a coat of arms portraying a sword and a Welsh motto, 'if this hold, woe to the Roundhead!'.[7] But no Welshman did more to ignite the loyalty of his countrymen into a dazzling royalist flame than Sir John Owen of Clenennau. Owen, according to the poet Huw Machno, was 'a bulwark to the crown'.[8] He threw himself, heart and soul, into the struggle on behalf of royal authority. Fired by a passionate loyalty to Charles, Owen laboured unstintingly to galvanize support for the king and to reassure his fellow royalists throughout the years of strife. A man of infinite courage, he sallied forth into battle 'to protect Wales from injustice and to defend his country and the true faith'.[9]

Charles relied heavily on the traditional rulers of society because, in

---

[7] Philip Jenkins, *The Making of a Ruling Class: The Glamorgan Gentry 1640–1790* (Cambridge, 1983), p. 104.
[8] A. H. Dodd, *History of Caerns.*, p. 106.
[9] N. Tucker, *Royalist Major-General Sir John Owen* (Denbigh, 1963), p. 16.

raising armies, they were able to call on age-old ties of loyalty and deference. Some of them retained sufficient power to cow the recalcitrant into submission. From June 1642 onwards commissions of array were issued by the king to individual officers, who were required to recruit able-bodied men and to organize them into troops and companies in order to prepare for the forthcoming crisis. Wales soon became 'the nursery of the king's infantry'.[10] John Corbet, chaplain to the Gloucester garrison, claimed that 'the common people addicted to the king's service have come out of blind Wales, and other dark corners of the land'.[11] During the first few months of the war, more than ten regiments of foot-soldiers, mostly tenants, trained-band soldiers, and labourers, were recruited in Wales. Few of them understood or cared about the political issues at stake, but rather slunk unwillingly to the battlefields at the behest of their masters. Charles's dependence on Welsh foot-soldiers provoked a flurry of anti-Welsh propaganda in the popular press in London. Parliamentary pamphleteers claimed that the Welsh gentry led the common people 'which way they please' and that the raw, ill-trained royalist levies were as 'moles who had no eyes'.[12]

Support for Parliament's cause in Wales came mainly from among those who had imbibed the Puritan faith in religiously minded enclaves along the Welsh borders, notably at Llanfaches in Monmouthshire and Wrexham in Denbighshire, and among those whose finely tuned commercial instincts had induced within them a fundamental mistrust of the king's financial policies. Economic considerations were of crucial importance to some. Merchants in Haverfordwest, Pembroke, and Tenby depended heavily for their livelihood on a substantial sea-trade with Bristol, which was renowned for its fervent Puritanism. Ties of kinship were of special importance in Pembrokeshire, where the rebel cause was favoured by families linked with the commander-in-chief of the parliamentary forces, Robert Devereux, earl of Essex, who owned extensive estates in south-west Wales. Two of the most prominent supporters of Parliament, Rowland Laugharne and Rice Powell, had served under Essex in the Low Countries and the German states. Elsewhere, too, there were influential landowners who sympathized deeply with Parliament's cause. In Glamorgan, Philip Herbert, the fourth earl of Pembroke, owner of Cardiff Castle and many large estates, despised the vanity and pretensions of the king and thus adhered to the rebel cause. Henry Herbert of Coldbrook in Monmouthshire nursed a profound contempt for the recusant king-worshippers at Raglan. In Denbighshire, Sir Thomas Myddelton, owner of

[10] N. Tucker, *North Wales in the Civil War* (Denbigh, 1958), p. 9.
[11] David Underdown, *Pride's Purge* (Oxford, 1971), p. 12.
[12] J. R. Phillips, *Memoirs of the Civil War in Wales and the Marches 1642-1649* (2 vols., London, 1874), i. 98.

the lordship and castle of Chirk, was the son of a former merchant and lord mayor of London and was well-known for his Puritan sympathies.

Welsh parliamentarians who opposed the king did not abhor the monarchy as such, nor did they wish to abolish it. None of them nursed truly revolutionary aspirations. The most they hoped for was a working relationship between king and Commons, based on the recognition of certain parliamentary privileges and the rule of law. They did not question Charles's right to rule, but they did resent his abuse of that authority. Clearly, however, the influence of Puritan ideas was more apparent in Wales than the demand for liberty. Ardent Puritans, like Morgan Llwyd and Vavasor Powell, went to war in order to rid their fellow countrymen of what they saw as the spiritual tyranny imposed upon them by zealous Laudians. To them, the war was a spiritual crusade; a campaign for Christ against the forces of evil and darkness, and an opportunity to prepare the way for a massive campaign to save men's souls. They fervently believed that they were fighting God's battles. Colonel John Jones of Maesygarnedd in Merioneth, a Puritan zealot and republican, saw the war as a means of advancing God's cause by force of arms. 'The Lord', he declared, 'is our man of war.'[13] Walter Cradock, one of the most winsome of Puritan saints, toured army camps, urging royalist captives in sonorous biblical tones to acknowledge that the Lord of Hosts favoured Parliament's cause. Civil strife, moreover, reawakened anti-Catholic prejudices that were never far below the surface. Welsh Puritans believed that it was their duty to set in motion a godly reformation and in so doing to strike at the very roots of Antichrist. Roman Catholicism, in their view, was a perverted form of Christ's teaching, a specious faith shot through with blasphemy and error. Moreover, it was corrupt and politically seditious. Not the least of their worries was the fear of an Irish invasion to stiffen the king's cause. The Welsh had long been conditioned to believe that the Irish were wild and savage barbarians, no better than the fearsome Turks. Protestant refugees had been pouring into Wales since the Irish massacres of 1641, bringing with them inflated accounts of the horrifying atrocities inflicted upon their brethren. Inhabitants of Anglesey and Pembrokeshire in particular were haunted by the nightmare of a popish invasion from Ireland. As coastal defences were hastily strengthened, a rash of rumoured popish plots convinced Puritans that Charles's dealings with the Irish were fraught with sinister implications. Indeed, Puritans were able to score heavily in the propaganda duel by stressing that establishing a Catholic despotism was one of the king's major priorities.

Even so, only a small minority of Welshmen was intransigently committed to radical Puritanism and parliamentary liberty. In the eyes of

[13] NLW MS 11440D, f. 178.

English Puritans, Wales was a pathetic backwater, sunk in superstition and ignorance. Remote from the main drift of political and intellectual currents, it was 'one of the barren corners of the land'.[14] Poor communications and transport, backward technology, scarcity of capital, and the smallness of towns were all indications of sluggish economic and religious growth during the early Stuart period. Puritanism was no more than a tender sapling. The middling sorts of small merchants, yeomen, and freeholders, who were providing so much of the Puritan thrust in English towns and ports, were few in number in Wales. Little effort was made by Parliament to set its case before Welsh people. John Lewis's *Contemplations upon these Times: Or The Parliament Explained to Wales* was not published until 1646 and served only to inform better educated, bilingual Welshmen. Over 22,000 sermons, speeches, and pamphlets were published in England during 1640–61, but little of this torrent of literature spread as far as Wales. Monoglot Welshmen knew nothing of the ferment of radical ideas being aired and discussed on the streets and in the taverns and coffee houses of London, and parliamentary pamphlets constantly made the point that the bulk of the Welsh nation had never been 'burdened' with arguments about 'nature, justice and reason'. Richard Baxter feared that there were multitudes in Wales who were 'scarce able to talk reason about common things'.[15] Small wonder that Roundhead soldiers despaired of convincing the common man in Wales of the legality and justice of Parliament's cause.

Not all Welsh citizens were prepared to fight. Charles's commissioners soon found that it was difficult to turn the Welshman's sentimental attachment to the Crown into an effective military instrument. Men shrank from the limelight, refusing to commit themselves to one side or the other until events drove them to make a decision. In south-west Wales, for instance, many of the gentry simply ignored the call to arms and remained studiously neutral. Fear of death and a desire for peace, order, and stability prompted many, as Clarendon put it, to sit still, whilst the more cynical counselled the wisdom of self-interest and self-preservation. Resentment, ambition, and greed drove small landowners to pay off old scores or resolve long-standing feuds with their more powerful neighbours. Beneath the ideological tensions there seethed a turmoil of personal vendettas, jealousies, and intrigues. As in most civil wars, there were heroes and cowards, men of conviction and self-seekers. As the war gathered momentum, men swayed to and fro in their allegiance, and there was some truth in the contemporary jibe that the only constant thing about the Welsh was their inconstancy.

[14] Christopher Hill, 'Puritans and the "Dark Corners of the Land"', *TRHS* 13 (1963), pp. 77–102.
[15] Richard Baxter, *A Holy Commonwealth* (London, 1659), p. 90.

Nevertheless, it was with zealous assurances of Welsh loyalty ringing in his ears that Charles Stuart raised his standard at Nottingham in August 1642. The quality of that support was another matter. No Welsh (or English) county was on an effective war footing and royalist commanders lacked both technical knowledge and professional experience. But Charles was in good spirits. Despite his flaws of character and limitations of intellect, he had a restless appetite for action and adventure. His major objective was to defeat the enemy as swiftly as possible, for Parliament could count on the support of the navy as well as of the affluent counties of south-east England. Crucially, too, the rebels controlled London. The king's initial strategy, therefore, was to assemble a huge army which would enable him to capture the capital. On 13 September Charles left Nottingham and made for the Welsh border, recruiting loyal subjects as he marched. He established his headquarters at Shrewsbury where, by mid-October, his army had swollen to respectable proportions. When he set off for London on 12 October his forces numbered some 12,000 men, many of whom were recruits from north and south Wales. *En route*, the king's army was intercepted by the earl of Essex's forces between Kineton and Edgecote. This led to the first skirmish of the war at Edgehill on 23 October, where Welsh levies, untrained and badly equipped, acquitted themselves poorly. Many of them turned tail and fled. Following the fray, Robert Evans contemptuously described the 1,200 Welsh royalists at Edgehill as 'poor Welsh vermin, the offscouring of the nation'.[16] Much blood was shed, but neither side gained a tactical advantage and the king's forces moved ponderously on to Oxford. By 4 November the marquis of Hertford and Lord Herbert of Raglan had amassed a 7,000-strong army at Cardiff and set off to assist the king. Hertford's ranks, however, were seriously reduced by the earl of Stamford's forces at Tewkesbury, where 2,000 men were killed and 1,200 taken prisoner. Overwhelmed by a superior fighting force, the untutored Welsh recruits distinguished themselves by fleeing hastily from the fray. The king's army eventually reached Brentford, on the outskirts of London, where, on 12 November, Welsh infantrymen redeemed themselves by courageously storming the barricades. Faced by determined trained bands at Turnham Green, Charles lost his nerve—fatally as it turned out—and retreated to Oxford, thereby losing his clearest opportunity of bringing the rebellion to a swift conclusion. His withdrawal signalled the beginning of a very long and weary struggle.

During the early months of 1643 the king's principal strategy was to launch a triple advance on London. The earl of Newcastle would bring his northern army southward through the Midlands, Sir Ralph Hopton would advance from the six western counties, and from Oxford Charles himself

---

[16] J. R. Phillips, *Memoirs of the Civil War*, i. 128.

would engage Essex's forces. The king's armies were in good heart, refusing even to contemplate the possibility of defeat. Meanwhile, strenuous efforts were made to demolish Parliament's control of the southern Marches in order to provide the Crown with an undivided line of royalist strongholds along the borders. When Bristol surrendered on 26 July, Parliament's cause reached its nadir. The sole major border stronghold left in parliamentary hands was Gloucester, garrisoned by troops under Colonel Edward Massey. Supported by Welsh troops, Prince Rupert and Prince Maurice were already besieging the city. Lord Herbert of Raglan had raised an army of over 1,500 foot and 500 horse during the early months of 1643 in order to support the besiegers; but his forces were surprised by Sir William Waller's Roundhead troops at Highnam in the Forest of Dean on 25 March, and a large proportion of his army was either captured or killed. Undaunted, the house of Raglan recruited fresh levies and Gloucester was put under siege once more on 9 August. As many as 1,500 Welsh armed volunteers, together with 2,000 clubmen, may have been involved in this assault. Against all the odds, Gloucester held firm, resisting bravely until the earl of Essex, supported by 8,000 foot and 4,000 horse, swept up from Oxford and marched unopposed into the city on 5 September. This spectacular intervention was a major set-back for the king. Indeed, his failure to win Gloucester was eventually to cost him the war. In a Welsh context, Gloucester was the king's Achilles' heel. Its loss permitted Parliament to move soldiers and supplies freely between Oxford and south Wales. No longer would Charles have a monopoly of the men and resources of the southern counties. There were clear signs, too, that he had lost the initiative, for Essex's success had strengthened Parliament's resolve and boosted its morale immensely.

Meanwhile, parliamentary forces in north-east Wales were poised to launch an offensive. If Gloucester was a vital strategic asset for Parliament, Chester was similarly prized by Charles: as the major port for Ireland, the security of north Wales depended upon its being securely held. Since north Wales was one of the king's most prolific recruiting grounds, Parliament was anxious to penetrate these 'dark corners'. In June 1643, Sir Thomas Myddelton of Chirk Castle, a devout, moderate Puritan and an intelligent military commander, was commissioned as major-general for the six counties of north Wales. Myddelton established an alliance with Sir William Brereton, who controlled the whole of Cheshire save for the city of Chester. Myddelton was acutely aware that north Wales and its coast constituted a vital sector of the royalist war machine, and he was determined to prevent the flow of men, munitions, and supplies from north Wales to the royalist armies in England. Charged with the task of waging war against 'many papists, notorious delinquents, and other ill-

MAP I. Wales and the Civil Wars

affected persons',[17] Myddelton and his forces, assisted by Brereton and his
men, made a sudden dart across the old medieval bridge at Holt on 9
November, before moving forward triumphantly into Wrexham. Within a
fortnight the Parliamentarians had overwhelmed most royalist strongholds
in Flintshire and east Denbighshire, thereby depriving Chester of supplies
of men and food. Their audacity threw the royalist command in north
Wales into disarray, and the sole obstacle to further parliamentary advance

[17] Ibid., ii. 71.

into Gwynedd was Conway Castle, manned by Archbishop John Williams, who had spared neither pains nor expense in restoring its fabric, stiffening its defences, and filling it with munitions and provisions. Williams was acutely aware that a crisis was at hand, and no one did more than he to rally the men of Gwynedd to defend their ports and to prepare the way for the landing of what he called an 'English–Irish army'. Williams maintained an effective liaison between Lord Byron in Chester, Lord Bulkeley in Beaumaris, and the duke of Ormonde in Dublin, and when some 2,500 Irish and English troops landed at Mostyn on the Flintshire coast, Myddelton's forays ended in ignominious retreat. As Myddelton's men scurried hastily back across the Dee, they demolished Holt bridge and left the garrison at Hawarden Castle to face the wrath of the advancing royalists. Following a three-week siege, members of the parliamentary garrison surrendered and were marched to Wrexham, where they were 'cruelly used by some Welshmen'.[18] Once the Parliamentarians had retreated over the Dee, Byron put Nantwich under siege, and only the intervention of Sir Thomas Fairfax's troops saved Brereton and his men from further ignominy. Even so, Myddelton's incursions had done much to undermine royalist morale, and the king's commanders were forced to tighten discipline and make even heavier demands on their men and supporters.

In south-west Wales, Parliament's cause was rather less buoyant at the outset of war. Each of the three south-western counties of Cardigan, Carmarthen, and Pembroke nominally supported the king, and the sole loyal bastion of parliamentary strength was the town and castle of Pembroke. In the summer of 1643, Richard Vaughan of Golden Grove, the second earl of Carbery, a man of overbearing mien and dilatory habits, had been appointed lieutenant-general of the king's forces in west Wales. Carbery advanced with his forces from his base in Carmarthenshire into Pembrokeshire, where he achieved a large measure of success in converting towns and country houses into royalist strongholds. By September, his troops held the upper hand over all but the citizens of Pembroke. Early in 1644, Carbery was poised to launch an assault on Pembroke itself when, by a dramatic twist of fate, pounding storms drove the parliamentary ships which had been policing the south-east coast of Ireland into Milford harbour. Captain Richard Swanley, the commander of parliamentary ships in the Bristol Channel, seized his opportunity and launched an enormously successful land and sea assault on the Pill at Milford. Swanley's assault released Rowland Laugharne, the parliamentary commander at Pembroke, to lead his forces out of the town, capture Stackpole Court and Trefloyne, and assist Swanley in scattering the

[18] A. H. Dodd, 'The Civil War in East Denbighshire', *Denbighshire Hist. Soc. Trans.* 3 (1954), p. 56.

opposition at Milford Pill. Laugharne had been thirsting for an opportunity to teach Carbery a lesson and, fortified by these unexpected successes, he now looked for juicier plums further afield. Haverfordwest capitulated without a shot being fired, Tenby provided dogged but brief resistance, Carew Castle surrendered, and by 10 March Laugharne had achieved direct control over the whole of Pembrokeshire. Still unsated, Laugharne raised a considerable army which cowed Carmarthen into obedience. Swansea proved more obdurate, scornfully disdaining Laugharne's call to surrender, but Cardiff was overrun by parliamentary forces entering from the sea.

Carbery's leadership had been irresolute and, having failed to persuade him to bestir himself, Charles dismissed him from his post as commander of the royalist forces in south-west Wales. His successor, Colonel Charles Gerard, was the very antithesis of the inept and timid Carbery. Gerard was a soulless, professional soldier; a man of demonic energy, given to moods of black rage and ruthless behaviour. He undertook a vigorous recruiting campaign and Laugharne swiftly realized that he was a formidable adversary. Gerard lost no time in recovering Cardiff and putting Laugharne firmly in his place. Pushing remorselessly westward, he established control over Cardiganshire and Carmarthenshire by recovering lost castles and inflicting a heavy defeat on a parliamentary force at Newcastle Emlyn. Laugharne's forces were cut to ribbons as Gerard's men bore down on Haverfordwest, and by midsummer 1644 only Pembroke stood firm in the rebel cause in the south-west. Even so, Gerard's marauding troops had made few friends in either camp. Gerard's unbridled appetite for aggressive warfare, together with his habit of turning a blind eye to the misdemeanours of his men, made him a much-hated figure. His armies, flouting local sentiments and despoiling property with shameless abandon, raised nothing but discord and hostility wherever they went. These reckless and indiscriminate excesses served in the long run to weaken Welshmen's faith in the royalist cause and to drive them to forge pacts of neutrality or else to vent their spleen on plunderers and swordsmen.

Meantime, the royalist cause was under heavy pressure in north-east Wales. Early in 1644, fears that Charles had entered into a pact with the barbaric Irish drove the Scots and Parliament together. In January, 20,000 Scottish soldiers under the command of the earl of Leven crossed the Tweed and changed the whole complexion of the war in the north. Charles was forced on to the defensive and he resumed feverish negotiations with the Irish. Desperately fearful of losing ground in the 'dark corners', Charles sought to strengthen his control over north Wales and the borders. On 5 February he appointed Prince Rupert President of Wales and Captain-General of the counties of Cheshire, Lancashire, Worcester, and

Shropshire. Rupert established his headquarters at Shrewsbury and set about appointing commissioners for the levy of taxes and the recruitment of troops. Professional commanders began supplanting local amateurs, and they imbued the royalist campaign with a far greater measure of cohesion and discipline than before. In fact, as the king's cause became increasingly hard-pressed, the general mood of royalist commanders became more determined and ruthless. Yet the demands of these 'foreign intruders' were icily received in north Wales, where the inhabitants, according to Arthur Trevor, 'love not a stranger longer than he can tell them the news'.[19] Rupert and Byron were sorely tried by the lack of response among the men of Gwynedd, and Archbishop John Williams was hard-pressed to smoothe the differences between them. The north Walians often reduced royalist officers to utter despair. Captain Thomas Dabridgecourt's *cri de cœur* to Prince Rupert was typical: 'if your Highness shall be pleased to command me to the Turk, or Jew, or Gentile, I will go on my bare feet to serve you; but from the Welsh, good Lord deliver me'.[20]

Sir Thomas Myddelton was anxious to take advantage of these divisions, but relations between him and Brereton had become strained. Both commanders were eager to show their mettle, but were being tugged in different directions. Brereton was largely preoccupied with the task of taking Chester, whereas Myddelton's burning ambition was to conquer north Wales. But Parliament, which had the last word, was determined to capture Chester at all costs. This left Myddelton severely handicapped, for supplies of cash, provisions, equipment, and reinforcements were not forthcoming. Without adequate financial support, Myddelton was unable to take the offensive. His superiors never truly appreciated his powers of leadership or his devotion to duty, and, considering that large numbers of his troops were unpaid and underfed, he did well to hold his ground against constant royalist challenge in north-east Wales.

In the summer of 1644, however, new opportunities arose for Myddelton. Having got wind of the weakness of royalist garrisons at Oswestry, a town which he believed was 'the key that lets us into Wales',[21] Myddelton seized his opportunity to capture the town and castle on 22 June. He now faced the mouth-watering prospect of penetrating deep into the Severn valley and driving a wedge between north and south Wales. Events elsewhere increased his confidence. The royalist defeat at Marston Moor on 2 July was a stunning blow for Charles. Parliament's jubilation knew no bounds as its enemies were decisively crushed. The débâcle left Rupert's forces in considerable disarray. Freed from his obligation to support the northern campaign, Myddelton resolved to aggravate the royalists' plight. A surprise raid on Welshpool in early August, when Rupert's troops were

[19] R. L. Lloyd, 'Welsh Masters of the Bench of the Inner Temple', *THSC* (1937–8), p. 195.
[20] J. R. Phillips, *Memoirs of the Civil War*, ii. 139.   [21] Ibid., ii. 181.

robbed of their horses and baggage, was followed in September by a sudden dart to Newtown, where barrels of gunpowder were seized from bemused royalists. On 18 September the first pitched battle on Welsh soil was fought at Montgomery. This was the biggest engagement of the First Civil War in Wales, and Myddelton achieved resounding success in a bloody encounter: some 1,200 royalist soldiers were captured, between three and four hundred were slaughtered, and a similar number was wounded. Casualties on the parliamentary side were slight. Myddelton's striking achievement sealed his authority along the line of the Severn and forced royalist commanders in Denbighshire and Flintshire to alert themselves to the parliamentarian threat from Powys. Flushed with success, Myddelton led his men on a moonlight march to capture Powis Castle on 2 October. Defections to his cause multiplied, with the gentry, led by the notorious trimmer, Sir John Pryce of Newtown, beginning 'to warp to the enemy'.[22] Myddelton moved northward to defeat royalist forces at Ruthin, and only the dogged resistance of the castles of Ruthin and Chirk prevented his men from swarming on to the major royalist citadels in Gwynedd. Smarting at this rebuff, Myddelton turned south to capture the fortified former abbey of Cwm-hir, the sole royalist garrison in Radnorshire. A final sally northward to Flint brought his incursions to an end. Myddelton's campaigns in mid-Wales had clearly damaged royalist morale. Many citizens were already utterly sick of war, and Wmffre Dafydd ab Ifan, sexton of Llanbryn-mair, was moved to compose a dozen anguished stanzas in 1644 pleading for peace. Yet Myddelton's plans of building on his successes in mid-Wales by moving into Gwynedd remained unrealized. Parliament was unmoved by his pleas for assistance, and Myddelton's discomfiture was scarcely eased by the preferential treatment accorded his ally, Brereton. Obsessed by the task of capturing Chester, Brereton had made it clear that he was not prepared to assist Myddelton in what were seemingly desultory campaigns in central Wales.

With the approach of winter the situation in south-west Wales had changed. Gerard was summoned to Bristol to strengthen Rupert's ailing cause. Having fidgeted restlessly long enough, Rowland Laugharne resolved to recoup parliamentary fortunes in the absence of his *bête noire*. The castles at Laugharne and Cardigan were recovered, and news of the adversary's effrontery prompted a furious Gerard and his forces to march a hundred miles at speed, ravaging as they went, to restore his authority and bring Laugharne to heel. On 23 April 1645, Gerard's army inflicted the sternest of military lessons on Laugharne's men at Newcastle Emlyn, and the royalist army proceeded to reassert its control over the castles of Cardigan, Picton, and Carew. Once Haverfordwest had been taken, the

---

[22] R. N. Dore, 'Sir Thomas Myddelton's Attempted Conquest of Powys, 1644–5', *Montgomeryshire Collections*, 57 (1961–2), p. 102.

king's banner again billowed proudly over the towns and castles of south-west Wales. Only Pembroke and Tenby remained in parliamentary hands. But royalist euphoria proved short-lived. The declining fortunes of Charles's armies in England necessitated the recall of Gerard. Deprived of 2,000 foot and 700 horse, the remaining royalist army was no match for Laugharne's forces. In Gerard's absence, Laugharne, who had a keen eye for the right terrain, avenged his defeat at Newcastle Emlyn by crushing the forces of Major-Generals Stradling and Egerton at Colby Moor, some three miles from Haverfordwest, on 1 August. 150 royalists were slain, 700 were taken captive, and four field guns, five barrels of gunpowder, and 800 arms were seized. Within a month, Laugharne had occupied Carmarthen and from there he advanced eastward into Glamorgan and then north to besiege Aberystwyth. By the spring of 1646 the whole of west Wales was in his hands.

While events moved swiftly in the south-west, Chester continued to resist heroically in the north-east. Slowly but surely, however, parliamentary forces tightened the noose around the city. In January 1645 parliamentary forces crossed the Dee, marched to Hawarden, seized Holt, and plunged north-east Wales into crisis once more. Prince Maurice was sent with 4,000 men to repel the enemy forces and to ensure that vital supplies were able to reach Chester unhindered. But while Chester was protected, other strategic centres were left vulnerable, and in February Colonel Thomas Mytton, Myddelton's replacement in north Wales, launched a surprise attack on Shrewsbury and forced the governor to capitulate. Shrewsbury was virtually the capital of north and central Wales and a vital link in the chain of communications between Chester and Oxford. As a result, further routes were opened into Wales. Flurries of activity focused on Holt bridge, where Sir John Owen and his levies were dispatched to repel further invaders and to harass the besiegers of Chester. Meantime, the counties of Flint and Denbigh were judged fair game by roving bands of soldiers and renegades, who rounded up sheep and cattle and pillaged homes and churches at will. The intervention of Rupert's men forced the Parliamentarians to retreat across the Dee, but the general mood of apprehension and unease returned when Rupert was called away to Hereford.

By this time it had become clear that Charles was simply muddling along, lurching from crisis to crisis as his adversaries grasped the initiative. In contrast, Parliament had devised an efficient administrative and financial system to ensure military success. New taxes, such as the excise and the assessment, raised enormous sums of money. Strategically, too, the rebel cause was gaining strength. In February 1645 the Parliamentary army was remodelled. With the creation of the New Model Army, the invertebrate armies of the early stages of the war found themselves supplied with the stiffest of backbones. The New Model Army was a highly trained, unified, disciplined, professional fighting machine, a national force unencumbered by local ties and constraints. From April onward, it provided Parliament with a superior army, capable of turning the tide irrevocably in its favour. Indeed, the intervention of the New Model Army was chiefly responsible for settling the issue. At Naseby on 14 June, the king's main field army was annihilated by Oliver Cromwell's Ironsides. All practical hopes of a royalist triumph vanished, and Parliament was now convinced that its success on the battlefield was irrefutable evidence of God's will. 'The favours of God have broke in upon our armies',[23] wrote John Lewis, Glasgrug. One of the most deplorable episodes in the famous encounter at Naseby was the iniquitous treatment inflicted upon Welsh women who were part of the royalist train. About a hundred of them were brutally slain, and the remainder had their noses slit or their faces slashed. Members of the New Model Army claimed that the women were Irish whores, armed with long knives, but it is more likely that they were Welsh-speaking wives or camp-followers of Welsh soldiers.

Following the crushing defeat at Naseby, Charles retreated to south Wales to soothe his ragged nerves, find time to think, and to recoup his forces through the good offices of his loyal friends at Raglan, Ludlow, and Cardiff. The Commissioners of Array for the counties of south Wales promised him 'mountains'[24] of support, and Charles withdrew to Raglan Castle, home of one of his most generous patrons, the marquis of Worcester, to await further news. It soon became clear that the spell cast by Charles over Welshmen was nothing like as potent as it had been when hostilities began. The traditional affection for the king had perceptibly cooled. During the battle of Naseby the king's secret correspondence had fallen into parliamentary hands, and this provided clear testimony that Charles had been intriguing with the forces of Antichrist–papist Irishmen. Nowhere was the ground swell of anti-Roman sentiment stronger than in Wales, and Welsh soldiers were simply not prepared to march cheek by jowl with Irish mercenaries in what was, in their view, an increasingly fruitless cause. Furthermore, the behaviour of Gerard and his men in riding roughshod over the sentiments and interests of local people still rankled. Indeed, the men of Glamorgan had formed a 'Peace Army' which complained loudly against excessive taxes, military burdens, and wanton pillage by troops. Committed to protecting its localities from military depredations and unpalatable centralist commands, this 'Army' achieved a surprising degree of success. It was made abundantly clear to Charles that no support would be forthcoming unless specific grievances were redressed.

---

[23] John Lewis, *Contemplations upon these Times: Or, The Parliament Explained to Wales* (London, 1646), p. 10.
[24] C. M. Thomas, 'The Civil Wars in Glamorgan' in *Glamorgan County History*, vol. iv, ed. Glanmor Williams (Cardiff, 1974), p. 267.

The king agreed to meet the Glamorgan forces at St Fagans on 29 July. In a polite but chilly atmosphere, Charles was pressed to eject papists from the county, remove the existing governor and English garrison at Cardiff, and remit £7,000 arrears demanded by Colonel Charles Gerard. The king's cause was so weak that he was in no position to bargain with such impassioned petitioners, and on the following day he bowed to their demands. Sir Timothy Tyrell was replaced as governor of Cardiff by a Glamorgan gentleman, Sir Richard Bassett of Beaupré, and Colonel Charles Gerard was stripped of his command in south Wales in favour of Sir Jacob Astley.

Such was the disaffection within royalist ranks in Glamorgan, however, that Sir Jacob Astley soon found his army melting away before his very eyes. Laugharne's decisive victory at Colby Moor and the capture of Bristol on 10 September showed that the king's cause was floundering on several fronts. Three days later, Montrose was soundly beaten at Philiphaugh. Rupert advised Charles to capitulate graciously in order 'to preserve his posterity, kingdom and nobility', but the king, myopic and stubborn to the last, refused to 'suffer rebels and traitors to prosper'.[25] On 14 September he left Raglan and journeyed north, his affection for the Welsh distinctly less than ardent. In his absence, the 'Peace Army' in Glamorgan seized the initiative. On 17 September Sir Richard Bassett was forced to surrender the town and castle of Cardiff to them. Bassett was replaced by a fervent parliamentarian, Edward Pritchard of Llancaeach. Other 'well affected' Puritans soon rose to positions of eminence: Philip Jones of Llangyfelach was appointed governor of Swansea and Bussy Mansell of Briton Ferry commander-in-chief of the Glamorgan forces. However, the rapid puritanizing which came in the wake of these changes was not to the liking of zealous royalists. Many of them were horrified to find 'base men' supplanting gentlemen of standing on county committees, honest clergymen being exhorted to preach undiluted Puritan doctrines, and unwelcome tax burdens increasing. The most vociferous dissenter was Colonel Edward Carne, who declared for the king in February 1646, claiming that oppressive financial exactions, the proscription of the Prayer Book, and the elevation of low-born men were portents of a fundamental and insidious shift within society. Carne marched with his men to Cardiff Castle and called on Edward Pritchard to capitulate. Pritchard refused and summoned help. Rowland Laugharne's forces arrived on 18 February, engaged the armies of Carne and Sir Charles Kemeys in battle, and won a resounding victory. Having seen his forces cut to pieces, Carne was forced to come to terms with the victorious parliamentarians. He himself was thrust into prison and fined for his part in the resistance, whilst Laugharne was rewarded with the post of commander-in-chief of Glamorgan. The royalist cause in south Wales was in total ruin and when Raglan Castle fell on 19 August, hostilities there drew to a close.

Meanwhile, royalists in north-east Wales were filled with gloom and despair following the crushing blow at Naseby. Royalist forces under Sir William Vaughan and Sir John Owen strove manfully to prevent Roundhead invaders from sealing off all likely landing-places for an Irish army in north Wales. Chester was still resisting bravely, postponing the fateful day as long as possible. But the rout at Rowton Heath on 24 September 1645, when some 600 royalists were killed, was the final straw which broke the camel's back. On 3 February 1646 long-suffering Chester finally capitulated. Parliamentary forces were now free to surge into Wales to mop up royalist castles. Meantime, Charles had fallen back on Denbigh Castle, which was in the stubborn hands of Colonel William Salusbury, popularly known as *Hen Hosanau Gleision* (Old Blue Stockings). Salusbury had remained a loyal friend to Charles in foul and fair weather alike, but he was sufficiently independent to take the opportunity of telling the king a few home truths as he sheltered within Denbigh's walls. Most Welsh royalist commanders realized the futility of further resistance and submitted peacefully. This meant that parliamentary forces were able to snuff out the last embers of royalist resistance at leisure. Welsh castles succumbed one by one. Chirk surrendered first, abandoned by Sir John Watts for a bribe of £200. Ruthin Castle fell in April, following a siege of eleven weeks. William Salusbury refused Colonel Mytton's call to surrender, vowing to defend Denbigh Castle to the last gasp and eventually relenting only at the written command of the king in October 1646. Meanwhile, as Mytton's men moved on remorselessly, the governors of Welsh fortresses decided that further resistance was pointless. On 4 June Caernarfon surrendered, and Beaumaris, Rhuddlan, and Flint quickly followed suit. Conway surrendered in November, Holt in January, and the last stronghold to fall was Harlech Castle in March 1647.

Although Charles had been decisively defeated on the battlefield, the First Civil War had failed to resolve the struggle to delimit the king's power and authority. Charles refused to bow to Parliament's demands, and chronic disagreements ensued as to the nature of the constitution and a religious settlement. He still believed himself to be more sinned against than sinning. Like Mr Micawber, he hoped that something would turn up, possibly a relieving force from Ireland or France. He knew well enough that his enemies were divided and that his chances of achieving a political victory, though admittedly slim, were not hopeless. In order to widen rifts among his opponents, he used all his powers of deception in playing off one group against another in a bid to gain time. The years from 1646 to 1648 were fraught with turmoil, unrest, and resentment. The conservative elements in society voiced their objections to radical committee-men, burdensome taxes, Puritan tub-thumpers, and military rule. Presbyterians were so fearful of the growing influence of radical sectarianism that they strove feverishly to come to acceptable terms with the king. Soldiers, too, were resisting plans for their disbandment and were clamouring for back pay and various indemnities. Many of them felt that the Civil War had ended in compromise and betrayal. Finally, reformers such as the Levellers and the Fifth Monarchists were determined to restructure society by guiding the country on a radical path. Levellers championed the democratic rights of free-born Englishmen, whilst Fifth Monarchists, represented in Wales by Vavasor Powell and Morgan Llwyd, laboured unceasingly to lay the foundations of a New Jerusalem.

These social, religious, and political divisions enabled royalists to marshal their forces and mount a further offensive in south-east England and in Wales in the spring of 1648. In Wales, curiously enough, the focus for rebellion was Pembrokeshire, a former parliamentary stronghold. The major instigator of it was John Poyer, governor of Pembroke Castle. A merchant and sometime mayor of Pembroke, Poyer had served Parliament faithfully during the First Civil War. Like most insurgents in the Second Civil War, Poyer was motivated less by concern for the fate of Charles Stuart than by local grievances and personal antagonisms. He nursed a deep-seated hatred for his neighbours, notably such adroit equivocators as the Lort brothers of Stackpole and John Elliot, who had trimmed shamelessly during the war and now seized every opportunity to shower allegations of public and moral impropriety upon Poyer. The nub of their case was that he had appropriated the profits of the demesne lands of Carew Castle. Some of his adversaries couched their enmity towards him in personal terms, calling him a self-seeking adventurer puffed up with dreams of self-aggrandizement, which ill-befitted a man who had sprung 'from a turnspit to a glover'.[26] Poyer was under so much pressure that he came to believe that 'men of blood' now 'thirsted after' his life.[27] Tensions seethed below the surface and, when he was ordered to surrender Pembroke Castle to a detachment of the New Model Army under Colonel Fleming, he refused to obey until arrears were paid to himself and his men, and a special indemnity awarded to them. Throughout the country, officers and soldiers were deeply troubled by issues such as disbandment, pay arrears, indemnity, and the projected expedition to Ireland. As time passed, Poyer became increasingly intransigent and his personal animosities and grievances escalated into a general antipathy towards Parliament.

[26] A. H. Dodd, 'The Pattern of Politics in Stuart Wales', *THSC* (1948), p. 62.
[27] A. L. Leach, *The History of the Civil War (1642–1649) in Pembrokeshire and on its Borders* (London, 1937), p. 139.

Royalist newspapers pinned fresh hopes of a renewal of their fortunes upon him. 'Great England's honour lies in the dust', exclaimed *Mercurius Aulicus*, 'and Little England lends a hand to raise it up.'[28] On 10 April 1648, Poyer burnt his boats by declaring for the king.

Poyer's apostasy may have been prompted by his anxiety to avoid a parliamentary inquiry into his financial dealings. There are good reasons, too, for thinking that he was irresistibly tempted by promises of local support and assistance from Prince Charles at St Germains. Whatever the truth may be, Poyer now found himself borne aloft by a heady wave of monarchical sentiment. His fellow insurgents, Rowland Laugharne (Poyer's brother-in-law) and Rice Powell, both veteran soldiers and former parliamentarians, were also no longer prepared to dance to the tune of Cromwell's generals. Laugharne's disillusionment with Parliament had deepened in the wake of a summons to London to answer allegations of involvement in royalist plots. His disaffected troops, now led by Colonel Rice Powell, forced their way into Carmarthen, seized Swansea and Neath, and speedily marched on towards Cardiff. Laugharne was forewarned of these plans and hastened from London to join the insurgents in south Wales. Powell's 'Welsh Army' of 8,000 men comprised Cavaliers, conservative Parliamentarians, disbanded soldiers, and former clubmen. Most of them were raw, untrained recruits, inadequately armed with pikes and bills. At St Fagans, near Cardiff, on 8 May, the insurgents' triumphant progress in south Wales was halted by Colonel Horton's seasoned Ironsides. Although Horton's 3,000 horse and foot were heavily outnumbered, they held the advantage, for they were better equipped, more experienced, and highly disciplined. A fierce and bloody contest lasted for two hours. It was the largest battle witnessed on Welsh soil in either Civil War. Laugharne's men fought bravely, but they were no match for the systematically trained parliamentarians; 200 royalists were slaughtered and 3,000 taken captive. The two leaders, Laugharne and Powell, fled back to Pembrokeshire. A day of thanksgiving was appointed by Parliament and was duly celebrated on 17 May by William Strong, whose sermon was based on the text, 'So let all thine enemies perish, O Lord'.

A week after the victory at St Fagans, Cromwell arrived in south Wales. Tenby was placed under siege by Colonel Horton and Rice Powell surrendered unconditionally on 31 May. Cromwell advanced on Pembroke, where the undaunted Poyer was declaring to all and sundry that he 'feared neither Fairfax, Cromwell or Ireton'.[29] Pembroke Castle was well-nigh impregnable, and nothing but a long and wearying siege or the use of massive guns would be likely to secure its fall. Cromwell relied on starving the garrison, but as the siege dragged on his own men were soon living on

---

[28] Ibid., p. 146.   [29] Ibid., p. 174.

little more than bread and water. Eventually, however, the further threat of heavy guns and mortars forced Poyer to yield. Pembroke's capitulation on 11 July, following a siege of eight weeks, saved the locality from the bloody excesses which were soon to characterize Cromwellian rule in Ireland.

In north Wales, similar grievances, aggravated by growing agitation among supernumeraries in the army, excessive fiscal exactions, and the economic results of the poor harvest of 1647, were smouldering fiercely during the early summer of 1648. Lord Byron was only too happy to flex his muscles once more and, when his commission as commander of the forces of Wales was renewed by the Prince of Wales, he scoured the counties of north Wales and Lancashire in a bid to attract fresh recruits and put new heart into disillusioned royalists. Byron believed that guerrilla-type forays in north Wales would provide a useful diversion which the Pembrokeshire rebels could turn to their advantage. Sir John Owen of Clenennau found untapped reserves of energy and set about collecting together small bands, which steadily grew into a fighting force of 150 horse and 120 foot by the end of May. Owen's immediate aim was to capture Caernarfon Castle, which was garrisoned by Thomas Mytton's men. Plagued by flurries of royalist attacks, Mytton appealed to Colonel George Twisleton, governor of Denbigh, for assistance. Twisleton assembled some 100 foot and 60 horse and, much to Sir John Owen's chagrin, captured several royalist detachments at Barmouth on 23 May. Even so, Owen felt sufficiently confident to take his chance against the parliamentarians in the open field. At Y Dalar Hir, near Llandygái, a fiercely passionate struggle was fought between the two armies on 5 June. Although Sir John Owen's bold tactics ensured that the royalists had the better of the exchanges, they failed to consolidate their position and eventually found themselves outmatched by the parliamentary reserves. Cruel and ruthless deeds were in evidence, for the skirmish allegedly witnessed the murder of the high sheriff and the cold-blooded killing of three parliamentary captives. Sir John Owen fought courageously but was wounded and unhorsed. Undaunted, he bade his captives heed the fact that 'there were three-score thousand men now in arms in Essex and Kent'.[30] Bent on revenge, the parliamentary forces plundered Clenennau and Owen was incarcerated in Denbigh Castle.

Six weeks after the defeat at Y Dalar Hir, Anglesey declared for the king. The crushing royalist defeat at Preston in August forced Lord Byron to retreat south-westward with his motley force of bedraggled and despondent men. On his arrival at Beaumaris Castle, he was rebuffed by the men of Anglesey. No longer prepared to entrust their cause to strangers, they pledged themselves to follow Richard, the vain and reckless

[30] J. F. Rees, 'The Second Civil War in Wales' in *Studies in Welsh History* (2nd edn., Cardiff, 1965), p. 111.

son of Lord Bulkeley. Full of cocksure arrogance, Richard Bulkeley paid no heed to Archbishop John Williams's warning that precipitate action on his part might turn Anglesey into a bloody battleground. Meanwhile, Thomas Mytton's troops were gathering, and Richard Cheadle, the son of one of Bulkeley's old enemies, seized the opportunity of paying off an old score by guiding the parliamentary forces across the Menai Straits at night. At Red Hill, Beaumaris, on 1 October, Bulkeley's men fought bravely but were outclassed by Mytton's well-trained campaigners. Two days later, Beaumaris Castle capitulated and Parliament reasserted its authority over the whole of north Wales.

The military efforts of Welsh royalists in the Second Civil War had been poorly co-ordinated and flaccid. The king's supporters were left in total disarray and Parliament ensured that the major insurgents were punished. Strenuous efforts, however, were made to free Sir John Owen. In June 1648 a daring group of royalists tried to seize Denbigh Castle and came within a hair's breadth of succeeding. Sixty men had already scaled the outer wall when the alarm was raised and the plot failed. Owen was then moved from Denbigh Castle to London to face charges of treason, violation of his articles of surrender, and the murder of the sheriff of Caernarfon. At a time when so many self-seekers postured as sincere royalists, Owen's shining courage and altruism left a lasting impression upon those who witnessed his defence. Even the stoutest of parliamentarians admired his unblemished record of honour and loyalty to the king. Nevertheless, he was sentenced to death. Yet the threat of execution failed to dampen his ardour, for Owen's spirited reaction was to declare that 'it was a very great honour for a poor gentleman of Wales to lose his head with such fine lords'.[31] For some unknown reason, however, Owen's life was spared; it may be that Ireton and others, who had warmed to the Welshman's gallantry, had pleaded on his behalf. At any rate, Owen was freed and allowed to return to his home at Clenennau. There, local bards worshipped him as a war-hero, and on his death in 1666 the poet, John Owen, penned an elegy to him which ran to 111 couplets. Parliament looked less favourably upon those of its supporters who had trimmed their sails to the royalist wind. Cromwell believed that Poyer, Powell, and Laugharne were more deserving of severe punishment than loyal royalists because they had 'sinned against so much light and against so many evidences of Divine Providence'.[32] The three ringleaders in Pembrokeshire were condemned to death by a military court in London, but Fairfax subsequently decided that only one should lose his life. Instructed to draw lots for their lives, the prisoners refused. A child, therefore, carried out the task. Fate smiled on Powell and Laugharne, and Poyer was shot by a squad

[31] N. Tucker, *Royalist Major-General*, p. 112.
[32] J. R. Phillips, *Memoirs of the Civil War*, ii. 397.

of musketeers at Covent Garden on 25 April 1649. The royalist cause in Wales was further weakened when Colonel Richard Bulkeley was slain in a duel with his bitter enemy, Richard Cheadle, at Traeth Lafan in February 1650. Within a month, Archbishop John Williams, too, was dead.

The conduct of Welshmen during the Civil Wars shows, above all else, that men are complex creatures, capable of widely differing responses. The most loyal royalists revealed their devotion to the king's cause by digging deep into their pockets. The marquis of Worcester's family at Raglan claimed to have contributed the enormous sum of £900,000 to Charles's campaign. The Mostyn family of Flintshire lost as much as £60,000 in fines, equipping soldiers, and fortifying castles. In Glamorgan, the Mansells contributed some £30,000 to the royal war chest, whilst the Stradlings brought virtual financial ruin upon themselves by supporting the king's cause. Many Welsh royalists were made to pay for their sins through loss of property by sequestration and confiscation, or by payment of fines through compounding with Parliament. Other fervent royalists suffered imprisonment. When the First Civil War broke out, James Howell, the Welsh correspondent and former government spy, was thrust into Fleet Prison by the Commons on suspicion of being a 'dangerous malignant'. He remained there for nine years, but he continued to publicize Charles's cause with such zeal that Carlyle was later to describe him as 'a quickwitted, loquacious, scribacious, self-conceited Welshman'.[33] Towards the end of the First Civil War, Judge David Jenkins of Hensol was charged with high treason and thrust into the Tower. A forthright, uncompromising royalist, Jenkins had fought valiantly for the king until his capture at Hereford in December 1645. He defied his accusers openly, declaring his readiness to be hanged with the bible under one arm and Magna Carta under the other. He was fined £1,000 for his temerity, and might have gone to the gallows had not Henry Marten reminded the House of Commons that *sanguis martyrum est semen ecclesiae*. Shut away in the Tower, Jenkins still waged a robust war of propaganda, championing the divine right of kings and accusing Parliament of exercising 'an arbitrary, tyrannical and treasonable power over the people'.[34]

Other Welshmen were rather more wary of committing themselves totally to Charles. As the war gained momentum, some of those who had promised to fight for the king to the last drop of their blood were found wanting. Local interests and personal rivalries provoked disharmony. The leading gentry of Caernarfonshire, for instance, were distinctly reluctant to release stores of munitions to help the king's cause on English soil. They were loath, too, to leave their localities, for fear of looting soldiers and

[33] J. D. H. Thomas, 'James Howell, Historiographer Royal', *Brycheiniog*, 9 (1963), p. 89.

[34] J. D. H. Thomas, 'Judge David Jenkins, 1582-1663', *Morgannwg*, 8 (1964), p. 29.

predatory Irishmen. In many ways, fear of a popish invasion from Ireland weighed far more heavily on the minds of the inhabitants of Anglesey and Caernarfonshire than the plight of the king of England. In these communities men and women tossed and turned restlessly at night, fearing that Irish barbarians might land on their shores and murder them in their beds. The sight of strange vessels evoked genuine alarm, and rumours and counter-rumours often spread like wildfire. Underpaid and underfed, Welsh foot-soldiers had little stomach for long marches and were often reluctant to replenish depleted royalist ranks on 'foreign' English soil. Petty squabbles among commissioners and local gentry vitiated many attempts to organize them into an effective fighting force. In many parts of Gwynedd the lukewarmness of magistrates and the recalcitrance of deputy-lieutenants drove Charles's commanders to distraction. The king himself berated those 'who prefer private ends before the public', but few heeded him; no amount of weeding out of disloyal commanders seemed to improve the situation, and Lord Byron despairingly concluded in 1645 that Charles could 'expect no good out of north Wales'.[35] Even so, one must not exaggerate. Throughout the wars, many thousands of common Welshmen fought boldly for the king, and the poetry of Henry Vaughan (himself a royalist officer) reveals the chains of friendship, the courage, and shared dangers which bound soldiers together in a common cause.

Provincialism, cravenness, jealousy, hypocrisy, and avarice were all in evidence during the strife. Like chameleons, Welshmen changed their colours according to changing circumstances and needs. Ambidexterity was a common weakness among the gentry of south-west Wales. Their sentiments found expression in Howell Gwynne of Glanbrân's declaration: 'Heigh god, heigh devil, I will be for the strongest side'.[36] David Evans of Gwernllwyn-chwith, one of Colonel Philip Jones's supporters in Glamorgan, was later described as 'a dark-lantern man that never stuck at anything in the ill times'.[37] Some shunned the royalist cause when the king's foolish attempts to forge an alliance with the Irish became common knowledge. Sir Trevor Williams of Llangibby changed his allegiance on more than one occasion. A fervent royalist in 1642, he took umbrage at the king's increasing reliance on Irish Catholic troops and was thrust into prison. Following his release he fought on Parliament's side, holding Monmouth Castle against the king and participating in the assault on Raglan Castle in 1646. However, subsequent land settlements in south-east Wales were not to his liking, and he returned to the royalist fold in 1648. Personal resentment and pique led Archbishop John Williams to trim his sails. Having spent heavily on repairing and fortifying Conway Castle on the

[35] A. H. Dodd, *History of Caerns.*, pp. 108–9.
[36] A. H. Dodd, *Studies in Stuart Wales* (2nd edn., Cardiff, 1971), p. 133.
[37] Philip Jenkins, *The Making of a Ruling Class*, p. 115.

king's behalf, Williams advised Charles not to make excessive demands on the Welsh. Rebuffed by his master, Williams began to resist the almost incessant demands for money. As a result, he was relieved of his command and unceremoniously bundled out of Conway Castle by Sir John Owen of Clenennau in May 1645. Owen's appointment was a severe blow to the archbishop's pride and the wound festered long. Williams came to terms with Mytton in 1646 and actually participated in the parliamentary assault on Conway in August 1646. There are grounds for thinking, however, that he later deeply regretted his apostasy.

Political weathercocks and opportunists were common enough. Notorious trimmers like Sir John Pryce of Newtown and Sir Hugh Owen of Orielton incurred the opprobrium of both camps. The formation of the 'Peace Army' in Glamorgan enabled dexterous royalists to abandon the king in order to further their careers. Bussy Mansell, the youthful Colonel-General of royalist forces in south Wales, quickly saw the wisdom of treating with the enemy. In so doing he evaded punishment by fine or sequestration, and by the end of the First Civil War he had emerged as one of the most powerful soldiers and administrators in Glamorgan. Some of the more shameless trimmers took pride in their duplicity. Roger Lort of Stackpole was said to have fought 'in preservation of no cause but his own'.[38] In his biting interlude on the Civil War, Huw Morys put these words into the mouth of the Fool:

> I'll turn like the wind for better wages
> I'll kill my own mother for twopence.[39]

Henry Vaughan of Derwydd was a man who, according to one of his neighbours, would do 'anything for money' and often boasted that 'he who knows not how to dissimulate knows not how to survive'.[40]

Preserving a haughty independence was not easy, but some individuals managed to opt out of the struggle altogether. Lord Herbert of Cherbury buried his head in his books and refused to be dragged out of his unworldly seclusion, while Sir Walter Lloyd of Llanfair Clydogau sheltered contentedly 'within the walls of his house'.[41] Once men had spilled blood on the battlefield or suffered at the hands of pillaging soldiers, the desire for non-involvement grew. Firm partisans became passive onlookers. As the war dragged on, neutralist movements achieved greater prominence and no small success. During the months from August to November 1645, associations of clubmen in south Wales and the borders made strenuous efforts to keep contending armies at bay. The 'Peace Army' of Glamorgan

---

[38] E. D. Jones, 'The Gentry of South West Wales in the Civil War', *NLWJ* 11 (1959-60), p. 143.
[39] David Jenkins, 'Bywyd a Gwaith Huw Morys, Pontymeibion (1662-1709)' (unpubl. University of Wales MA thesis, 1948), p. 473.
[40] E. D. Jones, 'The Gentry of South West Wales', p. 145.   [41] Ibid., p. 144.

claimed to have a force of 10,000 men. Like the *Croquants* and the *Nu-pieds* of France, Welsh clubmen clung tenaciously to time-honoured traditions, rights, and customs within their localities, and were prepared to expend much energy and ingenuity in staving off innovations and unwelcome intrusions of all kinds. Preoccupied with keeping violence away from their doors and with bringing strife to an end as quickly as possible, they banded together to shield themselves and their families from the depredations of both armies. Voicing their readiness to defend local liberties to the hilt, they cried out against 'the devouring sword' which was violating traditional rights and liberties. Their sentiments found focus in the heart-rending stanzas of Wmffre Dafydd ab Ifan of Llanbryn-mair: he pleaded with the Almighty to protect peasant peoples from 'the contempt of both armies'.[42] Sir Thomas Myddelton claimed that plundering armies had made the inhabitants of central Wales 'hate the very name of a soldier'.[43]

Rumours and counter-rumours of atrocities committed by soldiers were common during the Civil Wars, but there is little evidence of sustained brutality or vandalism. The royalist propaganda machine dredged up countless examples of infamous deeds alleged to have been committed by Roundheads, most of which were either exaggerated or false. Bishop Henry King accused the parliamentary forces of selling defeated Welsh soldiers as slaves to the Plantations, whilst Huw Morys believed that no Welsh virgin had been spared by ravaging Roundheads. But the truth is that parliamentary troops were generally more considerate towards civilians than their royalist counterparts, largely because they were better paid and more adequately equipped. Even so, not even parliamentary generals were prepared to spare Catholic Irishmen, especially when it became clear after the battle of Naseby that the king had been negotiating for papist forces to land in Wales. Captain Richard Swanley made a practice of tossing Irish captives overboard whenever he intercepted vessels bound for Bristol from Dublin. Anti-Catholic sentiment also induced Captain Rich at Conway to send Irish prisoners 'swimming towards the place whence they came'.[44]

It was generally agreed, however, that the most outrageous violations were perpetrated by royalist armies. Few of their commanders were sticklers for proprieties. Prince Rupert was known as 'the Duke of Plunderland' in north Wales, and Lord Byron was utterly contemptuous of the property and interests of private citizens. South Walians regarded Colonel Charles Gerard as the devil incarnate, and not even ardent

---

[42] NLW MS 19660B, p. 103.
[43] R. N. Dore, 'Sir Thomas Myddelton's Attempted Conquest of Powys', p. 116.
[44] Aled Eames, *Ships and Seamen of Anglesey 1558–1918* (Anglesey Antiq. Soc., 1973), p. 76.

royalists lamented his long absences, for his wilful draconianism had seared itself into the minds and hearts of friend and foe alike. Badly paid royalist soldiers seized every opportunity to win prizes and settle old scores. Colonel John Bodvel's mother complained bitterly that troopers collecting contributions levied by Lord Byron threatened to burn her house and carry her off unless she bowed to their demands. Some of Carbery's soldiers incensed the people of Pembrokeshire by threatening to manhandle the wives and children of Laugharne and Poyer, and by promising to roll Poyer into Milford Haven in a barrel of nails.

The behaviour of Welsh foot-soldiers on the battlefields had often evoked a mixture of mirth and contempt. 'Poor Taffy', claimed satirical parliamentarians, was living proof of the wisdom of the old proverb that one pair of swift heels equals two pairs of hands. But the bands of sick, wounded, and mutilated soldiers who limped back from the fray bore witness to the misery and anguish endured by many brave men on the battlefield. Some of those who suffered the most grievous injuries had served as far afield as Edgehill, Chichester, Oxford, Rathmines, and the Isles of Scilly. A flow of applications for pensions came from maimed soldiers, penurious mariners, and their wives, and many war casualties were forced to wait several years for relief. Magistrates needed to guard against malingerers and impostors, for among the genuine cases there were always rogues with hard-luck stories to tell. Nevertheless, deserving veterans were rewarded for their services over a long period of time. Among the Caernarfonshire veterans who presented petitions in 1661 were William Gruffydd of Llanllechid, aged 87, and Rhydderch ab Edward of Llysfaen, aged 76, who had loyally served Elizabeth, James I, and Charles Stuart, and had suffered physical injuries during the wars.

The wars clearly disrupted the functioning of local administration in the provinces. Roads and bridges were neglected, offices remained unfilled, funds and records went missing. Wild life flourished as never before. Local justices in Caernarfonshire were as much worried by the predatory habits of foxes, polecats, weasels, and stoats as by the declining fortunes of Charles Stuart. Country houses were looted and destroyed. Rowland Pugh, barrister and staunch royalist of Mathafarn, saw his house burnt down by parliamentary soldiers in 1644, and Rowland Vaughan's profound distaste for the rebel cause knew no bounds when his home at Caer-gai in Merioneth was razed in 1647. Sir Thomas Myddelton's troops plundered Sir John Vaughan's mansion at Trawsgoed 'to his great loss'.[45] Even so, rural Wales was not as deeply scarred as the towns. The bulk of the fighting occurred largely on the Welsh borders and in south Wales. Broad acres of the Welsh heartland never witnessed as much as a skirmish, and not until

---

[45] J. Gwynn Williams, 'Sir John Vaughan of Trawsgoed 1603-1674', *NLWJ* 8 (1953-4), p. 38.

the closing years of the First Civil War did the inhabitants of north-west Wales have to endure the bloodshed of civil strife. The people of Merioneth, for instance, suffered much less than those who lived in the Severn valley or the towns of Denbighshire and Flintshire.

Welsh towns suffered most. Deliberate punitive destruction by fire occurred at Wrexham and Oswestry. Many castles were reduced to a sorry state. John Taylor, the Water Poet, who rode through Wales on his patient nag 'Dun' in the summer of 1652, noted that many castles were in an advanced state of decay. Churches, too, had been desecrated. Sir Thomas Myddelton's troops were alleged to have wrecked the famous organ of Wrexham parish church and confiscated the pipes to make bullets. Direct taxation was a chronic grievance among town-dwellers. The excise on food and daily necessities was profoundly unpopular, especially among poor people, and it is difficult not to sympathize with the 'poorest sort of women'[46] who caused uproar in Haverfordwest in September 1644 by bullying and berating commissioners of excise in their lodgings. Endless hordes of soldiers seeking free quarter and food, fuel and horses, placed a considerable burden on Welsh towns. It was widely believed that soldiers carried the plague with them, and valiant efforts were made to keep them at bay. When Welsh reinforcements marched into Bath to assist Goring and Rupert during the royalist campaign in the south-west in July 1646 they were met with cries of 'No Welsh! No Welsh!' from fearful residents who were terrified by the prospect of a fresh outbreak of plague. Towns, moreover, were subjected to the privations of siege and to wearisome demands for refortification.

The war also brought economic dislocation and suffering in its wake. The 1640s were trying years for Welsh drovers and clothiers in north and central Wales, for they could find no vent for their cattle and cloth. Undernourished, marauding levies made merchants' lives a misery. In 1643, clothiers and drovers presented a petition to the king calling for free passage through his armies with their cattle, sheep, and cottons. Shorn of its export outlets, north Wales had become a stagnant hinterland. Archbishop John Williams complained bitterly that poor drovers—'the Spanish fleet of North Wales which brings hither that little gold and silver we have'[47]—were being denied access to essential markets. Farmers claimed that the prohibition of free trade prevented them from paying taxes and imperilled the lives of thousands of families. Ready cash was pitifully scarce in rural communities and a succession of harvest failures after 1646 drove up food prices and exacerbated the plight of the poor. Restrictions were imposed on the consumption of corn in the borough of

[46] B. E. and K. A. Howells (eds.), *Pembrokeshire Life: 1572–1843* (Pembs. Record Soc., 1972), p. 15.
[47] *Calendar of Wynn (of Gwydir) Papers 1515–1690* (Aberystwyth, 1926), p. 287.

Caernarfon. Walter Kyffin described Denbighshire in 1649 as 'destitute of all sorts of provision both for horse and man'.[48] In 1650, the inhabitants of Haverfordwest complained that Gerard's forces had 'so eaten, spoiled and made desolate'[49] the hinterland around the town that no profit could be gained from the land. Cromwell confirmed their story, finding the countryside around Pembroke 'miserably exhausted and so poor'.[50] Furthermore, crippling assessments provoked the council at Haverfordwest to complain that two-thirds of the inhabitants were impoverished and that its former manufacture of high friezes and winter coat liveries was in dire straits. A severe visitation of plague in 1652 brought further trials and tribulations.

The preparations for war, the sieges, skirmishes and battles, and the mopping up afterwards all took their toll, bringing misery, hardship, and a general sense of war-weariness. A wide range of authors, poets, clergymen, and antiquarians gave vent to their frustrations and fears. Robert Vaughan, the celebrated antiquarian of Hengwrt, found 'each minute of every hour so very long'.[51] Two of Wales's foremost poets, Huw Morys and William Phylip, dwelt in gruesome detail on the death and destruction wrought by war. Archibald Sparkes, vicar of Northop, believed that 'the vessels of wrath have poured themselves forth upon our earth, and have filled it with a deluge of devastations'.[52] More poignantly, Henry Vaughan wrote of the 'vile weed' which had 'cast down the sacred rose'[53] and filled a pleasant land with terrible afflictions. James Howell, whose *England's Teares for the Present Wars* (1644) was a heartfelt plea for peace, knew that the years of bloodshed would leave an indelible mark on men's minds: 'the deep stains these wars will leave behind, I fear all the water of the Severn, Trent or Thames cannot wash away'.[54]

In many ways, the Second Civil War sealed the king's fate, for it served to heal divisions within the army. The army had become a distinctive entity, with a will of its own. Feeding on the king's duplicity and its own material grievances, the army had transformed itself into an agent of revolution. Soldiers were now of the opinion that peace and stability could never be restored so long as Charles was allowed to live. Before the Second Civil War, only a small radical minority had dreamt of establishing a viable

[48] A. H. Dodd, 'The Civil War in East Denbighshire', p. 85.

[49] *Calendar of the Records of the Borough of Haverfordwest 1539–1660* (Cardiff, 1967), ed. B. G. Charles, p. 91.

[50] J. R. Phillips, *Memoirs of the Civil War*, ii. 393.

[51] E. D. Jones, 'Robert Vaughan of Hengwrt', *Journal Merioneth Hist. and Record Soc.* 1 (1949–51), p. 29.

[52] NLW MS 12463B, f. 70.

[53] Alan Rudrum (ed.), *Henry Vaughan: The Complete Poems* (Penguin, London, 1976), p. 64.

[54] James Howell, *England's Teares for the Present Wars* (London, 1644), p. 163.

political settlement without the king. Further hostilities had convinced many more parliamentarians that negotiating terms with the king was futile and meaningless. Radical army officers no longer conceived of Charles as a sacred person: he was a polluted 'man of blood' who had defiled the land and brought untold misery to his subjects. Swept to the forefront by the flow of events, army officers decided to purge the House of Commons. On 6 December 1648 and succeeding days, 231 members were removed, leaving a remnant of zealots who were believed to be sufficiently radical to bring the king to account. At his trial, Charles performed with a brilliance and assurance which astonished his friends and enemies alike. Nevertheless, he was sentenced to death and duly executed on a public scaffold outside Inigo Jones's splendid Banqueting House at Whitehall on 30 January 1649. A chorus of groans rose from watching crowds. Philip Henry, the Welsh Presbyterian, shuddered as the axe fell and was haunted ever after by a terrible sense of guilt and shame. Indeed, the majority of Welshmen abhorred the deed and were filled with grief and horror. They had been taught to believe that the king was the Lord's anointed and the monarchy an essential pillar of the social order. William Phylip's famous elegy on the death of Charles expressed the general sense of outrage. Huw Morys believed it was 'the coldest day for the kingdom', whilst James Howell, plunged into great depths of despair, claimed that 'the more I ruminate upon it, the more it astonisheth my imagination, and shaketh all the cells of my brain'.[55] The 'New Litany' of the bards voiced the deep sense of rage:

> From educating the killing of kings,
> From preaching this publicly,
> From the violence of soldiers and armies
> *Libera nos domine*.[56]

Every effort was made to create the legend of a royal martyr cut down by malevolent men. Within a year of Charles's death, Rowland Vaughan of Caer-gai had composed a Welsh version of the best-selling *Eikon Basilike*, the alleged thoughts and meditations of the late king. Works such as this not only ensured that the ghost of Charles I would continue to brood over the lives of many of his subjects but also helped to bring about the peaceful restoration of Charles II in 1660.

Yet, a small minority of Welshmen hailed the king's death as the dawn of a new era. John Jones, Maesygarnedd, and Thomas Wogan, MP for Cardigan boroughs, were among those who signed the death warrant which authorized the execution of the king. They believed that Providence had guided them and that they had fulfilled their duty to the people and to their

---

[55] D. Jenkins, 'Bywyd a Gwaith Huw Morys', p. 56; J. D. H. Thomas, 'James Howell', p. 94.
[56] *Hen Gerddi Gwleidyddol: 1588–1660* (Cardiff, 1901), p. 30.

Maker. Zealous Puritans had always viewed Charles as a tyrant with 'popish' sympathies. Morgan Llwyd fervently believed that Charles, 'the last king of Britain', had deserved no better fate: 'unhappy Charles', he wrote, 'provoked the lamb, to dust he must withdraw.'[57] Llwyd, in fact, was not unsympathetic to the cause of political radicals like the Levellers. His correspondence is littered with references to Lilburne's attempts to remodel society, and his colleague, Vavasor Powell, was counted by 'Honest John' Lilburne among his 'faithful and beloved friends'.[58] Even so, both Llwyd and Powell were more committed to establishing the saints' kingdom on earth than to the struggle on behalf of the birthright of free-born Englishmen. Their hopes rose as republicans threw off their political shackles. In March 1649 the monarchy and the House of Lords were abolished. On 19 May the Republic was proclaimed and the task of finding a workable and acceptable political settlement was set in motion.

From 1648 to 1653 Wales was governed by the Rump Parliament (a minority element of the Long Parliament), which governed largely by committee. The Rump, however, was so heavily burdened with administrative problems, and dogged by the innate conservatism of its members, that it failed to live up to expectations. Its piecemeal attempts to reform society, spread godliness, and prepare a new constitution did not commend themselves to Cromwell. Cromwell's major task at this time was to find a compromise settlement between radical sentiments and moderate voices. His desire for 'a government by consent' was genuine enough, but 'healing and settling' proved a difficult undertaking in such a divided land. The traditional members of the county community in Wales were deeply alienated from the republican regime, and Cromwell's support came largely from among small gentry, freeholders, merchants, and former soldiers. Those who endeavoured to fan royalist flames were swiftly suppressed. In June 1652, Christopher Love, a Presbyterian minister and native of Cardiff, was charged with plotting against the government and conspiring to revive the Stuart cause. At the outbreak of war, Love had declared for Parliament and had fulminated strongly against the king's misdeeds. But as the revolution took a leftward course, he came to despise the rampant sectarianism of the army. His outspoken criticisms of the new born republic were not well received and he was executed, at the age of 34, on 22 August. During a two-hour address from the gallows, he cryptically warned his hearers against mistaking old devils for new gods.

In April 1653, Cromwell brought the proceedings of the Rump Parliament to an abrupt end, thereby revealing that the army was the true power in the land. Carried forward on a heady wave of millenarianism, he was persuaded to convene a Nominated Parliament (popularly known as

[57] *Gweithiau*, i. 55.
[58] Hugh Bevan, *Morgan Llwyd y Llenor* (Cardiff, 1954), p. 11.

the 'Barebones Parliament') on 4 July. Composed of saintly and idealistic men, it was expected to map out a godly reformation according to God's will. Millenarian zealots were convinced that it heralded the birth of a totally new order. However, the radical sympathies which achieved prominence within the parliament of saints offended Cromwell's increasingly conservative tastes and in December the Barebones Parliament was forcibly dissolved. Cromwell's first experiment in godly rule had ended in ignominious failure. In order to prevent further damage to the fabric of law and property, Cromwell himself took on the headship of the state by accepting the office of Lord Protector, conferred upon him by the Instrument of Government. Fervent millenarians were infuriated by his betrayal of their cause: Vavasor Powell regarded him as an apostate and set about organizing full-scale resistance to the Protectorate along the Welsh borders.

During the years of the Protectorate, Cromwell's aim was to establish himself as a constitutional ruler, backed by popular support. Political and economic levelling was by this time as abhorrent to him as it was to the traditional ruling families whom he so assiduously courted. Few men of substance, however, were disposed to forget that he had been brought to power by the army or that his regime was based on the sword. Under the new constitution, each Welsh county, except Merioneth, was given two seats, whilst one borough seat each was allotted to Cardiff and Haverfordwest. The traditional forty-shilling freeholder franchise was replaced by a landed qualification of £200 real or personal property, thus narrowing the electorate considerably. The first Protectorate Parliament lasted five months only, with Cromwell still haunted by fears of a royalist revival. He relied heavily on the influence of key and trusted individuals, many of whom, having secured special privileges and offices on the strength of their war records, had risen from relative obscurity to positions of great authority. In Glamorgan, for instance, political power rested in the hands of a tiny caucus of 'well-affected' parliamentarians led by Philip Jones, Bussy Mansell, Rowland Dawkins, and John Price. Those who were faithful to Cromwell were duly rewarded for their services. Colonel John Jones of Maesygarnedd, husband of Cromwell's sister, became one of the members of the Protector's Council of State. In Caernarfonshire, Sergeant John Glynne became Lord Chief Justice in 1655, and when Sir Griffith Williams forsook his royalist sympathies he was created a baronet in 1658. In Glamorgan, Philip Jones became Comptroller of the Household and Evan Seys was appointed Attorney-General.

Cromwell's problem was to secure support in the localities. Disaffection was rife, and rumours of royalist plots were legion. Penruddock's rising in the south-west early in 1655 was a flaccid affair, but it prompted Cromwell to review security. Although plans had been laid in Wales to assist Penruddock, the government was forewarned and took steps to nullify the threat. According to Sir Thomas Myddelton, some 800 royalists had organized a rendezvous on the borders of Montgomeryshire and Shropshire, but these were routed at Welshpool by none other than Vavasor Powell and his followers. Given the choice of supporting Cromwell or the king, Powell could do no other than defend the Protector's cause. Even so, he still believed that Cromwell had betrayed Fifth Monarchist hopes of establishing a millennium on earth, and he was thus kept under close surveillance. Morgan Llwyd, too, was unimpressed by Cromwell's 'transient pebble-stones of governments' and believed that there were so many conflicting interests and divergent factions within society that the task of reconciling them was well-nigh impossible: 'to unite all these to a quiet life in one hand, or in one world, would be a wonder indeed, yea, a miracle in all Europe'.[59]

Fearful of insurrections, Cromwell urged his spies to exercise the greatest vigilance. In March 1655, groups of militia commissioners were appointed in Welsh regions, charged with the responsibility for stiffening defences and uncovering royalist plots. In a bid to make defence truly effective, Cromwell then proceeded to put England and Wales under the control of eleven Major-Generals, who were given the responsibility for securing the realm against plots and risings, establishing efficient rule, and enforcing a godly reformation. In August 1655, Wales was placed under the command of Major-General James Berry, a former clerk in a Shropshire ironworks, who treated north Wales as a single unit and, largely for administrative purposes, severed the six southern counties into two units. Much to his discomfiture if not embarrassment, Berry was invested with enormous powers and even more enormous tasks. He was expected to supplement and supervise the work of local authorities and county committees in Wales. In his dual capacity as administrator and policeman, he was expected to weed out conspirators, suppress riots, horse-racing, bear-baiting, stage plays, and illicit alehouses, collect taxes from delinquent royalists, implement the poor law, prod local magistrates, and generally promote due order, godliness, and virtue. Berry was a decent, well-meaning man, with a rough charm, a dry sense of humour, and a firm grasp of practicalities. He found the Welsh 'an affectionate, tender-spirited people' who had 'suffered much', and he did his best to treat them sympathetically and honestly. He toured the country and stuck diligently to his task, knowing full well that 'men will rule if they be not ruled'.[60] His rule was not a dictatorship, nor was it unduly harsh; but it did cause resentment. There was undoubtedly a strong antipathy towards the Puritan values of urban society which Berry and his colleagues sought to graft on to

[59] *Gweithiau*, ii. 224, 229.

[60] James Berry, *A Cromwellian Major General: The Career of Colonel James Berry* (Oxford, 1938), pp. 152, 167, 180.

undisciplined rural communities. Civilians, too, were outraged by military rule and all the petty interference and tensions implicit in government by the sword. Direct military rule from Westminster was anathema to Welshmen, and the regime of the Major-Generals not only left a bitter taste in men's mouths but also deepened the desire to return to more stable, traditional royalist government.

Even so, the elections for the second Protectorate Parliament during the summer of 1656 seemed to confirm that the power of the sword during the brief reign of the Major-Generals had bred loyalty and obedience to Cromwellian rule. Fourteen of the twenty-five members of parliament elected to the first Protectorate Parliament were re-elected, and most of their new colleagues shared their enthusiasm for the republican regime. But new divisions were appearing between Cromwell's civilian and military supporters. Republicans would have no truck with the Humble Petition and Advice, and once Cromwell had spurned the offer of a crown the Petition was revised in order to establish an Upper House (or 'other House') in Parliament. But the army was not appeased, and the regime remained fraught with ill-will and animosity until Cromwell's death on 3 September 1658.

One of the major reasons why Cromwell failed to establish a workable form of government was his inability to woo and win faithful support in the localities. At local level, Wales was governed during the Interregnum by a plethora of committees. These evolved out of those committees which had been established by Parliament during the Civil Wars. Two major committees had served the cause well. The Standing Committee had been charged with the task of mobilizing the resources of the country and imposing Parliament's will on the people following military conquest. The Committee of Accounts was set up to supervise war finances at county level and to exact appropriate financial penalties from recalcitrant royalists. During the war, however, Parliament lacked strong local support, especially in areas where fervent royalists vowed their undying allegiance to the king. Staunch parliamentary supporters, whose zeal had been proven, were in short supply. A dearth of men of wealth and status, notably in Gwynedd and west Wales, forced Parliament to rely on administrators who had not championed their cause and whose sympathies were in doubt. Between the end of the First Civil War and the execution of the king, most county committees were fairly broadly based, including traditional landed gentry, up-and-coming squires, and army officers. The precise mixture tended to vary from county to county, reflecting the ebb and flow of political currents during those troubled years. But, in the wake of the king's execution, a flurry of changes occurred in the composition of local committees. Royalist sympathizers lost their positions, whilst those who feared that Parliament was bent on destroying traditional values withdrew their support. Smaller gentry, freeholders, yeomen, tradesmen, and Roundhead soldiers filled many of the breaches. Not all the country gentry, however, shunned the loaves and fishes of office. Merioneth, for instance, had its share of prudent time-servers. Men of property like Owen Salesbury of Bachymbyd, Edward Vaughan of Glan-llyn, and John Vaughan of Caer-gai abandoned their loyalty to the throne by occupying a niche on the county committees. This meant that they were forced to rub shoulders with a 'meaner sort of people'. In Anglesey, political power was vested in the hands of a 'well-affected' caucus of military men, whilst local government in Caernarfonshire relied heavily on the contribution of rising families like those of Glynllifon, Talhenbont, Castellmarch, and Madrun. Since Denbighshire could boast a goodly number of fervent parliamentarians like Sir Thomas Myddelton and Sir John Trevor its post-war committees were not burdened by intrusive soldiers and 'foreign' bureaucrats.

Even so, local government in Wales was riven with prickly problems. Private feuds and personal antagonisms were pursued relentlessly and poisoned day-to-day administration in the localities. As early as August 1647 it was claimed that most county committees in Wales had 'grown contemptible in the eyes of the country'.[61] Many of the county gentry were hostile towards social upstarts and religious zealots who, in collecting taxes, assessments, and fines, rode roughshod over local sentiments and traditions. Few developments occasioned greater resentment among them than the elevation of those whom they contemptuously described as 'base and unworthy men' to positions of authority in local government. This had prompted many of them to retire from public life, to come to terms with being 'civilly dead'[62] and to hope for better days. However, when Cromwell adopted a more conciliatory approach from 1657 onwards, the Protectorate government consciously sought to widen the membership of assessment committees and commissions of the peace in the localities by tempting the older governing families, many of whom were sulking in the wings, to recover some of their offices and accustomed positions of authority. Throughout the years of the Interregnum, however, the traditional rulers of Welsh society looked askance at upstarts of lowly birth and little refinement, and Welsh bards voiced their version of the world turned upside down:

> Putting the head where the rump should be
> And putting the tail in the front, may be,
> Chopping and changing perpetually,
> Making great mock of each noble degree.[63]

[61] HMC, Egmont, i. 450–1.
[62] Calendar of Letters relating to North Wales 1533–circa 1700 (Cardiff, 1967), ed. B. E. Howells, p. 29.   [63] Hen Gerddi Gwleidyddol, p. 33.

If second-rate committee-men were the bane of Welsh royalists, heavy-handed sequestrators and excisemen were despised by all. From the outset of the wars, Parliament had been determined to ensure that 'delinquent' and 'malignant' royalists should suffer for their sins through sequestration of property and payment of fines. Rates varied in accordance with the importance of the victims, the degree of their delinquency, and the influence of friends in high places. Commissioners found great difficulty in extracting payments, and in 1649 statutory sequestration committees were set up for north and south Wales to levy collective fines of £24,000 and £20,500 imposed on the two communities for their participation in the Second Civil War. These area committees directed the daily business of the county committees. In January 1650, however, their powers were taken over by the central committee at Goldsmiths' Hall, London. All funds henceforward were to be directed to its coffers. This central authority, in turn, entrusted sequestering powers to three subordinate committees, representing north Wales, south Wales, and Monmouthshire. Further administrative changes occurred under the Protectorate. From February 1654 onwards, the power to sequester the estates of proven delinquents was transferred to a single official in each county. In south Wales, however, this task was entrusted to six men who, in the last resort, were answerable to the central committee for compounding in London.

Welsh gentlemen, notoriously hostile to social change and uncompromising in their belief in the sanctity of property, harboured deep-rooted resentments against sequestrators and tax-collectors. None of them paid up with a smile. Indeed, sequestrators found themselves inundated with claims from erstwhile supporters of the king, pointing out why their property should not be taken from them and sold. All possible means were used to avoid paying maximum fines. The work of commissioners was hindered so much that sequestration procedures became a chaotic maze of conflicts and disagreements. Indeed, in some instances, the actual task of collecting fines proved almost as much of a trial to sequestrators as to their victims. On balance, however, there were no large-scale and permanent confiscations of landed estates in Wales. Wales was a land of small owners, few of whom could afford to pay substantial fines without saddling themselves with heavy mortgages. James Berry found to his cost that it was easier to find fifty Welsh gentlemen with an income of £50 per annum than five with £100. Even so, sequestrators and excisemen were hated figures. Welsh royalists seethed with contempt at the exactions of 'the scum of the world', the people of Carmarthen never forgot the heavy-handed ways of those 'boars of the forest', and the citizens of north-east Wales yearned to be rid of 'the horrid plague of excisemen'.[64] Many tax-collectors were

[64] Ibid., p. 18; David Lewis, 'A Progress through Wales in the Seventeenth Century', *Y Cymmrodor*, 6 (1883), p. 146; *Calendar of Letters relating to North Wales*, p. 107.

roughly treated. Daniel Wise, an excise officer, was sentenced to death by a Welsh jury at Haverfordwest for killing a man whilst fulfilling his administrative duties. Wise earned a reprieve, thanks to the good offices of James Berry, but the episode reminded Whitehall of the Welshman's antipathy towards tax-collecting strangers. Legend has it that William Phylip, the royalist poet, whose property at Llanddwywe in Merioneth was confiscated, took refuge 'among the furze bushes and clefts of the rocks of the mountains of Ardudwy'[65] before taking up an appointment as tax-collector of Is-artro under the Protectorate. He, too, found it prudent to remind people of his royalist sympathies and his hopes of a restoration of the monarchy as he wheedled taxes from his neighbours. Minor riots against taxes or 'mises' occurred in Cardiganshire, Montgomery, Radnor, and Monmouthshire during the 1650s, and the literature of the period reveals how acutely sensitive people were to the demands of tax-collectors.

Following the Civil Wars, a wave of land sales was launched as Parliament strove to pay its debts and achieve solvency. Crown and church estates were placed on the market and swiftly snapped up by profiteers and speculators. Furthermore, the complex arrangements of sequestration and composition afforded unscrupulous administrators unlimited scope to feather their own nests. During the Interregnum, Cromwellian administrators were widely suspected by Welsh royalists of being a vulgar breed of money-grubbing opportunists and sycophants. Archibald Sparkes, vicar of Northop, believed that republicanism had thrown up 'a new brood of Iscariots minding profit more than credit'.[66] Colonel John Jones fervently hoped that Robert Owen of Dolserau was 'free from having the country's moneys sticking in his fingers',[67] but the Merioneth gentry believed otherwise. It was widely reckoned that the 'ambidextrous' Lorts of Pembrokeshire, Edward Vaughan of Llwydiarth in Montgomeryshire, and Henry Williams of Caebalfa in Radnorshire, were not averse from expropriating lands and profits for their own use. It would, of course, be grossly misleading to suggest that every administrator dipped freely into public funds, for there were clearly godly and fastidious men among Cromwell's chosen few in Wales. Some of them pursued their duties with vigour and zeal in extremely difficult conditions. Rice Williams, the radical Puritan from Monmouthshire, discharged his obligations meticulously and, according to Walter Cradock, had 'served the state in many places, but not gained a penny therefrom'.[68] Colonel John Jones, Maesygarnedd, was a shrewd bargainer who did well for himself by amassing estates in north Wales and Ireland. But, unlike many men in his position, Jones denounced greedy profiteers and had the interests of small freeholders at heart. His

[65] W. Ll. Davies, 'Phylipiaid Ardudwy', Y Cymmrodor, 42 (1930), p. 217.
[66] NLW MS 12463B, f. 70ᵛ.   [67] NLW MS 11440D, f. 45.
[68] G. E. Aylmer, The State's Servants (London, 1973), p. 69.

correspondence with his kinsman, Morgan Llwyd, also testifies to his personal piety and his genuine devotion to the Puritan cause.

Nevertheless, a small but powerful group of cynical adventurers and pragmatists, motivated largely by pecuniary considerations, was determined to make hay while the sun shone. Much to the embarrassment of their saintly colleagues and to the chagrin of royalist gentry, these adventurers were little troubled by Puritan scruples. According to John Jones, Sir John Carter, former governor of Conway Castle and MP for Denbighshire in 1654, 1656, and 1658–9, was 'an odd man who cares not whom he oppresses if it be to his profit'.[69] Carter was a former linen draper from Buckinghamshire who had lined his pockets by marrying (as local wiseacres observed) the best piece of holland in Denbighshire, Elizabeth Holland, heiress of Kinmel. Colonel George Twisleton, governor of Denbigh Castle, also had a keen eye for rich pickings. A Yorkshireman, he settled on extensive ex-royalist estates in Denbighshire and Flintshire, married the heiress of William Glynne of Lleuar, Caernarfonshire, and represented Anglesey in Parliament under the Protectorate.

It was galling enough for the Welsh gentry to be unseated by alien upstarts and low-born men, but to see them prospering mightily at their expense was scarcely bearable. The major villain, judging by contemporary testimony, was one of Cromwell's chief acolytes, Philip Jones of Llangyfelach. Jones's gifts as a soldier during the war years were far surpassed by his adroitness as a wire-pulling administrator during the Interregnum. Formerly a modest freeholder, his knack for being in the right place at the right time won him office and promotion in the local administration of Glamorgan. By 1650 he was virtually ruler of south Wales, assuming the powers of a dictator and using his authority to strip landowners of their acres, bring undue pressure to bear on the courts, and exploit the land market at will. At national level, he moved in exalted circles: he was one of Cromwell's most trusted councillors, acted as Comptroller of the Household, and was able to influence political affairs as a member of the inner circle of government. Jones had an appetite for work as gluttonous as that for land. It is estimated that during the Interregnum he spent more than £15,800 in land purchases alone, and his rapid rise to fame sent his political enemies into paroxysms of fury. Wronged gentry accused him of trafficking in sequestered lands, of receiving 'diverse rewards, bribes and gratuities'[70] and of recovering his expenses from the public purse. The well-orchestrated, and sometimes cacophonous, complaints of disenchanted royalists against Jones were endemic during the 1650s. Rumour bred rumour, innuendo followed innuendo, and Jones was never able to scotch the numerous accusations

[69] *Calendar of Wynn Papers*, p. 313.
[70] A. G. Veysey, 'Colonel Philip Jones, 1618–74', *THSC* (1966), p. 335.

made against him. How much truth lay in these allegations is hard to tell, for the evidence of injured parties is at best partial and at worst scurrilous. Even so, there is room to suspect the means by which a man of relatively humble birth and few connections had risen to such enormous wealth and influence so swiftly. Desperate attempts by aggrieved gentry to bring Philip Jones to justice proved fruitless, and he was eventually allowed to retire on his alleged 'ill-gotten moneys' to his estate at Fonmon in the vale of Glamorgan.

When Oliver Cromwell died in September 1658, Philip Jones declared: 'he is gone to heaven embalmed with prayers and tears'.[71] But not many Welshmen mourned his passing. His son Richard, though brimming with good intentions, was ill-fitted to the task of creating a workable and lasting political settlement. His rule witnessed a recrudescence of the old radical campaign for the 'Good Old Cause', and after a mere eight months in office 'Tumbledown Dick' resigned. His fall ushered in the Rump, made up largely of anti-Protectorate republicans and army leaders. But old civil and military tensions bubbled to the surface once more, and the political uncertainty of the day encouraged a growing conviction that only the restoration of the monarchy could save the country from anarchy. Commissions were issued in July 1659 to raise and reorganize the militia to repulse growing royalist sentiment and agitation. Experienced old colonels, such as John Jones, George Twisleton, and Thomas Madryn, strove to snuff out likely insurrections in north Wales, but the leading Cromwellian lights in the south, Philip Jones, Rowland Dawkins, and John Price, had faded from the scene. Only Bussy Mansell, who took over Philip Jones's position of authority, proved himself sufficiently adroit to survive the political turmoil of the day. As divisions among the revolutionaries deepened, the old governing families, together with moderate men, judged the time ripe to reveal their true colours. When the Rump was dissolved in the autumn of 1659, the general mood was in favour of restoring the king. The most prominent Welshman to conspire secretly on behalf of the king in exile was Sir Thomas Myddelton. He had been secluded from Parliament following Pride's Purge in 1648 and subsequently found himself out of sympathy with rampant sectarianism and republicanism. On 7 August 1659, at the ripe age of 73, Myddelton had drawn his sword in Wrexham market-place to proclaim Charles II king. Together with some 200 men from Flintshire and Denbighshire, he threw in his lot with Colonel George Booth in the famous, but poorly organized, Cheshire rising on 18 August. Booth's army was soundly thrashed by Lambert's troops at Winnington Bridge, Chirk Castle was forced to surrender, Sir Thomas Myddelton was

---

[71] A. G. Veysey, 'Colonel Philip Jones, 1618–74', *THSC* (1966), p. 326.

declared a traitor, and his lands were sequestered. 'When a kingdom is tossed in a blanket, happy are they who are out of it',[72] declared William Glynne of Lleuar.

Not all Welshmen, however, had abandoned the 'Good Old Cause'. In Cardiganshire, Merioneth, and Glamorgan, there were plots afoot to organize armed resistance to royalist plans to invite the Stuart king to return. At Haverfordwest, 'the fanatic parties' armed themselves and gathered cobblers, hatters, weavers, and tailors together under the slogan, 'No King, No Lord, We are Engaged!'[73] But when General Monck crossed the Tweed, the days of 'fanatical rule' were numbered. On 25 May 1660, the 'Merry Monarch' landed at Dover, and four days later triumphantly entered the capital to begin what royalists claimed was the twelfth year of his reign. Sir Thomas Myddelton's timing in proclaiming Charles II king at Wrexham was on this occasion impeccable. The return of the king occasioned scenes of great jubilation in many parts of Wales. Banquets abounded, wine ran freely, and bells chimed loudly. Wise old owls like Huw Morys and William Phylip smiled smugly in the knowledge that their prophecies and prayers had not been in vain. Throughout Wales, especially among royalist gentry and clergy, there was an enormous sense of release. No longer would fervent royalists need to move by stealth, for they had, according to John Roberts of Llanrhaeadr-ym-Mochnant, received 'a miraculous resurrection from the grave'.[74]

Whatever else he might have achieved, Cromwell had failed to establish an acceptable form of government in Wales. Indeed, few features of republican and Puritan rule had endeared themselves to the Welsh, and the rising tide of hostile petitions, pamphlets, poems, and ballads in the 1650s revealed widespread resentment. The overwhelming view was that the republic was 'a monster without a head'.[75] The execution of Charles I had clearly sent a shudder of horror and shame throughout the land, and enthusiasm for monarchical government remained very powerful. The proscription of church services had stirred the ire of devout Anglicans, and Puritan discipline, imposed by upstarts and aliens, had proved deeply unpopular. None had suffered more than the gentry: they were bitterly resentful at being elbowed roughly aside by men of inferior birth, rank, and station. Having been humiliated on the battlefield and bled white by sequestrators, they had good cause to despise 'base' men. To find yeomen sitting on the magistrates' bench, excisemen as smartly dressed as nobles, shoemakers discoursing in church pulpits, and unscrupulous foreigners

[72] *Calendar of Wynn Papers*, p. 352.
[73] *Calendar of the Records of the Borough of Haverfordwest*, p. 170.
[74] *Calendar of Letters relating to North Wales*, p. 241.
[75] Rowland Watkyns, *Flamma Sine Fumo* (1662), ed. Paul C. Davies (Cardiff, 1968), p. 9.

waxing fat on gentry lands was not only, in their eyes, a breach of the bounds of civility but also a blasphemy against God's appointed hierarchy. To William Price, squire of Rhiwlas, Merioneth, these were 'distempered and bedlam times'.[76]

The gentry, it is true, were men with axes to grind. Many of them sponsored the publication of scurrilous tracts designed to blacken the reputation of republican governors. But republican rule was also deeply repugnant to common people. They, too, viewed the rule of Puritan soldiers and saints as an incubus, and the boldest among them blurted out their resentments from time to time. Tongues warmed by ale often wagged freely. Lewis Morris, a former royalist soldier of Llanddeiniolen, declared publicly in an alehouse: 'a turd in the state's teeth and I care not if they and all Roundheads were hanged'.[77] When harassed citizens in Caernarfon manhandled a persistent bailiff and threw him to the ground, they cried loudly: 'there is no justice to be had now'.[78] More than anything else, people had resented the heavy-handed ways of Cromwellian 'swordsmen'. The Interregnum in Wales had been the child of the Civil Wars: it was founded and maintained by the power of the sword. Huw Morys might have claimed in 1660 that the wheel had turned full circle, but the experiences of civil strife and republican government, both real and imaginary, would not lightly be cast aside. Nor would the legacy of blood readily be forgotten.

[76] A. H. Dodd, *Studies in Stuart Wales*, p. 176.

[77] N. Tucker, *North Wales in the Civil War*, p. 167.

[78] J. Gwynfor Jones, 'Caernarfonshire Administration: The Activities of the Justices of the Peace, 1603–1660', *WHR* 5 (1970), p. 155.

CHAPTER 2

PROPAGATING THE GOSPEL

THROUGHOUT the early Stuart period, Wales's image among Puritans had been distinctly unflattering: it was seen as one of the dark corners of the land, a heathenish country riddled with the remnants of popery and paganism, and shot through with ignorance and profanity. The scandalous lack of preaching and the paucity of educational facilities meant that there were many hungry sheep unfed by the Word. In remote rural areas, where slender maintenances, pluralism, and non-residence sullied the image and effectiveness of the established church, a large proportion of society was still ignorant of basic Christian dogmas. Poor people may rarely have darkened the door of their parish church, save perhaps at Easter. Peasant peoples remained strongly wedded to superstitions and magical practices, and cunning men were often held in higher esteem than clergymen. During the reign of James I, the Welsh had been described in Parliament as 'an idolatrous nation and worshippers of Devils'.[1] Sir Benjamin Rudyerd had declared in 1628 that Wales was 'scarce in Christendom'.[2]

Ever since the reign of Elizabeth the backward nature of the Welsh economy had restricted the growth of Puritanism. In England, Puritanism drew much of its strength from serious-minded middling sorts in urban communities and from university-trained clerics. But in Wales, towns were small and impoverished, the middle class was miniscule, and penurious clergymen were ill-equipped to puritanize their flocks. Communications were difficult, news and ideas travelled slowly, and there were no national institutions or facilities to sponsor and nourish radical religious movements. As a result, Puritanism made progress only in those counties linked by trade to English towns and ports. It spread slowly along the trade routes leading from Bristol to Monmouthshire and Glamorgan, and from Chester to Denbighshire. It also took root among the flourishing merchant communities in Pembrokeshire. But the apparent docility, somnolence, and indifference of the Welsh still endured, thus inducing London merchants, many of them Welshmen or of Welsh descent, to enter the mission field by financing philanthropic schemes to help the poor and needy, and by publishing Bibles and popular devotional books in Welsh.

[1] J. Gwynn Williams, 'Witchcraft in Seventeenth-Century Flintshire', *Flintshire Hist. Soc. Journal* 26–7 (1975–6), p. 22.
[2] C. Hill, *Society and Puritanism in Pre-Revolutionary England* (paperback edn., London, 1966), p. 58.

These responses touched a nerve among earnest clergymen, who were equally determined to rescue their parishioners from ignorance and near-paganism. Rees Prichard, the celebrated vicar of Llandovery, penned rough and ready rhymes in order to instil basic Puritan tenets into the minds of semi-literate peasants. But, as the 1630s wore on, Puritan energies became increasingly committed to the task of defending Calvinist theology against the Arminianism of Archbishop William Laud and his acolytes. Attempts to buy up vacant livings and to endow lectureships had been thwarted by the vigilant Laud, who was determined to harry the Puritans into conformity. Some obeyed meekly. Others took flight to the remote and howling wilderness of New England or to Holland. A small minority, however, was prepared to suffer for the right to follow conscience.

Laud's reckless disregard for Puritan sentiments prompted a small band of Welsh saints to renounce the Church of England and establish voluntary associations of believers. Led by William Wroth, the aged and revered rector of Llanfaches in Monmouthshire, these separatists planted the seed-bed of Dissent in Wales. Most of those who were at odds with Laud were relatively well-to-do natives of the border counties. William Erbery, son of a Roath merchant, was the former vicar of St Mary's and St John's in Cardiff. His curate, Walter Cradock, a native of Llangwm in Monmouthshire, was an unusually gifted preacher who found joyful fulfilment in winning souls. Vavasor Powell, a freeholder's son from Knucklas in the parish of Heyop in Radnorshire, was one of Cradock's converts. So too was Morgan Llwyd, a native of Cynfal in the parish of Maentwrog, and the scion of an old and substantial Merionethshire family. The undisputed mainspring of their preaching missions was the Llanfaches congregation, founded according to 'the New England Way' in November 1639. The adoption of this particular policy meant that its members did not cut the cords which bound them to the established church, for they continued to worship as a church within a church (*ecclesiola in ecclesia*). Bound together by a sense of common purpose and shared dangers, they asserted that religion was a matter of personal faith. There may have been other separatist congregations besides Llanfaches in pre-Civil War Wales, fugitive affairs which are now virtually impossible to trace; but there is no doubt that in its day Llanfaches was acknowledged to be the 'mother church in that Gentile country'.[3] A tremendous vitality was sustained under Wroth's pastorate. He became known as 'the Apostle of Wales', saints flocked to his church in considerable numbers from contiguous counties, and 'all was spirit and life'.

The outbreak of civil war in 1642 was interpreted by many Puritans as an

[3] R. Geraint Gruffydd, *'In that Gentile Country': The beginnings of Puritan Nonconformity in Wales* (Bridgend, 1976), p. 16.

extension of the war of the spirit between Christ and Satan within their souls. Charles's absolutism and Laud's authoritarianism became twin symbols of the evils of Antichrist, and the Bible supplied all the proof that was needed that the demise of these evil agents was at hand. As Parliament hurried on with its programme of reformation, Welsh Puritans addressed themselves to the task of bringing their countrymen out of their spiritual bondage. Popular ignorance and spiritual torpor filled Puritans with horror and dread. They feared for the souls of the benighted and yearned to liberate them from the evils of popery. Some of them cherished grandiose ideals: nothing less than the building of a New Jerusalem would satisfy Colonel John Jones of Maesygarnedd in Merioneth. His priority was to form 'a Commonwealth out of a corrupt rude mass' by 'pulling down the works of Antichrist in the land'[4] and expelling idolatry, superstition, and ignorance. The Llanfaches saints dreamed of creating a literate, Bible-reading public, of imposing godly discipline, and, above all, of satisfying the deep spiritual needs of their 'beloved countrymen'. It was entirely natural for men who counted themselves among the elect to deplore the moral and spiritual failings of the unregenerate mass and to see Wales as an ideal field for missionary enterprise. They were prepared to devote all their energies to infusing new spirit into the religious life of Wales, and the fact that the mass of the people was as indifferent to the Puritan gospel as to the constitutional struggles of the day made their task all the more urgent and necessary. It was their privilege and duty to reveal the healing powers of redemption to their benighted brethren and to render them receptive to God's grace. In essence, theirs was a labour of love.

For the moment, however, such worthy ideals were cast aside as the outbreak of hostilities threw the Welsh saints into disarray. Gusts of pro-royalist fervour blew around their ears, forcing them to flee across the Severn to seek shelter among like-minded saints in Bristol. Further threats to the security of England's second largest city, however, left them with no choice other than to travel south-eastwards in search of parliamentary enclaves. London soon became a reception centre for Puritan ministers from all parts of the realm. But, although the saints were 'as scattered sheep', they were so convinced of the righteousness of their cause that their spirits remained high. God, they declared, had vouchsafed His favours to the godly cause, and no set-backs on the battlefields would prevent Him from rewarding the faithful and overthrowing evil. 'Be not sad on our account', wrote Morgan Llwyd to his mother, 'for great joy is near. In spite of men and devils, God will keep His word and His children.'[5]

Fired by their conviction that the righteous always conquer, most of the Welsh saints either preached vigorously or fought bravely during their

---

[4] NLW MS 11440D, f. 75.   [5] *Gweithiau*, ii. 243.

enforced exile. The glorious mission was essentially a young man's campaign. Their revered patriarch, William Wroth, had died before the drums of war began to beat; but, on the eve of the rebellion, his colleagues and disciples were full of youthful enthusiasm and ready for the fray: Erbery was 38, Richard Symonds 33, Cradock 32, Henry Walter 31, Powell 25, and Llwyd 23. Some of them established themselves in settled livings. Cradock was appointed to a lectureship at All Hallows the Great in Thames Street, a poor parish in London where, according to Thomas Edwards, he informed his congregation that 'the day was breaking out after a long night'.[6] Richard Symonds took up a Puritan lectureship at Andover and subsequently held the living of Sandwich in Kent. Vavasor Powell was appointed vicar of Dartford in Kent in 1644. Welsh saints were also closely associated with the parliamentary war effort as soldiers or chaplains. Cradock, who acted as chaplain to Sir Thomas Fairfax, used all his gentle powers of persuasion to win the allegiance of captured royalist prisoners. Llwyd preached vigorously against traditional forms of worship and caused a stir at Oxford by publicly tearing up and burning a copy of the Prayer Book. As army chaplains, Welsh saints were free not only to preach to soldiers but also to attend councils of war held by officers, where they were able to gather an intimate knowledge of military and political affairs. Moreover, by moving in the same circles as radical chaplains such as William Dell and John Saltmarsh, it was hard to avoid becoming intoxicated with the heady wine of religious and social radicalism. Morgan Llwyd and William Erbery, in particular, gained much from the intellectual energy and democratic convictions which animated the Puritan fighting forces.

Meanwhile, as Welsh Puritans stiffened the anti-Royalist cause, Parliament set about promoting the work of reformation in Wales. The influx of uprooted Puritan ministers into London prompted Parliament to establish a Committee for Plundered Ministers to safeguard the welfare of individuals and to distribute relief according to personal need. However, the dearth of preaching ministers in the dark corners of the land was so acute that the Committee's powers were widened to include the examination of witnesses against scandalous clergymen and the recommendation of 'godly and painful' ministers to fill vacant and sequestered livings. In order to measure the problem at grass-roots level, parliamentary committees were empowered to examine charges against scandalous clerics and to monitor local demands for more preaching. Those clergymen whose morals and integrity were above reproach were left alone; but their allegedly sinful colleagues were summarily removed from their livings. A fifth of the revenues of a sequestered living was awarded to the wife and children of each deposed

---

[6] J. M. Jones, 'Walter Cradock a'i Gyfoeswyr', *Y Cofiadur*, 15 (1938), p. 9.

incumbent. Most ejections occurred in south Wales: thirty-five unsuitable clergymen were unseated in Glamorgan and eighteen in Monmouthshire. Inevitably, there was only a small minority of fervent Puritans to take their place. Some 130 appointments were made to livings in Wales between 1644 and 1649, most of them godly but moderate men who were obliged to labour in harness with pluralists, opportunists, and time-servers. The great crusade had scarcely begun.

Whilst hapless clergymen were being put to flight, the military tide was turning in Parliament's favour. The royalist war effort was seriously weakened by a series of military disasters during the autumn and winter of 1644–5, and Parliament seized its opportunity to enfeeble further resistance, discredit the king's authority, and use its strategic gains as a spring-board for godly reformation. When parliamentary soldiers under the command of Sir Thomas Myddelton irresistibly surged up the Severn valley in the summer of 1644, they were accompanied by Welsh-speaking ministers sponsored by Parliament. Generous sums were set aside to enable itinerant ministers to spread the gospel and to undermine the morale of the enemy. From the summer of 1645 onwards, Walter Cradock, Richard Symonds, and Henry Walter were authorized to preach as itinerant ministers at a salary of £100 each, to be drawn from the ecclesiastical revenues of the bishoprics of St Davids and Llandaff. Three years later their counterparts in the north, Morgan Llwyd, Ambrose Mostyn, and Vavasor Powell, were commissioned on similar financial terms to win men's souls and to sap the moral and physical reserves of disillusioned royalists. No small success was achieved. People from 'far and near' pressed to hear the gospel. Walter Cradock joyfully claimed that 'the gospel is run over the mountains between Breconshire and Monmouthshire . . . as the fire in the thatch'.[7] His ardour is understandable. Glittering prizes had been won, both on and off the battlefield, but Cradock and his colleagues knew well enough that unless a more intensive spiritual campaign was mobilized the gospel would never blaze forth over the whole of Wales.

In fact, from 1646 onwards, an avalanche of petitions had been pouring into Westminster begging for scores of preaching ministers to be sent into Wales and the north of England to launch a truly powerful reformation. Clamant demands for 'saving knowledge' flow through these petitions and manifestos like heady wine. Tramping preachers were convinced that efforts to purge the church of malignant royalists and 'dumb dogs' had hitherto achieved only meagre results. Wales was still in the grip of fervent royalist clergymen, who carried out their ecclesiastical duties with

---

[7] C. Hill, 'Propagating the Gospel' in H. E. Bell and R. L. Ollard (eds.), *Historical Essays 1600–1750* (London, 1963), p. 42.

shameless lack of zeal, and 'the lax and compromising men of Meroz',[8] who cynically devoured the loaves and fishes of office. From 1643 onwards, the Assembly of Divines, a solid phalanx of Presbyterians, had attempted to impose a uniform discipline and cleanse the church of its iniquities. But its membership and resources were such that it was unable to produce the single-minded drive that would enable Puritanism to strike deep roots in the consciousness of Welsh people. As a result, more radical nostrums were being advanced by left-wing Puritans, who were out of sympathy with moderate Presbyterianism and deeply critical of the Assembly's attempts to defend the established ministry against sectarian incursions. Richard Symonds declared that Presbyterianism was 'a limb of Antichrist'.[9] In the vanguard of these radicals were former New Englanders who had been so disillusioned by the deadening theocracy established at Massachusetts that they had returned to England and Wales ablaze with enthusiasm for the campaign to liberate society in their homeland.

The most dynamic crusader in their midst was the godly Cornishman, Hugh Peter. He led the chorus of pleas for a bold, radical, and effective campaign to enlighten the rude, popish, royalist, and barren corners of the land. In April 1646, Peter preached a sermon before both Houses of Parliament to celebrate Sir Thomas Fairfax's success on the field of battle in Cornwall. He argued that the 'miserable, dark and ignorant parts' of the kingdom were 'ripe for the gospel' and that Parliament should not shrink from its duty to sow its 'timely seed' in the barren provinces by establishing an itinerant ministry and pooling tithes. Peter was shrewd enough to remind the authorities that preaching the gospel was the most effective means of winning political support in Wales: 'the people are desperately ignorant and prophane abroad: and from prophane priests and ignorant people you know the other party have fomented this war, and may begin it again, if the word prevent not the sword'.[10] John Owen, a leading Puritan divine of Welsh descent, echoed Peter's plea: 'doth not Wales cry, the north cry, yea and the west cry, "Come and help us"?'[11] Walter Cradock, too, recognized the importance of securing total political sway over Wales. In *The Saints Fulnesse of Joy*, a moving peroration preached in July 1646 to celebrate the surrender of Oxford, Cradock pleaded with Parliament to 'spend one single thought' on 'poor contemptible Wales' lest Satan should 'rage yet more then ever'.[12]

As we have seen, Parliament did respond, if half-heartedly, to these entreaties by financing small groups of itinerant ministers. But a posse of

[8] Thomas Richards, 'Nonconformity from 1620 to 1715' in J. E. Lloyd (ed.), *History of Carmarthenshire* (2 vols., Cardiff, 1939), ii. 137.

[9] T. Richards, *The Puritan Movement in Wales, 1639 to 1653* (London, 1920), p. 76.

[10] Hugh Peter, *Gods Doings, and Mans Duty* (London, 1646), pp. 43–4.

[11] C. Hill, 'Propagating the Gospel', p. 39.

[12] Walter Cradock, *The Saints Fulnesse of Joy* (London, 1646), pp. 34–5.

itinerant preaching ministers, trudging haphazardly along the Welsh borders, could never hope to overthrow Antichrist and build a new Zion. Doughty Puritan colonels, such as John Jones, Philip Jones, and Thomas Harrison, argued strongly that real progress could never be achieved among 'ignorant' and 'seduced' people unless a properly organized scheme of propagation was devised and, if need be, forcibly implemented. Such radical initiatives found scant sympathy among Welsh Presbyterians at Westminster, and troubled saints soon tired of looking to them for salvation. Both the army and radical sectarians grew more and more impatient with the dilatory ways and stodgy illiberalism of the Presbyterians. Emboldened by dazzling victories on the battlefield and fired by a burning desire to effect God's purposes, they resolved to undermine the monopoly of the Westminster divines. Pride's Purge in December 1648 and the execution of the king in the following January opened the way for long-delayed ecclesiastical reforms. Welsh Presbyterians such as Sir Thomas Myddelton, Sir Hugh Owen, and Sir Richard Wynn were removed from Westminster, thus ushering in new opportunities for radical enthusiasts to press their case for a more ambitious programme of evangelization.

Reformist zealots looked forward eagerly to the opportunity of remodelling Welsh society and lost no time in urging members of the Rump Parliament to 'sweeten your new government to the people'.[13] Major-General Thomas Harrison, a fiery millenarian and one of the leaders of the radical wing of the army, called on them to create a properly organized preaching ministry for the whole of Wales. Petitions from Wales calling for church reform strengthened his hand and the Rump eventually bowed to their demands. On 22 February 1650 Parliament passed the Act for the Better Propagation and Preaching of the Gospel in Wales. Similar acts were published around the same time for the propagation of the gospel, the advancement of learning, and the maintenance of godly ministers in Ireland, the north of England, and New England. The Act relevant to Wales closely followed the recommendations for church reform which had been advocated in Hugh Peter's *A Word for the Armie* (1647).

The Propagation Act shifted the initiative from the hands of individual Puritan missions to powerful, coercive authorities who became the instruments of the new political and religious regime. Wales was to be governed by a specially constituted commission of seventy-one members led by Thomas Harrison. Forty-three commissioners were made responsible for governing the counties of south Wales, whilst the remaining twenty-eight were to rule the northern counties. The overwhelming majority of the administrators were prominent officials who had faithfully supported Parliament's cause during the years of strife and pledged themselves to

---

[13] Blair Worden, *The Rump Parliament* (Cambridge, 1974), p. 235.

strife for a glorious reformation in church and state. English soldiers became major bulwarks of the scheme: George Twisleton of Yorkshire, John Carter of Buckinghamshire, and Hugh Courtney of Cornwall were rewarded for their devotion. Eleven commissioners hailed from the English border counties, and only two members, John Lewis of Glasgrug and James Phillips of Tre-gib, were called to represent thoroughly Welsh-speaking areas. Only a handful of traditional county families, led by Sir Erasmus Philipps of Picton Castle, Sir John Trevor of Trefalun, and John Puleston of Emral, found themselves a niche. Most commissioners were well-heeled yeomen, up-and-coming minor country squires, affluent lawyers, and local government officers. Since many of the commissioners had military and administrative duties to fulfil elsewhere, actual power and decision-making devolved into the hands of relatively small and select groups each with fifteen men in north and south Wales respectively. The most crucial decisions, however, were taken by smaller panels of six trusted and 'well-affected' men. In south Wales, the most powerful arbiters were radical squires like Philip Jones, Bussy Mansell, Rowland Dawkins, and John Price, whilst John Carter and George Twisleton held sway in the north.

The commission was empowered to act as a scourge of delinquent ministers in Wales. It was given full authority to eject clergymen for delinquency, scandal, malignancy, or non-residence, and to order pluralists to abandon all livings save one. Five or more commissioners were empowered to receive charges against clergymen wanting in piety, education, or acceptable political views, and it was possible for the accused to be condemned on the evidence of two credible witnesses. A panel of five or more would set its seal on the ejection, and a panel of twelve or more was to hear appeals. Furthermore, the Propagators were granted authority to act as commissioners for indemnity in Wales. They were empowered to hear complaints and to instruct defendants to appear before them to answer all charges. Appeals against their final decision were allowed to proceed to the parliamentary Committee of Indemnity in London.

The commissioners set about their tasks with brisk, unfussy zeal. Their brief was to rid Wales of the 'dumb dogs', drunkards, fornicators, pluralists, and malignants who had brought the ministry into disrepute. The number of ejections, and the speed with which they were carried out, varied from county to county. Appalled at finding so many people 'eaten up with ignorance through want of instruction', Hugh Peter actively assisted the commissioners to eject the unworthy in Pembrokeshire and was duly dubbed the 'bishop of Pembroke' by his enemies.[14] By October 1650, fifty clergymen had been thrust out of their livings in Pembrokeshire.

---

[14] R. P. Stearns, *The Strenuous Puritan* (Urbana, 1954), p. 362.

Within a month, Anglesey had lost most of its black sheep. In Flintshire, on the other hand, changes were slow and unremarkable. On the whole, however, the task of weeding out unworthy parsons was swiftly executed by the commissioners. Over a period of three years, 278 clergymen were deprived of their livings, 196 from south Wales and 82 from north Wales. Most of those who suffered ejection were judged guilty of moral lapses and political disaffection, and only a small minority was deemed unsuitable on religious grounds. The Propagation Act permitted the payment of a fifth of the revenue of a parish to the wife and children of an ejected clergyman. The entire ecclesiastical revenue of the church was placed in the hands of the commissioners in order to enable them to pay stipends and provide pensions. In view of the enormous financial and administrative problems confronting them, they were assisted in their tasks by county-based sequestrators and collectors who were empowered to gather in rents and profits.

The Propagation Act also established a body of Approvers to expedite the missionary campaign. Twenty-five moderate and godly ministers (including Cradock, Llwyd, Powell, and John Miles) were entrusted with the responsibility of appointing effective ministers of repute and good character to replace deprived clerics. The Approvers were men of profound Puritan convictions, but in terms of geography and background they were scarcely representative of the interests of the whole of Wales. Five counties—Anglesey, Caernarfonshire, Flintshire, Carmarthenshire, and Pembrokeshire—could not boast a single representative between them on the committee. Most members were natives of the Welsh borderland. Well-educated, moderate, and pious men, they were firmly committed to 'love, honour and receive saints *qua* saints'.[15] A determined drive was launched to recruit pious, preaching ministers. But, as in Ireland so in Wales, the Approvers were mortified to find that in spite of the prospect of a plenteous harvest the labourers were few. The number of candidates capable of passing muster proved small. Wales was not well-stocked with bountiful livings and many able and well-educated candidates, especially those who were unable to preach in Welsh, chose to reveal their talents in more lucrative benefices in south-east England. Many university graduates also judged that propagating the gospel in the dark corners of northern England was a less daunting prospect than bringing the light of the gospel to Welsh-speaking unbelievers. Recruiting settled ministers in Wales thus proved a painfully slow process; so slow that it became necessary to employ itinerant ministers to preach from parish to parish. In all, some ninety itinerant ministers, on salaries of £100 per annum, were at work in Wales during the Propagation years. Lay preachers, granted salaries of between

[15] Walter Cradock, *The Saints Fulnesse of Joy*, p. 3.

£17 and £24 per annum, were also allowed to minister in the more needy areas. The overwhelming majority of the evangelists preached in south Wales and along the borders. No more than a dozen were employed in north Wales.

Yet there were clearly powerful and creative influences at work in Wales during the Propagation period. The itinerant ministers, endowed with superb self-confidence, the gift of eloquence, and boundless energy, viewed their mission as nothing less than a spiritual renewal. Many of them attracted large audiences who were fascinated by their dexterous ability to interpret abstruse texts and unfold the mysteries of the gospel. The Propagators were imbued with 'a vital rage for utterance',[16] and there can be no doubt that they communicated far more directly and intimately with the people than the resident clergy had done under the early Stuarts. Vavasor Powell declared that he would rather preach one sermon than publish a thousand books. He and some of his colleagues often threatened to rupture the ear-drums of 'good men with their raucous preaching'.[17] Powell was evidently the driving force behind the Propagators and his sworn enemy, Alexander Griffith, dubbed him the 'metropolitan of the itinerants'.[18] His travels took him regularly through the counties of Montgomery, Radnor, and Brecon, and it was not uncommon for him to preach two or three times a day, often to captive audiences in churchyards, fairs, and markets. His colleagues strove hard to meet his exacting standards. Ambrose Mostyn flung himself wholeheartedly into the task of planting the gospel in Denbighshire and Montgomeryshire, while Henry Walter laboured without stint in the valleys of Glamorgan and Monmouthshire. Spurning sleep and defying enemies, Walter Cradock tramped up and down the Wye valley. Although Morgan Llwyd was based in Wrexham, he thought nothing of travelling as far as the Llŷn peninsula to exhort his countrymen to search their hearts for signs of divine grace. According to the eighteenth-century Welsh Methodist, Robert Jones of Rhos-lan, Llwyd used to preach at Pwllheli on market days, striding through the market brandishing a Bible, 'and the people would retreat before him, as though a chariot were rushing through the streets'.[19] Well-established saints such as these were also joined by talented young preachers and scholars like Charles Edwards, Richard Jones, and Jonathan Roberts, who would provide Welsh Dissent with much of its lustre and resolve during the persecution of later years.

In many ways, the Propagation period was the fulfilment of the aspirations and dreams of two generations of Welsh Puritans. John Penry's

---

[16] William Haller, *The Rise of Puritanism* (New York, 1938), Chapter 4.

[17] T. Richards, *Religious Developments in Wales 1654–1662* (London, 1923), p. 189.

[18] Alexander Griffith, *Strena Vavasoriensis* (London, 1654), title-page.

[19] Robert Jones, *Drych yr Amseroedd*, ed. G. M. Ashton (Cardiff, 1958), p. 3.

pleas in the 1580s that the 'public wants' of Wales be recognized were answered, for the state had acknowledged the need to throw its weight behind a powerful evangelical campaign in the dark corners. The exuberant self-confidence of the Propagators led them to eulogize their campaign and achievements. Having nursed the scheme through its embryonic stages into life and dedicated themselves to the task of seeing it grow, it was natural for them to sing its merits. 'Hath any generation since the Apostles' days had such powerful preachers and plenty of preaching as this generation?', asked Vavasor Powell. Oliver Cromwell himself believed that the preaching ministers had achieved brilliant success: God, he claimed, had kindled a seed in Wales 'hardly to be paralleled since the primitive times'.[20]

Powerful preaching was not the only means by which the Propagators hoped to win people's hearts. The Act also called for the extension of education. In spite of the charitable missions activated by Puritan merchants in the pre-war period, educational facilities, particularly for the poor, were appallingly sparse and inadequate in Wales. The grammar schools established in market towns catered mainly for the needs and aspirations of the sons of the lesser gentry and well-to-do yeomen. But the state's attitude towards popular education changed during the Interregnum. Scores of new elementary schools were founded in England, and the precepts of educational reformers, such as Dury, Hartlib, and Winstanley, helped to crystallize men's ideas about universal elementary education. Radical Puritans argued that the location of grammar schools was arbitrary and that their clientele was highly selective. More effort, they insisted, should be invested in educating humbler sorts. The Propagators were determined to dispel 'ignorance and profaneness' among the rising generation. Funds drawn from the sequestered revenues of the church enabled them to set up sixty-three schools in the larger towns and market centres of Wales. The distribution of these schools reflected the relative strength of the Puritan cause in Wales. Thirty-seven schools were established in the south, and twenty-six in the north. The border counties were better served than the western shires, where the Welsh language predominated. Schools were free and open to both sexes. Schoolmasters were paid a salary of some £20 or more per annum and were obliged to teach reading, writing, and arithmetic through the medium of the English tongue. In outlawing the Welsh language, Puritans were continuing a tradition, begun by Tudor grammar schools, which was to persist until the days of Griffith Jones, Llanddowror. Most schoolmasters were avowed Puritans, bent on inculcating the highest standards of moral probity in their pupils. Although a dearth of properly qualified masters led to a

[20] C. Hill, 'Propagating the Gospel', pp. 45-6.

deterioration in the quality of teaching and also in the number of schools after 1653, this scheme was noteworthy in that it represented the first attempt by the state to establish a subsidized system of primary education in Wales.

   In spite of the undoubted achievements of the Propagators in preaching the word and educating the poor, it is difficult to resist the impression that the Act promised more than it delivered. Almost from its inception, glaring deficiencies came to the surface and threatened to bring the well-laid plans of the Propagators to naught. The operation of the Act provoked bitter controversy and the administrators were forced to carry out their daily tasks amid a multitude of rumours, accusations, and animosities. Not surprisingly, deprived clergymen and affronted gentlemen worked in harness to thwart Puritan ambitions. The most unremitting foe of the Propagators who has left his views on record was Alexander Griffith, a clergyman who had been ejected from his livings at Glasbury and Llanwnnog in mid-Wales. A prickly, embittered man, he claimed that wholesale ejections had reduced the clergy to poverty and created a famine of the word, that the tramping itinerants were ignorant tinkers and rogues, that their insolent self-assurance had alienated the natural rulers of society, that Propagation was simply a cloak for personal and party advancement, and that its instruments had felt no compunction about forcing their principles down the throats of unwilling people. In almost all the hostile propaganda, Vavasor Powell was singled out for vilification. Alexander Griffith nursed an obsessional hatred of him and vented his spleen upon Powell in a series of petitions and defamatory tracts. The most vivid of these is *Strena Vavasoriensis* (1654), a catalogue of Powell's infamous deeds. Although it was hastily cobbled together by Griffith and his colleagues, scarcely a page is without a bitter and sharply etched vignette of Powell's villainies. In furious tirades of recrimination and revenge, Griffith claimed that Powell's professed aim was 'the destruction of the magistracy of England, as well as the ministry of Wales'.[21] He insisted that Powell had preached false doctrines and obscenities, vilified lawyers and clergymen, and oppressed widows, bailiffs, and gentlemen. Griffith's vitriolic attacks prompted Powell's friends and supporters, Edward Allen, John Griffith, James Quarrell, and Charles Lloyd, to publish *Vavasoris Examen et Purgamen* (1654), in which they attempted to expunge Powell's caluminators' 'monstrous draught' and draw out their hero 'in his proper colours'.[22]

   Although Alexander Griffith was no stranger to hyperbole and untruth, his criticisms of the Propagation Act, its operation, and its consequences were not without some foundation. He was right, for instance, to make the

---

[21] *Strena Vavasoriensis*, p. 5.
[22] Edward Allen and others, *Vavasoris Examen et Purgamen* (London, 1654), *passim*.

point that the lot of the ejected clergy and their dependants was hard. Prompt and regular payment of fifths to wives and children was not always forthcoming, and as a result many clergymen were forced to seek alternative means of subsistence. Some migrated to London, others remained in their parishes. Some earned a pittance by keeping 'petty' schools, whilst a handful found positions of trust as chaplains and tutors in country houses. A minority was reduced to a condition of extreme destitution and pathos. Nathan Jones of Merthyr, who was married with seven children, claimed that he had 'scarce a herb or root to dine or sup withal'.[23] Although few of them were harassed, theirs was an uneasy and deeply gloomy existence. The bravest of them continued to preach openly, whilst the more timid conducted services by stealth in private homes. A strong bond existed between them and their parishioners, a bond which Puritan newcomers failed to sever completely.

The sense of spiritual deprivation and desolation which overtook deprived clerics is best conveyed by Welsh poets. Tossed and buffeted by personal crises, appalled by the destruction of revered institutions, they aired their heavy affliction in verse. Rowland Watkyns, ejected from his living at Llanfrynach, chafed miserably:

> I like a sparrow on the house alone
> Do sit, and like a dove I mourn and groan.[24]

Henry Vaughan, Silurist, author of *Silex Scintillans* (1650), composed his finest religious verse in the wake of two cruel blows which shook him to the core: the death of his brother, William, during the Second Civil War, and the execution of the king. The fruit of his intense grief was a powerful religious experience and a poetical rebirth. Repining in solitude, he yearned for an end to the 'sad captivity' of his day. Puritan soldiers and itinerants had brought nothing but discord and vexation, and Vaughan longed to discover the 'sweet peace' which adorned the country 'far beyond the stars'. In the preface to *Flores Solitudinis* (1654), written in April 1652, he wrote poignantly 'out of a land of darkness, out of that unfortunate region, where the inhabitants sit in the shadow of death: where destruction passeth for propagation'.[25] Jeremy Taylor, too, conveys the sense of desolation felt by beleaguered churchmen in eloquent meditative prose. In 1645 Taylor had been captured by parliamentary troops at Cardigan, and following his release he became domestic chaplain to Richard Vaughan, earl of Carbery, at Golden Grove, Carmarthenshire. He remained at the Carbery home for ten years, profoundly disillusioned by the calamities of

---

[23] Charles Wilkins, *The History of Merthyr Tydfil* (Merthyr, 1908), p. 302.
[24] Rowland Watkyns, *Flamma Sine Fumo*, p. 103.
[25] A. Rudrum, *Henry Vaughan: The Complete Poems*, pp. 185–6; L. C. Martin (ed.), *The Works of Henry Vaughan* (2nd edn., Oxford, 1968), p. 217.

the age. During this period he composed his most popular books of devotion, *Holy Living* (1650) and *Holy Dying* (1651), both characteristically couched in limpid, sober prose designed to help readers to achieve holiness of life. In spite of the privations and humiliations suffered by the clergy, therefore, the Propagation period witnessed an efflorescence of High Anglican apologetic and propaganda. Churchmen were acutely conscious that they were living in perilous times. Since there were no indications that republican rule would be but a brief experiment, it was vitally important that the rites, ceremonies, and practices of the established church should not be allowed to fade away from people's minds and hearts. Appalled by the prospect of seeing the true practice of religion disappearing for ever, they supplied their scattered sheep with the essentials of Christian faith and piety.

The second charge levelled against the Propagators was that, having purged the church of its pastors, they had failed to find adequate replacements to minister to the spiritual needs of the people. The widespread use of itinerant ministers proved inadequate and often invited gibes such as 'the sinecure rector makes room for the fleeting preacher'.[26] There were frequent complaints that parishes were being woefully neglected. Many vacant livings in north Wales were left unfilled. Parliamentary officials at Brecon in October 1651 claimed that there were only two settled preaching ministers in the whole of the county. In 1654, Anthony Ashley Cooper travelled through Wales and found 'churches all unsupplied, except a few grocers or such persons that have formerly served for two years'.[27] In the same year, Alexander Griffith insisted that 700 parishes had been deprived of a resident minister and that a man could ride ten or twenty miles on the Sabbath and find twenty churches closed to worshippers. Although we may discount Griffith's wilder flights of fancy, it is none the less evident that, in many areas, wholesale rejection of clergymen had resulted in no ministry at all.

The elevation of 'lay ignoramuses and schismaticks' to the pulpit was deeply repugnant to churchmen. Their social background, unconventional methods, and style of preaching evoked unease and resentment among those who had traditionally occupied a position of leadership within society. In some places, unruly mobs were encouraged to upbraid, heckle, and beat the itinerants. At Dolgellau, a 'gifted brother'[28] was violently dragged from the pulpit and pummelled. Anglicized elements poured scorn on the Propagators for 'eternally thundering out in the ancient British tongue'.[29] Men of taste and discernment looked askance at their lack of

[26] David Walker (ed.), *A History of the Church in Wales* (Penarth, 1976), p. 76.
[27] C. Hill, *The World Turned Upside Down* (Penguin Books, 1975), p. 76.
[28] T. Richards, *Puritan Movement*, p. 174.
[29] *Hen Gerddi Gwleidyddol*, p. 28.

learning and poise. Widely reviled as 'hackney preachers' and 'journeymen pedlars', itinerant ministers became the butt of calumny and scorn. 'Preach they cannot unless they be sent', declared Nathan Jones of Merthyr, 'and teach they cannot what they never learnt.'[30] A rash of songs and pamphlets portrayed the itinerants beating the pulpit, frothing at the mouth, and twisting their tongues around unfathomable doctrines. A Wrexham Puritan was said to leap so feverishly from chapter to chapter in the Bible that his neck looked like 'a wrested text'.[31] Few believed that such firebrands were fit to teach and preach. Rowland Watkyns bewailed the emergence of the 'mechanic itinerants':

> The tinker being one of excellent mettle
> Begins to sound his doctrine with his kettle.
> And the laborious ploughman I bewail,
> Who now doth thresh the pulpit with his flail.[32]

'We are now', claimed Rowland Vaughan, 'in the hands of Alexander the blacksmith, Tom the mason and Dic the spayer.'[33] It is easy to imagine the chagrin felt by the judges and officials of the Court of Great Sessions who, clad in their finery in Beaumaris church, found that the Assize sermon was to be delivered by Benjamin, the local blacksmith. Such, in epitome, was the Welsh version of the world turned upside down.

Those who showered most contempt upon itinerant ministers were propertied men. Their sneers were born of fear. For many generations they had fulfilled their God-given roles as the natural rulers of society, and their social and political pre-eminence had never been questioned. The church, in their eyes, was a valuable buttress of the social order and it was only right that the dignity and the property of its clergy be safeguarded. The elevation of 'base men' to the pulpit filled them with dread and their apprehension led to constant gibes about the social origins and educational attainments of the 'mechanic preachers'. They might, it was claimed, bellow loudly in market-places, but their pedigrees were as threadbare as their sermons. How much truth lay in these deeply rooted prejudices is hard to tell. It is true that John Lewis, Glasgrug, nursed misgivings about dispatching inexperienced young men to the barren corners and that Richard Baxter was later to meet a former itinerant with whom it grieved him to converse. But what churchmen refused to acknowledge was that 'mechanic preachers' believed that they had been called to preach the gospel. The snobbish fulminations of dyed-in-the-wool churchmen roused the

[30] C. Wilkins, *History of Merthyr Tydfil*, p. 299.
[31] T. Richards, *Puritan Movement*, p. 174.
[32] Rowland Watkyns, *Flamma Sine Fumo*, p. 44.
[33] Rowland Vaughan, *Pregeth yn erbyn Schism* (London, 1658), p. 14.

Propagators to righteous indignation. They believed that the revolutionary decades had released in humble men energies and talents which would otherwise have remained latent or been frustrated. Walter Cradock was prepared to defend to the last the right of uneducated men to preach the gospel: 'hath he the spirit, or no?'[34] was the litmus test which he invariably applied in assessing candidates for the ministry. Morgan Llwyd likewise believed strongly in a calling open to all talents, whilst Vavasor Powell was moved to defend the right of godly men to exercise their gifts, especially since resident clergymen were content to keep 'poor alehouses in the mountains, where they and the people spend together the greatest part of the Sabbath in profaneness'.[35] Colonel John Jones was equally scathing towards 'dumb dogs' who were idle and silent: 'how many are there in poor Wales that think God sufficiently served by going once a week to hear a huddle of prayers delivered many times by a poor creature whose mind is in his alehouse, or rather in hell'.[36] Far better, he and fellow Puritans insisted, that Welshmen should be served by conscientious ministers who were rooted in the true faith.

Much of the abuse and odium heaped upon itinerants of humble stock was also the direct result of the allegedly offensive social doctrines which they drummed out from the pulpit. Itinerant ministers were singularly free from the social and political inhibitions which characterized and sometimes fettered resident clergymen. Powerful gentlemen were convinced that peripatetic preachers and middling sorts were threatening their hegemony. Their message was anything but other-worldly and much of what they had to say was extremely unwelcome to the establishment. John Miles bitterly denounced rapacious landlords and heartless usurers. Morgan Llwyd berated lawyers and priests, venting his spleen, too, on gentry, 'who lick up the very sweat of the poor, causing your tenants to groan and crushing their very bones'. Llwyd hoped that a more equitable distribution of land would ensure that 'no poor man shall have too little, nor the rich too much'.[37] Vavasor Powell informed the parishioners of Llansanffraid, Radnorshire, that all lawyers were 'thieves and pick-purses'.[38] William Erbery championed the lot of the poor, and in particular the plight of debtors and prisoners. In a petition on behalf of the poor inhabitants of Cardiff in July 1652, Erbery urged Oliver Cromwell to 'break in pieces the oppressor . . . [and] to relieve poor families with bread' by abolishing tithes and sharing out spoils gained from sequestered lands.[39] In sermons preached at Newport and

[34] G. F. Nuttall, *The Puritan Spirit* (London, 1967), p. 121.
[35] Thomas Rees, *History of Protestant Nonconformity in Wales* (2nd edn., London, 1883), p. 85.
[36] NLW MS 11440D, f. 123.   [37] *Gweithiau*, i. 237–8.
[38] *Mercurius Cambro-Britannicus* (London, 1652), p. 6.
[39] J. Nickolls, *Original Letters and State Papers Addressed to Oliver Cromwell* (London, 1743), p. 88.

Cardiff, Erbery told the poor that lawyers and clergymen 'oppress and plague the souls and states of men'.[40] To Welsh gentlemen and clergymen who lived in suspicious dread of the wretched multitude, such ideas not only challenged the concept of a state church but also threatened to undermine the social hierarchy.

One of the shrillest anti-Propagation cries was that the commissioners had feathered their own nests while religion decayed. This allegation found focus in a petition presented by Colonel Edward Freeman, Attorney-General of south Wales, and John Gunter, a lawyer of Tredomen, Breconshire, to Parliament in March 1652. Both petitioners ('prejudicated persons', according to Vavasor Powell) harboured personal grievances but claimed to represent the sentiments of 15,000 disaffected citizens in south Wales. The petitioners charged the Propagators, *inter alia*, with gross neglect, misappropriation of tithe revenues, and maldistribution of sequestered livings. There is no doubt that controlling the purse-strings proved a major problem for the commissioners. Collecting tithes and revenues was a cumbersome and time-consuming process, and the opponents of the regime were swift to notice that large sums of money remained unaccounted for. The Propagators were condemned by their adversaries as vulgar adventurers in pursuit of selfish ends. *Mercurius Cambro-Britannicus* (1652) claimed that the so-called Propagation of the Gospel was in fact 'a propagation of land and money', and went on to mock the godly party's new attire of 'rich scarlet and plush'.[41] Huw Morys bitterly castigated saints who 'played for bishops' sheaves':

> You saw, your honour, each one of the committee
> With the churches' rents on his sleeve.[42]

The rancorous Alexander Griffith alleged that the Propagators had disposed of £40,000 annually over a period of three years. Vavasor Powell and Hugh Peter were accused of having divided Propagation funds into two 'halves for themselves'[43] and of having bestowed their favours on ignorant sycophants and hypocrites.

It was widely agreed among gentry and clergy alike, however, that the main culprit was Colonel Philip Jones. A man such as he who had risen to high office and amassed lands so swiftly was bound to find himself under suspicion of having availed himself of every means of diverting money to his own advantage. The Welsh gentry laid about Philip Jones with obvious relish, portraying him as a vulgar peculator who had risen from obscurity by stealthily filching public moneys. Although many of the allegations

---

[40] *The Testimony of William Erbery* (London, 1652), pp. 152–82.
[41] *Mercurius Cambro-Britannicus*, pp. 6–7.
[42] D. Jenkins, 'Bywyd a Gwaith Huw Morys', p. 388.
[43] R. P. Stearns, *The Strenuous Puritan*, p. 362 n.

made against the Propagation commissioners in general, and Philip Jones in particular, were scurrilous, there is little doubt that the financial administration of the campaign had been both irregular and arbitrary. The anti-Propagation case advanced by the petitioners from south Wales was weakened by its heavy reliance on the partisan testimony of embittered clerics and aggrieved gentlemen. Many of their wilder charges were clearly based on gossip, hearsay, and rumour. The Committee for Plundered Ministers, which examined each allegation meticulously, exonerated Philip Jones from all blame and found no evidence of peculation or maladministration on the part of the commissioners. Philip Jones's keen eye for the main chance did not fail him: he ordered the arrest of the petitioners Gunter and Freeman, and the latter was later deprived of his post as Attorney-General of south Wales. The whispers and rumours proved harder to scotch and, from time to time throughout the Interregnum, voices were raised implying that Philip Jones had abused his public commission for private gain. In May 1659, Bledry Morgan, a former treasurer of sequestrations in Carmarthenshire, presented a petition to Parliament containing twenty detailed charges against Jones on behalf of many 'oppressed' citizens. Jones vigorously denied the accusations but prudently chose to retire from the political scene soon after May 1659. Undeterred, Bledry Morgan and his colleagues persisted with their campaign, and further exhaustive inquiries into the dealings of the Propagation commission were launched following the Restoration. By then, however, most commissioners had covered their tracks successfully and allegations of misconduct were never fully substantiated.

The final objection of the anti-Propagation lobby carries more weight. Wales, they insisted, was occupied territory, manned by a military middle-class. Their countrymen groaned under the yoke of armed rule. Some of the views advocated by leading Welsh saints lend substance to this charge. 'I had rather do a people good though against their wills, than please them in show only',[44] claimed Colonel John Jones, Maesygarnedd. He was prepared to liberate Welshmen from the fetters of superstition, sin, and neglect, by the use of military force if necessary. In his view, oppression, though cruel in the short term, would be seen to be kind and beneficial in the long term. Self-appointed servants of God believed themselves duty-bound to enlighten their benighted brethren by fair means or foul, and John Owen was later to confess ruefully that the Welsh Propagators had tended to impose their ideas by forcible means. It was clearly difficult for former Roundheads to shed martial postures when spreading the gospel among sullen and uncooperative people. Rightly or wrongly, Vavasor Powell's name was inextricably linked in Anglican minds with the use of

[44] C. Hill, 'Propagating the Gospel', p. 53.

the sword. Some of his most outrageous *obiter dicta* were long remembered by his enemies, many of whom had felt the rough side of his tongue. Likewise, Jenkin Jones, the militant Puritan of Llanddeti, won himself a place of singular unpopularity: his ways of hectoring and drilling the recalcitrant were judged especially obnoxious. Heavy-handed sequestrators and tax-collectors were widely despised. Edward Davies of Eglwysegle's blue coat and predatory hand earned him the nickname *y cneifiwr glas* (the blue shearer), while Jenkin Williams of east Glamorgan was believed to be capable of 'every villainy and barbarity'.[45] Even so, the excessive zeal which animated the Propagators was clearly over-coloured by partisan witnesses. To liken the Propagators to shameless brigands, badgering and bullying the ungodly at the point of a sword, is a travesty of the truth, and it must be said that Alexander Griffith's poisonous pen produced a caricature of the Welsh saints. The instruments of the Propagation in Wales, fired by the belief that they were fulfilling God's purposes, dedicated themselves to winning men's souls. There are no Welsh parallels to the infamous behaviour of Cromwell's troops in Ireland.

For a variety of reasons, the Rump chose not to renew the Propagation's commission in April 1653. But state-subsidizing of Puritanism did not perish in its wake. It now took on a different aspect, shedding its martial image and adopting a centralized approach to the religious problems of Wales. On 20 March 1654 the task of approving and appointing settled ministers was entrusted to the Commission for the Approbation of Publicque Preachers. Popularly known as the Triers, they constituted a body of thirty-eight worthy and distinguished ministers and laymen based in London. Two members only—Walter Cradock and Jenkin Griffiths—were Welsh. The itinerant system was allowed to lapse and every effort was now made to appoint men to settled livings. Four 'Receivers of Wales' were appointed, charged with collecting arrears of rents and profits from ecclesiastical and sequestered revenues in order that appointed ministers might be adequately paid. It was hoped to maintain ministers at an annual salary of £100, but few incumbents received as much and most had to make do with considerably less. Plans were also laid, but not fulfilled to any enduring degree, to unite small parishes and to divide and redistribute larger parishes in order to ease the problem of maldistribution of wealth and the lack of preachers.

The success of the venture depended largely on the enthusiasm and commitment of erstwhile itinerants who now found themselves in settled livings. But recruiting fresh faces still remained a problem, and some measure of pluralism was inevitable. Fashioning a collection of promising, but scarce, parts into a convincing whole was a daunting task. Indeed, it eventually proved impossible to abandon the old itinerant procedure completely. The rigorous standards applied by the Triers also narrowed the field of likely candidates. No minister might enter a living without their permission and no patron could install his own nominee without their consent. Inordinate emphasis was placed on securing watertight testimonials to the character of candidates: no one was admitted to a living unless his testimony was signed by at least three men of known godliness and integrity, including a settled minister. Even so, men of quality were recruited, and Richard Baxter rightly paid tribute to the Triers for saving many congregations from 'ignorant, ungodly, drunken teachers'. 'Many thousands of souls', he claimed, 'blessed God for the faithful ministers whom they let in.'[46] Among the most prominent were Marmaduke Matthews, who settled at St John's-iuxta-Swansea, Evan Roberts, who was appointed to Llanbadarn Fawr, Walter Cradock, who took up the living of Usk, and Henry Walter, who put down roots at Newport. James Davies at Merthyr, Stephen Hughes at Meidrim, and William Jones at Cilymaenllwyd were other gifted preachers who would figure prominently in the history of Welsh Dissent after the Restoration.

Other fertile schemes were mooted at this time in order to invigorate the Puritan campaign. The problem of recruiting able ministers provoked John Lewis, the Puritan squire of Glasgrug, Dr John Ellis of Dolgellau, and Richard Baxter, the Kidderminster divine, to discuss plans to establish a Welsh college in order to create 'a supply of able ministers'. John Lewis feared that the 'raw simple younglings' now being sent into remote parts of Wales were not intellectually equipped to wage a convincing campaign. The towns of Shrewsbury, Machynlleth, Aberystwyth, and Cardigan were all mooted as likely sites for the proposed college, and although the correspondents were well aware that their scheme was fraught with financial problems they believed that 'God can make way through all difficulties'.[47] But Cromwell's Protectorate was riven with so many constitutional and fiscal problems that this praiseworthy scheme virtually died of inanition. More important were the efforts made to provide Welshmen with bibles in their own tongue. Two editions of the Welsh New Testament had already been published in 1646–7, and Walter Cradock and Vavasor Powell were so moved by their countrymen's cries for bibles that an edition of 6,000 copies of 'Cromwell's Bible', as it was called, was

---

[46] *The Autobiography of Richard Baxter*, ed. J. M. Lloyd Thomas (London, 1925), pp. 70–1.

[47] G. F. Nuttall, 'The Correspondence of John Lewis, Glasgrug, with Richard Baxter and with Dr. John Ellis, Dolgellau', *Journal Merioneth Hist. and Record Soc.* 2 (1953–6), pp. 120–34.

published in 1654. This was by far the largest edition of the Scriptures hitherto published in Welsh.

The growth of Puritanism in Wales during the revolutionary period was not by any means wholly dependent on state initiatives. During the years after 1640, Puritanism broke into fragments and a multitude of radical sects emerged. Relishing their new freedom, they preached a wide range of radical doctrines and ideas. Books, pamphlets, and sermons poured from the presses. Unfettered by age-old constraints, sectarians aired their views on such burning questions as tithes, the state church and its ministry, the legal system, economic privations, the nature of the franchise, and any other subject which caught their fancy. The sects derived their inspiration directly from the Holy Spirit and were convinced that religious truth was revealed through grace and faith. They interpreted the Bible for themselves and campaigned strongly for liberty of conscience. No longer content to tarry for the magistrate, they were determined never to allow new presbyter to replace old priest. Presbyterians strove vainly to preserve their power and privilege against the rising tide of radical sectarianism. Sir Thomas Myddelton of Chirk was so concerned by the upsurge of sectarianism that he invited William Lilly, the most eminent English astrologer of the day, to calculate the likelihood of Presbyterianism enduring as the national religion. Similarly, the way in which mechanic preachers waged war on gentry, lawyers, doctors, clergymen, and university teachers filled the propertied classes with dread. James Howell doubted the sanity of tub-preachers: 'there's a worm got into their tongues as well as their heads', he declared.[48] Men of property were convinced that 'anarchical confusions and fearful calamities' would accompany the emergence of 'the giddy-headed multitude'. Rowland Watkyns threw up his hands in despair:

> Now in the temple every saucy Jack
> Opens his shop, and shews his pedlar's pack.[49]

Given the mobility of itinerant preachers and army chaplains, it was inevitable that many sects, together with their radical ideas, would take root in Wales. The most active and numerous Welsh saints were the Congregationalists, who rejected the arid rigidities of Presbyterianism and worked to establish a loose alliance of gathered congregations bound together by the fellowship of the Spirit. In Ulster, the Scottish Covenanters ensured that Presbyterianism established deep and tenacious roots, but in Wales the Congregational church order was the polity which commended itself to the Approvers who operated under the Propagation Act. Little

---

[48] James Howell, *A New Volume of Familiar Letters* (London, 1650), p. 47.
[49] Rowland Watkyns, *Flamma Sine Fumo*, p. 43.

sympathy was apparent for conventional Presbyterianism, and it is significant that when Philip Henry settled in Flintshire in September 1653 as tutor to the children of Judge Puleston at Emral and preacher in the chapel of Worthenbury, he chose to convey the essentials of Presbyterianism in a softer, more moderate way. Congregational churches in Wales were scattered, loosely knit affairs, dependent on the organizing genius of men like Vavasor Powell, Morgan Llwyd, Walter Cradock, and Jenkin Jones. Influential laymen were also key patrons. Colonel Philip Jones of Swansea used his considerable political influence to fortify Puritan causes in Glamorgan. In Caernarfonshire, minor gentlemen imbibed Puritan doctrines and sheltered preachers: Richard Edwards of Nanhoron succoured the Puritan minister, Henry Maurice, while Jeffrey Parry of Rhydolion in Llanengan, a former Roundhead cornet, was an enthusiastic tub-thumper known to all and sundry as 'a great heaven-driver in Llŷn'.[50] Tiny cells of visible saints thus met in private houses for mutual edification. Setting themselves apart from the unregenerate, they drew up appropriate rules and regulations in order to preserve their autonomy and unity.

Among the most vigorous and enterprising of the sects which emerged in Wales during these convulsive years were the Baptists. During the Civil War, army preachers had peddled Baptist doctrines along the Welsh borders. In 1646, a soldier was accused of preaching and dipping in Breconshire and Radnorshire, 'where he hath vented many doctrines of Antinomianism and Anabaptism and rebaptized hundreds in those counties'.[51] But the real Baptist thrust came when John Miles, a native of Newton Clifford in the Welsh-speaking part of Herefordshire, was dispatched to south Wales in 1649 to launch a missionary campaign on behalf of the Baptist cause. His energy and drive soon bore fruit. By October, Miles had established the first Particular Baptist church in Wales 'according to the primitive pattern' at Ilston, near Swansea. Soon he began to cast his net more widely. Early in 1650 Miles tempted several members among the Congregationalists of Llanigon in Breconshire to form a Baptist church at Hay-on-Wye. Llanharan in Glamorgan became the third 'golden candlestick set up in those parts'. In January 1651 a 'city of God' was established at 'Satan's seat' in Carmarthen, and by August 1652 thirteen Baptists were breaking bread together at Abergavenny in Monmouthshire.[52] All five churches were uncompromisingly Calvinist, insisting upon the principles of adult baptism and closed communion.

From 1654 onwards, Baptist church organization began to crystallize. A triumvirate, comprising a pastor, a teacher, and 'ordinary prophets', took on the burden of ministering to, and educating, Baptist flocks. Church

[50] A. H. Dodd, *History of Caerns.*, p. 144.
[51] T. M. Bassett, *The Welsh Baptists* (Swansea, 1977), p. 14.
[52] Mansel John (ed.), *Welsh Baptist Studies* (Llandysul, 1976), pp. 35-71.

discipline was entrusted to ruling elders and deacons. At Ilston, weekly meetings were held in the parish church on Wednesday at nine in the morning. Communion was held every third week. Sunday services were conducted at eight in winter and an hour earlier in summer. 'Ordinary prophets' held the reins during the first hour and non-members were excluded until the second hour, when they were ministered to by teachers and prophets. A third session was administered by Miles himself or one of his nominees. Miles's primary aim was to nurture effective preaching ministers and to promote united fellowship. He brooked no opposition to his plans and vigilantly ensured that no Antinomian blight was allowed to blemish Baptist vineyards. If he was rigorous in his enforcement of Baptist orthodoxy, he was also tireless in his efforts to persuade discordant brethren of the errors of their ways. Discipline was strict and uncompromising. Sinners were admonished and censured publicly, and if they remained manifestly unrepentant they were excommunicated.

The Baptist cause was not entirely dependent on John Miles's vigorous missionary campaigns. During the Propagation period, the Baptists made inroads into the border counties of Wales. The Congregational churches established in Montgomeryshire and Radnorshire by Vavasor Powell included Baptist members. Churches established by Jenkin Jones of Llanddeti and William Thomas of Llangwm practised open membership, that is, they practised believers' baptism but favoured free communion. Baptist churches were generally organized on lines similar to those of the Congregational churches. Churches covered a wide expanse of territory, and members were obliged to travel long distances to worship. The members at Hay-on-Wye, for instance, hailed from the area stretching from Olchon in Herefordshire to Llan-gors in Breconshire. Special arrangements were often implemented in order to accommodate those who lived far from Baptist focal points. Other problems also furrowed the brows of Baptist leaders. Finding adequate ministers to serve the spiritual needs of scattered Baptist flocks was a perennial source of anxiety. There were violent disagreements, too, over accepting public maintenance from the state. Unlike Miles, the overwhelming majority of Welsh Baptists bitterly opposed wedding themselves to the Cromwellian state church. In July 1655, the Abergavenny church resolved to 'withdraw from all such ministers that do receive maintenance from the magistrate',[53] and other churches loudly protested against the necessity of paying tithes and church rates. A host of diverse opinions raged among Welsh Baptists, and several wounding vendettas were waged both orally and in print.

The overwhelming majority of Welsh Presbyterians, Congregationalists, and Baptists subscribed to the orthodox Calvinist doctrines enshrined in

[53] Ibid., p. 64.

the Westminster Confession. Although John Calvin's rigorous doctrine of predestination was no longer preached in rigid fashion, it was still a basic tenet of the Puritan faith that a minority of men and women—the elect—had been chosen by God to live for ever, whereas the reprobate were foredoomed to eternal damnation. As the 1640s wore on, however, orthodox Calvinists were increasingly troubled by a host of heretical and divisive doctrines, most of which were faithfully recorded in Thomas Edwards's *Gangraena* in 1646. Turbulent and licentious Antinomians claimed that they had achieved assurance of salvation solely by the free gift of God's grace. They felt no need to obey the moral code, for they were free of sin. Some of these beliefs, widely canvassed in the taverns and alehouses of London, were also aired in Wales. At Merthyr, a group of Ranters publicly disdained the Puritan moral code and made their parson's life a misery. According to his biased testimony, they were strongly opposed to the clergy and the payment of tithes, and he alleged that they gathered together in the parish church on Sundays and weekdays to smoke tobacco, drink beer, sing rude songs, and indulge in blasphemous levity and profaneness. In their eyes, sin had no meaning. Heaven and Hell were simply a state of mind. Individuals elsewhere also anathematized strict Calvinism and rejected all visible forms and constitutions. In John Miles's Baptist church at Ilston, Colonel Thomas Bowen invited opprobrium by proclaiming that Heaven and Hell, and God and the Devil, simply did not exist. In 1655, Henry Hake, a humble corvisor of Haverfordwest and a man with a reputation for heretical views, was accused of declaring that 'God would not nor could not forgive a sinner'.[54] A small, but often vocal, minority was not loath to deny the essential tenets of the Calvinist faith.

The most bitter foe of orthodox Calvinists, however, was William Erbery. Ever since his ejection from his living in Cardiff in 1638, Erbery had earned notoriety as an individualist, if not a maverick. He absorbed radical ideals in the company of army chaplains like John Saltmarsh and William Sedgwick, he read the ideas of Brightman and Boehme, and picked up many subversive notions in the alehouses of London. The *enfant terrible* of the Welsh saints, Erbery became the scourge of Presbyterians and Congregationalists alike, preaching free grace and scorning Calvinist theology. 'The Presbyterians called the Independent churches whore', he declared, 'and the Independents called them whore again; and I say they are all whores together.'[55] He was even more hostile towards the established church and its 'antichristian' clergy. Erbery deeply regretted having been in receipt of public maintenance, claiming that God had driven him to near distraction for his cupidity. 'I then laboured to be rich', he said in 1652, 'I now learn to be poor.' Wales, he feared, was a 'poor

---

[54] Francis Jones, 'Disaffection and Dissent in Pembrokeshire', *THSC* (1946–7), p. 215.
[55] Clarke Papers (Camden Society), iii. 238.

oppressed people and despised also', and his powerful sermons touched chords among the poor of Cardiff and Newport. He became a spokesman for those 'poor families who cry for bread', and called on Cromwell to tax 'mighty moneyed men'. Eventually, Erbery rejected all forms of a visible church and took refuge in the doctrine of the everlasting gospel by joining the Seekers. He believed that the first dispensation had ended with the Incarnation. Christ's first coming began the second dispensation, which collapsed with the total apostasy of the Christian Church. Since the apostasy, all forms of Christian worship had been bereft of the Holy Spirit 'as the dry bones scattered in the open valley'. Erbery believed that no truly pristine church could be constituted until God chose to select a new race of apostles from the gathered churches. He expected a new and final dispensation when God would come forth in judgement 'to turn the earth upside down', to 'burn up all the flesh and forms' of the churches of Laodicea, and to roar in every man and 'make our flesh to shake, quake, and tremble'. By 1652, Erbery was convinced that the inner glory for which he yearned was at hand and was likely to be revealed in north Wales. Quoting the prophet Ezekiel, he declared: 'I looked and behold a whirlwind came out of the north, a great cloud and a fire unfolding itself'.[56] He now shunned involvement in matters of state and awaited deliverance. Whether his own death in April 1654 brought him peace of mind we cannot tell.

While William Erbery dreamed of a new dispensation, the Fifth Monarchy Men confidently asserted that the millennium was at hand. A powerful wave of millenarianism had developed during the 1640s and there was much talk of Doomsday and the Second Coming of Christ. Long before the outbreak of civil war, millenarianism was an essential element in the mainstream of religious and intellectual life. Many Puritans, following John Foxe's advice, believed that the monarchy and the bishops would prepare the way for the millennium by undermining the powers of Antichrist. But as radicalism burgeoned during the years of strife, it became more and more obvious that the path to the millennium would never be cleared by the Godly Prince and his prelates. The New Jerusalem would clearly have to be built by the people and for the people. Bizarre prophets and serious scholars set about teasing out the significance of biblical prophecies with astonishing mathematical ingenuity and finesse. Untutored men claimed that the Bible supplied irrefutable evidence that the last days were nigh. Prior to his arrival in London in 1629, Arise (formerly Rhys) Evans, a Merioneth tailor, had looked upon the Scriptures

---

[56] *The Testimony of William Erbery, passim*; A. L. Morton, *The World of the Ranters* (London, 1970), pp. 124–31.

'as a history of things that passed in other countries, pertaining to other persons'.[57] But as he increasingly delved into the Bible during the revolutionary years, he came to realize that the Word of God had a personal message for him. Like many untutored mechanic preachers, he found a niche among sophisticated publicists, journalists, and astrologers in London and duly informed them that he had been blessed with a monopoly of the truth. In 1647 he stood up in St Botolph's church, Bishopsgate, to proclaim that he was Christ.

But millenarianism was not a creed preached simply by cranks and imbeciles. Puritan saints were convinced that Antichrist's fall could no longer be delayed and that the reign of Christ was at hand. They saw themselves as God's agents engaged in warfare against the evil powers which raged in the latter days of the world. Victory on the battlefield, Pride's Purge, and the execution of the king raised their hopes and opened the way for new initiatives. Most Welshmen were repelled by the execution of the king, but Vavasor Powell, who believed that Charles Stuart had been the despicable tool of papist absolutism, swore his allegiance to King Jesus:

> But of all Kings I am for Christ alone,
> For he is King to us though Charles be gone.[58]

In the wake of Charles's demise, Powell's preaching became suffused with millenarian hopes and expectations. Morgan Llwyd, too, was unravelling the cryptic mysteries of the apocalypse for the benefit of his countrymen. Both men became the most active and vocal agitators on behalf of the Fifth Monarchy movement in Wales.

The Fifth Monarchists derived their inspiration from biblical texts, notably the seventh chapter of the Book of Daniel and the twentieth chapter of the Book of Revelation. The four beasts referred to in Daniel's prophetic vision were believed to correspond to four great kingdoms (the Babylonian, Persian, Grecian, and Roman kingdoms), whilst the ten horns of the fourth beast corresponded to ten kings. Daniel prophesied that, prior to the destruction of the fourth beast, three of the ten horns would be plucked up by a little horn which was the enemy of the saints. On the basis of these prophecies, it was widely believed that the downfall of the Pope was at hand and, with his demise, the Fifth Monarchy would arise. In his vision, John saw the angel descend from the skies, grasp the dragon, and cast him into the bottomless pit. Christ then descended to reign, with his saints, over the world for a thousand years. The only matter left for speculation was the precise date of the destruction of the fourth beast and the emergence of the kingdom of Jesus Christ.

[57] Arise Evans, *An Eccho to the Voice of Heaven* (London, 1653), p. 17.
[58] NLW, HM 2.14. f. 7a.

The expectations of the Fifth Monarchists knew no bounds. Their hearts beat faster at the promise of the Second Coming. Morgan Llwyd toyed with significant, if mystical, figures as he strove to forecast the timing of the momentous event. Several possibilities offered themselves: the year 1656 was widely canvassed in his writings, for this was the number of years believed to have elapsed between the Creation and the Flood. There was a strong possibility, too, that 1666 was the most probable date of the millennium since Revelation 13: 18 designated the Number of the Beast which had first to be destroyed as 666. It was then, more than likely, that 'the summer of the faithful'[59] would become a living reality. His Fifth Monarchist colleagues were determined to expedite Christ's triumph by brushing aside all impediments to the Second Coming, if necessary by force. They saw themselves as the engines of social and political change. Major-General Harrison, a doughty Roundhead zealot and one of the most active propagators of Fifth Monarchist views, quoted Daniel with evident relish: 'the saints . . . shall *take* the Kingdom'.[60] Pockets of Fifth Monarchists were established by Powell and Llwyd in Denbighshire, Montgomeryshire, and Radnorshire. Freeholders, artisans, and small traders, anticipating a democracy of the saints, protested vigorously against the burden of tithes, the oppressive ways of landed Titans, and the shameless depredations of lawyers. The coming of the millennium would extinguish these iniquities, for the reign of King Jesus, according to Vavasor Powell, would usher in peace, plenty, and prosperity.

The strong bonds which existed between the gathered churches in Wales and the army served to emphasize the military connections of the Fifth Monarchist cause. Welsh saints flocked to Thomas Harrison's aid when the call came to repel Scottish invaders in 1651. Troops were raised by Powell, Llwyd, Cradock, and Jenkin Jones, and these rode at speed to join Harrison's forces in Cumberland. Powell's followers in the counties of Montgomery and Radnor prayed for him and his troopers, and claimed that 'you are called to bring the King of Righteousness . . . to his Crown'.[61] When the Lord of Hosts intervened to scatter the Scots at the battle of Worcester, members of Llwyd's church at Wrexham exclaimed: 'who can be against us if God of heaven be for us?'. Many Welsh saints were now pinning their hopes on Oliver Cromwell. 'Great things God has done by you in war', said William Erbery, 'and good things men expect from you in peace.'[62] The Lord General was anxious to project his image as a social reformer, and Thomas Harrison constantly urged him to ignore the

[59] *Gweithiau*, i. 83.
[60] P. Toon (ed.), *Puritans, the Millennium and the Future of Israel* (Cambridge, 1970), p. 68.
[61] Bernard Capp, *The Fifth Monarchy Men* (London, 1972), p. 55.
[62] J. Nickolls, *Original Letters and State Papers*, p. 88.

counsels of patience advocated by John Owen and to join with the saints in hastening the kingdom of King Jesus.

From 1649 onwards, the saints had also entertained hopes that the Rump Parliament would initiate radical changes. The Rump, however, was soon seen to be riven by diverse interests and too deeply wedded to established forms of worship even to contemplate bowing to the saints' demands. The stubbornness of the members infuriated the Fifth Monarchists and they urged Cromwell to bring Parliament's desultory proceedings to a close. Radical agitation increased among the troops, and the disaffection of the saints turned to fury when the Rump resolved not to renew the Act for the Propagation of the Gospel on 1 April 1653. Cromwell shared their chagrin and, his patience exhausted, he forcibly dissolved the House on 20 April. The Rump's demise filled Vavasor Powell with joy: he proclaimed that henceforth 'law should stream down like a river freely'.[63] He and Morgan Llwyd lobbied Cromwell vigorously, urging him to further the privileges of the saints. One hundred and fifty-three members of Llwyd's congregation at Wrexham petitioned Cromwell, calling on him to 'suffer and encourage the saints of God in his spirit'[64] and to ensure a voice for the gathered churches in the election of representatives to a godly assembly.

Heavily influenced by Harrison and his radical followers, Cromwell eventually bowed to the demands of the saints. It was decided that a Nominated Assembly be established, made up of 140 members chosen by Cromwell and the Council of Officers, on the basis of recommendations submitted by the gathered churches. Major-General Harrison and Vavasor Powell used their good offices to secure the return of religious radicals of acknowledged piety and integrity. The six nominees from Wales were John Brown, Hugh Courtney, Bussy Mansell, James Phillips, Richard Price, and John Williams. All but Mansell were strongly in favour of the Fifth Monarchist manifesto. On 4 July the Barebones Parliament (baptized after a member named Praise-God Barebone) assembled to begin its task of preparing the way for the latter-day glory of the Church on earth. Cromwell reiterated his praise for the labours of the Welsh saints and reminded them of their awesome obligations. 'Truly you are called by God to rule with him and for him . . . . I confess I never looked to see such a day as this—it may be nor you neither—when Jesus Christ should be so owned as he is, at this day, and in this work.'[65] Colonel John Jones shared his enthusiasm. In his view, the Barebones Assembly was an instrument of God's purposes, 'the choicest and most singularly elected Parliament that ever was in England'. Morgan Llwyd believed that the climactic summer of 1653 was a watershed in the history of mankind. He was convinced that he

[63] R. Tudur Jones, *Vavasor Powell* (Swansea, 1971), p. 102.
[64] J. Nickolls, *Original Letters and State Papers*, pp. 120-1.
[65] Michael R. Watts, *The Dissenters* (Oxford, 1978), pp. 144-5.

was living in a time of religious and political change of potentially cataclysmic proportions. In *Llyfr y Tri Aderyn* (The Book of the Three Birds) and *Gwaedd ynghymru yn wyneb pob Cydwybod* (A Cry in Wales in the face of every Conscience), both published in 1653, he endeavoured to flesh out the significance of biblical prophecies, explain the nature of the millennium, and urge Welshmen to prepare themselves for Christ's return. 'There are terrible signs and wonders in the heavens, as though the end of all things were at hand', he claimed, 'there is some power among men just now that was not before present.' His overriding concern was that his beloved countrymen should help to throw off the Roman yoke and prepare themselves for the imminent glories of Christ's monarchy: 'Repent; the Kingdom of the Great King is at hand'.[66]

Very soon, however, deep divisions revealed themselves among 'the people of God' in the House. The members of the assembly committed to pushing through the radical revolution advocated by the Fifth Monarchists found their path blocked by obdurate moderates. Once the threat to propertied and clerical interests emerged, Cromwell's enthusiasm for the regime of the saints evaporated. Following a brief but tempestuous session of five months, Cromwell was relieved to accept the resignation of the moderate majority on 12 December. The remaining radicals were forcibly expelled by the army. Having already destroyed the Levellers in 1649, Cromwell had now smitten the saints hip and thigh.

On 16 December 1653 Cromwell was proclaimed Lord Protector. Howls of protest rang out from Fifth-Monarchist strongholds throughout the land. Cromwell's usurpation filled millenarians with horror and despair. Hugh Courtney declared that 'the people of God are highly dissatisfied';[67] Vavasor Powell was more than dissatisfied—he was outraged. Goaded into fury, he showered a torrent of abuse upon Cromwell, describing him as 'the dissemblingest perjured villain in the world'. No longer did he believe that Charles I had been the little horn: the real enemy of the saints was the newly installed Lord Protector. In a courageous, if not reckless, assault on Cromwell at Blackfriars, London, on 19 December, he likened him to the 'vile person' referred to in Dan. 11: 20, 21, and witheringly urged his disciples to go home and pray: 'Lord, wilt thou have Oliver Cromwell or Jesus Christ to reign over us?' Anticipating a fierce reaction from the authorities, Powell added boldly: 'we shall never give over, and God will not permit this spirit to go down'.[68] Before he was able to heap further obloquy on the Protector, Powell was arrested and imprisoned for three days. He then judged it prudent to seek refuge in Wales.

---

[66] *Gweithiau*, i. 177, 180, 265.   [67] B. Capp, *The Fifth Monarchy Men*, p. 101.
[68] R. Tudur Jones, 'Vavasor Powell and the Protectorate', *Trans. Congregational Hist. Soc.* 17 (1953), p. 43.

In Wales, the disciples of Powell and Llwyd were ranting furiously. John Williams, sheriff of Radnorshire and a former member of the Barebones Assembly, declared that Cromwell was as great a tyrant as the late-departed but unlamented king. Morgan Llwyd coyly observed that Harrison rather than Cromwell was probably God's chosen lieutenant on earth. Owen Lloyd, one of Llwyd's disciples, experienced a vision in which he saw four men—a soldier, a lawyer, a wealthy citizen, and a clergyman—all of whom declared 'we will not have this man to rule over us'.[69] This black mood persisted for many months. Several magistrates along the Welsh borders demonstrated their disaffection by joining Powell's entourage on his preaching tours. Powell duly informed his flocks that he would 'never submit to any government but that which is according to God's word'.[70] Rumours that arms were being collected were rife and Powell was hopeful that Cromwell's perfidy would contrive to turn some of his grudging allies in Wales into stubborn political foes. Cromwell's spies were kept on their toes, for Powell could clearly count on fairly substantial support within the Welsh Marches even if his claim that 20,000 Welsh saints were prepared to hazard their blood in defence of his cause was no more than pious bravado. John Thurloe, head of Cromwell's intelligence service, took Powell's threats seriously and kept him under close surveillance. He believed that Powell was heavily involved in intrigue and, haunted by the prospect of finding a flourishing network of Fifth-Monarchist cells along the Welsh borders, he was not disposed to underestimate reports of much cloak-and-dagger activity. In 1655, Powell was summoned to appear before the Council of State, but no charges were pressed. Powell's inflammatory perorations, however, continued to trouble Major-General James Berry, who called the Welsh firebrand before him in November and bade him draw in his horns. Powell assured him that his taste for intrigue and strife had been grossly exaggerated by his enemies and that his major concern was for the welfare of the poor people of Wales. Berry, who was deeply impressed by Powell's sincerity, let the matter rest.

Major-General Berry was soon to regret giving Powell the benefit of the doubt. In December, the latter published *A Word for God*, a strongly worded condemnation of the Protectorate in petition-form; endorsed by 322 signatures, it was a bold document, studded with rhetorical flourishes and real grievances. Powell had succeeded in combining a lively defence of the 'Good Old Cause' with a pungent indictment of Cromwellian government. Focusing on 'wickedness in high places', [71] the remonstrants protested against the maltreatment of God's saints, onerous taxes, nepotism and cupidity, and the Hispaniola fiasco. Like most disciples of

---

[69] Owen Lloyd, *The Panther-Prophesy* (London, 1662).
[70] B. Capp, *The Fifth Monarchy Men*, p. 110.
[71] A. H. Dodd, 'A Remonstrance from Wales, 1655', *BBCS* 17 (1958), pp. 279-92.

Powell and Llwyd, the majority of the signatories consisted of freeholders, artisans, tradesmen, or shopkeepers, from the counties of Denbigh, Montgomery, Brecon, and Radnor. Many of them had laboured faithfully during the Propagation period and more than thirty of them had agitated strongly for a Parliament of Saints in 1653. But if Cromwell's stock had declined markedly in north and mid-Wales, pro-Protectorate sympathizers in south Wales were more than ready to affirm their trust in the government. Unlike Powell, Walter Cradock had remained true to Cromwell, even to the extent of pandering to his vanity. In 1652, he had confessed to Cromwell that his heart was ready to burst with 'a flood of affections, a conjunction of love, joy, delight, and earnest desire to salute you'.[72] Outraged by his former ally's actions, Cradock immediately organized counter-propaganda in defence of the Protector. *The Humble Representation and Address* (1656), endorsed by 762 signatures, epitomized orthodox Puritan views. Most of the signatories were natives of Carmarthenshire, Glamorgan, or Monmouthshire, and they included men of repute such as Daniel Higgs, Henry Walter, Marmaduke Matthews, Henry Nicholls, and Rice Williams.

These petitions led to a parting of ways for old comrades. They also revealed that Welsh Puritanism was fatally split in its aims, outlook, and sympathies. Walter Cradock represented the moderate wing of the Puritan movement. Wroth's mantle had fallen upon him in 1642. He was much revered by his contemporaries as a riveting preacher of the gospel, capable of presenting the essentials of the Christian faith in simple, intelligible language. His warm piety and elegance of both tongue and pen won universal admiration. He was deeply sensible of the spiritual needs of Wales and worked assiduously to create an effective preaching ministry and to encourage religious toleration. Cradock did not possess the restless vigour of Powell and he had none of the imaginative powers of Llwyd. But he had a better grasp of political realities than either of his colleagues, and his judgement of men and moods was often more calm and balanced. If Powell attracted more attention in his day, it was Cradock who best represented the mainstream of Puritan thought in Wales.

By the mid-1650s, Morgan Llwyd was also distancing himself from the direct, anti-Cromwellian political stance favoured by Powell. Although Llwyd's name had figured among the signatories to *A Word for God*, he had refused to endorse Powell's petition. Llwyd had felt intense chagrin following the demise of Barebones, but prudently advised Powell to leave well alone. 'Let us then', he told Powell, 'say no more of others, but quietly without private mutterings tend our own work and wait within ourselves on God.'[73] Powell was both exasperated and dismayed, and upbraided Llwyd

---

[72] J. Nickolls, *Original Letters and State Papers*, p. 85.
[73] *Gweithiau*, ii. 222–3.

not only for deserting the millenarian cause but also for straying from the paths of orthodox Calvinism. In a way, there is no true label for Morgan Llwyd. Although there were clearly many ambiguities in his doctrines, Llwyd's gift for eclectic synthesis enabled him to evolve his own complex web of thought. He mined a wide range of orthodox and unorthodox ideas from men as varied in their opinions as Peter Sterry, John Saltmarsh, John Lilburne, William Erbery, Vavasor Powell, Richard Baxter, and George Fox, and succeeded in re-heating and refining them in the crucible of his own imagination. The major spiritual influence upon him, however, was that of the German mystic, Jacob Boehme. Llwyd's contact with European thinkers was limited, but he relished the complex, metaphysical ideas of Boehme. The essence of Boehmenism was that God was in everything and that the inner light was infinitely more important than the letter of the Bible. Boehme's *Mysterium Magnum* strongly influenced Llwyd's celebrated prose classic, *Llyfr y Tri Aderyn*, and two parts of *Der Weg zu Christo* were translated by Llwyd into Welsh and published in 1657. Thus, while Vavasor Powell continued to preach millennial doctrines with unflagging zeal, Llwyd withdrew more and more into himself, urging his readers to realize that 'we have the true preacher standing in the pulpit of our hearts'.[74]

Whereas the mercurial Powell was a born activist, Morgan Llwyd was an idealist who gave the saints' mission in Wales its intellectual distinction. Although he was a preacher of compelling artistry, he is best remembered for his literary gifts. Neither Cradock nor Powell wrote or published in Welsh and, apart from modest contributions by Evan Roberts, Oliver Thomas, Richard Jones, and Stephen Hughes, the Puritan literary output in Welsh during the revolutionary years was decidedly small. The signal exception is Morgan Llwyd. The period from 1653 to 1657 is his golden age: during those years he published nine major works, six in Welsh and three in English, each of which expressed a rich variety of intellectual ideas and political dialectic. Llwyd was a conscious stylist, a writer who mastered a variety of approaches, including experiments in the fields of metaphysics and human psychology, in an attempt to express his own spiritual experiences, celebrate the spirit, and awaken his countrymen from their slumbers. He possessed an unique mind and there is no doubt that he added new depth, grace, and distinction to Welsh literature. But although many of his vivid images and profound aphorisms linger long in the memory, it is difficult to measure how far or how permanently he influenced contemporary thinking. His complex prose often baffled and deterred his readers: Colonel John Jones chided him for his 'parabolical'[75] statements and urged him to feed babes with milk.

---

[74] *Gweithiau*, ii. 174-5.   [75] NLW MS 11440D, f. 149.

As Llwyd faded away into 'the inner world', Vavasor Powell continued to ride out every storm, revealing his deep instinct for survival and his devotion to duty. This diminutive, wiry, and cantankerous man was one of the most striking and pivotal Welshmen of his day. In many ways, he seemed to epitomize the virtues and defects of the archetypal Puritan saint. His closest colleagues warmed to his crusading zeal, his ability to communicate warmth, spontaneity and vigour, and his willingness to uphold orthodox Calvinism against all challengers. In an age of hypocrisies and self-deceptions, when trimmers and time-servers compromised and abandoned their principles, Powell clung unswervingly to his beliefs. A man of indomitable spirit, he 'feared not the face, nor yet the fury of the most menacing, most mighty mortal'.[76] He stamped his will on the campaign to puritanize Wales, cherishing the limelight and constantly urging his colleagues on to greater things. Unlike Llwyd's, his was a life of action rather than of contemplation. His enemies, however, formed a less than generous view of him. They found him an obsessive, even imperious, soul, stubborn to the point of bigotry and given to sweeping, emotional statements. His short temper, crass manner, and fondness for strong-arm tactics alienated many, and eventually provoked moderate Puritans to dissociate themselves from him.

Eventually, Powell's seditious attacks on Cromwellian government provoked a breach within Puritan ranks in Wales, a breach which was never healed. Although he himself would never have admitted it, Powell's millennial cause was in ruins by 1656. It had proved easier to pull Babylon down than to build a New Jerusalem. It is unlikely that even Powell's most myopic acolytes believed that enough support could be mustered to overthrow Cromwell's regime. The abortive Fifth Monarchist rising of 1657 did nothing but harm to Powell's cause and, after that, most millenarians travelled more in hope than in expectation. When Venner's futile rising in 1661 was ruthlessly put down, the vision of a New Jerusalem had long since faded in Wales.

The demise of the Fifth Monarchists led many disillusioned millenarians to seek refuge in the bosom of Quakerism. The Quakers were the most remarkable and potentially disruptive of all the radical sects which emerged in Wales during the Interregnum. The first Quaker sorties began in the autumn of 1653. Morgan Llwyd's burning curiosity about 'the Children of the Light' prompted him to send two members of his congregation to visit George Fox at his headquarters at Swarthmoor Hall, Ulverston, in order to learn more of the movement which was threatening to take the north of England by storm. One of them, John ap John, a Ruabon yeoman, fell under Fox's potent spell, returned to Wales a

---

[76] Thomas Rees, *History of Protestant Nonconformity*, p. 107.

convinced Quaker, and dedicated the remaining forty-four years of his life to making Quakerism a living force in his native land. In October, in response to Llwyd's enquiries, John Lawson and Richard Hubberthorne visited Wrexham to address members of Llwyd's church and, later, a group of separatists at Malpas in Cheshire. Soon, leading English Friends, such as John Audland, William Dewsbury, and Francis Howgill, were tramping Welsh roads in obedience to Fox's exhortation to 'sound ye the trumpets, the melodious sound abroad'.[77] By 1655, John ap John, already known as 'the Apostle of Quakerism in Wales', was in south Wales, preaching the indwelling of the Spirit, and he was joined by Thomas Holme, the Kendal weaver, and his wife, Elizabeth. Substantial inroads were made into Vavasor Powell's Baptist congregations in mid-Wales, and a marked surge of interest in the towns led to the foundation of Quaker meetings in Cardiff and Swansea.

In 1657, George Fox, the Quaker leader, embarked on his celebrated tour of Wales. Fox's visit was partly designed to heal the divisions which had been created in the wake of the celebrated case of James Nayler. In October 1656, James Nayler, a leading Friend, had re-enacted, in Bristol, Christ's entry into Jerusalem. Among the adoring women who sang 'Holy, Holy, Holy, Lord God of Sabaoth' and strewed garments and flowers before him was Dorcas Erbery, William's daughter. She claimed that Nayler was 'Jesus himself come again in the flesh' and that he had raised her from the dead in Exeter prison. Nayler was savagely punished for his temerity and Erbery, too, was pilloried alongside her hero at the Old Exchange in London. Nayler's sensational behaviour seemed to underscore Puritan warnings that an excess of spiritual enthusiasm and claims of infallibility would inevitably spill over into self-righteousness and libertinism. His extravagant deeds brought great discredit on the Quaker movement and allowed unruly elements, many of them Ranters, to interrupt Quaker meetings under the cloak of Naylerism. In Cardiff, Nayler's followers drove Thomas Holme to distraction by going about in sackcloth and ashes, interrupting meetings, heckling, singing, and tumbling on floors. In spite of Holme's efforts to keep Friends 'cool and quiet', the commanding presence of Fox was plainly needed in order to impose tighter discipline and to persuade Nayler's devotees that the day of their visitation was past.

Fox's arrival in Wales cheered beleaguered Friends enormously. His vigorous sermons and charismatic deeds were already a byword, and none of his fellow Quakers was as capable as he of winning and retaining men's undying love and devotion. During June and July, Fox visited each of the Welsh counties, accompanied by John ap John and, for parts of the journey, Thomas Holme and Edward Edwards of Denbighshire. He

[77] W. C. Braithwaite, *The Beginnings of Quakerism* (2nd edn., Cambridge, 1961), p. 206.

travelled from Bristol to Cardiff, Swansea, Brecon, and Shrewsbury before turning southwards through mid-Wales to Tenby and Haverfordwest. From there he made his way along the west coast, sounding the Day of the Lord in the major market towns, eventually moving into Gwynedd and then eastwards to Wrexham and the Welsh borders.

Fox met with a mixed reception. Many areas welcomed him warmly, but others were so hostile that he was obliged to reveal his unflinching courage and fidelity to truth. At Brecon, Fox was convinced that plans were afoot to murder him and his colleagues. At Tenby, John ap John was imprisoned. The people of Lampeter proved 'exceeding rude', whilst Fox's impression of the inhabitants of Aberystwyth was marred by an unscrupulous ostler who, determined to give the 'Cardi' a bad name, filled his pockets with oats bought for Fox's horse. When John ap John was again thrust into prison at Beaumaris, Fox marched up and down the streets, remonstrating with magistrates and local inhabitants. Hostile faces also greeted them at Wrexham, where Fox found Llwyd's followers to be 'very rude, and wild, and airy'. In many communities, however, Fox received a cordial welcome and made positive gains. Many thousands flocked to hear him preach and to experience the 'Lord's everlasting life and truth'. Many were turned to the Lord at Cardiff, a 'blessed meeting' was held at Swansea, and a large convincement was achieved at Pontymoel. In Radnorshire, Fox dazzled people by the force of his personality and hearers confessed that they had never heard such 'an opening of the Scriptures in their lives'. Recruits were enlisted in Carmarthenshire and Pembrokeshire, 'the seed was sown' in Cardiganshire, and upon Cadair Idris in Merioneth Fox exercised his remarkable gift of prophecy by foretelling 'in what places God would raise up a people to set under his teaching'. By 1660 Quakerism was winning substantial support in those very places he had named. Abusive citizens in Beaumaris and Caernarfon were shamed into silence and left to ponder the consequences of sin and wickedness. Finally, a glorious meeting at Trefor, John ap John's birthplace, rounded off a spectacular mission.[78]

Quakerism found its most fruitful recruiting grounds in counties where Puritan seeds had earlier been sown. Friends poached heavily among Baptist congregations in the counties of Montgomery, Radnor, and Brecon. Richard Davies of Cloddiau Cochion, near Welshpool, a tireless Quaker evangelist and author of a priceless account of early Welsh Quakerism, was plucked from one of Vavasor Powell's flocks. Quakerism was also a refuge for disillusioned Fifth Monarchists: Morgan Llwyd's liking for Friends was shared by many of his followers. Quakerism was also the final resting place for those travellers who had run through the whole gamut of doctrinal allegiance during the revolutionary years. There is some

---

[78] J. L. Nickolls (ed.), *The Journal of George Fox* (Cambridge, 1952), pp. 289–307.

truth in Huw Morys's gibe that the Puritan who was yesterday an
Independent is today an Anabaptist, and tomorrow a Quaker. Quakerism
touched genuine chords within those who had found the established
church, Presbyterianism, and radical sectarianism inadequate. One such
pilgrim was Thomas Wynne, a freeholder's son from Ysgeifiog in
Flintshire. Wynne was thrown into great depths of spiritual turmoil during
the 1640s. His spiritual overseers had left him 'to the mercy of the wolf' and
he found no succour either within the parish church or from tramping
itinerants 'of low degree'. Like many seekers of his day, he embarked on a
search for spiritual truth, wrestling furiously with his doubts and sins until,
sometime in the mid-fifties, he experienced a dramatic and pulsating
religious experience. By his own striking testimony, 'the heavenly power
wounded as a sword, it smote like a hammer at the whole body of sin, and
in my bowels it burned like fire'.[79] The divine light of Christ drew him out
of darkness and despair into light and hope.

Most Welsh Quakers during the Interregnum were freeholders, yeomen,
or craftsmen, men and women imbued with a spirit of independence and
self-will. By 1657, Quaker ranks had been strengthened by the convincement
of well-to-do yeomen from the arable communities of the vale of
Glamorgan. Former Commonwealth soldiers, like Francis Gawler, Matthew
Gibbon, and David Jones, were prominent Friends in Cardiff. Important
recruits were also found among the affluent. In Swansea, the most
prominent Friend was William Bevan, a wealthy merchant who donated
the site for a meeting-house. Justices of the Peace like Walter Jenkins of
Pontypool and Peter Price of Presteigne helped to shelter fellow Friends
from the rigours of the law and the abuse of their enemies.

Under Cromwellian rule, churches and congregations worshipped in
relative freedom, for the Protector was prepared to tolerate an enormous
diversity of Christian worship. The growth of rival theologies occasioned
much bitterness and strife which found their outlet in public disputes and
unseemly slanging matches. The three-hour public dispute between
Vavasor Powell and George Griffith at Newchapel, Montgomeryshire, in
1652 was accompanied by hissing, laughter, and tumult, as both sets of
supporters traduced each other. Having crossed swords with David Davies,
a hot-tempered Particular Baptist from Gelli-gaer, William Erbery, by way
of a parting shot, consigned his adversary to the impending fires of God.
But churchmen and Puritans alike shared a strident anti-Quaker animus.
Faced with such a menacing and fast-growing movement, they closed ranks
in order to defend what they believed to be the fundamental tenets of the
Christian faith and ordered society. In order to understand why Friends
aroused such fierce hostility, it is important to bear in mind that the

[79] Geraint H. Jenkins, 'From Ysgeifiog to Pennsylvania: The Rise of Thomas Wynne,
Quaker Barber-Surgeon', *Flintshire Hist. Soc. Journal* 28 (1977-8), pp. 39-40.

Quakers of the 1650s were quite unlike their quietist successors in Restoration Wales. The pacifist witness was not part of Quaker teaching in Cromwellian times; indeed, few of them were averse to violence. The Welsh Quakers of the Interregnum were deliberately militant and antagonistic towards traditional religious practices and social customs.

Quakerism aroused passionate opposition among the orthodox because the doctrine of the inner light was believed to be a grievous threat to the authority of the Scriptures, the efficacy of the Trinity, and the validity of the sacraments. Moreover, their subversive social habits made them a dangerous threat to social harmony, so much so that it was feared that their real aim was to eliminate both magistracy and ministry. Their customs defied age-old conventions of etiquette and accepted standards of decency and reverence. The use of the pronouns of address 'thee' and 'thou', the refusal to remove hats or acknowledge titles, the rejection of pagan names for days and months, and the refusal to swear oaths or pay tithes were all practices which carried sinister implications. Richard Davies, the felt-maker of Cloddiau Cochion, was violently beaten about the head with a stick by his enraged mistress for speaking 'the pure language' of 'thee' and 'thou'. When he appeared behatted before nonplussed Welshpool magistrates, 'the justices stood as people in a maze'. Deliberate provocation of priests and ministers was also seen as evidence of the Quakers' determination to undermine Christian institutions. Interrupting sermons rarely failed to set ministers' teeth on edge. Francis Gawler, a Cardiff hatter, interrupted the sermons of Joshua Miller, the Puritan incumbent of St Andrew's church, Cardiff, berating him with words 'that the Oyster women of Billingsgate would blush to name'. John ap John sent Morris Bidwell, the Puritan vicar of St Mary's church, Swansea, into paroxysms of fury by pressing him publicly to prove that he was a minister of Christ. Ministers were understandably resentful at being labelled 'hirelings', 'false prophets', and 'deceivers' in the presence of their flocks. Others feared the malign influence of Quakers, suspecting that their strange conduct was proof of diabolic possession. The natives of Welshpool were convinced that Richard Davies was in the hands of the Devil, Henry Walter of Newport lived in dread of being bewitched by Francis Gawler, and Joshua Miller was horrified to see Cardiff Quakers 'staring and raving like the men in Bedlam'. Ministers in Swansea urged local magistrates to whip John ap John so that 'the Devil might come out of him'.

Churchmen and Puritans alike bitterly condemned Quaker doctrines. Many Welsh Friends were beaten and stoned by hostile crowds and suffered grievously at the hands of unsympathetic magistrates and brutal gaolers. Travelling ministers were often confined to prison for long periods and Quaker meetings were broken up. Elizabeth Holme's biting criticisms of Puritan ministers earned her a lengthy imprisonment in Swansea's infamous 'dark house', where she was chained far from the door in order to prevent her from upbraiding ministers as they passed by. Francis Gawler was stoned in the churchyard of Llandaff cathedral, violently struck by a Cardiff clergyman, and called 'a flattering devil' by Walter Cradock. 'Get thee behind me Satan' was Cradock's usual retort to pestering Quakers. Some of his colleagues were more combative: Morris Bidwell pulled John ap John's nose, Marmaduke Matthews pinched Alice Birkett so spitefully that he drew blood, whilst that most gentle of Puritans, Stephen Hughes, was so mortified by a baiting Quaker that he struck him in the face. Hughes tarred the Quakers with a Ranter brush, claiming in 1659 that they had 'harshly shaken the foundations of true Protestantism'. Vavasor Powell, too, took them to task with relish, crossing swords in public dispute with Richard Hubberthorne at Chirk, Alexander Parker and John Moon at Old Radnor, and Morgan Watkins at Knighton. In characteristically pungent tones, Powell declared that Christians were in danger of being split between two rocks—the world and Quakerism—and that the worse fate was Quakerism. Similarly, Quaker assaults on Baptist citadels meant that John Miles could not ignore their presence: in a biting condemnation of 'railing Rabshakehs', he denounced Quakers as 'the infection of the times'. Amid these sonorous fulminations the still, small voice of Morgan Llwyd was barely audible. Although Fox's followers had drawn many of their converts from his congregation at Wrexham, Llwyd sympathized deeply with Friends and spoke well of their teachings. He maintained that Friends 'speak the truth, but not the whole truth'. In 1659, a year of mounting agitation and violence, Llwyd stood alone among Welsh Puritans in extending an olive branch to 'those that are called Quakers in scorn' and pleading for general liberty of conscience.[80]

The fear of radical sectarianism and of the social and political implications of Quakerism reached its peak in 1659. The return of the Rump in May was warmly welcomed by Friends, for they fondly expected it to expedite the 'Good Old Cause'. Their hopes were dashed, however, for after a few months of brief but chaotic rule, the Rump was forcibly dissolved by troops for the second time in its history. As the country drifted into anarchy, George Monck resolved to rid the land of the 'intolerable slavery of a sword government'. Events moved swiftly as the demand for the restoration of the monarchy grew. Charles Stuart was recalled and landed at Dover on 25 May 1660. His arrival was greeted with almost universal delight in Wales. The restored monarch was prepared to promise 'liberty to tender consciences', but defeat on the battlefield, the zeal of radical sectarianism, and heavy-handed republican rule had left a bitter legacy of resentment and humiliation among churchmen and royalists alike.

[80] For these, and other examples of brutality towards Welsh Quakers, see Geraint H. Jenkins, 'The Early Peace Testimony in Wales', *Llafur* 4 (1985), pp. 10-19.

The demise of the Puritan regime in 1660 was viewed as a merciful release by the overwhelming majority in Wales. Welshmen nursed many grievances, some of which found expression in pamphlets, lampoons, interludes, and songs of bitter invective. Both propertied and unpropertied elements in society disliked Puritan godly rule. The loss of such old familiar landmarks as the Prayer Book, the sacraments, creeds, feast days, and festivals was acutely felt, and even the Puritan, John Lewis, admitted in 1656 that a surfeit of sermons had deprived many thousands of people of their cherished festivals and ceremonies. Most Welshmen were as deeply attached to the Anglican church order as their forebears had been to the Roman Catholic order in the days of the Henrician Reformation. If Protestantism had been *ffydd Saeson* (the faith of Saxons) to the *cwndidwyr* of Mary's reign, it was now acknowledged to be *ffordd yr hen Gymry* (the path of the old Welsh). Indeed, one poet from Gwent, fired by patriotic zeal, believed that it was every Welshman's duty to defend the Anglican church against the violations of sacrilegious Saxon invaders. It is clear, too, that the Puritan moral code was as unwelcome as a run of bad harvests. The common man intensely disliked Sabbatarianism, the institution of civil marriage, the proscription of holy days, and the suppression of alehouses, revels, maypole dancing, and cock-fighting. Mechanic preachers were reviled as 'cuckolds', 'vermin', and 'scum', and there are grounds for thinking that large numbers of people stayed away from church services in protest. Many of them were totally bewildered by the more exotic doctrinal niceties unravelled in Puritan pulpits, and it was claimed that audiences had 'no more capacity to pry into them than a bat into the third heaven'.[81] The cry for liberty and reformation appealed little to the ungodly rabble. In 1654, Major-General Charles Fleetwood wearily confessed that 'the generality of the people . . . are little better than the Irish: they have envenomed hearts against the ways of God'.[82] Embittered churchmen likened themselves to spiritual captives in a desolate and empty land. In 1658, Rowland Vaughan of Caer-gai declared that he had lived 'like a pilgrim in a cell'[83] over the previous seven years, while Archibald Sparkes, deprived of his living in Northop, Flintshire, grieved inconsolably in 'this murmuring and unthankful, peevish land'.[84] Henry Vaughan, too, wrote of his 'sad captivity' in such 'foul, polluted' times, and yearned for a speedy release:

> Heal then these waters, Lord; or bring thy flock,
> Since these are troubled, to the springing rock.

[81] T. Richards, *Puritan Movement*, p. 215.
[82] T. Richards, *Religious Developments*, p. 147.
[83] Rowland Vaughan, *Yr Arfer o Weddi yr Arglwydd* (London, 1658), sig. A6^v–A7^r.
[84] NLW MS 12463B, f. 82.

> Look down, great Master of the feast; O shine,
> And turn once more our water into wine![85]

For many generations after 1660, Puritanism was inextricably linked in Welshmen's minds with heavy-handed soldiers, bullying commissioners, and the power of the sword. The period of Propagation and the rule of the Major-Generals left bitter memories and lasting divisions. Pro-church pamphlets and poems helped to perpetuate old hatreds: Huw Morys likened Cromwell and his saints to Herod and his servants, Vavasor Powell's name became encrusted with myths of dubious historical authenticity, and many other radical sectarians were called 'rogues and tinkers'. Many of these stereotypes were created by gentlemen and clerics. Fears of left-wing sectarianism and of a tyranny of the saints stalked their minds throughout the revolutionary years, and the prospect of a Puritan despotism led by the likes of Ananias the button-maker and Flash the cobbler filled them with such dread that muck-raking was rife. Sectarians were constantly accused of eroding the foundations of family life, challenging accepted sexual mores, and aspiring to turn the world upside down. Propertied men were never loath to revive the old *canard* of Münster: when Captains Jenkin Jones and John Morgan interfered in the election of the municipal officers of the town of Brecon in 1659, they and their followers were accused of seeking to 'erect a righteous government, after the mode of John of Leyden, and Knipperdolling'.[86]

If the revolutionary years were decades of strife, turbulence, and violence, they were also decades of experiment and idealism. In many ways, these were heady, intoxicating years, when men dreamed dreams and pursued spiritual goals with irrepressible enthusiasm. During twenty years of 'blood and confusion', Welsh Puritans had struggled to overthrow Antichrist, reform society, and win men's souls. John Miles was proud to have been among the faithful saints who poured an 'abundance of heavenly wisdom and grace' into the hearts of 'thousands of poor, ignorant and straying people'.[87] Philip Henry considered that 'in the matters of God's worship, things went well'.[88] Vavasor Powell was in no doubt that 'religion did grow', and could point to the many hundreds of members within the gathered churches who now walked 'in love and the fear of the Lord'.[89] Although only modest success had been achieved in north Wales, strong and determined pockets of Dissent had been established in the border counties and in south Wales. It is clear, too, that sectarians exercised an

[85] A. Rudrum, *Henry Vaughan: The Complete Poems*, p. 156.

[86] *An Alarum to Corporations* (London, 1659), p. 8.

[87] John Miles, *An Antidote against the Infection of the Times*, ed. T. Shankland (Cardiff, 1904), p. 16.

[88] M. Henry, *The Life of the Rev. Philip Henry* (London, 1825), p. 89.

[89] Vavasor Powell, *The Bird in the Cage Chirping* (London, 1662), sig. B3ʳ.

influence out of all proportion to their numbers. The star of Puritanism, however dimmed and tarnished by 1660, had not been extinguished.

Even so, the day of the saints was over. Morgan Llwyd died, at the premature age of forty, on 3 June 1659. Legend has it that a royalist soldier sought out his grave at Rhos-ddu burial ground and 'in great rage and malice thrust down his sword into it as far as it would go'.[90] Shortly before Llwyd's death, Vavasor Powell, filled with remorse, had sought to repair relations with his former colleague. The fact that his letter of apology arrived after Llwyd's death somehow lends an aura of pathos to the stricken millenarian cause. Powell himself was incarcerated in July 1660 and, save for a few months of freedom in 1667–8, was to remain in prison until his death in 1670. Undeterred, he still held his head high and voiced his undying commitment to the 'Good Old Cause': 'A Roundhead I will be'.[91] In a sense, however, it was Walter Cradock, who died in December 1659, who exercised the most abiding influence on the future growth of Welsh Dissent. His soul clearly went marching on. According to Joshua Thomas, doyen of Welsh Baptist historians, elderly Dissenters talked much of Walter Cradock in the 1730s, and when Methodists began penetrating the counties of north Wales they found the sobriquet 'Cradockites' bestowed upon them.

[90] A. N. Palmer, *A History of the Older Nonconformity of Wrexham* (Wrexham, 1888), p. 35.
[91] NLW MS 366A, p. 9.

PART II

THE RETURN TO STABILITY
1660–1730

CHAPTER 3

THE SOCIAL AND ECONOMIC STRUCTURE

HARDY English travellers who ventured beyond Offa's Dyke in this period were unimpressed by what they saw. Far from stirring their emotions, the Welsh landscape was judged wild, bleak, and joyless. Its terrain scarcely offered sufficient sustenance for man or beast. Wales, in Ned Ward's words, was 'the fag-end of Creation; the very rubbish of Noah's flood'.[1] The prim Celia Fiennes had little good to say of the land or its people: barefooted Welsh peasants were 'a nasty sort of people'.[2] Even Defoe, who commented favourably on the convivial hospitality of the Welsh gentry, confessed wearily that Hannibal himself would have found the mountains of Wales intimidating. Such jaundiced views were largely provoked by the hazards and inconveniences of travelling on paths and roads which were more often than not a risk to life and limb. In many ways, Wales was a remote and inaccessible federation of small communities, a mosaic of self-contained localities, cut off from each other by geographical division and poor communications, yet also bound together by ties of kinship, good neighbourliness, and language. Wales lay very much on the fringe of Europe and the life of its people was governed by the cycle of the seasons and the steady rhythms of age-old customs and traditions. The most isolated rural communities were content to shelter themselves from the madding crowd: as late as 1806 Dolwyddelan in Caernarfonshire was said to be 'out of the way from every intercourse with the world',[3] whilst, around the same time, Benjamin Malkin commented that Cardiganshire peasants gazed in wonder whenever strangers ventured into their midst.

Each locality had its own distinctive features and qualities, and to a large extent the social and economic history of Wales in this period is the sum of its local histories. There were marked physical and economic contrasts between the rugged uplands of Snowdonia and the fertile valley of the Severn, and between the bleak moorland plateaux of mid-Wales and the wide fertile cornfields of the vale of Glamorgan. In terms of wealth, there were striking differences between the impoverished counties of the north-west and the prosperous low-lying vales of the south-east. Even within

[1] Ned Ward, *A Trip to North-Wales* (London, 1701), p. 6.
[2] *The Illustrated Journeys of Celia Fiennes 1685–c. 1712*, ed. C. Morris (London, 1982), p. 159.
[3] William Williams, 'A Survey of the Ancient and Present State of the County of Caernarvon', *Trans. Caerns. Hist. Soc.* 34 (1973), p. 141.

counties, geographical and agrarian contrasts were apparent: in Glamorgan, the barren pastureland of the Blaenau, inhabited largely by peasants, was a world apart from the prosperous fertile plains of the Bro, where the gentry waxed fat. Historical traditions, architectural patterns, and communal obligations varied from place to place. Each locality had its own price structure, weights and measures, and agrarian customary laws. A mass of disparate accents and dialects bemused the untutored traveller. Indeed, there were wide regional variations in both spoken and written Welsh. Dissenting and Methodist preachers who ventured north found great difficulty in making themselves understood by the people.

Throughout this period Wales remained an overwhelmingly rural country. Its population was small: more people lived in London than in the whole of Wales. Prior to the first of the decennial censuses taken in 1801 it is impossible to venture a precise estimate of the population of Wales at any given time. The available data are so defective and unreliable that all estimates are subject to a wide margin of error. It seems probable, however, that Wales entered a relatively stagnant phase for at least two generations after 1640; the annual frequencies of both births and marriages fell, and it was not until the early eighteenth century that renewed population growth occurred as a result of both natural increase and the migration of English families into industrial communities. The population rose from around 371,000 in 1670 to 489,000 by 1750, with the period after 1710 seeing a more consistent tendency towards a surplus of births over deaths. Population density was low, and the physical pattern of mountains, moorlands, plains, and coasts dictated the location of settlements. In many parts of mid and west Wales there were fewer than fifty persons per square mile. The coastal plains and fertile valleys, notably south Pembrokeshire, the vale of Clwyd, the Tywi valley, and the vale of Glamorgan, were naturally more densely populated than the rugged uplands or the bleak, wind-swept moorlands. And although towns such as Brecon, Carmarthen, Swansea, and Wrexham were thriving economically, only about a sixth of the population lived in towns.

But, although the general growth in the population is clear, it would be wrong to presuppose a steady level of mortality. Local populations were clearly subject to considerable and sometimes even violent fluctuations in mortality rates. Short, sharp bursts of high mortality, usually provoked by harvest failures, food shortages, and the incidence of a host of diseases, severely pruned local populations. In a marginal subsistence economy, governed largely by the natural elements of sun, wind, frost, and rain, the annual harvest was crucial to the well-being of the overwhelming majority of the population. It was of vital consequence in every peasant's life. The quality of harvests, however, fluctuated from year to year and possibly as many as one harvest in four was deficient in this period. Crises at

Westminster or dramatic victories on the battlefield in Europe were of small account when the harvest failed. Even worse was a run of bad harvests. A series of poor harvests, usually caused either by cold springs or wet summers, deprived men, women, and beasts of adequate food supplies, drove up prices, and rendered the weak vulnerable to infectious diseases. Moreover, the shortfall in seed-corn automatically depleted the crops harvested the following year. It was also a grave but understandable temptation for hard-pressed families to consume part of the following year's supply of seed-corn, thereby seriously damaging their prospects of gathering decent crops in the future. Although farmers, both large and small, were dependent on good crops, the main burden of a harvest failure always bore most heavily on the poor. To them, a succession of poor harvests was as unwelcome as the plague, for it could ultimately be responsible for sending thousands of them to an early grave.

If a run of bad harvests might send mortality rates soaring, so, too, might the vagaries of infectious diseases. In 1652, Haverfordwest witnessed the terrible ravages of the bubonic plague. Whole families among the urban poor were wiped out and the resources of the town were stretched to breaking-point. Mercifully, however, the plague bade farewell to Wales and retreated eastwards into Europe. It was replaced, however, by a variety of less devastating but appallingly persistent killing diseases, notably typhus and smallpox. Although these virulent diseases never wrought such widespread and long-term devastation as the bubonic and pneumonic plague had done, their visitations, at least in the short term, were often shattering. By the early eighteenth century, smallpox had emerged as a major killer in both rural parishes and towns. No agent was more destructive of life and beauty. Although the citizens of south-west Wales strove to protect themselves from smallpox by practising the method of 'variolation' or 'buying the disease',[4] as Dr Perrot Williams of Haverfordwest called it, most people were vulnerable to its ravages. Smallpox seldom discriminated between the rich and the poor, the old and the young; its pock-marks scarred the complexions of famous Welshmen such as Griffith Jones, Twm o'r Nant, Williams Pantycelyn, and Iolo Morganwg. Advertisements for servants often contained the warning: 'must have had the smallpox'. People clearly lived in fear of its hideous ravages. In 1705–6, smallpox devastated the small community of Penmachno by killing sixty parishioners. Over a period of nine months in 1722–3, seventy-one citizens of Carmarthen died of smallpox.

In a land where so many undernourished and poor people depended on staple foods such as oats and bread, the combination of food shortages and infectious diseases periodically drove mortality rates upwards. Harvest

[4] G. Penrhyn Jones, 'A History of Medicine in Wales in the Eighteenth Century' (unpubl. University of Liverpool MA thesis, 1957), p. 317.

failures in 1667–9, 1678–83, 1694–1703, 1708–9, and 1722–3 brought grievous losses to farmers and serious malnutrition to peasants. This, in turn, lowered their resistance to disease and led to short-term surpluses of burials over baptisms. Most European countries, ranging from the Scottish highlands to the foothills of the Alps, were burdened during the 1690s by severe subsistence crises, caused largely by a series of cold, wet seasons. A third of the population of Finland was wiped out during the famine crises of 1696–7. The horrifying mortality crisis which struck Scotland, particularly during the period 1697–9, became embedded in the folk-memory of its people. These, too, were years of crisis in Wales. Deficient harvests and outbreaks of disease sent mortality rates soaring. In the parish of Wrexham, child burials increased from 210 per 1000 burials in 1670 to 610 per 1000 burials in 1695. In impoverished upland areas, where the margins of subsistence were always narrower, the crisis weeded out the weak. Many hundreds of widows, paupers, children, and beggars died as a result of either starvation or disease or a combination of both. The parish registers of rural Wales are littered with poignant references to poor beggars, many of them unnamed, who perished on the highways during the crisis years of the late 1690s.

Typhus triggered off another serious demographic crisis during the years 1727–31, one so severe that religious reformers were convinced that it was a divine punishment on a sinful people. In many towns and parishes the epidemic proved catastrophic, cutting down poor people with disconcerting speed. 'The gentry in general are pretty hearty in the country', wrote Owen Davies, curate of Bodewryd, in March 1729, 'it's the common sort that drop off.'[5] The cumulative effect of bad harvests and food shortages had rendered the undernourished poor a ready prey to sudden attacks of typhus, influenza, and smallpox. According to Griffith Jones, Llanddowror, the general sickness 'raged mightily'[6] in most counties, enfeebling or weeding out the weak. In March 1729 the overseers of the poor and the churchwardens of Wrexham were obliged to levy an additional rate owing to the sharp increase in the number of sickly paupers. All over Wales, poor people died almost like flies. In west Glamorgan there were 798 more burials than baptisms during the years 1727–31. In 1730, 123 people died in the hundred of Painscastle, the highest number of deaths in any single hundred in Radnorshire before 1800. No fewer than forty widows died in the parishes of Llanfechell and Llanbadrig in Anglesey in February 1730. Clearly, then, sharp and irregular fluctuations in local mortality rates temporarily affected the general growth in population. Yet, mortality caused by famine or infectious diseases was not sufficiently high to close

[5] Leonard Owen, 'The Letters of an Anglesey Parson, 1712–1732', *THSC* (1961), p. 89.
[6] *Correspondence and Minutes of the S.P.C.K. relating to Wales, 1699–1740*, ed. M. Clement (Cardiff, 1952), pp. 153, 163.

the overall gap between the birth rate and the normal mortality rate. Even in a year as severe as 1730, according to John Rickman's admittedly imperfect data, there were 522 more baptisms than burials in Wales.

Small households were the norm in Wales: a simple nuclear family of husband, wife, and children. Evidence provided in returns gathered by William Lloyd, bishop of St Asaph, from 109 parishes in north-east Wales between 1681 and 1686 suggests that the mean size of households was around 4.40, although larger households were of course common among the nobility and gentry. Families were small owing to the low expectation of life and the tendency to marry late. Although it is difficult to calculate the proportion of different age groups, it is likely that Welsh society was essentially a youthful population. In north Flintshire some 36 per cent of the population were under the age of 18, and children under 10 made up nearly a quarter of the population. At the age of 7, children began helping with menial tasks in the home or on the farm, and on reaching adolescence they either obtained apprenticeships or left home to serve as domestic servants or day labourers. High mortality rates, especially during sickly years or times of famine, kept families small. The expectation of life at birth during the 1690s was around 35. Many infants died during their first year of life, either as a result of malnutrition or infectious diseases. In 1685, no fewer than 56 of the 119 burials in Swansea were of infants. Even among the well-to-do, infants died in calamitous numbers. Sir Arthur Owen of Orielton and Robert Owen of Penrhos both shared the same fate of having to bury six of their twelve children. Sir Hugh Owen of Orielton's first wife, Anne, gave birth to thirteen children, including six sons and seven daughters, eight of whom died as infants or young people. Dissenting ministers, too, were well-acquainted with grief: five of Morgan Llwyd's eleven children died, whilst only two of seven children born to James Owen by his first marriage survived their infancy. If death cut down the babies of the well-to-do, mortality rates among the poor must have been alarming. The chances of infants born to humble parents avoiding or surviving infectious diseases were extremely slender.

It is significant, too, that contemporaries tended to venerate the old. The evidence collected by Edward Lhuyd during the 1690s suggests that, although a fair proportion of people survived to the age of 60 or even 70, few parishes could boast a sizeable number of adults above 80 years of age. When Rachel Whittingham of Montgomery died at the ripe age of ninety in 1716, her death was recorded in enormous letters in the parish register. Oracles with grey hairs were especially revered: Siôn Jones of Mold, aged 106, was dubbed 'Siôn Sufficient' by his fellow parishioners,[7] while the people of Gresford took great pride in the fact that Edward Allington,

---

[7] Edward Lhuyd, 'Parochialia', *Arch. Camb.* 1–3 (1909–11), pp. 98, 144.

aged 102, could walk, ride, and drink as well as the next man. Survival to old age usually betokened an unusually tough constitution. Nonagenarians in Trawsfynydd confidently attributed their longevity to honest, unremitting toil and a milk diet, whilst towards the end of the eighteenth century Iolo Morganwg claimed that his neighbours in the vale of Glamorgan lived longer than most owing to a full diet, abstinence from alcohol, flannel shirts, and clean stone cottages! For most people, however, life was extremely hazardous and insecure. In a society racked by dearth, illness, violence, and sudden death, it is not surprising that *ym mhob rhith y daw angau* (death comes in every guise) was a popular maxim. Even the rich were acutely aware of the brevity of human life.

Welsh society attached considerable importance to rank, title, and birth. The social hierarchy was based on widely accepted social conventions, durable and extensive family ties, and, most important of all, wealth and the possession of land. The clearest dividing line within society was that between the gentry and the common people. Maldistribution of wealth and inequality were evident everywhere. Whereas a small but highly influential minority of the population enjoyed the material benefits of life, the living standards of the overwhelming mass of the people were brutally depressing. In particular, the gulf in terms of wealth and comfort between the great landowners and the peasants was enormous. Whereas substantial landowners measured their fortunes in thousands of pounds, poor peasants did not even begin to measure theirs. The well-born and the rich governed Welsh society. At the apex of the social pyramid stood the nobility, a small, exclusive élite of prosperous and powerful men. These were followed by a county élite of baronets, knights, and squires, who, in turn, were followed by a more numerous but less affluent corpus of parish gentry. Within gentry families there were wide variations of income and wealth, especially between landed Titans and the smaller parish gentlemen, many of whom were very small beer indeed. In the economically less developed western counties, gentlemen were very much poorer than their counterparts in more progressive and advanced parts of Wales. An annual income of £600–£800 was the norm for gentry in Merioneth, whereas in prosperous Glamorgan at least fifteen estates brought in annual incomes of £2,000 by 1710.

There is no doubt that a decisive shift occurred in the pattern of Welsh landownership during the century which followed the Restoration. The economic climate favoured the prosperous, and property passed, almost inexorably, into the hands of the mighty. A much greater volume of land came on the market during this period, with the result that the rich became richer and the weak went to the wall. With remorseless determination, the great Leviathans extended and consolidated their estates. Managing large estates became big business and, by taking advantage of wider mortgage facilities, substantial landowners were able to invest heavily in industrial enterprises and the land market. Many applied the squeeze on vulnerable gentlemen and freeholders, men of diverse properties and fluctuating fortunes who were increasingly to find themselves caught in a web of mortgages, borrowing, and debt. As a result, families which had once held their heads high sank into obscurity. Whilst the behemoths went from strength to strength, the vulnerable either decayed or vanished. Some landowners—or 'potent men', as peasants often called them—were just as capable of encroaching on common lands and infringing the rights of peasants as they were of snapping up the estates of ailing squires. The popular verse of this period is studded with bitter references to hard-fisted gentlemen who acquired land with scant regard for the well-being of their helpless neighbours.

The economic gap between large estate-owners and the lesser gentry widened considerably for a number of reasons. Although the upheaval of the revolutionary years did not radically affect the distribution of landed estates, it is clear that the fortunes of many small landowners were seriously damaged by fines levied during the civil wars. Many of them had sought to keep their spirits buoyant by hoping for subsequent compensation for their wartime privations. Sir Henry Vaughan of Derwydd, for instance, convinced himself that 'God can restore the increase as to Job'.[8] However, few small landowners proved able to make good the ravages wrought by parliamentary sequestrators. Debts incurred during the wars continued to dog Welsh royalists after 1660. The legal bickering in which so many of them indulged bore witness to their battle to achieve solvency and ward off debt-collectors. Plagued by financial worries, many were forced to borrow money or mortgage their properties in order to keep their creditors happy. Some plunged ever deeper into debt. Sir Robert Thomas of Llanmihangel in Glamorgan, whose father had paid £2,195 in compounding his estate, ran up further debts and by 1683 was forced to beg his creditors to provide him with food and clothing for his wife and three children. Losses incurred by his father during the age of sequestration forced Edward Lloyd of Llanforda to lease and sell land, raise mortgages and loans, and transfer debts. He pleaded with his friends to save him from the jaws of his predatory neighbour, William Williams of Glasgoed. 'Suffer not me', he begged, 'to be a prey to this prodigious glutton who will not buy my land unless for sauce my discretion is served up to his taste.'[9] His efforts to stave off disaster proved fruitless, however, and his stricken estate was 'swallowed up by the great Leviathan'.[10]

[8] Francis Jones, 'Cadets of Golden Grove', THSC (1977), pp. 139–40.
[9] Brynley F. Roberts, Edward Lhuyd: The Making of a Scientist (Cardiff, 1980), p. 9.
[10] Askew Roberts, Wynnstay and the Wynns (Oswestry, 1876), p. 8.

Substantial landowners spared no pains in fostering and preserving their patrimonies. Entail settlements protected their estates from the follies of a spendthrift heir. An entail held estates together by ensuring that when the eldest son inherited his patrimony he became a life-tenant. Although he was entitled to enjoy the profits of his estate during his own lifetime, he was barred from alienating his estate or disposing of capital. On his death, the estate was entailed to his son. Even so, some heirs were spectacularly prone to extravagance. Smaller squires, anxious to emulate the expensive tastes of their superiors, were easily 'dragged into all kinds of idle doings',[11] often with disastrous results. The dissolute ways of Hugh Owen of Penrhos, a spoilt and hyperactive rake, weighed heavily on his family. 'The Lord help thee poor simpleton', his uncle rebuked him in 1730, 'why dost thou line thy clothes with silk and talk of buying globes etc. as if thou wert the son of an earl?'[12] Some squires bit off more than they could chew. Joshua Edisbury built Erddig between 1684 and 1687, but his capital soon ran out and his financial affairs deteriorated so swiftly that he was forced to flee to London to avoid his creditors even before the house was fully finished. The attractions of drink, the gaming-table, and the racecourse threatened the well-being of small estates. Thomas Lloyd of Danyrallt, Carmarthenshire, was so acutely distressed by his eldest son's addiction to alcohol that he took the unusual step, in 1720, of nominating his second son as the successor to his estate. William Brynker of Bryncir, Caernarfonshire, a handsome philanderer and a transparent rogue, borrowed money from his rich English wife, his friends, and his acquaintances, recklessly mortgaged his already burdened estate, and eventually sought refuge from his furious creditors by fleeing to France in 1731. Many small owners, crippled by debt, mismanagement, or extravagance, were forced to sell out to their more affluent neighbours.

The caprice of demography also provoked shifts in the balance of wealth and power. An extraordinarily high failure rate of male heirs characterized the history of estates in many Welsh counties during this period. In Montgomeryshire the fate of over 40 per cent of landed estates between 1690 and 1760 was decisively affected by the failure to produce male heirs. In Glamorgan the owners of Hensol in 1721, Dunraven in 1725, Cefnmabli in 1735, and Y Fan in 1736 died without issue and their properties either came into the possession of powerful Welsh landowners or of affluent English families. Indeed, of eighty-three resident or semi-resident families who owned landed estates in Glamorgan in the 1660s, at least forty-five had vanished as a result of the failure of the male line a century later. Estates in

---

[11] Ellis Wynne, *Visions of the Sleeping Bard*, tr. T. Gwynn Jones (Gregynog Press, 1940), p. 135.
[12] Emyr Gwynne Jones, 'Correspondence of the Owens of Penrhos, 1712-1742', *Trans. Anglesey Antiq. Soc.* (1954), p. 70.

north Wales experienced the same phenomenon. None of the owners of
the Madrun estate in Caernarfonshire produced a male heir between 1688
and 1758. When Sir William Williams, owner of the Faenol estate, died
without issue in 1696, his estate passed into the hands of John Smith, a
Whig politician, and was eventually inherited by the Assheton-Smith
family. The failure of the gentry to reproduce themselves in the direct male
line is one of the great mysteries of the period. It is puzzling since it seems
to reveal an extraordinarily heedless disregard for the morrow among a
class which, on the whole, devoted its energies to consolidating and
preserving its patrimonies. Hyde Hall, the topographer, attributed this
self-destructive impulse to the Welsh gentleman's love of tippling: 'the
women were sober; the men drank themselves into an early grave'.[13] There
was probably more than a grain of truth in his witticism but the answer
more probably lies in the exceptionally high mortality, the low fertility, and
the celibacy which characterized so many landed families in this period.
Fewer children were born to fathers who had themselves entered this world
between 1640 and 1680. Moreover, a number of heirs chose either not to
marry or to marry late. Some gentlemen were doubtless homosexuals,
whilst others preferred hard riding and hard drinking to chasing eligible
heiresses. Whatever the reason for such widespread biological failure,
these demographic misfortunes meant that more property came on the
market or passed into the hands of heiresses, collateral relatives, or
English families.

The pursuit of rich heiresses gathered pace during this period. Lucrative
marriages enabled traditional families to enhance their standing and
afforded those whose aspirations were greater than their fortunes with the
opportunity of replenishing their coffers and extending their territories.
Arranged marriages were complicated economic transactions which
involved an elaborate number of dowries, portions, jointures, and trusts.
Eligible heiresses were pursued simply for their property and wealth, for in
most gentry households the notion of romantic love was widely scoffed at.
Many Welshmen did well out of the marriage market. The substantial
dowry of £20,000 which came into the possession of Judge Marmaduke
Gwynne of Garth, Breconshire, following his marriage to Mary Gwilym, a
merchant's daughter of Glasgwm, Radnorshire, enabled him to buy
extensive territories in Radnorshire. His son, also called Marmaduke,
further consolidated his family's fortunes by marrying Sarah Evans of
Peterwell, Cardiganshire, in 1716; she was one of six co-heiresses, each of
whom was endowed with a handsome dowry of £30,000. When Watkin
Williams Wynn married Anne Vaughan of Llwydiarth, Montgomeryshire,
in 1719, extensive estates valued at between £15,000 and £20,000 were

[13] A. H. Dodd, *A History of Caerns.*, p. 183.

yoked together. Attractive marriages thus offered substantial landowners the opportunity to expand their empires and extend their economic and political sway over families in neighbouring counties. Small wonder that the Quaker Charles Lloyd of Dolobran warned his eligible daughter, Elizabeth: 'many eyes will be upon thee unawares to thyself, some for good and some for evil'.[14]

More sinister, at least in the eyes of Welsh poets, was the fashion for 'foreign' matches. The failure of male heirs meant that there were rich pickings available in Wales for opportunist English or Scottish gentlemen who were anxious to fill their purses and broaden their estates. Increasingly, Welsh estates were falling into non-Welsh hands. When Frances Williams of Penrhyn died without issue in 1716, her estate was divided between her sisters, both of whom married affluent Englishmen. In 1689, Elizabeth, sister and heiress of Sir Gilbert Lort of Stackpole Court, Pembrokeshire, married Sir Alexander Campbell of Cawdor in Nairnshire. Two years later, the Perrot estate at Haroldstone passed by marriage into the hands of Sir John Packington of Worcestershire. In 1705 Jane, sister of Sir Charles Kemeys of Cefnmabli, married Sir John Tynte of Somerset. When her brother, a bachelor, died in 1735 the estate came into the possession of the Tyntes. Absentee landlordism was a direct result of many such marriages. English landowners entrusted the day-to-day administration of their Welsh estates to a posse of agents and stewards, and many dignified family mansions were left to decay. In 1678 Lady Mary Wynn, heiress of Sir Richard Wynn of Gwydir, married Robert Bertie, Baron Willoughby d'Eresby of Lincolnshire, who gave his Welsh estates such a wide berth that Gwydir mansion became 'a museum of curios'[15] rather than a family home. When Anne Vaughan, at the age of 23, inherited Golden Grove, the largest estate in south-west Wales, in 1713, a clutch of affluent English suitors jostled for her hand in marriage. The marquis of Winchester, heir of the duke of Bolton, was the winner in the marriage stakes and took his rich young wife with him to London. Unfortunately, Anne had chosen a thoroughly bad lot. Her husband proved to be an incorrigible spendthrift who sought to wring as much money out of her as he could before deserting her and fathering two illegitimate sons. Meanwhile, Golden Grove was left without a resident owner. Heavily encumbered by mortgages and rent arrears, the estate was governed by a steward and, to make matters worse, the empty mansion was badly damaged by fire in 1729.

Furthermore, as the Welsh gentry themselves acquired town houses in London, embarked on tours of European countries or succumbed to the attractions of the racecourse and gambling table, their estates were left to

---

[14] Humphrey Lloyd, *The Quaker Lloyds in the Industrial Revolution* (London, 1975), p. 32.

[15] A. H. Dodd, *A History of Caerns.*, p. 180.

be administered in their absence by stewards or agents. By the early eighteenth century, the efficient management of Welsh estates depended largely on the integrity, resourcefulness, and business acumen of stewards. They were expected to collect rents and tithes, draw up tenancy agreements, hire labourers, prepare detailed accounts, organize the sale of farm produce, acquaint themselves with modern agricultural developments, supervise industrial enterprises, and round up voters at elections. Eternal vigilance was the principal maxim of the reliable James Pratt, steward of the Morgan family of Tredegar, who served for thirty-four years 'with the utmost integrity, exactness and fidelity'.[16] Many stewards, however, abused their office by appropriating tenant lands, raising rents and pocketing the extra revenue. Hugh Jones, steward of Y Ddôl in Merioneth, was reputed to have an 'eager and vast appetite'[17] for enclosing lands, while Gabriel Powell, a tucker's son and steward of the seigniory of Gower from 1706 to 1735, was known as 'Gabriel the Dark Angel'.[18] Powell was a tyrannical bully who protected the alleged rights and privileges of the duke of Beaufort by removing squatters from common lands, insisting upon prompt payment of rents and manorial dues, and obstructing the plans of industrial entrepreneurs. Stewards who administered estates which had passed into English or non-resident hands were greatly feared by tenants. When the Clenennau family settled at Brogyntyn in Shropshire, they left their Caernarfonshire patrimony in the hands of Griffith Parry, an unpleasant steward whose depredations soon became a byword in the locality. Parry built a stone wall along the river bank on the boundary with land owned by Anna Lloyd of Gesail Gyfarch, thus preventing her cattle from frequenting a common watering-place. Her complaints were drowned in a torrent of abuse from Parry, who warned her that if cattle were found cooling themselves in the river he would send dogs to tear them to pieces.

It is clear, then, that substantial landowners, both Welsh and English, succeeded in extending their territories during this period. Legal developments relating to marriage settlements and mortgages hastened the drift of property into the hands of the Leviathans and an entail served to hold their estates together. Conversely, the smaller gentry, burdened by financial woes, found their annual rent-rolls shrinking and were often forced to sell all or part of their estates to more affluent and stable neighbours. By the early decades of the eighteenth century, the size of houses and estates, together with annual income derived from rents, fines, and investments, provided an accurate index of the wealth, social status, and power of the

[16] J. Martin, 'Estate Stewards and Their Work in Glamorgan, 1660–1760', *Morgannwg* 23 (1979), p. 17.

[17] G. M. Griffiths (ed.), 'John Wynne, a Report of the Deanery of Penllyn and Edeirnion, 1730', *The Merioneth Miscellany* 1 (1955), pp. 37–8.

[18] J. Martin, 'Private Enterprise versus Manorial Rights: Mineral Property Disputes in Eighteenth-Century Glamorgan', *WHR* 9 (1978), p. 158.

Welsh Titans. The mightiest estate was owned by Sir Watkin Williams Wynn of Wynnstay: his acreage straddled county borders and was valued at £19,623 in 1736. In south-east Wales the concentration of landed wealth in the hands of the Morgan family of Tredegar afforded them with an annual income of around £10,000. Below them came prosperous landowners—the Myddeltons of Chirk Castle, the Mostyns of Mostyn, the Herberts of Powis, the Vaughans of Llwydiarth, the Vaughans of Golden Grove, the Mansells of Margam, and the Lewises of Y Fan—with incomes ranging from £1,000 to £5,000 per annum. The gap between them and the squires, lesser gentry, and freeholders had widened considerably. Incomes, however, varied widely from county to county. In prosperous Glamorgan, some sixteen families of squires derived annual incomes of between £500 and £1,000 from rents and fines. In rural Montgomery, on the other hand, squires were more likely to receive incomes ranging from £250 to £500. Similarly, the parish gentry of Glamorgan were able to boast far longer rent-rolls than their country cousins in the north. Over fifty lesser gentry families in Glamorgan received annual incomes of between £150 and £500. On the other hand, the median income of the lesser gentry in Flintshire and Caernarfonshire was £123 and £67 respectively. These were men of relatively modest means who lived in smaller houses, carried out the tasks of local government and prided themselves on their attachment to their native heath and culture.

In terms of their birth, affluence, life-style, and positions of authority, the gentry stood apart from the rest of society. They were the natural rulers of the countryside. Most of them had been educated and trained from their earliest years to fulfil their role as the rulers and guardians of society. Few questioned their God-given right to rule, to live in splendid mansions, to sport distinctive prefixes and suffixes, to wear expensive clothes, and to eat well. The most prosperous gentlemen were, in effect, rural patriarchs, lording it over the rest of society and insisting upon the punctilious observance of such social obligations as bowing, curtseying, and forelock-tugging. The pecking order at public ceremonies and strict seating arrangements in churches were clear indices of the deferential character of society. Indeed, the Welsh gentry were blessed with many privileges denied to the overwhelming majority of their countrymen. As a consequence of their privileged position, they were taller and generally more healthy than others. They wore swords, fought duels, possessed the right to hunt, owned a coach and carriage, and possessed considerable quantities of gold or silver plate. They cut elegant figures in their embroidered coats, waistcoats, plush breeches, satin stockings, buckled shoes, periwigs, and cravats. Maids and servants attended to their needs: there were thirty-three servants at Chirk Castle in 1683, forty-six (thirty-five men and eleven women) at Tredegar House, Newport, in 1674, and thirty-eight at Margam in 1712. Social and public events involving gentry families were celebrated with pomp, dignity, and display. When Sir Roger Mostyn, third baronet of Mostyn, married Lady Essex Finch in London in 1703, he and his bride were met on the borders of Flintshire by an escort of 300 horsemen who accompanied them to Mostyn Hall. During the funeral of Sir Thomas Myddelton of Chirk Castle in 1666 the procession of mourners stretched for over a mile, whilst on the death of John Morgan of Tredegar in 1719 the bells of Newport and Basaleg were rung for fifteen days and mourners were regaled with hams, tongues, macaroons, biscuits, and ale. The gentry were also, almost without exception, well-grounded in their ancestry. Their mansions were richly adorned with heraldic decorations, the family silver bore engraved arms, and mural tablets in churches and costly tombs in churchyards all bore witness to their lineage. And, even though pedigrees unsupported by broad acres counted for little in a period when power and influence were more firmly based than ever before on ownership of extensive lands, the smaller parish gentleman continued to flaunt an elaborate pedigree displaying his descent from the fifteen tribes or some other mythical progenitors.

The pursuit of pleasure filled many of the waking hours of the Welsh gentry. Recreations such as horse-racing, fox-hunting, hare-coursing, shooting, and fishing were pastimes exclusive to them. Many were connoisseurs of claret, wines, and punch, as well as home-made beer and ale. Drinking parties were common events and helped to relieve the tedium of rural life as well as to anaesthetize squires hard-pressed by financial worries. Indeed, many drank to excess. 'How does your head do this morning?', asked Sir Roger Mostyn in a letter to Piers Pennant in 1674, 'mine aches confoundedly.'[19] Pot-bellied gentlemen also gorged themselves, and some even took pride in their corpulence. Enormously fat gentlemen were often rudely satirized in contemporary cartoons and it is not surprising that they suffered from dental decay, gout, and the stone. Arthur Williams of Ystumcolwyn, Montgomeryshire, was so obese by his death in 1723 that he was buried with great haste, 'he being so corpulent he could not be kept'.[20] Others paid the penalty for loose living. John Lloyd of Rhiwaedog in Merioneth was scathingly described by his rural dean as 'a broken, decayed rake, and a mere skeleton . . . he justly labours under the effects of his unparalleled debaucheries'.[21] John Vaughan, second Viscount Lisburne, of Trawsgoed in Cardiganshire, embarked on an orgy of

[19] Lord Mostyn and T. A. Glenn, *History of the Family of Mostyn of Mostyn* (London, 1925), p. 146.
[20] T. Melvin Humphreys, 'Rural Society in Eighteenth-Century Montgomeryshire' (unpubl. University of Wales Ph.D. thesis, 1982), p. 273.
[21] NLW, Records of the Church in Wales, SA/RD/21, p. 68.

extravagant living which plunged his family so deeply into debt that he almost ruined the fortunes of his patrimony. The accomplishments of polite society and the sophisticated pleasures of London life appealed enormously to wealthy gentlemen. In winter they were only too pleased to forfeit the company of their 'rude' and 'clownish' country cousins for the concerts, theatres, balls, gaming-houses, and brothels of the metropolis. In summer, groaning with gout, they hastened to sample the purgative waters and hot springs of Bath, as well as the dubious pleasures provided by raffling shops and wandering prostitutes.

Some gentlemen, probably a minority, were contemptuous of the 'vulgar sorts' and treated them as serfs. When John Vaughan, third earl of Carbery, was appointed governor of Jamaica in 1674 he acquired considerable wealth by selling his own servants as slaves. Richard Parry of Pwllhalog, Flintshire, was a tyrannical landlord who maltreated his tenants, libelled his neighbours, and defamed his relatives. Evan Lloyd, a 'potent man'[22] of Llanfihangel Cefnllys in Radnorshire, was accused in 1691 of barbarously treating poor men and women in his locality by hauling them by the hair, beating them, burning their homes, and depriving them of food and shelter. Thomas Powell of Nanteos, Cardiganshire, thought nothing in 1731 of gathering a posse of servants and tenants together, arming them with guns, blunderbusses, swords, pistols, and staves, and using them to intimidate alleged trespassers. Wealthy gentlemen, as we shall see, enjoyed enormous electoral influence and only the brave or the foolhardy chose to challenge the control of the great magnates over their lives. As Lewis Morris tersely sang:

> Your landlord shall be your God
> Beside him you're a mere wren
> For you dwell on *his* land.[23]

But there were also, of course, humane, Christian gentlemen who were deeply disturbed by the plight of the underprivileged. Benevolent men, for a variety of reasons, relieved the poor, the sick, and the aged in times of emergency, provided funds in the form of bequests to set up children in apprenticeships, and established almshouses and charity schools. Substantial numbers of the lesser gentry also remained deeply proud of their roots and revealed their Welshness by collecting the literary treasures of the past, patronizing authors and poets, and subscribing to the increasingly rapid flow of Welsh printed books.

It is hard to generalize about the characteristics of the Welsh gentry, for

[22] E. D. Jones, 'Gleanings from Radnorshire Files of Great Sessions Papers, 1691-1699', *Trans. Radnorshire Hist. Soc.* 13 (1943), p. 25.

[23] Hugh Owen, *The Life and Works of Lewis Morris 1701-1765* (Anglesey Antiq. Soc., 1951), p. 256.

they were clearly a mixed group. Some were able to cultivate an extravagantly lavish life-style, whilst others were hard-pressed to stay solvent. Some were rakes and spendthrifts, while others were bookish, refined men. Some ruled their provinces with a rod of iron, whilst others were Christian gentlemen and men of honour. Their wives, on the other hand, were so closely confined to the drawing-room that their personalities and interests were rather more uniform. Women were not entitled or expected to voice an opinion on matters of public concern. Their lot was to obey, suffer in childbed, entertain guests, and manage the household. Gentlemen expected their wives to be modest, affectionate, dutiful, and submissive. For many years during early married life women were forced to suffer frequent and debilitating pregnancies. Mary Pryce of Gunley in Montgomeryshire gave birth to nine children between 1697 and 1710. In an age of arranged marriages it is not surprising that some wives were badly treated by their husbands. Mary, the wife of Sir Charles Kemeys of Cefnmabli, loved her husband deeply and spent long sleepless nights in his absence. Kemeys, however, worshipped the bottle rather than his wife and proved demonstrably neglectful of her feelings. The duke of Bolton, husband of Anne Vaughan of Golden Grove, abandoned his wife when he fell in love with Lavinia Fenton, a celebrated London actress. Plagued by the curse of boredom, gentry wives whiled away the hours by reading romantic novels, drinking tea, listening to minstrels, and playing backgammon or whist. It was said of Mary Price of Hengwrt, Merioneth, that the only means by which an angel could seek her out on Judgement Day would be by shaking a box of dice 'and she would come at a call'.[24] Others took refuge in pious literature: Mary Myddelton of Croesnewydd, Denbighshire, derived great comfort from reading the works of à Kempis, Pascal, and William Law.

The most wealthy and sophisticated gentlemen and women were also connoisseurs of fashion. This was an age of refined tastes, and owners of large estates were able to use their capital to build anew, according to Renaissance styles. Tredegar House, near Newport, rebuilt by Sir William Morgan in 1670, was one of the few Welsh houses to display baroque features. The largest Renaissance house in Wales, it contained opulent, stately rooms, elegantly panelled and decorated walls, lavish paintings, gilt leather chairs, velvet cushions, Turkish carpets, tiles from Holland, and marble fireplaces from Italy. Another outstanding three-storeyed edifice—the Great Castle House—was built within the grounds of Monmouth Castle in 1673. An enormous stone house, its classical frontispiece, stone-mullioned windows, and exquisitely decorated plaster ceilings made it both a dignified and a palatial home. At Powis Castle, the Dutch-trained

[24] P. R. Roberts, 'The Social History of the Merioneth Gentry, c. 1660–1840', *Journal Merioneth Hist. and Record Soc.* 4 (1961–4), p. 220.

architect, William Winde, introduced Dutch and Italian styles: the grand staircase, the state bedchamber, and the blue drawing-room were all decorated in opulent baroque style. In the same spirit, ornamental gardens, shrubberies, orchards, and lakes were designed in a style befitting gentlemen of rank and fashion. The famous orangery at Margam included orange, lemon, and citrus trees, whilst the superb hanging gardens and terraces at Powis Castle, inspired by Italian concepts, were astonishingly beautiful. At Llannerch, Mutton Davies installed intricate and expensive water-devices based on Italian models. The most outstanding examples of baroque art in Wales, however, are the magnificent wrought-iron gates and screens which embellish many estates and churches in north-east Wales, including Chirk Castle, Leeswood Park, St Giles's Church, Wrexham, and St Peter's Church, Ruthin. Inspired by the artistry of Jean Tijou, these splendidly elaborate gates were designed by Robert and John Davies, humble gatesmiths from Bersham, near Wrexham.

Lack of capital prevented more modest gentlemen from attempting much more than adapting, extending, or repairing their mansions. Most of the rebuilding occurred in the upper Severn valley, where many handsome half-timbered houses were constructed or extended. In general, however, there was a shift away from timber to stone, a much wider use of brick and glass, and a greater emphasis on privacy, comfort, and ornamentation. When Richard Vaughan redesigned Corsygedol in the early eighteenth century, he laid new floors, installed window sashes, and added several new rooms. Similarly, when John Meller, a prosperous London lawyer, took possession of Erddig in 1716, he redesigned the house by adding two wings at each end and replacing mullion and transom windows with sashes. Meller also equipped the house with superb silvered and walnut chairs, gilt girandoles, and pier-glasses purchased in London. Most modest gentlemen, however, furnished their homes with solid, enduring furniture made of seasoned oak, ash, or elm by local craftsmen. Welsh joiners were scarcely affected by London fashions and continued to supply the homes of the gentry with beds, tables, settles, chairs, dressers, chests, and press cupboards (*cwpwrdd deuddarn a thridarn*) which were essentially Welsh in character and design. Both in redesigning and furnishing homes, only the truly affluent were in a position to keep up with fluctuations of taste.

Whereas the gentry enjoyed seemingly endless privileges, the non-gentle or common peasantry, who formed the overwhelming majority of the rural population, were blessed with few comforts. Within this group, the economic circumstances of yeomen, husbandmen, craftsmen, farm servants, cottagers, labourers, and the poor varied considerably. The most prosperous peasants were yeomen. The term 'yeoman' was highly ambiguous and was increasingly becoming a suffix of social rather than economic significance. It is probably true to say that the tendency by the second half of the seventeenth century was for the term 'yeoman' to be used to describe farmers big and small. Some yeomen administered possessions which were larger and more prosperous than those owned by parish gentlemen and even more claimed to be able to boast a finer pedigree than their more privileged superiors. Judging by probate inventories, however, most yeomen in the poorer rural counties were small farmers: the median value of a yeoman estate ranged from £26 in Caernarfonshire to £37 in Flintshire. Even so, their mode of living generally set them well above husbandmen. Much of their assets was tied up in livestock, farm implements, and crops, but those who had some surplus funds were usually more prepared than most to respond favourably to new husbandry techniques. Yeomen were tolerably well housed, clothed, and fed. They lived in sturdy farmhouses, furnished with solid and durable furniture and equipped with the necessary household ware. To them, literacy was both a mark of social pride and an economic asset, and some of the well-to-do among them were well able to afford to send their sons to grammar schools and universities. Yeomen were also invaluable local administrators and men of influence, especially in open parishes where the power of substantial landowners was conspicuous by its absence. From their ranks were drawn high constables of the hundreds, overseers of the poor, overseers of the highways, and churchwardens. They were, for the most part, entitled to vote in county elections and were also eligible to serve on juries at both quarter and great sessions.

Below yeomen in the social hierarchy came husbandmen or small farmers. In almost all cases, these were farmers of small acreage and slender purses. Although their status varied—some were customary tenants whilst others were copyholders or tenants-at-will—they were obliged to live frugally and to produce most of their own food themselves in order to survive. Their life was a ceaseless and exhausting round of beaver-like toil from which there was no escape until death intervened. The fortunes of a husbandman were extremely fragile and unstable, and were generally dictated by the vagaries of the weather, the quality of the harvest, the buoyancy of local fairs and markets, and the financial burdens imposed upon him by the demands of central and local government. Small farmers were invariably obliged to acquire an alternative part-time occupation, such as spinning, weaving, or knitting, to help them make ends meet. Few could entertain hopes of accumulating a private reserve fund which might cushion them against misfortune or help them improve their lot. Saving money was simply out of the question, for any profits were swallowed up by rents, local rates, taxes, tithes, and debts. They lived on the knife-edge margin of penury; and flooded fields, rotten crops, or light yields were often enough to bring them crashing down into the ranks of the poor.

Rural craftsmen took considerable pride in their skills and were careful to hand them down from generation to generation. They were essential members of the local community. Blacksmiths were employed in shoeing horses and producing items made of iron for the farm and the kitchen. Carpenters fashioned tools, furniture, and domestic utensils, usually from local oak, ash, or elm, which were characterized by their durability rather than their sophistication. Weavers and tailors provided essential clothes. Many other skilled craftsmen, notably wheelwrights, saddlers, coopers, turners, and thatchers, produced a wide range of products both for domestic and agricultural purposes. The most highly skilled craftsmen usually shared the same living standards as small farmers. But since many of them required more than one source of revenue in order to survive, they also kept livestock, grew crops, or processed wool. Many craftsmen exercised a decisive influence on the cultural and religious life of their communities. Their workshops were often meeting-places for articulate and literate men. Unlike tenant farmers and labourers, most craftsmen could pursue their crafts indoors without wetting or tiring their bodies. This left them with the time and the opportunity to discuss religious and cultural matters, and even to read. A relatively high degree of literacy was evident among rural craftsmen: many subscribed enthusiastically to Welsh books and became the backbone of Dissenting and Methodist congregations. Some were unusually gifted men: Rhys Morgan of Pencraig-nedd, Glamorgan, was a carpenter, weaver, harp-maker, poet, and preacher. Narrow horizons did not dull their minds: Thomas William, a humble weaver who spent virtually the whole of his life on Mynydd Bach in rural Carmarthenshire, read Tudor chronicles, classical novels, and Welsh devotional books with voracious enthusiasm. Thomas Jones, Wales's first almanacker, was a tailor's son, whilst many ballad-mongers and poets were craftsmen.

By the later Stuart period, possibly as many as a third of the population were labourers, an amorphous mass of mobile, unskilled, and illiterate men and women, whose life was a daily struggle to keep body and soul together. Landless labourers earned a daily pittance—ranging from 6d. a day in Caernarfonshire to 1od. a day in Glamorgan—by the labour of their own hands and the dripping sweat of their own brows. These unsung, obscure Judes were the workhorses of the Welsh economy. When Griffith Jones, Llanddowror, argued in favour of education through the medium of Welsh, one of his major arguments was that instructing Welsh labourers through a foreign tongue might provoke them to rebel against their allotted life of unsparing toil, desert their callings, seek a new life in Pennsylvania, and thereby ruin the Welsh economy. The working hours and conditions of labourers were akin to those of serfs. They were employed in hedging, ditching, ploughing, sowing, weeding, reaping, harvesting, shearing, threshing, sawing wood, digging gardens, and cutting gorse and broom. Roughly clad and miserably fed, they worked from dawn to dusk, sometimes under a roasting sun but more often in pouring rain. None of them could rely on receiving regular work. Since employment fluctuated according to the rhythms of the season, they were obliged to get used to periods of enforced idleness. Labourers who had small gardens were able to grow carrots, leeks, peas, and cabbages. Some kept a pig or a cow, while many took advantage of the right to gather wood, gorse, and peat on their employer's land. Fresh seafood, such as eels, crabs, lobsters, herrings, and cockles, added variety to the diet of labourers who lived in coastal areas. Poor labourers in south Wales helped to keep body and soul together by collecting kelp (calcined ashes of seaweed), which was used in the manufacture of glass bottles, or soap ashes derived from fern-burning. Virtually every penny earned by labourers was used to buy food, drink, and clothing. They lived in small, squalid cottages of one or two rooms. Such mud-walled hovels were often utterly wretched. Those at Walwyn's Castle in Pembrokeshire were described as 'a sort of extempore erections of dirt and clay called *clom*, and very uncertain being though but lately built [and] suffered after to fall into ruins'.[25] Pinched by hunger and want, labourers found life harsh and hard to bear. They lay at the mercy of demanding landlords and stewards, tyrannical bailiffs, and hounding justices. For them, life offered no comforts and very little hope.

At the foot of the social pyramid lay substantial numbers of paupers. Society divided the poor into two groups: the deserving poor of old, orphans, sick, and disabled people, and the undeserving—thriftless vagrants, rogues, and vagabonds. Hearth tax returns for the 1660s and 1670s reveal a high proportion of paupers in most counties. Even in the prosperous county of Glamorgan, 60 per cent of the population lived in houses of one hearth and 30 per cent of households were inhabited by paupers. A third of the households of Montgomeryshire sheltered paupers. In 1681 it was estimated that 38 per cent of all heads of households in the parish of Whitford in Flintshire were paupers. Such people lived a hand-to-mouth existence. Undernourished and emaciated, they were a ready prey for infectious diseases and were always the first to perish of famine and cold during severe winters. Although they have left few personal testimonies of their thoughts and feelings, court and borough records are studded with heart-rending petitions for relief from the sick, the unemployed, and the homeless. The loss of the principal wage-earner, either through illness or death, could prove a shattering blow to a poor

---

[25] 'Parochialia', *Arch. Camb*. 3, p. 24.

family. When Eleanor Eckley of Presteigne lost her husband in 1697 she
was unable to pay four shillings to the collector of burials and was forced to
live 'in a poor cot without any shelter of walls and almost exposed to all the
weather'.[26] In fact, most poor people lived in primitive, single-roomed
hovels which appalled and disgusted travellers. Walled with clay or turf
and roofed with rushes, these flimsy cottages lacked chimneys or fireplaces.

Apart from a scatter of wooden lumber, the poor had few possessions:
they sat on stones or stools, slept on beds of hay or straw, and ate meals on
floors strewn with earth, rushes, or bracken. Parishes strove to supply the
needs of the deserving poor: church collections were donated to the needy,
benevolent men fed and clothed pauper children, and wealthy testators
remembered the distress of the poor in their wills. Conversely, local
communities were haunted by the fear of homeless men and women—the
'undesirables' who wandered the country. The vagrant poor were believed
to be such an acute threat to local resources, as well as a potential source of
disorder, that they were liable to be arrested, whipped, thrust into houses
of correction, or marched summarily back to their native parishes.
Whenever little work was available, hordes of labourers joined droves of
unemployed and destitute people who had no choice but to roam the
countryside and towns in search of food, shelter, and employment. Many
simply did not survive. On a bitterly cold winter's night in 1739, Owen
Humphreys, a poor youth from Llanwrin, Montgomeryshire, who walked
from parish to parish begging for bread, perished from want of food and
shelter. He was simply one of many who died from cold and starvation.

It is much harder to penetrate the mentalities of unsophisticated peasant
people than to discover the characteristics of the gentry. Patterns of
thought and practice probably differed from ours in a thousand little ways
of which we know little. Most peasants spent virtually the whole of their
lives in their native parish, and although they also had detailed knowledge
of surrounding villages and parishes they identified themselves primarily
and proudly with their native heaths. Community ties were strong and it
was not only poets who were capable of tracing the history of families in
vivid detail over several generations. 'His memory is astounding', said
William Morris of his aged father, Morris Prichard, a carpenter and
cooper, 'it is wonderful to hear him recount hundreds of events which have
befallen since his boyhood.'[27] Farmers tended to store the past in the
memory in terms of good and lean years. Much emphasis was placed on
memory and oral testimony both as a source of knowledge and as a means
of settling disputes concerning land or voting rights. Edward Lhuyd, the
scholar and scientist, preferred to trust the memory and the oral evidence
of an illiterate shepherd rather than the pious observations of a bishop in

---

[26] E. D. Jones, 'Gleanings from Radnorshire Files', p. 32.
[27] *Morris Letters*, ii. 517.

matters of 'mountainous and desert places'.[28] Indeed, the invaluable
evidence assembled by Lhuyd's correspondents reveals clearly that common
people were so closely tied to the soil that they were extraordinarily well-
versed in the physical features, climate, flora and fauna, marine and animal
life, place-names, local customs, and dialects of their communities. Most
peasants clung happily to age-old habits of thought. The world, in their
eyes, was a solid, motionless focal point around which all else moved. The
influence of fate was 'as natural and unavoidable as the course of the sun
and river, or the growth of the grass in the field'.[29]

Yet it would be wrong to suppose that peasant communities were havens
of bliss, good humour, and bland stoicism. From time to time, seemingly
harmonious communities were torn by petty criminal deeds, family
quarrels, and cases of assault and riot. As we shall see, court records are
replete with cases of assaults in churchyards, alehouses, and private homes.
Tensions were often provoked by the hazards and insecurities of the
environment. Generally, the labouring classes were a constant prey to
disease, for they ate badly, dressed shoddily, and lived in wretched hovels.
Few people bothered with personal hygiene, medical knowledge was so
rudimentary that physical pain and suffering were endemic, and the
disgusting concoctions peddled by doctors, apothecaries, and quacks were
exotically named but ultimately useless. Most peasants preferred to rely on
age-old herbal remedies or take their chance with the local wise woman or
cunning man, some of whom were revered for their extraordinary gifts of
healing. The lack of nourishing food not only weakened the resistance of
common people to coughs, colds, agues, fluxes, and killing diseases such as
typhus and influenza, but also made them tetchy and irritable. Whilst the
tables of affluent gentlemen were decked with salmon, venison, mutton,
beef, oysters, herrings, and fruit, peasants lived chiefly on a diet of milk,
flummery, bread made of oats or barley, together with occasional supplies
of vegetables and fruit. Although Lewis Morris liked to claim, in nostalgic
vein, that 'a man would not die for a hundred years, if he could eat a bellyfull
of bubbling gruel',[30] there is no doubt that liquid foods such as flummery,
porridge and gruel offered a monotonous surfeit of carbohydrates but few
vitamins. Few members of the labouring classes ate meat unless they
owned a strip of land on which they might keep a cow, a pig, or poultry.
Some intrepid poachers also risked their lives by catching rabbits, ducks, or
pheasants on gentry estates. 'The vulgar', it was claimed in 1684, 'are most
miserable and low as the rich are happy and high, both to an extreme.'[31]
During periods of dearth and increases in the price of bread, hungry people

[28] F. V. Emery, *Edward Lhuyd F.R.S. 1660–1709* (Cardiff, 1971), p. 27.
[29] NLW MS 10B, p. 80.   [30] *Morris Letters*, i. 320.
[31] T. Dineley, *The Account of the Official Progress of the First Duke of Beaufort through
Wales* (1684), ed. R. W. Banks (London, 1888), p. 249.

protested vigorously. Following the famine years of 1708–9, colliers in south-west Wales were living on cockles. 'I'm sure some of them look more like skeletons than men', observed the steward of the Briton Ferry estate, 'the poor children being almost famished, their case being so miserable.'[32] Nothing infuriated the hungry poor more than the export of priceless supplies of corn during periods of dearth and distress. In May 1709 furious mobs in Wrexham bayed for the blood of local badgers who, in obedience to instructions received from Lords Powis and Molyneaux, had purchased supplies of corn in bulk and transported it to France. In June 1728, hungry women in Beaumaris, armed with stones and broken glasses, sought to prevent Sir Roger Mostyn's servants from shipping corn.

The presence of immigrants also often provoked economic tensions. Strangers, or 'foreigners' as they were called, were regarded with chilly suspicion, especially if they knew no Welsh. During the civil wars, royalist commanders found the Welsh at best truculent and, at worst, fiercely uncooperative. Lord Willoughby's agent in north Wales beat his head in frustration as he desperately tried to gather in rents 'amidst as many enemies as I had men to deal with'.[33] Land-hungry speculators were 'knaves' who denuded forests, trampled on the rights of commoners and 'undid the country by making lands dearer to the natives'.[34] English merchants in Pembrokeshire in 1684 were described as 'the strangers who come thither to eat the countrymen's bread out of their mouths'.[35] Widespread resentment was aired in Neath when Sir Humphrey Mackworth staffed his mines and smelteries with skilled English workers, many of whom, it was alleged, were profane, loose livers who wallowed in drink and led fair maidens astray. In a society in which the margin between sufficiency and dearth was extremely fine and where employment was at best irregular, the arrival of English workers was always likely to occasion resentful protests.

On the other hand, few witchcraft trials were held in Stuart Wales. The stresses and strains which were provoked as English society moved from a highly integrated, neighbourly community to a more individualist or commercial economy were not evident in Wales. Welsh society remained strongly wedded to the traditional pattern of mutual obligation, hospitality, and good neighbourliness. Yet, belief in witchcraft still remained deeply woven into the fabric of peasant life; and malevolent women, who often lived alone on the fringes of society and were believed to be endowed with ample powers of mischief, were occasionally brought before the courts.

---

[32] A. H. John, *The Industrial Development of South Wales 1750–1850* (Cardiff, 1950), p. 18.

[33] P. R. Roberts, 'The Decline of the Welsh Squires in the Eighteenth Century', *NLWJ* 13 (1963–4), p. 158.

[34] NLW MS 120406E, p. 15.

[35] T. Godwyn, *Phanatical Tenderness* (London, 1684), pp. 24–5.

Anne Ellis, a widow of Penley, Flintshire, who was accused of practising witchcraft in 1657, reputedly lived 'by begging and knitting of stockings . . . and many people used to give more [to her] than to any other beggar out of fear'.[36] Most of these poor creatures were believed to be responsible for causing accidents to persons, the death of animals or, most commonly, the souring of butter, cheese, and beer. In 1693, Catherine Rees of Nancwnlle in Cardiganshire was accused of cursing the local clergyman and paralysing a young child. Some of the more superstitious labourers at Jefferston coalworks in Pembrokeshire during the 1690s used to say 'there comes Olly' and 'fall atrembling all over'[37] whenever Olly Powell muttered dark curses in the direction of those who refused to supply her with coal or food. The alleged ability of eccentric and bad-tempered women to do harm by occult means made them figures to be respected and feared. However, few were brought to book. Witchcraft prosecutions were declining swiftly by the later Stuart period and it was more common for society to prosecute malicious sowers of discord and strife than eccentric old women.

Those who found life both cruel and capricious continued long after this period to find an explanation for their misfortunes in the belief in witchcraft. Moreover, beneath the 'orthodox' culture of Protestant Christianity there lurked a thriving subculture founded on superstition, magic, and 'popish beliefs' which was to linger on in peasant communities well into Victorian times. Common people carried charms and amulets to ward off evil, engaged fairies, spirits, and goblins in conversation, travelled long distances to wells and shrines to seek the blessing of saints and restored health, visited the cottages of cunning men and wise women with boundless faith and optimism, and remained convinced that their lot in this world was bound up with the constellations of the stars, the movement of the planets, and the phases of the moon. Peasants were traditionally conservative and gregarious in their habits, and successive generations of religious reformers found that the task of eliminating the notion that the destiny of men and women was in the hands of powerful supernatural forces was well-nigh hopeless. 'People will not be taken off their old groundless observances',[38] complained Philip Henry mournfully in 1671. Scores of religious reformers long after his death were still echoing his lament.

While some took refuge in superstition and magic, others delighted in participating in the simple games and recreations of the countryside. Between the twin pivots in the Welshman's calendar—*Calan Gaeaf* (1 November) and *Calan Haf* (1 May)—a wide range of festivities and

---

[36] J. G. Williams, 'Witchcraft in Seventeenth-Century Flintshire', p. 33.

[37] Geraint H. Jenkins, 'Popular Beliefs in Wales from the Restoration to Methodism', *BBCS* 27 (1977), p. 447.

[38] M. H. Lee (ed.), *Diaries and Letters of Philip Henry* (London, 1882), p. 240.

customs was observed. The heavy burdens of sustained agricultural labour forced peasants to seek relaxations and distractions from care on Sundays, holy days, or wakes. On Sundays, peasants threw aside traditional restraints and scandalized earnest Dissenters by drinking, dancing, and feasting. In 1679, Thomas Wynne, a Quaker, inveighed against the 'great meetings' held on Sundays in Flintshire, 'with fiddlers, to revel and roar, swear, dance and sing, yea, the same up and down the country, and Morris dances, wakes, interludes, football, ninepins and tennis'.[39] The *gwylmabsant* (wake), a parochial festival normally held in spring, was often the scene of heavy tippling, riotous behaviour, and debauchery. Political elections and public ceremonies were also opportunities for licentious behaviour and turbulence. For those who were sunk in misery, alcohol offered a temporary means of escape from their poverty and frustration. Beer was drunk in such substantial quantities at fairs, markets, and festive gatherings that whipping-posts, ducking-stools, and stocks were habitually needed to bring drunkards to heel.

Since peasants were unable to enjoy the county pursuits or the whirl of city amusements which occupied the leisure hours of the landed classes, their recreations were simple, informal events held on the village green, in open fields, or outside taverns and churches. Few games were governed by specific rules and if violence and bloodshed were inevitable at least this often served as a safety-valve for inter-parish hostility. A football match, involving twenty-four players, between the parishes of Llanbadrig and Llanfair-yng-Nghornwy in Anglesey in April 1734 drew cheering crowds of 500 people, who warmly appreciated the 'courage, skill and resolution'[40] of both teams. Not many participants in the game of knappan, traditionally held on Shrove Tuesday and Easter Monday in the counties of south-west Wales, returned home without blackened faces, bruised limbs, or broken bones. On the village green, recreations such as running, wrestling, cudgelling, and hurling the stone placed much emphasis on physical vigour and courage. Griffith Morgan (Guto Nyth-brân) of Llanwynno, Glamorgan, became a legend when he dropped dead in 1737 following an astonishing cross-country run from Newport to Bedwas church, a distance of twelve miles, which he was said to have completed in fifty-three minutes. No sport was more popular than cock-fighting: these dramatically exciting contests, held either in churchyards or in specially designed cockpits built in towns, were violent, bloody affairs held before baying crowds. Whatever their shortcomings, however, village sports helped to strengthen community ties and brought a dash of colour, warmth, and joy into the lives of people whose solaces and delights were few. If only briefly, such relaxations

[39] Thomas Wynne, *An Antichristian Conspiracy Detected* (London, 1679), p. 17.
[40] Hugh Owen, 'The Diary of William Bulkeley of Brynddu', *Trans. Anglesey Antiq. Soc.* (1931), p. 29.

provided peasants with moments when they might forget the penury, squalor, and tedium of their daily lives.

Although there was a good deal of migration to English cities and towns like Bristol, Chester, Hereford, and Shrewsbury, the city of London offered the most attractive escape-route to humble men and women who were driven from their native parishes by the pressure of over-population, dearth, and unemployment. With a population of 575,000 by 1700, London dwarfed every other English city, let alone Welsh towns. Thanks to Welsh poets, word soon got around that London was the fairest city on earth: its streets, sang Ellis ab Ellis, ran with gold. Its colour, turbulence, and boundless attractions clearly offered men and women of humble stock much wider scope for their enterprise and ambitions. Many Welsh gentlemen, merchants, and scholars prospered in London and confessed, as did James Howell, to being 'habitually in love with her'.[41] By this period, however, London was as much a Mecca for craftsmen, servants, and labourers as it was for affluent gentlemen, merchants, and drovers. It welcomed an annual stream of young migrants, many of them masterless men of wit and enterprise. Some of the luckiest profited financially, others fell by the wayside. A handful even achieved fame. Arise Evans, a native of Llangelynnin, Merioneth, settled as a tailor in Blackfriars and styled himself a prophet. Determined to become famous come what might, Evans thrust himself into the presence of Charles I, Charles II, Oliver Cromwell, and Henry Ireton, and succeeded in intriguing them, and many other eminent men, with his prognostications. Thomas Jones, another tailor from Merioneth, joined the hurly-burly world of the Grub Street fraternity during the 1680s and by dint of unwearying labour became a successful bookseller and almanacker. It was, therefore, possible for colourful and determined characters to emerge from total obscurity.

Others, moved less perhaps by the hope of financial gain than by the spirit of adventure, entered service in the army or navy. Sir Thomas Morgan of Llangatwg, Monmouthshire, a diminutive, semi-literate man, began a celebrated military career as a volunteer in the Thirty Years' War. During the Civil Wars he won a knighthood for his service to the republican cause in Scotland, and he ended his days as the governor of Jersey. Richard Philipps, the younger son of a Pembrokeshire clergyman, joined the king's army in 1678 and by 1717 had become governor of Nova Scotia. Scaling rope ladders as a pirate helped Henry Morgan, a Monmouthshire labourer, to climb the social ladder and to win fame as Wales's most illustrious buccaneer. Morgan ran away to sea at the age of nineteen and became a swashbuckling privateer of rare daring and prowess. From his base at Barbados, he led brilliant forays to Panama and

---

[41] James Howell, *Londinopolis* (London, 1657), sig. A3ʳ.

Venezuela, where he snapped up rich spoils and enchanted beautiful women. He was knighted by Charles II and appointed deputy-governor of Jamaica in 1674. He died there in 1688, worn out by his amorous adventures and his addiction to drink. Equally flamboyant was Bartholomew Roberts (*Barti Ddu* or Black Bart, 1682–1722), a Pembrokeshire man of exceptional courage and daring. The first pirate to hoist the 'Skull and Crossbones' flag, Roberts captured and plundered ships from Barbados to Newfoundland, and earned a reputation as the terror of the Spanish Main.

Differences in topography, soil, climate, and wealth, accentuated by poor communications, dictated variations in farming patterns in Wales. Wales was a collection of fragmented regional economies and there were, as Edward Lhuyd pointed out in the 1690s, particularly clear contrasts between patterns of upland and lowland farming. In the rugged, precipitous Welsh uplands and the desolate, wind-swept moorlands, only coarse grass, bracken, and heather grew. In these areas, poor soils, a high incidence of winter snow and year-round rainfall, and a restricted number of sunshine hours offered little scope outside sheep farming. On the other hand, there were greater possibilities in the broad fertile valleys and coastal plains. Lower rainfall, more agreeable temperatures, and relatively rich and fertile soil provided a more appropriate environment for farming. Whereas corn, oats, and rye formed the staple cereal crops in the more impoverished upland regions, wheat, barley, oats, rye, peas, and beans were grown on the broader and more fertile lowland plains and river valleys. However, many thousands of acres of valley marshlands, marginal mountain pastures, and coastal bogs and dunes remained open and unenclosed until the end of the eighteenth century. Most enclosures were carried out piecemeal and were confined to the valleys and to tracts of land surrounding villages and farmsteads. In 1795 it was estimated that 1,696,827 acres of common and waste lands were still unenclosed.

Growing cereal crops was no easy task and most upland farmers devoted their energies mainly to rearing lean cattle. Pasture of good quality was always scarce and only on the more prosperous lowland farms was a surplus of grain available for fattening cattle. In early May, in accordance with the ancient practice of transhumance, sheep, cattle, and goats were driven from their winter quarters up to the summer pastures on the hills, where they were guarded by their owners who dwelt in *hafotai* (upland shelters). Cattle were the linchpin of the Welsh economy. The prosperity and well-being of small communities were heavily dependent on the livestock trade. Wales was a major breeding ground for those who fattened cattle in English counties; and the growth in the population of London and other leading English cities, together with the Irish Cattle Act of 1666, which prohibited the import of livestock from Ireland, created an insatiable demand for Welsh meat. Tens of thousands of cattle were driven out of Wales by drovers each year. Travelling a steady twenty miles a day, drovers and their animals trekked eastwards along ridge-top routes and old mountain paths to the lusher pastures of the Midlands and the southern counties of England. Suitably fattened, they were then driven on to the lucrative markets of Barnet and Smithfield. Most drovers were well-to-do men. On his death in 1736, Thomas Lewis of Trefeibion Meyrick in Anglesey left nearly £1,500 in money and stock. In order to qualify for an annual licence to trade they were required to be literate, numerate, married householders aged above 30. But they also needed to be rugged, hard-fisted, and intrepid men. Little romance belonged to droving. It was a filthy and dangerous occupation—but clearly a necessary one. For drovers were 'the Spanish fleet' of Wales,[42] providing farmers with much-needed currency and acting as local bankers and investors on behalf of landowners. Popular rhymesters believed that drovers were a roguish breed and although Edward Morris, the poet of Perthillwydion, and Dafydd Jones, the celebrated hymnologist of Caeo, were drovers of unimpeachable character, many of their colleagues were not overburdened with scruples. A cloud of witnesses variously described the drover as 'a dirty conditioned fellow', 'the very worst kind of highwayman', and 'an old thief'.[43] Court records reveal several cases of betrayal of trust, with many drovers succumbing to the temptation to abscond to Ireland with sums of money entrusted to their care by hard-pressed farmers. Nevertheless, the cattle trade remained a powerful stimulant to the Welsh economy and enabled farmers both large and small to keep body and soul together.

Welsh estates were units of ownership which supplied landowners with an annual income from rents and fines paid by tenants. Welsh tenant farms were generally small, ranging from ten to sixty acres. Work carried out on such farms was always arduous and seldom profitable. Tenants were granted leases for a term of three lives or for twenty-one years. Such leases stipulated the prompt payment of food and service rents over and above normal money rents. These burdens tended to vary from estate to estate, but the general demands were for reaping, ploughing, harrowing, digging, and carting coal, together with the supply of gifts such as eggs, capons, geese, or hens on specified feast days twice a year. William Edwards of Bryn-coch, Whitford, was obliged to keep a greyhound or a spaniel for the use of Sir Roger Mostyn and his heirs. Obedient and industrious tenants were generally treated with consideration by their masters. Most were assured of a reasonable measure of tenure and their relationship with their

[42] *Calendar of Wynn Papers*, p. 287.
[43] *Calendar of Letters relating to North Wales*, p. 133; Ellis Wynne, *Visions of the Sleeping Bard*, pp. 21–5; G. M. Griffiths, 'Glimpses of Denbighshire in the Records of the Court of Great Sessions', *Denbighshire Hist. Soc. Trans.* 22 (1973), p. 100.

landlords was, on the whole, harmonious. During periods of economic hardship, sensible landowners tempered strictness with mercy by permitting their tenants to pay rents in kind, to perform extra labour services, or by allowing their arrears to accumulate and, in some extreme cases, to be written off. Many landlords were reluctant to evict tenants, partly because of a genuine concern for their well-being but more often lest they should find difficulty in securing suitable farmer's to replace them. However, whenever their own debts mounted swiftly they took action with a vengeance. During the 1720s the Powis family, deep in debt, ordered its agents to collect all rent arrears 'or else drive the people out of the country, for my lord had as good be without tenants as to have such as pay no rents'.[44] There were other potential flash-points too. A landlord's greed for land often soured relationships, whilst bullying stewards were much vilified in verse.

Farming was still essentially a manual art. Simple hand tools, a wooden plough, a harrow, and a cart were virtually all the implements which the farmer had at hand. Farm implements were rough-hewn, cumbrous, and old-fashioned. Wooden ploughs, drawn by a team of four or six hardy oxen, tore rather than cut the ground, whilst wooden triangular harrows rarely succeeded in pulverizing the soil thoroughly enough to produce a finely wrought tilth. Seed was sown by hand and crops were cut with scythes and reaping-hooks. Land was cleared by folding or by beating and burning, and good soil was rapidly exhausted owing to the lack of sophisticated methods of crop rotation. Innovations in cropping remained thinly spread, partly because farmers remained wedded to well-tried and familiar farming practices hallowed by centuries of use.

Even so, recent scholarship has revealed that, from the 1680s onwards, the livelier spirits within the farming community were becoming more responsive to new techniques in husbandry. A significant number of forward-looking landlords and farmers on the principal estates of Wales, including Erddig, Lleweni, Mostyn, Nannau, Picton, and Margam, were cultivating legumes and improved grasses, such as clover, sainfoin, perennial ryegrass, and trefoil, in order to improve the quality of their livestock and raise yields. There are unmistakable signs that in the fertile lowlands, where the soil and climate were favourable, agriculture was becoming more productive. More extensive use was made of lime, marl, sand, dung, and muck as manures, whilst near the coast seaweed, shells, and sand were also profitably used. In 1704 Henry Rowlands of Llanidan completed his pioneering *Idea Agriculturae* (published in 1764), which included current agricultural theories, accounts of local experiments, and cogent arguments in favour of a more widespread use of shelly sand, white

---

[44] T. M. Humphreys, 'Rural Society in Eighteenth-Century Montgomeryshire', p. 111.

marl, and lime. Enterprising stewards, who kept themselves well informed of current farming ideas, adopted more flexible and efficient methods on their estates. Watkin Owen, steward of the Gwydir estate in the 1680s, owned a copy of John Worlidge's *Systema Agriculturae* (1669), while at Bodewryd, Edward Wynne possessed copies of Richard Bradley's *A Compleat Body of Husbandry* (1727) and Edward Laurence's *The Duty of a Steward to his Lord* (1731). Wynne, in fact, was a shrewd practical farmer who employed progressive techniques, including a crop rotation of wheat, barley, peas and beans, barley and clover, mowing clover, grazing clover, and wheat. In 1728 he was cultivating potatoes and by 1737 he was growing small quantities of turnips.

Yet, new developments such as these were not extensive, nor did they lead to striking increases in agricultural output. Only in the more fertile arable areas were agricultural improvements a practical proposition. Much of upland Wales was unsuited to modern husbandry and landlords were still reluctant to plough their profits back into land or to stimulate improved methods of husbandry. Furthermore, since a growing number of Welsh estates were in the hands of absentee landowners, few progressive ideas were being pressed upon tenant farmers. Travellers were prone to ascribe the backward state of Welsh agriculture to the incorrigible idleness of tenants, but Moses Williams was probably closer to the truth when he rebuked Welsh landowners for gadding about in English cities rather than improving their estates. Lack of capital resources severely restricted the opportunity of most farmers to implement new ideas and embrace the spirit of enterprise. They were so hard put to subsist that they were never in a position to experiment with new seeds or animal stock. The volume of printed material on modern husbandry was still small and of marginal significance only, while for Welsh-readers it was virtually non-existent. Force of custom hampered new developments: tenants were suspicious of newfangled methods and preferred to work the land as their fathers and forefathers had done. The truth is that most of them were too impoverished, downtrodden, and demoralized to carry out improvements.

There were no clear-cut boundaries between towns and the surrounding countryside in this period. Town and country were indivisible, for there was no hard and fast line between rural and urban life any more than there was between agrarian and industrial occupations. Rural labourers were often also urban weavers, cloth and leather workers depended on the surrounding countryside for their raw materials, yeomen owned tanyards in towns, and small farmers often found work as hauliers for furnaces. Wales had no capital and no cities. Bristol was the metropolis of the counties of south Wales; Shrewsbury functioned as the economic capital of mid-Wales to such a degree that on market day its streets echoed loudly to the sound of the Welsh language; the economic prosperity of north Wales was closely linked with that of Chester; and the people of Anglesey looked upon Dublin as their capital.

Welsh towns were small, modest, and unprepossessing units. By European standards they were little more than glorified villages. Small market towns were simply a collection of two or three principal streets, an assortment of houses, lanes, workshops, orchards, crofts, and gardens. A leisurely stroll from one end to the other took a matter of minutes only. Craftsmen and tradesmen kept sheds, workshops, kilns, and tanyards, while substantial householders owned tracts of grazing or cultivable land within town walls. Cattle and swine roamed the unpaved, undrained, and unlit streets. Diseases spread swiftly in towns owing to the dirt, squalor, and lack of hygiene. Butchers slaughtered animals in the streets, and the stench from malt-kilns, tanyards, and dye-houses was often overpowering. Churches and taverns reeked of stale sweat. Householders dumped rubbish and human excrement in the streets and kept dung-hills in their gardens. Celia Fiennes found Flint a 'very ragged place',[45] while the dirt and smoke of Aberystwyth offended the eyes and nose of Daniel Defoe. Prostitutes flourished in the towns of Dolgellau and Llanrwst, prompting Edward Morris, the drover, to dub the former 'a smoky Gomorrah' and the latter 'a second Sodom'.[46] If towns were insanitary, they were also a prey to fire, for flames spread alarmingly swiftly through timber-framed and thatched buildings. A quarter of the houses of Wrexham were burnt down in 1643, while Builth Wells was almost wholly destroyed by fire in 1681.

Even so, Welsh towns were of far greater significance to the economy than their modest size and shabby appearance might suggest. They offered not only employment and generally higher wages to migrants but also greater variety and excitement. Towns were the locations of fairs, markets, shops, schools, inns, and taverns. A host of entertainments—cock-fighting, wrestling, horse-racing, bowls, ninepins, puppet-shows, and dancing minstrels—attracted people from near and far. The colour and pageantry of public celebrations brought life and gaiety to the streets. Crowds flocked to see thieves and murderers hanged or convicted felons and whores stripped to the waist, flogged, and publicly humiliated. Inns and taverns were convenient centres of refreshment for travellers and local tradesmen, and were often the focal points for county business, local administration, and politics. These wider range of facilities made them, in many ways, the hub of the social and economic life of the surrounding countryside. They were vital centres for the distribution and sale of

[45] *The Illustrated Journeys of Celia Fiennes*, p. 158.
[46] Gwenllian Jones, 'Bywyd a Gwaith Edward Morris, Perthi Llwydion' (unpubl. University of Wales MA thesis, 1941), pp. 325-6.

agricultural produce. Markets attracted merchants, wayfaring traders, drovers, and pedlars as well as local farmers. Fairs, too, were visited by hundreds of people from far and near. Fairs were held at least twice a year, usually in spring and summer, and customers were able to buy a wide variety of miscellaneous items, including dairy produce, hides, sheepskins, ironware, refined metal goods, cloth, and linen. Weekly or monthly markets provided facilities to sell local surpluses of cheese, butter, corn, wheat, rye, meat, poultry, fish, and fruit. By the latter half of the seventeenth century, moreover, a much wider range of goods and commodities was available in shops. This reflected the growing importance of maritime trade and the developing links between shopkeepers and travelling pedlars, colporteurs, and chapmen. Mercers, acting as general retailers, were able to titillate affluent customers with window displays revealing gaily patterned textiles, expensive silks, lace, ribbons, hats, and buttons. Indeed, mercers stocked an extraordinarily wide range of miscellaneous goods, including linen, tapestry, calico, sugar, raisins, spices, dyes, cocoa, tobacco, soap, candles, powder, buttons, collars, locks, looking-glasses, spectacles, razors, scissors, and much else. Griffith Wynn of Caernarfon stocked haberdashery, grocery, ironmongery, stationery, tobacco, and spirits; George Buttall of Wrexham supplied sheet lead and iron girders; while Dawkins Gove of Carmarthen sold a variety of Welsh and English books as well as paper, primers, and parchment.

Welsh market towns were, therefore, increasingly valuable stimuli to the growth of the rural economy. The more thickly peopled and prosperous towns, usually located in relatively rich farming areas and closely linked to the principal roads, were clearly thriving. According to John Taylor, Carmarthen, the commercial capital of south-west Wales, lacked nothing but tobacco pipes. A plentiful, populous town of some 3,000 inhabitants, it was referred to by an early eighteenth-century traveller as 'the London of Wales'.[47] In north-east Wales, Wrexham's increasing prosperity was based on the woollen industry and its role as a centre for the exchange of goods between north Wales, the north of England, and the Midlands. The major growth areas, however, were industrial towns such as Neath and Swansea. New enterprises in the coal and copper industries, together with the opening of new port facilities and overseas markets, meant that Swansea in particular had acquired an industrial profile by the 1720s. Defoe was greatly impressed by Swansea: he described it as 'a very considerable town for trade',[48] where as many as a hundred ships could be seen loading coal.

The largest Welsh towns were sufficiently thriving to attract men of

[47] H. Moll, *A New Description of England and Wales* (London, 1724), p. 258.
[48] Daniel Defoe, *A Tour through the Whole Island of Great Britain*, eds. G. D. H. Cole and D. C. Browning (2 vols., London, 1962), ii. 54.

wealth and talent as well as the inevitable stream of masterless men. They offered expanding opportunities for ambitious men in search of commercial success. The younger sons of landed families, for instance, saw opportunities for entry into the ranks of prosperous merchant classes. Community life was governed, as in rural areas, by a small but powerful élite of wealthy gentry, comprising town gentry and professional classes, many of whom were bound together by personal and business ties. In effect, this ruling minority dictated the fortunes of the whole community. Their solid, handsome homes gave the impression of sober prosperity and provided an accurate index to their power, wealth, and discrimination. Most towns boasted a handful of professional men, notably lawyers, doctors, apothecaries, merchants, clergymen, and schoolmasters. Small-time lawyers such as Hugh Price, a pedlar's son, and David Williams, a weaver's son, both of Beaumaris, were busily climbing the greasy pole by the early eighteenth century. Town attorneys were increasingly being called upon to search for titles, prepare debt and credit transactions, mortgages, and entails, as well as to cope with the perennial flow of litigants. Doctors, apothecaries, and barber-surgeons dispensed potions and medicaments, reduced fractures and purges, and bled ailing patients. Hard-headed merchants expedited local trading developments and kept a sharp eye open for lucrative deals. Many town clergymen enjoyed fat incomes, whilst schoolmasters, printers, and booksellers prospered, as the demand for education and printed books grew. These middling sorts were a small but acquisitive group, as yet perhaps unaware of their corporate identity but wielding a growing influence in town corporations or parish vestries. Many of them deliberately aped the social manners and customs of their superiors, knowing that sheer hard work, determination, and just a little luck might one day bring them into the charmed circle of the privileged élite.

Tradesmen and skilled craftsmen also formed substantial and influential elements in Welsh towns. Most thriving towns had their maltsters, millers, brewers, tanners, cobblers, saddlers, glovers, hatters, fullers, weavers, and blacksmiths. In 1664, Brecon, a country town of some 2,000 inhabitants, had seventy tradesmen, including mercers, hosiers, butchers, glovers, corvisors, curriers, saddlers, and tanners. Denbigh boasted a high proportion of tanners, corvisors, and glovers. Such men put great trust in skilled craftsmanship and application. Tradesmen and master craftsmen were relatively well-to-do men who were able to furnish their houses well, and eat and drink in comfort. Unskilled craftsmen, on the other hand, were impoverished people who lived in sparsely furnished houses and eked out a miserably precarious living. Below them came the urban poor: the sick, the disabled, the old, beggars, vagrants, and vagabonds. The latter, in particular, were feared and despised by their betters. Hordes of masterless, unemployed persons were believed to be at the root of crime and disorder. In 1681 'sturdy beggars'[49] in Ruthin were said to be prone to 'debauchery and insufferable idle behaviour'. Nowhere was the stark contrast between the living conditions and well-being of rich and poor more evident than in the towns.

The decisive influences in determining trading conditions within towns were those of the burgesses. Burgesses were enfranchised citizens who were able to trade freely within the borough without having to pay tolls. They also enjoyed long leases, reasonable rents, and rights of pasturage on extensive common lands. The status of burgess was thus an important economic privilege to which admission was rigorously controlled. Tradesmen and craftsmen protected their rights and interests by controlling entry to full membership of a guild and by regulating the supply of labour. In 1665, Denbigh had seven trade companies—mercers, farmers, shoemakers, weavers, hammermen, tailors, and glovers. Strict enactments were made to prevent the violation of borough regulations either by inhabitants of the town or by foreigners. At Ruthin the company of fullers and dyers insisted that no 'foreigners' be allowed to trade within the corporation upon penalty of distraint of goods. They did not hesitate to prosecute transgressors: in 1693 William Carlisle, a Scottish pedlar and 'an intruder', was fined £10 for illegally selling his goods in public.[50] At Neath, non-residents were required to obtain licences from the corporation to open a shop or to sell their wares upon pain of prosecution and a fine of 6s. 8d. Throughout this period, therefore, commercial activities and exclusive rights of trading were tightly regulated within the towns.

Just as Welsh towns underwent a period of expansion and growth after 1660, so, too, were the manufacturing and industrial resources of Wales developed to a much greater degree than ever before. Ever since the later Middle Ages, the woollen industry had been an essential complement to farming in rural Wales. As a source of employment it was vital to the well-being of small communities. Production was concentrated mainly in the three counties of Montgomery, Merioneth, and Denbigh. Here, the woollen trade bulked large in the local economy. Few farmhouses and cottages were without hand cards, hand looms, and small spinning wheels. Cottagers in Montgomeryshire, for instance, were able to buy hand cards for 4d. and spinning-wheels for 5s. Since weaving looms were more expensive at around £2, much of the weaving was carried out during slack winter months by more substantial farmers, helped by skilled farm labourers, in outhouses or sheds known as *tai gwŷdd* (loom houses).

[49] D. Gareth Evans, 'The Market Towns of Denbighshire 1640–1690' (unpubl. University of Wales MA thesis, 1978), p. 22.
[50] N. Tucker, 'The Councell Booke of Ruthin, 1642–1695', *Denbighshire Hist. Soc. Trans.* 11 (1962), p. 45.

Woven cloth was finished at the countless number of *pandai* (fulling mills) which dotted the countryside, especially in Merioneth.

Scarcely a parish in mid and north Wales was without its spinners, carders, weavers, and fullers. Sheep provided a copious supply of raw wool, rivers and streams supplied swiftly flowing water, and there was an abundance of domestic workers whose principal skill was the art of manufacturing woollen cloth. In hundreds of Welsh farmhouses, families spent long evenings carding, spinning, dyeing, and weaving wool. During winter months, men, women, and children regularly assembled in cottages to hold *nosweithiau gwau* (knitting evenings) or *cymorth gwau* (knitting assemblies), where, to the accompaniment of traditional songs and ballads, recitations, gossip, and banter, copious supplies of socks, gloves, caps, and wigs were knitted and prepared for the market. Although the quality of wool varied from county to county, Welsh cloth was generally coarse, poorly made, and expensive. Each county specialized in its own brand of webs, friezes, and flannels: whereas the weavers of Montgomery produced flannel, those in neighbouring Merioneth and Denbighshire prepared thick white woollen cloths. Moreover, compared with that of the English textile industry, gross output was small. Units of production were small, under-capitalized, and almost totally at the mercy of the whims and prejudices of the Shrewsbury Drapers' Company, whose middlemen controlled the fortunes of Welsh trade in flannel and cloth and gobbled up the profits.

Significant developments occurred during this period in mining and the primary metal industries. The return of stability and order during the Restoration years boosted business confidence and stimulated a renewed desire among Welsh landlords and industrialists to invest in both old and new enterprises. The tapping of new resources, the growth in demand (especially during the war with France after 1689), and the emergence of new markets enabled industry to expand and diversify. One of the most vital triggers to new developments was the successful challenge to the monopoly of the Mines Royal Society of all mines which contained an admixture of precious metals and ores. In 1690 a shepherd discovered a fabulously rich lead and silver mine at Esgair-hir, on the Gogerddan estate of Sir Carbery Pryse in Cardiganshire. Dubbed the 'Welsh Potosi',[51] the mine was reputed to be capable of yielding 60lb. of silver to each ton of lead. Such a treasure trove provided frustrated landowners with a heaven-sent opportunity to challenge the right of the Crown or its agents to regard such a mine as royal. In this case, the Pryses of Gogerddan insisted that minerals discovered on their estate were their property, and Sir Carbery Pryse travelled to London to argue his case at the Bar of the Court of Exchequer. The Crown's case was duly defeated and in 1693 an act was

---

[51] William Rees, *Industry before the Industrial Revolution* (2 vols., Cardiff, 1968), ii. 492.

passed which entitled all owners of copper, tin, lead, or iron mines to work their own deposits, provided the Crown or its agents were granted the right to buy the ore at fixed prices within thirty days after it was raised. This act kindled a quickening realization that fat profits were available. By freeing industry to private enterprise, it ushered in a new era of prospecting. Terminating the rights of the Mines Royal thus helped to revive confidence in mining. No longer would landlords be inhibited by frustrating legal niceties or interfering Crown agents.

The principal beneficiary of the successful challenge to the monopoly of the Mines Royal Society was Sir Humphrey Mackworth, a native of Shropshire, who settled in Neath and became the most outstanding entrepreneur of his day in Wales. Mackworth was a resourceful Tory industrialist, lawyer, and philanthropist whose marriage in 1686 to Mary Evans, daughter and sole heiress of Sir Herbert Evans of the Gnoll at Neath, provided him with sufficient financial security to enable him to invest heavily in a number of truly spectacular ventures, the like of which had never been seen in Wales. Mackworth, a man whose self-confidence bordered on conceit, used his considerable energy and flair for administration to revive the industrial fortunes of Neath. His success was based on the development of coal-mining and the smelting of imported lead and copper. A number of eye-catching developments were carried out at Neath. Mackworth introduced the latest and most sophisticated engines, which facilitated the raising of coal and water from the base of mining shafts. War with France had provided a growing demand for coal, and Mackworth was the first to introduce a coal-fired reverberatory furnace in Britain. At Neath, coal-pits were no longer shallow holes: mines were worked to a depth of sixty fathoms, thus enabling increasing amounts of coal to be used for industrial as well as domestic purposes. Soon Neath began to echo to the noise of engines, wagons, and ships. Mackworth ingeniously devised Wales's first tramway—a wagon-way which travelled on wooden rails from his coal-pits to the wharf at Neath Bank. By fitting sails to coal-trucks, Mackworth relieved his horses of the burden of dragging coal on windy days. One of Mackworth's admirers described the tramway as 'the wonder of the world', with 'one horse doing the work of ten and, if the wind was good, even twenty'.[52] Regular supplies of coal were thus swiftly loaded on to vessels bound for the West Country, Ireland, and France. Mackworth's enterprise brought speedy rewards: average profits of £700 per annum from the sale of coal increased his private fortune and brought Neath out of industrial stagnation.

If Mackworth was the architect of Neath's industrial fortunes, he was also the driving-force behind the emerging lead industry in Cardiganshire.

---

[52] Moelwyn I. Williams, *The South Wales Landscape* (London, 1975), pp. 197–8.

Although the mines of Cardiganshire had resumed production shortly after the Restoration, the boom period in the lead industry did not arrive until Mackworth purchased Sir Carbery Pryse's wealthy mines of pure lead and silver ore at Esgair-hir in 1698. William Waller, steward of the lead-mines on the Gogerddan estate, had been so deeply impressed by Mackworth's successful schemes at Neath that he was convinced that the Shropshire entrepreneur was just the man 'to set the wheels a-going with us in Cardiganshire'.[53] From 1690 onwards joint-stock enterprises had begun to proliferate and in 1700 Mackworth established the Company of the Mine Adventurers. His aim was to raise funds to develop mineral deposits, establish charities, and cater for the well-being of poor miners and their dependants. For a short period, Cardiganshire felt the breath of change and prosperity. At Neath, Mackworth had established smelting furnaces for imported lead and copper, and placed skilled workmen from Germany and other parts of Britain in charge of operations. Between 1698 and 1708 he spent nearly £17,000 on developing smelting and refining processes, as well as improving transport and marketing facilities in Neath. In spite of Mackworth's ingenuity and profit-making ability, however, his mines in Cardiganshire proved extraordinarily expensive and failed to live up to expectations. He was scarcely helped by the inefficiency of his manager, Waller, whose inexperience prevented him from coping with serious drainage problems and other technical difficulties. By 1703, only 1,500 tons of ore had been raised. Not surprisingly, the shareholders rebelled as the Company's financial position deteriorated alarmingly.

Mackworth was also at loggerheads with his neighbours in Glamorgan. His drive, flair for profit-making, and ambition had brought him into conflict with the powerful Mansell family of Margam. Whig industrialists believed that Mackworth's principal aim was 'nothing less than universal monarchy in Glamorganshire',[54] and the political differences which divided them brought an even sharper cutting edge to their violent rivalry in the coal trade. Although the Mansell collieries at Swansea and Briton Ferry were probably worth between £800 and £900 per annum, the Mansell family was so deeply resentful of Mackworth's industrial success and political ambitions that they employed violent ne'er-do-wells to molest his workmen, damage vital equipment, and inflame local feelings by spreading false rumours. Mackworth's troubles deepened when a Committee of the House of Commons held an inquiry into the financial affairs of the Company of the Mine Adventurers. He strove valiantly to maintain the Company's credit, but his enemies in the Whig camp seized every opportunity to blacken his name and take revenge for the slights and

[53] D. R. Phillips, *A History of the Vale of Neath* (Swansea, 1925), p. 272.
[54] Richard D. Till, 'Local Government in the Borough of Neath: A Study in Urban Administration, 1694-1884' (unpubl. University of Wales MA thesis, 1970), p. 20.

injustices which Mackworth had perpetrated in the past. In March 1710 Mackworth was found guilty of 'many notorious and scandalous frauds and indirect practices'.[55] Undeterred by this set-back, he had no intention of fading from the limelight. He returned to his estate at Neath and set about rebuilding his shattered fortunes. He remained extremely popular among the mercantile and wage-earning elements in Neath: a local ballad-monger, Dafydd Evan, hailed him as 'the saviour of Wales',[56] a sentiment provoked largely, perhaps, by the acute fear of the effects of unemployment. Mackworth, however, never recovered his former wealth: his debts totalled more than £17,000 at his death in 1727.

As Mackworth's fortunes in the Cardiganshire lead-mining industry took a downward turn, vigorous new ventures were successfully launched in north-east Wales. During the latter half of the seventeenth century, landowning families such as the Grosvenors, Mostyns, and Myddeltons invested considerable sums in lead-mines located near the coast at Halkyn, Holywell, and Mostyn, with such success that Thomas Williams of Broncoed, Mold, confessed that they had been 'so enriched by this sort of treasure that it makes our teeth run'.[57] So promising were the omens that the Quaker Company, one of the best organized and most sophisticated chartered companies in London, secured a forty-two-year lease which enabled them to invest heavily in the richly endowed mining areas of Diserth and Halkyn. Guided by prudent Friends and administered by vigilant professional managers, the Company invested wisely. A smelting-house was built at Gadlys, near Bagillt, in 1704. This highly efficient mill provided the foundation for two decades of expansion and prosperity. A flurry of leases was taken out, more mines were sunk, and dividends increased sharply, especially when the Company's products were bought by the Board of Ordnance and the East India Company. By 1724 the annual yield from lead and silver ore was more than £14,000—a success story which bore witness to the foresight, technical knowledge, and efficiency of the Company. During the late 1720s, however, profits dwindled sharply. By 1729 the annual financial yield had plummeted to £5,493. The death in 1728 of Dr Edward Wright, the Company's gifted pioneer, was a serious blow. So, too, were serious flooding problems in the lucrative Trelogan mine in the parish of Llanasa. As a result, the Company was obliged to withdraw so much of its investment that it never recovered its former prosperity. Elsewhere, however, enterprising individuals grasped their opportunities. In 1703, George Wynne inherited a tract of freehold land, worth £30 per annum, on Halkyn mountain, which, twenty years

---

[55] William Rees, *Industry before the Industrial Revolution*, ii. 561.
[56] D. J. Davies, *The Economic History of South Wales Prior to 1800* (Cardiff, 1933), p. 131.
[57] NLW MS 120406E, p. 24.

later, supplied him with annual profits of £22,000 from lead-mining. Similarly, when the rich vein at Llangynog, Montgomeryshire, came into the possession of William, marquis of Powis, in 1725, the family's fortunes were boosted by profits of £142,000 over the following two decades.

Rapid progress was made in this period, too, in the smelting of copper and tin. The most successful developments were carried out in the Neath–Swansea area, where the proximity of navigable rivers, advantageous harbours, cheap supplies of anthracite coal, and an abundance of skilled labour were important advantages. War with France after 1689 stimulated demand and domestic needs also provided a spur. Indeed, by the later Stuart period there was a widespread demand for a range of copper and brass products, notably coins, buckles, buttons, guns, and kitchen utensils. At Neath, Sir Humphrey Mackworth used local coal for smelting copper at his furnaces at Melincryddan. As his influence declined, however, Swansea emerged as the leading centre of the metallurgical industry. In 1717 Dr John Lane, a Cornish entrepreneur, established a new lead- and copper-smelting mill at Landore, in the parish of Llangyfelach. Lane's personal fortunes, however, were ruined when the South Sea Bubble burst, and the works passed into the hands of Robert Morris of Swansea, founder of the Lockwood and Morris Company and the man who gave his name to the village of Morriston. Morris made use of abundant supplies of local coal and persuaded Cornish mineowners that copper smelting in the parish of Llangyfelach could prove at least forty per cent cheaper than in Cornwall.

Significant developments were also evident in the iron industry. The location of ironworks was largely determined by the availability of timber, cheap charcoal, and a regular water supply. Whilst water-wheels provided power to drive bellows and tilt-hammers, charcoal was indispensable for smelting and refining processes. At least until the end of the seventeenth century, units of production were generally small and widely scattered, and the average annual output was around 100–150 tons. The most significant development was sponsored by Charles Lloyd, an enterprising Quaker, who took a lease for twenty-one years on the forge at Mathrafal in Montgomeryshire in 1697 and built his own forge at Dolobran. In 1717 Lloyd entered into a partnership with three ironmasters from Wolverhampton to develop an iron furnace at Bersham, near Wrexham. Lloyd was closely connected by marriage with the leading ironmasters and merchants of the West Midlands and he was also keenly aware of the growing demand for bar iron. His scheme, however, ended in disaster. In October 1727 Lloyd was declared bankrupt, much to his own personal distress and the shame of the Quaker fraternity, which promptly disowned him. At Bersham he had used methods which had been perfected at Coalbrookdale by his friend, Abraham Darby. However, Darby's discovery of how to smelt iron with coked coal proved only of limited significance during this period, for charcoal remained the principal fuel of the iron industry until the middle of the eighteenth century. Welsh woodlands were reduced piecemeal by countless encroachments carried out by landlords in search of wood for charcoal-burning. By the second decade of the eighteenth century, more extensive operations increased the annual output of small furnaces. In 1717, furnaces at Pontypool and Llanelli were producing 400 tons of pig-iron per annum, whilst John Hanbury's forges at Pontypool produced 300 tons. The furnace at Caerphilly yielded an annual output of 200 tons of pig-iron, and two forges at Machen and Tredegar produced 200 tons and 180 tons respectively. By 1720 there were sixteen furnaces scattered throughout south Wales. These gains were also accompanied by radical developments in the manufacture of tinplate, an infant industry pioneered by John Hanbury, the vigorous, enterprising Quaker industrialist of Pontypool. The proximity of supplies of iron and coal, swiftly flowing water, and a fund of unskilled labour enabled him to establish a rolling-mill which produced thin, malleable, and relatively cheap sheets, which were used to make furnaces, pots, kettles, and saucepans.

Finally, the portents of large-scale industrial developments were also evident in the slate industry of north Wales. Here, the industry was very much in its infancy during the early decades of the eighteenth century. It was largely confined to a scatter of tiny quarries at Cilgwyn in the Nantlle valley, Caernarfonshire. These enterprises were small-scale, poorly financed ventures, for local demand for roofing slates was small. Even so, exports of slates were picking up by the end of the 1720s. Over two and a half million slates were exported between June 1729 and December 1730, over a million of which were shipped to Ireland.

Although resident landowners and smaller gentry were heavily engaged in mining activities, many industrial enterprises launched during this period were funded or managed by Englishmen: Mackworth hailed from Shropshire, William Waller was a native of Westmorland, and John Lane was born in Cornwall. The scattered iron enterprises established in early eighteenth century Carmarthenshire were sustained by capital provided by English ironmasters, such as Zachary Downing and Thomas and Peter Chetle. The Lloyds of Dolobran and the Hanburys of Pontypool were closely linked with Quaker merchant dynasties in the Midlands and the West Country. Capital from Bristol financed thriving copperworks in the Swansea area. Even at this early stage, therefore, there was truth in John Campbell's dictum: 'the Welsh have the labour, and strangers the profit'.[58] Wages, of course, varied from industry to industry and from season to season. Some miners were paid in cash, others received part of their wages in kind. Miners in the lead-works of Cardiganshire and Montgomeryshire

---

[58] John Campbell, *The Political Survey of Great Britain* (2 vols., London, 1774), i. 189.

were often paid piece-work rates weekly or through open 'bargains', which involved miners in selling their 'venture' ore to the Company. Labourers who received daily wages were paid between 6d. and 8d. a day at Llangynog in the 1730s, whilst skilled masons, sawyers, and carpenters received 1s. 2d. a day. Women miners, who were reputedly every bit as industrious as men, earned 9d. a day. In Glamorgan wages were generally higher. Cutters, hewers, and colliers earned between 10d. and 12d. a day. During the early decades of the eighteenth century, mine-burners and fillers at Melin-y-cwrt furnace received 7s. a week, whilst a founder and an under-founder were paid 10s. and 8s. respectively. Some of the refiners at Aberafan forge in 1725 received 10s. a week, together with a house and firing. Working conditions were deplorable and fraught with hazards. In coal-mines, miners were expected to cope with defective winding gear, rickety ladders, unsafe roofs, and constant flooding. The effects of choke damp were often horrendous. Ignited gas in the Mostyn collieries in February 1673 caused such an enormous explosion that one miner's body was hurled a hundred yards. The blast tore off other miners' clothes and singed their bodies so fiercely that their skin appeared 'as if they had been whipped with rods'.[59] Industrialists who were anxious to secure quick returns were reluctant to improve working conditions. The use of adits for drainage and the installation of engines sent costs soaring and dissuaded them from acquiring new techniques and equipment. Shifts were long and arduous. At Gadlys in Flintshire, drum-beats summoned workers to their tasks at 6 a.m. for a twelve-hour shift, interrupted only by an hour's break for a midday meal. Many colliers in Glamorgan began work at 3 a.m. in order to complete an eight-hour shift by midday, which would enable them to swell their wages by loading ships during the afternoon. Work at Sir Humphrey Mackworth's mines in Neath was so exhausting that even hardened criminals whom Mackworth shipped in from English cities were appalled. At Esgair-hir in Cardiganshire, miners and their families were housed in purpose-built barracks and, on pain of a shilling's fine, labourers there were prohibited from swearing, cursing, quarrelling, drinking, and neglecting their Sabbath duties. Not surprisingly, therefore, Mackworth's employees nursed ambivalent feelings towards him: it was said that 'the miners both love him and fear him'.[60]

As yet, of course, there were few indications of the massive transformation which was to occur in the social and economic life of Wales. Industrial concerns were so small and widely scattered that the landscape barely revealed their existence. Welsh industries remained labour-intensive, and large-scale units of production were still a thing of the future. Lack of

---

[59] Adrian Teale, 'The Economy and Society of North Flintshire, c. 1660–1714' (unpubl. University of Wales MA thesis, 1979), p. 127.

[60] D. J. Davies, *Economic History*, p. 81.

capital was a constant stumbling-block which caused many potentially lucrative projects to be abandoned. Conscious of the friction and envy which prospecting brought in its train, some landowners chose not to exploit mineral deposits. In 1692 Owen Wynne of Brogyntyn reacted to the news of the discovery of minerals on the Merioneth estate of Sir Robert Owen by advising that the find should be left 'to sleep on its dross and dust than rouse it to make war against its proprietor'.[61] Poor communications, rising costs, and lack of technical expertise and skilled labour also combined to frustrate the best endeavours of enterprising industrialists. As late as the 1750s Lewis Morris complained that 'the art of mining is but in its infancy'.[62] On the other hand, there is no doubt that industrial developments gathered pace during this period. An increasing number of landowners, prospectors, and surveyors, undaunted by technical problems and primitive transport facilities, were searching for mineral wealth and tapping promising veins of coal, iron, and lead. Individual entrepreneurs were more than willing—indeed anxious—to invest capital and set up permanent units of production. Moreover, the formation of joint-stock companies, run by men of considerable administrative experience, made a signal contribution to the development of Welsh industry. A much greater volume of broadly based industrial production was evident by 1730 than had been the case a century earlier. It is true that progress had been gradual and patchy, but industrial enterprises, together with the variety and volume of extracted minerals, had clearly expanded.

Significant advances in Welsh industry were accompanied by the expansion of trading horizons. Small communities in Wales were heavily dependent on the extensive trade in livestock and the buying and selling of grain, wool, and minerals. The carriage of goods by road, however, was costly and dangerous. Although the principal arterial roads which ran along the north and south coasts were reasonably well maintained, most Welsh roads were simply atrocious. No actual roads had been constructed in Wales since Roman times. Many of them were simply grass tracks and bridle-ways riddled with ruts, boulders, and puddles. Although overseers of the highways were entitled to call upon the unpaid services of parishioners for six days each year, local inhabitants were reluctant to bear the responsibility of repairing roads and often did little more than fill in holes and remove obstructions. Only when magistrates imposed fines did they exert themselves. The lack of adequate foundations or surfaces to roads meant that they swiftly fell into disrepair. Following periods of heavy rain, many roads were so badly ploughed up by the increasing volume of traffic of

[61] P. R. Roberts, 'The Gentry and the Land in Eighteenth Century Merioneth', *Journal Merioneth Hist. and Record Soc.* 4 (1961–4), p. 338.

[62] A. H. Dodd, *The Industrial Revolution in North Wales* (3rd edn., Cardiff, 1971), p. 24.

cattle, horses, sledges, and wagons that travellers could make little or no progress, except on foot. During his gruelling journey through Wales in 1652, John Taylor and his faithful nag, 'Dun', found themselves up to their knees in a quagmire on their way to Carmarthen. Journeys by road were hazardous enterprises, not to be lightly embarked upon. Sir John Wynn of Gwydir used to describe the route from Llanrwst to Llanberis as 'the devil's bowling-green',[63] whilst Breconshire was known to the English as 'Breakneckshire'.[64] It is hard to believe the contemporary tale that Sir Carbery Pryse galloped from London to Esgair-hir in Cardiganshire in a mere forty-eight hours in 1693. For travel, either by foot or on horseback, was arduous and slow. Even coaches drawn by six strong horses seldom travelled at more than three miles an hour. Indeed, coaches in Wales were something of a novelty. Hordes of bemused onlookers lined the route from St Asaph to Conway in December 1685 as the Lord Chancellor took five hours to complete his journey by coach. A coach journey from Chester to London—a distance of some 180 miles—took six days. Strangers who ventured without guides across swollen rivers or the shifting sands of the Dee estuary or the Menai Straits did so at their peril. Many found to their cost that ferry services were subject to serious delays and were not without their hazards. In 1664 the Abermenai ferryboat capsized, following an argument over an extra penny added to the fare levied on passengers; seventy-nine passengers died and only one survived. Small wonder that 'God be praised' was a common sigh of relief among weary travellers as they reached their destinations safely.

Clearly, therefore, it was impossible to carry substantial quantities of goods on Welsh roads. In the absence of railways, tramroads, and canals, small farmers were forced to convey their produce to fairs and markets on wagons, carts, and pack-horses—a distressingly slow and costly process. Where possible, therefore, landowners, farmers, and industrialists preferred sea carriage. Since trading patterns were necessarily governed by available transport facilities, the sea was the principal highway in Wales. Coastal shipping was not only more suitable for transporting bulky goods but also less expensive and time-consuming. A growing number of ships plied along the Welsh coasts, carrying coal, grain, dairy produce, copper, and slates, all of which were more easily and cheaply carried by water than by road. Although the volume of exports in this period is not quantifiable, the indications are that markets were expanding. Basic raw materials and unprocessed goods formed the bulk of Welsh exports. In north Wales the ports of Beaumaris, Caernarfon, and Conway exported small quantities of livestock, dairy produce, timber, and slates to Ireland. In south Wales,

---

[63] F. V. Emery, 'A New Account of Snowdonia, 1693, Written for Edward Lhuyd', *NLWJ* 18 (1973–4), p. 409.

[64] D. Defoe, *A Tour through the Whole Island of Great Britain*, p. 53.

coal was the most valuable export commodity. The rapid growth in the coal and copper industries, together with its convenient harbour facilities, enabled Swansea to develop new markets in southern Ireland, the Channel Islands, Brittany, Spain, and Portugal. Following the long period of foreign wars, trade picked up swiftly. Swansea's export of coal to ports such as Cork, Waterford, and Kinsale in Ireland increased from 2,532 tons in 1709 to 7,528 tons in 1719. Shipments of grain, fish, woollen goods, and lead were also exported to Bordeaux, Lisbon, Bilbao, and San Sebastian. The economic life of south Wales, especially Glamorgan, was also closely associated with Bristol. With a population of 20,000 in 1700, Bristol was England's second largest city. A bustling city of trade and commerce, its expansion as a port had been hastened by its participation in the tobacco and sugar trades, the African slave-trade, and the Newfoundland fisheries. It was also a vital factor in stimulating the economy of south Wales, for this period witnessed a considerable increase in cross-channel trade. Bristol harbour was constantly thronged with large vessels, small coasting craft, and market boats from Wales. Apart from dairy produce, ships from south Wales brought coal, tallow, leather, wool, stockings, hats, lead, copper, and iron to Bristol and other West Country ports, such as Minehead, Bridgwater, and Ilfracombe. In return, the ports of Glamorgan received supplies of iron, soap, alum, grocery, haberdashery, fruit, wine, beer, and tobacco. In February 1700, for example, the *William* docked at Aberthaw, bringing from Bristol a cargo which included 108 hides and bends of leather, half a ton of soap, forty trusses of linen, 200 shot, two dozen chairs, ten bags of tobacco, and supplies of brandy, vinegar, and wine. Coastal trade was clearly acquiring greater variety in the nature and volume of its cargoes.

As new markets were acquired, a wider range of raw materials, foodstuffs, and table delicacies was imported. In south Wales, shipments of cloth, linen, tallow, hides, soap, timber, and linseed oil were brought into Swansea from Cork and Dublin, together with salt, oil, brandy, almonds, figs, prunes, and lemons from Spanish ports. Few ships from foreign ports docked in the ports of Wales, although Beaumaris acted as an entrepôt for exotic goods such as tobacco, ginger, and red sugar, which were transferred from Caribbean vessels to smaller ships which sailed to Chester and Liverpool. General cargo, such as coal, iron, spades, saucepans, cork, paper, leather, soap, treacle, sugar, alum, and hops, was also shipped into the ports of Caernarfonshire by vessels sailing from Flintshire, Chester, and Liverpool. The import of a much wider range of raw materials, manufactured goods, and luxury items, such as exotic foodstuffs and spices, undoubtedly helped to stimulate the retail trade in particular and the economy as a whole.

Yet there were many risks and disadvantages involved in shipping goods and raw materials by sea. Like farmers, sailors were at the mercy of the weather. Inclement weather either drove small vessels to port or tore them asunder on rocks. The violent storm of November 1703 wrecked several hundred ships off the coast of Wales. Wicked currents and shifting sandbanks deceived unwary skippers, and the graves of mariners in the churchyards of coastal parishes bear witness to the persistent danger of shipwreck caused by storms and high winds. There were also other problems: maritime trade was mostly seasonal and ports were often so heavily silted that they were unable to handle large vessels. Most ships were small and seldom ventured far from home. The average burthen of local ships was around twenty tons, whilst those which carried coal and other raw materials to foreign ports ranged from eighty to a hundred tons. Sailors also faced the unnerving prospect of being waylaid by privateers, who sailed in small squadrons in search of plunder. In particular, during the war with France, Welsh ships needed to be on their guard for enemy ships bent on hampering maritime trade. Indeed, trade with foreign ports came virtually to a standstill during the campaign against the forces of Louis XIV, and in 1709 a Glamorgan steward declared that 'peace is the prayer of the whole country'.[65] Finally, as maritime trade began to prosper following the cessation of hostilities, smuggling reared its ugly head. In Caernarfon bay, the celebrated *lladron creigiau Crigyll* (robbers of Crigyll rocks) plundered vessels with reckless abandon during the early eighteenth century. Manufactured articles, tea, brandy, and coffee were often hidden by Swansea traders under fish piled in large baskets. Catherine Lloyd, landlady of the Ferry Inn in Briton Ferry, earned fame for her prowess in smuggling wines, spirits, and tea, robbing customs officials of their booty and selling her ill-gotten gains to her customers. Excise officers were widely detested: 'those damned waiters', thundered Robert Wynne of Garthewin, 'always on the watch, the bane of humankind'.[66] All these factors proved inimical to highly successful and profitable maritime trade.

The seventy years which followed the Restoration in 1660 evidently witnessed significant social and economic changes. Although many farmers continued to till the soil according to the dictates of tradition, an enterprising minority had seen the wisdom of adopting new crops and techniques. Industry, too, not only embarked on a period of expansion but also acquired a greater degree of diversification. Entrepreneurs of wit and imagination, such as Mackworth, Hanbury, and Lloyd, had introduced advanced technical and scientific methods which helped to increase production. Internal and overseas trade also witnessed a period of modest

[65] A. H. John, *Industrial Development*, p. 11.
[66] D. L. Davies, 'Miss Myddelton of Croesnewydd and the Plas Power Papers', *Denbighshire Hist. Soc. Trans.* 22 (1973), p. 152 n.

expansion. Yet it is important not to exaggerate. The economy, bereft of large-scale capital, was still backward and underdeveloped. The majority of the population lived at subsistence level and were periodically burdened by harvest failures, local famines, and vicious assaults by infectious diseases. Sluggish communications served to perpetuate insularity, inhibit mobility, and hamper the development of trade.

CHAPTER 4

THE PATTERN OF POLITICS

WHEN Charles II stepped nimbly ashore at Dover on 25 May 1660 he was assured of a warm welcome from his Welsh admirers. Lady Grace Wynn of Gwydir believed that the king's arrival had delivered the land from slavery. Leading Welsh poets were beside themselves with joy: gone were the austerities and oppressions of Cromwellian times, and the colourful processions and merry clamour which accompanied Charles's return, even the extravagant life-style and fulsome promises of the restored monarch himself, seemed to presage happier times. Bonfires were lit, wine flowed freely, and grateful loyal toasts were offered to the heir of Brutus, the legendary progenitor of the British people. John Roberts, vicar of Llanrhaeadr-ym-Mochnant, looked forward with almost childlike pleasure to tucking in to a piece of beef and being 'civilly merry' with old friends who had been 'civilly dead for so many years'.[1] More than anything, there was a widespread yearning for peace, unity, and stability.

For the most part, royalist families were able to regain their offices and recover their former prominence and prestige in local affairs. They were joined by those who had served in Cromwellian times in order to preserve some kind of constituted authority and public order. A powerful majority of Welsh royalists and churchmen was returned to Parliament in spring 1661. Many old faces returned, weary and battle-scarred, but relieved to be rid of the yoke of republican rule. At least two-thirds of the Welsh members were men who had sat in the Long Parliament prior to the civil war. But although the monarchy, the established church, and the administration were safely and peaceably restored, things could never be the same again. In particular, civil strife and the attempts of propagators and major-generals to dragoon the populace into obedience had left a legacy of bitterness and recrimination which would colour the character of Welsh politics for the next two generations. Too many people had suffered, too many wounds refused to heal, and too many painful memories remained. As William Lloyd, bishop of St Asaph, observed, the revolutionary years had bequeathed 'an odious scent to posterity'.[2]

Within the minds of property-conscious gentlemen there lurked an abiding dread of further turmoil and violence which might irrevocably destroy their authority and rights. Memories of the Puritan sword died

[1] *Calendar of Letters relating to North Wales*, p. 241.
[2] NLW MS 11302D, p. 29.

hard in Welsh country homes and dexterous Puritan administrators and republicans who made their peace with the new government were sneered at in a spirit of jealousy and vindictiveness which boded ill for old Roundheads. Great resentment was harboured towards an upstart like Colonel Philip Jones, who was allowed to seek refuge at his estate in Fonmon, Glamorgan, and thrive on what many considered to be ill-gotten gains. John Glynne of Glynllifon, Caernarfonshire, a wily lawyer who had served as Lord Chief Justice under Cromwell's administration, abandoned his republican sympathies when the tide turned against Puritan rule. His volte-face was viewed with considerable distaste, and when he fell from his horse during Charles's coronation procession not a few hardened royalists rocked with laughter. Samuel Pepys noted how people 'do please themselves to see how just God is to punish the rogue at such a time as this'.[3]

The fate of Charles I had been the cause of much bad blood. No fewer than eighty-nine lords, knights, and gentlemen of north Wales subscribed to a loyal address to Charles II on his restoration, urging him to ensure that 'all those who assisted in the murder of the late king should be delivered over to public justice'.[4] Many of them were fearful that the Act of Indemnity and Oblivion, passed in August 1660, would, in practice, mean indemnity for the king's enemies but oblivion for his friends. They were determined, therefore, to avenge themselves on old enemies. Proceedings against the regicides began in October 1660. Colonel John Jones, Maesygarnedd, had been arrested in Finsbury in June and was sentenced to death. On the gallows at Charing Cross on 17 October he bore himself with conspicuous dignity and courage. His mangled body was carried in a basket and buried, with the remains of three fellow regicides, in a single grave. His descendants found to their cost that their good name had been besmirched. His son was removed from the shrievalty of Merioneth within a week of his appointment in January 1687 and was replaced by a royalist Tory. During Anne's reign, Thomas Jones the almanacker unashamedly exploited past grievances by rattling some of the skeletons in the cupboard of his great rival, John Jones of Caeau. By exposing his adversary's damaging family associations with the Merioneth regicide, Thomas Jones was able to taunt him, claiming that his hands were stained with the blood of Charles I. Thomas Wogan, the other Welshman who had signed the death warrant of Charles I, was imprisoned in the Tower of London, whence, in circumstances which have never been properly explained, he escaped to Holland.

To loyalist Welshmen, the name of Oliver was anathema. When Cromwell's decomposed bones were dug up and hanged in public,

[3] Glyn Roberts, *Aspects of Welsh History* (Cardiff, 1969), p. 165.
[4] *Calendar of Wynn Papers*, p. 362.

Welshmen remembered him as a destroyer of sacred places and country homes. Huw Morys, Wales's most popular bard, likened Cromwell to Herod, and, in a spate of lampoons, interludes, and songs of bitter invective, he censured arrogant soldiers, greedy adventurers, and low-born preachers. William Roberts, bishop of Bangor, could hardly bring himself to mention the 'usurper Oliver',[5] whilst in Ellis Wynne's *Gweledigaetheu y Bardd Cwsc* (1703) the very name 'Cromwell' carries a sinister ring. John Burchinshaw poked fun at Cromwell's family connections with brewing, whilst Theophilus Evans icily dismissed him as a hardened reprobate. Those who had expressed admiration for Cromwell or sympathized with his aims paid the penalty: in 1683 the hopes for promotion of a candidate in the diocese of St Davids were thwarted when it was revealed that he had figured among the mourners at Cromwell's funeral.

While Cromwell was vilified as a usurper, Charles I was extolled as a pure and upright saint. To most Welshmen the execution of Charles I had been a monstrous deed, and memories of his unhappy fate were not permitted to die. Each year on 30 January, the anniversary of the death of the 'royal martyr', Welsh clergymen bade their parishioners beat their breasts in shame and humiliation. 'The guilt of innocent blood', lamented Humphrey Humphreys, bishop of Bangor, 'leaves a deep and lasting stain.'[6] The cult of the royal martyr was assiduously fostered in Wales. Rowland Vaughan of Caer-gai, whose veneration for the monarchy was second to none, was convinced that 'old Charles' had been safely delivered to 'a saint's place'.[7] An anonymous genealogist-cum-herald went to considerable pains to copy William Phylip's elegy upon the death of Charles I, surrounding it with a decorative border and a pedigree tracing Charles's descent through Gwladus Ddu from Llywelyn ab Iorwerth (Llywelyn the Great). Commemorative sermons were also used to vilify Dissenters. Forced to defend themselves against old aspersions, Dissenters were particularly resentful of clergymen who used the anniversary of Charles's death to 'sow the seed of bigotry and abuse their hearers'.[8] Poets, too, lost few opportunities to remind their audience of the evil deeds committed by 'king-killers' and 'sons of Belial'. In his elegy to William Owen of Brogyntyn, who was buried at Llangollen on 30 January 1678, Huw Morys recalled the day when Charles had fallen innocent victim to rebellious subjects:

> Let Wales remember the burial
> on the anniversary of the bitter pang

[5] Bodleian Library, Tanner MS 45, f. 21.
[6] Humphrey Humphreys, *A Sermon Preach'd before the House of Lords* (London, 1696), p. 2.
[7] E. D. Jones, 'The Brogyntyn Welsh Manuscripts', *NLWJ* 7 (1952), p. 166.
[8] NLW MS 17054D, p. 203.

when the traitors cut off
the golden head of a king without need.[9]

The horror and shock of the deed thus lingered on in the minds of Welshmen, and it is not surprising that so many devotional books peddled by churchmen were designed to re-implant the belief that rebellion against the Lord's anointed was a heinous sin and that every citizen was in duty-bound to be pious, holy, humble, faithful, and obedient. Even in Anne's reign, landed gentlemen were still terrified of rebellion. In the wake of the Sacheverell affair, Tory parsons and gentlemen were convinced that republican spirits were bent on reviving 'those pernicious and fatal doctrines that paved the way to the execrable murder' of Charles I.[10]

The Restoration did not simply witness the return of the king; it also heralded the return of the devout sons of the established church. Churchmen and royalists were swift to pounce on men or sons of men who had taken up arms against the king and undermined the authority of the Anglican church. Although the king discouraged private vendettas, there were many resentful royalists in the provinces with old scores to settle. Dissent was associated in the public mind with disloyalty to the Crown and local authorities lost no time in taking action against notorious sectarians, notably Baptists and Quakers. By midsummer 1660, Welsh gaols were crowded with Dissenters. Twenty-eight Quakers were under lock and key in Denbighshire and Flintshire, and forty were incarcerated in Cardiff. Many Friends were detained indefinitely in wretched prisons for refusing to tender the oath of allegiance. Puritan ministers were cowed by bullying parishioners. In December 1660, Ellis Rowlands, vicar of Clynnog Fawr, was violently manhandled by two furious parishioners who locked the doors of his church, tore bibles from the grasp of worshippers, and cried: 'we demand to see all bibles without the prayer book burnt'.[11] Militant Anglicans joined together in defence of royal and episcopal authority and called for strong measures to ensure that the enemies of the church were deprived of their rights to worship freely or hold public office.

Even in remote Welsh provinces news of Thomas Venner's abortive rising in London in January 1661 chilled the marrow of men's bones. The constant flow of missives sent by the earl of Carbery, President of the Council of Wales, to deputy-lieutenants, high and petty constables, and the militia bears witness to the fears of central government. In the absence of an adequate army the Crown was obliged to press deputy-lieutenants to apprehend known vagrants, dissidents, and mischief-makers, and to keep trained bands on their toes. In Caernarfonshire, nineteen Dissenters and

---

[9] E. D. Jones, *NLWJ* 5 (1948), p. 244.

[10] Geoffrey Holmes, *The Trial of Doctor Sacheverell* (London, 1973), p. 250.

[11] J. Gwynfor Jones, 'The Caernarfonshire Justices of the Peace and their Duties during the Seventeenth Century' (unpubl. University of Wales MA thesis, 1967), pp. 179–80.

republicans from Llŷn and Eifionydd were thrust into prison. Among them were Richard Edwards of Nanhoron and Jeffrey Parry of Rhydolion. Officers of the king searched Edwards's home and found two cases of pistols. Six pistols were found in Parry's house and one of his neighbours insisted that he had concealed cases of arms in a gorse field. Throughout Wales former parliamentarians were kept under surveillance and were relieved of their pistols, rapiers, and swords. Major suspects were periodically rounded up and interrogated, their letters intercepted and opened, their homes searched, and their hours of worship disturbed. The haunting fear that republicans might once more unsheathe their swords provoked acts of petty malice. The corpse of John Williams, Vavasor Powell's faithful ally, was dug up by his enemies shortly after burial and Williams's friends were obliged to rebury the corpse in his own garden. There remained an abiding fear of those whom Bishop Lucy called the 'old leaven'[12]—former soldiers and sectarians who still nursed dreams of turning the world upside down. With hindsight we can see that the threat to civil peace in Wales was more apparent than real, but the authorities of the day were faced with conventicles which were riddled with army officers, radical veterans, and republican magistrates, many of whom still proudly sported titles such as 'captain' and 'major'. In 1668 Vavasor Powell was accused of preaching to a thousand hearers, many of whom were allegedly armed, at an unlawful conventicle in Merthyr. Small wonder that every Dissenter was considered a potential rebel. Vengeful royalists and churchmen were determined to harry sectarians who had for so long harried them and the discomfiture of old enemies often brought them great satisfaction: when Colonel John Carne was challenged by conventiclers at Merthyr to declare by what authority he acted against them, he smugly laid his hand upon his sword. 'We thank God we have the sword of power in our hands, and by the grace of God, I will root you out of the country',[13] declared a furious Welsh magistrate to stubborn Presbyterians at Oswestry in 1681.

Whenever the authorities smelt rebellion on the wind during the years of the penal code, Dissenting preachers were molested, worshippers were abused, and prisoners beaten. Leading churchmen often made considerable capital out of their adversaries' past records. Bishop William Lucy's tenure of St Davids' diocese was virtually governed by his fear that religious and political malcontents were lurking undetected in secret meeting-places. In March 1666 he sought the support of local justices in suppressing Dissenting conventicles at Llangyfelach which, he claimed, were 'dangerous

---

[12] Philip Jenkins, ' "The Old Leaven": The Welsh Roundheads after 1660', *Historical Journal* 24 (1981), p. 809.

[13] D. Walker (ed.), *History of the Church in Wales*, p. 91.

to the king and kingdom and an affront to the established religion'.[14] Like the reigning monarch, Lucy believed that towns were nests of sedition and he was deeply disturbed to find radical sympathizers sponsoring local schools within his diocese. Itinerant preachers found themselves hounded by fear-ridden bishops and magistrates. Humphrey Lloyd, bishop of Bangor, remained haunted by the spectre of the Cromwellian regime. His instinctive reaction when Thomas Gouge began collecting subscriptions in his diocese for a new edition of the Welsh Bible was to murmur *timeo Danaos et dona ferentes*.[15]

The political turbulence and mass hysteria which accompanied the Popish Plot deepened anti-papist sentiments and brought a brief measure of relief to beleaguered Dissenters. However, the Tory reaction after 1681 unleashed a period of draconian persecution, with many Dissenters, having forfeited the goodwill of the Crown, suffering severely as a result of their association with Whig exclusionists. When details of the Rye House Plot of June 1683 were revealed, the shadow of civil war fell across the land once more. Dissenters and Whigs were denounced as dangerous enemies of the state and many of them were openly accused by their enemies of complicity in the plot. William Lloyd, bishop of St Asaph, condemned those 'atheists and fanatics'[16] who were resolved to cut the throats of innocent men. Leading Dissenters were kept under surveillance and their houses were searched for arms. In Monmouthshire, magistrates claimed that former Roundheads were stockpiling arms in Abergavenny, that John Arnold and Sir Trevor Williams—bitter foes of the marquis of Worcester—were plotting over barrels of ale, and that the king had become the subject of mirth and ribaldry. Fulsome loyal addresses were delivered to the Crown, many of them recalling the blood-drenched strife of the revolutionary years. Fervent royalists used the occasion of the colourful progress of the duke of Beaufort (formerly the marquis of Worcester) through Wales in 1684 to remind the forgetful of the heinous deeds committed during the years of upheaval by 'boars of the forest' and 'arbitrary and republican hoghens moghens'.[17]

The accession of James II in May 1685 ushered in further violent changes of fortune and almost continuous political instability and turbulence. During the abortive Monmouth rebellion, prominent Dissenters and republicans found themselves marked men. Bussy Mansell, the former parliamentary commander, and Rowland Dawkins, who had served as one of Major-General James Berry's deputies, figured among eight men who

[14] Glanmor Williams, 'The Dissenters in Glamorgan, c. 1660–c. 1760', in *Glamorgan Co. Hist.* 4 (1974), p. 471.
[15] Tanner MS 40, f. 18–19ʳ.
[16] A. Tindal Hart, *William Lloyd 1627–1717* (London, 1952), p. 47.
[17] David Lewis, 'A Progress through Wales', *Y Cymmrodor* (1883), p. 146.

were briefly detained by the governor of Chepstow Castle as 'disaffected and suspicious persons'.[18] Further cause for alarm was provided when James II sought to woo Dissenters by elevating them to the bench in 1687–8. Tory loyalists were not only horrified by the king's indifference to the prejudices and interests of his subjects, but also by their discovery that the 'Good Old Cause' was seemingly still alive and well. The new justices included some of Vavasor Powell's former disciples, Richard Edwards of Nanhoron ('a man of close and shrewd parts and of dangerous principles'),[19] and old republican soldiers such as Henry Williams of Merthyr and Thomas Evans of Gelli-gaer. In withering satirical verse, Philip Williams of Dyffryn Clydach portrayed the new magistrates as 'the old gang' of 1641[20]—low-born fanatics, hypocrites, and traitors who threatened to turn the world upside down once more. Faithful churchmen seethed with rage and indignation and gentry parlours echoed to cries of 'no Presbyterian rebellion'.

As the popish threat receded temporarily following the overthrow of James, old fears of republicanism resurfaced. The chief threat to the established order was now thought to be those rapidly increasing numbers of Dissenters who had torn themselves away from the Church of England following the Toleration Act of 1689. In the eyes of resentful churchmen, the Toleration Act had been perilously charitable to Dissent and clearly boded ill for the future of Anglicanism. The number of church communicants would begin to dwindle, Dissenting academies would poison the minds of talented young men, and the greater measure of freedom enjoyed by Dissenters would embolden many of them to flout the remaining penal restrictions. Dyed-in-the-wool Anglican clergymen still viewed the established church as an indivisible body and believed that 'schismatics' were a potential threat to the well-being of Anglicanism and the fabric of society. Theophilus Evans and Ellis Wynne, for instance, emptied the vials of their wrath on all Dissenters, claiming that they posed a threat to internal peace and order. Fearful of the consequences of swelling Dissenting congregations, Anglican clergymen were prepared to fight tooth and nail against their sectarian neighbours. No opportunity was missed to blacken the name of a Dissenter or to subject him to pressure. The Dissenting chapel at Chwarelau-bach, near Neath, was built some distance from the main road in order to protect its windows from a stone-throwing rabble. Fears of harrassment prompted several Baptist members of the Rhydwilym church to abandon their homeland and set sail for the

---

[18] A. M. Johnson, 'Bussy Mansell (1623–1699): Political Survivalist', *Morgannwg* 20 (1976), p. 27.
[19] *Calendar of Letters relating to North Wales*, p. 149.
[20] Philip Jenkins, 'Two Poems on the Glamorgan Gentry Community in the reign of James II', *NLWJ* 21 (1979–80), p. 176.

Welsh Tract on the banks of the Delaware in 1701. A group of Welsh Baptists, having arrived in Swansea in 1706, escaped the clutches of a press-gang only by the skin of their teeth. Matthias Maurice, a tailor's son from Llanddewi Felffre and a rousing Calvinist preacher, was less fortunate: he was betrayed by one of his enemies into the hands of a press-gang at Haverfordwest and sent to London in a man-of-war.

For zealous Anglicans, the reign of William had proved a deeply depressing period. However, the accession in 1702 of Anne, the last of the Stuarts, filled them with hopes of reviving the influence and authority of the established church. It also presented Tory incendiarists with the opportunity to exact vengeance on old enemies. Militant parsons raised the cry 'The Church in danger'. Much of their resentment was provoked by the cynical practice known as 'occasional conformity'. In order to qualify themselves for public office a growing number of Dissenters adopted the practice of attending church and taking the Anglican sacraments, thus evading the obstacles enshrined in the Test and Corporation Acts. In 1697, Sir Humphrey Edwin, the son of a Carmarthenshire felt-maker and now an affluent wool-merchant and Lord Mayor of London, made a public spectacle of the practice by attending, in full mayoral regalia, Anglican communion on a Sunday morning and a Dissenting service in the afternoon. Undeterred by Anglican gibes, he repeated this display on the following Sunday. High Churchmen were outraged and even a Dissenter like Defoe was so embarrassed by the Welsh merchant's cynicism that he accused Edwin and his fellows of 'playing Bo-peep with God Almighty'.[21] James Owen, the brilliant academy tutor of Oswestry, argued that occasional conformists were men of piety and moderation and that the practice had a long and venerable history. The case for occasional conformity, however, was slender and churchmen made much of the claim that it reduced the sacrament to the level of a passport to office. Occasional conformists were especially vulnerable to charges of whiggism, ambition, and hypocrisy. Their religion, claimed Sir Humphrey Mackworth, was a moral sham, a mischievous practice designed to ruin the church and increase the strength of Whigs and Dissenters in the corporations. Between November 1702 and December 1704 three bills designed to eliminate the practice of occasional conformity were foiled by Whig peers and bishops in Parliament. Not until 1711, following the Tory victory in the general election of 1710, did the Bill for Preventing Occasional Conformity enter the statute-book.

To many High Churchmen in Wales, Dissenters were fanatics and traitors who were still wedded to the principles of sedition, regicide, and anarchy. Their passions were further excited when Henry Sacheverell

[21] Geoffrey Holmes, *Religion and Party in late Stuart England* (Historical Assoc. pamphlet, London, 1975), p. 16.

delivered his notorious sermon, 'In Perils among False Brethren', at St Paul's Cathedral on 5 November 1709, the twenty-first anniversary of William's landing at Torbay. Using inflammatory language, Sacheverell castigated Dissenters as purveyors of false doctrine, heresy, and schism, and urged fellow churchmen to close ranks against this 'brood of vipers'.[22] According to William Fleetwood, bishop of St Asaph, Sacheverell's sermon was 'a rhapsody of incoherent, ill-digested thoughts, dressed in the worst language that could be found'.[23] The decision to impeach Sacheverell served only to rouse the deepest Tory passions and news of his release heralded astonishing scenes of tumult and celebration. Tory and High Church prejudices were rampant on the Welsh borders. Sir Joseph Jekyll, Chief Justice of Cheshire and one of the managers of Sacheverell's impeachment, was mortified by the behaviour of 'a great rabble' of perhaps 500 rioters in Wrexham, who, carrying burning barrels and staffs, ransacked the meeting-house and homes of Dissenters. Cries of 'Down with the Manager'[24] and a volley of curses and abuse greeted Jekyll as he travelled the legal circuit of north-east Wales. Sacheverell's scurrilous address also provoked a flurry of sermons denouncing schismatics, occasional conformists, and Dissenting academies. On 25 March 1710 a querulous parson named Cornwall ascended Welshpool pulpit on the occasion of the Assize sermon to rant against 'evil-doers' and 'the workers of iniquity'.[25] A month later, the sermon preached at Cardiff Assizes by Thomas Hancorne, rector of St Donat's, was filled with muted echoes of Sacheverell's celebrated theme. Every opportunity was seized by high-flying divines to whip up passions against Dissent and to take advantage of their opponents' confusion.

The zeal of Tory parsons was shared by many of the Welsh gentry. During his trial Sacheverell had received the substantial living of Selatyn from an admirer, Robert Lloyd, a High Tory from Shropshire. On 1 June 1710 Sacheverell embarked on a triumphal tour of the Welsh borders. The journey to Selatyn, deliberately conducted at a snail's pace, took him four weeks. The Welsh received him with joyous rapture: the gentry treated him in princely fashion, whilst his supporters ensured that streets were strewn with flowers; windows were festooned with bunting and bells were rung incessantly. At Wrexham—where Walter Cradock and Morgan Llwyd had laboured so diligently sixty and more years previously—the tide of High Church sentiment ran particularly strongly. Doting maidens and matrons vied with one another to kiss their hero, while Robert William,

[22] Henry Sacheverell, *In Perils among False Brethren* (London, 1709), *passim*.

[23] J. P. Kenyon, *Revolution Principles: The Politics of Party 1689–1720* (Cambridge, 1977), p. 130.

[24] E. Hughes, 'The Letters of Chief Justice Spencer Cowper from the North Wales Circuit, 1717–19', *THSC* (1956), p. 53.

[25] G. Holmes, *The Trial of Doctor Sacheverell*, p. 237.

the local blacksmith, sang appreciatively of Sacheverell's steadfast espousal of the 'true faith'.[26] Dissenters were mortified by the enormous upswell of Tory and High Church sentiments. John Kelsall, the Quaker, considered that many people had been 'infected by that malignant comet bursting its orb', whilst an anonymous Dissenter heaped abuse on Sacheverell for having 'spewed fire from his mouth' and invited unruly mobs to kiss his feet as though he were the bishop of Rome.[27]

To most Welsh churchmen, however, Sacheverell was a popular hero. The flood of loyal addresses which the affair provoked revealed that Welsh Tories were still haunted by the spectre of rebellion and regicide. During the hustings prior to the general election of 1710, cries of 'No Forty Eight' and 'No Presbyterian Rebellion' rang out resonantly. Favoured by the queen, the Tories sought to destroy Dissent. The Occasional Conformity Bill was passed in 1711 and this was followed by the Schism Act of June 1714, an odious measure which declared that no person might keep a private or public school without having first subscribed to the contents of the Prayer Book and secured a bishop's licence. By a curious quirk of fortune, however, Anne died on 1 August and the act lost its cutting edge. Following Anne's death, Welsh Baptists designated the first Sunday in August a day of prayer and thanksgiving. Similar sentiments were expressed at prayer meetings held on the first Wednesday of each month. Not unexpectedly, therefore, Welsh Dissenters hailed George I as their deliverer. A deputation of leading Dissenters, headed by Dr Daniel Williams, the celebrated benefactor of Wrexham, waited on the new monarch to express their loyalty to the House of Hanover. Even under the Hanoverians, however, the deeds and misdeeds of prominent sectarians and republicans in 'Oliver's times' remained green in the memory. Old antipathies, only partly interred, were swiftly dug up whenever popular movements threatened the status quo. 'Down with the Rumps' was a common cry during closely fought parliamentary elections, and by dubbing itinerant Methodist preachers 'Cradockites' and 'Roundheads' the people of north Wales revealed that the myths and terminology of the 'unhappy times' were still very much alive.

If anything, the threat posed by popery was believed to be even more real than the likelihood of renewed civil conflict. During the Restoration period, there were widespread fears that the number of Catholics was increasing. Catholic priests had taken advantage of the confusion which had followed the clerical ejections of the Propagation period so that, according to one observer, 'people were choosing to go to Rome rather

---

[26] Geraint H. Jenkins, *Hanes Cymru yn y Cyfnod Modern Cynnar 1530–1760* (Cardiff, 1983), p. 207.
[27] Friends House Library, Kelsall MSS, ii. 88–90; NLW MS 9167A, pp. 82–3.

than to Bedlam'.[28] Far from having been prostrated by the civil upheaval, Catholics, so it seemed, were winning ground. By the 1670s Welsh Protestants were convinced that a covert Catholic campaign was gathering momentum. The secret inclinations of Charles II, the conversion of James, duke of York, the heir presumptive, to Catholicism, the laxity of local justices of the peace, and the busy activities of Jesuit priests prompted Stephen Hughes to preface his Welsh tracts with increasingly alarmist and despairing remarks. In 1671, Sir Trevor Williams informed the House of Commons that half the population of Monmouthshire was Catholic and that priests outnumbered Protestant ministers. The religious census of 1676 clearly revealed that Monmouthshire possessed the lion's share of priests and worshippers. Protected by the House of Raglan and succoured by the Jesuit mission at Cwm in Herefordshire, groups of closely knit gentry, farmers, craftsmen, labourers, artisans, widows, and spinsters clung stubbornly to the Catholic faith and asked for nothing more than to be left alone to practise their religion in peace and quiet. Protestants, however, firmly believed that Catholicism was an imposture, a delusion based on ignorance, superstition, and image-worship. Whereas the Protestant religion came from the God of Truth, they claimed, Catholicism came from the Father of Lies. But Catholicism was reckoned to be more than an abhorrent faith: it was an evil political menace. Seen as led by Louis XIV, the ambitious French autocrat, popery was believed to be a scheming, aggressive power which threatened the liberty of Protestant Europe. Ellis Wynne was convinced that Belial had commanded the Pope, Louis XIV, and the Turks to burn the Bible, destroy the Church of England, and slay her members. Protestant propagandists, in fact, were so adept in exploiting the credulity and fears of the populace that, at times of political crisis, there was almost nothing Protestants would not believe about the wickedness of their Catholic enemies. The shadow of popery fell so heavily across the pages of Welsh literature that readers had no doubts that Catholicism fostered and gave its blessing to deeds of barbaric ferocity.

Anti-papist passions were heightened enormously in 1678 when Titus Oates revealed detailed plans of an alleged plot by Catholic activists to murder the king, replace him with his brother James, dismiss Protestant leaders, and dragoon the country into Catholicism. Protestants were horrified and their outrage knew no bounds when, shortly afterwards, the body of Sir Edmund Berry Godfrey, the London magistrate to whom Oates had presented his testimony, was found murdered in a ditch. More informers surfaced with wild stories to tell. Among them was William Bedloe, a native of Chepstow. Bedloe was a professional criminal and confidence trickster who embellished Oates's story and revelled in his

[28] M. M. C. O'Keeffe, 'Three Catholic Martyrs of Breconshire', *Brycheiniog* 17 (1976–7), p. 62.

newly discovered role as the saviour of the Protestant cause. He gave evidence before the House of Lords of a proposed rising, led by Lord Powis and involving Charles Price, steward of the marquis of Worcester, and other close associates and friends in the Catholic community of south-east Wales. The rebels, according to Bedloe's perjured testimony, proposed to seize Chepstow Castle and then march to Milford Haven to rendezvous with an invading force of 20,000 soldiers from Spain. Although Bedloe's testimony was full of errors and contradictions, it fuelled the notion of a Jesuit conspiracy. A wave of anti-Catholic hysteria, buoyed up by crude anti-popish propaganda which poured from the presses, enveloped many parts of Wales. The south-east, in particular, was swept by gusts of fear and anger.

Tension had been rising in Monmouthshire for some time. The root of the troubles lay in a bitter and long-standing feud between the marquis of Worcester and John Arnold, a Whig MP and lord of the manor of Llanfihangel Crucornau. Although the marquis had renounced the faith of his forefathers, he was widely suspected of being a crypto-papist who protected priests, retainers, and tenants from the rigours of the penal code. His appointment as President of the Council of Wales in 1672 awakened much ill-feeling and trepidation, for many Protestants were convinced that he would use his political position not only to mitigate the sufferings of his Catholic neighbours but also to cow his enemies into submission. John Arnold was a headstrong Protestant who nursed a paranoiac hatred of Rome. He had been the victim of several personal slights and injustices at the hands of Worcester and was now bent on revenge. In a bid to counter the growth of recusancy and besmirch Worcester's reputation, Arnold and his ally, John Scudamore of Kentchurch, Herefordshire, presented copious evidence to a parliamentary inquiry into the growth of militant popery in Monmouthshire and Herefordshire in the spring of 1678. According to their testimony, at least twenty-eight priests were active in the area, celebrating mass openly in the homes of Catholic gentlemen, whilst Catholic worshippers regularly frequented ancient shrines 'with beads in their hands'.[29] Oates's revelations provided Arnold and the anti-Catholic lobby in south-east Wales with a long-awaited opportunity to wreak their revenge on old enemies. Blinded by fear and anger, Protestants raised the cry of 'no popery' and rallied to the defence of the Protestant faith in its hour of need. Anti-Catholic passions were whipped up and a vigorous campaign of intimidation and persecution was launched. As a result, the Jesuit community at Cwm was dispersed, five innocent priests were barbarously executed and several more died after having gone to ground in caves, barns, and pigsties. Every opportunity was seized to bring the

[29] M. M. C. O'Keeffe, 'The Popish Plot in South Wales and the Marches of Hereford and Gloucester' (unpubl. University of Galway MA thesis, 1969), p. 50.

religion of Rome into disrepute. At Abergavenny in 1679 a pope-burning procession was led by a 50-year-old dwarf, carrying a brass blunderbuss and followed by guards, cardinals, Jesuits, monks, two 'lusty sow-gelders', and a richly adorned effigy of the Pope. Pardons and indulgences were sold *en route* and eventually the effigy was burnt on 'a stately pile of faggots and bavins'.[30]

Meanwhile, Arnold and Scudamore proved a persistent pair of avengers. Their denigration of Worcester never faltered: no opportunity was lost to publicize his arbitrary deeds and his dangerously close links with the apostate duke of York, the heir apparent. In their eyes, Worcester was the embodiment of evil, cruelty, and deceit. The propaganda which Arnold and Scudamore peddled was doubtless exaggerated, but it was close enough to reality to strike a responsive chord in the hearts of those Welshmen who believed that the Protestant cause was in dire peril. Arnold, in particular, knew how easily popular opinion was inflamed against Catholicism. In April 1680 he was the victim of an alleged attack by an unknown assailant in Jacknapes Lane, near Fleet Street. His wounds were probably self-inflicted, for Arnold was anxious to revive flagging anti-popish passions and to bring down his autocratic overlord. At any rate, Thomas Giles, a friend of Thomas Herbert of Usk, another of Arnold's enemies, was found guilty of the alleged crime and Arnold was hugged and mobbed by his relatives and friends on his return to Monmouthshire. Nevertheless, Worcester was a resolute, strong-minded politician who had, over the years, developed a remarkable political staying-power. A born survivor, he emerged unbruised from the Exclusion crisis, as did those whom Bedloe had implicated. Worcester continued to bask in the king's favour and was rewarded with the dukedom of Beaufort in 1682. The pro-royalist feeling which followed the discovery of the Rye House Plot in 1683 strengthened his position and enabled him to turn the tables on his antagonists. In November 1683 John Arnold and Sir Trevor Williams were summoned to appear before the Court of King's Bench to answer charges of *scandalum magnatum*, and were heavily fined. Like King Charles himself, Beaufort proved sufficiently resilient and flexible to ride out periods of unpopularity and to triumph in the end.

Most Welshmen greeted the accession of James II in 1685 with joy and expectation. The new king was well liked by most of the gentry, many of whom served him with unswerving fidelity during his brief reign. Little or no support was forthcoming when the duke of Monmouth launched his rebellion in the summer of 1685. The rebels were ruthlessly suppressed and, during the 'Bloody Assizes' which followed, Judge George Jeffreys, a native of Acton Park near Wrexham, earned notoriety not only for the

---

[30] Anon., *The Popes Down-fall at Abergavenny* (London, 1679), *passim*.

brutal sentences which he imposed on the rebels but also for the verbal abuse and bullying tactics with which he treated witnesses. Unlike his brother, James II failed to recognize the folly of openly embracing Catholicism. Driven on by his mistaken belief that a Catholic minority was capable of winning over the Protestant majority, he appointed fellow Catholics to high office in government and to key posts in the army and navy. His main ambition was to repeal the penal laws and Test Acts, advance the interests of Catholicism, and eliminate the powerful anti-Catholic animus which dominated Protestant thinking. James's catholicizing policies proved both provocative and foolhardy, particularly in view of the excesses committed in the course of Louis XIV's dragonnades in France. In October 1685 Louis had revoked the Edict of Nantes and some 200,000 Huguenots had fled abroad. Hundreds of refugees flooded into Wales. William Lloyd welcomed many of them to his diocese of St Asaph and endeavoured to mitigate their sufferings. Many Huguenots doubtless brought with them stories of popish cruelty and absolutism which convinced Protestants that James, too, was laying plans to establish an arbitrary popish government. 'For aught I know', cried John Freeman, a husbandman from Bosherston, 'he will have our throats cut shortly.'[31] Conscious, perhaps, of the need to publicize his aims and curry favour with his Welsh subjects, James ventured in August 1687 on the last royal pilgrimage in these islands, to the celebrated well of St Winifred in Holywell, Flintshire. There he paid his respects to St Winifred, presented gold rings to some of his loyal followers, and prayed for a son by the influence and intercession of the local saint.

In April 1687 James followed in his brother's footsteps by suspending not only the penal legislation but also the Test Acts of 1673 and 1678. Having alienated leading Anglicans, he now aimed at wooing support from among Dissenters by offering them a general toleration. Some Dissenters eagerly welcomed what they supposed to be a new dawn. 'King James, God keep him, is an instrument in God's hand to give us a lovely, likeable freedom by a strong unshakable declaration',[32] sang Richard Thomas Pugh, a Baptist miller and poet from Tredwstan, Breconshire. Most Dissenters, however, were rather more cautious in their approval. Although anxious to take advantage of the grant of toleration, they feared that James's primary goal was to encourage a faith which was abhorrent to the overwhelming majority of the Welsh people. No true Welsh Protestant would ever wish to be associated in the public mind with Catholicism. Nevertheless, the duke of Beaufort, who had remained loyal to James II, endeavoured to persuade the gentry of the merits of the king's plans for

---

[31] F. Jones, 'Disaffection and Dissent', p. 216.

[32] R. Tudur Jones, 'Religion in Post-Restoration Brecknockshire, 1660–1688', *Brycheiniog* 8 (1962), p. 62.

toleration. In October 1687 the deputy-lieutenants and justices of Wales were summoned to Ludlow to answer three questions tendered by Beaufort regarding James's policy of granting liberty of worship to Catholics and Dissenters. If they were elected to the next Parliament, would they pledge themselves to vote for the repeal of the Test and Corporation Acts and the penal laws? If not intending to offer themselves as candidates, would they pledge themselves to support a candidate who had given such an undertaking? Were they prepared to promise to live peacefully and tolerantly with men of all persuasions? Some 320 magistrates were expected to attend the inquisition at Ludlow, but half of them stayed away. Many of them brandished the Stuart equivalent of sickness notes. Sir Edward Mansell of Margam pleaded infirmity, claiming that he had not ridden ten miles during the previous four years. The third Viscount Bulkeley of Baron Hill feigned sickness, whilst Nicholas Bagnal of Plas Newydd was 'ill of the spleen to so high a degree he could not come'.[33] Fear of floods kept William Jones of Monmouth at home, while David Evans of Glamorgan was so unnerved when his horse threw him that he abandoned his journey to Ludlow. Those wily foxes who did heed the royal summons provided Beaufort with such vague, ambivalent, or negative answers that the whole exercise was rendered meaningless. It was clear, however, that James could not expect uncritical acceptance of his propaganda or unconditional obedience to his policies from his Welsh subjects.

With mulish obstinacy, James continued to cultivate his unhappy knack of alienating Protestant support. No argument, however enlightened, could reach or affect him. He went on to pack Parliament with his supporters and remodel local government. His enemies within the commissions of the peace were put out of office and replaced by Dissenters. These expedients, implemented by fraud and force, served only to create bitter resentment within the established church. When James commanded his bishops to order that a second Declaration of Indulgence, proclaimed on 27 April 1688, be read in every parish church on two successive Sundays, several leading bishops decided to resist the royal command. Among the seven bishops who were imprisoned in the Tower on 1 June was William Lloyd, bishop of St Asaph. Nine days later, St Winifred's supernatural powers were revealed when Queen Mary gave birth to a healthy son, James Francis Edward, Prince of Wales. Little public joy was apparent, for hatred of popery had driven Anglicans and Dissenters into each other's arms. Not a single candle was lit and not a single bell was rung by Welsh students at Jesus College, Oxford. Edward Morris, the drover and poet, dubbed James a 'cruel persecutor' who had,

[33] Thomas Richards, 'The Puritan Movement in Anglesey', *Trans. Anglesey Antiq. Soc.* (1954), p. 57.

by his despotism, incarcerated 'seven wise men'.[34] Tensions mounted and there were real fears of civil strife. Amid scenes of great delight, however, the seven bishops were acquitted on 30 June. In his fury, James dismissed two of the presiding judges, Sir Richard Holloway and Sir John Powell, a native of Carmarthenshire. Following his release from the Tower, Bishop Lloyd hurried north to preach in churches and dine in country mansions in Wales in order 'to incense the people against the king and dispose them to what followed'.[35] Leading churchmen like Lloyd were convinced that the king no longer believed himself to be accountable to mere mortals.

The revolt against James grew apace and his reign ended in defeat and humiliation. A few weeks prior to Prince William of Orange's landing at Torbay on 5 November 1688, the duke of Beaufort was commissioned to raise 10,000 men in Wales, including a special Prince of Wales Regiment to be recruited in south Wales by Colonel Thomas Carne of Glamorgan. Sir Robert Owen of Clenennau and Thomas Mostyn also volunteered to raise local levies in order to sustain the king's cause. After an initial show of force, however, James decided that discretion was the better part of valour. Looking back from the vantage point of 1696, James Owen saw James's precipitate flight to France and the arrival of the Dutch redeemer as a major turning-point in the history of Welsh Protestantism: 'we were upon the brink of ruin, and knew it not . . . this island might have been swimming in a deluge of innocent blood and become the sad monument of French and popish cruelties'.[36] For a brief period, fears of bloodshed frayed Protestant nerves. James's flight provoked fears that disbanded Irish troops would terrorize the land, indulging in the bestial conduct for which they were believed to be notorious. Several Irish soldiers in Pembrokeshire were thwarted in their attempts to cross the Irish Sea to their homeland. As in 1641–2, a rash of extravagant and improbable rumours of Irish atrocities broke out. At Dolgellau an unruly mob attacked the prison and freed the prisoners; on the following day, excise commissioners found themselves under fire from villagers who had mistaken them for Irish soldiers. In Caernarfonshire, Robert Pugh of Penrhyn Creuddyn stood by helplessly as local constables defaced his private Catholic chapel. The citizens of Wrexham were filled with horror when reports filtered through that papist incendiarists had razed Bangor to the ground, but it later transpired that the conflagration was simply an accidental fire in a bakehouse. Protestants and Catholics fought furiously on the streets of Welshpool and Powis Castle was ransacked and badly damaged.

Most Welshmen, however, were suing for peace. 'I pray God restore our

---

[34] Gwenllian Jones, 'Bywyd a Gwaith Edward Morris, Perthi Llwydion', pp. 319–21.

[35] A. H. Dodd, *Studies in Stuart Wales*, p. 224.

[36] James Owen, *Salvation Improved* (London, 1696), p. 19.

religion, liberties and properties with a happy peace',[37] was Sir Robert Cotton's fervent prayer on 7 December 1688. His prayers were answered: the so-called Glorious Revolution passed peacefully, with neither tumult nor bloodshed, in Wales. Whigs hailed the arrival of the Dutch liberator as a victory for parliamentary monarchy. Dissenters, too, welcomed William with open arms, for he had spared Britain from 'Sicilian vapours or a Bartholomew supper'.[38] Although William was a morose, asthmatic man, he possessed great inner resources and determination which endeared him to men who had suffered cruelly in defence of their faith and liberties. Following the rout of James and his followers at the battle of the Boyne on 1 July 1690, Welsh Dissenters and poets eulogized 'King Billy' as the saviour of the Protestant cause in Europe. However, many Tory and Country members, who were still wedded to the theories of divine right and passive obedience, remained deeply suspicious of the new monarch, if not downright hostile to him. Edward Llewelyn, a gentleman from Newton Nottage, voiced his belief that Parliament had arrogated unto itself illegal powers and that 'there was never such a fool of a king as this'.[39] Abergavenny forfeited its charters when the town's burgesses doggedly refused to swear the oath of allegiance to the new sovereign. Diehard Tories and churchmen refused to recognize any other monarch but James II. Bishop William Lloyd of Norwich, a native of Llangywer and formerly bishop of Llandaff, Bishop William Thomas of Worcester, formerly bishop of St Davids, and eighteen Welsh clergymen joined the ranks of the non-jurors. They remained convinced that William was a usurper and that James II was their rightful monarch. In 1691 Humphrey Collins, a clergyman from Narberth, declared forebodingly: 'rebellion is worse than the sin of witchcraft and the judgement of God will fall upon all disobedient children'.[40] Such men were not afraid to declare where their loyalties lay. Others, emboldened by a surfeit of alcohol in taverns, drank regular toasts to James and his family and discussed the possibility of his return. Still others spat their venom publicly on William and his advisers. In 1695, Ned Carne, Francis Gwyn's Tory agent at Cowbridge, was prosecuted for 'speaking contemptuous words'[41] of William III and his government.

Welsh Protestants lived in mortal fear of the possibility that an assassin's bullet or knife might remove William and usher in arbitrary popish government. In February 1696 a plot to assassinate William came close to success and Whigs and Dissenters were clearly shaken. In a solemn

[37] A. L. Cust (ed.), *Chronicles of Erthig on the Dyke* (2 vols., London, 1914), i. 69.
[38] James Owen, *Salvation Improved*, p. 19.
[39] J. H. Matthews (ed.), *Cardiff Records* (6 vols., Cardiff, 1898–1911), ii. 178–9.
[40] F. Jones, 'Disaffection and Dissent', p. 218.
[41] Philip Jenkins, 'Francis Gwyn and the Birth of the Tory Party', *WHR* 11 (1983), p. 291.

thanksgiving sermon preached at Oswestry, James Owen maintained that
William's deliverance indicated that he was precious in the sight of the
Lord. The court Whigs swiftly produced an 'Association' paper, which
called on Members of Parliament, lords-lieutenant, and justices of the
peace to recognize that William was the rightful and lawful king of England
and binding them to disavow James and his adherents. Some prominent
Welsh politicians could not bring themselves to subscribe to the document.
Among those displaced for refusing to subscribe to the oath were Sir
Richard Myddelton of Chirk Castle and Sir William Williams, one of the
prosecutors of the seven bishops. Sir Thomas Mansell of Margam refused
to sign, stoutly claiming that he 'would not do such a thing for all the kings
in Christendom'.[42] More significant, however, is the fact that 760 leading
citizens in Glamorgan signed the document with some alacrity. Following
the plot, anti-Jacobite passions ran high, for it was widely believed that the
exiled Stuart was heavily implicated. Although not all Welsh Tories
identified themselves with the exiled Stuart cause they were vulnerable to
the charge of Jacobitism, and Whigs and Dissenters, playing on popular
fears of arbitrary Catholic rule, branded them as traitors. Just as 'Dissent
and Sedition' had been synonymous in the reign of Charles II, so now did
'Toryism and Jacobitism' acquire a resonant affinity.

With the accession in 1702 of Anne, James II's daughter, the Stuart
cause entered a new phase. Anne's emergence clearly boosted the morale
of those country gentlemen who had pledged themselves to the Jacobite
cause. Among those who were known publicly to toast the Pretender were
the fourth Viscount Bulkeley of Baron Hill, Lewis Pryse of Gogerddan,
Colonel William Barlow of Slebech, Sir Edward Stradling of St Donat's,
Thomas Lewis of Y Fan, and Sir Charles Kemeys of Cefnmabli. In a
deferential society, such men wielded powerful influence and they were
optimistic of paving the way for the return of the exiled dynasty. Leading
Tories gathered in Lewis Pryse's town house in Aberystwyth to drink the
Pretender's health and roar Jacobite slogans during their roisterings. The
major bastion of Welsh Jacobitism, however, was north-east Wales. In
1710 the Cycle of the White Rose was founded on 10 June, the birthday of
the Old Pretender. The moving spirit behind the society was Watkin
Williams Wynn, Tory MP for Denbighshire from 1716 to 1749 and the
most powerful landowner in north-east Wales. Members of the society—
Tory gentlemen to a man—frequented private gatherings every three
weeks and behind closed doors drank the health of 'James III' in exquisitely
engraved wine glasses, decorated with the white rose. Thunderous roars
accompanied toasts of loyalty and rousing Jacobite songs such as 'Robin
John Clerk' were declaimed with great gusto.

[42] Philip Jenkins, *The Making of a Ruling Class*, p. 142.

Jacobite expectations, however, were rudely shattered when the elector of Hanover was proclaimed king of England in 1714. Lewis Pryse, the young Jacobite firebrand of Gogerddan, refused to take his seat in the House of Commons following his election in 1715. Messengers were sent to order him to attend, but Pryse went to ground; found guilty of contempt, he was expelled from the House. Sir Charles Kemeys of Cefnmabli reacted to a royal invitation to attend George I at court with a petulant outburst: 'I should be happy to smoke a pipe with him as Elector of Hanover, but I cannot think of it as king of England'.[43] Such men were seemingly prepared to raise the standard of the exiled dynasty, but when the acid test came in 1715, they were not prepared to endanger themselves or their families. The Jacobite rebellion of September 1715 was a largely Scottish affair. Badly planned and catastrophically executed, it came to grief with depressing inevitability. The southern Jacobite army surrendered at Preston, while the Scottish Jacobites were deserted by the Pretender and the earl of Mar following the battle of Sheriffmuir. This débâcle proved a bitter blow for those Welsh Jacobites who were extremely reluctant to accept with good grace a dull, indolent foreigner, who spoke no English, as their monarch. Judicial records reveal that impudent and disaffected tongues often wagged, and acts of wanton damage were committed. On 16 July 1715 bands of rowdy craftsmen and labourers roamed the streets of Wrexham, chanting slogans and ransacking Dissenting meeting-houses. On the following Monday, local colliers, spoiling for a fight, entered Wrexham in their dozens. Local Dissenters pleaded with Watkin Williams Wynn to protect them, but the violence continued for most of the week. On 1 August, the anniversary of the Hanoverian succession, no bells were rung in Wrexham, no bonfires were lit, and only Dissenters closed their shops. Conversely, on the birthday of James Stuart in the following year, the bells of Wrexham rang incessantly from eight until dusk and devout Jacobites wore feathers in their hats and carried oaken boughs. In Cardiff, two barbers, a glover, and a cordwainer were prosecuted for wearing oaken boughs on the Pretender's birthday, while Thomas William was punished for declaring publicly 'that King James would come to rule and order him [i.e. his opponent, one Thomas Evan] and the rest of the shit sacks as he thought fit'.[44]

The truth is, however, that few Welshmen were able or prepared to offer support on any significant scale to the ailing Stuart cause. Times were changing and even the most highly committed Welsh Jacobites could do little more than hope, pray, and bide their time. Meanwhile, Whigs and Dissenters made the most of their opportunities to exploit anti-Catholic prejudices, besmirch Toryism, and unite the Welsh behind the Hanoverians.

[43] P. D. G. Thomas, 'Jacobitism in Wales', *WHR* 1 (1962), p. 282.
[44] J. H. Matthews, *Cardiff Records*, ii. 189.

Members of the Society of Antient Britons, founded in London in 1715, vowed their undying support for the House of Hanover. Children in Welsh charity schools were commanded daily to pray for King George and the royal family. In a rousing sermon, preached in 1717, on the text, 'For consider how great things he hath done for you', Jeremy Owen maintained that the blood of the Tudors flowed in George's veins and that he could be relied upon to bring strong government and greater security to the Protestant cause. Owen found it hard to believe that 'stark mad' Welshmen were prepared to entertain the idea of bringing back a Catholic dynasty and turn their thoughts to rebellion. 'We should strive unto blood against Popery', he declared, 'and against all such that would bring in one of that bloody religion into the government.'[45]

It is difficult to judge how far the Jacobite cause enjoyed mass support in Wales. Not all Welsh Tories by any means identified themselves with the exiled Stuart cause. Powerful Tory families, such as the Mansells of Margam, the Mostyns of Flintshire, and the Myddeltons of Chirk, had rid themselves of the taint of Jacobitism by loyally defending the principles of the Glorious Revolution and proclaiming their enthusiastic support for the Hanoverian succession. Some families who still hankered after the Stuarts took refuge in violent, diehard rhetoric. Others lost heart for the struggle following the Pretender's ignominious flight back to France in 1715. Lewis Pryse and Lord Bulkeley retained their contacts with the exiled dynasty, but several crackbrained invasion schemes brought the Jacobite movement into further disrepute. Without significant assistance from the major Catholic powers in Europe, the movement could scarcely hope to topple the House of Hanover. Disheartened and disorganized by their rural isolation, leading Welsh Jacobites either daydreamed or shrouded their activities in secrecy. From time to time they boosted their morale by burning pictures of George I and other members of the royal family. Members of the 'Cycle Club' continued to gather over dinner, toast the Pretender, and sing romantic songs in a haze of nostalgic sentiment. In 1725 the Society of Sea Serjeants, a clubbable gathering of fully fledged Tory squires, was founded in south-west Wales. Members met annually and, like their northern counterparts, developed a taste for esoteric symbolism and empty ritual. For obvious reasons, clandestine societies leave few records behind them, but however hard it may be to believe that these Jacobites were not committed to some intrigue, it is unlikely that they were able to improve the political prospects of the Pretender. Welsh Jacobitism survived not as an effective political force but as a waning romantic ideology embraced by economically powerful but politically impotent landowners. Long before the ultimate disaster on the battlefield of Culloden in 1746, Welsh

---

[45] Jeremy Owen, *The Goodness and Severity of God* (London, 1717), p. 27.

Jacobites had decided not to risk their necks or their estates on behalf of the Stuart dynasty. Welsh Jacobitism is the tale of the dog that barked but never bit.

Throughout this period the system of parliamentary representation was designed to ensure that political power remained in the hands of men of substance. Politics and its practice were the preserve of rich men. It is difficult to judge, however, how far Welsh Members of Parliament were political animals. Some shared Bishop Burnet's view that tarrying long in London both wasted their estates and corrupted their morals. Some, choosing a life of frivolous consumption, neglected their parliamentary duties and exhausted themselves by falling prey to the gaieties of London life. Some enjoyed moving among people who mattered in the exclusive dining clubs and coffee houses of London. Most Welsh members, however, were basically home-loving men. Their parliamentary duties sat lightly upon them, and only during years of acute political crisis did they trouble to attend to their chores at Westminster. They all believed that a parliamentary seat was a prized social asset, but few of them were prepared to serve on committees or participate in debates.

The 'Welsh interest', which, to some extent, had provided Welsh members with a common identity under the early Stuarts, dissolved after 1660. Members who attached themselves to the court divorced themselves not only from their constituents but also from Welsh interests as a whole. Some were showered with rewards: Sir Herbert Price allegedly received a salary of £10,000 per annum as Master of the Household at Charles II's court, and Lord Vaughan of Golden Grove one of £1,000 per annum on his appointment as governor of Jamaica in 1674. Other willing hands were kept happy with offices, emoluments, and favours. In this way, many Welsh members became tied to the British establishment, on whose patronage they largely depended. Unlike the Scots, who formed a distinctive body of opinion in the House, Welsh members acted and voted as individuals. Only crucial matters, such as the prohibition of imported Irish cattle or the bill for burying in woollens, brought them together to vote as a united group. Bored and sometimes befogged by parliamentary proceedings, many country members remained tongue-tied even during heated debates and seldom stood up for the interests of their constituents. Rarely did the House resound to the stirring rhetoric of a Welshman. The most celebrated peroration by a Welshman occurred in 1695 as a result of William III's grant of the lordships of Denbigh, Bromfield, and Yale to his foreign favourite, William Bentinck, earl of Portland. In a memorable speech delivered before a spellbound House, Robert Price of Giler, MP for Weobley, launched a blistering assault, on behalf of 'thousands' of like-minded people, on William's attempt to reduce the country to 'a colony of the Dutch'. His speech, however, was less an expression of Welsh national sentiment than an exercise in xenophobia. 'I would have you consider we are Englishmen', declared the Welsh-born Price, 'and must, like patriots, stand by our country, and not suffer it to be a tributary to strangers.'[46] Ever since the Acts of Union, the influence of Welsh national sentiment upon Welsh members had declined perceptibly. In their eyes, Wales meant England.

Although only a minority of ordinary members was either capable of or interested in energetic political activity, a surprising number of Welshmen rose to positions of dizzy eminence during this period. During the reigns of Charles II and James II, Wales produced a number of gifted lawyers who gained preferment in their profession and political office as a result of their fidelity to the Crown. Sir John Vaughan of Trawsgoed, Chief Justice of Common Pleas from 1668 to 1674, was an icy, sardonic man whose arrogance was not to all men's taste. But he was a brilliant debater in Parliament, a man of integrity, and a scrupulously fair judge who championed the cause of parliamentary privilege and the freedom of the individual. Vaughan is remembered principally for his decision in Bushell's case in 1670, when he pronounced that a jury whose verdict was at variance with the evidence or the direction of the judge should not be subject to any penalty. Sir Leoline Jenkins, the son of a minor squire from Glamorgan, pulled himself up by his own bootstraps, becoming President of the Admiralty Court and Secretary of State from 1680 to 1684. Whereas Jenkins won respect as a man of learning and probity, Judge George Jeffreys became a legend in his own lifetime, on account of his unbridled temper and judicial brutalities. Jeffreys was an uncommonly able man whose rise to fame was meteoric. He was called to the bar at the age of 24 and by 1685 he had become the youngest Lord Chancellor in English history. By implementing James's asinine policies and intimidating witnesses in court, however, Jeffreys earned the implacable hostility of Anglicans and Dissenters alike. Few mourned when this vindictive bully died (in excruciating pain resulting from severe attacks of the stone) in the Tower in April 1689.

Throughout this period there were rich pickings available for the lackeys of the Crown and for time-servers and sycophants who were prepared to trim or moderate their principles. 'Politicians are like watermen', declared Thomas Bulkeley, 'who look one way and row another.'[47] Artful opportunists were able to exploit their own talents and the political flux of the times to make a career for themselves. Sir John Trevor of Bryncunallt was particularly adept at devious manœuvres and intrigues; grotesquely

---

[46] Francis Jones, *The Princes and Principality of Wales* (Cardiff, 1969), pp. 95–7.
[47] B. D. Henning, *The House of Commons 1660–1690* (3 vols., London, 1983) i. 746.

cross-eyed, he was known to his many enemies as 'squint-eyed Jack'.[48] An unscrupulous political adventurer, he was chiefly animated by naked self-interest. He wormed his way into high office as Speaker and Master of the Rolls under James II and his ingratiating manners later earned him the favour of William III. Eventually, however, his venal practices were exposed. In 1695 Trevor was expelled from the Speaker's chair for having received a bribe of a thousand guineas for expediting a local bill. His removal from office elicited the venomous observation that no longer would he be able to 'take an oblique view of every question from the chair'.[49] Sir William Williams, a native of Anglesey, was also an eloquent debater and a skilful intriguer who manipulated political situations for his own ends. He abandoned the Whig cause for that of the court and was appointed Speaker of the House in 1680 and 1681. During James's reign he supported the Crown's catholicizing policies even to the extent of leading the prosecution of the seven bishops. A further volte-face during William's reign enabled him to return to office once more. The careers of Trevor and Williams exemplify the peculiar skills of malleability and survival which marked the lives of so many Stuart politicians. And although they were detested by many of their contemporaries, they were politicians of no mean ability.

Although there was little enthusiasm for politics among Welsh members after 1689, talented men continued to reach positions of political eminence during the reigns of William and Anne. One of the key figures in the Tory party was Francis Gwyn, a native of Llansannor in Glamorgan. Having served twice as Under-Secretary of State during the reign of Charles II, Gwyn immersed himself in the ins and outs of party politics. He married well, inherited massive estates in Glamorgan and Dorset, and established close connections with Robert Harley and Lord Rochester. In spite of an obsessive interest in racing, gambling, women, and wine, Gwyn was a dexterous political animal who helped to knit together the Tory party during the crisis years of 1690 and 1710. Robert Harley, MP for Radnor borough from 1690 to 1711, served as Speaker of the House and Secretary of State under Anne and, as earl of Oxford, became prime minister of England in all but name from 1710 until 1714. Sir Thomas Mansell (Lord Mansell from 1711 onwards) of Margam held office under Tory governments in 1704–8 and 1710–14 and, by a shrewd use of patronage, he secured prestigious offices and sizeable pensions for his kinsmen and neighbours. Once the Hanoverian dynasty had established itself, however, Welsh Tories were excluded from political office and were replaced by ambitious, rising Whigs like Thomas Wynn of Glynllifon, who was appointed Equerry

[48] R. J. Lloyd, 'Welsh Masters of the Bench of the Inner Temple', THSC (1937–8), p. 191.
[49] A. L. Cust, Chronicles, i. 51.

to the Prince of Wales in 1714 and Clerk to the Board of Green Cloth ten years later.

A highly select and affluent circle of county gentlemen dominated parliamentary representation in Wales. As Titans, by fair means and foul, concentrated landed wealth into their own hands, the gulf between them and the smaller gentry families widened considerably after 1660. Whilst the weak fell by the wayside, the great Leviathans went from strength to strength, both economically and politically. Those who represented Wales at Westminster were increasingly drawn from a narrow circle of famous county families—the Bulkeleys of Baron Hill, the Myddeltons of Chirk, the Mostyns of Flintshire, the Vaughans of Corsygedol, the Vaughans of Golden Grove, the Harleys of Radnorshire, the Mansells of Margam, the Morgans of Tredegar, and their like. Such families believed that they had been blessed with a God-given right to represent and govern their inferiors. Virtually no one questioned that right. A gentleman who possessed neither substantial estates nor extensive commercial interests could entertain few hopes of gaining a parliamentary seat. Politics was the preserve of the wealthy. From 1711 onwards, membership of Parliament was further restricted by the Property Qualifications Act, which obliged candidates to possess real estate worth £600 per annum for the county seat and £300 for the borough seat.

As single families rose to positions of undisputed economic supremacy within their shires, they laid claim to the county seat and treated it as their own property. John Morgan of Tredegar referred to the shire of Monmouth as 'my neighbourhood'[50] and regarded the affairs of the community as his exclusive concern. A county seat carried considerable prestige and power. The county member was in a position to offer advice regarding the nomination of the lord-lieutenant and the *custos rotulorum*. He was able to dispose of civil offices and church livings. Neither the aspiring middle classes nor the disenfranchised masses were in a position to challenge the great families' monopoly of parliamentary representation. Those who held the longest rent-rolls were the natural rulers of the countryside; and smaller squires, often seriously burdened with heavy mortgages and debts, yielded precedence to them. In many counties seats were family heirlooms to be passed on, as a matter of course, to sons, relatives, or clients. Seats were often kept warm until an heir came of age. As a result, leading families were able to maintain an unbroken hold on their seats for many generations. In those counties where landed gentlemen vied with one another, deals were struck in advance. In 1671 a dozen of the leading gentry of Merioneth agreed that Edward Vaughan of Glan-llyn and William Salesbury of Rug should draw lots in order to decide

[50] W. T. Morgan, 'County Elections in Monmouthshire, 1705–1847', *NLWJ* 10 (1957), p. 169.

who should serve as knight for the county. Families often came to a gentleman's understanding regarding the division of political power, thus enabling seats to be rotated among aspiring candidates. Acquisitive gentlemen who broke unwritten rules by seeking to gain further power at the expense of others were often cut down to size. In 1705 John Morgan, a merchant of Ruperra and the borough member for Monmouthshire, declared his intention of standing for the second county seat, together with his nephew, John Morgan of Tredegar. The Beaufort family and their satellites were infuriated by the temerity of the Tredegar family. The duke of Beaufort threateningly declared that 'the gentlemen of the county will not like two out of the same house'.[51] So it proved: John Morgan of Ruperra came third in the poll. Similarly, the leading Welsh families and the electorate at large generally looked askance at carpet-baggers and men of low birth. Sir Robert Needham, MP for Pembrokeshire, was left in no doubt by the citizens of Haverfordwest in 1660 that 'nothing will satisfy them but the choosing of a native of the country to be their representative'.[52] When a prominent Whig, Admiral Thomas Matthews of Llandaff, was nominated for the borough election in Glamorgan in 1727, Bussy Mansell loftily declared: 'I would not for a thousand pounds be thrown out by *such* a gentleman'.[53]

The constitution and the system of parliamentary representation enabled the leading families to rule almost as feudal barons over the rest of society. In the shires, the franchise was vested in those who owned freehold property valued at 40s. per annum. The actual size of the county electorate in early eighteenth-century Wales ranged from 360 in Anglesey to 2,000 in Monmouthshire. Five Welsh shires (Anglesey, Caernarfonshire, Cardiganshire, Flintshire, and Merioneth) had fewer than a thousand voters. The overwhelming majority of these voters were tenants or dependants of the ruling gentry families. In Glamorgan, for instance, one-sixth of the electorate was under the direct control of the powerful Mansell family of Margam. In the boroughs, the situation was rather more complex. Here, the electorate was small and was often deliberately kept so. The franchise in eleven Welsh boroughs was held by freemen, who had acquired their privileges either through inheritance, apprenticeship, marriage, residential qualifications, or membership of the corporation. Beaumaris was unique in that it was a corporation borough in which the mayor, two bailiffs, and twenty-one capital burgesses elected the member. In the boroughs of Flint and Haverfordwest, inhabitants paying scot and lot—generally the poor rate and church rate—were able to vote. Six Welsh boroughs were deemed small (i.e. fewer than 500 voters), the boroughs of Montgomery and Flint

[51] W. T. Morgan, 'County Elections in Monmouthshire, 1705–1847', *NLWJ* 10 (1957), p. 168.
[52] *Calendar of the Records of the Borough of Haverfordwest*, pp. 166–7.
[53] P. D. G. Thomas, 'Glamorgan Politics, 1700–1750', *Morgannwg* 6 (1962), p. 64.

had electorates of between 500 and 1000, whilst five boroughs (Caernarfon, Cardigan, Denbigh, Monmouth, and New Radnor) were deemed large, since their voters exceeded a thousand. It is not possible to be precise about the actual size of the electorate in early eighteenth-century Wales, but it is likely that around 21,000 (4 per cent of the population) were entitled to vote.

Ever since Tudor times, Welsh freeholders and tenants had considered the vote as an extension of older rights based on feudal loyalty. Habits of deference and submission were deeply ingrained, for the mass of the Welsh people had been conditioned to accept social distinctions, and the inequalities which sprang from them, as belonging to the nature of things. Untutored in their political rights, the majority were apolitical and utterly apathetic. Few tenants were disposed to disobey the wishes of their landlords, for those who were bold or foolish enough to refuse to render instant obedience to their political masters often found themselves threatened with increased rents, feudal exactions, or even eviction. Generally, most leading families could rely upon the unwavering support of those freeholders and tenants who came under their economic sway. Some Leviathans made sure of support by governing their territories with an iron fist. In December 1718, Watkin Williams, grandson of Sir William Williams, solicitor-general to James II, inherited the estates of Llwydiarth in Montgomeryshire, Glan-llyn in Merioneth, and Llangedwyn in Denbighshire. A month later the extensive Wynnstay estate in Denbighshire and Rhiwgoch in Merioneth came into his possession. Williams Wynn (as he was now known) swiftly used his considerable economic influence to build up a wide following in Denbighshire. So dominant did he become among the Tories of north Wales that he was called 'Prince of Wales'. John Meller of Erddig was appalled at the way Wynn arbitrarily exercised his authority over magistrates, stewards, agents, smaller squires, and tenants. 'This whole country [i.e., north-east Wales] is governed by fear', wrote Meller in 1720, 'and the lesser gentry are as much awed by those of better estate as the poor people are; and those of large estates do as much awe and tyrannize over the lesser gentry as they do over the poor.'[54] Wynn was a bitter foe of Dissenters, Whigs, and Hanoverians, and fear of reprisals prompted many of them to join his campaign against Chirk Castle during the election of 1722. A poor lame woman whom Wynn had failed to cajole or coerce into obedience was deprived of her allowance on his estate for failing to rally to his cause.

As the arts of political management became more sophisticated, landowners used every possible means to promote their own interests. During or immediately prior to elections, landlords often prepared new

---

[54] A. L. Cust, *Chronicles*, i. 230.

leases in order to increase their voting strength. A common stratagem was to create a number of freeholds by leasing pieces of property to tenants which they were entitled to use to claim a vote during the election but were to surrender immediately afterwards. Candidates bargained, canvassed, and bribed with shameless insouciance. Many months before the election of 1701, Sir Humphrey Mackworth began nursing his constituency in Cardiganshire. He ordered William Waller, the manager of his mines, to allow Lord Lisburne to name his own price for coal supplies and pressed him to fly a few kites such as setting up a fishery, a woollen mill, or an almshouse in the community. 'These thoughts being well spread beforehand', wrote the crafty Mackworth, 'will prepare the way better than if they did suspect there was any design in it.'[55] Craft and chicanery were not foreign to Sir Thomas Mansell of Margam either: he spent lavishly during the 1708 election, winning the burgesses of Aberafan to his cause by sending them gifts of coal. On polling day, contingents of voters were provided with free transport to the polling booths, lavish suppers and barrels of ale in local inns, and beds in private homes. Horses were accommodated with hay, corn, and bedding. Bell-ringers, drummers, sheriffs and agents all needed to be paid. Electoral costs, therefore, often ran into hundreds of pounds, especially following the passing of the Septennial Act (1716), which, by diminishing the number of polls, sent the price of a seat soaring. Many years after a bitter electoral contest in Anglesey in 1722, it was alleged that Lord Bulkeley's success had cost him £10,000. The cost of fighting an election was so prohibitively high that candidates, particularly those with hidden financial problems, sought to reconcile differences whenever possible and avoid a challenge at the polls which might lead to possible ruin.

Leading families did not scruple to use every conceivable weapon in their armoury to maintain their control over boroughs and corporations. Their control was usually so tight that they were free to employ every known subterfuge. The art of increasing the electorate, fixing seats, and bribing voters was part and parcel of the politics of local oligarchy. During elections, boroughmongers often paid the expenses of voters out of corporation funds. More critically, they controlled the electorate by restricting the number of burgesses or swamping the electorate on the eve of an election. In most boroughs, residence was not a condition for the admission of burgesses. Any number of voters might be created prior to an election and it was possible for a single borough, however puny, to outvote more populous and powerful boroughs within the constituency. In 1715 it was claimed that the mayor of Haverfordwest had declared that 'he would

---

[55] M. Ransome, 'The Parliamentary Career of Sir Humphrey Mackworth 1701–1713', *University of Birmingham Historical Journal* 1 (1948), p. 236.

make as many new burgesses as would serve his turn'.[56] In the 1722 borough election in Caernarfonshire, 1,281 out of 1,553 voters in the constituency were non-resident. Borough elections were riddled with malpractice, bribery, and corruption. During the 1729 election in Cardiganshire, Thomas Pryse, mayor of Cardigan, was offered a bribe of £500 by one of the supporters of Thomas Powell of Nanteos. It transpired, however, that Richard Lloyd of Mabws, the opposing candidate, had already offered a plumper *douceur*. One of the most celebrated and bitter campaigns to protect the exclusive rights of boroughs occurred in Montgomeryshire. There, the borough constituency comprised Montgomery and the three out-boroughs of Llanidloes, Llanfyllin, and Welshpool. Each of these was controlled by Tory patrons: Llanidloes was in the possession of the Llwydiarth estate, Llanfyllin and Welshpool were under the sway of Lord Powis, while the town of Montgomery was controlled by the Whig family, the Herberts of Oakley Park. From the Restoration period onwards, disgruntled representatives of the disenfranchised out-boroughs claimed the right of their burgesses to cast their votes. Matters came to a head in 1727 when Llwydiarth and Powis Castle put forward Robert Williams, the younger brother of Watkin Williams Wynn, as a candidate against William Corbett, a Whig from Shropshire, who was supported by Henry Arthur Herbert, the patron of Montgomery town. Williams swept to victory at the polls, but Corbett claimed the seat on the grounds that he had secured a majority of seventy-eight votes in Montgomery town itself. Both parties submitted petitions to the House of Commons which, to the undisguised fury of Welsh members, confirmed Corbett's victory by disfranchising the three out-boroughs. As a result, Montgomery became a prized pocket borough in the hands of Henry Arthur Herbert and his heirs for the next hundred years.

Parliamentary candidates were well advised to cultivate the friendship or good humour of the county sheriff prior to an election. In his capacity as returning officer, a sheriff could either make or break a candidate. A cussed or unscrupulous sheriff might employ all kinds of ruses. He might inconvenience either one or both candidates by advancing or retarding the date of an election. He might choose an awkward venue or change it at the eleventh hour. He might delay the poll or close the proceedings abruptly. He might even arbitrarily reject votes and deny candidates the right to demand a scrutiny. In the stormy Denbighshire election of 1681, the sheriff disqualified Richard Myddelton of Chirk on the grounds that an ancient statute passed during the reign of Henry V had declared that a candidate for a shire seat was required to be resident in the constituency on the day when the election writs were issued. In April 1685 the bailiffs who acted as

---

[56] R. Sedgwick, *The House of Commons 1715–1754* (2 vols., London, 1970), i. 379.

returning officers in the borough constituency of Montgomeryshire proclaimed the time of the election in such hushed tones that it was barely audible to passers-by, and the actual poll was conducted at six o'clock in the morning. During the election in Anglesey in 1708, the sheriff, John Sparrow of Red Hill, wound up the proceedings at such an unexpectedly early hour that Sir Roger Mostyn of Flintshire, who had rallied to Lord Bulkeley's cause, marched off in disgust.

Stewards and land agents were also key figures during elections. It was their task to press tenants to obey the will of their landlords and to round them up on election days. Many of them were prepared to browbeat defenceless as well as truculent tenants. Prior to the 1722 election in Glamorgan, John Watkin and his wife, aged tenants of Lord Mansell of Margam, were so violently treated on four separate occasions by Thomas Morgan of Tredegar and his draconian agents that they failed to obey the wishes of their lord. Stubborn tenants were often left to digest the bitter fruits of their insubordination after receiving notices of eviction or increased rents. At the poll, either the candidate or his steward would usher forward his supporters, often in batches of twenty. During the turbulent county election of 1681 in Denbighshire, voters were herded like cattle to the booths and they stretched in a long queue from the bridge to the horse market in Wrexham. Many stewards made their presence felt whenever candidates were running neck and neck, and it was not unusual for them to employ mobs to intimidate voters. In 1714, John Barlow of Lawrenny, Pembrokeshire, accused Sir Arthur Owen of Orielton of arming his servants with halters in order to dissuade voters from abandoning their allegiance to Orielton.

It is not surprising, therefore, that electoral contests often suddenly erupted into violence. Fisticuffs, private duels, and pitched battles were commonplace. Queries and rejections at the poll, together with complaints of corrupt and illegal practices, provoked ill-tempered jostling and arguments. In 1715 the supporters of Richard Fowler of Abbey Cwm-hir used such violent methods to deter Thomas Harley's supporters at the county election in Radnorshire that several freeholders informed the sheriff that since the county was 'full of threats and bloodshed to terrify the freeholders',[57] they were not prepared to cast their votes. During polling for the borough seat in Flintshire in August 1727, George Wynne, a well-to-do industrialist and political adventurer, stiffened his cause by flooding the town with raucous and intimidating lead-miners from his estate at Halkyn. During the borough election of 1729 in Cardiganshire, Thomas Powell of Nanteos ushered several hundred alcohol-sodden burgesses from Tregaron into Cardigan. There, many of them behaved outrageously

[57] D. R. Ll. Adams, 'The Parliamentary Representation of Radnorshire 1536-1832' (unpubl. University of Wales MA thesis, 1970), p. 221.

during the poll, presenting themselves twice or even thrice as voters and forcing the petrified sheriff to register their votes. When Richard Lloyd of Mabws, the wronged candidate, demanded a scrutiny of the poll, Powell called the mayor a fool, his brother threatened to shoot him, and his brother-in-law bloodied the town clerk's nose. Sir Thomas Longueville of Prestatyn freely admitted to the Committee of Elections in 1728 that 'there never was any election in Wales without mobbing and tumults'.[58] Fear of the 'manifold inconveniences and disorders'[59] which attended contested elections, together with prohibitive costs, prompted the gentry to avoid going to the polls whenever possible. Prestige, too, was at stake. To lose the day at the polls was considered a personal slight as well as a blow to the good name of a family. Few gentlemen in this period suffered defeat at the polls with good grace. Candidates whose pride had been dented invariably petitioned Parliament (which was the final arbiter of disputed elections), claiming that they had fallen victim to malpractice. But, since the number of petitions against election returns was so great, many pleas were never heard, let alone granted.

Politics in England, at least until the Hanoverian period, were a colourful and turbulent affair, with Whigs and Tories divided over policies and principles. In Wales, however, election contests were, for the most part, untouched by the ideological principles which caused such deep divisions beyond Offa's Dyke. Although some degree of principle and ideology was involved in the stormy elections held during the Exclusion crisis and during the reign of James II, most contests were provoked by either local jealousies or a desire to protect territorial interests. The struggle for mastery between Whigs and Tories was more apparent than real in Wales, for rarely did outward labels reflect party interests at Westminster. Strict party discipline and organization did not exist in rural Wales. Indeed, many constituencies prided themselves on their independence. Only on rare occasions did the counties of Wales echo to the stormy political controversies of Westminster. Local elections were usually a trial of strength between rival personalities or factions. Yet, it would be wrong to assume that Welsh voters were totally ignorant of the political issues and constitutional principles of the day. In fact, they were better informed than ever before. Information and ideas were spreading, thanks largely to the development of postal services, improved stage-coaches, and the liberation of the press in 1695. News-letters, journals, periodicals, and newspapers, used to spread propaganda, to publicize elections, and influence popular opinion, were bought regularly by educated landed gentlemen and squires. The popularity of Welsh almanacs from 1680 onwards also suggests a

---

[58] P. D. G. Thomas, 'Sir George Wynne and the Flint Borough Elections of 1727–1741', *Flintshire Hist. Soc. Journal* 20 (1962), p. 5.

[59] P. D. G. Thomas, 'Glamorgan Politics', p. 58.

growing interest in politics among the reading public. In particular, Thomas Jones the almanacker strove assiduously to ensure that his readers were kept informed of Britain's role in Europe and the conflict of ideology and interest which separated Whigs and Tories. Most ordinary Welshmen, however, acquired information through overhearing gossip in gentry parlours or in taverns, heeding the proclamations of town-criers, absorbing church sermons, or boggling at eyewitness reports of dramatic conflicts abroad retailed by former soldiers and sailors.

Although party passions did not run high in Wales, the reign of Anne, in particular, witnessed a flurry of general elections which must have helped to create a wider body of informed opinion. During the period 1701–15, twenty-nine contests were held in Wales, the majority of which were won by candidates affecting Tory labels. Yet there were clear signs that the Whig cause was gaining ground in traditional Tory bastions. Ever since the Restoration, the ruling power in Anglesey had been the Bulkeley family of Baron Hill. By the end of William's reign, however, this hegemony was under challenge from a group of active and aggressive Whigs led by Owen Hughes. Known as 'Yr Arian Mawr' (Moneybags), Hughes was a well-connected Beaumaris attorney. He was also a man of vaulting ambition, and he and his faction were determined to challenge Baron Hill's control over the pocket borough of Beaumaris. As mayor of Newborough, Hughes claimed a lineage for Newborough which antedated the claims of Beaumaris. During the election of 1698 he gathered together a caucus of burgesses to challenge the existing franchise and to revive his town's claims to participate in borough elections. His hopes were dashed, however, for the Bulkeleys chose not to contest the seat. Hughes was returned unopposed but lost his seat to the third Lord Bulkeley in 1701. Local grievances became more acute when Richard, son of the third Lord Bulkeley, entered into his inheritance on the death of his father in 1704. The fourth Lord Bulkeley was a fervent Jacobite whose strident and aggressive ways provoked violent resentment among his enemies. Bulkeley acquired an imposing array of influential offices and used his privileged position in the judiciary and in local administration to increase his authority. His contemptuous despotism and extravagant tastes lost him the trust and confidence of many of his kinsmen. His enemies openly despised him. Lloyd Bodfel of Boduan, Caernarfonshire, was alleged to have threatened to run him through with his sword should he happen to meet him. Local Whigs, led by Owen Meyrick of Bodorgan and John Hooke, a Chief Justice on the legal circuit of north-west Wales, launched a propaganda campaign of vilification against Bulkeley. His deeds and movements were subjected to watchful scrutiny, and evidence of his heavy-handed dealings with colleagues and tenants was collected and magnified. Eventually, the anti-Baron Hill faction presented the Lord High Treasurer with a printed memorial, charging Bulkeley with having appropriated lead, timber, and stones from Beaumaris Castle, neglected the defence of the Menai Straits, and of having favoured his friends and overtaxed his enemies within the courts of law. Amidst mounting agitation, the Whigs came close to ousting Bulkeley in the general election of 1708. In 1715, however, Bulkeley withdrew from the county seat in the expectation that Owen Meyrick would resign later, at Bulkeley's request. But Meyrick refused to honour his pledge to resign. Seething with rage, Bulkeley bared the iron fist in the face of such impudence. His malign influence over the landowners, freeholders, and tenants of Anglesey proved so far-reaching that Meyrick was defeated by sixty-nine votes in the bitterly contested election of 1722. A further attempt was made to extol the historic distinction of Newborough in 1727, but the House of Commons ruled in favour of the exclusive rights of the mayor, bailiffs, and capital burgesses of Beaumaris. Beaumaris thus remained a pocket borough of the Bulkeley family until the Reform Act of 1832.

An even more tenacious, and ultimately successful, anti-Bulkeley campaign was sustained in Caernarfonshire. During Anne's reign the Whigs of Glynllifon emerged as major challengers to the powers of Baron Hill. When Frances Glyn, heiress of Glynllifon, married Thomas Wynn of Boduan in 1700, two substantial properties were merged, which helped to propel the Wynn family to the front rank among the gentry families of north Wales. Wynn promoted the Whig cause with great vigour and sought to gain political advantage in the borough seat of Caernarfon by remoulding the electorate. He created a mass of non-resident burgesses in the out-boroughs which lay under his control. Between 1707 and 1713, 689 new burgesses were admitted at Nefyn and 174 at Pwllheli. Their votes proved decisive in the general election of 1713. Wynn secured the borough seat and William Griffith of Cefnamwlch, who had been tempted by Wynn to repudiate his Tory friends and hitch his wagon to the rising Whig star, defeated Sir Roger Mostyn in the county election. By the end of 1713 the political influence of Baron Hill in Caernarfonshire had suffered a total eclipse. Glynllifon retained its hold on the borough seat for over seventy years.

Yet, Toryism was still a powerfully effective force in Wales even after the Hanoverian succession. In the 1715 election, Wales returned fifteen Tories and twelve Whigs; in 1722 the Tories gained an extra seat from the Whigs. Not until 1727 did the balance change: in the general election of that year, Wales returned sixteen Whigs and eleven Tories. Clearly, the Whig government was beginning to create powerful interests in traditional Tory territories. In Monmouthshire, the Morgans of Tredegar were active supporters of the Whig cause and, by the 1720s, nine of the twenty leading gentry families in Glamorgan were Whigs. In Carmarthenshire, the influence of the third earl of Carbery of Golden Grove created a Whig tradition which was sustained under George I by the marquis of Winchester and the dukes of Bolton. Too much, however, should not be made of party labels. Although parliamentary candidates and landed families sported Whig or Tory colours, there was little practical or ideological difference between them. Their attitudes to politics and religion were remarkably similar and, as far as the electorate was concerned, economic power and personalities counted for more than party labels.

At least until the Glorious Revolution in 1688, central government exercised a powerful influence over local affairs. Although local communities jealously cherished and defended their independent rights, the Crown and central government, especially during periods of crisis, intervened at local levels by determining the composition of the commission of the peace and the charters of the boroughs. During the Exclusion crisis, Charles II sought to gain supporters in the provinces and control over elections to future Parliaments by removing allegedly disloyal and untrustworthy magistrates from the county benches and replacing them with men who were sympathetic to his aims. The marquis of Worcester, President of the Council of Wales, was the moving spirit behind the Welsh proscriptions in 1680. He provided the Privy Council with detailed information on the background and predilections of potential troublemakers in Wales. Twenty-seven magistrates were removed from the bench, most of them thoroughgoing Protestants from Montgomeryshire, Breconshire, Monmouthshire and Glamorgan. Using his vast experience and authority to the full, Worcester picked off old enemies and suspects with unerring ease. Griffith Bodwrda of Caernarfonshire, having served under Cromwell, was irrevocably smeared with the taint of republicanism. Rowland Laugharne of Pembrokeshire was penalized for his father's record of political dissidence and unreliability. Sir Robert Thomas of Llanmihangel in Glamorgan was blacklisted for serving on Commonwealth committees and advancing rigorous Puritan values. City connections counted against Marmaduke Gwynne of Garth, Breconshire. Other cases, too, revealed that Worcester was determined to avenge himself on old enemies.

Since the Corporation Act of 1661 had failed to curb the growth of Dissent in Welsh towns, Charles II compelled several boroughs either to substantiate the legality of their charters or surrender them to the Crown. By 1686 the corporations of Cowbridge, Swansea, Neath, and Cardiff had been remodelled, potential dissidents had been removed, and loyal supporters of the Crown insinuated into key positions. As a result, the ability of these towns to control their own affairs and to elect anti-court candidates was drastically reduced. James II pursued the same course, blindly striving to manufacture a packed Parliament in order to secure the repeal of anti-Catholic legislation. By interfering with borough charters, James succeeded in blunting anti-royalist opposition, but he alienated those who cherished the independent rights of corporate boroughs. Moreover, the admission of Catholics and Dissenters to the commissions of the peace aroused deep resentment among traditional ruling families.

Following the Glorious Revolution, electoral tactics were by no means as crude. Even so, successive governments continued to manoeuvre shifts in the balance of local power by shrewdly tampering with the composition of the commissions of the peace. Sometimes local pressure stirred governments into action. When Lord Lisburne informed Robert Harley that the people of Cardiganshire were subject to 'violent humours'[60] following the elevation of several non-jurors to the bench, sweeping changes were ordered: in February 1706 nine justices were put in and two were removed. Often, too, the commission of the peace was manipulated in order that candidates who had earned the approval of the government might stiffen their cause during elections. Some shrewd reshuffling at local level enabled Tories to consolidate their power in 1702 and 1710, and Whigs likewise in 1705–6 and 1714–15. Following the accession of George I, however, local government was left to put its own house in order and was happy to do so.

Throughout this period, in fact, central government played relatively little part in determining the destiny of the ordinary citizen. Of greater significance in the preservation of law and order were the local governing bodies. Following the abolition of the Council of Wales in 1689, the Courts of Great Sessions became the sole remaining superior court of justice and administration in Wales. Two judges held Great Sessions twice yearly in four separate circuits in each corner of Wales for six days, usually in spring and autumn. The court possessed considerable powers, including civil and criminal jurisdiction over the whole of Wales (except Monmouthshire). Most of the court's business focused on criminal cases and disputes between landlords and their tenants over issues such as tenures and debts. More people, however, came face to face with the law at the Court of Quarter Sessions, which was the main instrument of local justice and administration. In a sense, the Court of Quarter Sessions was a local parliament held in a noisy and informal atmosphere in Welsh county towns. Justices of the peace were required by statute to hold four sessions each year. The court was summoned formally by the high sheriff and legal proceedings were preceded by an elaborate procession to the shire hall with magistrates, clad in gold-laced coats and full-bottomed wigs and three-cornered hats, the focus of attention. The streets were normally thronged with justices, clerks, jurors, constables, bailiffs, attorneys,

[60] L. K. J. Glassey, *Politics and the Appointment of Justices of the Peace 1675–1720* (Oxford, 1979), p. 177.

burgesses, prisoners, witnesses, scriveners, petitioners, suitors, and many others. The Sessions dealt with civil and criminal cases as well as administrative matters. Magistrates were expected to deal with cases of assault and petty theft, unlawful assemblies, forcible entry of lands, encroachment on common land, raising false hue and cry, keeping disorderly alehouses, the settlement of bastard children, the relief of poor persons or maimed soldiers, and the repair of bridges and highways. Private manorial and hundred courts had also survived and were not without influence. Courts leet, acting as disciplinary institutions, governed the dos and don'ts of everyday life: the removal of obstructions from roads and rivers, the repair of hedges, ditches, pounds, and pillories, the prevention of straying animals, selling bad meat or illegal ale, overcharging customers, and the illegal erection of cottages on common land.

The dominant figure within the county was the lord-lieutenant, whose office was a Crown appointment. Although his post carried few day-to-day duties, the lord-lieutenant possessed great powers of patronage and controlled appointment to a wide range of offices in the shires. The office of sheriff, however, had lost its status and had become little more than a ceremonial post. Only during elections did a sheriff emerge from the shadows and exercise powerful influence. As the shrievalty declined, so the magistracy acquired greater prestige. From 1543 until 1693, the statutory limit upon justices of the peace was eight per county. Most counties, however, sported many more justices than the law demanded, and from 1693 onwards the reigning monarch was empowered to appoint as many justices as he pleased. Most justices were drawn from the ranks of wealthy gentlemen and well-to-do squires, with a leavening of legal experts. Ruling families were always loath to welcome 'mean men' to the bench and from 1731 onwards a candidate for office was required to own land worth at least £100 per annum. Always mindful of the grave social disadvantages of exclusion, aspiring justices were sometimes moved to violence whenever the door to office was closed. When the commission of the peace was remodelled in Radnorshire in 1692, Thomas and Nourse Lewis of Harpton Court terrorized the county, assaulting the bailiff of New Radnor, breaking the jaw of a female bystander, and precipitating an unsavoury affray (involving Robert Harley) on the streets of New Radnor. Since no financial rewards were involved, most justices sought office in order to acquire prestige for themselves and their families and to consolidate their own local power by preserving the social and political fabric.

Within his own community the justice of the peace was a police chief, a tax-assessor, a magistrate, a road-surveyor, a recruiting-officer, a censor, an inquisitor, and a licensor. His office, therefore, conferred upon him a considerable measure of local power and prestige. Unpaid and grossly overworked, the justice of the peace was showered with a host of administrative and judicial duties. A single justice was entitled, within his own home, to administer oaths, issue warrants against suspected persons, investigate criminal cases and minor misdemeanours, take sureties for good behaviour, punish petty offenders, and send serious miscreants to prison. Two justices acting together in petty sessions were empowered to license alehouses, enforce the poor law regulations, inflict fines on persons using unlawful weights and measures, remove paupers to their native parishes, and order constables to ensure that roads and bridges were kept in decent repair. Like their Tudor forebears, the justices of the peace were 'maids of all work', the linchpins of local government. The administrative and judicial commission which they exercised was wide, ambiguous, and onerous; and their stamina and probity were tested by constant cares and calls of duty.

Justices of the peace were a mixed group. Some suffered from poor health. Others were over-fond of tippling: the Glamorgan magistrates who tried Vavasor Powell in 1669 were as drunk as lords. Many were apathetic and bone idle. One of Robert Harley's correspondents in Radnorshire in 1690 complained that one of the seven justices in his county was superannuated and another 'so fat that he can hardly ride three miles to the sessions and when he is there does only sleep'.[61] Some justices refused to act against offenders because of ties of kinship, whilst others used their privileged positions to confer favours on their friends, shield miscreants, or ride roughshod over the weak. A few were unscrupulous rascals who, by their misconduct and petty tyranny, embarrassed their fellows. In 1711 Robert Ingram, a Llanidloes justice, was accused of physical assault and false imprisonment. Lewis Owen of Peniarth, *custos rotulorum* of Merioneth, was indicted in 1725 for having committed persons to prison without cause, favouring a suspect who was his friend, stifling the examination of a sheep-stealer, and generally using his authority to obstruct the course of justice. It was said of William Humphreys, a squarson of Corwen, that 'neither preaching nor beer, nor ale could melt the villain into justice'.[62] By the early eighteenth century, the chief problem was persuading justices to bestir themselves. Only a small minority pulled their weight, and attendance at Quarter Sessions was poor and erratic. It proved virtually impossible to persuade justices to attend to their magisterial duties by attending sessions. Only a faithful few—on average between three and six justices—bothered to frequent Quarter Sessions. Most of them excused themselves by pleading the costs of travel, the deplorable state of Welsh roads, the multiplicity of arduous and time-consuming obligations expected of them, and the sullen hostility of parishioners. Yet, in spite of the complex and taxing nature of their work,

[61] Ibid., p. 16.
[62] G. M. Griffiths, *The Merioneth Miscellany* (1955), pp. 45–6.

an active minority of justices carried out their duties competently and conscientiously. They leaned heavily on the administrative skills of the clerks of the peace who were, in the main, efficient salaried officials. Each county could depend on a faithful band of willing workhorses, who were prepared to devout toilsome hours in the performance of what were, for the most part, excruciatingly tedious duties.

Under the supervision of the justices of the peace, officials such as the overseers of the poor, the surveyors of the highways, and parish constables regulated village life. Overseers of the poor were empowered to set able-bodied paupers to work out of funds levied by the poor rate. Surveyors of the highways were entitled to demand six days' unpaid labour from parishioners for repairing roads. For each hundred there were two high constables, normally drawn from the ranks of fairly well-off yeomen, who were charged with a host of routine transactions, such as collecting county rates, apprehending criminals, and surveying bridges. Petty constables, normally recruited from among smaller farmers, acted as policemen and tax-collectors in the parishes and townships. Constables were often obliged to enforce laws which were extremely unpopular among common people, and a persistent or callous officer could easily find himself the target of abuse or violence. Having to carry out commands which were at odds with the wishes of their neighbours often led to conflicting loyalties and obligations among constables, and it is not surprising that so many of them had little taste for their duties. The most that justices could expect from them was that they might act as mediators between the demands of the Quarter Sessions and the wishes of local parishioners. Much laziness and malpractice were doubtless to be found in their ranks, but the best of them understood the needs of common people and somehow managed to maintain the peace as well as could be expected.

Justices of the peace and their fellow officers were conscious of the fact that the threat to good order often arose from hunger and poverty. Their tasks were eased to some degree, however, by the readiness of the affluent to relieve the condition of the distressed. The Poor Law Act of 1601 was based on the principle of setting able-bodied paupers to work and alleviating the distress of the old, sick, and disabled, who were unable to support themselves, by ensuring the provision of either food, clothing or money. These arrangements were to be financed by a compulsory poor rate. Ever since its inception, however, this legislation had proved difficult to enforce in Wales. Whereas rate-financed poor relief was in operation in most parts of England under the early Stuarts, the remoter parts of Wales did not levy poor rates until the early decades of the eighteenth century. The practice in many rural communities was to adopt the system of outdoor relief based on church collections, door-to-door visits, charitable donations, and communal efforts such as raffles and *cymorth cwrw* (beer-relief). John Jones, dean of Bangor, declared in 1716 that since poor rates had not been settled in Caernarfonshire, it was 'the constant method to relieve the poor at their doors'.[63] Looking back, sentimentally perhaps, to the days of his youth in the early eighteenth century, Thomas Pennant maintained that 'filial piety had at that time full possession of the breasts of children, or great affection on the part of more distant relations, and the pangs of poverty were as much as possible alleviated'.[64] As a result, few parishes felt the need to impose compulsory poor rates, and even in those parishes where it was levied it was rare for the rate to exceed 4d. to 7d. in the pound before the middle of the eighteenth century. The incidence and rate of local taxation varied from place to place, and it is probable that only in the towns was the problem of the poor forcing itself constantly on the attention of justices. In the towns the principal items of expenditure under outdoor relief were maintenance grants to widows, orphans, expectant mothers, and the aged. Paupers were provided with corn, clothes, shoes, candles, tools, and coffins. Unemployed or maimed soldiers and former mariners also received financial support, as did those who had lost their belongings through misfortunes such as fire or theft.

Justices were able to cope with the settled poor without recourse to repression. But itinerant vagrants, rogues, vagabonds, and ne'er-do-wells were another matter. Much time and energy were expended in removing chargeable newcomers from a parish and in the general administration of the settlement laws. The Settlement Act of 1662 was the direct result of the growing need to rid parishes of unwanted immigrants who threatened to become an unmanageable financial burden. Newcomers were to be removed within forty days of their arrival and escorted back to their native parishes or previous abode. Justices of the peace found themselves regularly obliged to arbitrate between warring parishes that were reluctant to accept the financial burdens which destitute people brought with them. Vagrants and sturdy beggars were whipped out of parishes by constables. Nor did parishes welcome unmarried pregnant women without a settlement, and Quarter Sessions regularly ordered the parents of bastard children to be whipped. In 1685, Margaret Rees, a prisoner in Brecon's house of correction and the mother of an illegitimate child, was ordered to be whipped on market day. Her child was to be maintained by her labour, and she and the reputed father were ordered to pay 4d. per week to maintain the child.

In 1697 steps were taken to guard against the abuse of outdoor relief. It was made compulsory for each recipient of parish relief to wear a badge bearing the letter 'P', together with the initial of their native parish. The

[63] *Correspondence and Minutes of the S.P.C.K. relating to Wales*, p. 86.
[64] Thomas Pennant, *The History of the Parishes of Whiteford and Holywell* (London, 1796), p. 100.

aim was to ensure that false claims could be more easily detected. Those who refused to bear the stigma publicly were often committed to the house of correction, where they rubbed shoulders with persistent vagrants, mischief-makers, debtors, and lewd women. Many of these houses were deplorable hovels and it is not surprising that many inmates died of malnutrition and fever. Among those held in custody in Carmarthen's house of correction in July 1729 were disorderly persons and thieves accused of stealing blankets and coal. In theory, those who were committed to these foul institutions were to be taught the virtues of hard work, thrift, and moral probity, but confinement in houses of correction seldom deterred or improved miscreants.

Justices of the peace were also obliged to pursue the often depressingly fruitless task of suppressing unlicensed and disorderly alehouses. The proliferation of alehouses was a very real problem: unlicensed alehouses in towns and remote rural areas were multipying at an astonishing rate. By 1672 there were 107 alehouses in Gwyrfai, Caernarfon, and Bangor alone. Taverns and alehouses were seductive and popular social centres which inevitably tempted the lower orders. Didactic tracts and ballads are riddled with cautionary tales of poor labourers who drank their wages and left their wives and children unprovided for. Preaching the virtues of thrift and moderation, religious reformers painted lurid portraits of the self-indulgence and licentiousness of the alehouse. Local authorities believed them to be squalid dens of mischief, the abode of idle, disorderly, and violent persons. 'Could you not live without abetting waste and gambling, harlotry, drunkenness, oaths, quarrels, slander and lying?',[65] the alehouse-keeper was asked by Lucifer in one of Ellis Wynne's famous 'Visions'. Quarter Sessions records reveal that alehouse-keepers were frequently punished for selling ale without licence, cheating customers by selling short measures, and encouraging drunkenness on their premises. In 1708 six magistrates in Carmarthen resolved to reinforce the moral sanctions of the church by publicly declaring their determination to execute the statutes against drunkenness, immorality, and profanity, a decision which, according to Bishop George Bull, had 'a wonderful influence upon the lives and manners of the people'.[66] Since the number of alehouses was high and the consumption of alcohol even higher, however, justices enjoyed little success in enforcing the licensing laws and were often reluctant to inflame local opinion by suppressing unlicensed houses.

In the absence of detailed local studies and reliable statistical evidence, it is impossible to assess what place crime and violence had in society at this time. It is fairly clear that most communities were riven with petty animosities and fierce disputes, but the indications are that justices of the

[65] Ellis Wynne, *Visions of the Sleeping Bard*, p. 165.
[66] Robert Nelson, *The Life of Dr. George Bull* (2nd edn., London, 1714), pp. 451–5.

peace were not overwhelmed with problems of serious crime. Cases of homicide were rare. The fact that Welsh ballad-mongers, who always preferred the unusual to the mundane, chose to sing of murderous deeds suggests that they were relatively rare events. Homicides were seldom premeditated affairs and brutality was often the result of sudden aggression rather than cold-blooded design. Whenever short-tempered or drunken people quarrelled, violent blows were often struck, sometimes with fatal consequences. At an inn in Dolanog, Montgomeryshire, in 1690, Ellis David and Francis William consumed large quantities of ale and then quarrelled and fought furiously. During the fracas William was kicked in the belly and subsequently died. In August 1696 the wife of John Whitney of Llanbedr Painscastle, Radnorshire, visited Charles and James Phillips and was so grievously abused and beaten by them that she died later that night. The assailants sought to stifle the matter by offering Whitney £30 for holding his tongue. Since Whitney, according to his own testimony, was not worth five shillings in the world, he petitioned the Court of Great Sessions, begging that the overseer of the poor be ordered to prosecute on his behalf. Cases of homicide were always hard to conceal and violent murderers were shown no mercy. When Robert Owen of Llanrwst was hanged for murder at Shrewsbury in April 1717 his cries of remorse from the gallows sent shivers of apprehension down the spine of onlookers.

Many proceedings at Great Sessions and Quarter Sessions came about as a result of charges of assault and battery, which were themselves usually the outcome of family squabbles or disputes over property. Countless petitions were presented by poor men who had suffered wrongs at the hands of acquisitive landlords, lawyers, and creditors, and it is significant that many cases of assaults were directed against bailiffs and constables. More serious was the problem of theft. Most indictments, especially against labourers and vagrants, were for petty larceny. Offences in this category often resulted from high grain prices and a dearth of food. In times of acute poverty, thieves stole food, livestock, and clothing. Pilferers who were apprehended and found guilty of petty larceny were sentenced to be stripped and severely whipped until the 'body be bloody'. In 1692, Elizabeth Lewis of Merthyr was sentenced to be whipped for stealing a petticoat, valued at 11d. In 1723 Gwenllian Jenkin of Neath, convicted of stealing a silver spoon, was sentenced to be publicly whipped between ten and twelve in the morning from the Neath gaol to the mill-gate and back. The same penalty was administered to Jenkin at Caerphilly on the following Thursday.

The available evidence suggests, however, that only those who persistently pilfered or disturbed the peace were brought to justice. These were the offenders who threatened social harmony within the local community. Many miscreants were never prosecuted, for justices of the peace and constables, preferring to use their discretion and common sense, chose to admonish rather than to punish the petty criminal and urge him to mend his ways. A wide range of informal sanctions was available to the justices of the peace. By mediation and arbitration, justices were able to secure extra-judicial settlements between parties and thus smoothe over local differences of opinion. Petty offences were winked at. Malefactors who threatened to become nuisances were bound over to be of good behaviour by justices acting in petty sessions. Sureties for good behaviour were believed to be infinitely preferable to burdening local gaols with hordes of petty offenders. Justices were also mindful of the fact that there were fifty capital offences by 1689 and that a stolen petticoat or silver spoon valued at more than a shilling could send a thief to the gallows. It was common, therefore, for them to undervalue stolen goods in order to spare the accused the horrendous consequences of an indictment for grand larceny. And just as justices were reluctant to institute criminal proceedings against individuals down on their luck, so were juries loath to indict. In all these ways, therefore, the brutality of the system was tempered.

The system of local administration, law enforcement, and public order was thus heavily dependent upon the diligence, shrewdness, and common sense of amateur and unpaid officers. Central government could not function effectively without their co-operation, whilst securing order, peace, and harmony within the provinces depended on their authority and zeal. The conduct of these untrained officials was often erratic and rarely above reproach, but they implemented the policies of government and maintained public order. Following the accession of the House of Hanover, moreover, the rulers of local government in the Welsh counties and boroughs were more than ever before at liberty to administer local affairs as they saw fit.

CHAPTER 5

RELIGION, EDUCATION, AND LITERACY

FOLLOWING the storms and tempests of the previous two decades the arrival of the Merry Monarch in May 1660 was welcomed by jubilant churchmen. Indeed, a great wave of relief rippled across Wales as news of the return of the exiled sovereign filtered through to the localities. By 1660 most Welshmen were heartily sick of Puritan rule and the noisy acclamation which greeted Charles II in London was echoed in many Welsh towns. William Phylip declared that the descendant of the last of the Celtic kings had arrived through divine intervention: 'God of Heaven by his power has brought the bones of Cadwaladr home'.[1] Conversely, Puritan saints feared the worst. Jenkin Jones of Llanddeti, a former captain in the parliamentary army and a fervent propagator of the gospel, was so discomfited by news of Charles's landing at Dover that he mounted his horse, rode furiously through Llanddeti churchyard, and fired his pistol at the church door, declaiming, 'Ah, thou old whore of Babylon, thou wilt have it all thy own way now'.[2] He knew full well that those who had suffered cruel injustices at the hands of Puritan soldiers and zealous sectarians would be loath to extend the hand of friendship to old enemies.

Welsh churchmen were acutely aware that a critical phase lay ahead. Following two decades of civil strife, military occupation, and social upheaval, they yearned for a period of stability and peace. But old animosities and grievances were not easily forgotten and the Restoration years were riven with fear, suspicion, and uncertainty. The ruling classes lived in mortal fear of another civil war and were haunted by the ghost of millers-turned-Roundheads. Lucifer himself shuddered when confronted by Cromwell in the vivid portrait of hell etched by Ellis Wynne in 1703. As late as 1752 Theophilus Evans described the Civil War as a period when the gates of hell had opened and when Satan, with his 'infernal crew', had broken loose.[3] Old wounds stubbornly refused to heal.

The traditional rulers of the countryside were convinced that more tranquil, settled times could only be achieved by reimposing Anglican discipline and reinstilling the need to revere the monarchy, obey the law of the land, and submit to the authority of gentlemen and parsons. Driven on by a desire to restore the Church of England to its former glory, an

---

[1] E. D. Jones, 'The Brogyntyn Welsh Manuscripts', *NLWJ* 8 (1953), p. 9.
[2] C. Wilkins, *The History of Merthyr Tydfil*, p. 303.
[3] Theophilus Evans, *The History of Modern Enthusiasm* (London, 1752), p. 26.

irresistible tide of Anglican sentiment swept through Wales. The nobility and gentry of the six counties of north Wales petitioned Charles II, complaining bitterly of their sufferings under the iron rule of Puritan propagators and pressing hard for the restitution of episcopal authority. Although Charles had vowed to protect 'tender consciences', his promises were drowned by clamant demands from zealous Cavaliers, who insisted upon establishing a church edifice on traditional lines. Nor were common people unsympathetic to this call, for many of them had not abandoned their old religious practices. Welsh poets claimed that their countrymen yearned for 'the way of the old Welsh',[4] the traditional Anglican church order which had been such a cherished part of their lives before Puritan rule. Intransigent Cavaliers won the day in Parliament: the use of the Anglican liturgy was swiftly revived and Puritan incumbents who refused to obey the doctrine and discipline of the Church of England were ejected from their livings. When the Act of Uniformity entered the statute-book on 19 April 1662, Anglicans and Dissenters went their separate ways.

The most immediate task facing churchmen, however, was to rebuild Zion. Many churches were in a grave state of dilapidation and the traditional system of ecclesiastical administration had fallen into disarray. Later commentators were to claim that the church had been torn asunder and ravaged by Puritan zealots. Theophilus Evans exercised his gift for hyperbole by insisting that Puritans had 'defiled the very churches with their excrements, and gloried in their beastly nastiness'.[5] But it is impossible to estimate how far diocesan and parochial organization had been disrupted during the years of flux. What is clear is that throughout this period the ecclesiastical system stood in need of drastic and extensive reform. The church was paralysed by crippling administrative and financial problems. Most of its defects stemmed directly from its impoverished condition. Following the dissolution of the monasteries, the bulk of church spoils had fallen into the hands of landowning families. Expropriation of tithes and endowments by lay impropriators had particularly weakened the economic resources of the southern dioceses. By this period the dioceses of St Davids and Llandaff were valued at £900 and £500 respectively. In 1721 Erasmus Saunders's sombre document, *A View of the State of Religion in the Diocese of St. David's*, revealed a church which had been 'robbed and pillaged' of its wealth.[6] Half the livings in the rambling diocese of St Davids were in the hands of impropriators; a quarter of them were valued at less than ten pounds. However, the northern sees had not been robbed of their wealth and resources to the same degree. The dioceses of Bangor and St

---

[4] See *Hen Gerddi Gwleidyddol*, passim.

[5] Theophilus Evans, *History of Modern Enthusiasm*, p. 21.

[6] Erasmus Saunders, *A View of the State of Religion in the Diocese of St. David's* (London, 1721), p. 5.

Asaph were each valued at £1,400. Here, livings were distinctly richer. In 1707 it was estimated that only ten livings in the diocese of Bangor and only four in the diocese of St Asaph were valued at less than ten pounds.

The penury of the church, especially in south Wales, hampered efforts to restore or refurbish churches. Throughout this period, many parish churches, notably in remote rural areas, were in a deplorable condition. Clergymen constantly complained to unheeding ears of leaking roofs, mouldering walls, broken windows, unpaved floors, and encroaching ivy. At Llanfair-ar-y-bryn and Llanegwad in 1710 it was reported that 'men's skulls and bones are piled up against the church wall about six foot high and exposed to the open air'.[7] Rural deans and churchwardens often reported that churches were 'out of repair', and Erasmus Saunders claimed that some were so ruinous that even Turks and Saracens could not have wrought such devastation. Generally, the maintenance of the church fabric was dependent on funds accruing from the church rate, but the truth is that large capital sums were not available to protect churches from the ravages of the elements. Urgent repairs were, therefore, often long delayed or simply neglected. In northern dioceses, however, the situation was more hopeful. Royal briefs for building and restoring churches in the diocese of St Asaph increased sharply in the 1720s as churchmen strove to refurbish existing churches and accommodate more worshippers. In many parts of the diocese of Bangor, too, parish churches were in sound repair. The parish church of Llanfechell, Anglesey, for instance, resplendent with its gilded weathercock and silk-fringed table cover, was a world apart from the dilapidated and ruinous 'habitations of owls and jackdaws'[8] in the diocese of St Davids.

Poverty was also the root cause of most of the familiar weaknesses of the established church—absenteeism, non-residence, pluralism, nepotism, and neglect. But although the administrative shortcomings of the church were patently obvious, they were not easy to remedy. In fact, such abuses, because they were reckoned to be well-nigh insoluble, seldom aroused deep passions. They were simply accepted as a fact of life. Radical plans to refashion the administrative machinery of the church ran counter to the conservative instincts of the age and were doomed to remain stillborn. Save for the partially effective Queen Anne's Bounty, no real attempt was made to eradicate abuses within the church or to reform its anomalies. The established church was still essentially a medieval institution, lacking the means to reform itself. Impoverished, unwieldy, and cumbersome, it was a rickety, scarcely seaworthy vessel, and it made impossible demands on its servants.

[7] G. M. Griffiths, 'A Visitation of the Archdeaconry of Carmarthen, 1710', *NLWJ* 18 (1974), pp. 292–3.
[8] E. Saunders, *A View of the State of Religion*, p. 24.

Welsh sees were pitifully poor and it is not surprising that they were the least prized dioceses in the kingdom. Many English bishops simply viewed them as the first rung on the ladder of episcopal preferment. They accepted their appointments 'in expectation of a sudden remove',[9] and their precipitate departure seldom occasioned either surprise or resentment. Those who yearned for more lucrative sees elsewhere were ill at ease in the Welsh fastnesses. Life for William Beaw, the quixotic bishop of Llandaff, was one long vexation: marooned in his 'little bishopric'[10] for twenty-six years, he chafed and fretted miserably. Since there was no obligation to labour in one's appointed vineyard for twelve months a year, many bishops augmented their incomes by holding other ecclesiastical offices and livings in plurality. Increasingly, too, the demands of the affairs of state deflected them from their pastoral concerns in Wales. Bishops were expected to attend the sessions of the House of Lords, and these wearisome obligations often prevented them not only from discharging their episcopal duties effectively but also from forging close links between themselves and their clergy. There were also daunting social problems with which to grapple. Welsh dioceses were rambling, unwieldy structures, and roads were so poor that portly prelates blanched at the prospect of having to embark on their visitations. Some excused themselves by pleading old age and infirmity, whilst others ventured out only when the butterflies were in season. However, it was the crippling poverty of the Welsh church which frustrated the best endeavours of bishops. To a large extent their hands were tied, for they possessed neither the legal authority nor the financial means to launch large-scale reforming movements.

Appalled by the daunting problems which faced them, some bishops preferred to rest their idle bones on the plush ermine of the House of Lords rather than venture into one of the barren corners of the land. Some developed a taste for factional intrigues, others saw themselves as political animals rather than spiritual leaders. Glaring scandals were sometimes exposed. Thomas Watson, bishop of St Davids (1687–99), was deposed for simony and corruption, whilst in 1701 Edward Jones of St Asaph was suspended for six months for gross simony and scandalous behaviour. During his six-year tenure of Bangor, Benjamin Hoadly, a controversial cripple, never once set foot on Welsh soil. But it would be wrong to judge the Welsh episcopate on the performance of such notorious black sheep; most Welsh bishops in this period took their spiritual duties very seriously indeed and served their dioceses with a diligence and devotion which compel admiration. Many of them were men of true learning who prided

[9] Norman Sykes, *Church and State in England in the Eighteenth Century* (Cambridge, 1934), pp. 63, 65–6.
[10] Lambeth Palace MS 930, f. 49.

themselves on their ability to provide their clergy and their flocks with a convincing spiritual leadership.

The dioceses of Bangor and St Asaph were particularly well served. In Gwynedd, William Roberts (1660–5) and Robert Morgan (1666–73) were zealous churchmen who reasserted episcopal authority and recruited able incumbents. Morgan's successor, Humphrey Lloyd (1674–89), a scholar of some distinction, also proved a stickler for the rights of the Anglican church. But the most vigorous and efficient bishop of Bangor was Humphrey Humphreys, who was dean of the diocese for nine years and bishop for twelve years until his translation to the diocese of Hereford in 1701. Humphreys was a distinguished scholar, steeped in the history, antiquity, and literature of his native land. He enjoyed a cordial relationship with his clergy, urging them to spare no pains in beating down the strongholds of Satan and advancing 'the Kingdom of Christ in the hearts of our people'.[11] Humphreys was the moving spirit behind many of the advances made in north Wales by voluntary societies, notably the campaign for the reformation of manners and the SPCK. In spite of his lofty position and considerable learning, the common touch never deserted him. Humble clerics and poets received his counsel and encouragement in abundance. He once told Owen Gruffydd, a blind poet from Llanystumdwy: 'You have God's gift, Owen bach; but I have nothing except that which I received for my money'.[12] Humphreys's translation to Hereford was widely regretted throughout the diocese, even though his successor, John Evans (1701–16), enforced church discipline and provided enthusiastic support for charitable ventures.

In the diocese of St Asaph, George Griffith (1660–6), erstwhile foe of Vavasor Powell, was the architect of the revised edition of the Welsh Prayer Book in 1664. Standards fell under the indolent Glemham (1667–70), but the appointment of William Lloyd in 1680 proved a turning-point in the fortunes of the diocese. An energetic administrator and stern disciplinarian, Lloyd wielded his authority in no uncertain manner. He was not a man to be trifled with, as many errant pastors and stubborn Dissenters found to their cost. 'I will not', he declared, 'like old Eli see the Ark of God lost for their sakes.'[13] Lloyd drove out scandalous incumbents, replaced them with conscientious Welsh clergymen, and increased the revenues of his diocese. Highly adept in the art of oral combat, he was prepared to intimidate as well as persuade truculent Dissenters in public conferences. Lloyd established such a sound and efficient administration at St Asaph that it survived the maladministration of his successor, Edward Jones. St Asaph

---

[11] E. G. Wright, 'Humphrey Humphreys, Bishop of Bangor and Hereford', *Journal Hist. Soc. Church in Wales* I (1950), p. 75.

[12] For his patronage of Gruffudd, see ibid., pp. 78–9.

[13] NLW, Lloyd-Baker Letters, No. 6.

was also fortunate in its early eighteenth-century bishops. William Beveridge (1704–8) was a man with an unquenchable thirst for learning and a deep desire to nurture a sense of holiness and devotion among his flock, whilst his successor, William Fleetwood (1708–14), was a rigorous overseer of his clergy, who rooted out the lazy and the dissolute, and urged faithful pastors to promote practical piety. Similarly, John Wynne (1715–27) established an effective pastoral relationship with his clergy, co-ordinated the reforming endeavours of philanthropic societies, and tenaciously defended the rights of the church.

Since the southern dioceses were in more straitened circumstances, prelates of quality were less often nominated to them. Following William Lloyd's translation to Peterborough in 1679, Llandaff found itself deprived of a Welsh-speaking bishop for over two hundred years. William Beaw was the last bishop of Llandaff to reside at Mathern palace, and only Robert Clavering (1724–8) won the respect and support of his flock. Although the diocese of St Davids was saddled with more than its share of birds of passage, most of its bishops did not neglect their spiritual and administrative duties. William Lucy (1660–77) might have been an incorrigible nepotist, but no bishop in the Restoration period laboured harder than he to rid the land of 'scandalous schisms'. Lucy conceived of the established church as an indivisible body and he was more than happy to lead the drive to restore church unity. His successor, William Thomas (1678–83), was Lucy's antithesis: a man of integrity, goodwill, and genuine piety, he provided Stephen Hughes with the financial means and connections which enabled him to publish edifying literature. His translation to Worcester ushered in a series of undistinguished bishops, whose indolence was exposed by the exemplary zeal and diligence of George Bull (1705–10). A frail, saintly man of ten and three score years, Bull gave no hint of feeling his age during his sojourn at St Davids. He resided within his diocese, kept a watchful eye on errant clergymen, encouraged local branches of the societies for the reformation of manners, and earned the undying admiration of so stern and resolute a critic as Griffith Jones, Llanddowror. Some of his successors, notably Adam Ottley (1713–23) and Richard Smallbrooke (1724–31), promoted a godly reformation by urging clergy and laity alike to bestir themselves in the name of Christianity, advancing the careers of talented Welshmen within the church, and insisting upon strict discipline.

A similar north–south dichotomy was evident in the quality of cathedral dignitaries. In the dioceses of Llandaff and St Davids, the higher échelons of the church were occupied by Englishmen who neglected their cures and grew fat on the spoils of more profitable preferments in England. 'Englishmen who creep in', declared Browne Willis, 'care for nothing but the pence.'[14] Many were cynical opportunists, caring only for the loaves

---

[14] E. D. Evans, *A History of Wales 1660–1815* (Cardiff, 1976), p. 72.

and fishes of office and unwilling to involve themselves actively in the social life of their communities, let alone carry out their pastoral duties effectively. Thomas Davies denounced those 'strangers and foreigners' whose 'ravenous and greedy temper'[15] had robbed the diocese of Llandaff of its wealth and influence. Climbing the ladder of advancement depended heavily on patronage and influence, and those who viewed the church as a career rather than as a vocation were often promoted at the expense of learned and deserving Welshmen. In the dioceses of Bangor and St Asaph, however, the situation was quite different. Cathedral dignitaries were mostly native Welshmen of learning and distinction who discharged their duties vigorously and kept a firm hand on the clergy. John Jones, dean of Bangor (1689–1727), was a virtuous and generous man who encouraged clergymen to adopt stricter moral standards and laboured without stint to provide religious and educational facilities for the poorer sorts. Similarly, John Wynne, chancellor of St Asaph (1690–1743), was an energetic administrator who purged his diocese of abuses, taught by example as well as precept, and initiated several successful educational and philanthropic enterprises. Their assiduity often compensated for episcopal neglect elsewhere in Wales.

It is hard to generalize about the mass of the parish clergy. Many were evidently not saints. Some were lazy, others were immoral. Some, like Fielding's Parson Trulliber, cared more for their pigs than for their parishioners; others were simply indifferent. But it is easy to exaggerate the lethargy, rogueries, and sexual peccadilloes of the clergy. Many of them were genuinely pious and hard-working. Erasmus Saunders and Griffith Jones, Llanddowror, were agreed that many honest clergymen, by dint of innate ability and dogged persistence, rose above severe financial handicaps and proved an active leaven in the lump. A large proportion of them were graduates. Obliged to undertake daily tasks which were unglamorous and time-consuming, they earnestly ministered to the spiritual and material needs of their parishioners, devoted time to charitable enterprises, translated devotional and doctrinal literature, and generally stuck to their tasks with enviable determination. An age which produced such unusually talented clergymen and authors as Griffith Jones, Ellis Wynne, Edward Samuel, Thomas Williams, Samuel Williams, Moses Williams, and Theophilus Evans was hardly one of spiritual darkness. Clergymen such as these shunned the unseemly scramble for preferment, choosing instead to concentrate on their parochial duties and to foster sober piety, godliness, and sound learning. Many of them were contemptuous of the behaviour of profligate colleagues, believing that nothing was more unacceptable to their flocks than 'the moral lessons of an immoral man'.[16]

[15] L. J. Hopkin James, *The Soul of a Cathedral* (Cardiff, 1930), p. 63.
[16] Erasmus Saunders, *The Divine Authority and Usefulness of the Pastors of the Christian Church Vindicated* (London, 1713), p. 28.

At the lowest levels in the ecclesiastical hierarchy, the financial plight of penurious curates was deplorable. Ill-paid, poorly housed, overworked, and much-abused, their lot was undeniably hard. A yawning gulf separated them from the privileged minority of well-paid churchmen and most of them had no hope of advancement. Thomas Price of Merthyr claimed that many of these 'mountain clergymen' were unable to 'purchase more than bare food and raiment for their families'.[17] Some were no better than peasants. Tithes had fallen into the hands of niggardly lay impropriators, who guarded their rights jealously and expected poor curates to subsist on a mere pittance. Although the impropriator of Llanddewibrefi in Cardiganshire received over £400 per annum, he offered as little as £8 to his curate. According to Sir John Philipps, the duke of Somerset received tithes worth £900 per annum from a number of parishes in Carmarthenshire but spared no more than £70 to the six curates who served his cures. Sometimes meanminded impropriators withheld payment altogether, and it is significant that the proverb 'as ragged as a Welsh curate' achieved currency during this period. 'Pinched with poverty',[18] they were obliged to serve three or four churches in order to make a living. Covered in sweat and grime, they hurried feverishly from church to church on Sundays in order to minister to the needs of their parishioners. Small wonder that many of them sought solace in the local tavern. 'Disorderly living and drinking' was a common charge brought against impoverished curates in church courts, whilst rhymesters dubbed them 'sow-gelders and alehouse-keepers'.[19] 'Hedge-parsons' wandered the countryside, officiating at clandestine marriages in order to win a few shillings but bringing their calling into disrepute in the process. Yet, although unbeneficed clergymen were held in low esteem by their superiors, they were none the less needed to serve as curates for absentees and to minister in the most poorly endowed livings.

Although the established church was riddled with defects and abuses, the majority of the Welsh people evidently held it in great affection. The local parish church was the hub of village life, around which a host of social activities revolved. The rites and traditions of the church were bound up with the daily lives of parishioners. Therein were enacted intimate personal events such as the baptism of infants, marriage, and burial. The Anglican liturgy, too, was deeply grounded in the Welshman's consciousness, and authors and poets never wearied of affirming their love and devotion for the 'best and purest church upon earth'.[20] Dissent had scarcely begun to

---

[17] E. T. Davies, 'The Church of England and Schools, 1662–1774', in *Glamorgan Co. Hist.* 4 (1974), p. 438.
[18] NLW, Ottley Papers, No. 100.
[19] Anon., *North Wales Defended or an Answer to an Imodest and Scurrilous Libel* (Shrewsbury, 1701), p. 5.
[20] Geraint H. Jenkins, *Literature, Religion and Society in Wales, 1660–1730* (Cardiff, 1978), pp. 169–70.

sever the bonds which had traditionally tied the mass of the people to the Anglican edifice. Nine out of every ten Welsh men and women still believed that the established church was the sole vessel of salvation. Yet, although people would not lightly abandon the Anglican framework into which they had been born, this did not necessarily mean that regular Sunday worship was part and parcel of their lives. The poorer orders seldom darkened the door of their parish church, unless doles of bread or similar largess were there to tempt them. A decline in Anglican observance was an inevitable result of the Toleration Act of 1689, for the legal and social pressures upon people to attend church on Sundays were no longer so powerful. Sunday was as much a day of merriment as of devotion. Curates catechized children during Lent only, and although the monthly celebration of communion was not uncommon, the general practice after 1689 was to celebrate communion quarterly, on the occasion of the three great festivals of the church and following the gathering of the harvest.

On the other hand, there was clearly a popular demand for sermons. Clergymen were exhorted by their superiors to preach clear gospel truths in the practical, unambiguous style of John Tillotson. Not all of them succeeded in presenting their material winningly. Griffith Jones, Llanddowror, had cause to chastise clergymen who suffused their discourses with abstruse doctrines, 'empty speculations', and 'lofty phrases'[21] which were far above the level of common understanding. George Bull, too, rebuked those preachers who were prone to deliver 'frothy and trifling sermons'.[22] Most preachers, however, adopted a didactic approach, lacing their homilies with scriptural references and moral imperatives, and pressing home their message in a homespun, often colloquial, style. Many contemporaries noted the Welshman's love of sermons, and by the eve of Methodism the general rule in rural areas was for sermons to be preached, if not each Sunday, then at least on alternate Sundays. William Richards, a satirist who normally poked fun at the Welsh, was impressed by their 'pretty glowing zeal'.[23] In a much-quoted passage, Erasmus Saunders maintained that humble parishioners in the diocese of St Davids were so anxious to deepen their religious knowledge that they were prepared to travel several miles in order to hear sermons preached in damp and remote churches. Many of them were anxious to fill their hours of worship profitably. Whenever clergymen neglected to preach they sang or chanted *halsingod* (religious carols) during church services as well as at wakes, funerals, and festivals, and on holy days. *Halsingod* were enormously popular in the vale of Teifi during the years between the Restoration and Methodism. Composed by local clergymen and laymen, they were invaluable means of

---

[21] NLW, Ottley Papers, No. 100.
[22] Robert Nelson, *Life of Dr. George Bull*, p. 492.
[23] William Richards, *Wallography* (London, 1682), p. 103.

implanting scriptural knowledge and moral values. Moreover, they filled a spiritual void by providing a popular medium of instruction and entertainment in churches where sermons were seldom heard. It is significant that early Methodism drew much of its vitality and strength from the lively and enterprising communities of the Teifi valley and south Cardiganshire generally.

Griffith Jones's astonishing success in attracting hundreds of hearers from Herefordshire, Monmouthshire, and north Wales, as well as from neighbouring counties, to Laugharne and Llanfihangel Abercywyn also testified to the widespread desire for 'plain, practical, pressing and zealous preaching'.[24] A native of the parish of Pen-boyr in north Carmarthenshire, Griffith Jones had received a 'heavenly call' while tending his sheep on the hillsides of Cilrhedyn. He became convinced that God had singled him out to rid Wales of its 'miserable blindness'.[25] Consumed and fired with a sense of mission, he resolved to be of service to 'myriads of poor ignorant souls'[26] who were starved of saving knowledge. He preached, like the early Puritan itinerants, in churchyards, fairs, and market-places, and throngs of pilgrims flocked to Carmarthenshire to hear his rousing sermons. Griffith Jones cut an impressive figure in the pulpit and contemporaries were convinced that he was the finest preacher in Wales. George Whitefield claimed that, of all the 'burning and shining lights' in the Anglican and Dissenting ministry, Griffith Jones 'shines in particular'.[27] His eloquent, sonorous sermons forced his hearers to 'feel their blood thrill within them',[28] whilst his lurid descriptions of hell's fires filled them with apprehension and terror. Griffith Jones cursed sinners publicly, venting his wrath 'like a flaming meteor'. 'Consider what it will be like to be boiled in the huge cauldron of God's wrath', he warned, 'what it will be like to burn in the unquenchable fire, in the fiery furnace, in the lake which burns with fire and brimstone.'[29] Calling for unqualified repentance, Griffith Jones begged sinners to renounce their evil ways and 'flee to Christ'. This 'busy enthusiast', as his enemies called him, warned his hearers that those who had not been 'born again' were 'feeding on husks with pigs'.[30] Griffith Jones seldom minced his words in the pulpit and it is not surprising that multitudes of churchmen and Dissenters flocked to his services. Long before the dawn of Methodism, Griffith Jones's gifts as a preacher had

[24] Griffith Jones, *Welch Piety* (London, 1742), p. 13.

[25] Geraint H. Jenkins, '"An Old and Much Honoured Soldier" Griffith Jones, Llanddowror', *WHR* 11 (1983), pp. 449–68.

[26] *Welch Piety* (London, 1740), p. 32.

[27] *George Whitefield's Journals* (London, 1960), p. 231.

[28] Henry Phillips, *A Sketch of the Life and Character of Mr. Griffith Jones* (London, 1762), p. 7.

[29] Griffith Jones, *Cyngor Rhad yr Anllythrennog* (London, 1737), sig. A4^r.

[30] Ottley Papers, No. 139; Griffith Jones, *Cyngor Gweinidog o'r Wlad i'w Blwyfolion* (London, 1769), p. 14.

become a legend. Moreover, his influence on the development of the Methodist movement itself was crucial, for in a sense Llanddowror was as much a breeding-ground for Methodism as were Llangeitho and Trefeca. It was Griffith Jones who secured the conversion of Daniel Rowland. Howel Harris revered—even loved—him as 'an old saint, an old minister and a Father in Israel',[31] whereas Williams Pantycelyn readily admitted that the fruitful soil in which Methodism grew had been prepared by the rector of Llanddowror.

If poverty was the major canker in the body politic of the established church, Dissent was also a prickly thorn in its side. Almost as soon as Charles was safely crowned, churchmen in gentry mansions and episcopal palaces set about paying off old scores. Rumours of plots were rife and soldiers scoured the country in search of dissidents and caches of arms. Many Puritan ministers lost their livings immediately. Others chose to quit their incumbencies of their own accord rather than violate their consciences. Many sectarians became the victims of violent retribution: dozens of Quakers and Baptists were placed under lock and key. Stones were hurled at Jenkin Jones, Llanddeti, as he was led—with head unbowed and spirit unquenched—to Carmarthen prison. Vavasor Powell, the sole survivor of the first generation of major Welsh Puritan saints, was also clapped in prison and was destined to see no more than ten months of liberty during the last ten years of his life. It was in Fleet prison that he wrote *A Bird in the Cage, Chirping* (1661), a vivid testimony to the ideals and sufferings of a man of stunning fortitude.

Hopes of accommodating Dissenters within a broad church were swiftly abandoned, for uncompromising Anglicans and Cavaliers would have no truck with old enemies. Churchmen felt desperately insecure and were gripped by fears of the consequences of another popular rebellion, especially when Thomas Venner's abortive Fifth Monarchist rising in January 1661 revived fears that the 'Good Old Cause' was alive and well. The 'late unhappy times' had left a legacy of bitterness which found its sharpest focus within the Cavalier Parliament. Not only were its members determined to establish an intolerant church settlement, but they were also bent on drastically curtailing the civil rights of Dissenters. The Act of Uniformity of April 1662 declared that all ministers were required to give their unfeigned assent to the rites and liturgy of the Church of England before St Bartholomew's Day on 24 August 1662. In a Welsh context, however, this statute simply brought down the curtain on a drama which had been played out since 1660. Out of 130 Puritan ministers ejected from their livings, ninety-five had already left prior to the implementation of the

---

[31] Tom Beynon, *Howell Harris's Visits to Pembrokeshire* (Aberystwyth, 1966), p. 12.

act. Nevertheless, the Act of Uniformity ushered in a lasting and painful social division between Anglican and Dissenter and between Church and Chapel.

In order to arrest the growth of Dissent and undermine the spirit of its members, a series of repressive measures, usually called the 'Clarendon Code', was passed. The clear intention of this legislation was to silence the voice of Dissent by imposing severe penalties on those who chose to follow their consciences by refusing to conform to the established church. The Corporation Act (1661) demanded that those who held public office were obliged to subscribe to the Anglican communion and swear loyalty to the king. A special Quaker Act (1662) was designed to make life intolerable for Friends. In May 1664 the first Conventicle Act prohibited dissidents from worshipping in defiance of the liturgy of the Church of England in groups of more than five persons. Offenders were liable to a fine of £5 or three months in prison. A second offence doubled the penalty, whilst a third transgression was punishable by either a fine of £100 or transportation for seven years. The Five Mile Act, passed in October 1665, bound Dissenters by oath to attempt no alteration in church or state. Those who refused to vow to support the government of church and state were forbidden to come within five miles of any parish, conventicle, town, city, or borough where they had previously ministered. The penalty was a fine of £40. The Conventicle Act expired on 1 March 1669, but within a year a second, and far more savage, act was passed. Worshippers who defied the law were liable to a fine of five shillings for a first offence and ten shillings for a second. Preachers and owners of meeting-places were liable to a stiff fine of £20 for a first offence and £40 for a second. A third of these fines was to be paid to informers, and magistrates who neglected to convict offenders were liable to find themselves subject to a fine of £100. Finally, the Test Act of 1673 disqualified Dissenters from office under the Crown unless they complied with the sacramental test.

In a bid to restore the authority of the church in their dioceses, Welsh bishops led the drive to enforce the penal code. Some of them were implacably hostile towards Dissent. The ghost of William Laud lived on in the shape of William Lucy, bishop of St Davids, a man of violent prejudices who made no concessions to erstwhile enemies as he strove to coerce Dissenters into conformity. Nor were olive branches forthcoming from Humphrey Lloyd, bishop of Bangor. He, too, nursed old grievances and was determined to check the growth of radical sectarianism. Lloyd was even suspicious of the motives of the supporters of the Welsh Trust: he ranted furiously against Thomas Gouge's annual tours through Wales and accused him of stuffing seditious notions into the heads of 'credulous common people'.[32] William Lloyd of St Asaph was far more fair-minded in

---

[32] Tanner MS 40, f. 18–19^r.

his dealings with Dissenters, but even he was prepared to wield a heavy bludgeon whenever 'bloody wretches'[33] refused to heed his counsels and threatened to make serious inroads into his flock.

Clergymen and magistrates who had suffered in the past were also disinclined to let former Puritans off the hook. The penal code offered them a golden opportunity to settle old scores, and Dissenting records of this period testify to the frustrations and indignities of the daily life of dissidents, the petty and malicious deeds perpetrated against them, and the constant threat of harassment, imprisonment, or personal ruin. Gone were the days of Cromwellian toleration. Dissenters who flouted the penal code drew a nest of hornets down upon their heads and were often forced to endure acts of unspeakable cruelty. Vavasor Powell claimed that many Dissenters in 1662 were dragged from their beds and forced to walk twenty miles to prison, 'receiving many blows and beatings'[34] from their captors *en route*. Some punishments were astonishingly mean-minded. The authorities took away the last cow owned by Henry Gregory, an Arminian Baptist of Llanddewi Ystradenni in Radnorshire, thereby depriving his children of milk. Even the dead were not permitted to lie in peace. The body of the daughter of a former Puritan itinerant was dug up from the churchyard of Llanfihangel Brynpabuan in Breconshire and reinterred like a common criminal or suicide at the crossroads. Quakers were men and women of exceptional honesty and integrity, and since they made little effort to avoid persecution or to evade the rigours of the law they suffered more than most. Even the smallest transgressions were sometimes punished by vigilant persecutors: Owen Lewis of Tyddynygarreg was excommunicated for refusing to pay 2d. cheese-tithe. In Penllyn, Elinor Ellis, a poor widow dependent on alms, was deprived of her bedclothes, waistcoat, apron, smock, stockings, and books for refusing to abandon her convictions.

The treatment meted out to Dissenters in prisons varied from place to place. Much depended on the attitude of the gaoler: he was often empowered to allow prisoners to visit their families or fulfil long-standing preaching engagements. William Jones, the Baptist minister of Cilymaenllwyd, was released on parole through the good offices of an influential gentleman who also lent him his horse and top coat. Richard Davies of Cloddiau Cochion was set at liberty for short periods and was even permitted to travel as far afield as London. Other prisoners were less fortunate, finding themselves incarcerated for many months or even years in dark, crowded, dirty holes, where spiteful felons and brutish gaolers made their lives a misery. Many Welsh prisons were in appalling condition. In 1662 Quakers in Montgomeryshire were imprisoned in a filthy stable where they were periodically showered with fellow prisoners' excrement that fell from an

[33] Lloyd-Baker Letters, No. 20a.
[34] Michael R. Watts, *The Dissenters*, p. 233.

upstairs chamber. Only the fittest survived such traumas. Five Welsh
Quakers perished in prison during the period of the 'Great Persecution'
from 1660 to 1689, and many of those who were released were never the
same again. Left to rot in the capital, Vavasor Powell, the most heroic
Welsh Dissenter, eventually died, aged 53, in Fleet Prison in October 1670.

Yet, even though Dissenters lived constantly in a climate of fear and
uncertainty, it must be emphasized that they did not suffer anything like
the fierce and barbaric atrocities which befell the Huguenots in France.
The application of the penal legislation varied both in incidence and
severity from place to place. Persecution and harassment were fitful rather
than endemic, and much depended on the animus of prelates, priests, and
magistrates or on the current political climate. External stimuli, such as
fears of an advancing popish army, or an internal domestic crisis like the
Rye House Plot, often stirred reluctant magistrates to apply the full rigour
of the law. Persecution was at its sharpest during the years 1662–6, 1670–2,
1678–9, and 1681–6. At such times, the fortitude and stoicism of suffering
Dissenters were often remarkable. Nourished by their belief that theirs was
a favoured cause, they assigned each calamity which befell their persecutors
to the Lord's providential will. David Maurice, a magistrate of violent
prejudices who came from Pen-y-bont, Montgomeryshire, was drowned
when he was thrown from his horse into Tanat brook near his home. John
Swayn of Tywyn, a bitter foe of Merioneth Friends, was struck down 'by
the Lord' in 'a most strange and terrible manner'.[35] As news of such
providences filtered through the localities, long-suffering Dissenters
thanked the Lord for his mercies. Providential deliverances also confirmed
their belief that their faith and fortitude would receive just reward. When a
bullet grazed Daniel Phillips's head as he preached in Pwllheli, he declared
loudly: 'in the shadow of His hand hath He hid me'.[36] Peregrine Phillips,
'the apostle of Pembrokeshire', was saved, at the eleventh hour, after
falling into a coal-pit at Freystrop. While Henry Williams of Ysgafell,
Montgomeryshire, languished in prison, his enemies set his house on fire,
murdered his father, abused his pregnant wife, seized his stock, and
plundered his goods. But a newly sown wheat field was left untouched and,
much to the amazement of local people, it produced such an abundant crop
that Williams's financial losses were more than amply redeemed. The tale
of *Cae'r Fendith* (the Field of Blessing) duly entered the annals of
Dissenting hagiography.

But the ability of Dissenters to rise above their sufferings was not simply
due to their faith and the intervention of providence. They were shrewd
and resourceful men. At times of draconian persecution they were thrown

[35] J. Gwynn Williams, 'The Quakers of Merioneth during the Seventeenth Century',
Journal Merioneth Hist. and Record Soc. 8 (1978–9), p. 138.
[36] Thomas Rees, *History of Protestant Nonconformity*, p. 159.

on to the defensive and forced to worship covertly. Apart from the Quakers, most Dissenters did not advertise their activities; indeed, they used all kinds of elaborate devices to avoid discovery. Some, like Philip Henry, the Flintshire Presbyterian, displayed a keen awareness of the loopholes in the legal system, whilst others revealed unusual flair and expertise in devising stratagems to escape the severities of the law. Preachers met their flocks in desolate spots—Stephen Hughes and Rees Prydderch worshipped in caves—and took care to cover their tracks. Times of services were changed regularly and hawk-eyed guards were appointed to inform preachers of the movement of informers and constables. It was not easy for magistrates and informers to keep a close watch on nimble and industrious evangelists. Preachers travelled, preached, and instructed with distracting persistence, especially when the law granted them brief moments of respite. Although Dissenters viewed with suspicious eyes the indulgence granted by Charles II in 1672 they could not resist taking advantage of the breathing-space. Ministers coyly embraced their new liberty by taking out 185 preaching licences (136 in south Wales and 49 in north Wales) and by organizing their scattered flocks. Bishop William Lucy was soon at his wit's end: 'preach these fellows do everywhere',[37] he whined to Archbishop Sheldon in February 1673, and his problems did not vanish when the king was forced to revoke his declaration a month later.

Fleet-footed Dissenters were not without friends. Wealthy and respectable men opened their doors to beleaguered Dissenters. According to Lucy, 'great purses'[38] were lending funds and authority, as and when necessary, to Dissenters in the major market towns of his diocese. Although Stephen Hughes was kept under close surveillance by court officials, he was befriended by William Thomas, Lucy's successor at St Davids, shielded from the consequences of the law by powerful local gentlemen, and allowed to preach in parish churches which were 'much thronged by the vast numbers that came to hear him'.[39] Henry Maurice, a man of gentry stock, had friends on the bench who used their good offices on his behalf, while Peregrine Phillips enjoyed the patronage of the Perrots of Haroldstone and the Owens of Orielton. In north Wales, William Jones, the ejected minister of Denbigh, found his asylum at Plas Teg, home of Sir John Trevor, while the Puritans of Llŷn were harboured by Richard Edwards of Nanhoron. It is clear that not all magistrates were prepared to execute the penal legislation. Many were reluctant to proceed against men of repute,

[37] Tanner MS 146, f. 113.

[38] W. T. Morgan, 'The Prosecution of Nonconformists in the Consistory Courts of St. David's, 1661–88', *Journal Hist. Soc. Church in Wales* 12 (1962), p. 44.

[39] Edmund Calamy, *An Account of the Ministers . . . Ejected after the Restoration in 1660* (2 vols., London, 1713), ii. 718.

close neighbours, or old friends, while others were already so burdened with time-consuming chores that pursuing Dissenters held few attractions for them. Local constables, too, tended to turn a blind eye, sometimes because of ties of kinship but also sometimes out of sheer indolence. Prosecution was often a protracted, shambling process and the opportunities for prevarication, especially for those Dissenters who were capable of exposing obvious lacunae in the legal process, were so frequently made use of that the diktats of the law often went unheeded. Few Dissenters were obliged to do public penance. The sentence of excommunication was a light cross to bear, except when it was stiffened in the civil courts by a writ *de excommunicato capiendo*, issued by the Court of Chancery at the instigation of a bishop. But such a writ was so expensive that it was rarely invoked. In practice, therefore, most Dissenters feared neither episcopal censures nor the sheriff's writ.

Yet it must be emphasized that the brunt of persecution was borne largely by Roman Catholics and Quakers. These brave dissidents suffered grievous hardships. In Restoration Wales there existed an irrational, almost pathological, fear of Catholics. The popish threat seemingly hung over people's lives like a dark cloud, for it was widely believed that Catholics were bent on destroying the Protestant religion and constitutional liberties. Every Protestant was taught to believe that Catholicism was a blasphemous, tainted faith. Moreover, it was reckoned to be a political threat. A Catholic, by definition, was base and untrustworthy: it was unthinkable that any papist could be considered a faithful and upright citizen. The territorial ambitions of 'the French monster',[40] Louis XIV, were well-known, and fears of popery intensified following the conversion to Catholicism of James, duke of York, heir apparent and future James II, in 1673. Welsh literature reveals the almost hysterical fears which bubbled to the surface at times of national crisis. Almanacs were riddled with anti-popish sentiments, whilst Protestant authors, such as Charles Edwards and Stephen Hughes, portrayed the Catholic as a bloodthirsty foe who fed on people's ignorance, peddled a specious faith, and practised the most unheard-of cruelties. These writers, and many others, were convinced that Jesuit priests were proselytizing with no small success and were threatening to transform the old faith into a living force. In truth, however, the popish threat was a myth. The handful of Jesuit priests who ministered to tiny flocks in remote enclaves on the Welsh borders were hardly political subversives. Nor were those nobles and gentlemen who clung steadfastly to the old faith seriously committed to turning the world upside down in the name of the Pope. Indeed, as far as the whole of Wales was concerned, Roman Catholicism was a sleepy, unmilitant, even innocuous, religion

---

[40] Thomas Jones, *Newyddion Mawr oddiwrth y Ser* (London, 1691), sig. A2ʳ.

practised by a hard core of gentry and yeomen and supported by craftsmen, wives, spinsters, and widows.

Even though Catholics were a tiny minority in Wales, their very presence, especially at times of political crisis, exercised a disproportionate influence on people's minds. Monmouthshire was the strongest pillar of the old faith. According to the religious census of 1676 there was a resistant core of 541 popish recusants in the county. These were being served by fifteen priests and succoured by the highly influential Somerset family of Raglan. South-east Wales was an area of extreme religious instability and was also characterized by an atmosphere of suspicion and mistrust. The root of the trouble by the mid-1670s lay in the rapid deterioration in relations between the marquis of Worcester and John Arnold of Llanfihangel Crucornau. Arnold viewed the Catholic magnate's policy of local aggrandizement with growing fury and vowed to root out papists from Gwent. Fired largely by personal grievances, Arnold and John Scudamore presented a parliamentary inquiry with secret information regarding the activities of Catholic priests in Monmouthshire. As a result, in the autumn of 1678, Herbert Croft, bishop of Hereford (a relatively recent convert from Catholicism), together with his servants, ransacked the Jesuit College at Cwm in the parish of Llanrothal in Herefordshire. Ever since its foundation in 1622, St Francis Xavier's college at Cwm had been a haven for Jesuit priests on the Welsh borders. Within hours, it was shattered by Croft's servants, who made off with several loads of secret papers, devotional literature, and relics. This raid coincided with the publication of Titus Oates's ingenious revelations of a Popish Plot to murder the king, subvert the government, and uproot the Protestant religion. A massive scare swept the country. Preachers conjured up horrifying images of Catholics as barbarous fifth-columnists. 'God keep England from your bloody religion',[41] declared Bishop William Lloyd, whilst John Thomas, vicar of Penegoes, peppered his *Unum Necessarium* (1680) with virulent assaults on the ritualism and barbarism of the 'devilish' enemy.

In such a fevered atmosphere, no self-respecting Protestant could remain blind to the presence of Jesuit proselytizers on Welsh soil. Memories of the Smithfield Martyrs, the Gunpowder Plot, and the Irish Massacre came flooding back, and local magistrates rigorously sought to dragoon errant papists into conformity. A furious priest-hunt was launched in south-east Wales and a pope-burning ceremony at Abergavenny helped to fan anti-papist sentiments. Five priests (Philip Evans and John Lloyd at Cardiff, David Lewis at Usk, Charles Meehan at Ruthin, and John Kemble at Hereford), who had ministered to the needs of recusants in Wales and the Marches, were found guilty of high treason and barbarously executed

---

[41] A. Tindal Hart, *William Lloyd 1627–1717*, p. 29.

in 1679. They suffered their grisly fate of hanging, dismemberment, disembowelling, and quartering with great dignity and fortitude. When Philip Evans was informed of his impending execution, he insisted on completing a game of tennis and then took up his harp to play a joyful refrain. David Lewis, popularly known as 'Tad y Tlodion' (Father of the Poor), insisted to the last that no man could move him 'one hair's breadth'[42] from the true faith. Anti-popish hatreds raged as never before during these troubled years, and these harrowing executions not only accelerated the number of defections to Protestantism but also consigned Catholicism to a long period of decay in Wales.

Since Quakers were considered to be the most radical survivors of the 'late wretched times', they, too, were widely feared and severely persecuted. Friends ruffled the tempers of the authorities by disturbing the peace, refusing to pay tithes, church rates, and levies, defying the legal requirement to take the oath of allegiance or swear oaths, absenting themselves from church, and meeting in unlawful conventicles. Thus, not only were they believed to be a threat to the well-being of the established church but also an even greater menace to the social and political fabric. Churchmen and orthodox Dissenters alike avoided them like the plague, dubbing them 'giddy-brained'[43] dealers in heresy and witchcraft. Quakerism, they claimed, was a noxious, tainted faith, espoused by fanatics whose aim was to demolish existing social values and conventions. Their apprehension deepened as Quakerism spread swiftly in the Welsh-speaking communities of rural Wales. The counties of Merioneth, Montgomery, and Radnor proved an extraordinarily fertile soil for the Quaker faith, with the doctrines of George Fox winning a considerable following among substantial freeholders and yeomen, who were linked both by economic ties and bonds of kinship. A special Quaker Act, passed in May 1662, sought to silence Friends by making it an offence to refuse to swear an oath and for more than five persons to assemble for conventicle worship. Yet Quakers continued to plague the clergy and confound the authorities. Many of them were repeatedly fined, distrained upon, or thrust into prison. The penal code, however, held few terrors for them, for they had vowed to suffer passively for their faith. From 1661 onwards, Friends renounced carnal weapons and preached the virtues of pacifism. They suffered nobly, enduring each adversity with patience, courage, and resolution. In the words of Charles Lloyd of Dolobran, Friends 'hated none but Satan, sin and self'.[44] Sustained by a strong collective identity and

---

[42] T. P. Ellis, *The Catholic Martyrs of Wales 1535–1680* (London, 1933), p. 137.

[43] NLW, Records of the Church in Wales, SD/Archdeaconry of Carmarthen churchwardens' returns 1684, No. 79.

[44] Humphrey Lloyd, *The Quaker Lloyds*, p. 36.

their common experience as a persecuted minority, they retained an unwavering conviction in the rightness of their cause.

During the first two decades of the penal code, the rocklike fortitude of Quakers was a source of despair to their most bitter foes. But there was a limit to the patience and fixity of purpose even of Friends. Having weathered early storms, they faced the nightmarish prospect of further harassment and persecution in the 1680s. Small wonder, then, that many of them were tempted to sail to America. In May 1681, a dozen prominent Welsh Quakers, led by John ap John and Thomas Wynne, were interviewed by William Penn in London. Seven Welsh companies were formed, and 30,000 acres of land, lying chiefly in the Haverford, Merion, and Radnor counties, on the west side of the Schuylkill river and to the north-west of Philadelphia, was bought. 'The Lord', declared Thomas Ellis of Is Cregennan in Merioneth, had opened 'a door of mercy'[45] to beleaguered Friends. From 1682 onwards, boatloads of independent, cultured, Welsh-speaking Friends journeyed westwards across the stormy Atlantic seas in search of a New Jerusalem. The cumulative effects of years of persecution compelled them to seek asylum in Penn's promised land. One of them, Hugh Roberts of Bala, insisted that it was fear of further persecution which persuaded them to pack their bags. William Penn's spellbinding personality and idealism had also allayed their initial fears and persuaded them that freedom of worship and conscience would be the hallmark of his experiment. There is no doubt, too, that some of the smaller gentry and yeomen, notably those who had suffered ruinous forfeitures at the hands of their foes, were tempted by alluring reports of the salubrious climate, fertile soils, and abundant crops of Pennsylvania. Between 1682 and 1700, some 2,000 individuals, including 900 from Merioneth, set off for America. For the sum of £20, a man could take his wife, two children, and a servant, and expect to receive 500 acres of 'good and fruitful land' on arrival. 'This is the place', enthused Thomas Wynne, a former barber-surgeon of Caerwys, 'for soul and body.'[46]

The sudden exodus of whole families of sturdy, independent members proved a grievous blow to the Quaker cause in Wales. Had not Welsh Quakers abandoned their bastions in their native land, the history of Welsh Dissent might have been very different. As it was, meetings collapsed with alarming swiftness and by the early decades of the eighteenth century the Quaker faith was at a low ebb in Wales. John Kelsall, a schoolmaster at Dolobran in Montgomeryshire, was mortified to witness 'a spirit of ease' spreading 'like a hidden leprosy'[47] among his brethren. Old enemies (save for irremediable diehards like Ellis Wynne and Theophilus Evans) had

[45] J. Gwynn Williams, 'The Quakers of Merioneth', p. 328.

[46] NLW, Rhual MS 106.

[47] Kelsall MSS, vol. ii, A Book of Letters, dated 8 mo. 1701.

become forbearing, even loving, towards them—clear testimony that
Quakerism had entered its quietist phase and become innocuous.
Throughout the eighteenth century, Welsh Quakerism survived only in
small isolated groups, insulated by their clannish marriage customs and
their curious patterns of behaviour. Equally disappointing to Welsh
Friends was the discovery that Penn's experiment was a flawed Utopia. In
many ways, the hopes of Welsh emigrants remained unfulfilled, for the
dream of establishing an autonomous Welsh settlement in Pennsylvania
proved a snare and a delusion. By the 1690s, Pennsylvania was riven by
intense political conflict, and many Welsh colonists were bitterly critical of
Penn's iniquitous quitrent scheme and his reluctance to uphold their
baronial rights of self-government. Although Welsh Quakers struggled
valiantly to maintain a separate sense of identity in the Welsh Tract, this
proved impossible when the boundaries of their lands were refashioned.
Thus, while Dissent in Wales was acutely impoverished by the exodus of
Quakers, the cause of Welsh Friends in America would also, in time, be
much the poorer for losing its distinctive Welsh identity.

Meanwhile, the number of orthodox Dissenters was steadily increasing.
Although the returns supplied by the Compton census of 1676 were
massaged by the Anglican authorities in such a way as to play down the
growth and influence of Dissent, it is clear that the coercive power of the
state had not wiped out sectarianism. The census claimed that Welsh
Dissent could boast merely 4,248 members, but this figure seriously
underestimated the strength of the Dissenting cause. Ministers had
evidently preserved the fellowship of their churches and old Puritanism
was still very much alive, notably in the counties of Brecon, Glamorgan,
and Monmouth. It was particularly strong in parts of the diocese of St
Davids, especially in the archdeaconries of Brecon and Carmarthen, and at
its most slender in north-west Wales. Congregationalists made up the
overwhelming bulk of its numbers, followed by the Baptists, with the
Presbyterians a poor third. Members of Dissenting churches were scattered
far and wide over many parishes or even counties, and it was not
uncommon for some members to travel over forty miles to attend monthly
communion services or preaching meetings. The general practice was to
worship in private dwelling houses—'the good old way',[48] as Joshua
Thomas, the Baptist historian, was later to describe it.

The growth of Dissent was fostered by the itinerant evangelism of a
remarkably hardy group of preachers who ministered to the spiritual needs
of small but highly resilient flocks in clandestine services. Although
traditional accounts of these early ministers carry more than a strong whiff
of hagiography, there is no doubt that the growth and influence of Dissent

⁴⁸ T. M. Bassett, *The Welsh Baptists*, p. 58.

depended heavily on their labours and bravery. Dissenting preachers saw themselves as 'stars in the right hand of Christ', a chosen few who were privileged to bring the gospel into a 'benighted and frozen world'.[49] Some of them were extraordinary men. In the summer of 1671 Henry Maurice experienced a dramatic conversion which prompted him to forsake the Anglican ministry and join the ranks of Dissent. Maurice evangelized far and wide, infusing fresh vigour into Dissenting causes and defying ecclesiastical censures. Widely known as 'the Apostle of Breconshire', he was chiefly responsible for recruiting and shepherding the 682 Dissenters who were numbered in the county of Brecon in the religious census of 1676. His aristocratic mien and brisk temper often concealed his essentially humble and compassionate nature. A naturally gregarious man, he never passed a poor person or child during his travels without discoursing with them about the state of their soul. His diary honestly mirrors the fears, dreams, passions, and rages which enlivened and bedevilled the life of a travelling evangelist. Stephen Hughes, 'the Apostle of Carmarthenshire', was also a man of great warmth and humility. Few Dissenting ministers were more highly revered and loved than Hughes. His aim was to provide his countrymen with saving knowledge, and his fear that Jesuits were sowing their 'poisonous seeds'[50] throughout Wales drove him to defend the Protestant cause by publishing and distributing pious books. Hughes's extraordinary capacity for work enabled him to establish eight gathered churches in south-west Wales and to nurture many of the most gifted young ministers in the ranks of Welsh Dissent. No less indefatigable was Hugh Owen of Bronclydwr in Merioneth, a modest man of low estate who lived on milk, slept on straw, and often rode far into the night in order to serve the spiritual needs of his scattered flocks in Merioneth, Caernarfonshire, and Montgomeryshire. When John Miles, the Baptist leader, left for America, the Baptist cause in Wales found a worthy standard-bearer in William Jones, Cilymaenllwyd. Blessed with a seemingly inexhaustible reservoir of energy, Jones founded a new Baptist ministry at Rhydwilym in Pembrokeshire in 1667 and, almost overnight, turned it into a new Ilston. Single-handed, William Jones succeeded in multiplying the number of Baptist communicants from 33 in 1668 to 113 by 1689, in a church which covered thirty-eight parishes in south-west Wales. Undisturbed by violent persecution, these 'men of Macedonia' (as Joseph Alleine called them)[51] put their consciences above principles of state and safeguarded the progress of Dissent.

The period from 1660 to 1689 was, truly, the heroic age of Welsh

[49] Charles Owen, *Some Account of the Life and Writings of Mr. James Owen* (London, 1709), p. 136.

[50] *Gwaith Mr Rees Prichard*, ed. Stephen Hughes, Part 4 (London, 1672), sig. A5^r.

[51] Charles Stanford, *Joseph Alleine: His Companions and Times* (London, 1861), p. 308.

Dissent. In spite of being subjected to severe physical and psychological strains, Dissenters were determined to maintain the distinctiveness of their faith and to prosper. Only men endowed with great resilience and faith could have borne such burdens for so long. But, as James Owen insisted, 'if the gospel was not worth suffering for, it was not worth preaching'.[52] Even the most implacable enemies of Dissenters grudgingly admired their courage and fidelity to truth. Persecution had clearly thinned their ranks of time-servers, trimmers, and waverers. Pliable and Worldly-Wiseman had been weeded out. In short, Dissent was here to stay.

By the mid-1680s, moreover, there had been a widespread shift in the centre of gravity of opinion. More and more churchmen were anxious to heal rifts within the religious community. It was fairly clear that coercive powers were not likely to make Dissenters accept the Anglican church as the sole true faith, and the accession of James II to the throne in 1685 sharpened anti-popish feelings and helped to drive moderate Anglicans into the arms of Dissenters. James II naïvely strove to remove all penal laws against Roman Catholics and to restore the religion of Rome as the official national religion. In so doing he seriously underestimated his subjects' attachment to the Protestant faith and their deeply felt antipathy towards popery. Bishop William Lloyd of St Asaph led the seven bishops who petitioned against James's Declaration of Indulgence in 1687 and was consigned to the Tower. Faced by the threat of arbitrary popish government, Lloyd had mellowed a good deal in his attitude towards Dissenters and was anxious to repair relations with them. James Owen, the learned Presbyterian tutor, was summoned to meet him at Oswestry, and Lloyd, to his credit, expressed his remorse: 'we have indeed been angry brethren, but we have seen our folly, and we are resolved if we ever have it in our power that we will treat you as brethren'.[53] With the arrival of William III, a broadminded Calvinist, in 1689, the old ideal of comprehension was abandoned. Those who believed in re-establishing the unity of the national church were now a small minority and the new Protestant king was not disposed to support an Anglican monopoly. Laudianism was a dead letter and Dissent had become a permanent feature of religious life in Wales.

The Toleration Act of May 1689 permitted Dissenters (except Roman Catholics and Socinians) to worship freely in meeting-houses, provided they were duly licensed and their services conducted behind unlocked doors. The act offered much-needed relief to Dissenters and helped to soften the hard shell of Anglican prejudice against them. The persecuting spirit of old enemies had not entirely abated, but at least Dissenters were now free to advance their cause publicly, to worship in peace, and to build

---

[52] Thomas Rees, *History of Protestant Nonconformity*, p. 167.
[53] D. Walker, *History of the Welsh Church*, p. 94.

chapels. Yet they still carried badges of inferiority: excluded from municipal government and the universities, they remained second-class citizens until the repeal of the Test and Corporation Acts in 1828.

The Toleration Act undoubtedly weakened the position and authority of the Anglican church in Wales. Slowly but surely, Dissent began to take advantage of the administrative weaknesses within the established church by recruiting members in large parishes and scattered rural communities where church discipline was weakest. High Tories and churchmen were fearful that zealous sectarians were undermining the authority of the church and breeding tumult and sedition. They ranted furiously against 'the flagrant sin of schism',[54] poured scorn on the pretensions of base-born Dissenting ministers, and urged their parishioners to remain faithful to 'the most excellent liturgy in the whole Christian world'.[55] Anglican diehards were fearful that a tidal wave of Dissent would engulf the Anglican community, but Dissent, in fact, was still a tiny movement. By c. 1715–18, there were some eighty-nine Dissenting congregations in Wales (mostly Congregationalists) with a total membership of 17,770, i.e. less than 5 per cent of the country's population. These statistics were collected at the request of members of the Committee of the Three Denominations, who were anxious to measure the strength of Dissenting causes in England and Wales. Although the Welsh statistics are highly suspect, largely because Dissenting numbers were magnified by the inclusion of hearers as well as actual members, they reveal that Welsh Dissent was a small but influential minority. Dissent was strongest in the six counties of south Wales, notably in Glamorgan where it had won the hearts of some 12 per cent of the adult population. In north Wales, however, the established church still held massive sway.

Dissent thrived in commercial communities and in prosperous, anglicized towns such as Wrexham, Cardiff, and Swansea. It boasted substantial numbers of tradesmen, artisans, and craftsmen. Half the members of the Congregational church at Haverfordwest in 1706–11 were textile tradesmen, tailors, and shoemakers. Leading Quakers were often successful business-men. When Charles Lloyd married Sarah Crowley of Stourbridge in 1693, he forged the first link in a celebrated chain which united the Lloyd dynasty of Dolobran to the great ironmaster families of the West Midlands. Richard Hanbury, the ironworks master of Pontypool, was a tower of strength to Quaker causes in south Wales. Although some causes in rural areas were bolstered by the patronage of wealthy gentlemen, most Dissenting members were freeholders, craftsmen, and labourers. Many of the well-to-do middling sorts were sufficiently independent to be able to divorce themselves from the social hierarchy of the established church and

---

[54] Griffith Jones, *A Letter to a Proselyte of the Church of Rome* (London, 1731), p. 24.

[55] G. H. Jenkins, *Literature, Religion and Society*, pp. 169–172.

follow their consciences without fear of undue harassment from the local squire and parson. In rural Aberystruth and Mynyddislwyn in Monmouthshire, Dissenting congregations were made up of 126 yeomen, 98 farmers, 54 tradesmen, and 113 labourers. In south-west Wales, the majority of Welsh Baptists at Rhydwilym were humble farmers and craftsmen like Thomas Parry, who was described as 'a simple countryman holding a little farm and sometimes following a trade'.[56]

Some Dissenting ministers eked out a living on miserably small stipends. James Owen of Oswestry was sustained by 'a small pittance',[57] whilst Marmaduke Matthews of Swansea depended entirely on the goodwill of his family. Edmund Jones, the colourful Dissenting minister of Pontypool, lived 'very low' on £10 per annum, sustained largely by his conviction that 'the Lord will provide'.[58] Many ministers were so poor that they were obliged to draw on funds made available by the Congregational and Presbyterian boards from the 1690s onwards. However, following the passing of the Toleration Act, Welsh Dissent began to nurture a new generation of gentlemen-preachers. Most ministers were self-sufficient men of private means who held freehold or tenant land. Some won the hand of affluent heiresses, whilst others inherited substantial estates. Many of them had been trained at Dissenting academies. When Dissenters were excluded from the universities, private academies were established in order to equip the movement with a learned ministry. Early Welsh academies were private, self-sufficient institutions, set up in the homes of individual tutors and frequented by relatively well-to-do students. The first and probably the most celebrated academy was founded by Samuel Jones, a distinguished scholar, at Brynllywarch, Llangynwyd, in Glamorgan in 1672. Academies tended to migrate from place to place, according to the personal circumstances of tutors. In 1690, James Owen, a learned disputant and an outstanding theologian, opened a highly successful academy at Oswestry where he ruled his students with a canny mixture of discipline and affection. James Owen had few equals as a tutor and he devised a rigorous course of lectures which rivalled any syllabus which the universities of Oxford and Cambridge could provide. Most academies, in fact, offered a progressive and inventive curriculum which not only nourished the faith and learning of prospective ministers but also encouraged freedom of thought and inquiry.

Dissenting services were plain, simple, and dignified occasions consisting of psalm-singing, a fairly lengthy sermon, and a closing prayer. Communion was celebrated monthly. Family worship was encouraged, and sermons were repeated within the household, either from memory or from notes,

[56] T. M. Bassett, *The Welsh Baptists*, p. 66.
[57] Charles Owen, *Some Account . . . of Mr. James Owen*, p. 77.
[58] Thomas Rees, *History of Protestant Nonconformity*, pp. 405–6.

on Sunday evenings. Sermons were clear, practical discourses, heavily soaked in scriptural references, methodically organized, and precisely delivered. It used to be argued that Dissenting ministers preached in dry, rational vein, squeezing all traces of emotion from their homilies. But many of them were skilled practitioners in the art of probing the inner recesses of man's soul. They deliberately chose 'awakening texts' and strove to exhort inwardly and touch the affections of their hearers. Henry Maurice was renowned for his skill in anatomizing men's souls; Stephen Hughes's ability to draw tears from his hearers and melt their hearts was proverbial; whilst Enoch Francis seldom preached without shedding tears. All of them would have agreed with James Owen that the conversion of 'one poor sinner' was 'worth an age's preaching'.[59] Their members were devout, serious-minded, responsible men and women who placed a high premium on piety, theological knowledge, and literacy. Rigorous standards of church fellowship were set and each new member was carefully vetted before being admitted to the fold. Those who neglected worship, blasphemed, tippled, committed sexual misdemeanours, or peddled unorthodox doctrinal views were summarily expelled.

The notion that Dissent was withering by the eve of the Methodist revival still finds favour with some historians. But, far from being torn apart by sterile theological disputes and fractious schisms, Dissenting churches were experiencing a modest and encouraging growth. Numbers increased steadily at Pen-maen, Monmouthshire, at Capel Isaac, Llandeilo, and within the five churches under the ministry of Phylip Pugh in south Cardiganshire. A separate Welsh Baptist Association was founded in 1700. By 1723 the Rhydwilym congregation had swollen to 220, and steady gains were also recorded at Cilfowyr, Hengoed, and Blaenau. By dint of patient labour, application, and boundless enthusiasm, ministers like James Davies, Enoch Francis, Miles Harri, Edmund Jones, and Lewis Rees ensured that the voice of Dissent was heard. Even so, their tendency to separate from the world meant that a new lease of life was required in order to capture the hearts of the majority of the Welsh people. The Methodist revival was to provide that fillip.

Although religious animosities and the spirit of persecution were clearly evident in this period, especially prior to the Toleration Act, it would be wrong to assume that all Anglicans and Dissenters harboured grievances against each other and were divided into two implacably hostile camps. Many men of goodwill—both churchmen and Dissenters—were anxious to build bridges and to focus on those elements which they held in common, rather than the theological dogmas which kept them apart. The Latitudinarian

[59] Charles Owen, *Some Account . . . of Mr. James Owen*, p. 72.

school, for instance, dispensed with narrow theological creeds and argued in favour of catholicity and forbearance. Its dearest wish was that men of all religious persuasions (except papists) should live together in amity and concord. Fear of popery also drove moderates on both sides into each other's arms. All good Protestants accepted without demur their obligation to man the barricades against 'the mother of superstition and sedition'.[60] At local level, too, ties of neighbourliness and a common desire to root out evil and raise moral standards meant that churchmen and Dissenters were often happy to work in harness. This period, moreover, was extraordinarily fruitful in good works. A powerful Puritan ethos prompted Anglicans and Dissenters to prize charity above rubrics and to encourage collective endeavours. Affluent men were called upon to loosen their purse-strings and to do good 'to the souls and bodies of men'.[61] No man could consider himself a philanthropist unless he felt a genuine sense of pity for the underprivileged and unless the practice of piety was writ large in his daily conduct. All these factors helped to contribute towards a marked advance in the provision of educational facilities, the publication of religious books, and the growth of literacy.

One of the earliest enterprises designed to foster a common Protestant Christianity was the Welsh Trust (1674–81), a charitable body which reflected the Latitudinarian ideals of disparate individuals. Among the major patrons were stout prelates such as Patrick, Stillingfleet, and Tillotson, and doughty Dissenters like Baxter, Bates, and Firmin. Many of them saw Wales as a *tabula rasa*, a mission field for the gospel. Charles Edwards, one of Stephen Hughes's colleagues, joyfully confessed that erstwhile foes had now become generous benefactors: the English, who had once been 'ravenous wolves', had become 'as embracing shepherds, almost as dear to us as we are to each other'.[62] Owain Glyndŵr, he declared, would never have credited such a transformation. The moving spirit behind the foundation of the Welsh Trust was Thomas Gouge, the ejected minister of St Sepulchre, Southwark. Gouge became so passionately interested in the spiritual welfare of benighted Welshmen that he adopted Wales as one of his special 'livings'. He wheedled substantial funds from wealthy London gentlemen and merchants, many of whom were of Welsh origin, and their affluent counterparts in Wales responded in kind. The funds were used to establish charity schools and to publish pious books. Gouge's earnestness and piety were infectious and he persuaded Stephen Hughes to help him build a literate, God-fearing society. Hughes was a man of such sagacity, patience, and courtesy that he was able to charm those of all religious persuasions (except Catholics), win commitment from

---

[60] J. Miller, *Popery and Politics in England 1660–1688* (Cambridge, 1973), *passim*.
[61] M. G. Jones, *The Charity School Movement* (Cambridge, 1938), p. 3.
[62] Charles Edwards, *Y Ffydd Ddi-ffvant* (Oxford, 1677), p. 210.

the equivocal, and disarm his enemies. Sustained by the wisdom and money of his well-to-do wife, 'the Apostle of Carmarthenshire' set up a close working relationship with Gouge based on mutual respect and agreed goals.

Stephen Hughes used his flair for organization to ensure that both children and adults were supplied with edifying reading material in their native tongue. His publications included a new edition of the New Testament in Welsh, a substantial edition of 8,000 copies of the Welsh Bible in 1678, and editions of the works of John Bunyan, Rees Prichard, and William Perkins. No one laboured harder than he to ensure that the Welsh Trust disseminated pious literature for use in the family household as well as in schools. In 1678 alone the Trust was responsible for distributing 5,185 Welsh books among poor but deserving readers. The need for charity schools was even more acute. The primary school structure established under the terms of the Propagation Act had crumbled shortly after Charles II's accession. Grammar schools served the needs of the sons and daughters of affluent men. Such institutions were inaccessible to the poor boy and girl who, in any case, were scarcely interested in acquiring a good classical education. Gouge filled the void with a network of charity schools. For a short while his labours produced handsome dividends: by the autumn of 1675, 2,225 children were being taught to read, write, and cast accounts in eighty-seven schools in the major market towns of Wales. Schools were established in every Welsh county, save Merioneth, though there was a heavy preponderance in south Wales and along the Marches. The size of classes ranged from ten to sixty pupils, and schoolmasters were provided with bibles, catechisms, prayer books, and devotional books such as *The Practise of Piety* and *The Whole Duty of Man*. It was the fervent wish of the Trust's patrons that by learning to read the English tongue Welsh children would become 'more serviceable to their country and live more comfortably in the world'.[63] Such pious sentiments might have won roars of approval from thrusting middling sorts in Victorian Wales, but they were far removed from reality in impoverished and largely monoglot Stuart Wales. Stephen Hughes was clearly unhappy about the language policy of the Welsh Trust and voiced his misgivings publicly to unheeding ears. The Trust was also under fire from other quarters and the fact that only thirty-three schools were still open in 1678 indicates that it was the target of much resentment and malice. Embittered bishops such as William Lucy and Humphrey Lloyd were deeply suspicious of Thomas Gouge's motives and seized every opportunity to vent their anti-Puritan animus. The politico-religious crisis which came in the wake of the Popish Plot also produced rifts within the movement. By 1681 the

[63] M. G. Jones, 'Two Accounts of the Welsh Trust, 1675 and 1678', *BBCS* 9 (1937–9), p. 72.

attitude of High Tories towards the ideals of the Trust had cooled considerably. Following Gouge's death in the same year the Welsh Trust was wound up, a sad ending to a laudable, if flawed, enterprise.

Another feature of the age of benevolence was the campaign to raise moral standards by eliminating wickedness and vice. During the reign of William III the drive for a national reformation of manners gathered pace. Enforced by statute, encouraged by royalty, Parliament, magistrates, and the church, the campaign aimed to declare war on vice, improve manners, and encourage a moral revival. During the 1690s branches of the Society for the Reformation of Manners were established, with some success, in Caernarfonshire, Carmarthenshire, and Pembrokeshire. In 1701, Thomas Thomas of Carmarthen declared that 'drunkenness, swearing, profanation of the Lord's Day, etc. are generally suppressed, and the state of religion very much mended'.[64] Plans were also laid by the Society for the Propagation of the Gospel to export the Christian faith to the colonies and other parts of the world where the gospel was either unknown or inadequately preached. Many of these fruitful activities, however, were generally absorbed by the most successful voluntary society in the late Stuart period, the Society for the Promotion of Christian Knowledge.

The educational scheme launched under the auspices of the SPCK in March 1699 was heavily influenced by the pioneering work of the German pietists, Philip Jacob Spener and August Herman Francke. The aim of the founders was to rescue the Welsh peasantry from the clutches of Rome and the thraldom of ignorance, superstition, and magic. Education was to be the tool of conversion. Some critics, however, were dubious of the wisdom of educating the lower classes. Bernard Mandeville entertained fears that educating the poor would make them dissatisfied with their lot and invite social tumult. Far from being a means of social control, he argued, education might instil into the illiterate ideas above their station. But religious reformers in Wales welcomed the new scheme with open arms. John Jones, dean of Bangor, was convinced that the provision of charity schools and saving literature would help to reduce the 'reigning diseases'[65] in Wales—ignorance and poverty. Indeed, it was widely prophesied that the knowledge and virtue generated by the schools would 'produce a plentiful harvest in the next age'.[66]

In rapid succession, charity schools were established throughout Wales in private houses, parish churches, and vestries, where poor children were instructed in the basic skills of reading, writing, and casting accounts. In some schools, older pupils who had acquired the basic skills of literacy were instructed in more practical subjects, such as farming, seamanship, knitting, weaving, and spinning. By focusing on the Bible, the Prayer

---

[64] *Correspondence and Minutes of the S.P.C.K.*, p. 11.
[65] Ibid., p. 2.   [66] M. G. Jones, *The Charity School Movement*, p. 59.

Book, the church catechism, and devotional books, it was hoped to stiffen the Anglican faith and promote a moral regeneration. Schoolmasters were urged to combat profanity, sloth, and disobedience, and to plant within young children the virtues of obedience and common decency. The Catholic threat also loomed large in the minds of founders: thus, charity schools were designed to be not only nurseries of piety, but also 'little garrisons against popery'.[67] Even the underprivileged child had a role to play in the remorseless campaign against the common enemy.

Impoverished curates, tempted by the prospect of adding five or ten pounds to their miserable stipends, were only too happy to act as schoolmasters. Some of them were unusually talented men, notably the fervent young preacher, Griffith Jones, at Laugharne, the assiduous grammarian, William Gambold, at Puncheston, and the gifted translator, Lewis Evans, at Carmarthen. Few schoolmasters were able to rest on their oars, for their daily round of schooling was time-consuming and arduous. Schools were open from seven until eleven in the morning and from one until five in the afternoons during the months of summer. In winter, lessons began an hour later and ended an hour earlier. Schools were chiefly dependent on the largess of local baronets, gentlemen, and clergymen. Sometimes, funds were available from private endowments or parental contributions. The most outstanding philanthropist in early eighteenth century Wales was Sir John Philipps of Picton Castle, Pembrokeshire. Wherever and whenever philanthropy was required, Sir John Philipps's paternal hand was in evidence. He was the great driving force behind the successes of the SPCK in south Wales. A man of truly evangelical piety and unflagging zeal, Sir John took an active interest in charitable work both at home and abroad. He was a leading light in all the major philanthropic and spiritual movements of his day, he befriended the early Methodists, and carved an opening for Griffith Jones by offering him the rectorship of Llanddowror in 1716 and the hand of his sister, Margaret, in marriage. Sir John cherished a genuine sympathy and affection for the poor and used his considerable wealth to feed, clothe, and educate poor children in south-west Wales. He established twenty-two schools in his native county and several others in Carmarthenshire. He also gently persuaded affluent ladies, who were blessed with an abundance of leisure time, to co-operate in his philanthropic ventures by knitting or sewing caps, handkerchiefs, aprons, shifts, and skirts for poor pupils in his charity schools. John Vaughan of Derllys Court, Carmarthenshire, father of Madam Bridget Bevan, was also a liberal patron who plied the SPCK headquarters in London with fertile and adventurous schemes. Vaughan was anxious to promote a scheme of local taxation to fund charity schools. Moreover, he

[67] Ibid., p. 14.

pioneered the notion of setting up free libraries and children's libraries. Sir John Philipps also launched a campaign to set up a training college for teachers, whilst Thomas Price of Merthyr successfully persuaded the Society of the merits of distributing godly books among prisoners in the county gaols of Wales.

In the initial stages the schools prospered. By 1715, sixty-eight schools had been established, thirty of them in towns and villages where Thomas Gouge's schools had been located in the 1670s. However, the coming of the Hanoverians ushered in a period of alarming decline. The Schism Act of 1714 generated such bitter controversies that Dissenters promptly withdrew their support; patronage was also lost because the schools were believed to be seminaries of Jacobitism. Since the SPCK had neither the resources nor the stomach to embark on a bitter sectarian campaign, it devoted its energies mainly to the task of publishing Welsh literature. Only twenty-eight new schools were opened between 1715 and 1727. Of the ninety-six charity schools established by the SPCK, fifty-eight were set up in the diocese of St Davids, including thirty-one in Pembrokeshire and fourteen in Carmarthenshire. Only fourteen charity schools were established in north Wales. The political storms which accompanied the arrival of George I did nothing but harm to the SPCK. The work languished as the number of subscribers fell away and other privately endowed schools emerged. In a passionate and often emotional sermon preached before members of the Society of Antient Britons in London in 1717, Moses Williams, the SPCK's most indefatigable agent, pleaded with prosperous London Welshmen to solve the social and economic problems of Wales by building charity schools, universities, almshouses, and hospitals for the benefit of his underprivileged countrymen. His pleas went unheeded and by the late 1720s the SPCK was a spent force in Wales.

The charity schools clearly prospered best in the anglicized market towns of Wales. Most pupils who acquired their schooling under the auspices of the SPCK were the sons and daughters of relatively prosperous merchants, traders, and craftsmen. These were families who could afford to send their children to day-schools and who were more likely than most to consider literacy a social necessity. Many tenant farmers and small labourers, traditionally indifferent to education, were averse to releasing their children from daily chores. They argued, with some justice, that charity schools diverted children from more gainful and necessary duties at home. To humble folk, education for their children was neither necessary nor desirable. The poverty of the Welsh countryside and the pressing need for infant labour in the domestic economy meant that penurious parents were reluctant to invest in education. Poor children were often required to perform menial tasks such as herding sheep and cattle, scaring crows, and picking stones. Others, notably in rural Caernarfonshire, were sent from door to door to beg for victuals. An even more crucial drawback to the success of the charity schools was the adoption of the English language as the medium of instruction. The society made no secret of its contempt for the Celtic languages and refused to be swayed from its objective of rearing a new generation of English-speakers. Such a myopic and fruitless policy often roused the wrath of benefactors and schoolmasters alike. In parts of south Wales, monoglot Welsh children were forced to learn their catechism by rote. Sir John Philipps was mortified to find children in his locality who could recite the catechism perfectly but had simply mastered the sounds and echoes of words rather than their actual meaning. In many schools in north Wales, clergymen and schoolmasters cocked a snook at the follies of their distant rulers by teaching their pupils through the medium of their native tongue. John Morgan, a native of Merioneth and vicar of Matching in Essex, revealed the absurdity of the SPCK's language policy by pointing out that monoglot Welsh children were 'as wise after five or six years' schooling as they were before'.[68]

Even so, the SPCK schools helped to broaden social and educational opportunities for young children and to stimulate the growth of literacy. Their contribution was bolstered by private endowments and educational charities. John Jones, dean of Bangor, established a dozen Welsh schools at his own expense and provided for their continuance in his will. In 1719 John Davies of Neath bequeathed £200 to the minister, churchwardens, and overseers of his parish to educate twenty poor children. Sir Humphrey Mackworth, Wales's leading industrial entrepreneur, sponsored works schools at Esgair-hir and Neath for the benefit of miners and labourers employed by the Company of Mine Adventurers. An annual grant of £40 from the Company enabled poor children to acquire the basic skills of literacy. There were also many local reading schools, kept by impoverished curates or poor widows, who used alphabets and syllable tables in primers and hornbooks in order to provide the poorer sorts with a rudimentary schooling. There was clearly a widespread thirst for education in some communities. Archdeacon Edward Tenison estimated in 1710 that 760 of the poorer sort were capable of reading in twenty-nine parishes in the archdeaconry of Carmarthen. Erasmus Saunders saluted those shepherds and peasants who held informal reading schools in their homes. In 1699, thirty-eight parishioners (some of them illiterate) of Cwm-du in the Teifi valley petitioned the bishop of St Davids, imploring him to grant a licence to one Edward Williams to enable him to teach the three 'Rs' and the principles of the Christian religion to their children. Although the educational curriculum in these petty schools was seldom ambitious, their very presence provided a valuable stimulus to the growth of literacy. In

[68] NLW MS 17B, pp. 12–13.

1714, William Lewis, curate of Margam, declared that there was scarcely a parish in Glamorgan 'where there is not a private school for teaching children to read'.[69] A much wider range of educational facilities existed in Wales than ever before and the overwhelming impression is that standards of literacy were improving.

This period also witnessed the first intensive campaign to disseminate the cardinal doctrines of the Protestant Reformation by means of printed books in Welsh. Years of experience of preaching the gospel to sleepy and unresponsive congregations had convinced many religious reformers that the eye was a more faithful guide than the ear. Unless people were provided with printed books, they argued, sermons would have but a fleeting influence. Books could provide worshippers with a basic grounding in Christian truths and a deeper awareness of their religious obligations. By making the household a focal point of religious inculcation, readers could be persuaded to pore over printed books in their native tongue and meditate upon their contents. The number of printed books in Welsh multiplied dramatically during this period. At least 545 Welsh books were published between 1660 and 1730, i.e. over five times as many as had been published between the printing of the first Welsh book in 1546 and the accession of Charles II. In a sense, Wales moved from an oral culture to a print culture in this period. The initial thrust was provided by the philanthropic work of the Welsh Trust, and especially the ceaseless toil of Stephen Hughes. The passing of the Toleration Act in 1689 was also a turning-point since it encouraged Dissenters to popularize their faith in print. More crucial still were the abolition of censorship with the lapsing of the Licensing Act in 1695, the formation of the SPCK in 1699, and the emergence of the first printing-presses on Welsh soil, at Trerhedyn in 1718 and at Carmarthen in 1721. The pressing demand for saving literature meant that many books were translations of English best sellers. Churchmen and Dissenters alike were chiefly concerned with eliminating ignorance by instilling the basic tenets of Protestantism, achieving a deeper respect for the moral laws of Christianity, and encouraging a greater degree of piety and a more immediate, subjective commitment towards religion. Much of the literature was aimed at the family unit, for private worship and prayers were judged to be as important as public worship. Moreover, cultivating the tender minds of young children was a fundamental priority. 'Babes must be fed with milk'[70] was a favourite aphorism among Welsh authors in this period.

The task of creating a literate, bible-reading society was made easier by the publication of six major editions of the Bible—a total of 40,000

---

[69] *Correspondence and Minutes of the S.P.C.K.*, p. 63.
[70] NLW MS 11440D, f. 149.

copies—in this period, many of which were distributed cheaply or freely among the deserving poor. After Thomas Gouge and Stephen Hughes had stumped the countryside in search of subscriptions, an edition of 8,000 copies of the Bible, sold at 4s. 2d. each, was published in 1678. Financial support for this venture was forthcoming from 'men of quality' in London, as indeed it was for an even bulkier edition of 10,000 copies in 1689–90. The organizing genius and unremitting toil of Moses Williams, vicar of Defynnog, were largely responsible for the publication, under the auspices of the SPCK, of sizeable editions of the Welsh Bible in 1718 and 1727. Sold at 4s. each, they were eagerly welcomed by bible-starved readers. Copies were distributed gratuitously among the poor and, according to Griffith Jones, Llanddowror, poor tenants were thereby encouraged 'to learn to read that before could not, and in some respect to reform'.[71] Many people went to some pains to secure copies of the Welsh Bible and the number of individuals who mentioned their personal copy in their wills suggests that it was viewed as a precious and sacred possession. Bibles were richly prized by farmers, craftsmen, and even humble labourers, and the contents of the scriptures were clearly becoming an intrinsic part of their daily vocabulary. Many young people acquired the basic skills of literacy by learning words from the Bible or by listening to verses read aloud to them by the head of the household. For the first time in the history of Wales, Welsh bibles were in the hands of laymen in large numbers. Like Howel Harris, humble Welshmen developed 'a very great love to the bible as God's Word'.[72]

Cheap octavo editions of the Welsh Prayer Book and thousands of catechisms and primers were also published in order to foster an understanding of the rudiments of the Christian faith within charity schools and the household unit. Although riddled with printing errors, pocket-sized prayer books, published largely at Shrewsbury, were cheap and popular. More and more stress was laid upon the need for private devotion and regular attendance at Holy Communion. 'Sums of divinity' or expositions of the church catechism were published in their thousands in order to further popular understanding of the basic principles of the Christian religion and to guide young children along the path of literacy. Most catechisms and primers were aimed at 'babes in Christ' and sought simply to instil the rudiments of Christianity. Many religious reformers were acutely aware that their hearers were unable to digest sermons properly because they were inadequately versed in first principles. In preparing material for the 'uneducated peasantry', authors took pains to present Christian knowledge in a style and manner which were intelligible and attractive. In 1700, David Maurice confessed that there were 'more sparrows than eagles, more bruised reeds than cedars, and more babes in

[71] Correspondence and Minutes of the S.P.C.K., p. 103.
[72] T. Beynon, Howell Harris's Visits, p. 5.

Christ than strong, well-grown Christians in God's family'.[73] Eschewing doctrinal niceties and abstruse controversies, authors focused on the fundamentals of religion as they strove to establish a sound catechetical base, especially among children and young people. Special stress was laid on the need to plant the Christian faith early. Solomon's wisdom rang down the decades: 'Train up a child in the way he should go, and when he is old he will not depart from it'.

Books, too, were used in the national war against wickedness and profanity. A steady flow of moralizing literature inveighed against the 'popular' sins of rural Wales, notably drunkenness, swearing and cursing, and Sabbath-breaking. Churchmen and Dissenters alike sought to enforce the conception of a biblical Sabbath and to implant the duty of restraint and moderation in the minds of their flocks. Authors emphasized the duties implicit in the fourth commandment, calling on readers to respect the Lord's day as a day of spiritual harvest. Insobriety was judged to be the mother of sin, a wasteful, ruinous habit which could reduce whole families to misery and want. Similarly, vain swearing and cursing were horrid practices 'fatal to the souls of men'.[74] Reformers preached the virtues of moderation, frugality, thrift, and sobriety, not only in order to eliminate wickedness but also to guard against social tumult and disorder. The Puritan moral code also reminded men that the wicked never went unpunished. Graphic examples of God's judgement on unrepentant sinners were chronicled in James Owen's *Trugaredd a Barn* (Mercy and Judgement, 1687), a work which left many of its readers with chronic insomnia. Similarly, Ellis Wynne's celebrated *Gweledigaetheu y Bardd Cwsc* (Visions of the Sleeping Bard, 1703), with its tormenting visions of hell, sent shivers of apprehension down the spine of readers. Lurid focus on the 'four last things'—death, judgement, heaven, and hell—was a deliberate ploy in the campaign to deter people from sin. A spectacular event like the great storm which swept across Wales in November 1703 prompted Samuel Williams, vicar of Llandyfrïog, to translate *Time and the End of Time* into Welsh in order to remind sinners of the eternal torments of the yawning, bottomless pit. When south-west Wales was stricken by an attack of typhus, fever, and smallpox between 1726 and 1729, Jenkin Jones seized his opportunity to focus on the harrowing fate which awaited the reprobate in his *Dydd y Farn Fawr* (Day of the Last Judgement, 1727). Thomas Richards of Llanfyllin also viewed the epidemic as a function of the wrath of the Almighty, and 4,000 copies of his translation of *Advice to Persons Recovered from Sickness* were distributed in 1730 to sick people who had experienced both the goodness and the severity of God. Authors never shied away from warning sinners of the fragility of man's existence

---

[73] David Maurice, *The Bruised Reed* (Oxford, 1700), p. 26.
[74] William Fleetwood, *A Sermon upon Swearing* (London, 1721), sig. A2ʳ.

and the physical torments of hell. Like preachers from medieval times to the early Methodists, they were convinced that the notion of an eternal hell served to deter people from sin.

The overwhelming majority of Welsh books published in this period consisted of practical works of piety couched in plain, intelligible language. Welsh translations of popular English devotional tracts, notably Bayly's *Practise of Piety*, Allestree's *Whole Duty of Man*, and Rawlet's *Christian Monitor*, nourished the devotions of a wide cross-section of society. Popular manuals such as these stressed the crucial importance of individual, private worship, outlined the right way of living and preached the virtues of a holy, pious life. Book subscription lists clearly reveal that these books were warmly received by yeoman-farmers and husbandmen, who used them as 'home-helps' to godly living. Thousands of copies of smaller devotional books and primers were also widely sold among humble folk with slender purses and a limited number of leisure hours. Books which provided compact family units, mainly in rural areas, with guides to prayer and devotion were avidly read in farmhouses. Humble yeoman-farmers and craftsmen formed a sizeable portion of the 689 subscribers to *Trefn Ymarweddiad Gwir Gristion* (The Order of Living of the True Christian, 1723–4) and the 352 subscribers to *Defosiwnau Priod* (Appropriate Devotions, 1720). This kind of literature proved remarkably successful in promoting piety and devotion within the domestic circle.

A growing corpus of literature was also available for men and women who wrestled to attain salvation. Many awakening tracts called on readers to deplore the flaccid piety of the 'almost Christian' and the hypocrisy of the bible-carrying bigot. Works such as *Galwad i'r Annychweledig* (A Call to the Unconverted, 1677), *Cyfoeth i'r Cymru* (Wealth to the Welsh, 1688), and *Dwys Ddifrifol Gyngor* (A Serious Exhortation, 1713) offered the view—echoed later by many Methodists—that a heart full of grace was a greater asset to an individual than a head full of knowledge. Readers were constantly urged to embark on a programme of exhaustive inward scrutiny in order to explore the recesses of the soul, to become aware of the perils of sin, and the overwhelming need for repentance, faith, and regeneration. In calling for an unrelenting dissection of the soul, authors emphasized the value of a subjective personal experience in spiritual matters. Welshmen developed a special taste for Bunyan's stress on justifying faith. *Pilgrim's Progress* was published in a Welsh garb in 1688, 1699, 1713, and 1722, and many more times during the eighteenth century. Anglicans and Dissenters alike professed a warm admiration for Bunyan's works and many of them made a point of recording their debt to him. Iaco ab Dewi's translation of *Come and Welcome to Jesus Christ* in 1719 was a strikingly influential work which, by all accounts, drew many men from darkness into light. Edmund Jones of Pontypool confessed that many others besides himself had good cause 'to bless God that such a book was wrote'. Howel Harris found it an 'extraordinary book', while David Jones of Llanlluan testified that while reading a copy of the book in a field, 'God Almighty pleased to show me a great light . . . and the voice was, I am willing to receive thee, come to me'.[75] This type of literature of inward experience, with its emphasis on the awareness of sin, the cleansing powers of grace, and justification by faith alone, was afforded a prominent position on the godly Welshman's 'five-foot shelf' of religious treatises. In a period when godly, literate people reflected deeply upon the written word, saving literature of this kind helped to prepare them for the Methodist message. Many features of early Welsh Methodism—the emphasis on subjective, inward religion, the preoccupation with self-scrutiny and personal piety, and a strongly developed sense of evangelical fervour—were to be found in these awakening tracts. Not only did they, in Edmund Jones's words, 'do good to many souls in Wales',[76] but they also enabled many to identify themselves with the desires and longings of the Methodist leaders.

Like the Methodists, too, religious reformers in this period were acutely aware of the mnemonic merits of rhythm and rhyme. Religious verse served an invaluable function in communicating the doctrines of the Christian faith to those underprivileged people who derived more benefit from learning edifying verses than from listening to tedious homilies. In particular, carols and godly poems, drenched in scriptural allusions and moral imperatives, supplied spiritual guidance and consolation to humble folk. However, the most effective and popular publication of this period was Rees Prichard's *Canwyll y Cymry* (The Welshmen's Candle), a collection of catchy, homespun popular verses which contained the sum and substance of Christian faith and morality. Fourteen editions of 'the Vicar's Book' were published between 1658 and 1730. It proved a vital weapon in the campaign for godly reformation, for the old moralist of Llandovery had striven earnestly in his poems to show readers how to wage war on the world, the flesh, and the devil. In rough and ready verses, he preached the merits of public and private worship, spelt out the implications of sin and the frailty of life, and nurtured a greater awareness of individual responsibility in spiritual matters. It is no exaggeration to say that *Canwyll y Cymry* became the common Welshman's song-book of the Reformation. Contemporaries were impressed by its influence on the growth of literacy and religious awareness. Stephen Hughes believed that 'the Vicar's Book' had fortified the reforming cause by persuading readers to worship more frequently and to cherish their bibles. Many people read and reread Vicar Prichard's homely, rugged rhymes and learned to repeat

[75] G. H. Jenkins, *Literature, Religion and Society*, pp. 130–1.
[76] Edmund Jones, *A Sermon Preached . . . Occasioned by the Death of Mr. Evan Williams* (London, 1750), p. 82.

large portions of them by heart. Robert Nelson was astonished to find that even illiterate folk were able to recite verses as proof of their faith and scriptural knowledge. Before the publication of the hymns of Williams Pantycelyn, Rees Prichard's popular rhymes were closer to the Welshman's heart than any other manual of religious verse. His influence on the growth of scriptural knowledge and spiritual awareness in this period is incalculable.

Most of these books were much cheaper and far more widely accessible than ever before. This was partly because charitable bodies like the Welsh Trust and the SPCK published sizeable editions at cheap rates and distributed many of them free of charge to the deserving poor. But the most influential factor was the relaxation of the licensing laws in 1695. This offered enterprising printers and publishers a long-awaited opportunity to forsake the capital and establish printing-presses in the provinces. First off the starting-blocks was Thomas Jones, a Corwen-born almanacker, whose commercial instincts led him to set up a pioneering Welsh printing house in Shrewsbury, the natural capital of mid-Wales. By publishing a wide range of pious literature and more popular reading matter, 'the Sweating Astrologer'[77] (as he was called) made Shrewsbury the headquarters of the printing trade for Wales. Since the vale of Teifi was highly regarded for the vigour of its spiritual life and the richness of its literary tradition, it is not surprising that the first official printing-press on Welsh soil was established by Isaac Carter at Trerhedyn or Atpar in south Cardiganshire in 1718. Hard on its heels came another press, set up in Carmarthen by Nicholas Thomas in 1721. These printers and publishers were highly adept at catering for, and fulfilling the desires of, the Welsh reading public. Most of them adopted the subscription method of publishing books. This was a practice whereby the printer or his agent collected half the cost of a book from each subscriber beforehand and the other half on handing over a copy of the printed work. This enabled publishers to produce bulky editions ranging from 500 to 5,000 copies at prices which were within the means of all save the most deprived orders of society. Books were sold by mercers, grocers, and ironmongers in market towns, and by pedlars and chapmen in fairs and markets. Churchmen and Dissenters alike acted as local agents for publishers, distributing copies among their flocks and lending literature to the literate poor. Parcels of books were sent from London by land and sea to a network of agents in each Welsh county. Under the auspices of the SPCK, lending libraries were established at Bangor, St Asaph, Carmarthen, and Cowbridge between 1708 and 1711, where book-starved clergymen and schoolmasters were able to browse and borrow religious literature. These facilities were further augmented by a series of parochial libraries which were delegated to the care of the incumbent of the parish.

[77] Geraint H. Jenkins, 'The Sweating Astrologer': Thomas Jones the Almanacer' in R. R. Davies and others (eds.), *Welsh Society and Nationhood* (Cardiff, 1984), pp. 161–77.

Literacy rates varied according to the economic circumstances of individuals and their personal aspirations. Not unexpectedly, illiteracy was highest among labourers, cottagers, and paupers. The gentry and clergy were, of course, literate in the sense of being able to read and write. The same was true of the emerging professional classes, for there was clearly a significant difference in literacy rates between the occupants of market towns and remote highland communities. But one of the most significant features of this period was the growing appetite of middling sorts, notably yeoman-farmers, craftsmen, and artisans, for pious literature. As in many parts of Europe, standards of literacy were rising swiftly among men of independent means. There was a growing demand for edifying reading material among farmers and craftsmen whose economic independence enabled them to share the spiritual and cultural interests of educated classes. The parish of Cellan in Cardiganshire was reported in the 1690s to have smiths, joiners, bookbinders, glovers, weavers, tuckers, harp-makers, and shoemakers, all of whom were perceptive and literate men and able to give a 'very good account of their faith'.[78] The middling sorts among Dissenters in rural Carmarthenshire were reputedly so well-read that Methodist evangelists hesitated before crossing swords with them over doctrinal issues. As we have seen, yeoman-farmers prized pious books, subscribed to them regularly, and ensured that their sons and daughters availed themselves of the growing range of educational facilities. Early Methodism was to feed avidly on the support of these enterprising and pious farmers and craftsmen.

Reading was also, of course, an oral activity. Prior to the growth of compulsory education and mass literacy, people were blessed with excellent memories and learned simply by listening to others reading aloud. Printed books brought the literate and illiterate together in informal reading groups within the domestic circle. During the 1680s the youths of Llanfihangel Tre'r Beirdd in Anglesey used to flock to the home of the only literate parishioner, Siôn Edward, a cooper, in order to learn to read books published by Thomas Jones the almanacker. The father of the celebrated Morris brothers of Anglesey was one of these precocious youths and William Morris later speculated to his brother Richard: 'who knows but that you and I would be illiterate were it not for that old fellow of Clorach who taught our father . . . and so started the blessed gift'.[79] Within the family household, the paterfamilias was expected to read aloud from the Scriptures and from devotional books for the benefit of illiterate members. Both Stephen Hughes and Erasmus Saunders were impressed by the eagerness of shepherds and servants to imbibe religious knowledge by instructing one another in their homes.

---

[78] 'Parochialia', *Arch. Camb.* (1909-11), 3, p. 68.   [79] *Morris Letters*, i. 198.

In Welsh historiography, the period from the Restoration to Methodism has long lain under a dark shadow of reproach. In Erasmus Saunders's view, the church in Wales was so riven with weaknesses and abuses that the cardinal doctrines of the Reformation were unable to take root. Methodists, too, believed that this was an age of spiritual torpor when Wales lay in 'some dark and deadly sleep'.[80] But it would be a mistake to take Saunders's lamentations and the Methodist calumnies at face value. As we have seen, there were seminal forces at work in this period which helped to nourish the religious, educational, and cultural revivals of the eighteenth century. Genuine improvements had been carried out and Wales was far more thoroughly protestantized in 1730 than it was in 1630.

Given the evils of non-residence, pluralism, and nepotism, it is to the credit of the established church and its servants that so much was achieved. Most bishops, at least until the Hanoverian period, were deeply concerned with the well-being of the Anglican church and strove to protect its interests by purging their dioceses of abuses. Many of them were men of true learning who prided themselves on their ability to provide genuine spiritual leadership. Although poverty often prevented many clergymen from exercising effective pastoral oversight, others among them had admirable qualities. It is true that some of them were idle or dissolute, but the mass of the parish clergy were decent, conscientious men who endeavoured to fulfil their onerous duties to the best of their ability. Church sermons were not only extraordinarily popular but also more frequent in number by the eve of the Methodist revival. Moreover, the spiritual thirst of common people was clearly evident, with many commentators endorsing Gerald of Wales's verdict in an earlier age regarding the Welshman's desire for spiritual edification. Dissent, too, was a highly influential leaven in the lump. Although Catholicism and Quakerism had been reduced to pale shadows of their former selves, Dissent in general had not lost momentum. Following the Toleration Act, Dissenting ministers were given their head and began to make modest inroads in those communities where standards of clerical discipline were slack. Far from disintegrating into impotent factional strife, Dissent in Wales, especially in the south, was a significant force. Early Methodists would depend heavily on the knowledge, connections, and vitality of Dissenting ministers. Again, striking advances had been made in the provision of educational facilities, the number of printed books available, and the growth of literacy in general. By the 1730s a much wider range of elementary schooling and edifying literature was available than ever before. The fundamental doctrines of the Protestant Reformation were far more deeply understood and appreciated, notably by those farmers and craftsmen who had acquired a degree of economic

[80] Gomer M. Roberts (ed.), *Hanes Methodistiaeth Galfinaidd Cymru, cyfrol 1, Y Deffroad Mawr* (Caernarfon, 1973), p. 71.

independence and could read. The mass of printed books in Welsh had helped to awaken within them an awareness of the evils of sin and the joys and terrors of eternity. The need for individual accountability and inward scrutiny was more widely accepted, whilst both individual and collective piety were encouraged.

Both Anglican and Dissenting ministers were convinced that they lived in privileged times. In the preface to his translation of Hugo Grotius's *De Veritate Religionis Christianae* in 1716, Edward Samuel, vicar of Betws Gwerful Goch, spoke enthusiastically of the many gains which had been achieved: 'To God be the thanks that the light of the gospel now shines as brightly in Wales as in almost any other country; there are more edifying, godly books more frequently printed, and undoubtedly better preachers among us than existed in any age for more than a thousand years'.[81] Two years later, Simon Thomas, a Presbyterian minister, enthused by quoting Ovid: *Ego me nunc denique natum/Gratulor.*[82] Neither of them, nor indeed the overwhelming majority of their colleagues, would have subscribed to the view that pre-Methodist Wales languished in a Slough of Despond. On the contrary, they considered themselves fortunate to be alive in that dawn. There is no doubt that early Welsh Methodism would never have flourished as it did had not growing numbers of literate men and women been intensively prepared to respond favourably to the soul-stirring message of its leaders. John Wesley was right: Wales was 'ripe for the Gospel'.[83]

[81] Edward Samuel, *Gwirionedd y Grefydd Grist'nogol* (Shrewsbury, 1716), p. 5.
[82] Simon Thomas, *Hanes y Byd a'r Amseroedd* (Shrewsbury, 1718), sig. A2ʳ.
[83] A. H. Williams (ed.), *John Wesley in Wales 1739–1790* (Cardiff, 1971), p. 5.

CHAPTER 6

CULTURAL AND INTELLECTUAL LIFE

THROUGHOUT this period there were many intelligent Englishmen who believed that the Welsh were a rude, uncouth, and dishonest people. In refined English circles, the archetypal Welshman was seen as a rustic, slightly quaint figure, with a hook on his shoulder, a leek in his hat, and a piece of cheese on the point of his knife. In his mock-heroic poem, *Muscipula* (1712), Edward Holdsworth held up Taffy, the inventor of the mousetrap, to ridicule. Welshmen were thought of as emotional, excitable people whose taste for toasted cheese and metheglin was matched only by their devotion to their tedious native patois and their even more tedious pedigrees. To an irreverent scribbler like Ned Ward, Wales was a squalid land where peasants spoke an inarticulate, guttural language which sounded 'more like the gobbling of geese or turkeys than the speech of rational creatures'.[1] Some argued that the extirpation of the Welsh language would be a service to the civilized world. William Richards nursed hopes of seeing the old British tongue 'English'd out of Wales, as Latin was barbarously Goth'd out of Italy'.[2] Charitable men were convinced that English was the language of economic opportunity and advancement. Philip Bisse, whose tenure as bishop of St Davids was mercifully brief, offered the view that supporting the Welsh language was a misguided exercise which would serve only 'to obstruct the English tongue'.[3]

Conversely, Welshmen nursed ambivalent views regarding their assimilation with the English. Welsh poets had clearly not forgotten the centuries of spoliation, neglect, and contempt which had blighted the lives of their forefathers. Well-versed in the disastrous episodes of their past, notably the Treason of the Long Knives and the Edwardian Conquest, Welsh bards were reluctant to abandon their ancestral hatred of the Saxons. Successful Welshmen, however, were less concerned with the rights or wrongs of the past. To progressive landlords, entrepreneurs, merchants, and even religious reformers, belief in the merits of political assimilation with England was a *sine qua non*. In their eyes, the Union of 1536–43 was 'a remarkable deliverance': far from engendering strife and resentment, it had brought Wales unmixed blessings. Charles Edwards, who never veered

---

[1] Ned Ward, *A Trip to North-Wales*, p. 3.
[2] William Richards, *Wallography*, p. 124.
[3] *Correspondence and Minutes of the S.P.C.K.*, p. 42.

from the view that God was the driving force of history, believed that the Lord had planned the marriage between England and Wales just as he had watched over Israel in the days of Ahasverus and Esther. Old antagonists had now become allies, English wolves had become shepherds. His fellow Dissenter, Jeremy Owen, claimed that recent Welsh–English relations offered a splendid paradigm of Samson's riddle: 'out of the eater came forth meat, and out of strong sweetness'. 'I must speak to you no more as a particular nation', declared Owen in a sermon preached to Welsh Protestant Dissenters in 1716, 'but as one and the same people and body politic, happily incorporated with the English.'[4] Although many Welshmen cherished a passionate nostalgia for the heroic, distant past, they no longer entertained dreams of recovering Welsh independence. Indeed, there was a strong tradition of loyalty to the English Crown.

More pressing was the need to maintain a distinctive cultural identity. Wales was a land of small towns and had the reputation of being economically backward and archaic in its attitudes. It possessed no institutions of statehood. Unlike Scotland, it could not boast its own independent legal system or a national church. Nor were there national foci such as a court, an academy, a university, or a major library to nourish indigenous cultural pursuits. These were grave handicaps at a time when more and more poets and scholars were beginning to appreciate that their native culture was on the run. One of the dominant themes in Welsh literature in the late Stuart period is the plight to which Welsh culture had been reduced. Men of letters feared that the Welsh language lacked status and prestige. In the eyes of the influential ruling classes it was a vulgar, unrefined patois. Many poets had seen noblemen, on whom they depended for patronage, abandon their heritage and ape the speech and habits of their English counterparts. Welsh translators, groping for appropriate words, confessed that their native language was as though enslaved. Pessimism was the leitmotiv of so much that was written by poets, scholars, and savants in this period: 'the Almighty', claimed Thomas Jones the almanacker, 'had almost blotted us out of the Books of Records.'[5]

During the second half of the seventeenth century, Welsh scholars and poets were acutely aware that several honourable literary traditions had either disintegrated or were visibly crumbling before their eyes. The glorious years of Renaissance scholarship had faded away. The professional poet and the *clerwr* (itinerant poet), starved of noble patronage, disappeared. The few remaining practitioners of the old ways, sunk in gloom, brooded miserably over these losses and blamed the ruling classes for failing to honour their obligations. But, as the old perished, a new generation of poets, authors, and scholars resolved to rebuild old traditions

---

[4] Jeremy Owen, *The Goodness and Severity*, pp. 16, 23.
[5] Thomas Jones, *The British Language in its Lustre* (London, 1688), sig. A3ʳ.

and invent new ones. Public tastes and sensibilities were changing, and two major elements helped to inject new life into the cultural life of Wales: the development of the provincial printing-press and the scholarly zeal of Edward Lhuyd, the versatile Oxford scholar.

'The printing-press', declared Lewis Morris, 'is the candle of the world, the freedom of Britain's sons.'[6] When the Printing Act of 1662 was allowed to lapse in 1695, a new era beckoned. Prior to 1695, printing had been confined to London and the two university towns. No one had been permitted to set up a printing-press elsewhere. Zealous publishers of Welsh books, such as Charles Edwards and Stephen Hughes, chafed miserably under such restrictions and had been obliged to spend weeks in London supervising the work of compositors, correcting proofs, and disseminating books. Communications with Wales were sluggish and arduous, and distributing Welsh books was often a source of despair to publishers. But after 1695 there was no looking back. The first Welshman to take advantage of the liberty of the press was Thomas Jones, a native of Tre'r-ddôl, near Corwen, in Merioneth. A self-taught tailor, Jones had settled in London during his youth. He saw little improvement in his fortunes and therefore turned to Welsh publishing as a means of livelihood. In 1680 he became Wales's first almanacker, and he briefly enjoyed the glamour of friendship with famous men, such as Tom Brown, Francis Moore (of *Old Moore's Almanac* fame), and Tom D'Urfey. Having been schooled in Grub Street circles, Jones found to his cost that most booksellers and agents were shameless cheats and liars. He became increasingly disenchanted with the seedy and devious world of printers, scribblers, and hacks, and yearned for the opportunity to return to the provinces. By the winter of 1695 Jones had abandoned the metropolis and had moved to the bustling provincial town of Shrewsbury. There he was to find success and fulfilment. Jones settled in Hill's Lane and embarked on a career of beaver-like toil. It was his restless energy and inventive mind which gained for Shrewsbury an unchallenged pre-eminence as the printing capital of early eighteenth-century Wales. Jones was a sharp administrator and publicist, with a keen eye for cost and detail as well as a shrewd appreciation of the needs of the reading public. As long as the financial risk was not too great, he was always prepared to experiment, and in the cut-throat world of printers, publishers, and pirates he showed an astonishing aptitude for survival. A fretful, acrimonious, but basically solitary man, he hungered for attention and the prefaces to his books and almanacs reveal all too clearly the jealousies, intrigues, and vendettas which pervaded his life. But Jones brought more than colour to the Welsh publishing trade.

[6] Lewis Morris, *Tlysau yr Hen Oesoedd* (Holyhead, 1735), p. 3.

Fired by ardent patriotism, he was determined to inject new life and vigour into 'the old and most excellent British language'[7] by providing humble readers with attractive and stimulating material. Literacy was increasing by leaps and bounds during this period, and there was clearly a popular demand for cheap literature.

Thomas Jones was animated by a genuine desire to instruct, edify, and amuse humble readers. His almanacs and ballads claimed a wide circulation among the lower classes and every effort was made to provide common people with attractive literary material at a price they could afford. In the absence of popular fiction in Welsh, almanacs and ballads offered exciting tit-bits of esoteric information, as well as poetry and literature. Jones ceaselessly searched for new material and devices in order to maintain the interest of his readers and to steal a march over his rivals. He never lost sight of the fact that literate or semi-literate farmers, craftsmen, and peasants were his most avid readers and, in spite of the malicious gibes of cultivated scholars, he made a valuable contribution to popular culture. He widened the range of popular culture among humble people who, but for him, would have been denied a taste of poetry and prose in print. No one did more than Thomas Jones in this period to ensure that literacy was no longer the preserve of the affluent and leisured classes. He devised an efficient system of book distribution, based on a network of booksellers, agents, and clergymen, which ensured that his publications were available in remote and thinly populated communities as well as in market towns. By modern standards, of course, the circulation was modest, but there is no doubt that Thomas Jones spread the reading habit simply by adapting his material to popular tastes. His life must be accounted one of the success stories of late Stuart Wales.

During and after Thomas Jones's day, several flourishing and durable printing enterprises were established in Shrewsbury. John Rogers, an inveterate pirate, set up a press in 1707 and Thomas Durston, printer and bookseller in Shoemaker's Row, succeeded Thomas Jones in 1715. Jones's true successor, however, was John Rhydderch, a native of Cemaes in Montgomeryshire. Rhydderch was a versatile printer, poet, grammarian, and almanacker who battled heroically against personal penury and public apathy to ensure that Welsh poetry and literature were addressed to a more general audience. He was one of the moving spirits behind the resuscitated Welsh *eisteddfod* in this period, and few publishers were as aware as he of the printed word's ability to revive ailing traditions. These early Welsh printers were scarcely sophisticated craftsmen. The presentation and binding of their books left much to be desired and it is not surprising that cultivated scholars gave their presses a wide berth. William Morris

---

[7] Thomas Jones, *Almanac am y Flwyddyn 1681* (London, 1681), sig. A2ʳ.

found their workmanship intolerable: 'bad paper, bad print, bad orthography, bad everything, except the subject matter'.[8] To these printers, however, selling books at cheap rates to an expectant public was more important than producing lavishly bound works of art. The subscription method, moreover, eased the worries of Welsh publishers and enabled them to respond to popular tastes.

As Shrewsbury established its name as a printing centre, new ventures sprang up elsewhere, sponsored by practical men of enterprise who were keen to stimulate and satisfy the demands of the swelling ranks of the Welsh reading public. The demand for Welsh books was nowhere greater than in the Teifi valley, a progressive community where indigenous literary traditions stretched back over the centuries and where readers, especially clergymen, ministers, farmers, and craftsmen, devoured whatever Welsh books publishers could issue. The first printing-press on Welsh soil—other than the clandestine Catholic presses of the Tudor period—was established in 1718 by Isaac Carter at Trerhedyn (or Atpar) in the parish of Llandyfrïog. Carter printed five books at Trerhedyn before transferring his press to Carmarthen in 1725. Meanwhile, Nicholas Thomas, a native of Cenarth and one of John Rhydderch's printing apprentices, had already set up a flourishing press at Carmarthen in 1721. In spite of his antiquated typographical equipment, Thomas fared rather better than Carter and succeeded in publishing a crop of popular works. Carmarthen was an affluent provincial town of some 3,000 inhabitants, many of whom were enjoying rising material comforts. It prided itself on its economic role as the chief marketing centre for the vale of Tywi and also on its celebrated grammar school and Dissenting academy. It was the centre of gravity for middling sorts, who attached great importance to self-improvement, theological debate, and even heterodox religious belief. However resourceful and enterprising these early Welsh printers and publishers were, they were heavily dependent on the largess of local dignitaries. Since they possessed few friends in high places, their most enthusiastic supporters were lesser squires and scholarly clerics and ministers who were eager to satisfy the growing demand for books. The growth of the provincial press in Wales, therefore, not only enabled religious reformers to nurture the fundamental doctrines of Protestantism but also to revivify Welsh culture and foster the growth of literacy in general.

Whilst the Welsh press provided native culture with a new momentum, Edward Lhuyd, the Oxford scholar, was seeking to broaden the intellectual horizons of his countrymen. There is no doubt that Lhuyd was one of the great minds of the age. Although his short-term influence on Wales was not

[8] *Morris Letters*, i. 82.

profound, he sowed the seeds of ideological concepts which would grow
and blossom luxuriantly in the future. Born around 1660, Edward Lhuyd
was the illegitimate son of Bridget Pryse of Glanfrêd, Cardiganshire, and
Edward Lloyd of Llanforda, near Oswestry. His father was a quixotic,
profligate man who soon went bankrupt; and the formative influence on
the young Lhuyd was Edward Morgan, botanist and gardener at
Llanforda, who took him under his wing and trained him in scientific
method. When Lhuyd entered Jesus College, Oxford, in 1682, he was a
sensitive, bookish young man with a growing interest in the methodology
of the new experimental science. During that same year the Ashmolean
museum was opened, and Lhuyd was soon moving freely among enthusiastic
scholars and antiquarians whose interests included the study of ancient
remains and records. Within five years, Lhuyd had been appointed assistant
Keeper to Dr Robert Plot at the Ashmolean. He thus embarked on an
illustrious, but all-too-brief, career which earned him an international
reputation as a scientist and scholar. At the age of thirty-one, Lhuyd
succeeded Plot (whom he despised) as Keeper of the Ashmolean Museum
and he held this influential post until his death in 1709. 'You live at the
fountain', Hugh Thomas told him, 'from whence all the learning of our
land flows.'[9]

At Oxford Lhuyd became initimate with many leading English scholars
whose labours made the late Stuart period a golden age of English
historical scholarship. Men of the calibre of Dugdale, Gibson, Hearne,
Hickes, Tanner, and Wanley were noted for their intellectual vigour and
their deeply held regard for the past. But Lhuyd was never overawed by
these great names. Indeed, his own polymathic learning and critical spirit
soon commanded respectful attention in scholarly circles. He won
distinction in a wide range of disciplines and his expertise as a botanist,
chemist, archaeologist, philologist, historian, and antiquarian was an
inspiration to a host of clergymen, squires, yeomen, and craftsmen in his
native land. His encyclopaedic mind and infectious enthusiasm were a
source of wonder to his adoring disciples. Lhuyd was acutely interested in
the antiquity, geography, archaeology, natural features, language, and
culture of Wales, and it was his leadership and energy which kindled the
enthusiasm of Welsh antiquarians to study the past, visit sites, tombs, and
stone circles, and rescue priceless manuscripts. He was an outstanding
Celtic scholar who radiated new respect for the study of philology. His
Archaeologia Britannica (1707) ranks alongside Bentley's *Dissertation* and
Hickes's *Thesaurus* as one of the major achievements of the age in the
fields of philology and antiquity. Inspired by the highest ideals, Lhuyd
infused the study of languages and culture with renewed purpose and

vitality. In his versatility he was a truly Renaissance figure and his many-sided pursuits reveal that he was blessed with a wider breadth of vision than any other Welshman of his day. Lhuyd's desire to re-examine and revise ancient truths was boundless, and his research was marked by a healthy distrust of received wisdom, a rigorous attention to detail, and careful, sometimes agonizing, thought. His conclusions, though not always correct, were the product of meticulous study and deep meditation. His work opened up rich new seams in the world of Welsh scholarship.

These influences in the late Stuart period were especially timely since the Welsh language, at least in gentry circles, was not deemed to be appropriate for people with social pretensions. The gentry with the longest rent-rolls were invariably the first to be absorbed into English civilization, but the speed with which the Welsh language vanished from the lips of the ruling classes varied from county to county. The most prosperous and powerful gentry, who dwelt in economically developed counties like Glamorgan and Monmouth, were among the first to deride their native tongue, suppress their dialects, and imbibe 'plum' English accents. Many of them believed that the cultivation of the English language and polished manners was the mark of a true gentleman. Increasingly, the most anglicized Welsh gentry took a lively interest in the content of literary journals such as the *Tatler*, the *Spectator*, and *The Gentleman's Magazine*. English magazines, periodicals, and newspapers helped to create new tastes and to wean affluent gentlemen from their local culture and traditional loyalties. By abjuring the tongue of their fathers and forefathers, the landed classes widened the cultural breach between themselves and the rest of society. In their eyes, the Welsh language was an eminently dispensable patois, fit only for the kitchen and market-place. In parts of Glamorgan, 'Welsh' was a synonym in fashionable gentry parlours for drunken, ignorant, and superstitious. Children of gentry stock were sent to private schools in order to acquire a polished English accent and thus immure themselves from the 'clownish' speech of their inferiors. It became fashionable to abandon Welsh patronymics based on the particle *ap* (son of) in favour of the dull, monotonous English model, a shift which Thomas Jones of Oswestry deeply regretted, not least because witnesses who sported the old Welsh patronymics had often reduced many judges in the Courts of Great Sessions to a state of bewilderment. Ancient baptismal names passed out of circulation among the gentry, and only among the families of farmers and peasants were enchanting names such as Angharad, Cynwrig, Dyddgu, Ednyfed, Gwenhwyfar, Lleucu, and Llywarch preserved.

As a result, by the early eighteenth century, the language and culture of a small squire in the Welsh heartland were a world apart from those of an affluent Glamorgan gentleman. Not all the Welsh gentry, of course, welcomed the new metropolitan values. The lesser gentry of north and west Wales, sheltered against the winds of change in culture and fashion, remained fundamentally Welsh in their speech and outlook. Many of them revealed their concern for the plight of their native tongue by subscribing regularly to Welsh books. On the whole, however, the influence of the Welsh language and its culture on the ruling landed classes became weaker with each passing year in this period. The same trend was evident in other Celtic countries, as well as in many parts of Europe. In Ireland, for instance, the Irish language was no longer patronized by the older nobility and gentry and it was left to the masses to preserve the Gaelic culture. In Languedoc, the nobility and bourgeoisie adopted French, leaving craftsmen and peasants to speak Occitan. In Bohemia, German-speaking noblemen affected to despise Czech, which was spoken only by peasants.

It was becoming clear, too, that the English language was gaining ground in Wales. There had long been established Englishries, of course. Upland Gower, with its single farms and hamlets, was Welsh, whilst peninsular Gower, with its compact nucleated settlements dating from Norman times, was predominantly English. According to Isaac Hamon, one of Edward Lhuyd's correspondents, English was spoken throughout the whole of west Gower, Ilston, Pennard, Oystermouth, most of Bishopston, and part of Llanrhidian. Similarly, whereas the vale of Glamorgan had lost its Welshness during the seventeenth century, the Blaenau had retained its Welsh complexion. In Pembrokeshire there were two distinct linguistic heritages: the 'Welshry' of the north and 'Little England beyond Wales' in the south. More serious was the fact that the linguistic frontier was gradually moving west in mid-Wales in this period. The English language was clearly moving up the Severn to Welshpool and Newtown. John Catlyn, vicar of Kerry, complained to the SPCK that Welsh books would 'stick upon his hands',[10] since Welsh was held in low esteem in his locality. Dafydd Manuel of Trefeglwys, Montgomeryshire, referred to his locality as 'our ignorant parts, where Hengist and Horsa and Rowena have settled their affairs'.[11] In Radnorshire and north-east Breconshire, too, the Welsh language was slowly retreating westwards. In some border communities the ebb and flow of economic prosperity created artificial linguistic boundaries. In the wake of industrial developments in north-east Wales in the late seventeenth century, miners and colliers migrated from Welsh communities in west Denbighshire and from English communities in east Denbighshire and met on or near Offa's Dyke. Bilingual zones were constantly shifting, and Welsh enclaves were still to be found on the eastern side of Offa's Dyke.

It is easy, however, to exaggerate the degree of anglicization. The Welsh

[10] *Correspondence and Minutes of the S.P.C.K.*, p. 77.
[11] 'Parochialia', *Arch. Camb.* 3, p. 64.

language, as the everyday medium of communication for 90 per cent of the population, was not in jeopardy. It was much stronger than any other Celtic language at that time. In Scotland the drive to destroy the clan system was accompanied by the outlawing of the Gaelic language, and the Cornish language, too, was in a state of advanced decay and would die out as a spoken language in the early eighteenth century. In Wales, however, the native language was firmly entrenched: it was the prevailing language in the home, fair, market, church, and chapel. Welsh was strongest, as a living language spoken by monoglot people, in the rural counties of north and west Wales. In recounting his early education, Lewis Morris claimed that there were whole parishes in the mountainous regions of Wales 'where there is not a word of English spoken'.[12] Few of these inhabitants felt handicapped by their ignorance of the English tongue. The quality of spoken Welsh varied, of course, from place to place. In the absence of a metropolitan standard, a court, or some kind of national cultural centre, the proliferation of local dialects was inevitable. Contemporaries were acutely conscious of differences in vocabulary, syntax, dialect, and accent. Thomas Baddy of Denbigh was discomfited to find that visiting Dissenting ministers were 'differing much in their dialect from us',[13] while Lewis Morris was disdainful of the 'hodge-podge' spoken in Glamorgan. With tongue in cheek, Thomas Jones the almanacker once declared that a closer affinity existed between Hebrew and Welsh than between the Welsh of Gwynedd and the Welsh of south Wales.

Even though the Welsh language was not in any way imperilled in this period, it was evidently undergoing change. English words and idioms were not confined to the vocabulary of the gentry and the middling sorts. English was 'the genteel and fashionable tongue' and, as the years rolled by, more and more people became bilingual. As the proportion of monoglot Welsh-speakers declined, valuable Welsh words and figures of speech were abandoned, becoming, in Henry Rowlands's words, 'obsolete and useless'.[14] Many of Edward Lhuyd's correspondents confirmed that when words and phrases were abandoned by common people, they swiftly dropped out of memory. Traditional Welsh idioms were often impenetrable to newcomers: David Lewis of Llanboidy claimed that several old men in his parish used ancient Welsh words and idioms which were a mystery to the young. Stephen Hughes of Meidrim was acutely conscious of the fact that penetration by the English tongue had been a salient factor in the alarming deterioration of spoken and written Welsh in south Wales, and Alban Thomas, curate of Blaen-porth and Tre-main, prepared a lengthy

[12] *Add. Letters*, ii. p. 511.
[13] W. A. Evans, 'Thomas Baddy ac Ymddiriedolwyr Cronfa Dr. Daniel Williams', *Y Cofiadur* 27 (1959), p. 25.
[14] Henry Rowlands, *Mona Antiqua Restaurata* (Dublin, 1723), p. 38.

list of English words which had warped the language of the inhabitants of south-west Wales. In the preface to his English–Welsh dictionary in 1725, John Rhydderch revealed how the common Welshman's daily speech had become riddled with words such as *iwsio* (use), *mendio* (mend), *dangerus* (dangerous), and *repento* (repent). By the late Stuart period, too, more and more Welsh poets were borrowing words from the English language.

In the eyes of many Welshmen, therefore, the Welsh language lacked status and lustre. Many of the gentry and *nouveaux riches* affected to despise it. 'Why should we use or think in such a poor, anonymous tongue', they declared to Lewis Morris, 'English is the language of this kingdom.'[15] Pessimism was the hallmark of much of Edward Morris's poetry by the 1680s. He compared his mother tongue to a gentle peacock 'in grey hairs':

> Britain's bright tongue today despised
> Lies unrewarded and unprized;
> Men pass it by with scornful brow,
> And none will bring it succour now.[16]

The general fear was that the Welsh tongue was not attuned to the fashions and sensibilities of the modern age. Thomas Jones of Oswestry believed that its decay would be rapid unless the ruling classes, a prince, or even Parliament adopted it as an official, respectable language. Griffith Owens of Pwllheli echoed his plea, arguing that the Welsh language required nothing 'to make it famous save a king to speak it'.[17]

It was against this background that religious reformers and men of letters fought to ensure that Welsh would be the language of religion and education in Wales. Ever since Elizabethan days, Protestantism had taken root in Wales as a result of the special relationship, based on a common language, which had developed between clergymen and their parishioners. Even the infiltration of 'mercenary remote English clergymen'[18] had not, as yet, opened up fissures in the bonds which united common people to the church in Wales. There was a powerful and abiding connection between language and religion, and by ensuring that their countrymen had access to vernacular Scriptures, men such as Stephen Hughes, Charles Edwards, Moses Williams, and Griffith Jones not only reinforced the Protestant faith but also buoyed up the Welsh language. They also protected the interests of the Welsh language in educational circles. Stephen Hughes pointed out to the governors of the Welsh Trust the folly of instructing monoglot Welsh pupils through the medium of English. He understood better than most that the majority of his countrymen, subconsciously perhaps, revered their

[15] Hugh Owen, *The Life and Works of Lewis Morris*, p. 332.
[16] Thomas Parry, *A History of Welsh Literature*, tr. H. Idris Bell (Oxford, 1955), p. 221.
[17] UCNWL, Penrhos (VII) MS 933.
[18] Christ Church Library, Oxford. Arch. W. Epist. 22, item xxx, f. 42.

mother tongue because it was the language of their homeland and of their kin. 'If, over many ages', he claimed, '13,000 learned and conscientious Englishmen were to keep schools at the same time in the thirteen counties of Wales in order to teach English to our countrymen . . . it would still be impossible for the common people of our land to lose their mother tongue over the ensuing 500 years.'[19] John Morgan, vicar of Matching, shared Hughes's views, arguing that teaching through the medium of a foreign tongue would result in greater barbarism, ignorance, and irreligion. Thus, by encouraging the use of Welsh in schools and by making a mass of scriptural and devotional literature widely available, religious reformers helped to preserve the Welsh language.

Earnest efforts were also made to swell the pride of the Welshman in his native language. Nothing provoked Welsh patriots to greater wrath than attempts by the ruling classes to demean or stigmatize the Welsh language. Much was made of the belief, first mooted by Dr John Davies, Mallwyd, that the Welsh language was a sister language of Hebrew and that it had figured among the primitive languages of mankind in the period before the Tower of Babel. In a highly idiosyncratic pamphlet, *Hebraismorum Cambro-Britannicorum* (1675), Charles Edwards pointed to the phonetic parallels between Welsh and Hebrew, and reiterated his view in *Y Ffydd Ddi-ffvant* (The Unfeigned Faith) in 1677. Thomas Jones found the notion irresistible. In his popular dictionary, *Y Gymraeg yn ei Disgleirdeb* (The British Language in its Lustre, 1688), and in his eagerly thumbed almanacs, Jones thundered against ambitious gentlemen and middling sorts who aped their English counterparts and consigned their mother tongue to the dunghill. 'Can a man own God', he railed, 'and yet be ashamed of that language which God himself chose first? It would far better become the Welsh men to uphold and extol their own language than to cast it away through undervaluing of it.'[20] Since Welsh was a God-given language, declared Lewis Morris, it was a grievous sin for Welshmen to abandon their mother tongue and embrace 'the English concubine'.[21] Divine providence, it was argued by countless authors, had protected and preserved the Welsh language throughout the ages. God had vouchsafed His favours to the Welshman's native tongue: 'the rust of time', claimed Jeremy Owen, 'is not like to devour or wear it out.'[22] Such a view achieved particularly wide currency following the publication of Paul-Yves Pezron's *L'Antiquité de la nation et de la langue des celtes* (1703). Pezron, a cultured Breton monk, advanced the view that the Welsh were directly descended from Gomer, son of Japhet, son of Noah. This thesis conferred upon the

---

[19] *Gwaith Mr Rees Prichard*, sig. A3ᵛ.
[20] Thomas Jones, *Newydd oddiwrth y Seêr* (London, 1684), sig. A3ʳ.
[21] Hugh Owen, *Life . . . of Lewis Morris*, p. 339.
[22] Jeremy Owen, *The Goodness and Severity*, p. 8.

Welsh the most distinguished ancestry. Pezron traced the common origins of the Welsh and Breton peoples to the Celts, whose dominion in ancient times had extended from Gaul to Galatia. This notion ran counter to Edward Lhuyd's discoveries but it gained wide credence. Pezron's book was translated into English by David Jones in 1706 and subsequently found focus in a Welsh setting in Theophilus Evans's *Drych y Prif Oesoedd* (A Mirror of the First Ages, 1716). Evans and others were captivated by the romantic lucubrations of the 'learned Pezron',[23] and thus many Welshmen came to believe that they were the descendants of Noah's sons and that they spoke one of the original languages of mankind.

Less exciting and far less tendentious, however, were the sober comments of Edward Lhuyd. Of all the rich seams which Lhuyd opened up, none was more vital than his contribution to Welsh philology. By Lhuyd's day, the study of philology was in vogue. Studies in Anglo-Saxon etymology had made notably rapid advances. In 1705, George Hickes's massive three-volume *opus*, *Thesaurus of the Northern Tongues*, was published, and Mabillon and Montfaucon were engaged in similar work in France. But Lhuyd's expertise lay in the field of Celtic philology. Although he had always been proud of his roots—he once declared, 'I don't profess to be an Englishman, but an old Briton'[24]—it was not until after 1692 that Lhuyd developed a consuming interest in Welsh culture and acquired in particular a new awareness of the significance of language. He soon became a Celtic scholar of astonishing distinction. He mastered each of the Celtic languages, except Manx, and learned to understand the origins and cognates of words as well as kinships among languages. *Archaeologia Britannica* (1707), his major contribution to Welsh scholarship, stands as his abiding memorial in print. It demonstrated as never before that the Breton, Cornish, and Welsh languages enjoyed a common Celtic origin. The volume included an essay in comparative etymology, a Latin–Celtic dictionary, a Breton grammar, a Breton–English vocabulary, a Cornish grammar, a brief and imperfect catalogue of Welsh manuscripts, a study of the relationship between Welsh words and Greek, Latin, and Teutonic words, and, finally, an Irish grammar. Like all pioneer works, it was open to criticism on points of detail and interpretation, but it established Lhuyd's reputation as the founder of Celtic comparative philology. In particular, Lluyd broke new ground in discovering the significance of Old Welsh. By burrowing deeply into private collections, he discovered several rare manuscripts which contained specimens of the oldest written Welsh, and he was engaged on a study of their orthography when he died. Lhuyd was the first Welshman to master the science of comparative philology and no Welsh scholar was to address himself to similar philological research until

[23] Henry Rowlands, *Mona Antiqua*, p. 316.
[24] B. F. Roberts, 'Edward Lhuyd Y Cymro', *NLWJ* 24 (1985), p. 65.

the advent of Sir John Rhŷs at the end of the nineteenth century. It was Rhŷs, in fact, who described Lhuyd as 'in many respects the greatest Celtic philologist the world has ever seen'.[25]

Although few of Lhuyd's Welsh contemporaries were capable of digesting his rigorous philological theories, he did inspire them to expand the Welsh vocabulary by searching for old Welsh words and phrases. He was deeply interested in a bulky collection of Welsh words which Thomas Jones the almanacker had received from William Lloyd, bishop of St Asaph. William Gambold, one of Lhuyd's acolytes, felt impelled to prepare an English–Welsh dictionary which would provide translations of English idioms and expressions as well as Welsh equivalents of English words. Gambold began work on his project in 1707 but, gravely handicapped by a serious chest complaint, he wheezed over his dictionary for fifteen years and, having completed his task, was mortified to find that no funds were forthcoming to enable him to publish his 'Lexicon Cambro-Britannicum'. Another Welsh lexicographer, Thomas Lloyd, was fired by Lhuyd's enthusiasm. Lloyd, a graduate of Jesus College, Oxford, and chaplain to Mary Myddelton at Croesnewydd in Denbighshire, crammed his copy of John Davies's *Dictionarium Duplex* with thousands of additional words and citations. Lhuyd's inspiration lay behind much of this activity. No one did more than he to persuade literary-minded gentry, clergymen, freeholders, and craftsmen to seek out the language of the bards and to cherish their mother tongue.

Just as Welsh scholars strove to infuse new life and vigour into an ailing tongue, so, too, did Welsh poets endeavour to revivify the ancient craft of poetry. During the middle of the seventeenth century the Welsh bardic tradition, having declined markedly from its late medieval pinnacle in the days of Tudur Aled (d. 1526), finally collapsed. Deprived of their traditional patrons, Welsh poets were plunged into despair. Profound social and economic changes were chiefly responsible for the decline of the traditional Welsh patron. The pressure of inflation, coupled with the conservatism of patrons and the inadequacies of the poets themselves, had sapped the strength of the poetic craft. From 1660 onwards, Welsh landed estates gravitated to the hands of the great Leviathans, who increasingly shared the cultural tastes of their English counterparts. Many of them avidly pursued the manifold pleasures and temptations of sophisticated life in London, and as the century unrolled they became indifferent or even hostile towards Welsh culture. Since many of them spent many months of the year either in London or in Europe, the ancient ties which had bound them closely to their communities became looser. Ellis Rowland, the poet, was convinced that nothing had weakened Welsh culture more than a surfeit of footloose heirs chasing rich English heiresses. In 1703, the satirist Ellis Wynne mourned the loss of some of the strands which had been deeply woven into the fabric of Welsh society before the ruling classes took the high road to London—social harmony, ties of kinship, genuine public spirit, and generous largess. In the Street of Pride in his 'Vision of the World', Wynne discovered 'a straggling mansion, large and roofless, robbed of its eyes by birds and beasts, its owners having gone to England or France . . . and so, instead of the old family of former times, benevolent, good and homely, there is now in charge but the silly owl, or greedy crows, or proud magpies, or the like, to sing the praises of the present owners'.[26] However nostalgic Wynne's portrait may have been, there is no doubt that a growing proportion of the most influential landed proprietors was no longer prepared to fulfil its cultural obligations to the Welsh-speaking community. In particular, these people no longer shared the zeal of their forefathers for the preservation of the bardic craft. The days of the family bard were now over. Siôn Dafydd Las, family bard at Nannau, near Dolgellau, who died in 1694, was the last of his type. The *clerwr* was also a figure of the past. When Gruffydd Phylip, a member of the illustrious Phylip family of Ardudwy, died in 1666 he was described as 'the last of the old bards'.[27] No longer would Welsh poets peregrinate the length and breadth of Wales to sing for their supper.

Not surprisingly, embittered professional poets bemoaned the loss of old patrons. The destruction of the poetic craft, with its dire implications for cultural life, was a central theme in their writings. Like their Irish counterpart, Ó Bruadair, Welsh poets deplored the philistinism of families who had come up in the world and developed a liking for things English. A deep mood of pessimism and despair gripped Edward Dafydd, the last of the professional bards in Glamorgan. 'This world is not with the bards',[28] was his anguished cry in 1655. 'Wales is failing', wailed an anonymous poet, 'the bards have been buried.'[29] Largess from the pockets of the gentry had dwindled alarmingly and, by the end of the seventeenth century, poets were invited to celebrate special ceremonial occasions rather than provide regular entertainment throughout the year. No longer, complained Hugh Cadwaladr to William Owen of Brogyntyn, were itinerant bards assured of 'rivers of wine and beer'[30] within the portals of a gentleman's home. Owen Gruffydd of Llanystumdwy, who was born in 1642 and died in his 88th year in 1730, witnessed the decline in the system

[26] Ellis Wynne, *Visions of the Sleeping Bard*, p. 13.
[27] W. Ll. Davies, 'Phylipiaid Ardudwy', *Y Cymmrodor* (1931), p. 157.
[28] C. W. Lewis, 'The Literary History of Glamorgan from 1550 to 1770', in *Glamorgan Co. Hist.* 4, p. 540.
[29] E. D. Jones, 'The Brogyntyn Welsh Manuscripts', *NLWJ* 6 (1950), p. 236.
[30] *NLWJ* 8 (1953), p. 12.

of patronage. During his life, this weaver-poet had probably composed 150 *cywyddau* and *englynion* in praise of gentry families in Caernarfonshire and Merioneth, and in his twilight years he yearned for the palmy days when bards had been welcome guests in country homes. Sweeping economic changes and shifts in taste and fashion had squeezed the professional bard out of existence. In Gruffydd's poem, 'The Men that Once Were', we read the words of an old man clearly at odds with the world around him:

> Today my frozen cheek lacks cheer,
> I don't see any that call me near,
> Nor banquet, nor profit, nor a full meal.[31]

It is important to stress that although the gentry had withdrawn their patronage, the cultivation of the ancient strict metres persisted in many parts of Wales. The initiative passed from the hands of the gentry and a professional order of poets to literate, enterprising farmers, craftsmen, clergymen, and publishers, who were acutely sensitive to the cultural needs of ordinary people. Welsh poetry might no longer flourish in the halls and parlours of the landed classes, but it was alive and well in the smaller manor houses, vicarages, farmsteads, and cottages of rural Wales. It had become the hobby of enthusiastic amateurs, men 'whose gift of song to none was hired'.[32] By the late Stuart period, Welsh poetry was the leisured accomplishment of amateurs who had no commitment to fulfil to patrons nor any duty to cultivate men of consequence. The new Welsh poets were men of humble stock: Huw Morys was a freeholder's son who served an apprenticeship as a barker; Edward Morris was a farmer-cum-drover; Matthew Owen was a cottager; and Owen Gruffydd, Michael Pritchard, and Siôn Tomos Owen were weavers. Dozens of clergymen, craftsmen, and peasants ventured an ode or *englyn* which sometimes saw the light of day in printed miscellanies but few of them are remembered today. To such people, Taliesin, Aneirin, Myrddin, and Cynddelw were simply names; they might mention them fleetingly in their poems but they knew nothing about them.

Although the new generation of Welsh poets were pale shadows of their illustrious professional forebears, their poetry fulfilled a much wider social function. Welsh poetry became an open rather than a closed shop. Poets were less secretive and less jealous of one another; more able to relax, they sought to provide a wider and humbler audience with edifying, entertaining, and relevant material. The old strict metres were being elbowed aside by free-metre poetry. Poets now cut their cloth to suit the tastes of humbler

---

[31] Gwyn Jones (ed.), *The Oxford Book of Welsh Verse in English* (Oxford, 1977), pp. 110–11.
[32] Thomas Parry, *History of Welsh Literature*, p. 221.

folk. They had no wish to be trammelled by the inflexible demands of strict metres, *cynghanedd*, and formal syntax. The very notion of praising unworthy gentlemen in fulsome strict-metre verse was repugnant to many of them, for they had no sympathy for bloated squires who abandoned their homes for the flesh-pots of London. Penning a *cywydd* to profligate rakes held no attraction for humble craftsmen or farmers who were forced to practise their talents during valuable leisure hours. Some poets, however, successfully straddled the old world and the new. Huw Morys of Pontymeibion, Llansilin, Denbighshire—Wales's leading poet in the late Stuart period—was capable of composing sophisticated poetry in the older strict metres and experimenting in free metres. Morys succeeded in fusing old and new conventions by setting free accented metres to *cynghanedd*. He was a prolific poet who was more liberally patronized than his fellow poets and received due recompense for his labours from gentry families in north-east Wales. Morys addressed the Mostyns and the Myddeltons with graceful elegies and *cywyddau*, and although his work was erratic, he was capable of emulating standards set by fifteenth-century bards. But Morys preferred the freedom of the new measures, for they enabled him to convey the ideas, fashions, and preoccupations of his age. He established a sympathetic rapport with the common man by reflecting in his poetry the daily trials and tribulations which beset the lives of humble neighbours such as Siôn Elis, Lystan Owen, and Morys Siôn. Common folk were especially fond of his May or summer carols. Religious reformers were convinced that his poetry exerted a beneficial influence on the morals and manners of the Welsh people, and many of his poems were still in oral circulation in the vale of Clwyd in the mid-Victorian period. At his death, aged 87, in 1709, a sheaf of elegies bore witness to Huw Morys's standing as Wales's premier bard.

As noble patronage ebbed, the tide of print flowed. Poetry was no longer held to be simply an oral art. Welsh poets in the sixteenth century had viewed the printing-press as a newfangled design fraught with risk rather than pregnant with opportunity, but their successors harboured no such fears by the late Stuart period. Indeed, they understood only too well that the Welsh press could help to infuse new life into Welsh poetry, strengthen the language, and preserve manuscripts against loss, miscopying, or even plagiarism. Thomas Jones and John Rhydderch helped to generate new interest in poetry by enabling poets to publish collections of free-metre carols, as well as *cywyddau* and *englynion*, in anthologies and almanacs. A crop of popular anthologies were addressed to a wide audience. Thomas Jones's *Y Gwir er Gwaethed Yw* (The Truth be it never so Bad, 1684) included a number of *cywyddau* by Wales's most famous medieval poets as well as free-metre verses. Jones's *Y Gymraeg yn ei Disgleirdeb* (1688) and John Rhydderch's *The English and Welch Dictionary* (1725) provided poets with pocket-book editions of the old bardic vocabulary. Popular anthologies such as Foulke Owen's *Cerdd-lyfr* (Songbook, 1686), revised and enlarged by Thomas Jones in 1696 and again by John Rhydderch in 1720, were suffused with popular religious carols. Dafydd Lewys's *Flores Poetarum Britannicorum* (1710), at 4d. a copy, was a book for Renaissance amateurs: it contained a collection of poetry by Dr John Davies, Mallwyd, and a reprinted edition of Wiliam Midleton's *Bardhoniaeth, neu brydydhiaeth* (Bardism, or poetry, 1594). One of the most influential publications was John Rhydderch's *Grammadeg Cymraeg* (A Welsh Grammar, 1728), which served as a latimer for aspiring poets throughout Wales. Based on the celebrated *Pum Llyfr Cerddwriaeth* (The Five Books of Poetic Art) and Siôn Dafydd Rhys's famous grammar, it provided Welsh poets with the intricate secrets of the bardic freemasonry. Since oral instruction was a dying function, Rhydderch's grammar fulfilled a crying need. Its publication prompted Lewis Morris to christen its author 'King of *cynghanedd*', and the spate of exemplifying odes produced during the eighteenth century testifies to the influence of the work. The publication of annual Welsh almanacs from 1680 onwards also ensured that the springs of Welsh poetry did not dry up: Thomas Jones and John Rhydderch used the almanac as a means of popularizing Welsh poetry, both old and new. Promising apprentices and wise old poets were given the opportunity to show off their skills in print and this stimulated a greater desire among them to cultivate and refine the art of poetry. By providing them with a public focus for their muse, the Welsh almanacs bound together poets from all parts of Wales.

Thomas Jones and John Rhydderch were also instrumental in reviving the Welsh *eisteddfod*, which had been sorely neglected since the early years of Elizabeth's reign. Convinced that *eisteddfodau* could prove an effective means of fostering Welsh poetry and culture in general, Welsh almanackers published printed advertisements of forthcoming *eisteddfodau* from 1700 onwards. Rhydderch, in particular, nursed a burning desire to revive the rules and regulations which had governed the bardic fraternity in its palmy days. His aim was to organize assemblies on the lines of *eisteddfodau* held at Caerwys in 1523 and 1567–8. Early eighteenth-century *eisteddfodau* did not open their doors to the public at large: they were assemblies organized by, and for, accredited poets and grammarians and were normally held in taverns in small rural market towns. Plentiful supplies of ale and wine kept the muse refreshed, as nostalgic bards dreamed of past glories, exchanged manuscripts, tested their skills in classical measures, and publicly recited their songs around a long table. At the end of the competition, the 'president' declared the winner's name and he was duly chaired. His colleagues toasted his health and each placed sixpence in a jug in order to ensure that the chaired bard's glass remained full until the end of the proceedings. We have no means of knowing how successful these early *eisteddfodau* were. Some were clearly gimcrack affairs, patronized by a handful of bards. Only five poets arrived at Machynlleth in 1701. In 1734, John Rhydderch was mortified to find fewer than six poets in Bala and, all around him, 'signs of indifference, faint-heartedness and cowardice'.[33] On the other hand, the poetic fraternity in north-west Wales could boast a number of triumphs. An *eisteddfod* attended by more than a dozen poets in a tavern in Llannerch-y-medd in 1734 proved a highly successful and convivial affair: the highlights of the proceedings were forty *englynion* composed to celebrate the success of Richard Evans, the local doctor, in removing a plague of warts from the feet of Owen Gronw, Goronwy Owen's father. Many assemblies must have degenerated into raucous beer-swilling sessions and slanging matches, and religious reformers and savants often heaped ridicule on the allegedly thriftless, indolent 'besotted swine' who frequented them. 'If one can patch up any kind of a ditty', was Ellis Wynne's mordant comment, 'then he is a chaired bard.'[34] Nevertheless, the revived *eisteddfod* provided Welsh poets with the stimulus to master the rules for metres and alliteration and to practise their craft.

It is evident that, in spite of the demise of the traditional bardic order, knowledge of the rules of *cynghanedd* and the twenty-four metres was communicated either by word of mouth or via manuscript and printed book from poet to poet and from tutor to pupil. In the Teifi valley, one of the last remaining centres of Renaissance learning, poets learned their craft by sharing secrets and ideas with each other. They also developed their expertise by copying old manuscripts of the work of the poets of the nobility. Samuel Williams and Iaco ab Dewi collected and copied—in superb handwriting—scores of old *cywyddau* and odes. By the late 1720s, the uplands of Glamorgan could boast a thriving fraternity of cultured artisans and craftsmen, led by Lewis Hopkin, John Bradford, Wil Hopcyn, Rhys Morgan, and Dafydd Nicolas. These active and many-sided men mastered the poetic craft by circulating poems, grammars, and dictionaries among themselves as well as among like-minded friends. In north-west Wales lively poetic jousts were common. Even as a youth, Lewis Morris of Anglesey spent his leisure hours collecting poetry and composing carols, dialogues, maxims, and epigrams in both Welsh and English. He corresponded and conversed with veteran poets like Owen Gruffydd and Siôn Tomos Owen and derived great benefit from his contacts with the guardians of the old heritage. All the signs are that Welsh poetry was widely practised. Up and down the country humble poets composed hundreds, if not thousands of *englynion*, many of which were jotted down on the flyleaves of bibles, prayer books, and devotional tracts. In 1728 a lively bardic contest between Siôn Tomos Owen of Bodedern and Michael

[33] Prys Morgan, *The Eighteenth Century Renaissance* (Llandybïe, 1981), p. 63.
[34] Ellis Wynne, *Visions of the Sleeping Bard*, p. 85.

Pritchard of Llanllyfni (both weavers) developed into a lengthy fray in which both participants contributed over fifty *englynion* and 750 lines of *cywydd*, many of which included *sangiadau* (parentheses) and *cymeriadau* (repetition of the same word) after the manner of the ancient bards. Undoubtedly, the development of the printing-press and the revived *eisteddfod* had given Welsh poetry as a whole a fresh lease of life.

Similarly, at a time when traditional Welsh music was in retreat, there was an increasingly brisk market for Welsh ballads. During the Restoration period many traditional Welsh instruments, notably the *crwth* (crowd) and *pibgorn* (hornpipe), were replaced by flutes, fiddles, and harpsichords in gentry parlours. By the beginning of the eighteenth century, the traditional single harp had been supplanted by the Italian triple harp. Even the content of Welsh music was vanishing from memory. When the musically minded Morris family of Anglesey was confronted with a manuscript prepared by a kinsman, Robert ap Huw (d. 1665), a native of Bodwigan, Llanddeusant, and court harpist to James I, they were totally bewildered by its contents. Lewis Morris had been born and bred a stone's throw from Robert ap Huw's birthplace, but he could make nothing of it. Part of the reason for the musical amnesia of the Welsh was that English and French melodies had been pouring into Wales, especially from 1660 onwards. Many of them were carried from the taverns and theatres of London by printers, drovers, merchants, and sailors. In 1717, Richard Morris of Anglesey compiled a collection of popular tunes sung to the viol in his native country: five of every six tunes bore English titles such as *Pudding Pie*, *Soldier's Life*, and *Queen's Dream*. Welsh harpists and minstrels avidly copied the catchy musical styles emanating from the metropolis. Not all of them, however, were disposed to follow English models. Two of the most haunting Welsh airs, *Dafydd y Garreg Wen* (David of the White Rock) and *Codiad yr Ehedydd* (The Lark's Ascent) were composed in the early eighteenth century by David Owen of Ynyscynhaearn in Caernarfonshire, while Wil Hopcyn of Llangynwyd is believed by some to have composed the lovely lyrical song, *Bugeilio'r Gwenith Gwyn* (Tending the White Wheat). But, since few traditional Welsh melodies were committed to paper, there was a heavy demand for Welsh ballads. Many thousands of copies of Welsh ballads were sold during this period. Composed or translated from English best sellers by farmers and craftsmen, ballads were the cheapest and most entertaining commodities on the market. Many of them carried exotic English names such as *Janthee the Lovely*, *Crimson Velvet*, and *Moggy Ladder*. Readers never wearied of highly coloured tales of scandals, courtships, executions, murders, and disasters. Although religious reformers were deeply suspicious of 'the devil's catechism',[35]

[35] E. Saunders, *A Domestick Charge*, p. 135.

most Welsh ballads carried a moral sting in the tail. Rees Prichard had employed homely, colloquial verses as a means of bringing home to common people the essence of Puritanism, and many popular carols and godly poems, penned specifically for seasonal feasts and festivals, were also invaluable means of spreading scriptural knowledge and moral imperatives.

A small minority of Welsh poets also wrote for the benefit of leisured and educated gentlemen, clergymen, physicians, and lawyers who could read English. Although Henry Vaughan, the Silurist, spoke Welsh, acquired a rudimentary knowledge of Welsh poetry, and spent all but six of his seventy-four years in Wales, he exercised his craft as a poet in the English language. His most notable works, especially the celebrated *Silex Scintillans* (1650), were composed during the troubled revolutionary years. Following these vexations, Vaughan lived a secluded life in his beloved Usk Valley and his sole published work after 1657 was *Thalia Rediviva* (1678). Vaughan's neighbour, Rowland Watkyns, rector of Llanfrynach and author of *Flamma Sine Fumo* (1662), was a cultivated poet who sang for the benefit of a bilingual clientele on the Welsh borders. Some poets made their mark outside Wales. George Stepney (1663-1707), a native of Prendergast in Pembrokeshire, composed poems in his youth which, according to Samuel Johnson, made 'grey authors blush'. Stepney was a minor poet of no great talent and his later work possessed 'little either of the grace of wit or the vigour of nature'.[36] David Lewis (*c.* 1683-1760), another Pembrokeshire man and a graduate of Jesus College, Oxford, was more gifted than Stepney: he published a selection of miscellaneous poems in 1726 and, a year later, a tragedy in blank verse, *Philip of Macedon*, which he dedicated to Pope. The most celebrated Welsh Augustan poet, however, was John Dyer (1700?-1758), an attorney's son from Aberglasney in Carmarthenshire, who became a pioneer of descriptive landscape poetry. Although Dyer relished the company of artists, poets, and savants, such as Aaron Hill, Martha Fowke Sansom ('Clio'), Richard Savage, and James Thomson, who met in fashionable homes in London, he yearned for the pastoral simplicity and serenity of his native country. Dyer was a good and honest man who believed that 'knowledge is much to be prized, but peace of mind more'.[37] His quest for inward peace is best found in his most celebrated poem, *Grongar Hill* (1726), a poem inspired by the scenery in his native parish. A Miltonic piece in octosyllabic couplets, *Grongar Hill* was later much admired by Wordsworth. A few Welsh poets, too, saw themselves as connoisseurs of wit and humour. Thomas Richards of Llanfyllin was described by his Oxford tutor as the best Latin poet since Virgil: Richards produced a mock-heroic poem, *Hoglandiae descriptio*

---

[36] Samuel Johnson, *The Lives of the Most Eminent English Poets* (4 vols., London, 1783), i. 423-4.
[37] Belinda Humfrey, *John Dyer* (Cardiff, 1980), p. 56.

(1709) in answer to Holdsworth's *Muscipula*, a satire on Taffy's proverbial
love of cheese. The young Lewis Morris, too, was familiar with the work of
Congreve and Steele, and was capable of penning verses, dialogues, and
epigrams in the Augustan fashion.

The development of Welsh prose was hampered by the widespread feeling
that the Welsh language was not sufficiently flexible or modern to
encompass all branches of learning. Thomas Williams of Denbigh believed
that his native language was 'enslaved'[38] and was thus not conducive to
rational or philosophical discussion. Others were convinced that the Welsh
language was not attuned to the fashions and sensibilities of the modern
age. It is true that the masterful prose of the Welsh Bible and the inspiring
work of Welsh Renaissance scholars were still guiding influences, but the
view remained that Welsh, as a literary medium, lacked flexibility, lustre,
and prestige. Ever since the Union, English had been the language of law
and administration in Wales. English and Latin were the twin media in
Welsh grammar schools. English had supplanted Welsh as the first
language of the upper classes, and those who acquired education at public
schools, universities, and inns of court corresponded with each other in
English, read English books, and ensured that their sons and daughters
were duly educated in polite and civilized institutions. There was some
truth in Goronwy Owen's complaint: 'if our countrymen write anything
that is good, they are sure to do it in English'.[39]
    Even the deluge of Welsh books which were published in this period
were restricted in content. The overwhelming majority of prose writers
channelled their energies into producing godly, devotional manuals
couched in simple, unadorned language. The traditional emphasis on *dysg*
(learning) had been supplanted by the desire to win men's souls and to
place bibles, prayer books, and devotional tracts in the hands of God-
fearing householders. Since authors were anxious to 'edify spiritually', they
adopted a functional, didactic approach. The plain style became the
norm simply because it was best suited to the needs of the vulgar sorts.
Rhetorical flourishes and arcane classical phrases were frowned upon, for
clear gospel truths, couched in limpid prose, were the goal. As a result, a
large majority of Welsh books consisted of devotional manuals and
practical treatises designed to foster personal piety, godliness, and good
works.
    Yet it would be a mistake to believe that pragmatic religious reformers
were insensitive to the richness of Welsh prose. Stephen Hughes urged the
speedy reprinting of *Llwybr Hyffordd i'r Anghyfarwydd* (The Plain Man's

[38] Thomas Williams, *Ymadroddion Bucheddol ynghylch Marwolaeth* (London, 1691), sig.
A2^r.
[39] J. H. Davies (ed.), *The Letters of Goronwy Owen (1723–1769)* (Cardiff, 1924), pp. 7–8.

Pathway) and *Llyfr y Resolusion* (The Book of Resolution) 'for the sake of the very excellent language wherein they are written'.[40] Best sellers such as *Yr Ymarfer o Dduwioldeb* (The Practise of Piety) and *Holl Ddyletswydd Dyn* (The Whole Duty of Man) were often reprinted not only because of their proven record in aiding men's search for salvation, but also for the merits of their prose. Charles Edwards's *Y Ffydd Ddi-ffvant* (The Unfeigned Faith, 1677) is a truly outstanding work. The first edition, published in 1667, was little more than a ramshackle patchwork of fact and opinions pieced together from a variety of sources. Four years later, a fuller and a more animated edition appeared, in which Edwards traced the history of the unfeigned faith in Wales and invested his writing with a sturdy patriotic flavour. During the period 1667–71 he had immersed himself in the spiritual and martial glories of his forebears and his dearest wish was that his compatriots should reavail themselves of the Christian virtues which their ancestors had bequeathed to them. Edwards believed that he inhabited a sinful, godless world and, like his hero, Gildas, he was especially fond of drawing parallels between the fate of the Israelites and the fate of the Welsh. God smote sinners, he insisted, and favoured only the righteous. It was thus the duty of all Welsh Christians to rediscover 'the pure evangelical faith and power of godliness'[41] which was their rightful inheritance. Edwards's gifts as a writer also blossomed during the 1670s. By the third edition in 1677 (when the author was nearing his 50th year), a further transformation had been wrought: a powerful, resonant section, entitled *Rhinwedd y Ffydd* (Virtues of the Faith), subtly mapped out the regeneration of the human soul. Thus, the work had not only grown in size—from 90 pages in 1667 to 427 pages by 1677—but had also been transformed into one of the masterpieces of Welsh prose literature. Charles Edwards was acutely aware of the need to convey his Christian message in artistic, graphic prose. He had mastered the art of rhetoric and, in its logical, dialectical discipline, his metaphysical style owed much to the influence of Ramist ideas. *Rhinwedd y Ffydd*, in particular, is shot through with striking images of poetic brilliance and reveals that Edwards's prodigious literary gifts had reached their full maturity. Charles Edwards may not have been a thinker of great power or originality, but his command of graphic metaphors enabled him to create a literary masterpiece.

The most ambitious original prose work composed in this period was Ellis Wynne's *Gweledigaetheu y Bardd Cwsc* (Visions of the Sleeping Bard, 1703). Born at Y Lasynys, near Harlech, Merioneth, in 1671, Wynne was a cultivated, Oxford-trained cleric. His work is a racy, vivid, and satirical commentary on the follies and iniquities of Welsh and London life. The first of three visions, the Vision of the World, is located in the City of

---

[40] Stephen Hughes (ed.), *Tryssor i'r Cymru* (London, 1677), sig. A5ᵛ–A6ʳ.
[41] Charles Edwards, *Y Ffydd Ddi-ffvant*, pp. 198–214.

Doom, where sinners frequent the streets of Pride, Pleasure, and Lucre. The Vision of Death unfolds the ineluctable fate of each sinner, whilst the Vision of Hell provides a graphic account of the torments and sufferings of those consigned to the eternal flames down below. Wynne was a rather forbidding reforming cleric who nursed a black-humoured suspicion of men's professed virtues. He viewed all religions, save Anglicanism, with a cynical eye and, by means of a combination of irony, parody, and ridicule, he exposed the vanity, hypocrisy, and baseness of society. In waspish tones, Wynne scorned the vile enchantments of London, lashed the greed of the impropriating landlord, and berated the ruling classes and middling sorts for 'looking up to the pomp of the English'. His work teems with scurrilous character sketches. His vignette of an aspiring society woman is particularly striking: 'many a horned wench I beheld, like a ship in full sail, walking as it were in a frame, with quite a pedlar's shop about her, and dangling from her ears the price of a goodly farm in pearls'. Wynne cut like a whip through the pretensions of gentlemen who surrounded themselves with 'all manner of armorial bearings, banners, escutcheons, books of pedigrees, poems of antiquity, *cywyddau* . . .'. Nor did he recoil from smut and profanity. Some of his coarser touches echoed the irreverent tones of Grub Street scribblers: 'next to the Kings came the courtiers and flatterers, many. Each of these was thrown under the seat of his own King, as the Kings were under the devil's buttocks in Lucifer's stool of office'.[42] Small wonder that later Methodists felt obliged to avert their eyes from some of Wynne's more vulgar passages.

Ellis Wynne owed a heavy literary debt to Milton's *Paradise Lost* and Bunyan's *Pilgrim's Progress*. He also plucked the flavour of Stuart London from the effervescent prose style of the 'Cockney school of writers of Burlesque'. Wynne was the first Welsh author to bring the scabrous and immoderate language of Grub Street hacks to the notice of the Welsh reading public, and in a sense it is remarkable that a man in holy orders, who inhabited one of the least developed counties of the British Isles, should have taken an intelligent interest in the vulgar and hedonist life of the metropolis. He pilfered material freely from adaptations by Sir Roger L'Estrange and John Stevens of Quevedo's celebrated *Los Sueños* and made no secret of his dependence on the work of others. His success lay in his ability to 'adapt all to the humour of the Welsh'.[43] Wynne was deeply versed in the Welsh prose tradition and possessed an effortless command of the native idioms, proverbs, and phrases which were still alive on the tongues of his friends and kinsmen in the vale of Ardudwy. By merging these contrasting styles, he created a minor classic which has no parallel in Welsh literature. The strength of Wynne's book lies in its finely wrought

---

[42] Ellis Wynne, *Visions of the Sleeping Bard*, pp. 189, 15, 21, 165.
[43] Gwyn Thomas, *Y Bardd Cwsg a'i Gefndir* (Cardiff, 1971), p. 232.

structure, its vigorous narrative style and management of dialogue, and, above all, its sharp-edged satire. Wynne created a new form of prose narrative which had a hypnotic effect on generations of readers and was also to have a lasting influence on several literary schools that came after him. By 1932 at least thirty-two editions of his work had been published.

The popular press also endeavoured to provide the reading public with material which was quite different from the staple fare of didactic religious prose. Both Thomas Jones and John Rhydderch were aware of the demand for ephemeral reading matter. There was clearly a widespread hunger for news, information, and entertainment, and Thomas Jones was well aware that English almanacs sold like hot cakes and were more widely dispersed than any other form of literature. Never one to shun bold adventures, he lobbied furiously until, in January 1679, he gained sole rights for the compilation, printing, and publishing of an annual Welsh almanac. By 1702, John Jones, a Dissenter of Caeau near Wrexham, had begun publishing a rival almanac and, following Thomas Jones's death in 1713, John Rhydderch entered the field with some success.

To humble readers, the Welsh almanac represented the only suitable reading matter of any sort available. It was an amalgam of miscellaneous information designed to be read over a twelve-month period. It was used as a calendar, a diary, and a reference book, and it was avidly thumbed by many people who read little else. The most popular sections of the almanac were the astronomical and astrological guides, which often reflected the superstitious and magical beliefs that were deeply woven into the social fabric. Most prognostications advanced by Welsh almanackers were obscure, enigmatic, and confusing. Much of the data was deliberately designed to puzzle as well as impress readers, and it is small wonder that almanackers were often portrayed as plausible rogues who earned a dishonest living by gulling innocent readers. Yet, by offering graphic accounts of political crises and military affairs, the almanac helped to stimulate the reader's interest in political affairs and to widen his horizons. The almanac, moreover, provided a fund of useful information, notably a table of ebbs and floods, rules for blood-letting and purging, advice on agricultural matters, lists of fairs and markets, a chronology of salient historical events, samples of Welsh poetry, and a host of curious advertisements. Many underprivileged people found the almanac attractive since it articulated their resentments and grievances. Welsh almanackers were patriotic men who possessed a sharp awareness of right as opposed to wrong. It was common for them to criticize the vanity of the gentry, the affectations of *Dic Siôn Dafyddion*, and the avarice of landlords and lawyers. Thomas Jones, in particular, was a hard-hitting critic who knew how to strike both above and below the belt. Jones prided himself on his disrespectful tongue, impenitently confessing his penchant for being 'too saucy' towards pompous gentlemen. In many ways, he was the Welsh counterpart of Tom Brown or Ned Ward, for his almanacs were studded with nuggets of wry humour and mordant satire. Moreover, his graphic accounts of running battles with rival almanackers helped to satisfy the popular craving for entertainment and scandal. Like their English counterparts, Welsh almanackers were seemingly constantly engaged in scoring points off each other and their rivalries helped to keep. sales buoyant.

For all these reasons, Welsh almanacs commanded a wide readership and were valuable stimulants to the growth of literacy. Cheap, lively, and entertaining, they were deliberately tailored to the needs of the growing numbers of literate farmers, craftsmen, and peasants who, according to Thomas Jones, were 'too poor to enter the market of English and Latin to double their caps with learning'.[44] The almanac, in fact, was the first Welsh publication to provide humble readers with a happy blend of instruction and entertainment. In its many-sided role as diary, calendar, astrological guide, periodical, newspaper, primer, and songbook, it helped to instil the reading habit among lower social groups.

The restricted nature of the Welsh literary tradition, together with the absence of national institutions, prevented the development of new and original ideas in the field of *belles-lettres*, biography, autobiography, comedy, drama, and fiction. The obsession with saving literature, which poured out so prolifically during these years, was partly responsible for the lack of new genres. Whenever Welsh authors turned to fields other than popular religious literature they invariably expressed themselves in English. Welsh Dissenters, for instance, couched their autobiographies in the English tongue. *The Life and Death of Mr. Vavasor Powell* (1671) contains selections from Powell's diary, a fragmentary autobiography, and pieces of poetry. Powell was less concerned with creative self-expression than with nourishing the faith of his brethren, but his account of his youthful indiscretions, conversion, providential escapes, and ceaseless labours is an invaluable looking-glass into the soul of a Welsh Puritan. Although it does not rival Bunyan's *Grace Abounding*, Powell's work is a winsome account of a man of indomitable spirit who struggled as much against his own weaknesses as against the hostility of his enemies. Whereas Powell's spirit remained unquenched until his death, Charles Edwards's twilight years were desperately lonely and insecure, and his *An Afflicted Man's Testimony* (1691) is the pitiful valediction of a paranoiac. One of the most spirited autobiographies was written by Richard Davies, the Welshpool hatter. His *An Account of the Convincement . . . of Richard Davies* (1710) is a moving portrait of beleaguered Quaker communities in

---

[44] Thomas Jones, *Y Lleiaf o'r Almanaccau Cymraeg* (London, 1692), sig. A8[r].

mid-Wales and of the faith practised and cherished by men and women of unflinching tenacity. Davies had a keen eye for observation and an acute ear for dialogue, and his memoirs are crowded with dramatic incidents of journeys, meetings, and sufferings.

Expanding academic opportunities enabled many ambitious Welshmen to achieve literary fame by writing in English or Latin. Sons of gentlemen, clergymen, and yeomen were only too glad to avail themselves of the widening range of new careers which beckoned men of talent. English was the language of advancement and the prospects of pecuniary rewards for university-trained men of letters were far greater in London than elsewhere. Many of them either settled in church livings in England or found enhanced opportunities for advancement in the metropolis. This trend served to weaken both ethnic and linguistic bonds. When William Baxter (1649–1723), a native of Llanllugan in the heart of rural Montgomeryshire, was sent to Harrow at the age of eighteen, he understood no language other than Welsh. At Harrow he developed a flair for languages and lost no opportunity to parade his fund of classical learning. Baxter's edition of *Anacreon* (1695) earned him European fame and an edition of Horace in 1701 confirmed his reputation as a specialist in Latin grammar. But, as far as we can tell, although he studied Welsh he was never tempted to publish in his native tongue. Yet several Welshmen who attained a considerable reputation in the world of letters were not insensible of their roots. James Howell, of Llangamarch in Breconshire, prided himself on his mastery of English prose and his Welshness. The author of the celebrated *Epistolae Ho-elianae* (1645), Howell was a man of considerable knowledge and broad horizons. In 1661 he was appointed Historiographer Royal by Charles II, a post which he held until his death five years later. Although Howell pursued his career as a professional writer in England, he remained well informed about the language, literature, and antiquity of his native land. One of his last works, *Lexicon Tetraglotton* (1659–60), contained a collection of Welsh proverbs. Myles Davies of Tre'rabbat, Whitford, Flintshire, was a former Catholic priest who dreamt up many grandiose projects, the most notable of which was his six-volume *Athenae Britannicae* (1716–20), an extraordinary compendium of learned and esoteric information. Although Davies immersed himself in the critical writings of English scholars, he quoted his mother tongue frequently in his works. One of his more controversial aphorisms was that 'the truest common Cambrian idiom is best spoken in Denbighshire, as the Welsh poetic bardism is best cultivated by the ionics of Merionethshire, but the British atticisms are most frequent in Flintshire'.[45]

Many Welshmen made a genuine contribution to English letters. John

---

[45] Myles Davies, *Athenae Britannicae* (6 vols., London, 1716–20), i. 191.

Davies (1627–93), a yeoman's son from Kidwelly, Carmarthenshire, was a self-effacing scholar who moved in literary circles which included Elias Ashmole and John Aubrey. Davies steeped himself in the classics and made his livelihood by translating French books, notably Scarron's novels, on behalf of English booksellers. David Lloyd, a native of Trawsfynydd, Merioneth, a graduate of Oxford and sometime canon of St Asaph, was a prolific royalist historian and biographer. He published a large number of weighty tomes, notably *The Statesmen and Favourites of England* (1665) and *Memoirs of the Lives . . . of Noble Personages* (1668), which were widely read in their day. Owen Price, an Oxford-trained native of Montgomeryshire, ventured into the field of pedagogy: his text-books, *The Vocal Organ* (1665) and *English Orthographie* (1670), were widely used in private schools. William Jones, a farmer's son from Llanfihangel Tre'r Beirdd in Anglesey, seized the opportunity for self-betterment by moving to London to serve in a merchant's counting-house and subsequently as an instructor on board a man-of-war. Jones was a brilliant mathematician: his *New Compendium of the Whole Art of Practical Navigation* (1702) earned him repute in scholarly circles, while his *Synopsis Palmariorum Matheseos* (1706) attracted the attention of Halley and Newton. Jones edited some of Newton's work and was elected FRS in 1712. Finally, a small number of Welshmen rubbed shoulders with some of the most eminent men in the land. Among them was Erasmus Lewis, a native of Abercothi, near Carmarthen. Lewis was a purveyor of news-letters who wormed his way into a charmed circle of scholars, savants, and politicians which included Swift (who called Lewis 'a cunning shaver'),[46] Pope, Gray, Arbuthnot, and Harley.

Antiquarians and historians in this period were obsessed with the fear that the Welsh were losing their historical consciousness. Many of the wealthiest landowning families had lost interest in the Welsh past and believed that the study of Welsh history was a monstrous waste of time. In 1674, Nicholas Roberts, headmaster at Carmarthen, declared that Welsh manuscripts housed in private libraries were simply fossils 'of little use . . . to the advancement of the commonwealth of real learning'.[47] William Wynne feared that even learned scholars were 'so great strangers' to the study of Welsh history that they were virtually ignorant of the existence of 'such a history'.[48] Faced with the dire prospect of historical amnesia, antiquarians and genealogists (many of them parish squires, clergymen,

[46] L. T. Davies and A. Edwards, *Welsh Life in the Eighteenth Century* (London, 1939), p. 85.
[47] Eiluned Rees, 'An Introductory Survey of Eighteenth Century Welsh Libraries', *JWBS* 10 (1971), p. 202.
[48] William Wynne, *The History of Wales* (London, 1697), sig. A3ʳ.

yeomen, and craftsmen) pursued their studies with astonishing zeal, often neglecting their personal health and welfare in their anxiety to unlock some of the keys to the mysteries of the past. They laboured in the teeth of many frustrations. Often they were unable to discover the location of manuscripts or were prevented from obtaining a sight of the documents which they required. Even accredited scholars who sought admission to private libraries were often turned away. Moreover, much valuable historical material had not survived the storms and tempests of the revolutionary years. Nevertheless, our knowledge of the past would be immeasurably poorer had not a small group of scholars deliberately striven to preserve priceless literary treasures by rescuing, copying, and preserving ancient manuscripts.

Countless generations of Welsh scholars have to this day acknowledged their debt to Robert Vaughan, a modest gentleman and scholar of Hengwrt in Merioneth. Vaughan devoted his life to the study of Welsh antiquities. Fired by warm-hearted patriotism, he searched far and wide for literary and historical manuscripts and copied many of them with the meticulous care of a skilful penman. Among the priceless treasures which had come into his possession prior to his death in 1667 were the 'Black Book of Carmarthen', the 'Book of Taliesin', the 'White Book of Rhydderch', and the 'Black Book of Chirk'. Two thousand printed books also embellished his splendid library. The Hengwrt library was later to become one of the foundation collections of the National Library of Wales and no serious student of Welsh history, particularly medieval history, can afford to neglect the fruits of Robert Vaughan's labours. Collecting and preserving Welsh manuscripts were also a lifelong passion for William Maurice of Llansilin, Denbighshire. Maurice devoted years of labour to copying and editing texts and documents. He employed his own amanuenses to assist him in transcribing and cataloguing the copious material which he stored in his 'study'—a purpose-built three-storey edifice beside his home at Cynllaith. The study of Welsh antiquities and genealogies also preoccupied Humphrey Humphreys, successively dean and bishop of Bangor. Humphreys was always accessible to even the humblest poets and antiquarians, and was held in the deepest affection as much for his love of Welsh culture as for his spiritual leadership. Edward Lhuyd believed him to be 'incomparably the best skilled in our antiquities'.[49]

An immense amount of genealogical work was also undertaken. According to Jacob Quaint, a genealogist in Sir John Vanbrugh's play *Aesop* (1697), Wales was 'a country in the world's backside, where every man is born a gentleman and a genealogist'.[50] The smaller Welsh gentry were still inordinately fond of emblazoned rolls which revealed their

    [49] E. G. Wright, 'Humphrey Humphreys, Bishop of Bangor and Hereford', p. 81.
    [50] Francis Jones, 'An Approach to Welsh Genealogy', *THSC* (1948), p. 429.

descent from the fifteen tribes or the sons of Noah. John Owen of Manorowen, Pembrokeshire, traced his pedigree back to the fictitious Pwyll Pendefig Dyfed. 'I could go farther', he claimed, 'placing one end of the chain in Pembrokeshire, and fastening the other to Mount Ararat.'[51] Welsh genealogists fed the appetite of local gentlemen for family pedigrees. Many of them were skilled professionals: David Edwards of Rhyd-y-gors, Carmarthenshire, was appointed deputy herald for the six counties of south Wales in 1684, and in 1703 Hugh Thomas of Brecon, a merchant's son, was appointed deputy to Sir Henry St George, Garter King-at-Arms. Thomas was an accomplished herald who embellished his manuscripts with skilful pen-and-ink sketches. One of the most creative and influential genealogists and antiquaries was William Lewes of Llwynderw, Llangeler, in Carmarthenshire. Lewes took his craft seriously, lavishing great care on his manuscripts, heaping scorn upon charlatans in the trade, and claiming proudly that no person in south Wales possessed a finer collection of genealogies than he. Theophilus Evans was filled with wonder when he visited Lewes's library.

Many of these scholars turned to Edward Lhuyd for guidance in tracing confusing genealogies and deciphering obscure manuscripts. With infinite patience and magisterial skill, Lhuyd answered their queries and shed fresh light on their researches. One of his most cherished ambitions by the 1690s was to write a history of the geography, natural history, and antiquities of Wales. In 1695 he contributed a mass of detailed information on Welsh counties to Edmund Gibson's edition of Camden's *Britannia*. Lhuyd translated Camden's Latin text of 1607, which dealt with the thirteen Welsh counties, and also supplied the editor with an abundance of supplementary material which he had either accumulated by personal field-work or elicited from friends and correspondents in Wales. In 1695, too, he advertised his intentions of preparing a comprehensive work on the antiquities of Wales by widely distributing printed sheets, in the form of a questionnaire, among well-informed local correspondents. These 'Parochial Queries' contained thirty-one questions concerning the geography, natural history, and antiquities of Wales. Lhuyd knew that a multitude of squires, clergymen, farmers, and craftsmen in Wales were well-versed in local lore, and he directed their curiosity by soliciting detailed information. His brief immediately seized the imagination of a widely scattered community of local scholars, who duly plied him with an enormous corpus of notes, letters, maps, and drawings on natural history and geography, pre-historic remains, commercial activities, magical beliefs, linguistic divisions, popular diets, recreations, and much else. Humphrey Foulkes, vicar of Abergele, was deeply impressed by the way in which

---

[51] *The Cambrian Register*, 2 (1796), p. 65.

'young novices in the Welsh tongue'[52] responded enthusiastically to Lhuyd's researches by yielding up a store of hitherto undiscovered information.

Lhuyd's friends, many of whom were graduates of Jesus College, Oxford, found him an agreeable and attentive correspondent. A warm, often jocular relationship developed between them. Lhuyd was endearingly addressed as 'dear Ned' or 'honest Gabriel' by some of his correspondents and fellow students at Oxford, and it is clear that he was capable of inspiring lasting friendships. His letters to John Lloyd, Blaenyddôl, Corwen, are peppered with boyish jokes and secrets. Not the least of Edward Lhuyd's attributes was his ability to wear his great learning lightly. He was fortunate in the quality of his field-workers: many of them were shrewd and knowledgeable men who did their homework thoroughly before sending him information. Philip Williams of Dyffryn tramped the length of a Roman road before providing Lhuyd with a detailed report. John Lloyd of Blaenyddôl hired local guides (including an octogenarian) in order to acquire oral testimony handed down from their forefathers as well as first-hand knowledge of rare plants, leaves, flowers, fortifications, tombs, and inscriptions. John Williams of Swansea helped Lhuyd to test his theories by providing a detailed description of the intriguing remains of the megalith known as Arthur's Stone and the Worms Head blow-hole in Gower. Elsewhere, many devoted helpers (many of them industrious rather than erudite) provided Lhuyd with detailed descriptions of curious specimens, effigies, brass pots, catapults, silver daggers, brass rings, wooden vessels, primitive leather shoes, skeletons, and inscriptions on tombstones. Many answers to his queries were wry and humorous: Llandderwen's parson was reputed to burn 'as much coal as the whole parish'; the inhabitants of Coychurch complained that increased trade with the West Country 'spoils our Welsh'; the citizens of Llancarfan were 'very subject to toothaches and rheums'; and an inhabitant of Llangynidr was deemed worthy of note since his hair stood on end whenever he was near a hare 'though he sees him not'.[53] Such material, however esoteric, was food and drink for Lhuyd, for it helped him to understand the seemingly impenetrable secrets of local communities. No one was more eager to rescue and cherish the deposits of the past—be they words, habits, or relics—than Lhuyd.

But Lhuyd also realized that as long as he was permanently ensconced in Oxford he would remain isolated from what he called 'observables' and over-dependent on material supplied by his correspondents. Personal field-work was a necessity, and in May 1697 Lhuyd set out from Oxford, in the

---

[52] G. J. Williams, *Agweddau ar Hanes Dysg Gymraeg*, ed. Aneirin Lewis (Cardiff, 1969), p. 210.

[53] 'Parochialia', *Arch. Camb.* (1909–11), 1, p. 120; 3, pp. 14–15, 23, 105.

company of three trained assistants (William Jones, David Parry, and Robert Wynne), on a four-year journey through the Celtic nations. The sheer logistics of this marathon undertaking were daunting: a journey of at least three thousand miles in an age when travel was indescribably cumbrous, tedious, and expensive was fraught with difficulties. Apart from Wales, Lhuyd's perambulations took him as far as Iona and Mull, Killarney and Sligo, and parts of Cornwall and Brittany. He and his entourage must have resembled a moving library, with their reference books, manuscripts, and scientific instruments. Thomas Tonkin has a nice description of Lhuyd and his companions, with knapsacks on their backs, 'prying into every hole and corner'[54] in Cornwall. Ambulatory research of this kind, involving long months of travel, cold, and hunger, imposed a heavy burden on Lhuyd. On his return, John Lloyd of Blaenyddôl confessed that, given Lhuyd's poor health, the varying climates of the Celtic countries, and the appalling terrain, 'we gave you for gone in a manner'.[55] *En route*, Lhuyd steered a wary course through Celtic minefields. Not even his charming manner could beguile suspicious Cornishmen, hostile robbers in Killarney, and belligerent Bretons in Brest. Yet Lhuyd and his small band of scholars emerged unscathed. Through their collective labours, they accumulated a rich harvest of priceless material, including meticulously compiled drawings of plants, fossils, and minerals, which were loaded into enormous boxes and shipped to the Ashmolean. On his return to Oxford Lhuyd set about marshalling and digesting his information and shaping his volumes for publication. But his trials and tribulations were not over. The publication of his first volume hung fire. Lhuyd was not a wealthy man and having to solicit financial aid was a constant source of vexation and embarrassment to him. The manuscript of the first volume, entitled 'Glossography', was ready by 1703, but the snail-like progress of the university printers meant that four years passed before it was published. Within two years of the publication of *Archaeologia Britannica* (1707), Lhuyd was dead. An attack of pleurisy had cut short his illustrious career. He died, aged forty-nine, in Oxford in June 1709. His untimely death robbed Welsh scholarship of its most outstanding figure and we can only speculate what he might have achieved had he lived longer.

Edward Lhuyd was the only Welshman of his day to dedicate his life to pushing back the frontiers of scientific knowledge. He gave his life to the service of meticulous scholarship, and his colleagues were stunned by his capacity for work, his emphasis on exact record, and detailed draughtmanship. Like all self-respecting experimental scientists, he insisted on collecting first-hand information by visiting sites, perusing manuscripts, and analysing 'observables' with fastidious care. If his comments on earlier toilers in the

[54] R. T. Gunther, *Early Science . . . Edward Lhuyd*, p. 31.
[55] B. F. Roberts, 'Llythyrau John Lloyd at Edward Lhuyd', *NLWJ* 17 (1971), p. 197.

field (notably Gerald of Wales and George Owen) seem unnecessarily harsh, this was less because of his desire to pick out flaws and inconsistencies in their work than his eagerness to probe beneath the surface of current axioms. His distaste for hearsay and dogmatism was a byword. He held in contempt those scholars who 'never as much as stooped in a gravel pit',[56] and his rare talent for winning the affection of peasants enabled him to tease out extraordinary information from illiterate shepherds. Lhuyd moved easily among common people, benefiting as richly from his correspondence about 'old Welsh writings' with Thomas Dafydd, a Cardiganshire day-labourer and autodidact, as from his links with professional scholars. A cautious man by nature, Lhuyd would accept no theories 'for which I have no warrant from my own reasoning'.[57] The hypotheses of other scholars, however soundly based, were always put to the test by Lhuyd. Nor did he shirk from seeking answers to questions which seemingly defied analysis.

There is no doubt that Lhuyd, by dint of his unflagging energy and force of personality, stimulated and canalized scholarly activity in Wales. The talented and busy circle of authors, antiquarians, scholars, and poets in the Teifi valley was heavily influenced by his work. Iaco ab Dewi (James Davies) lived in semi-seclusion in a cottage in the parish of Llanllawddog, Carmarthenshire, where he eked out a living by meticulously copying old manuscripts and translating the works of Bunyan, Beveridge, and others; Samuel Williams, vicar of Llandyfrïog, was a cultivated man who laboured ceaselessly to rescue literary treasures and translate godly books; Theophilus Evans, author of *Drych y Prif Oesoedd* (1716), was a brilliant stylist and translator; whilst Alban Thomas, curate of Blaen-porth and Tre-main, a poet and translator, was privileged to be the author of the first Welsh book—*Cân o Senn iw hen Feistr Tobacco* (A Song of Rebuke to His Old Master Tobacco, 1718)—to be published by an accredited press on Welsh soil. The links between them and Edward Lhuyd were Moses Williams, son of Samuel Williams and a highly gifted scholar, and William Gambold, rector of Puncheston. Both Williams and Gambold were graduates of Oxford and two of Lhuyd's most promising protégés. Moses Williams shared many of Lhuyd's literary aspirations, while Gambold was an experienced lexicographer, grammarian, and antiquary, who supplied Lhuyd with detailed accounts of historical remains in Pembrokeshire. Although the other members of the circle had not darkened the doors of a university they felt no sense of educational inferiority. They had no need to, for, as Lhuyd discovered, they were extraordinarily well-versed in their literary and historical inheritance. Samuel Williams and Iaco ab Dewi

---

[56] F. V. Emery, '"The Best Naturalist now in Europe": Edward Lhuyd, F.R.S. (1660–1709)', *THSC* (1969), p. 60.

[57] F. V. Emery, *Edward Lhuyd*, p. 27.

burned the midnight oil for months in order to copy and preserve some of the richest literary treasures of the past. A gem of a manuscript, now known as Llansteffan 133 in the National Library of Wales, bears witness to their scholarship, craftsmanship, and perseverance. Reverence for scholarship and patriotic pride were binding forces among these men of letters. They vowed their undying love for 'the country and nation of the Britons'.[58]

Lhuyd's studies also stimulated the interest of antiquaries in Glamorgan and helped to bring them together as a team. Led by Francis Gwyn, John Williams, and Philip Williams, a knowledgeable and enthusiastic school of scholars responded vigorously to Lhuyd's promptings and plied him with drawings, maps, charters, and manuscripts. Sir Thomas Mansell of Margam, to whom Lhuyd dedicated his *Archaeologia Britannica*, was among his doughtiest supporters. Many magistrates and petty squires joined in the hunt for the Welsh past. Even after Lhuyd's premature death, a bevy of churchmen, antiquarians, and scholars, including James Harris of Llantrisant and Thomas and Francis Davies of Llandaff, continued to study wills, letters, chronicles, and inscriptions with boundless curiosity and shrewdness. Harris sketched the fifteenth-century tomb of Sir David Mathew, while Francis Davies prepared a survey of the parish of Llandaff in the manner of Lhuyd's 'Parochial Queries'.

The many-sided activities of these groups of scholars reveal that Edward Lhuyd stamped his convictions on a whole generation. Yet it would be a mistake to overestimate his influence. Although Dean Hickes informed Lhuyd that *Archaeologia Britannica* had been 'worth all your labour and pains',[59] it is unlikely that it was widely read. Many of the gentry were puzzled and bewildered by Lhuyd's scholarly rigour. One of Lhuyd's acquaintances in Glamorgan reported that *Archaeologia Britannica* 'had not the reception in these parts as it deserved, not one in twenty that I conversed with giving it any tolerable character'.[60] Many landed gentlemen, of course, had abandoned their roles as the traditional guardians of Welsh culture. Nor were they familiar with the new world of scientific learning. Such were the depth and rigour of Lhuyd's thought that it is unlikely that many of his countrymen were capable of grasping the full sweep, let alone the detail, of his arguments. Outside Dissenting academies in Wales, scientific discoveries were scarcely a staple of conversation. Prominent men of letters had failed to absorb the essence of Newtonianism: Charles Edwards and Ellis Wynne clung valiantly to the Ptolemaic notion that the sun moved round the earth, and Welsh almanacs reaffirmed the traditional

---

[58] Geraint H. Jenkins, 'Bywiogrwydd Crefyddol a Llenyddol Dyffryn Teifi, 1689–1740', *Ceredigion* 9 (1979), pp. 460–4.

[59] R. T. Gunther, *Early Science . . . Edward Lhuyd*, p. 43.

[60] C. W. Lewis, 'The Literary History of Glamorgan', p. 608.

belief in geocentrism. 'The world stands in the middle of the heavens like the yolk in the middle of an egg', declared Thomas Jones the almanacker, 'and the sun and moon and stars in the heavens turn constantly around it.'[61] Attempts to draw attention to the changing intellectual temper of the times were not outstandingly successful. In his *Hanes y Byd a'r Amseroedd* (History of the World and Times, 1718), Simon Thomas sought to advertise the scientific discoveries of Galileo, Huygens, and Newton, but his tract swiftly degenerated into a whining anti-Catholic threnody. *Golwg ar y Byd* (A View of the World, 1725) by Dafydd Lewys, vicar of Cadoxton, was modestly described by its author as 'some crumbs from the table of the learned'.[62] Lewys plied his readers with anatomical, biological, philosophical, and astronomical tit-bits, but by including an abundance of lively but credulous anecdotes and by seeking (under the influence of William Derham's works) to reconcile science with revelation, he failed to convey the essence of the new scientific spirit.

In the field of historical inquiry, too, Lhuyd's rigorous methods were not widely evident. Welsh history was still thick with myth and legend, with historians rarely rising above the recital of old familiar notions. In Lhuyd's eyes, Geoffrey of Monmouth's extraordinarily influential work, *Historia Regum Britanniae* (*c.* 1136), was riddled with fable and error. But the 'British history' remained the cornerstone of the common Welshman's sense of identity. If Geoffrey's colourful tale had not survived intensive scholarly scrutiny in Restoration England, it was still alive and well in learned circles in Wales. Patriotic Welshmen simply ignored the claims of sceptical English scholars. William Maurice of Cefn-y-braich declared that whereas Camden was 'at the autumn of his fame', the British history was in the 'spring of its credit', whilst James Owen, a learned academy tutor, saw no reason why Geoffrey 'should be so run down'.[63] Although William Wynne's natural reflex, in his revised version of David Powel's *History of Wales* in 1697, was to err on the side of caution he still chastised those who treated Geoffrey's tales with contempt.

Lhuyd's sober and prudent comments on 'the British history' proved less popular and acceptable than the romantic lucubrations of Paul Pezron and the vibrant tales published in Theophilus Evans's *Drych y Prif Oesoedd* (1716). With this book, Theophilus Evans, a native of Penywenallt in the parish of Llandygwydd in south Cardiganshire, embarked on a prolific career of writing which spanned forty-five years. *Drych y Prif Oesoedd* is an epic story written by a young man of 23, full of nervous energy and

[61] NLW MS 6146B, pp. 179–86.
[62] Aneirin Lewis, 'Llyfrau Cymraeg a'u Darllenwyr 1696–1740', *Efrydiau Athronyddol*, 34 (1971), p. 67.
[63] B. F. Roberts, 'Ymagweddau at Brut y Brenhinedd hyd 1890', *BBCS* 24 (1971), p. 126; Charles Owen, *Some Account . . . of Mr. James Owen*, p. 109.

anxious to secure a niche for himself in the world of letters. Evans was driven to write partly by his devotion to the Church of England. He celebrated Anglican values in all his works and maintained a fierce loyalty to the established church long after the Toleration Act had put an end to hopes of achieving uniformity enforced by the law. Above all else, however, Evans was a patriot who was anxious that his countrymen should feel able to hold their heads high. He remained stubbornly wedded to ancient myths, notably the link between the ancient Britons and the classical world. Although he was familiar with Edward Lhuyd's ideas, he could not bring himself to reject tales and legends which redounded to the credit of his forebears. Evans was proud to count himself a *defensor Gallofridi* and he was determined to ensure that the 'British history' survived the scepticism and obloquy heaped upon it by English scholars. He cared little for the icy detachment of self-styled 'non-Brutans' and found the cynicism of English antiquaries both painful and humiliating. In *Drych y Prif Oesoedd*, therefore, he unashamedly extolled the glorious origins of the Welsh, giving wide currency to the views of Pezron by associating his people with the Celts. Evans believed that Welsh history was a pageant of colourful episodes, of battles and conquests, of epic victories and bitter defeats. In recalling the past, he saluted famous Welshmen, delighting in particular in the prowess of Brutus and Arthur, and rejoicing in Welsh victories on the battlefield against Saxons, Picts, and Normans.

In its reliance on legend and history, myths and fables, Theophilus Evans's work was not unlike Séathrún Céitinn's *Foras feasa ar Éirinn*, which proved immensely popular in Gaelic circles during the seventeenth century. Although he took himself very seriously indeed, Evans made little attempt to distinguish between fact and fable. His knowledge of the past was both derivative and superficial, and his Latin phrases and copious footnotes were simply a pretentious parade of learning. Untrained in essential historical methods and working largely on his own initiative, Evans pursued his studies with a youthful disregard for current scholarly and scientific views. It is not surprising, therefore, that his work abounds in dogmatic assertions, rhetorical flourishes, and youthful blunders. Yet Evans wielded a lively pen, and the literary merits of his book far outweigh its historical defects. Some critics have described him as a verbose chatterbox whose mannered turns of phrase reveal a man preoccupied with eloquence for its own sake. But there is no doubt that Evans was a superb raconteur who garnished his colourful tales with memorable images. Like Homer and Virgil (on whose work he depended heavily), he reserved his grandest similes and metaphors for the epochal moments in Welsh history. As a result, in spite of its *naïveté* and verbosity, *Drych y Prif Oesoedd* exercised an extraordinary influence on the ordinary Welshman's view of his nation's past. By opening the eyes of Welsh readers to the glories of the past, it had a tonic effect on the nation's morale. At a time when Welsh scholars were scarcely able to sustain a decent argument in favour of the 'British history', Theophilus Evans provided them with a memorable epic couched in attractive prose. By defending Wales's glorious origins, he moulded the historical outlook of his countrymen. *Drych y Prif Oesoedd*— republished and refined in 1740—caught the imagination of the reading public. Indeed, it is scarcely an exaggeration to say that it became the most popular history book in Welsh prior to the twentieth century. At least twenty editions were published before 1900.

In the field of Welsh scholarship, Edward Lhuyd had blazed several new trails. Few of his colleagues and successors, however, took up his torch. At Oxford, Lhuyd had gathered around him a number of able pupils and inspired their interests; but, deprived of his guiding hand after 1709, many of them were reluctant to bestir themselves. John Morgan of Matching complained bitterly in 1714 that 'there peeps not a penny paper from Jesus College for the use of their country' and Thomas Hearne lamented that 'good letters miserably decay everyday'.[64] Some of Lhuyd's apprentices failed to live up to the glorious promise of their early years. David Parry, Lhuyd's most accomplished disciple, spent more time in the tippling house than at his desk and died of drink in 1714. In a sense, too, Moses Williams, another of Lhuyd's protégés, is one of the most eminent might-have-beens in the history of Welsh scholarship. A product of the fecund literary circle in the vale of Teifi, Williams was a scholar, translator, collector, and editor of immense energy and determination. In an age of honest toilers, none laboured more assiduously than he. Williams's zeal for scholarship and his eye for significant historical and literary material led him into several fields of inquiry. Following Lhuyd's death, he dreamt of publishing a collection of the most priceless ancient Welsh manuscripts and went to extraordinary pains to examine literary treasures in countless libraries. He published works by the Tudor scholar Humphrey Llwyd, the linguist William Baxter, and the antiquary William Wotton. His *Cofrestr o'r Holl Lyfrau Printiedig* (Register of all Printed Books, 1717) is the foundation-stone of Welsh bibliography, whilst *Repertorium Poeticum* (1726) provided a useful alphabetical list of the first lines of celebrated odes and *cywyddau*. Moses Williams was also one of the few Welsh scholars of his day to nurse dreams of an economically developed Wales. His heart bled for his country and, in a moving peroration delivered to members of the Society of Antient Britons in London in 1717, he urged exiled Welshmen to raise Wales from its provincial torpor and penury by investing huge capital sums to facilitate the building of universities, charity schools, workshops, almshouses, and

[64] Prys Morgan, *Eighteenth Century Renaissance*, p. 21; Lawrence Stone, *The University in Society* (2 vols., Princeton, 1975), i. 56.

hospitals. His blueprint was shrewd and full of common sense. But it fell on deaf ears, for Williams possessed neither the social connections nor the necessary financial support to enable him to fulfil Edward Lhuyd's dreams. He also lacked Lhuyd's tact, charm, and *bonhomie*. His forthright tongue led him to chastise dissipated gentlemen and indolent clerics and, as a result, few were prepared to assist him to realize his ambitions. Moreover, since Williams was not prepared to cultivate friends in high places or sacrifice his convictions, he failed to climb the ladder of advancement. There is no doubt that he failed to receive the patronage that his labours deserved. The Morris brothers of Anglesey contrived to destroy his reputation by sneering at the quality of his editorial work and Williams may well have spent the last years of his life in despair. Frustrated and lonely, he died in Bridgwater, Somerset, in March 1742.

Some of Lhuyd's disciples and fellow scholars were reluctant to follow his footsteps, often with catastrophic results for Welsh scholarship. William Baxter, who had plagued Lhuyd with bizarre philological speculations, published a dictionary of place-names and their derivations—*Glossarium Antiquitatum Britannicarum* (1719)—which was riddled with woolly conjectures and theories far removed from the rigorous, systematic work of Lhuyd. It is significant, too, that William Stukeley, the charming but credulous English antiquary who grappled with the mysteries of the Celtic languages, preferred to rely on Baxter's speculations rather than on Lhuyd's sober judgements.

Others went astray in the dense undergrowth of archaeological studies. In spite of Lhuyd's efforts in laying the foundations for a deeper understanding of the past, few heeded his call for more rigorous archaeological study. Many of his countrymen were obsessed with those whom Elias Ashmole called the 'mysterious Druidae'.[65] The coming of the Renaissance in sixteenth-century Wales had stimulated an upsurge of interest among serious students in the history of the Druids. The classical texts of Caesar, Pliny, and Tacitus became widely available to scholars. As Welsh humanists absorbed classical evidence of Druid activity in Gaul, they came to suspect that Welsh poets were directly descended from the learned Druids. This theory acquired respectability when Milton endorsed it in *Lycidas*, and by the Restoration period more and more books were being published on the subject of the Druids and British antiquities in general. Some were more bizarre than others. In his enormously entertaining, but vacuous, *Britannia Antiqua Illustrata* (1676), Aylett Sammes claimed that the Welsh were 'prodigiously addicted'[66] to Druidism. In his massive tome, Sammes included a stirring portrait of a venerable Druid, bearded and barefoot, clad in a hood and a knee-length tunic,

[65] A. L. Owen, *The Famous Druids* (Oxford, 1962), p. 1.
[66] Aylett Sammes, *Britannia Antiqua Illustrata* (London, 1676), p. 101.

holding a staff in one hand and a book in the other. But the most notable serious contribution to the study of Druidism came from the amiable and eccentric antiquary, John Aubrey. Aubrey was obsessed with the Druids and carried out considerable field-work into prehistoric monuments and antiquities. Although his celebrated discourse on Stonehenge and Avebury remained unpublished, Aubrey influenced many of the leading scholars of the day, notably Lhuyd, Plot, and Toland. Aubrey's tentative theories on stone circles were noted by Lhuyd and the two scholars discussed the possibility of publishing Aubrey's 'Monumenta Britannica'. Nothing came of the scheme, but Lhuyd did not abandon his interest in Druidism. The fairy bolts and snake-beads (*glain y neidr* or *maen magl*) which he found in some profusion in Wales, Scotland, and Cornwall drew wry comments from him, since they resembled the *ova anguina* attributed to the Druids by Pliny.

Interest in Druidism gathered pace during the early eighteenth century. Gaulish Druids were invented by Paul Pezron, Jean Martin, and Simon Pelloutier; and Henry Rowlands, one of Lhuyd's correspondents, found the clarion call of the Welsh Druids irresistible. Rowlands, vicar of Llanidan in Anglesey, prided himself on being almost entirely self-taught. While Lhuyd was alive, Rowlands did not stray from the straight and narrow path of serious scholarship. Indeed, he compiled some of the shrewdest and most detailed replies to Lhuyd's parochial queries and also wrote accomplished essays on agriculture in Anglesey. Following Lhuyd's death, however, he fell completely under the spell of the Druids. His major work, *Mona Antiqua Restaurata* (1723), sponsored by 347 subscribers and published in Dublin, reveals that although Rowlands was endowed with splendid imaginative powers he was no longer able to reason in a systematic fashion. Druidism had become a profound obsession which filled his waking hours and disturbed his sleep. His preconceptions, unlike those of Lhuyd, were essentially backward-looking: an avowed diluvialist, he clung stubbornly to the theory of divine revelation, focusing his attention on three cardinal fixed points—the Creation, the Deluge, and the dawn of Christianity. By conflating scriptural and classical evidence, Rowlands provided himself with a theoretical framework for his research. He firmly believed that the Welsh were descended from the sons of Japhet—'the first planters of Europe'—and that it was possible to trace their footsteps from Armenia through Europe. These earliest settlers, he argued, ended their post-diluvian travels in Britain, inhabiting clusters of huts which were to be found in 'prodigious plenty' in many parts of Anglesey.

With charming *naïveté*, Rowlands focused his wildest theories on the Druids. He fondly believed that Anglesey was the ancient seat or the 'Canterbury' of British Druidism. The appellation 'Môn Mam Cymru' (Anglesey, the mother of Wales) had persisted through the ages simply because Anglesey was the 'mother church' of Druidism. Rowlands produced a more advanced engraving, after the manner of Sammes, of a wise-looking Head Druid, clad in flowing robes and sandals, carrying a plain staff in one hand and a spray of oak leaves in the other. He believed that the priestly hierarchy had contained three elements: the Druids (*Derwyddon*), Ovates (*Ofyddion*), and Bards (*Beirdd*). The abundance of prehistoric tombs, stone circles, and cairns dotted about the landscape of Anglesey were evidently the remains of 'druidical territories'. The tombs were Druid altars, and ritual sacrifices had been performed on top of the denuded capstones of the burial chambers. Rowlands was convinced that the Druids had flourished mightily in his beloved Anglesey until Roman centurions ravaged the island, drove out the Druids to Ireland, and deprived Britain of a unique cult.

Henry Rowlands was a diligent, observant man who gathered a wealth of data on the physical and historical remains, customs, laws, and language of his native island. His theories, however ingenious, were nevertheless ultimately vacuous. His attempts to trace the derivation of Welsh words were unsuccessful. In fact, he muddied the waters of Welsh philology. He maintained, for instance, that *Môn* meant *Y Fon Wlad*, that is, 'the furthest land'. *Gwyddel*, he insisted, came from *Gwydd* and *hela*, that is, 'wood rangers' or 'forest hunters'. Most ludicruous of all was his claim that Abaris, the Hyperborean servant of Apollo, had acquired his name from someone bearing the surname 'ap Rees'.[67] In struggling to formulate new certainties, Rowlands found that his theoretical perceptions did not match his powers of observation. Although he was a pioneer in some respects, his work promised more insights than it delivered. A blinkered enthusiast, Rowlands's propensity to fantasy led him astray. He might refer to Edward Lhuyd as 'our exquisite antiquary', but his true sympathies, especially by the 1720s, lay with the romantic notions of Pezron and his like. Modern historians have rightly christened this enthusiastic but misguided man 'the Welsh Stukeley'.[68]

In a Welsh context, Lhuyd's scientific and scholarly ideas were clearly in advance of their time. Had his work been systematically studied and properly assimilated by Welsh scholars, many of the bizarre ideas which gained currency in eighteenth-century Wales might have been scotched at birth. Several quirks of fate also conspired to rob scholars of the opportunity to examine Lhuyd's massive corpus of unpublished material. Four years after his death, Lhuyd's voluminous collection of manuscripts was bought by Sir Thomas Seabright. Some of these manuscripts were later purchased by Thomas Johnes of Hafod, Cardiganshire, and were consumed

[67] Henry Rowlands, *Mona Antiqua*, *passim*.
[68] J. Gareth Thomas, 'Henry Rowlands, the Welsh Stukeley', *Trans. Anglesey Antiq. Soc.* (1958), pp. 33–45.

by a fire which destroyed his elegant mansion in 1807. Other manuscripts which came into the possession of Sir Watkin Williams Wynn suffered a similar fate in a fire at Covent Garden. The loss to Welsh scholarship was incalculable. Yet Lhuyd's career proved to be a source of inspiration for succeeding scholars. The Morrises of Anglesey were his most ardent admirers: they judged him 'inferior to no man in natural history, and had a prodigious knack of languages'.[69] It was Lhuyd's example which persuaded Lewis Morris to embark on a quest for Celtic remains in Europe. It is significant, too, that Lhuyd's dreams were echoed in the Cymmrodorion Society's *Gosodedigaethau* (Constitutions) and were eventually realized in the *Myvyrian Archaiology*, published in three volumes by the Gwyneddigion in 1801 and 1807.

During this period, two major factors came into play to determine the nature and quality of Welsh cultural life. The growth of the Welsh press was the first motor for cultural change. Thanks to the enterprise and initiative of a small group of printers, Shrewsbury and Carmarthen became important publishing centres which nourished spiritual and cultural needs. The marked increase in the volume of Welsh books enabled a wider circulation of ideas and provided a stimulus to literacy. Although the printed output of publishers like Thomas Jones and John Rhydderch lacked subtlety and refinement, it was a commercial success which left an indelible mark on Welsh cultural life. William Morris grudgingly admitted that Welsh publishers had opened up new frontiers and that Thomas Jones, in particular, was 'an old fellow who, in spite of his ignorance, did a lot of good'.[70] The increasing influence of the press enabled authors to remind their countrymen that their language was one of the mother tongues of Europe. By extolling the virtues of the Welsh language and arguing a seductive case for its primeval origins, authors helped to swell the Welshman's pride in his native language. Strenuous efforts were made, too, to foster a continuing interest in Welsh poetry, especially free-metre poetry, the content and temper of which were refashioned according to the demands of the reading public. Moreover, *eisteddfodau* and bardic contests helped to preserve and extend knowledge of the arcane lore of ancient bards. Although religious reformers were heavily preoccupied with the need to produce treatises of moral suasion and practical devotion, they were not insensitive to literary values. Charles Edwards, Ellis Wynne, and Theophilus Evans were all reformers who sought either to coax or frighten readers into moral conduct and repentance. Yet they were imaginative artists who produced extraordinary masterpieces which retained a hold on

[69] R. T. Jenkins and H. M. Ramage, *A History of the Honourable Society of Cymmrodorion* (London, 1951), p. 43.
[70] *Morris Letters*, i. 198.

the public taste down to the twentieth century. An instructive and entertaining fare of almanacs and ballads was also made available to humbler readers who had not hitherto been able to afford printed literature. More and more people were learning to read and asserting their right to have popular literature presented in attractive packages.

The second telling influence was the towering scholarship of Edward Lhuyd. Lhuyd was a man of true greatness who exercised a profound influence on Welsh scholarship. His sagacious grasp of an awesome range of intellectual and scientific subjects stimulated the curiosity of a whole generation of Welsh antiquarians, historians, archaeologists, and philologists. Lhuyd not only fostered a spirit of critical inquiry but also inspired fellow Welsh scholars to respect the past and to study it with genuine sympathy and understanding. Although Lhuyd's grandiose schemes did not come to full fruition in his own day, *Archaeologia Britannica* was a seminal work which established ideas from which were to spring many of the later developments of the eighteenth century. In many ways, the initiative for the cultural revival launched by London-based savants and littérateurs in the mid-eighteenth century was provided by the labours of Welsh scholars in this period. Given the absence of national institutions, a cultural capital, scientific academies, learned periodicals, and focal points such as salons and coffee houses, it is surprising that so much had been achieved.

PART III

THE AGE OF IMPROVEMENT
1730–1780

CHAPTER 7

SOCIAL AND ECONOMIC PROGRESS

ONE of the principal pace-setters of economic growth in mid-eighteenth-century Wales was the rising trend of the population. Although the absence of precise data makes it impossible to reconstruct the demographic structure before 1801, the population of Wales probably rose from around 489,000 in 1750 to 530,000 by 1780. By the time of the first census in 1801, demographic growth was well advanced and Wales's population stood at 587,000. Although demographic trends in this period fluctuated from region to region and even from parish to parish, the decisive upward movement seems to have occurred after 1750. Less prone by then to interruptions caused by mortality crises, population growth became normal and sustained. As famine years dwindled, the gap between the number of births and the number of deaths widened. In rural Radnorshire birth rates drew sharply away from death rates between 1750 and 1770, whilst in Caernarfonshire burials exceeded baptisms in two years only—1762 and 1769—in the period after 1740. In the parish of Aberdare, the excess of burials over baptisms had halted by 1750 and over the following three decades baptisms exceeded burials by twelve, eleven, and twenty-four respectively.

The most notable upsurge of population growth occurred wherever there was quickening economic activity. The counties of Denbigh, Flint, and Glamorgan, in particular, experienced unusually rapid numerical expansion as the birth rate accelerated and as increasing numbers of migrants were attracted to new and wealthy industrial communities. The swiftest growth rates in industrializing counties were found in Flintshire and Glamorgan. Between 1750 and 1801 Flintshire's population increased from 29,700 to 39,622 (an increase of 33.4 per cent), and Glamorgan's population grew from 55,200 to 71,525 (29.5 per cent) in the same period. From the mid-1740s, particularly, substantial increases occurred in the population of west Glamorgan: the most vital growth-centres were communities such as Llangyfelach, Llansamlet, Cadoxton, Neath, and Swansea, where numbers were rising as a result of considerable developments in the copper and coal industries. Marriage and baptism aggregates increased significantly and the ratio of baptisms to burials rose from 472:346 in 1750 to 710:499 in 1780. Even the epidemic diseases which continued to ravage Wales from time to time were no longer capable of checking the general upward turn in demographic patterns after 1750.

Few subjects remain so poorly documented and understood in the history of eighteenth-century Wales as the relative roles of birth rates and mortality rates in the general expansion of the population. The slender number of local studies on this hazardous subject, however, suggests that a rising birth rate was the primary factor in the upturn of the population. In both rural and industrial counties a variety of factors forced the population upwards. Women of child-bearing age tended to be more fertile. Earlier marriages were encouraged by the popular social custom of bidding (young couples were able to acquire smallholdings on the basis of loans, donations, and gifts contributed by their neighbours) and this, too, served to increase the size of families by extending the child-bearing period. Improved economic conditions also helped to keep the birth rate buoyant, and, as the number of crisis years dwindled, the ability of children and adults to survive, marry, and bear more children was enhanced. Improvements in nutrition may have helped to build up resistance to illness and enable more children to survive the first years after birth. The potato, in particular, became a crucial element in the diet of common people. Potatoes were extensively cultivated in fields and gardens after 1750 and they became either a supplement to or a substitute for bread, porridge, and oatcakes. Thomas Pennant believed that potatoes were 'a great support'[1] among labouring people and by raising standards of nutrition they clearly helped to encourage parents to raise larger families. A rising birth rate and a quickening tempo in industrial change also went hand in hand in this period: the most populous counties were those where economic expansion pushed up the birth rate and attracted the parents of young families in search of regular employment.

The significant rise in the birth rate, however, was not accompanied by a decline in the mortality rate. Wales was still not free of the scourge of epidemic diseases, many of which rampaged through counties, from time to time, with devastating results. It is not easy to diagnose or identify diseases which distressed and bemused contemporaries and were referred to as 'malignant fevers' and 'agues'; but it would seem that the most terrifying killers were diphtheria, smallpox, typhus, and measles. Smallpox continued to wreak havoc, bringing disfigurement, blindness, and death to many people, especially in 1747, 1752, 1759, and 1763. Its incidence among children was particularly high. Howel Harris's grief knew no bounds when smallpox cut down his 'loving, winning, sharp and amiable'[2] two-year-old daughter, Anne, in 1749, and memories of her death came flooding back when the same disease took its toll of children at his settlement in Trefeca in 1759. During the same period many of Griffith Jones's pupils died in excruciating pain. Impoverished people, too, were always at risk. Of the

---

[1] Thomas Pennant, *Tours in Wales* (2 vols., 1783), i. 15.
[2] Gomer M. Roberts, *Portread o Ddiwygiwr* (Caernarfon, 1969), p. 111.

fifty or so who died of smallpox in Holyhead in the early months of 1762 'there were hardly any but what lived in a poor way . . . It seems there are some constitutions more apt to receive it than others.'[3] Typhus was also capable of sweeping away the poor and most vulnerable members of society in a matter of days, especially during years of dearth and famine. It caused widespread dislocation and suffering in 1740–2, 1752, 1757–9, and 1762. Nor should we forget that people struggled daily to combat common colds, coughs, asthma, toothache, and stomach pains. Lewis Morris graphically recorded the miscellaneous ailments of his household in mid-Cardiganshire in February 1760:

My wife and I cough for the most; Jenny my little girl in a chincough; Siôn the sheep in a violent cough and a swelled head, bled this morning. Siôn the cowman . . . in an intermittent fever . . . coughs much. Will the Gifft a cold in his head, can hardly speak. Arthur the plowman barks like a lion.[4]

Mr Peswch (Mr Cough) was Lewis Morris's closest companion and not even ample supplies of garlic and honey could induce him to move on.

There are few signs of improved medical skills in this period. Few medical graduates or licentiates returned to Wales, and most rural practitioners earned a not altogether undeserved reputation for killing more people than they cured. During the 1730s a Dr Bates of Cardiff advised patients who had contracted smallpox to take a 'decoction of snails with cows' milk'[5] every morning and evening, as well as an assortment of drops, pills, and liniments. Well-meaning squires helped to diffuse knowledge of inoculation techniques with some success, notably in dispersed rural communities. But, in the towns, inoculation against smallpox may have spread the disease by causing secondary infections. Common people preferred to entrust their bodies to the tender mercies of lay healers, bone-setters, and cunning men, who, as ever, called on a rich fund of domestic remedies and herbal medicines. But even their fabulous nostrums were useless when deadly epidemics struck. Mortality rates remained high, and infants and young children, in particular, were highly vulnerable whenever infectious diseases raged. A tomb in a Monmouthshire churchyard records the death of four infants who, before reaching two months, 'shrank back from such a world as this/to live in realms of endless bliss'.[6] In Anglesey, a bleak gravestone in Trefdraeth churchyard marks the grave of the seven children of Edward and Gwen Williams who died between 18 December 1769 and 2 January 1770. Appropriately,

---

[3] *Morris Letters*, ii. 594.

[4] *Morris Letters*, ii. 178–9.

[5] Iolo Davies, 'A Certaine Schoole': A History of the Grammar School of Cowbridge (Cowbridge, 1967), p. 46.

[6] Charles Wilson, *England's Apprenticeship 1603–1763* (London, 1965), p. 368.

perhaps, it was in 1770 that Edward Richard composed his famous epitaph, *In Sepulchrum Infantuli.*

From time to time, periods of dearth and disease continued to prune local populations. The worst crisis occurred in 1739-41, when a combination of terrible weather, harvest failures, food shortages, high prices, and disease caused widespread misery and calamitous mortality rates. During the winter of 1739-40 the ground over most of Wales remained frozen hard until April. Wine froze in cellars, birds dropped dead from the skies, and snow was still falling in May. The cold and the drought stunted the growth of grass and caused appalling mortality among cattle and horses. In June 1740 William Bulkeley of Llanfechell noted that meadow grass looked 'frightful' and that 'poor cattle are almost starved'.[7] Farmers were left with no alternative but to slaughter their skinny beasts. A wet winter in 1740-1 deepened the crisis. By the spring, the price of wheat and barley was the highest in living memory and tons of grain were imported into north-west Wales in order to feed starving families. In Flintshire soaring prices forced the London Quaker Company to import large quantities of grain to feed workers who threatened to abandon their labours. Many parts of Wales were aflame with food riots: in Pembrokeshire furious mobs attacked the ship of the notorious smuggler, William Owen, and stole his mainsail, whilst in Denbighshire and Flintshire crowds of angry colliers, craftsmen, and women strove so ferociously to prevent the export of precious grain that soldiers were called in to restore order. Many tenants found themselves in arrears and a rash of petty thefts kept magistrates busy. Smallpox, typhus, and measles—those deadly killers—seized their opportunity to cut down the weak and the vulnerable. By March 1741 poor people were dying 'very fast' in Anglesey and, a month later, James Baker, agent of the Powis Castle family, declared that 'the misery the poor endure here is not to be expressed'.[8]

Once this crisis had been weathered, however, the population began to rise steadily and the risk of famine following harvest failures was not as great. There were, nevertheless, years of food shortages, distress, epidemics, and tumult, notably in 1751-3, 1756-7, and 1766-7, when mortality rose sharply and riotous mobs ransacked mills, granaries, and ships. But actual famine years were infrequent, partly because the development of maritime trade and improved transport facilities enabled local authorities to import or move grain more easily. Localities were becoming ever less dependent on domestic markets and their own produce. As the economy in general grew stronger, the short- and long-term

[7] J. Oliver, 'The Weather and Farming in the Mid-Eighteenth Century in Anglesey', *NLWJ* 10 (1957-8), p. 308.
[8] *Morris Letters*, i. 42-51; T. M. Humphreys, 'Rural Society in Eighteenth-Century Montgomeryshire', p. 17.

consequences of harvest failure were more easily borne. Moreover, since the overwhelming trend of the population was markedly upward, mortality spasms were quickly made good. Thus, although burial rates remained high throughout this period, the significant rise in the rate of natural increase, aided by sustained economic growth, ensured an excess of births over deaths.

One of the most striking features of society in mid-eighteenth-century Wales was the concentration of property within the grasp of powerful landowners. The shift of property into fewer hands had been under way since the Restoration, and wealthy landlords continued to seize their opportunities to expand their acreage, often at the expense of less affluent gentry who were badly crippled by heavy mortgages and taxation. Land was the most lucrative and prestigious form of investment and it enabled those Leviathans whose estates yielded annual rentals of well over £3,000 to enjoy unrivalled economic power and security. They possessed capital assets which insulated them from the financial ups-and-downs which plagued the lives and prospects of smaller neighbours. Rising rentals, mineral profits, and expanding trade yielded handsome returns which excited the envy of declining squires and the growing disapproval of common people. For affluent landowners, life was comfortable and assured. The eighteenth century was truly the golden age of the prosperous Welsh landlord.

The richest landowners lived in a grand manner. When Sir Watkin Williams Wynn came of age in April 1770, the landmark was celebrated on an unprecedented scale with a banquet of gargantuan proportions at Wynnstay Park. A bevy of cooks was brought in from London and Chester to prepare food for 15,000 guests; church bells rang; harpists, fiddlers, and morris dancers entertained the throng; and lamps and fireworks illuminated the gardens. Grandees with incomes large enough to fortify their tastes acquired handsome houses in Mayfair and squandered their liquid assets in the metropolis. Thousands of pounds were spent on concerts, masquerades, balls, and parties at Vauxhall and Ranelagh Gardens. According to John Byng, estate revenues were frittered away 'in the prodigalities of London, and in driving high phaetons up St. James's Street, whilst the glories of their country seats are neglected'.[9] No one was more willing to be drawn to the seductive pleasures of London than Sir Watkin Williams Wynn. Unlike his abrasive and unsophisticated father, Wynn became something of a dandy: he sold his horses and hounds, liked to dress up as a Druid, joined the Society of Dilettanti, and threw himself wholeheartedly into the social whirl of London life. Wynn spent hefty sums on fashionable clothes and

[9] John Byng, *The Torrington Diaries*, ed. C. B. Andrews (4 vols., London, 1934), i. 138.

wigs, spared no expense in decorating and furnishing his lavish London home, and purchased many rare paintings and *objets d'art*. His life of ease and luxury was shared by many fellow Titans.

But even many of these great magnates were heavily in debt. Many families incurred massive debts by embarking on furious but often fruitless attempts to win political influence. In a vain bid to undermine the political power of Wynnstay, members of the Myddelton family of Chirk Castle encumbered themselves with debts which forced them to raise new mortgages and to deal harshly with tenants who fell into arrears. Extravagant life-styles left others in a parlous state: Robert Jones of Fonmon owed debts of £50,000 in the 1760s, whilst Lord Grosvenor's liabilities stood at £151,000 in 1779. Even the mighty Sir Watkin Williams Wynn discovered that his life of conspicuous consumption placed a severe strain on his purse. Much to the chagrin of his patient steward, Wynn spent so freely that by 1789 his debts amounted to £160,000. Two marriages, six children, a Grand Tour, repairs and additions to Wynnstay, a stylish house in London, election costs, and a myriad other outgoings had sent his liabilities soaring, and he was obliged to avoid his creditors in Wales by spending most of his time in London or at popular spas and seaside resorts. However, powerful landowners such as he were better equipped to carry their debts than were their more slenderly endowed neighbours. Their property was invariably tied up in strict settlement or heavily mortgaged. Complex land settlements served to obstruct or delay the sale of their lands and many behemoths were sufficiently powerful to silence or bully their creditors.

For many stay-at-home gentlemen, life was a ceaseless round of drinking, gambling, fox-hunting, hare-coursing, cock-fighting, and shooting. The Welsh gentry were as capable as ever of swilling down large quantities of alcohol. Exclusive drinking parties became the rage as cellars were stocked with smuggled wines and spirits, terrifyingly potent home-brewed ale, and cunningly flavoured gooseberry or cowslip wines. Corsygedol's home-brewed beer was known as 'the Caesar's blood'.[10] Food was even more plentiful and varied than before. Gentlemen's tables groaned under the weight of venison, mutton, veal, beef, pork, poultry, game, salmon, trout, potatoes, beans, peas, carrots, turnips, plums, pears, apples, peaches, and gooseberries. Metropolitan fashions were spreading swiftly into the provinces and even modestly placed gentlemen were happy to welcome the wind of change. Thomas Johnes's country mansion at Llanfair Clydogau was a gambling centre not only for Cardiganshire gentry but also for politicians and diplomats from London who were rather shrewder at the tables than their untutored hosts. Even in the fastnesses of Merioneth

---

[10] B. B. Thomas, *The Old Order* (Cardiff, 1945), p. 19.

there was a flourishing 'Lunatick Club', and John Pugh Pryse, heir to the estates of Gogerddan, Mathafarn, and Rug, acquired the nickname 'the Merionethshire Macaroni'.

Fashion-conscious landowners also lavished considerable pride and affection on their country mansions and the surrounding environment. As the demand for comfort and privacy increased, gentlemen of taste began to pay even more serious attention to house-designs and interior furnishing. While some landowners built anew, others gave their homes a face-lift. The new trend was to build compact, square houses, according to Palladian tastes: the functional mansion at Nanteos in Cardiganshire, built in 1739, and Wynnstay, rebuilt by Francis Smyth in 1736–9, are particularly fine examples. Stone and brick were new alternatives to timber and Plas-gwyn (built of red brick) at Pentraeth in Anglesey is a splendid example of an early Georgian brick house. Spacious entrance halls and staircases, sliding sash windows, wooden wainscoting, heraldic decoration, and plaster ceilings all became more popular. During the 1760s splendid stucco ceilings were constructed at Chirk Castle and a magnificent Rococo plaster ceiling at Fonmon Castle. By the 1770s the rooms at Erddig were adorned with Chinese wallpaper as well as an exquisite Chinese pagoda and a model of the ruins of Palmyra, designed by Elizabeth Ratcliffe, a maid-servant of considerable artistic gifts. Libraries were enlarged and enriched, many more fine portraits were commissioned and bought, and a wide variety of elaborate hangings and tapestries was introduced. More sophisticated comforts were now available: as tea-drinking became universal, china and silver ware replaced earthenware and wooden utensils in modest country homes. Elegant mahogany furniture was imported from London, and chairs bearing the influence of Chippendale, Hepplewhite, and Sheraton began to displace the more solid and traditional oak chairs. Harpsichords replaced the virginals and the spinet. From 1771 onwards the leading families of north-east Wales flocked to the private theatre of the fourth baronet of Wynnstay.

Gardens, too, were adapted, modified, or redesigned in accordance with contemporary fashions and tastes. Many agreeable features beckoned discerning travellers: the hanging beechwoods at Erddig were a sight to behold, Powis Castle's famous terraces and loggia were still a delight to the eye, and the orangery at Margam invariably drew admiring comments. New initiatives were also launched by men of substantial means. 'Capability' Brown, the outstanding exponent of scenic architecture in the eighteenth century, was commissioned by Williams Wynn of Wynnstay to prepare designs for the grounds and the lake. William Emes, one of Brown's disciples, designed a cylindrical waterfall known as the 'Cup and Saucer' at Erddig and drew up for Gregynog a garden design based on informal groves, drives, pools, and lakes. On many estates, landowners sought to maintain appearances and emulate their neighbours by commissioning landscape gardeners to design flower-beds, winding paths, fishponds, scenic bridges, waterfalls, lakes, shrubberies, orchards, and sinuously contoured belts of trees.

There is no doubt that the gulf, in terms of wealth, life-style and sentiments, between the richest gentry and the common people widened considerably as the eighteenth century wore on. Demographic changes which had occurred since the late Stuart period were seen to have critical implications for the disposition of landed property in Wales and the general harmony and well-being of society. In many counties the extraordinary failure of the male line brought about fundamental structural changes. In Monmouthshire, failure to produce a male heir accounted for most of the nine long-established families who disappeared between 1700 and 1750; six more vanished between 1751 and 1805. In neighbouring Glamorgan the traditional dynasties continued to perish with lemming-like regularity: the families at Hensol, Dunraven, Cefnmabli, and Y Fan had died out by 1736, and they were followed by those of St Donat's (1738), Friars (1738), and Margam (1750). Other counties were also stricken by the prevailing propensity to biological failure. Around 40 per cent of the estates of Montgomeryshire vanished during the seventy years prior to 1760, and the high failure rate of male heirs accounted for many of them. In Pembrokeshire, well-known families such as the Barlows of Slebech, the Stepneys of Prendergast, and the Wogans of Wiston either failed to produce a male heir or sank under the burdens of mortgage and debt; whilst in Caernarfonshire the estates of Cefnamwlch and Madrun foundered.

The significance of these profound changes was not lost upon contemporaries. 'Alas, what will become of the good old breed once famous for getting sons and daughters?',[11] was John Garnons's plaintive cry in 1759. Over a relatively short period a remarkable metamorphosis had occurred in the character of landed property in many parts of Wales. In Glamorgan, for instance, failure in the main line led to changes of ownership in nineteen out of thirty-one estates between 1670 and 1770. Old and highly respected family names like Bassett, Carne, Herbert, Mansell, and Turberville simply vanished and their lands were transferred through a daughter or daughters to English families. A dozen of the most affluent and prominent Glamorgan gentlemen in the 1750s were men who belonged to families who could not boast any obvious Welsh connections before 1680; seven of them had not acquired Welsh lands until after 1735. The ruling élite now bore strange and un-Welsh names such as Plymouth, Talbot, and Bute. Elsewhere, too, prevailing demographic trends had robbed Wales of many of its native gentry and encouraged acquisitive

---

[11] J. Glyn Parry, 'Stability and Change in Mid-Eighteenth Century Caernarfonshire' (unpubl. University of Wales MA thesis, 1978), p. 18.

newcomers to snap up encumbered properties or marry eligible heiresses. In Caernarfonshire, strangers with double-barrelled names such as Assheton-Smith, Douglas-Pennant, and Wynne-Finch came in search of high yields on their capital and prompted Hyde Hall to pin-point the menace posed by 'English names' which were 'creeping everywhere in the Principality'. Many observers who were by no means interested parties were convinced that the demise of 'a very useful order of society' was regrettable.[12] Some claimed, with inevitable nostalgia in such troubled times, that the traditional Welsh families had always taken care to display a genuine concern for the well-being of their communities and had exercised the most profuse hospitality to those in greatest need. Cultural patriots bemoaned the rise of new ruling classes who found Welsh culture risible and its language beneath contempt. For the new Titans viewed 'Welsh ragamuffins' and 'the foul language of Taffydom' with studied disdain.[13]

By the middle of the eighteenth century many Welsh estates had fallen into the hands of absentee English or Scottish landowners who seldom visited their patrimonies, had no great liking for the Welsh people, and little sense of obligation towards their tenants. Absentees treated their estates as sources of revenue and not much else. Few of them devoted part of their disposable income to encouraging agrarian reforms, and they were certainly less disposed than their predecessors to identify people in need and to set aside sums of money for charitable purposes. Lacking a lineage rooted in the area, they were generally contemptuous of old values and obligations. As the traditional county community broke up and as the old, relatively cordial order of things was undermined, class divisions began to emerge. Resident gentlemen and freeholders were bitterly resentful of the ruthless power of distant aristocrats and the means by which their stewards exercised their will. According to one Glamorgan Whig, 'the honest feelings of the injured glow with indignant detestation at the very name of Windsor'.[14] Bitter disputes during political elections in the 1770s sprang from the fear and confusion which followed the end of the old order. Religious reformers aired their conviction that the motives of absentee magnates were transparently selfish, and a host of poets, ballad-mongers, and rhymesters told the same embittered tale. William Jones of Llangadfan believed that the new ruling classes held the view that the common people of Wales could 'scarcely be distinguished from brutes' and that their language was 'an incoherent jargon'.[15]

The growth of the great estates and the power of absentee landlords

---

[12] E. Hyde Hall, *A Description of Caernarvonshire (1809–1811)*, ed. E. Gwynne Jones (Caernarfon, 1952), p. 43.

[13] Philip Jenkins, *The Making of a Ruling Class*, p. 214; Geraint H. Jenkins, *Thomas Jones yr Almanaciwr 1648–1713* (Cardiff, 1980), pp. 107–8.

[14] John Davies, *Cardiff and the Marquesses of Bute* (Cardiff, 1981), p. 87.

[15] NLW MS 13221E, f. 377.

were inevitably accompanied by a corresponding decline in the number of the smaller gentry. All the evidence suggests that this was not an easy time for them. Perpetually short of funds, mortgaged to the hilt, buffeted by land taxes and county rates, they were extremely vulnerable. It was not as easy for them as it was for their affluent superiors to raise loans or live on credit, and during periods of economic crisis many of them were sucked into 'the gulphy vortex of our Leviathans'.[16] Some families inherited encumbrances which were too crippling to bear, whilst others struggled in vain to survive on limited financial resources. In Caernarfonshire the Coetmor-Pugh, Bryncir, Bodidda, and Ystumllyn estates went under because their owners' incomes were insufficient to meet increasing expenditure. Others frittered away their revenues through mismanagement, extravagance, or fecklessness. At Madrun, William Bodfel's extravagant style of living brought disaster in its train, while at Marl, Ann Williams had the misfortune of marrying, in turn, two ne'er-do-wells who spent money as though there were no tomorrow. Many small gentlemen overreached themselves not only by living beyond their means but also by aping the social habits of affluent English landowners. Hugh Vaughan of Hengwrt was an irremediable spendthrift who, having dissipated his fortunes at the gambling table and racecourse, fled his estate in 1778 as the bailiffs closed in.

Even so, it would be foolish to claim that most of the smaller gentry sank without trace. By adopting a policy of strict financial stringency and moderating their ambitions, some of them were able to swim successfully against the tide. Times were hard and few of them could afford to indulge their taste for risk and adventure; not for them the gaieties of the London season or the hazards of the turf. It was possible, therefore, for the sober, the cautious, and the persevering squires to survive. At Trawsgoed in 1741 Wilmot Vaughan inherited an estate on the verge of bankruptcy, but he managed to retrieve the situation by thriftily husbanding the resources of his patrimony and, above all, by marrying well. However frustrating that might have been, families were obliged to come to terms with their reduced social status and humdrum way of life. The epitaph to Simon Yorke of Erddig, who died in 1767, epitomizes the virtues of the frugal backwoods gentleman: 'a pious, temperate, sensible country gentleman, of a very mild, just and benevolent character . . . an advantage which amiable men have over great ones'.[17] Arthur Blayney of Gregynog, partly through necessity and partly through choice, dressed like a farmer who had seen better days. A benevolent and well-liked bachelor, he preferred local food to 'far-sought delicacies' (save for port, to which he was rather partial)[18]

[16] NLW MS 5A, pp. 102, 211; NLW MS 609A, pp. 82-5.
[17] Merlin Waterson, The Servants' Hall (London, 1980), p. 35.
[18] Glyn T. Hughes and others (eds.), Gregynog (Cardiff, 1977), p. 38.

and scorned current fashions in clothes. Blessed with a deeply-ingrained sense of financial responsibility and family duty, Blayney simply resolved to make the best use of his limited financial resources. Frugal gentlemen of this kind were better equipped than their prodigal neighbours to survive in such an exceptionally testing period.

Nevertheless, many of the lesser luminaries floundered from crisis to crisis and their decline had profound effects on the nature of Welsh society. All over Wales country houses which had once been of critical importance in their communities lost their status as *plasau* (mansions) and either became farmhouses or fell into ruin. In Caernarfonshire William Wynn of Wern married the heiress of Peniarth and left his ancestral home to crumble. When Anna Lloyd of Gesail Gyfarch died without issue in 1784, her home was let as a farmhouse. Thomas Pennant found many cheerless and neglected mansions during his tours in the 1770s and Richard Morris mournfully noted in 1779 that newspapers were 'shamefully stuffed with continual advertisements for sale of Welsh estates; several of which I remember to have seen in a flourishing condition'.[19] In north-east Wales, John Powell, a Llansannan weaver, yearned for palmier days: 'where there were once many handsome halls, there is now worse than cowhouses, without a resident to give either food or bedding'.[20] Meanwhile, the estates themselves either fell into the hands of distant relations or were snapped up by predatory Titans. When the once proud estate of Peterwell in Cardiganshire came under the hammer and passed to a London lawyer, the melancholy sight of the crumbling mansion moved Dafydd Dafis, Castell-hywel, to record the end of an era in elegy:

> To the dust it went when its time came,
> And its great merriment ended.
> The silent owl breeds in its walls.[21]

Scores of dilapidated or deserted country homes bore silent witness to the irrevocable decline of the Welsh squires.

As the smaller gentry—their pockets in tatters and their pride badly bruised—slipped down the social scale, the relationship between the bigger landlords and their tenants worsened. Several economic changes helped to loosen ties of mutual regard, especially on those estates where absentee landowners sought to tighten administration and increase their rent-rolls by entrusting the active running of their properties to stewards. In particular, the commutation of traditional services, duties, and gifts into

[19] D. W. Howell, 'Landlords and Estate Management in Wales', in J. Thirsk (ed.), *The Agrarian History of England and Wales, vol. v: 1640–1750* (Part 2, Cambridge, 1985), pp. 262–3.
[20] G. J. Williams (ed.), 'Llythyrau at Ddafydd Jones o Drefriw', *NLWJ* Suppl. 3 (1943), p. 22.
[21] Bethan Phillips, *Peterwell* (Llandysul, 1983), p. 225.

money payments and changes in the pattern of leaseholding provoked tension and disharmony. During periods of slump and depression it had behoved landlords not to bear down too heavily on tenants who had built up rent arrears, since undue pressure might lead to untenanted farms and depleted rent-rolls. Sympathetic local landowners, mindful of the interests of the community at large, were prepared to rescue hard-pressed tenants by permitting, on a short-term basis, rent abatements and payment of manorial dues in kind. More exacting landlords, however, especially absentees who worked through their stewards, made few concessions to tenants in financial trouble and were prepared to evict those whose farms were in serious disrepair or whose debts had multiplied too swiftly. As stewards strove, by fair means and foul, to obey the wishes of their masters, tenants found that prompt payment of rents, entry fines, heriots and other ancient dues was expected. Patterns of leaseholding were also changing in some of the more advanced Welsh counties. Throughout much of Wales, tenant farmers were normally granted leases for three lives, a practice which, if John Vaughan of Golden Grove is to be believed, they were 'well pleased with'.[22] But, as the demands for food grew, enterprising landlords were increasingly disposed to abandon three-lives leases on the grounds that they prevented them from raising rents, improving their properties, and increasing their yields. On many large estates, from the 1760s onwards, leases for three lives were replaced by shorter leases (usually of twenty-one years) or tenancies-at-will, which gave landlords absolute control over rents, improvements, and their tenants. Shorter leases enabled stewards to exercise a much tighter grip on day-to-day affairs on their estates and allowed them, by inserting appropriate 'improving' clauses, to urge tenants to be more industrious and enterprising. The tenant, on the other hand, was racked by fears for his future and, especially during the troubled inflationary years of the American War, he lay at the mercy of bullying masters. As Twm o'r Nant noted:

> Between the laws of stewards and the vanity of great men
> A tenant is caught between the devil and his tail.[23]

Soaring rents were a second source of grievance. For two or three decades after 1730 rents had remained fairly stable, but expanding population, rising food prices, agricultural improvements, and developing trade provoked substantial rent increases from around 1760 onwards. In south-west Wales rents nearly doubled during the forty years after 1760, whilst in Caernarfonshire they rose by 54 per cent between 1750 and 1790. On the largest and best-managed estates the steepest rises occurred during the crisis-ridden years of the 1770s: rents on the Wynnstay estate, for

[22] D. W. Howell, 'Landlords and Estate Management', p. 280.
[23] Thomas Edwards, *Tri Chryfion Byd*, ed. N. Isaac (Llandysul, 1975), p. 23.

instance, rose by 37 per cent between 1775 and 1780. During his journey through north Wales in 1776, Joseph Cradock found that the 'exorbitant demands' of landlords were provoking 'great complaints',[24] and in the same year Evan Evans denounced inhuman landlords who set extortionate rents: 'Great self is the object of all their aims and wishes, and thousands load them with curses for raising exorbitant rents'.[25] As rents doubled or trebled with disconcerting speed, a spate of songs and ballads aired the resentments of impecunious tenants. 'We are the slaves', cried one, 'and you great men are proud, cruel and oppressive.'[26] Hugh Jones of Maesglasau was convinced that the great landowners were prepared to squeeze every penny from their tenants in order to add to their wealth:

> We shall do as we please,
> And we'll make you suffer for us;
> We'll raise rents, and we'll rant,
> And we'll keep you awake
> In order to please us in every parish.[27]

Substantial rent increases had the effect of widening the gulf between powerful gentry families and impoverished tenants. Most absentee land-owners worried little about harming the image of their class, and want of mutual confidence between landlord and tenant lay at the root of the storm of protest which characterized much of rural Wales in the early nineteenth century.

As the number of small gentry families declined and as their influence naturally waned, an amorphous body of moneyed men, comprising substantial farmers, stewards, lawyers, attorneys, squarsons, merchants, tradesmen, doctors, and customs officials, began to play a more significant role in Welsh society. By the middle of the eighteenth century the *nouveaux riches* were increasing appreciably in numbers and were, to some degree, filling the gap which separated the privileged world of the gentry and the plebeian world of small tenants, labourers, and paupers. The Welsh middling sorts were essentially the product of agrarian improvements, urban development, and mercantile growth. Men who were maliciously described as 'brindled Jews' in the *Morris Letters* might have lacked pedigrees and social graces, but they were not short of energy and ambition. In their pursuit of worldly happiness, they agreed wholeheartedly with Richard Morris that it was money which set 'all the wheels in motion'.[28] Lacking truly powerful economic influence and as yet not strong

---

[24] Joseph Cradock, *An Account of Some of the Most Romantic Parts of North Wales* (London, 1777), p. 144.
[25] Evan Evans, *Casgliad o Bregethau* (2 vols., Shrewsbury, 1776), i. sig. B3.
[26] J. H. Davies (ed.), *A Bibliography of Welsh Ballads* (London, 1911), p. xxv.
[27] Hugh Jones, *Gardd y Caniadau* (Shrewsbury, 1776), p. 71.
[28] *Morris Letters*, ii. 607.

enough to exercise an effective curb on the political power of big landowners, the middling sorts sought compensation in making money. Although their incomes of around £100 to £125 per annum in rural counties such as Anglesey, Caernarfonshire, and Montgomeryshire were relatively modest, their eye for profitable deals seldom failed them. In commercially more advanced counties like Flintshire, Denbighshire, and Glamorgan they were more affluent and more determined to keep up with the Joneses of Wales and, given the chance, the nobs of England too. Twm o'r Nant, who invariably reserved his sharpest barbs for the self-seeking bourgeoisie, singled out some of those who had succumbed to the lure of profit:

> Attorneys and parsons
> Shopkeepers and apothecaries
> Steal as much good land as they can
> So that their finger nails can squeeze the weak.[29]

Many of them aspired to the living standards of the gentry and their comfortable and well-furnished homes contained visible signs of affluence such as desks, books, rugs, mirrors, clocks, and musical instruments. For a variety of reasons, however, these enterprising and often unscrupulous people were deeply unpopular among their less privileged inferiors.

From around 1750 a marked upturn in prices brought new opportunities of affluence to substantial farmers. Those whose purses were sufficiently long and whose confidence was sufficiently high were active in the land market and used their surplus capital to invest in agricultural improvements in order to meet growing demands for more food. Many of them owned livestock and household goods which were valued far in excess of those owned by neighbouring gentlemen. During lean years those who farmed fertile, grain-producing lands seized their opportunity to establish a monopoly of local markets and strike secret bargains with badgers, dealers, and ships' captains in order to export grain at a profit. Hoarding and exporting grain in times of dearth were major causes of the riots which flared from time to time in market towns and ports. The enrichment and avarice of big farmers who forsook age-old obligations in order to fill their own pockets caused bitter resentment among poorer farmers and common people. Small farmers were much more at the mercy of the weather than their larger neighbours and many of them, dogged by lack of capital, restricted acres, inefficient agricultural methods, and defective markets, eked out a bare and miserable subsistence. It was natural for families who found intolerable the pressure of having to pay rents, taxes, tithes, and dues (as well as to raise enough food to live on) to feel enraged on discovering that prosperous farmers were conspiring with others against them. Fortune rarely smiled on poor farmers in this period and many of

[29] J. Glyn Parry, 'Stability and Change', p. 150.

them went under. William Morris told the not untypical tale of the fate which befell his cousin, Margaret Salbri: 'She had six or seven children when she died. The father was a drunkard, the children scattered here and there, some gone to sea and some to the mountain. They lived quite respectably when she was alive, but afterwards all the property was swept away.'[30] Such anecdotes could easily be multiplied.

Estate stewards and agents, too, were in bad odour. Charged with the responsibility for increasing efficiency and maximizing profits, they were busy, influential, and well-paid men. In the mid-eighteenth century their annual salaries ranged from £50 in Montgomeryshire to £100 in Glamorgan. By the 1780s, however, stewards on the Powis and Wynnstay estates could boast annual incomes of over £500. For a variety of reasons, they were becoming highly unpopular. Many of them were practising attorneys who were well-versed in the art of provoking needless lawsuits and serving more than one master. Some unscrupulous knaves took advantage of the distance between themselves and their absentee masters to embezzle large sums of money entrusted to their care, and they used it to purchase land or to invest in commercial enterprises. Philip Williams of Dyffryn in Glamorgan was alleged to have decupled the value of his £40–£50 patrimony at the expense of the lords of Neath Abbey. In the lead-mines of Cardiganshire, stewards abused the truck system by paying subsistence rates in kind to miners, stealing goods at extortionate prices, and cheating the miners at the weighing of ore. Their frauds and tricks brought ruin to many investors in Cardiganshire and Montgomeryshire. John Paynter, an agent who 'drove ten times hotter than Jehu',[31] was a notorious embezzler and thief, while the Powells, who were known as the 'Kings of Swansea', were noted as much for their ruthlessness as for their vigilance. Many stewards practised their petty tyrannies with relish. Welsh-speaking tenants found themselves browbeaten by men bearing names like Durbrow, Pratt, and Robotham, and squires and freeholders who transgressed against property rights were intimidated and cowed into submission. On estates where tenancies-at-will were common, or where manorial and commercial rights were disputed, stewards were able to exercise considerable pressure. It was not only a 'hot-arsed'[32] Leveller like William Jones, Llangadfan, who found them arrogant, supercilious, and oppressive. Freeholders, tenants, labourers—even Methodist reformers—were often terrorized by them. 'Thou shalt worship the estate agent', wrote Lewis Morris, 'for he is the graven image of thy master and a demi-god. Obey him through fire and water, watch lest thou offend him, and woe be to thee if he frown upon thee.'[33]

---

[30] *Morris Letters*, i. 254–5.   [31] *Morris Letters*, ii. 48.
[32] Gwyn A. Williams, *The Search for Beulah Land* (London, 1980), p. 40.
[33] Hugh Evans, *The Gorse Glen*, tr. E. M. Humphreys (Liverpool, 1948), p. 31.

Lawyer-agents and attorneys, some of them of 'mean' birth and average talents, were also advancing and consolidating their wealth and status by investing in land and developing lucrative practices. The well-to-do town of Carmarthen, for instance, was copiously supplied with sixteen attorneys or lawyers by 1790. Many of them were engaged by substantial families or by stewards to prepare deeds, to draft and execute wills, pronounce on matters of custom and procedure, arrange mortgages, and tie up marriage settlements. Few commentators enthused over them. The Morris correspondence abounds with memorable vignettes of 'driving' attorneys and 'damned voracious' lawyers, whilst Twm o'r Nant held the view that hell was probably full of lawyers and parsons. Common people were convinced that bewigged lawyers, who only spoke English, offered no protection for the poor and the weak, and the allegedly villainous deeds of Anthony Maddocks, the 'very proud and rich' lawyer from Cwm Risga, were preserved for posterity in the celebrated folk-tale of the 'Maid of Cefn Ydfa'.[34]

The number of wealthy and influential squarsons was also increasing significantly. As land values rose, church livings, especially in north Wales, began to yield sizeable incomes. In parts of Anglesey and Caernarfonshire pluralist clergymen were receiving incomes in excess of £250 per annum and were much better off than parish gentry. Incumbents in rich country benefices were often good and conscientious men; but there were also some who hunted by day, drank until the small hours, and shared spoils at cock-fights with dissolute gentlemen. As the number of non-Welsh-speaking appointments to plum livings increased, popular rhymesters launched scathing attacks on the greed of lazy English pluralists and their lay masters. 'Many a fat parson', wrote Lewis Morris, 'makes the earth groan under him when he treads it, because he hath some hundreds a year for not keeping a school or serving his church.'[35] When Thomas Rogers, rector of Egiwysilan, died in 1769, it was widely believed that a surfeit of juicy steaks had hastened his departure.

Tithes were burdensome and unpopular impositions, and a growing number of disputes and quarrels found their way to the consistory courts, local assizes and even the Court of Arches. As crop yields increased, embittered farmers argued that bloated squarsons were robbing them of their profits. In those parishes where the alienation of tithes to lay impropriators was a running sore, farmers were incensed to find valuable tithe money collected by distant landowners who felt no obligation to ensure that those who held livings in their gift served their parishioners efficiently. Many people bitterly resented the obligation to pay church

[34] Philip Jenkins, *The Making of a Ruling Class*, p. 35; G. J. Williams, 'Wil Hopcyn and the Maid of Cefn Ydfa', Stewart Williams (ed.), *Glamorgan Historian*, 6 (1969), pp. 228–51.
[35] *Add. Letters*, i. 113.

rates and tithes to a church, led by absentee bishops and mercenary nepotists, which was supported by landowners who zealously guarded not only their tithing rights but also their claims over pews. Clergymen used their best endeavours to persuade recalcitrant parishioners to part with a tenth of their produce, but they found that the more pressure they exerted the greater the number of defections to Methodism or Dissent. Indeed, Dissenters were protesting loudly at having to pay compulsory church rate to an institution to which they no longer belonged. Nor were matters helped by the fact that growing numbers of well-to-do clergymen were now sitting side by side with the gentry on the commissions of the peace. Although clerical justices generally proved to be more efficient than most squires who sat on the bench, they must have found it hard to serve their political masters faithfully and provide for the needs of their flocks. For, in their capacity as magistrates, clergymen issued orders for the maintenance of bastards, removed widows to their native parishes, and sentenced vagrants to severe whippings, and it was perhaps natural for those who came under the lash of the law to gain some measure of retribution by stirring up anti-clerical sentiments.

Other members of the new moneyed class normally dwelt in expanding commercial towns. Welsh towns were developing and they now offered a much wider range of commercial and professional services to consumers. Tradesmen, merchants, and shopkeepers benefited from the upturn of agrarian production, the expansion of trade, and improvements in communications. Towns acquired specialisms—butchers, grocers, vintners, stocking merchants, periwigmakers, and booksellers began to proliferate —and the number of general and particular retail shops grew. Some tradespeople became remarkably affluent: Edward Jones, a Caernarfon shopkeeper, owned goods valued at £5,877 in 1741, whilst Richard Lloyd, a mercer's son, did so well as a flannel merchant that he became a pioneer banker at his house in Chester Street, Wrexham. As tradesmen became more affluent and assertive, they seized opportunities of marrying into the gentry class. One striking example is Elizabeth Bold, daughter of a Beaumaris shopkeeper, who married Hugh Owen, squire of the celebrated Penrhos family. Elizabeth was hailed as one of the seven 'Pretty Peggies' whose beauty (and wealth) helped to breach social barriers in Anglesey.

Much to public disgust, the number of salaried government officials was also increasing appreciably. Among the busiest but least-liked (at least within the smuggling fraternity) were customs and excise agents. Greater numbers of them were recruited in a bid to reduce illicit trade and to dissuade those who preyed on rich cargoes. By the mid-eighteenth century there were eleven customs agents stationed at Beaumaris alone. The most accomplished and efficient officers earned sizeable incomes: James Briscoe, Controller, Deputy Customer, Salt Collector, and Coal Duty

Collector at Beaumaris, earned £120 per annum. Lewis Morris earned £100 per annum as Collector of Dyfi, whilst his brother William, Deputy Controller at Holyhead from 1737 to 1763, received an annual salary of £80.

Although there was a dearth of qualified medical men, most towns had a resident physician of some sort and those which were prospering had many more: by 1790 Brecon had four surgeons and a druggist, and Carmarthen had ten surgeons and apothecaries. Even Llandovery had four apothecaries by 1761, a fact which prompted a surprised Lewis Morris to exclaim: 'London come almost to our doors'.[36] However, most of those who aspired to climb over social barriers were required to practise in London or join the Navy. Noah Thomas, son of a master mariner from Neath, had the dubious honour of serving as physician to George III, a disagreeable task which earned him a knighthood in 1775. David Samwell (Dafydd Ddu Feddyg) was a naval surgeon who sailed with Captain Cook on the *Resolution* and the *Discovery*, and witnessed his master's violent death on one of the Hawaiian Islands. Among others who broke through social barriers and acquired landed wealth was Herbert Jones of Llanengan in Llŷn: he served a medical apprenticeship in Anglesey, went to sea, served as a surgeon in the Navy, and accumulated an astonishing fortune of around £8,000 which enabled him to buy the estate of Llynone in Anglesey.

It is not hard to understand why the burgeoning numbers and wealth of the middling sorts earned the disapproval, envy, scorn, and hatred of plebeians. To those who were determined to obtain 'just' prices, defend common and waste land, worship according to their conscience, or smuggle goods freely, the *nouveaux riches* were tangible symbols of the unacceptable face of commercialism. A spate of ballads, interludes, and squibs bears witness to popular resentments over rents, engrossing and forestalling, petty tyranny, costly lawsuits, and tithes. From time to time disgruntled peasants vented their spleen on 'cheats, broils, sharking ministers, highwaymen, pick-pockets, villainous stewards, bloodsuckers etc.',[37] and characters in interludes such as 'Reginald Money-Bags' and 'John Eye-of-the-Penny' came to epitomize the priorities of moneyed men. Moreover, the fact that middling sorts placed heavy emphasis on diligence, thrift, and prudence, and consequently recoiled from those 'turbulent' and 'wasteful' rituals, customs, and recreations which common people held so dear, meant that they consciously and deliberately distanced themselves from plebeian culture. Affluent, ambitious, and well-educated, these groups were not only scaling the social ladder but were also helping to transform old ways of life.

---

[36] *Morris Letters*, ii. 393.
[37] *Add. Letters*, i. 144.

As we have seen, whereas farmers who possessed capital prospered, smaller tenant farmers began to feel the pinch. Stewards had become a force to be reckoned with and, as the process of consolidating farms and enclosing common lands quickened, small farmers found it difficult to survive. Troubled by rising rents and bitter competition for farms, they were often obliged to seek by-employments as craftsmen, colliers, or carters. From the 1770s onwards, their position was parlous: Hugh Jones, Maesglasau, maintained with pardonable exaggeration that for every one stubborn tenant who contemplated quitting his farm, there were eighteen others desperately seeking a tenancy. Popular ballads complained of soaring rents, high taxes and a general fund of resentful bitterness:

> You [the gentry] squeeze and moan and grow fat,
> We, dazed, fare poorly.[38]

According to Twm o'r Nant, gentlemen and stewards treated their dogs better than their tenants.

Demographic changes also imposed new strains on craftsmen. As their numbers swelled and competition for work increased, many shoemakers, corvizors, cordwainers, and weavers experienced a drop in living standards. On the other hand, as prospering towns began to respond to developments in local manufacturing and industrial and maritime trade, a greater number of craft specialisms became available. Tanners, saddlers, hatters, curriers, glovers, and tailors prospered in well-to-do towns, and shipbuilding in Cardigan bay, notably at Barmouth, Aberdyfi, and New Quay, offered wider opportunities of employment for ship's carpenters, shipwrights, nailers, ropemakers, and sailmakers. Unusually talented and inventive craftsmen also did well, none more so than William Edwards, an extraordinarily gifted stonemason and engineer who built (at the third attempt) a magnificent arched bridge across the Taff at Pontypridd in 1756. The single arch had a span of 140 feet—the widest in Europe—and astonished travellers dubbed it one of the wonders of the world. At the Methodist settlement founded at Trefeca, a plethora of arches, Venetian windows, balconies, dials, clocks, and mathematical instruments which were displayed for public view bore witness to the skills of the specialist craftsmen whom Howel Harris and his colleagues had recruited. Of all the highly skilled handcrafts in mid-eighteenth-century Wales, however, none carried greater prestige than the thriving business of clock-making. A growing demand for domestic clocks provided new opportunities for skilled craftsmen, and Samuel Roberts of Llanfair Caereinion and John Tibbot of Newtown became particularly famous clock-makers. The mechanical ingenuity involved in making long-case clocks made it one of the finest expressions of the true craftsman's art. Working in harness with skilled

[38] J. Glyn Parry, 'Stability and Change', p. 76.

cabinet-makers and joiners, clock-makers became busier and far more consumer-conscious. The number of recorded clock-makers in Wales rose from 72 in the period between 1700 and 1750 to 238 by 1800, and the demand for clocks reflected growing prosperity. There were eight clock-makers at work in the town of Wrexham alone in 1750, and many others carried on a lively trade in sheltered rural villages as well as in thriving towns.

Many such craftsmen were self-taught and bilingual men who were strongly committed to religious or cultural causes. Some were Methodist exhorters, while others were pillars of the Dissenting movement. Those among them who were most anxious to learn not only subscribed regularly to Welsh books, but also borrowed medieval chronicles, English novels, and popular classics from book clubs and circulating libraries. The development of independent thinking, the growth of scriptural knowledge, and the general spread of literacy were all causes to which they were deeply committed. They undoubtedly played a significant part in the campaign to rouse the conscience of the Welsh nation and to make good the lack of books and cultural activity.

As the gulf which separated the propertied from the unpropertied widened, agricultural labourers probably experienced a fall in living standards. Save for meagre portions of potatoes, fish, and bacon, their diet remained largely unchanged. Poorly dressed and often barefoot during the summer, rural labourers continued to live a life of dependence, exhausting toil, and drudgery. More than ever, too, they were chronically vulnerable to the effects of demographic growth, increases in food prices and fluctuations in employment. It is true that daily wages increased gradually as the century wore on—rising from 6d. to 8d. a day in the 1740s to 1s. a day in the 1770s in rural areas (it was a few pennies more at harvest time) and from 8d. a day to 1s. 4d. in industrial communities—but when prices of grain rose sharply after 1760 and especially during the inflationary years of the American War, the real wages of labouring people were eroded and their living standards deteriorated. Growing numbers of them either sought to cushion themselves against adversity by depending more than ever on by-employments such as spinning, weaving, or fishing, or, as happened more frequently, simply fell into the swelling ranks of paupers.

The loss of customary rights accelerated this process. Much to the vexation of local magistrates, Crown agents, gentlemen, and stewards, growing numbers of labouring families had been driven by demographic pressures and rural unemployment to encroach on common lands. By appealing to ancient custom and traditional rights of usage, poor labourers and cottagers were able to supplement their paltry wages by growing vegetables, gleaning, collecting peat and wood, picking wild fruit, and grazing sheep or cows. When it dawned on landlords and stewards that squatters had deposited themselves on lands which were ripe for enclosure or industrial development, they declared war upon people who were described by one surveyor as 'the very scum of the earth'.[39] As the nature of the Welsh economy began to change, the old paternalist view withered. Hundreds of labouring people were robbed of their immemorial right to enjoy the benefits of common land. Their eviction was fiercely resented, not only because it gravely affected their ability to cope with seasonal unemployment or periods of slump, but also because it robbed them of a certain measure of independence. Denied access to common pasture and supplies of fuel, they had to struggle even harder to survive. Many of those forced to quit the land joined the growing numbers of unemployed and destitute people who roamed Welsh towns in search of casual or permanent employment. Many others sank without trace.

Another reliable index of increasing distress and falling living-standards was the swelling number of labouring people who migrated to London and other English cities. Throughout the eighteenth century, of course, London's population was constantly being topped up by a wide cross-section of Welsh people. But, as times became harder around 1760, large numbers of labouring women also migrated to London during the summer months. Young women—known as *Merched y Gerddi* (The Garden Girls)—set off in groups of six from as far west as Cardiganshire and trudged over two hundred miles in search of employment in the gardens and parks of the capital. Others earned precious shillings by harvesting hay, grain, hops, and fruit in Middlesex and Kent. Severe economic pressures at home, together with the expansion in market gardening and a dearth of labour in London, offered these girls new opportunities which they were glad to accept. Indeed, they acquired a well-deserved reputation for honesty, cleanliness, and diligence.

Rural distress was also driving labouring people to both old and youthful industries where wages were more attractive. At Esgair-mwyn, Cardiganshire, in the mid-eighteenth century, lead-miners earned 1s. or 1s. 2d. a day. At Briton Ferry colliery, towards the end of the 1770s, colliers earned 1s. 4d. a day, whilst women earned 8d. per day for driving a gin-horse and 6d. per day for unloading wagons. At some works there was a wider range of comforts. Robert Morris built a block of flats known as Y Castell (The Castle) to house forty families of colliers and copper smelters employed at the Forest works in Glamorgan, whereas employers at the Melingriffith tinplate works provided amenities such as a company shop, a reading room, and a benefit club for working people. But in most industrial communities employment was irregular and conditions were harsh.

---

[39] A. Eurig Davies, 'Enclosures in Cardiganshire, 1750–1850', *Ceredigion* 8 (1976), p. 105.

278 THE AGE OF IMPROVEMENT 1730-1780

Industrial labourers were allowed to share only the minutest portion of the considerable wealth and benefits which their masters derived from the exploitation of industrial resources.

The rapid growth of population also created such enormous pressure on the land that small cottagers and labourers were forced to try to set up tiny *tai unnos* (one-night houses) on moorland and mountain. These pitifully small and makeshift houses, hastily built in a single night in order to enable occupants to establish freehold rights over plots extending from three to ten acres, were thrown up in the most rudimentary fashion. Walls were built with mud, clay, loose stones, rubble, or *clom* (earth compacted with straw) and roofs were thatched with straw or rushes. These miserable, smoking hovels, lacking sanitation, warmth, or comfort, became a familiar sight in isolated upland regions. Common people in Llŷn, according to Pennant, lived in houses 'made with clay, thatched, and destitute of chimneys',[40] and as late as 1810 Walter Davies described the cottages of north Wales as 'truly the habitations of wretchedness'.[41] Iolo Morganwg liked to believe that the whitewashed cottages of Glamorgan housed neat, clean, and gentle people, but travellers believed that the interiors of such premises stood in dire need of a tub of hot water. The homes of labouring people at Caerphilly were likened to the hovels of 'Hottentots or wild Tartars'.[42]

If the condition of the labouring classes was in many cases deplorable, the fortunes of paupers, squatters, and vagrants at the foot of the social scale were even worse. The pressure of rising population, land hunger, and soaring prices, especially after 1760, swelled their numbers and worsened their plight. All over the country growing numbers of poor people were claiming relief in the form of rents, pensions, food, and clothes, thereby imposing an intolerable burden on the meagre financial resources of parishes. Hitherto, families had always struggled to support their penurious relations and neighbours in order to avoid the stigma and opprobrium which were cast upon those in receipt of poor relief. But the traditional doctrine of paternalist support for poor people by their social superiors or well-to-do relatives was cracking under the weight of strong economic pressures. As Pennant noted, 'the warmth of natural affection'[43] had disappeared. Faced with the appalling prospect of large-scale pauperism, local authorities enforced Poor Law statutes rigorously, increased levies, and addressed themselves to the problem of settlement and removal. Churchwardens and overseers of the poor swiftly discovered that private

[40] Peter Smith, *Houses of the Welsh Countryside* (London, 1975), p. 310.
[41] Walter Davies, *General View of the Agriculture and Domestic Economy of North Wales* (London, 1810), p. 82.
[42] G. Nesta Evans, *Social Life in Mid-Eighteenth Century Anglesey* (Cardiff, 1936), p. 24.
[43] T. Pennant, *The History of the Parishes of Whiteford and Holywell*, p. 100.

almsgiving and charitable donations by rich individuals were insufficient to deal with the problem. In those communities where the population was thickening swiftly and where labourers had experienced a dramatic fall in living standards, there was a particularly pressing need to provide impoverished and disabled people with the basic necessities of life. Paupers were badged, orphans and idiots farmed out, apprentice schemes launched, and almshouses, houses of correction, and workhouses built. Every available means at the disposal of local authorities were employed to restrict the mobility of the landless poor. Large sums of money were spent on identifying unwanted strangers, vagrants, and pregnant women, and effecting their speedy removal to their place of birth lest they become chargeable to the parish. Harsh measures such as these brought great hardship to families and individuals. As paternalism declined, the poor suffered more than ever before. Driven from parish to parish and never likely to acquire gainful employment, paupers and beggars lived truly wretched lives. The well-groomed aesthete, William Gilpin, was shocked to encounter paupers occupying makeshift huts amid the ruins of Tintern Abbey; one old and disabled woman who lived in the remnants of a shattered cloister had no possessions, except a ragged bed, in her 'cell of misery'.[44]

Faced with these misfortunes, common people clung stubbornly to old habits and ways of life which had always helped them to cope with poverty, distress, and deprivation. Superstition and magic remained vital components of their culture, and despairing religious reformers beat their heads in frustration as plebeians heaped scorn on their sermons and insisted that their destiny was in the hands of powerful supernatural forces. Almanacs sold like hot cakes, cunning men were in constant demand, and the diabolic results of witchcraft were plain to see. When in 1752 eleven days were excised from the month of September in order to conform with the Gregorian Calendar, superstitious peasants resisted the changes and ascribed the floods, thunder, and hail which followed 'to the changing of Christmas'. Festive events such as wakes and May-Day celebrations continued to provide opportunities for communal fun, sexual encounters, and what Iolo Morganwg called *llamhidyddiaethau* (gambols). Bandy-playing or *bando* (a primitive form of hockey which was extremely popular on the sandy shores of south Wales) was added to the myriad games which encouraged broken heads and hacked shins. Alcohol was a lubricant as well as an anaesthetic, interludes offered fun and vulgarity in equal doses, and ritual dances and folk-songs brought a touch of gaiety to humdrum lives. Even so, those moments of joy and excitement which helped to loosen the vice-like grip of poverty and deprivation were essentially short-

---

[44] William Gilpin, *Observations on the River Wye . . . made in 1770* (London, 1782), p. 35.

lived. Travellers to Wales in this period do not convey a sense of joyousness among the lower orders.

There is no doubt that the middle years of the eighteenth century witnessed a new interest in ways and means of developing the considerable economic and strategic resources of Wales. Much greater vitality and an enthusiasm for change are detectable. A number of shrewd writers, with several worthwhile schemes and suggestions to offer, put pen to paper in order to encourage the spirit of improvement and to persuade investors to embark on modernizing enterprises. Some of them, perhaps, were over-optimistic and rhapsodical, but they were evidently conscious that Wales stood on the threshold of major social and economic changes. Whatever other faults he may have had, Lewis Morris was a particularly well-informed and constructive critic who was anxious to strengthen the economic infrastructure of Wales. In his *Plans of Harbours, Bars, Bays and Roads in St. George's Channel* (1748), Morris assembled a mass of written and cartographical evidence to show how well endowed Wales was. He did not gloss over the principal weaknesses of the economy—the lack of large-scale capital, the retarded state of technology, and the lack of domestic markets—but he was convinced that the environment was congenial to rapid growth and improvement. He upbraided Welsh landlords for preferring 'to rummage the East and West Indies for money, rather than to go fifty or a hundred yards underground in our own island'; and having drawn attention to the superb natural resources of his country he expressed the fervent hope that soon 'our manufactures of our own natural commodities may one time or other flourish for the benefit and honour of the nation'.[45]

Similarly, in *Proposals for Enriching the Principality of Wales* (1755), an author who wrote under the pseudonym of 'Giraldus Cambrensis' was deeply conscious of the colonial drain of wealth to the economy of England and of the need to modernize Wales by encouraging greater prosperity. In offering new approaches to agrarian betterment, he pressed landowners to enrich their estates and pockets by claying and marling their lands, sowing clover and turnips, and fattening bullocks, sheep, and pigs on available grazing-land. The opportunity for economic expansion in Wales was also a theme taken up by John Campbell in his survey of Britain in 1774. Campbell believed that the ruggedness of the soil, the harsh climate, and the dearth of indigenous capital were trivial handicaps as compared with the extraordinary assets and potential which Wales possessed:

The produce in all kinds of necessaries is a proof of this, as it makes the greatest part of their exports. Sheep, goats, black cattle, horses, they have in abundance.

---

[45] Lewis Morris, *Plans of Harbours, Bars, Bays and Roads in St. George's Channel* (London, 1748), p. 11; Part 2, p. 12.

Fish excellent, and in vast variety. Game, and all sorts of tame fowl, in plenty. Neither are they deficient in metals; silver, copper and lead especially are drawn from their mountains.[46]

In his view, no country in Europe was better equipped to encourage manufacturing industries, increase its productive capacity, and strengthen its domestic and overseas markets.

However exaggerated these hopes might have been, there were growing indications that the spirit of improvement was alive and well in rural communities. The growing trend was towards stock-raising and the production of meat. In most parts of Wales farmers continued to depend on their stock rather than their crops for profits. This made good sense, especially in the unenclosed upland and moorland regions, where it was much more appropriate to rear herds of hardy Welsh cattle than to experiment wildly with newfangled ideas better suited to the soil and climate of East Anglia. Sensible farmers relied on proven and generally profitable methods of pasturing cattle and used local lime, manure, clover, and perennial rye-grass to maintain the fertility of their fields. The well-being of the cattle trade remained of vital importance in a land where liquid assets were never regularly available. As London's population increased massively, the demand for Welsh beef was insatiable. By the middle decades of the eighteenth century, over 30,000 lean cattle and sheep were driven annually across windswept and rain-sodden moorlands through Herefordshire (and were even shipped across the Bristol Channel) and on to the fairs and markets of south-east England. Intrepid drovers continued to render valiant service to local communities by making substantial profits in the English market and by bringing badly needed currency into rural Wales.

These stimulants were accompanied by two significant changes in the nature of livestock farming. Firstly, the time-honoured, but declining, practice know as transhumance—whereby owners of sheep and cattle moved with their families to live in summer dairy houses in order to attend to their flocks, make cheese, and manufacture cloth before returning in winter to their lowland dwellings—perished during the latter half of the eighteenth century. Except in some of the drowsier parts of Caernarfonshire, few *lluestai* (summer homes) were now in use since most cattle were pastured on farms, whilst sheep were left to graze the mountain pastures and waste lands. Secondly, there was a growing tendency in many counties for sheep-farming to expand at the expense of rearing dairy cattle and goats. Much larger flocks of sheep were kept on farms and communal pastures. Farmers in Cardiganshire, according to Lewis Morris, kept 'many thousands, even to fifteen or twenty thousand, which is more than Job

---

[46] John Campbell, *The Political Survey of Great Britain*, i. 191.

had'.[47] These enormous flocks were kept as much for their meat as for their wool. William Williams of Pantseiri, Carmarthenshire, owned such large flocks of sheep and herds of wild horses that he was known as 'King of the Mountains' and 'Job of the West'![48]

Rising population, urban growth, and the accumulation of capital in commerce and industry undoubtedly stimulated agricultural change. Since there were growing numbers of people to be fed, land needed to be cultivated more efficiently. As the eighteenth century progressed, many 'spirited landowners' took a keener interest in new scientific methods and resolved to reclaim unenclosed land, introduce new breeding methods, and popularize crop rotations. The diffusion of agricultural improvements depended heavily on the initiative and enterprise of individuals. In Anglesey, Edward Wynne of Bodewryd and William Bulkeley of Bryn-ddu sanded and dunged their fields, watered meadows, and adopted progressive crop rotations. In Montgomeryshire, where it was the general practice to grow clover by the 1740s, Arthur Blayney of Gregynog was an enterprising improver who urged his tenants to vary their crops and use effective manures. Charles Powell of Castell Madoc in Breconshire toiled selflessly in order to break down old prejudices and pursued the path of agrarian betterment with a zeal ahead of his time, whilst, under Howel Harris's watchful eye at neighbouring Trefeca, more clover, fallow, hay, and turnips than corn were being grown by the 1770s and counsel was being offered to improvers at Leominster and Bristol. In Glamorgan, John Franklen of Llanmihangel reclaimed waste lands, popularized the use of the threshing-machine, and exemplified the new spirit of improvement in both deed and precept. Such men bought, borrowed, and read books on efficient husbandry, discussed new ideas with like-minded improvers, and influenced the habits of their tenants and neighbours.

Further spurs to improvement were provided by a number of enterprising agricultural societies which were established in a bid to encourage progressive landlords to improve methods of husbandry, develop manufacturing industries, reclaim undrained and unenclosed land, and generally foster 'a spirit of universal benevolence'.[49] The first county society— established in Breconshire in 1755—showed the way by awarding attractive premiums to progressive farmers for growing potatoes and turnips, and for spinning yarn and woollen cloth. Free turnip seeds were provided and an itinerant instructor was employed to offer practical guidance. Spinning schools were set up, trees were planted, tended, and

[47] F. V. Emery, *The World's Landscapes, 2: Wales* (London, 1969), p. 74.
[48] F. V. Emery, 'Wales', in J. Thirsk (ed.), *The Agrarian History of England and Wales, vol. v: 1640–1750* (Part 1, Cambridge, 1984), p. 420.
[49] H. Edmunds, 'History of the Brecknockshire Agricultural Society, 1755–1955', *Brycheiniog* 2–3 (1956–7), p. 36.

protected, and local roads were widened and improved. These improvements persuaded the county gentry of Carmarthenshire, led by Watkin Lewes, to establish their own society in 1772, and Glamorgan, too, followed suit shortly afterwards. By 1784 similar county societies, designed to encourage agriculture and industry, had been founded in Cardiganshire and Pembrokeshire. Subscribing members of these societies became more deeply aware of the financial benefits to be gained from adopting favourable cropping rotations, improving waste lands, growing potatoes, winter cabbage, and turnips, raising clover seed and whitethorn plants, spinning yarn, and knitting stockings. Although county societies did not, perhaps, work the wonders which were expected of them—many members still preferred to quaff wine, hunt foxes, and shoot pheasants rather than engage in agrarian improvements—they did help to speed up the diffusion of new scientific ideas and improve the quality of arable and agrarian husbandry.

Many obstacles to rural improvements, however, continued to handicap even the most fervent disciples of the new husbandry. Most Welsh farms were small (ranging from 30 to 100 acres) and fragmented, and capital resources were severely limited. As Walter Davies later observed, 'want of capital in the farmers is the obstacle of obstacles'.[50] Small farmers also lacked the necessary technology to put new ideas into practice, and without the mechanized facilities of modern farming the work of ploughing, harrowing, seeding, and harvesting was laborious and time-consuming. Many tenants tended to view all innovations (especially those canvassed by unpopular stewards) with a cynical eye and remained devoted to age-old habits. There was still much ignorance and inertia. In 1778 a surveyor of the Ashburnham estate in south Wales discovered 'a total aversion to exchange and every sort of innovation in this country'.[51] In many ways, however, it was far easier for agriculturalists and travellers to expose and ridicule the follies of poor Welsh farmers than to suggest ways of improving the quality of their life. In many parts of north-west Wales, where most landowners were absentee and where agents did little more than gather rents, tenants were not encouraged to carry out improvements. Apart from the occasional Welsh almanac, little literature on farming was available in Welsh. Moreover, many of the new ideas advanced in 'improving' manuals were totally inappropriate to the needs of farmers in rugged pastoral communities. The heavy, acidic soils of west Wales, for instance, did not encourage good husbandry and were especially inimical to turnip-growing. Sensible farmers thus grew hardy and dependable crops like oats and barley. Inevitably, therefore, standards of crop husbandry varied according to the nature of the soil and local climatic conditions.

[50] Walter Davies, *General View*, p. 460.
[51] D. W. Howell, 'Landlords and Estate Management', p. 294.

Nevertheless, those farmers who were able to adjust themselves to changing economic conditions and were prepared to invest portions of their capital resources undoubtedly benefited as progressive farming techniques began to spread more widely. Enterprising gentlemen and substantial tenant-farmers were particularly successful in the more fertile lowland valleys and coastal strips. More affluent and secure than hill farmers, they were in a position to bring more land into productive use, invest in arable activities, make use of the lighter Rotherham swing plough, apply regular manures and fertilizers (including lime, marl, ashes, and seaweed), adopt improved courses of cropping, and breed livestock for dairy and fattening purposes. In the fertile lowlands of counties such as Denbigh, Glamorgan, and Pembroke, clover, perennial rye-grass, sainfoin, trefoil, and vetches were widely grown grasses. Larger crop yields were gained by the extensive application of a wide variety of fertilizers, and selective breeding helped to improve the quality of livestock. In such communities, rising land values and agricultural prosperity often went hand-in-hand. A Wynnstay agent observed in 1776 that 'the value of land has been increasing this many years owing, among other things, to the plenty of money and great improvements in husbandry'.[52]

While the improvement in agriculture turned out to be of benefit principally to small landowners and rich freeholders, small farmers, starved of capital and finding it increasingly hard to make ends meet, were forced to rely on self-help in order to improve their social and economic circumstances. To them the woollen industry was a lifeline and its importance, particularly in mid- and north Wales, can hardly be over-estimated. Although the woollen industry was still run on cottage lines in this period, it not only expanded but also proved highly adaptable. In response to domestic and foreign demand, the volume of production and business increased and hundreds of tenant and labouring families who lived almost constantly on the edge of subsistence had cause to be grateful for the extra pennies and shillings which accrued from spinning and weaving wool. Long after sunset most cottages in the counties of Denbigh, Merioneth, and Montgomery echoed to the sound of spinners turning their wheels and weavers throwing their shuttles.

Three significant elements helped to bring new vigour to the Welsh woollen industry. The demand for what London drapers called 'Welsh plains and cottons' increased sharply as markets were extended to the slave plantations of America and the West Indies. Welsh wool was used to clothe the negroes of America and the slaves of the West Indies, as well as the peasants of Flanders. In response to this stimulus, weaving became a specialized craft in Merioneth, notably around Dolgellau, where there

---

[52] T. M. Humphreys, 'Rural Society in Eighteenth-Century Montgomeryshire', p. 104.

were fifteen fulling mills by the 1770s. Secondly, the monopoly of the dictatorial Shrewsbury Drapers' Company, which had for so long dictated prices and gobbled up profits, was undermined by the growing number of factors from Liverpool who poured into Wales in search of cheap cloth. No longer compelled to tramp to Shrewsbury and bow and scrape before Shropshire drapers, Welsh merchants were free to choose their own markets and, to some degree, control their own destiny. Fullers and weavers were given a new lease of life and textile manufacturing began to develop into an organized and profitable industry. Substantial amounts of Welsh webs and flannels were exported from Barmouth and Aberdyfi, and during the American War the woollen trade experienced years of unparalleled prosperity.

Finally, the expansion of the knitting industry helped to improve the living-standards and purchasing-power of poor families. The manufacture of multi-coloured stockings, caps, gloves, socks, and wigs flourished in an area stretching from Dinas Mawddwy to Corwen and from Trawsfynydd to Llanrwst. Large profits were made. In 1747 Lewis Morris calculated that stockings to the value of £200 were sold weekly at Bala market. By 1781 that figure had nearly doubled. The sale of knitted products accounted for a fifth of the estimated woollen manufacture of Merioneth, and Barmouth alone was responsible for shipping stockings to the value of £10,000 per annum. The discovery of new markets and wartime demand for uniforms also brought prosperity to woollen towns such as Llanybydder, Tregaron, and Llantwit Major in south Wales. At Cowbridge John Franklen launched a March fair in order to provide local farmers with the means of raising money to pay rents by selling knitwear. Regular supplies of 'fardles' and 'bags' of stockings were shipped by Welsh hosiers from Cardiff, Aberthaw, Newton, and Sully to ports in the West Country. In times of hardship, therefore, the domestic stocking industry enabled whole families to gain an extra source of revenue. Wayside knitters and barefooted urchins offered their stockings for sale on village greens and at roadsides, while the well-established nightly knitting assemblies were now often enlivened by the presence of revivalist ministers. Perhaps some of them knew that George III and Robert Clive counted themselves among the admirers of Welsh stockings.

Urban growth in Wales was also a central feature of social and economic change in this period. Agrarian improvements, the stimulus of rising prices, industrial investment, and more efficient trading networks all meant that the proportion of town-dwellers was increasing and that the vigour and variety of urban life were much more apparent. Although the social and political dominance of the leading gentry families was as great in the towns as in the countryside, there were new opportunities for affluent middling sorts to expand and prosper. In particular, those towns which were industrial or manufacturing centres, together with those which were strategically placed closer to fertile valleys or commercial centres, began to exercise a much greater influence on the nature of the Welsh economy.

Expanding industrial activity and the quickening pace of economic change were the most significant stimuli. Although none of Wales's industrial towns could stand comparison with those of England, they were growing swiftly. Swansea's heavy reliance on industry enabled it to emerge as the centre of gravity of the economy of south Wales. Following an act of 1760 which permitted the enclosure of 700 acres of Townhill and 50 acres of sand burrows between the town and the sea, its population began to soar. Often shrouded by billowing smoke and grime issuing from its numerous copperworks, Swansea became the first industrial town of consequence in Wales during the second half of the eighteenth century. Its population of around 3,000 in 1760 was twice as large by 1801, and the intensive economic development which accompanied and accelerated this growth enabled the town to overtake Bristol as the commercial capital of south Wales. Cardiff at this stage lay very much in the shadow of Swansea, and its fisheries, malthouses, and brewhouses bore witness to its rustic character. It was still, as Iolo Morganwg admitted, an 'obscure and inconsiderable town'.[53]

Elsewhere, too, industrial advance brought urban expansion. New towns began to emerge: as major new ironworks began to proliferate within the parish of Merthyr after 1760, the population of the town grew appreciably. In north-east Wales, the success of textile and metallurgical industries enabled Holywell's population to soar dramatically after 1765. Several travellers found it a rich and thriving town and by 1790 its brass, copper, and cotton works were judged to be scarcely inferior to any in Britain. Wrexham, the most populous town in north Wales, owed its growing prosperity partly to its location on a major thoroughfare, but increased economic activity, in the coal, lead, iron, leather, and brewing industries as well as the woollen trade, was the major trigger for growth.

A significant number of market towns were also fulfilling vital commercial functions. They became expanding processing centres dealing in a wide range of imported goods as well as food and raw materials drawn from the surrounding countryside. The growing volume of trade ensured not only that market and fair days were busy and noisy but also that more and more people were employed in the victualling and distributive trades. Towns which possessed lucrative specialisms did particularly well. Retailing and innkeeping were Cowbridge's forte, the stocking trade proved the salvation of Bala, while Dolgellau (described as 'no despicable little town for these parts')[54] had become a centre of the weaving trade. Thriving commercial towns could offer a much wider range of skills and services than had been the case in the early eighteenth century. The professional middling sorts offered specialist services in law, education, medicine, and banking. As consumer demands grew, shops became larger and offered a more enticing array of wares. Printers published and sold books, bookbinders were in surprising demand, postal services were available, and growing numbers of inns offered lodgings to gentlemen, travellers, and carriers. Not all market towns, of course, were happily placed or endowed with commercial advantages. Those smaller towns which lacked lucrative specialisms tended to stagnate, especially if the general improvement in communications had passed them by. Caerwys, eclipsed by nearby Holywell, was described by Pennant as 'a town mouldering away with age'.[55]

Several ports, too, were expanding rapidly. The expansion of maritime trade and the upturn in imports of foodstuffs and luxury goods helped many of them to grow. Along the Welsh coast swarms of seamen, merchants, traders, and labourers bore witness to the expansion of commerce, the growing size of ships, and the availability of stocks of raw material. Some ports grew, whilst others fell away so badly that they scarcely merited the name. The growth of slate exports from Caernarfon, for instance, meant that trade at Conway shrivelled to nothing. In spite of its first-rate harbour facilities, Beaumaris proved unable to compete successfully with Liverpool and Chester. Elsewhere, however, the story is one of growth. The improvement of the route over Penmaen-mawr, which enabled passenger and mail traffic to be directed through Holyhead after 1772, proved a considerable stimulus to the development of the port: facilities were improved and the number of sailing packets multiplied. The copper industry on Parys mountain brought vigorous expansion to the tiny port of Amlwch, whilst the increasing traffic in woollen goods kept ports such as Barmouth and Aberdyfi busy. Aberystwyth was given a new lease of life when the Customs House was transferred there from Aberdyfi in 1763. Boosted by the considerable herring trade, the port became a major depot in the maritime trade of west Wales. At Swansea, which was the liveliest and busiest port in Wales, a considerable number of wharves, coal banks, and large and small vessels provided evidence of the thriving export trade in copper, coal, lead, tinplate, zinc, and iron.

The burgeoning wealth and influence of the middling sorts, as well as the fashionable tastes of gentlemen, turned many well-to-do provincial towns into polite centres. A wide range of newspapers, journals, and novels helped to spread metropolitan fashions and values into well-developed

[54] J. Geraint Jenkins, *The Welsh Woollen Industry* (Cardiff, 1969), p. 182.
[55] T. Pennant, *Tours in Wales*, i. 244.

urban locations. Towns such as these became hives of intellectual activity, as printing-presses, book societies, circulating libraries, private schools, masonic lodges, assembly rooms, and coffee houses helped to diffuse the English language and current fashions, as well as to enable citizens to keep abreast of political developments. A diversity of pleasures was available. Travelling theatre companies enjoyed good houses in makeshift theatres, cock-fights drew throngs of rich and poor, and subscription concerts were timed to coincide with race-meetings. From time to time visits by bands of comedians, conjurers, lecturers, mountebanks, and dwarfs were arranged for the delectation of townsfolk. Even the factional strife which bedevilled Carmarthen's local government did not prevent it from acquiring a reputation as the politest town in Wales. Its well-regarded academy and grammar school, as well as its administrative and commercial advantages, made it an attractive venue for public lectures, fiery sermons, and travelling shows. Dafydd Thomas, a poet, believed that bagpipes were heard at fashionable weddings more often in Carmarthen than any other Welsh town.

As affluent men became increasingly determined to participate as fully as possible in the world of leisure, a growing number of towns, inland spas, and seaside resorts offered a sophisticated range of recreational facilities and entertainment. Although it was difficult to resist the charms of London, and although Bath was still an attractive venue for people of rank and fortune, the landed gentry and the middling sorts were spending more of their time in several attractive Welsh towns. Sizeable and prosperous towns consciously created facilities designed to suit the tastes of the leisured classes. At Brecon, where sixteen families owned coaches or chaises by 1760, there were flowered gardens, picturesque walks, bowling greens, and tea houses. At Chepstow, wealthy families formed picnic clubs and voyaged in pleasure boats down the river Wye. Saline and sulphur springs were discovered at Llandrindod in 1732 and by the middle of the century the mansion at Llandrindod Hall had been converted into a hotel, which boasted a wide range of popular amenities. Every year from spring onwards, gout-ridden gentlemen, free-spending heirs, and asthmatic middling sorts travelled to Llandrindod to sample the chalybeate waters, embark on long mountain walks, and catch up with the latest gossip. Lewis Morris, who went there armed with a microscope and other apparatus in order to examine the springs, found that facilities were excellent: he drank the medicinal waters at breakfast, dinner, supper, and even in bed, and departed feeling twenty years younger. Seaside towns were also becoming important leisure centres. The Jacobites of south-west Wales made it a practice to set aside a week annually for feasting and recreation at a fashionable seaside resort. As the quality of communications and the range of facilities improved, a craze for sea-bathing gripped the leisured classes.

Those with aches and pains found the sea water at Abergele, Rhyl, and Aberystwyth enormously soothing and beneficial.

It must be said, however, that most of the smaller towns of Wales were still shabby, dirty, and foul-smelling places, where dung-hills proliferated and pigs, sheep, and boars roamed the streets. Few of them caught the eye of visiting artists or map-makers. Rubbish, dung, and slops were regularly thrown into mounds in backyards, gardens, and streets. In Aberystwyth stinking fish was often left to rot in major thoroughfares, and Dolgellau's dark, damp streets reminded Joseph Cradock of a labyrinth of dungeons. Yet the prospering towns were by no means gloomy or shabby. Henry Penruddocke Wyndham found the streets of Caernarfon neat and clean, while Pennant praised its handsome buildings, notably the castle ('the most magnificent badge of our subjection') which he believed was 'the boast of north Wales'.[56] Wrexham, with its splendid church and prosperous streets, was described by Samuel Johnson as a 'busy, extensive and well-built town',[57] whilst Brecon drew a host of admiring comments from Methodist evangelists. In many such towns, basic utilities were either provided or improved as the century wore on. Streets were paved and widened, scavengers were employed, and street lights and names became more common. When efforts were made in 1774 to build a new market in Swansea, among the principal motives were the need to rid the town of obstructions in the street and the growing demand for higher standards of cleanliness. In the wake of a private act passed in the same year, Cardiff Street Commissioners also strove to improve their town: scavengers were appointed, roads resurfaced and paved, oil-lamps placed on street corners, and protruding signs, waterspouts, and penthouses removed. Such developments betokened a growing commitment on the part of the urban élite to a certain measure of civic improvement.

The most interesting and innovatory feature of the Welsh economy in this period, however, was the accelerating pace of industrial change. A combination of factors served to make Welsh industry more productive and diversified than ever before. The wider diffusion of new technology was the first spur. Although industry was still heavily dependent on the contribution of human muscle and animal power, the emergence of new inventions quickened the rate of production and lowered labour costs. The use of steam-power brought improved efficiency and greater profits. The installation of Newcomen engines enabled shrewd investors to exploit hitherto hidden coal-seams and to mine at considerable depths. From 1775 onwards, methods of hauling and improvements in the blast in smelting followed the invention of the Watt steam-engine. By the mid-eighteenth

[56] T. Pennant, *Tours in Wales*, ii. 214.
[57] A. H. Dodd, *A History of Wrexham* (Wrexham, 1957), p. 99.

century, too, Abraham Darby's method of using coal to smelt pig-iron in blast furnaces was more widely and effectively used. The transition from charcoal to coal enabled the volume of iron production to increase sharply, and improvements in techniques such as the use of blowing cylinders and leather bellows sent output soaring in the Merthyr area. In 1774 John Wilkinson, whose fertile brain made Bersham a centre of European importance in the iron industry, took out a new patent which enabled his work-force to bore iron cannon from solid castings, thus providing British forces with superior arms. Cylinders for Boulton's and Watt's engines were also made at Bersham. Finally, the most critical turning-point in the iron industry occurred with the momentous discovery of the puddling process by Henry Cort in 1783-4. This process was so eagerly adopted by Welsh ironmasters that it became known in south Wales as 'the Welsh method'.

The second critical factor was the inflow of substantial capital. Most of the capital requirements for new and profitable ventures, especially in the iron and copper industries, were provided by English adventurers. Merchants from Bristol, Cornwall, London, and the Midlands, utilizing profits raised from the exploitation of India and the inhuman traffic in negro slaves, invested substantial sums of money which helped to quicken the pace of industrial production appreciably. Excited by the prospects of securing land on favourable leases and capturing sites which were rich in mineral wealth, affluent and ambitious entrepreneurs found ample scope for their energies in north-east Wales and the Merthyr and Swansea areas. As such men vied with one another in the race to achieve greater prosperity, they became responsible for expanding industries in a major way. Many of them obtained a head start by forming partnerships and pooling expertise, money, and talent. This enabled them to ease the burden of raising capital, to regularize prices of products, negotiate suitable trade sales, and ride out financial storms. They were assertive, self-reliant, diligent men who had served a hard apprenticeship in the world of industry. With the exception of the Quaker Lloyds and the equable Thomas Williams (Tom Fairplay), the Anglesey 'Copper King', most of the new entrepreneurs placed profit and material success above all other considerations. In spite of his appealing streak of unconventionality (the sexual prowess of 'mad Iron John' was apparently legendary), John Wilkinson of Bersham was a tyrannical master who ruled his ironworks like a martinet. Similarly, John Guest, the Broseley-born manager of the flourishing Dowlais ironworks, was noted for his parsimony, acquisitiveness, and lack of humour. In the process, large sectors of the industrial economy of Wales became semi-colonial in character: large sums of capital were supplied by English entrepreneurs, land was provided at peppercorn rents by local landowners, and a reservoir of cheap labour was available to serve the needs of a powerful moneyed class.

It would be wrong to assume, however, that Welsh landowners were not interested in the pursuit of mineral profits. While absentee landlords tended to put their immediate pleasures before long-term profits, resident landowners and enterprising stewards developed a keen interest in industrial enterprises. Families whose purses were sufficiently long found that industrial and commercial projects were useful means of enhancing estate revenues, and stewards, smaller squires, and freeholders, conscious of what was at stake, were prepared to become involved in fractious and time-consuming disputes over mineral rights. Moreover, Welsh-born members of the industrial middle classes—Robert Morgan, Thomas Lewis, and Thomas Price—showed an eye for business and profit. By the end of the century, Thomas Williams, the Anglesey-born solicitor who made the copper industry at Parys one of Wales's biggest enterprises, was a millionaire.

War was the third major stimulus. Although the seemingly endless number of wars after 1739 had some adverse effects, in that trade was handicapped, markets lost, and men sacrified at sea and on the battlefield, there were also undeniable rewards. Wars not only helped to call forth new inventions but also stimulated new demands for iron, copper, lead, tinplate, and coal. The voracious needs of the British army and navy proved to be the salvation of some landowning families plagued by money troubles. Sales of timber and iron to the Navy Office in the 1740s rescued the Mansell family from financial ruin. But it was the iron industry which prospered best under the stimulus of successive wars. The Seven Years' War provided John Wilkinson of Bersham with the opportunity of manufacturing cannon, grenades, shells, and piping, and once hostilities had ceased he used his profits to purchase new furnaces and corn and fulling mills. It is no accident, either, that the most dramatic enterprises were launched in the Merthyr area once the war with France had begun in 1756. Units of production at Welsh ironworks were greatly extended after 1775, when the American War provoked further demands for arms and ironmasters at Bersham and Merthyr gained lucrative government contracts for the large-scale production of cannon.

These stimuli presented entrepreneurs in Wales with new challenges and opportunities and also sharply affected the rate of industrial progress. The most decisive expansion occurred in the iron industry. The first stirrings were witnessed in the 1740s, when Thomas Lewis and Thomas Price rebuilt the Pen-tyrch furnace and forge and revived the forge at Melingriffith. As the scale of these enterprises grew, interest switched to north-east Wales, where Isaac Wilkinson took over the famous Bersham ironworks in 1753 and expanded the firm by manufacturing a wide range of products, including cannon, water-pipes, and box-heaters. These successes persuaded several English entrepreneurs to take advantage of the buoyant and developing market in pig-iron. A series of highly promising ventures was launched along the north-eastern outcrop of the south Wales coalfield, where there were abundant supplies of timber, coal, ironstone, and water, as well as co-operative landowners ready to grant long-term leases at favourable rents. In 1759 the Dowlais Iron Company was formed by a partnership of nine entrepreneurs, the majority of whom were English merchants but who also included Thomas Lewis of Llanishen, Thomas Price of Watford, near Caerphilly, and Isaac Wilkinson of Bersham. Having raised capital of £4,000, the company leased extensive lands on the banks of the Dowlais river on highly favourable terms from Lady Windsor, and two air furnaces and a blast-furnace were built. As other investors discovered that cheap raw materials and attractive leases were available, a scramble for land followed. In 1763 John Guest of Broseley (who was later appointed manager of Dowlais) and Isaac Wilkinson took out a lease on the Plymouth ironworks. Two years later, Anthony Bacon and William Brownrigg, both natives of Cumberland, leased 4,000 acres (for a fixed annual rent of £100 for ninety-nine years) from Lord Talbot of Hensol and set up a furnace and a forge at Cyfarthfa. Bacon was joined in 1777 by Richard Crawshay, the first of the famous Crawshay iron kings, who expanded the works by exporting enormous quantities of cannon. The profits which accrued enabled Bacon to take over the Plymouth and Hirwaun works and to establish himself as the major manufacturer of iron, coal, and cannon in the 'mineral kingdom' around Merthyr. The iron industry in south Wales had entered a period of unprecedented expansion: pig-iron production had risen from 4,850 tons in 1720 to 12,500 tons by 1788.

The tinplate industry also grew by leaps and bounds during this period. The stimulus of war with France and America helped to stave off competition from Germany and encourage large-scale production of bar iron and japanned and tinned ware. Following the pioneering activities of John Hanbury at Pontypool, the manufacture of tinplate migrated westwards from the 1740s onwards. In 1747 the Caerleon works at Pont-hir turned from coppermaking to tinplate, but more thriving concerns were established at Ynys-pen-llwch in the Tawe valley, Ynysygerwn at Neath and at Melingriffith. The most significant advances, however, occurred in Carmarthenshire, where Robert Morgan took advantage of wartime demand for ordnance to expand his enterprising iron forges, rolling-mills, and tinplate works. On the eve of the war with France he owned a blast-furnace at Carmarthen, two air furnaces and four forges at Whitland, Kidwelly, Cwmdwyfran, and Blackpool, and a tinplate works at Kidwelly. Once hostilities had begun, these concerns developed swiftly and Morgan was able to set up self-contained and highly profitable tin-mills in Carmarthen. The American War provided a further stimulus to the industry and Welsh tinplate workers began to acquire an international reputation for their skill in the precision rolling of iron into sheets prior to tinning them. Two plate-mills were added to the forge at Melingriffith and substantial export markets were secured in France, Holland, Portugal, and Spain. As a result, output at Melingriffith increased from 4,201 boxes in 1771 to 18,194 boxes in 1800.

The turmoil of major wars, as well as growing domestic demand, also offered new opportunities for production and profit in the copper industry. Large quantities of copper, copper-zinc alloy, and brass were required for the manufacture of munitions, steam-pumps, engines, tools, machinery, coinage, and household utensils. From the 1740s onwards, diverse groups of adventurers, including Bristol merchants and Tory industrialists, developed non-ferrous smelting industries in west Glamorgan and south-east Carmarthenshire. The largest and most flourishing works were established between Landore and Morriston on the lower reaches of the Tawe river. Abundant supplies of cheap coal were available and the superb geographical and geological advantage of Swansea's location made for easy access to ores from Anglesey and Cornwall. By 1750 around half the copper produced in Britain came from the Swansea area. Fifty years later, west Glamorgan was the principal centre of copper smelting in the world. The export of copper rose from around 9,000 tons in 1750 to over 47,000 tons in 1780 and this, in turn, led to a sizeable influx of labour. The number of employees in the copper, lead, and tin works around Swansea rose from 200 in 1740 to 500 in 1770.

By that time Anglesey was staking a powerful claim to a share in the copper market. Following years of largely fruitless exploratory work, remarkably extensive and lucrative deposits of copper-ore were discovered in 1768 on Parys mountain, near Amlwch in Anglesey. Protracted legal disputes over the right to work the land ensued, however, and all attempts to mine the resources intensively were frustrated until Thomas Williams, an ambitious county solicitor, established the Parys Mine Company in 1778 and began to develop, with the help of a substantial work-force of 1,500 men, what Pennant judged to be 'the most considerable body of copper ever known'.[58] Within a year Williams had established large-scale smelting works in Flintshire, Lancashire, and south Wales, and by undercutting prices he undermined the monopoly of Cornish master-smelters and developed an unusual flair for promoting his own products. In particular, he seized on the advantages of being able to produce cheaper ore and to ship it conveniently and swiftly to his copperworks at Swansea. By 1790 this 'Copper King' had acquired a monopoly over British copper and a secure niche for Wales in the world copper market.

[58] J. Rowlands, *Copper Mountain* (Llangefni, 1966), p. 40.

In spite of problems of drainage and ventilation, as well as high overland costs, the overall trend in coal output was also upwards. In north Wales, productivity increased from 80,000 tons in 1750 to 110,000 tons in 1775, whilst in south Wales it rose sharply during the same period from 140,000 tons to 650,000 tons. Rapidly rising coal output was stimulated by the more widespread adoption of the Newcomen steam-pump for the purposes of pumping and winding, by the use of coal as a substitute for charcoal in the smelting of pig-iron, and, later on, by Cort's invention of the puddling process. The development of the non-ferrous metal industries in the Swansea area created a growing demand for coal, whereas after 1760 the intensive exploitation of iron-ore on the northern rim of the south Wales coalfield offered further opportunities for expansion. Coal was required in the malting and lime-burning trade and the growth of urban communities meant that more coal was being burned in private dwellings. Foreign demand was also rising and a sizeable coal trade was established with southern Ireland, the Cornish copper-mines, and the ports of the West Country.

On the south-western rim of the coalfield, where reserves were close to the sea, shrewd and wealthy landowners went to great lengths to affirm their right to mineral deposits which were located on copyhold or common land. The duke of Beaufort, the principal landowner in the seigniory of Gower, exercised a powerful influence over coal-bearing lands in west Glamorgan, while the marquis of Bute possessed extensive privileges over freehold and copyhold property in the eastern sector of the coalfield. Smaller local families, too, were not unmindful of the value of coal: the Prices of Penlle'r-gaer and the Popkins of Fforest did well in the Swansea area. Wealthy merchants were also attracted by the presence of coal: Chauncy Townsend, a London entrepreneur, opened collieries at Llansamlet near Swansea, and Charles Raby worked anthracite coal in the Gwendraeth valley. As they explored these new possibilities, investors utilized new technology in order to develop workable seams and mine deeper shafts. Miners at Sir Herbert Mackworth's pits in Neath were descending eighty yards in 1751 as opposed to thirty yards in 1705. Safety standards did not improve, however, and there is reason to believe that by the 1770s the production of coal had become more costly in terms of human life. There were nineteen fatalities in Glamorgan between 1770 and 1779, most of them presumably caused by explosions, roof falls, or poisonous vapours. Yet although it was a perilous occupation, coal-mining offered employment to growing numbers of full-time and part-time labourers, especially in the Tawe and Neath valleys. Sir Herbert Mackworth's collieries at Neath employed around 400 men in the 1760s, and more than twenty years later John Byng could hail Mackworth as one of 'the most extraordinary and enterprising geniuses in this kingdom' when he discovered 'colliers digging—copper works smoking—a domain of parkish ground—and about 300 men in daily pay' at Neath.[59]

The lead industry, on the other hand, experienced mixed fortunes. Shortage of capital, drainage problems, and rising transport costs inhibited large-scale expansion and several old ventures decayed. The principal casualty was the London Quaker Company which, having enjoyed unprecedented success during the early decades of the eighteenth century, found itself plagued by financial and technical problems. When the value of its shares began to plummet, the Llangynog mine (which was likened in 1740 to a 'dying man')[60] was abandoned and other ventures were set aside. Forced to embark on a period of retrenchment, the Company leased out mines to local landowners and transferred much of its dwindling capital to the north of England. When the Company finally wound up its activities in Flintshire in 1792, the Gadlys works were sold for a paltry £700.

Even so, other schemes prospered. As investors strove to meet domestic demands as well as the needs of foreign markets, the output of lead ore increased. Fresh discoveries kept hopes buoyant. The collapse of the Mackworth enterprises in Cardiganshire was followed by a frenzy of speculation. In 1751 a staggeringly rich vein was discovered at Esgair-mwyn in the upper reaches of the Teifi valley and, during the boom period which followed, over 2,000 miners were engaged in boosting levels of production. Lewis Morris, who was heavily and often painfully involved in protecting the interests of the Crown in the area, believed that Cardiganshire was 'the richest county I ever knew'.[61] In the north-east, too, enterprising landlords worked local lead-mines profitably. In 1761 the Minera mines in Denbighshire were rejuvenated when Chester Corporation leased lands to a silversmith who made substantial profits by producing over 10,000 tons of ore during the twenty years which followed. Bengt Ferrner, a Swedish industrialist, described the abundant lead and calamine mines in the possession of the Grosvenor family as 'the richest place of such scope in the world'.[62] Elsewhere, too, there were fat profits to be made. At Rhandirmwyn in Carmarthenshire, where 400 men were working in 1770, the Campbells of Stackpole Court amassed profits of over £300,000 over a period of sixty years.

Other industries progressed only modestly during these years. The slate industry, for instance, had yet to reach its maturity. The ports of Caernarfonshire were best placed to exploit the gentle expansion which occurred as the century wore on. The demand for slate for roofing

[59] J. Byng, *Torrington Diaries*, i. 298–9.
[60] W. J. Lewis, *Lead Mining in Wales* (Cardiff, 1967), p. 153.
[61] *Add. Letters*, i. 113.
[62] W. Linnard, 'A Swedish Visitor to Flintshire in 1760', *Flintshire Hist. Soc. Journal* 30 (1981–2), p. 149.

purposes was increasing in the towns and cities of England as well as on the Continent, and most of the products of the slate ranges of Snowdonia were transported by sea. Groups of quarrymen in parishes such as Llanberis and Llanddeiniolen formed small-scale partnerships, worked shallow quarries, and used blasting powder to increase their yields. But profits were generally small. Large-scale changes were delayed until the arrival of Richard Pennant, later Lord Penrhyn, who established a monopoly of quarrying in 1782 and invested his Jamaican income in developing mineral reserves.

Few industries, therefore, stood still. Some experienced modest advances, but most progressed swiftly and confidently. One especially noteworthy feature of this growing confidence was diversification. The shrewdest entrepreneurs developed a wide variety of pursuits. In Glamorgan, Thomas Price of Penlle'r-gaer set up an alum works around 1747 and Sir Herbert Mackworth of Neath successfully maintained a salt-works, first established by Charles Cotes in 1733. In north-east Wales entrepreneurial initiative was not the monopoly of the Wilkinsons of Bersham. Around 1750 the Cheadle Brass Company began smelting copper near Holywell, thereby establishing a thriving concern which became known in 1765 as the Greenfield Copper and Brass Company. Increased demand for calamine attracted a large number of brass manufacturers to the Holywell area. Investors from Bristol used local calamine for making brass and smelting blackjack, while the Smedleys—father and son—built a plant at Greenfield which manufactured white and red lead. In 1757 Jonathan Catherall began manufacturing firebricks on Buckley mountain and within two decades fourteen separate potteries, producing a variety of bricks, tiles, and mugs, had been established in the Hawarden area. Welsh industry was clearly more highly developed and diverse by the 1780s than it had ever been before.

A further index of the growth of the economy was the availability of larger amounts of capital which, in turn, led to more confident and sophisticated entrepreneurial activity. The general expansion of trade and capital, together with the need for credit facilities, led to the emergence of small-scale banks. *Banc y Llong* (the Ship Bank), established in Aberystwyth in 1762, was a natural concomitant of the considerable wealth which shipping and mercantile interests had generated in the town during the mid-eighteenth century. Similarly, increasing wealth produced by the intensive exploitation of the iron and copper-smelting industries prompted industrialists and traders to establish banks at Swansea and Merthyr in 1770. Banks such as these owed their existence to the initiative and expertise of manufacturers, merchants, and drovers who possessed the necessary credit and connections to conduct their financial affairs efficiently.

Improved transport facilities also reflected economic growth. As agricultural yields increased, industrial output grew, and domestic and foreign trade expanded, the case for improving communications in Wales became overwhelming. Industrialists, improvers, landlords, and many others were eager to improve economic links with English markets by establishing a comprehensive system of transport. Most public roads were not equipped to cope with heavy industrial traffic and the mud-tracks and bridle-paths so common in upland rural areas were scarcely conducive to economic progress. Parishioners were increasingly reluctant to obey the requirements of the statute of 1555, especially since roads in the localities often crumbled as a result of constant use by vehicles driven by outsiders who contributed nothing to the upkeep of road services. In many counties, the presentment of defaulting parishes had become a formality, and wherever piecemeal private improvements had been carried out little lasting success had been achieved. The extension of the turnpike movement into Wales from 1750 onwards was, therefore, warmly welcomed by self-interested and public-spirited parties alike. A series of turnpike acts, passed in swift succession, brought about extensive improvements. By 1770 a well-integrated and reasonably efficient network had been established. Extensions from trusts in Cheshire and Shropshire had penetrated deeply into north Wales, while in mid- and south Wales the formation of county trusts enabled seven counties to bring 1,185 miles of road under their control. The system was not without its defects—many steep gradients remained, roads in remote upland communities continued to be unspeakably poor, and materials used for surfacing roads were of dubious quality—but the dividends were soon apparent. The turnpiking of major roads undoubtedly accelerated expansion in agricultural and industrial marketing and stimulated the swifter movement of inland and coastal traffic. The volume of wheeled traffic increased, heavier loads could now be carried, carriage costs were lower, and ports and markets were more accessible. Coaching inns began to prosper, smoother rides won the goodwill of travellers, and faster and more regular services were provided by stage-wagons, flying wagons, stage-coaches, and mail coaches.

In many ways, too, the turnpiking of the principal arterial routes from west to east helped to dismantle parochial and geographical barriers and to break down the isolation of Wales. The spirit of improvement manifested itself in better transport facilities. Wales became more accessible to discerning travellers who discovered, much to their relief, that a journey west of Offa's Dyke was no longer comparable to an expedition to the Andes. From around 1770 onwards an army of pencil-and-brush artists and inquisitive travellers set off on extensive tours of Wales and proved themselves to be (with the signal exception of the choleric John Byng) less disposed to decry the manners of the people and to despise things Welsh. Since their journey was no longer simply a test of nerve and stamina, they took considerable delight in discovering the romantic beauty of the Welsh landscape. Tours by Cradock, Wyndham, and especially Pennant did much to create a lively interest in the notion of romantic Wales, and growing numbers of travel guides and water-colour views helped to encourage a wider appreciation of the beauty and diversity of the landscape.

The development of maritime trade also helped to increase prosperity and widen horizons. Although we have no means of measuring its extent in statistical terms, all the signs point to increasing maritime activity. In the absence of canals, the Welsh economy still depended heavily on sea transport which was generally cheaper and often more comfortable than road transport. Ships were increasing both in size and tonnage, and were venturing further from port. Hundreds of small vessels traded along the Welsh coast, carrying butter, cheese, oats, herrings, salt, coal, tin, iron, lead, and copper to and from Dublin, Liverpool, and Bristol. Larger vessels shipped raw materials to new markets in western Europe and the Mediterranean, and wherever local industries prospered there was brisk activity. Shipping tonnage at Swansea increased from 30,631 in 1768 to 120,852 in 1793. By the 1760s around 30,000 chaldrons of coal were being shipped annually from Glamorgan, mostly from Swansea. In the north-east, the ports of Chester and Deeside shipped and exported 92,000 tons of lead and lead ore between 1758 and 1777.

The prosperity of ports such as Beaumaris, Barmouth, and Swansea was closely associated with the new Atlantic trade. Barmouth's growth was spectacular. When jobbers from Liverpool undermined the monopoly exercised by the Shrewsbury Drapers' Company, a depot was established in 1772 at Barmouth in order to export webs to shareowners in America and the West Indies. Pennant estimated that, prior to the American War, Barmouth exported annually £40,000 worth of web or flannel and £10,000 worth of stockings. So lucrative was this trade that Barmouth began to rear its own seafaring families and expand as a shipbuilding centre. During the boom years of the 1770s, fifty-two sloops, four brigs, and two brigantines were built on the Mawddach estuary.

Elsewhere, too, there were signs of expansion in Cardigan bay. In spite of its seasonal nature, *sgadana* (herring-fishing) became a particularly valuable commercial activity during the mid-eighteenth century. During the 1740s there were as many as fifty-nine small sloops engaged in the herring-fishing trade at Aberystwyth and thirty-eight more at Aberdyfi, Borth, Aberaeron, and New Quay. Some extraordinarily large catches were made: during a single night in October 1745, forty-seven boats caught 1,386,500 herrings valued at £1,400. Fishermen returned to port with huge shoals of herrings, mackerel, whiting, ray, cod, skate, mullet, crabs, eels, lobsters, and periwinkles. The industry was further boosted by the Act for the Encouragement of the British White Herring Fishery in 1750, which offered a substantial bounty of thirty shillings per ton to every decked vessel of between thirty and eighty tons. Seafaring became a full-time occupation as the fishermen of west Wales became involved in unprecedented commercial activity. The port of Aberystwyth, in particular, reaped the benefits. By the time it acquired Aberdyfi's Custom House in 1763, it was the principal fishing port in Cardigan bay and a major depot in the maritime trade of Wales.

The import of a wide range of luxury goods for home consumption also assumed significant proportions in the mid-eighteenth century. One sure sign of prosperity was the prevalence of smuggling. In many coastal communities, smuggling became a way of life in this period. The volume of illegal trade in spirits, coffee, tea, and tobacco soared as hard-pressed customs officials strove in vain to combat the depredations of quickwitted and often ruthless smugglers. William Morris likened the role of a customs officer to that of 'a grey cat watching a hundred mouse holes at once'.[63] Smuggling was a lucrative practice and one which invariably commanded popular sympathy. Many bibulous gentlemen were well-disposed towards smugglers, common people devised ingenious stratagems which threw officers off the scent, and even clergymen were not above lending a hand. Customs officers at Cardiff reported that smuggled goods were sold in dozens of small shops in rural districts along the coast of Glamorgan. But the profits made by common people were small compared with the riches which professional smugglers such as Thomas Knight, William Owen, or the Crigyll robbers gained.

Clearly, therefore, a number of significant developments had stimulated economic growth and the spirit of improvement in Wales. Demographic growth set the pace and made new demands on society. Agrarian improvements and swelling trade stimulated economic expansion, urban life had become more vigorous, and new investors had supplied greater enterprise and purchasing-power. Improved communications not only influenced economic development but also hastened the arrival of new fashions, tastes, and ideas, which, in turn, encouraged more modern attitudes. Most of all, the way had been prepared for Wales's industrial take-off. The economic changes wrought by industrialization, though by no means revolutionary, had been considerable. The Welsh industrial economy was more soundly based, more diverse, and more confident than it had ever been before. The impetus provided by new investment, technical developments, and the demands of war had served to accelerate the pace of industrial growth. By 1780 it was possible to see the shape of things to come.

[63] *Morris Letters*, ii. 599.

CHAPTER 8

POLITICAL CONFLICT AND CHANGE

MORE than ever before, men who counted in Welsh politics in this period identified themselves closely with England. Landowners, especially those who had no roots in Wales, had no conception of a Welsh national interest or any memory of past glories. Wales as a nation was a concept foreign to those who identified native Welsh culture with social degradation and who spoke of the Welsh language in derisory terms. They often styled themselves 'true Englishmen' and during periods of war they became as aggressively patriotic as any John Bull. When Sir John Philipps of Picton Castle spoke of 'the honour of the nation' and 'the country's wish',[1] he was assuredly not referring to Wales. Sir Charles Kemeys-Tynte viewed his candidature on behalf of the Tory cause in Glamorgan as an opportunity to 'serve poor England'.[2] It is significant that, at the annual race-meeting at Lichfield in 1748, Sir Watkin Williams Wynn of Wynnstay entered a horse called 'Old England'. Even Welsh libertarians campaigned on behalf of 'free-born Englishmen'. When Evan Lloyd of Fron Dderw, Bala, threw in his lot with the Wilkesite cause, he cried 'joy to old England'.[3] Eminent Welsh radicals such as Richard Price and David Williams, too, promoted the cause of 'English liberty'. Not even cultural patriots conceived of Wales as a distinct and separate political entity. However much the Morris brothers might have loathed the Welsh gentry's propensity for whoring after the English tongue, they shared the same values as far as the constitutional relationship between Wales and England was concerned. Lewis Morris, who was no Anglophile, spoke in fulsome terms of the 'happy union with the valorous English',[4] whilst Richard Morris declared that 'there should be no distinction between an Englishman and a Welshman in our days'.[5]

What William Warrington called the 'wild spirit of independence'[6] had clearly long vanished. Since Wales possessed no powerful political institutions to lend support to a sense of national identity it could not, as was the case in Ireland, produce politicians of the calibre of Henry Flood or Henry Grattan to campaign for its constitutional rights as a separate

[1] L. Namier and J. Brooke, *The House of Commons 1754–1790* (3 vols., 1964), iii. 274.
[2] P. D. G. Thomas, 'Glamorgan Politics 1700–1750', p. 76.
[3] E. A. Jones, 'Two Welsh Correspondents of John Wilkes', *Y Cymmrodor* 29 (1919), p. 126.
[4] *Add. Letters*, i.39. [5] *Add Letters*, i. 322.
[6] William Warrington, *The History of Wales* (London, 1786), p. 556.

nation. It is evident that articulate Welshmen were fully convinced that the political incorporation of England and Wales in 1536–43 had been a conspicuous success story. Whereas many Scots believed that the recent Union of 1707 had proved a disastrous shot-gun marriage, affluent and educated Welshmen confidently declared that the assimilation of England and Wales had been a happy and gladsome marriage of equals. For from entailing political subjugation, union had served to promote the best interests of the public at large by granting Welsh people the full privileges of English citizenship and by conferring upon them untold economic blessings. Integration between England and Wales reached its political apogee in this period. 'Union and affinity', rejoiced Griffith Jones, Llanddowror, 'do increase more and more.'[7]

Furthermore, those who held the highest offices and who owned the broadest acres in Wales never tired of expressing their profound veneration for the English constitution. Durable, stable, just, and virtuous, it was, in their eyes, a pattern of perfection. Notions such as stability, liberty, and deference were deeply coloured by bitter memories of Roundhead violence. No inch was to be given to potential rebels, were they bloody papists or subversive Levellers. The principal concern of the political leaders of Wales was, therefore, to protect property and to preserve the traditional governing institutions, both at central and local level, from the threat of subversion from within and invasion from without. The political system itself was weighted even more overwhelmingly than before in favour of privileged men who protected a minority interest under the cloak of defending ancient liberties and a God-given social system. To those who believed that it was their right to preside over a deferential people, the very word 'reform' was anathema.

As a result of what William Jones, Llangadfan, called 'insatiable avarice',[8] thousands of acres had been remorselessly accumulated by landed Titans. As we have seen, many Welsh counties had experienced demographic crises which had enabled the biggest fish to swallow smaller ones. Having consolidated and extended their landed estates, the great Leviathans—who were now a privileged caucus of powerful families—exercised massive and undisputed sway over the economic and political life of Wales. Families such as the Wynns of Wynnstay, the Morgans of Tredegar, the Vaughans of Corsygedol, and the Mostyns of Mostyn ruled almost by hereditary right and did so virtually without challenge. They never invited or sought the political views of people below their station in life and parvenus who threatened to disturb 'the peace of the county' incurred instant displeasure. There were, however, few prospects of undermining their economic and political authority. The Welsh electorate

[7] Griffith Jones, *Welch Piety* (London, 1740), p. 55.
[8] NLW MS 13221E, f. 343.

was still small and inadequate. At most, no more than 25,000 adult males were deemed to be within the pale of the constitution. The mass of the populace did not possess the necessary wealth, the appropriate education, or the leisure time to engage in the practice of politics. Few peasants questioned the norms of society and they were little interested in the dealings of either their elected representatives or other faraway politicians at Westminster. Similarly, they cared little about the public or private affairs of the Crown. The feeling was clearly mutual: no Hanoverian sovereign ever bothered to visit Wales during the eighteenth century.

Although politics at Westminster were largely irrelevant to the bulk of the population, voting for one's political master was, in many cases, a time-honoured practice, even an act of homage, performed by tenants. Habits of deference were deeply ingrained in rural communities and even families such as the Hanburys, the Mackworths, and the Morgans, who accumulated substantial profits from industry, were as capable of drawing on old loyalties to landlords as on new industrial connections. It was a matter of regret for David Williams, the Welsh philosopher, that as late as 1796 the 'feudal ideas and habits of an oppressed and degraded peasantry' were 'not wholly abolished'.[9] Some of the movements which gathered strength in this period served to reinforce rather than undermine the deferential structure of society. The circulating schools, the Methodist societies, and the Sunday schools strengthened the power of ruling landowners by insulating the peasantry against the contamination of disloyal or subversive thoughts. Small wonder that frustrated libertarians spoke derisively of the 'sleeping sickness'[10] which had gripped Welsh people.

Given the nature of Welsh society, it is not surprising that most parliamentary seats became self-perpetuating gifts in the possession of landed Titans. Many of them regarded their seats as their own inalienable property. Families whose only abiding principle was a strong instinct for self-preservation often sat continuously for three or even four generations at Westminster. The middling sorts were as yet too small and frail to intrude upon their monopoly, whilst men without wealth or connections could never hope to mount a serious challenge to their authority. In some counties, parliamentary seats were objects in a kind of pass-the-parcel game. Leading landowners engineered amicable *ententes* in order to minimize contests or else employed suitable surrogates until an heir came of age. As a result, electoral contests were remarkably rare events. Generations of men lived out their whole lives without ever having the opportunity to cast their votes. In 1734 in Welsh counties and boroughs there were only four and five contested elections respectively. In 1747 only two counties witnessed a contested election, whilst silence reigned in the

---

[9] David Williams, *The History of Monmouthshire* (London, 1796), p. 348.
[10] Thomas Roberts, *Cwyn yn erbyn Gorthrymder* (Cardiff, 1928), p. 42.

boroughs. Not a single contested election was held in Cardiganshire, Denbighshire, or Flintshire between 1754 and 1790. The celebrated Montgomeryshire election of 1774 was such a rare and bitterly contested affair that it was deemed to have robbed the county of its political virginity. Contested elections in eighteenth-century Merioneth occurred as frequently as did oaths from the lips of its Quakers. Indeed, only the failure of the male issue ended the monopoly of the Corsygedol interest in 1791. In Pembrokeshire, Sir William Owen of Orielton sat continuously in Parliament for a period of fifty-two years, while a member of the Mostyn family represented Flintshire in every Parliament between 1747 and 1837.

Borough seats were even more easily managed and in many of them the number of voters was shrinking. In the borough of Brecon the number of voters dwindled from 180 in 1723 to 69 in 1744. In Glamorgan eight boroughs were controlled by four powerful patrons who ensured that only some 500 burgesses were eligible to vote. When commissioners inquiring into the condition of the municipal corporation visited Beaumaris in 1834, they found that the number of burgesses on the electoral roll had shrunk to five. Borough corporations became more élitist and restrictive as their governors closed doors to aspiring freemen, exercised regulatory powers over inhabitants, and used fair and foul means to protect their own privileges. Posturing as overlords, members of the powerful Mackworth family viewed the borough of Neath as an extension of their own private property and ensured that even the most obdurate elements submitted themselves to their rule. Borough members thus successfully retained their seats for long periods. The Wynns of Glynllifon retained a monopoly over the Caernarfonshire boroughs, save for a brief interlude in 1754 when Robert Wynn of Bodysgallen, a kinsman, was permitted to keep the seat warm for a brief period. Thomas Lewis of Harpton Court served for such a long period as member for New Radnor Boroughs (1715–61) that he was known locally as 'Old Burgess'.

The costs of fighting an election were also a major deterrent. Parliamentary contests became such a serious financial burden on candidates that all but the fabulously wealthy or the foolhardy strove to avoid them. The preparations involved during pre-polling months were often enormous and there is abundant evidence of the 'Eatanswill' character of elections. Tables groaned under plates of food, drink flowed freely, ribbons were sported by partisans, and celebrations went on far into the night. During the county election in Glamorgan in 1768, Morgan Thomas of Bridgend suffocated and died following a surfeit of food and drink. Sir Watkin Williams Wynn's expenses may well have exceeded £20,000 during the county and borough elections in Denbighshire in 1741. Some candidates came to grief at the polls, with calamitous financial consequences. Sir George Wynne of Leeswood's stubborn pride led him to embark on political campaigns which left him insolvent and friendless. John Owen of Prysaeddfed, Anglesey, paid dearly for toppling the Baron Hill interest at the polls in 1741: much to the amusement of his enemies, he was obliged to sell a portion of his estate in order to defray his expenses. The same fate befell William Mostyn Owen who, having defeated the powerful Wynnstay family in the Montgomeryshire election of 1774, found himself presented with a crippling bill. Faced with the prospect of miserable failure and bankruptcy, therefore, most hard-pressed gentlemen chose to forgo the opportunity of challenging the local Titan's right to a seat at Westminster.

Powerful families closed ranks against those who deigned to challenge their prospective rights to govern. Only occasionally were they forced to defend their honour, as well as the peace and harmony of the county, against nabobs—usually merchants, lawyers, or industrialists—who sought to gain prestigious parliamentary seats as a mark of recognition of their newly acquired wealth. 'Vulgar intruders' of this kind were beaten off without great difficulty. In 1771, Valentine Morris of Piercefield summoned up the courage to challenge John Morgan of Tredegar for the county seat in Monmouthshire. Morgan and his supporters were outraged to find an 'upstart Creole' (Morris's father had made his fortune in the West Indies) threatening to disturb the calm of the countryside, and no pains were spared to denigrate the low-born stranger:

> In a far distant land, my friends, as I hear,
> He keeps many slaves, and I own that I fear
> He who makes men slaves there, would make them so here,
>   Go Massa, and drive you negroes,
>   We've no slaves in Monmouthshire.[11]

Nevertheless, on occasion electoral contests were precipitated by clashes of personality, petty intrigues, and family feuds. Short-term opportunism rather than an enduring commitment to political principles governed the practice of politics in gentry circles and this meant that, from time to time, peace in the countryside and in the boroughs was disturbed by what Henry Richard called 'clansmen vehemently battling for their respective chieftains'.[12] Such battles were normally local trials of strength, for provincial factions seldom bore much relation to divisions found at Westminster.

In order to retain their political control and dissuade independent spirits from acting in defiance of their wishes, parliamentary candidates or their patrons employed a variety of malpractices. Although elections in Wales were not as corrupt as those held in England, reprehensible tactics were in

---

[11] W. T. Morgan, 'County Elections in Monmouthshire', p. 173.
[12] Henry Richard, *Letters on the Social and Political Condition of the Principality of Wales* (London, 1866), p. 80.

constant evidence. At the county election in Glamorgan in 1745, Lord
Mansell of Margam took steps to ensure that 216 of his tenants (nearly a
sixth of the electorate) cast their votes in a proper fashion at the polls and
subsequently assured his candidate, Sir Charles Kemeys-Tynte, that—given
the word—he would 'punish with the utmost severity all my tenants that
have either voted against you or refused to vote at all'.[13] Fear of
dispossession (what Lord Newborough of Glynllifon called a 'disagreeable
necessity')[14] or other penalties darkened the lives of voters. Only the
courageous or the foolhardy voted in accordance with their conscience and
against the wishes of their landlords. In north-east Wales, peasants used to
commit themselves to action only if it pleased God and Sir Watkin
Williams Wynn. The role of stewards in applying overt and covert pressure
on recalcitrant tenants was also a growing feature in Welsh political life.
The steward of Sir William Irby's estate compelled Morris Prichard, the
aged and infirm father of the Morris brothers of Anglesey, to attend the
polls in 1761 by sending a chaise to fetch him and spelling out in no
uncertain terms the consequences of voting against the interests of the Bayly
family of Plas Newydd. During the fiercely contested election in Montgomeryshire in 1774, Sir Watkin Williams Wynn's agents launched a vigorous
campaign of coercion and intimidation. Small freeholders who favoured
the Powis Castle cause were bluntly reminded of the burdensome duties
involved in seeking assessment for the land tax or were threatened with the
withdrawal of age-old rights to cut peat or graze sheep on common lands in
the possession of the Wynnstay estate.

Landowners and their stewards also exercised control over freeman
boroughs either by strict examination of admission of candidates to a
burgess-ship or by the practice of flooding the poll with honorary freemen
prior to an election or even on the eve of the poll. The Wynns of Glynllifon
were past masters at creating new burgesses: between 1757 and 1799, 1,800
new burgesses were admitted in the borough of Caernarfon, of whom only
160 were resident. In a bid to rid Cardiganshire of the tyrannical Herbert
Lloyd of Peterwell as the elected representative of the borough constituency,
John Pugh Pryse of Gogerddan created a thousand new burgesses in
Aberystwyth and Cardigan during the preliminary skirmishes prior to the
election of 1768. Undeterred, Lloyd simply admitted over 1,200 new
burgesses in Lampeter.

Foul play and unblushing partisanship on the part of sheriffs also
continued to vitiate parliamentary contests. According to the number of
votes cast at the shire election in Glamorgan in 1734, Bussy Mansell had
won the day by a majority of 145 votes. However, an unscrupulous sheriff,
duly bribed by the powerful Talbot family, disqualified 246 of Mansell's

[13] R. Grant, *The Parliamentary History of Glamorgan 1542–1976* (Swansea, 1978), p. 125.
[14] K. Evans, 'Eighteenth Century Caernarvon', *Trans. Caerns. Hist. Soc.* 8 (1947), p. 57.

voters and declared William Talbot the winner by a majority of 81 votes. In New Radnor boroughs in the same year, Thomas Lewis was returned by the bailiff (who happened to be his brother-in-law) when only seventy freemen had been permitted to cast their votes and no more than one vote had been registered for the opposing candidate. Blood ran thicker than water in the celebrated county election of 1741 in Denbighshire. As sheriff and returning officer, William Myddelton made no secret of his animus against the Wynns of Wynnstay. His shady manœuvres and partisanship constantly thwarted the Wynnstay supporters at the polls, and their fury knew no bounds when Myddelton disqualified 549 of Wynn's voters and declared his relative, John Myddelton, elected. An apoplectic Wynn lost no time in successfully petitioning Parliament and the hapless sheriff was both stripped of his office and committed to Newgate prison for seven weeks.

Over most of this period, however, contested elections were few and far between, and many electorates were never offered the dubious honour of going to the polls. Welsh politics resembled a gentlemanly game of cricket, with powerful landowners occupying the crease for long periods, their agents or sheriffs acting as umpires, the lesser gentry tossing up 'donkey drops' and enfranchised freeholders and tenants chasing leather in the outfield.

As a group, Welsh Members of Parliament in this period have few claims upon the curiosity of posterity. Indeed, seldom, if ever, has Wales produced such an uninspiring clutch of politicians. Few of them were stirred by exalted political principles and since there were no specific Welsh causes which they felt impelled to plead in the House, they used what little energy and lobbying powers they possessed to promote the interests of their kinsmen and dependants. Although candidates continued to sport the 'Whig' and 'Tory' colours at elections, such badges reflected family divisions rather than party differences. For the most part, party heats had abated and religious passions (at least outside Methodist circles) had cooled. Most members did not believe in undue exertion. Bereft of constructive thoughts, dilatory in their attendance and voting habits in the House, untroubled by critical affairs of state, many were more interested in the affairs of the turf or roistering with boon companions than political issues. William Talbot of Hensol, MP for Glamorgan in 1734–7, acquired a reputation as a rake; Horace Walpole maintained that he was 'better known as a boxer and a man of pleasure than in the light of statesman'.[15] Sir Nicholas Bayly of Anglesey lost his seat in 1761 after it was revealed that he had seduced the young daughter of a fellow gentleman. Some

[15] R. Sedgwick, *The House of Commons 1715–1754*, ii. 463.

members were understandably reluctant to be distracted for long from their estates or their cultural interests. Sir Thomas Mostyn, fourth baronet of Mostyn, preferred handling ornate manuscripts to political news-letters, whilst Sir Watkin Williams Wynn, fourth baronet of Wynnstay and a lover of the arts, did not inherit his fearsome father's passion for political intrigue and intimidation.

Since many members stubbornly refused to be sucked into the vortex of parliamentary life, it is hardly surprising that their influence on the pattern of politics at Westminster was negligible. The attendance record of some individuals was lamentable. Only rarely did the Vaughans of Corsygedol venture as far as London and none of them ever stood up to speak in the House of Commons. The performance of William Edwardes, MP for Haverfordwest in 1747–84, gives the impression of creeping sclerosis: he never spoke in the House, never begged for any favour or office, and never voted against a single government after 1760. Although Sir Herbert Mackworth made over a hundred speeches in Parliament between 1768 and 1774, neither he nor his fellow Welsh members ever dazzled an audience in the Commons. Most of them were extraordinarily dull dogs. Even Sir Watkin Williams Wynn, third baronet of Wynnstay and a fiery Jacobite, lacked oratorical graces, while Sir John Philipps of Picton, who huffed and puffed a good deal in advancing the cause of the exiled Stuarts, had the reputation of being insufferably dull. Between 1754 and 1790 only four Welsh members held political office. The most able of them was George Rice of Newton, MP for Carmarthenshire in 1754–79, who aligned himself with the 'King's Friends' during the reign of George III, held office at the Board of Trade (1761–70), and became a Privy Councillor and Treasurer of the Chamber in 1770. Nepotism enabled Whitshed Keene, MP for Montgomery borough in 1774–1818, to climb the greasy pole: he was said to have 'screwed himself into being much trusted by Lord North'[16]—to whom he was related by marriage—and thus became Secretary to the Lord Chamberlain (1772–82) and Surveyor of the Board of Works (1779–82).

A seat at Westminster enabled a Welsh member not only to boost his standing locally but also to place members of his family and his servants in line for preferment. There were many lickspittle lackeys who strove to charm their way into the favour of the ministry. In his copious correspondence with the duke of Newcastle and Lord Hardwicke, Sir William Owen, fourth baronet of Orielton, Pembrokeshire, was so preoccupied with currying favour on behalf of his sons, brothers, and kinsmen that he never mentioned critical political or international issues. Similarly, Sir John Wynn of Glynllifon's correspondence with the duke of

[16] D. A. Wager, 'Welsh Politics and Parliamentary Reform, 1780–1835' (unpubl. University of Wales Ph.D. thesis, 1972), p. 51.

Newcastle is littered with tedious requests for offices 'agreeable to my station in life',[17] minor posts for his sons and kinsmen, and favours which would promote the Whig interest in north Wales. The ministry devoutly looked after its friends, showering them with commissions, offices, sinecures, and salaries in order to determine and control the distribution of local power. Among the chief beneficiaries in Wales were Sir Thomas Wynn of Glynllifon, who held the post of Clerk of the Green Cloth, with a salary of £1,000 per annum, from 1724 to 1749, and his successor, Sir John Wynn, who held the office of Deputy-cofferer of the Household in 1743 and Deputy-treasurer of Chelsea Hospital (1744–54).

There were also Welsh members whose attitudes were not determined by strict party considerations and who remained either indifferent or hostile to Whig blandishments. Country gentlemen jealously guarded their independence and viewed distant political leaders with a healthy mixture of suspicion and contempt. The country interest often led the clamour against corruption within the political system, wasteful foreign wars, and the burdens imposed upon them by the ruling dynasty's Hanoverian possessions. Walpole's much reviled Excise Bill of 1733, for instance, aroused a storm of bitter protest among country gentlemen and a powerful anti-Walpole animus characterized the elections held in the following year. Non-aligned gentlemen refused to bow down to Baal and prided themselves on their independence. When William Edwardes, MP for Haverfordwest, applied for a British peerage in 1779 he claimed proudly that he had 'never asked or received place, pension or other emolument for himself'.[18] William Bulkeley of Llanfechell, who at least felt free to speak his mind in his diary, declared contemptuously in 1758 that venality was to be found 'in all orders of men, divines, Court of Justice, the Army and Navy in so much as we are become the contempt and derision of all the world'.[19]

Although no fundamental upheavals occurred in the structure of oligarchic government during this period, new patterns were emerging. Firstly, in spite of the largely personal political rivalries, the Whig interest was clearly gaining ground in Wales. Gains which had been achieved during the election of 1727 were consolidated. In 1734, seventeen Whigs and three Opposition Whigs were returned as against seven Tories. In 1747 there were sixteen Whigs and two Opposition Whigs as opposed to nine Tories. Although the Tory cause remained strong in Wales, the Whigs held all the levers of power in central government and they used their considerable advantages to tighten and consolidate their control over the political

[17] G. Roberts, 'The Glynnes and the Wynns of Glynllifon', Trans. Caerns. Hist. Soc. 9 (1948), p. 31.
[18] D. A. Wager, 'Welsh Politics' (thesis), p. 53.
[19] Hugh Owen, 'The Diary of William Bulkeley', p. 85.

system. Whig ministries sought to undermine Tory interests by offering a variety of lucrative pensions, benefices, and perquisites. As we have seen, leading Whigs profited from these douceurs, especially those whose fidelity was not in doubt. But many opponents of the Whig cause were also wooed and tempted with the spoils of privilege. Frustrated by proscription, many supporters of the Tory cause forsook their principles and their rooted enmity towards Whiggery in order to gain preferment. Social and economic changes also favoured the Whig cause. In Glamorgan, for instance, they took advantage of fortuitous demographic changes which had the effect of weakening Tory interests.

The second major change was the final collapse of Jacobitism. Although the proscription of the Tories after 1714 robbed them of positions of power and profit at Westminster and prevented them from dispensing local patronage, they remained a highly disciplined and durable force in Welsh politics. In particular, many of them enabled the cause of Jacobitism to survive for at least thirty years after the rising of 1715. Although there was considerable hatred towards the House of Hanover within gentry mansions such as Baron Hill, Gogerddan, and Nanteos, the most weighty and committed supporters of the Stuart cause were Sir Watkin Williams Wynn, third baronet of Wynnstay, Sir John Philipps, President of the Society of Sea Serjeants, and the third duke of Beaufort. Each of these laboured assiduously to maintain a stubborn opposition to the Whig ministry and to support the Pretender's ambitions. Such powerful men were capable of using their territorial strength and family connections to bring considerable pressure to bear on their dependants. The 'Great Sir Watkin', for instance, ruled the inhabitants of his 'province' in north Wales with a rod of iron, partly by employing hard-headed stewards and agents to advance his political interests by fair means and foul. Wynn also provided active leadership for the Tory cause in the House of Commons. Welsh gentlemen in exile used to gather together to meet him at Finchley and escort him to the Commons. Jacobites like Wynn and Philipps resolved tactical problems in favoured clubs and taverns in London as well as within semi-secret societies such as the Cycle of the White Rose and the Sea Serjeants.

Whigs were convinced that Williams Wynn was the most dangerous ally of the Stuart cause south of the Tweed. They had good cause to watch him carefully. In 1735 the Pretender was informed that Wynn had vowed his readiness to serve him 'both with his life and fortune'.[20] By 1743–5 the Tory front bench at Westminster was deeply embroiled in detailed negotiations with the French government. But although Wynn pressed the Pretender to launch an invasion, he was never informed in full of his would-be sovereign's military plans. In the upshot, Wynn and his fellow

[20] P. D. G. Thomas, 'Jacobitism in Wales', p. 295.

Welsh Jacobites were taken completely by surprise when Prince Charles Edward landed on the west coast of Scotland in July 1745. When the inevitable invitation was received to join the Jacobite army in its bid 'to shake off a foreign yoke',[21] Wynn had few men or ready cash at his disposal. Almost certainly sore at not having been consulted, Wynn continued to ply the Pretender with buoyant promises rather than concrete support.

Indeed, only a handful of Welshmen displayed their chivalrous devotion to the Stuarts by proving stronger in deed than in words. Among those who committed themselves to unseating the Hanoverians by armed rebellion were William and Richard Vaughan, members of an old Welsh Catholic family from Courtfield, Herefordshire, who fought at Culloden before escaping to the Continent and entering the service of the Spanish crown. The most zealous Welsh ally of the Pretender, however, was David Morgan of Pen-y-graig Tâf, Glamorgan, a barrister at Westminster and a prominent member of the Association of Independent Electors. Morgan boldly set off to the north, armed with pistols and a broad sword, and sporting a white cockade in his hat. He joined the Jacobite army at Preston, where Prince Charles Edward was gratified to welcome at least one Welshman who was not only every bit as zealous as he but in every way an agreeable and sympathetic man. During the march south, Morgan urged the prince and his commanders to head for Wales in order to muster greater support. But such an itinerary was judged impracticable. Scottish chieftains prevaricated at Derby and, once the retreat of the Jacobite army began, Morgan deserted the prince and made for Wales. His gamble had failed. Moreover, he was not able to make good his escape. He was apprehended at Stafford, brought to trial, and sentenced to death, a fate which he bore with admirable dignity. In his final statement prior to his execution on 30 July 1746 he seized the opportunity to publicize his loathing of the appalling deeds committed by the duke of Cumberland, the stupidity of the Lord Chief Justice, and the callousness of a dynasty which fleeced and impoverished its subjects. His bravery ensured that Welsh Jacobitism did not collapse in total ignominy and shame.

When news filtered through of the Pretender's landing in July 1745, Welsh Jacobites had been torn between their traditional loyalty to the royal dignity and authority of the House of Stuart and their understandable instinct for self-preservation. They knew that fortune had never smiled upon the exiled Stuarts and that there were enormous personal risks involved in an anti-Hanoverian rebellion. The Jacobite cause in Wales had never really possessed a credible ideological framework or a coherent military strategy. It was easier for its supporters to vow behind closed doors to fight to the death for the Pretender than to flex their muscles

---

[21] E. Cruickshanks, *Political Untouchables* (London, 1979), Chapter 6.

publicly on the battlefield. Even as they offered wistful toasts and loyal assurances, few truly could have believed that their cause would ultimately be successful. When put to the test in the summer of 1745, they resolved their dilemma by lying low. The Pretender had more than enough justification for believing that his Welsh allies had let him down. The funds, arms, munitions, and soldiers he had been led to expect never materialized, and it was with justifiable feeling that he subsequently declared: 'I will do as much for my Welsh friends as they have done for me; I will drink their healths'.[22] Recriminations flowed thick and fast after 1745 and Sir Watkin Williams Wynn's record of irresolution and delphic pronouncements led many to lay blame at his door. Wynn claimed—probably truthfully—that he had been caught unawares, but it is also likely that he privately believed that the whole expedition had been suicidally ill-advised. He was a wily old bird and it was entirely in character for him to wait upon events following the arrival of the Pretender's forces. We shall probably never know the whole truth on this matter, for Wynn was wise enough never to commit much to paper. It was rumoured, too, following his death in 1749, that his wife hastened to burn all incriminating correspondence involving her husband 'lest half Wales should be hanged'.[23] Most Welsh Jacobites, however, had neither preached sedition nor developed an appetite for military involvement. They were simply not prepared to risk their lives and security on behalf of a cause clearly doomed to failure.

Although Welsh Jacobites were, in a sense, their own worst enemies, they were also confronted by formidable adversaries. Whigs in great houses such as Chirk, Glynllifon, Margam, and Mostyn were hostile to the Jacobite cause and were implacably opposed to any attempt to put back the clock. The fidelity of gentlemen, freeholders, and clergymen to the House of Hanover was beyond question. Political prizes which had fallen into the laps of hopeful candidates had served to sap old allegiances to the exiled Stuarts. French envoys had always exaggerated the loyalty of Welshmen to the Pretender and there is little proof that Jacobitism had struck deep roots in the country as a whole. The anti-Jacobite mood in 1745 was unmistakable. A mounting wave of indignation and fear spread throughout Wales, especially along the coasts, as news arrived of the French landing. Troops were placed at the ready, known Jacobites were kept under surveillance, and the anthem 'God Save the King' acquired instant popularity. The spirit of loyalism blew irresistibly through Methodist society and prayer meetings. Howel Davies, the Pembrokeshire evangelist, confidently claimed to be able at need to mobilize fifteen hundred armed men in Pembrokeshire to do battle against invading enemies. Churchmen and Dissenters alike organized demonstrations of loyalty to the Hanoverian

---

[22] P. D. G. Thomas, 'Jacobitism in Wales', p. 298.
[23] D. Nicholas, 'The Welsh Jacobites', THSC (1948), p. 472.

regime and tapped old veins of popular anti-Catholicism. Memories of past atrocities committed in the name of popery were revived as Welsh people were reminded in no uncertain terms that Jacobitism was committed to the destruction of the Protestant religion and civic liberties.

There was intense relief all over Wales, therefore, when news of the Pretender's ignominious retreat and the subsequent horrors of Culloden filtered through. None was more grateful than Griffith Jones, Llanddowror, who had lived in dread of hearing 'the noise of the trumpet, clashing of swords and stampings of the horses' hoofs'.[24] Jacobitism's demise was now inevitable. Sir Watkin Williams Wynn, the stormy petrel of Welsh politics, died following an accident whilst hunting rabbits in 1749. His death must have convinced even the most stubborn Stuart loyalist that the Jacobite cause was irrevocably lost. Echoes of Jacobite songs and toasts to the king over the water were still to be heard in gentry parlours, but the harmless conviviality which characterized genteel Tory clubs never constituted a threat to the Hanoverian dynasty. Times were changing. The Seven Years' War (1756–63) once more stimulated anti-popish passions, the accession of George III in 1760 emancipated disaffected Tories, and Charles Edward himself, having become an alcoholic, perished in 1788.

A third significant change which became increasingly apparent after 1760 was the growing and bitter resentment felt by independent country gentlemen and freeholders. Their fury was roused by the arbitrary power gained and exercised by absentee landed Titans. Some of the enthusiasms which had sustained erstwhile Jacobites were channelled into freemasonry or Wilkesite radicalism, each of which offered means by which the interests of upright freeholders might be protected against domineering magnates. Not all secret societies, of course, espoused the cause of reform. Members of the Society of Sea Serjeants used their considerable political clout to support the Tory cause in elections in south-west Wales. Thomas Wynn, third baronet of Glynllifon, acquired a taste for pseudo-military pageantry and in 1761 founded on his estate 'The Society or Garrison of Fort Williamsburg', a loyalist institution designed to glorify the Hanoverian dynasty and to rejoice in the coronation of George III. But in most of the masonic lodges, which multiplied rapidly during the 1760s, ritual and ceremony were accompanied by a commitment to free inquiry and radical politics. Richard Price, Glamorgan's most celebrated champion of liberty, served as Grand Master of the Bridgend Lodge in 1777.

Families which had been high Tories in the 1730s became fervent supporters of John Wilkes in the 1760s. Wilkes had particular cause to be grateful for the support of radicals of industrial stock in Glamorgan. Robert Jones of Fonmon, an enthusiastic supporter of the Bill of Rights

---

[24] Griffith Jones, *Welch Piety* (London, 1747), pp. 16–17.

Society, was prepared to champion the rights of free-born Englishmen against a tyrannical executive. Robert Morris, a Swansea-born barrister, was captivated by Wilkes's rugged charm and soon shared his taste for radical politics and fast women. In 1769 he was appointed secretary of the Society of the Supporters of the Bill of Rights, but three years later he fell from grace by eloping to the Continent with a fourteen-year-old heiress. Sir Watkin Lewes, a barrister, industrialist, and second president of the Cymmrodorion, was also a prominent campaigner on behalf of the Bill of Rights. In 1771 he presented to Wilkes and his fellow prisoners in the Tower addresses from the three counties of south-west Wales.

Elsewhere in Wales, however, the cry of 'Wilkes and Liberty!' aroused few answering echoes. Although Evan Lloyd, the Merioneth-born poet and satirist who shared the same gaol as Wilkes following his conviction for libel and became charmed and excited by his hero's fervent libertarianism, liked to boast that Wilkes had 'a thousand well-wishers among the hills of Wales',[25] the Wilkesite cause made little or no impression on the mass of the Welsh people. Yet, by the 1770s, the signs were that many gentry families, aided by freeholders, were increasingly resentful of the monopoly which absentee families had gained over parliamentary representation. Traditional families were clearly at odds with those powerful newcomers whom David Williams, the philosopher, called 'little Lords'.[26] In many Welsh counties the power exercised by absentee Titans, who normally governed their extensive acres by means of stewards and agents, was causing tensions. In Glamorgan, for instance, failure in the male line of the principal native families had meant that the county's Members of Parliament during the second half of the century were drawn from English families. When the duke of Beaufort nominated Charles Edwin of Llanmihangel for the vacant county seat of Glamorgan in 1780, an 'independent' faction, led by the Morgans of Tredegar, Robert Jones of Fonmon, and Robert Morris of Clasemont, launched bitter attacks on the growing influence of 'villainous', 'despotic', non-resident potentates. 'From all such lords', they cried, 'the Lord of all deliver us.'[27] Their fury stemmed not only from their anxiety to secure a resident member of integrity to support the county interest, but also from their resentment over the concentration of supremacy in the hands of a ruling clique. Under such aliens, they claimed, the freeholders of Glamorgan were 'mere abject slaves'.[28] Similar struggles were sustained elsewhere by county gentlemen and freeholders who were sufficiently affluent or courageous to act

[25] E. A. Jones, 'Two Welsh Correspondents', p. 130.
[26] David Williams, *History of Monmouthshire*, p. 346.
[27] Ll. B. John, 'The Parliamentary Representation of Glamorgan, 1536–1832' (unpubl. University of Wales MA thesis, 1934), p. 108.
[28] Ibid., p. 105.

independently without fear or favour. During the Monmouthshire election campaign of 1771 the supporters of John Morgan of Tredegar proclaimed that their 'gracious and bountiful master'[29] was defending the liberties of the citizens of Monmouthshire against the tyrannies of absentee Goliaths such as the duke of Beaufort, Lord Abergavenny, and Sir Charles Kemeys-Tynte. In the 1774 election in Montgomeryshire, William Owen, the Powis Castle candidate, called on the gentry, freeholders, and clergy of the county to defend their 'free-born bosoms' against the alien yoke of Wynnstay lest they become as miserable as the peasants of Poland. During public dinners sponsored by the Powis family, toasts were offered to the independence of the county of Montgomeryshire and the right of freeholders to stand up against 'all arbitrary power' which robbed them of their liberties and right to prosper.[30] In spite of an alarming variety of electoral malpractices carried out by Wynnstay agents, William Owen carried the day by seventy-six votes. Although it is hard to detect genuine traces of political radicalism or Wilkesite fervour in these campaigns, they did represent increasingly clamant protests against the unloosening of old ties and the arbitrary power of absentee landowners.

A strong ferment of more radical opinion was forming in Dissenting and nationalist circles. Many Welsh academies were fostering a critical spirit and a desire for free inquiry. They not only educated ministers, scholars, and theologians of distinction but also, by extending their curricula to include many innovative subjects which remained untaught within the universities, they ushered in a clash between the old and the new by encouraging independent and unorthodox thought. The academy at Carmarthen played a critical role in this development. Under the influence of Thomas Perrot, who succeeded the founder of the academy in 1718, the Carmarthen seminary became increasingly liberal in character. Indeed, it acquired a reputation as a nursery of heterodoxy. Many disaffected Calvinist students were searching for a less exacting and rigorous theology, and by allowing them the freedom to exercise their own independent judgements, Perrot enabled some of them to desert orthodox paths and to espouse the cause of Arminianism. Jenkin Jones, a blacksmith's son from Llanwenog, caused flutters of apprehension within Calvinistic dovecots in south-west Wales by using his considerable preaching gifts to persuade disillusioned Calvinists to defect to Arminianism. His labours led to a series of secessions and splits during the 1730s. In a bid to counter the growing influence of the Arminian faith, the academy was moved from Carmarthen to Llwyn-llwyd in 1733. It returned to Carmarthen ten years

---

[29] W. T. Morgan, 'County Elections', p. 171.
[30] P. D. G. Thomas, 'The Montgomeryshire Election of 1774', *Montgomeryshire Collections* 59 (1965–6), p. 123.

later, only to find that Samuel Thomas, its new tutor, was also a lively advocate of free inquiry and unorthodox theology.

From the 1730s onwards, students and ministers who found Calvinist doctrines unpalatable drifted towards Arminianism. Between 1750 and 1780 many of them, believing that Christ was not divine and was subordinate to God, were converted to Arianism. After 1780 Unitarianism became the logical culmination of this odyssey. Anti-trinitarians of this kind made no secret of their debt to the liberal thinking of Locke and the scientific rationalism of Newton. Love of learning and a taste for experiment flourished within their circles. At his celebrated academy at Pentwyn, Llan-non, Samuel Jones used to nurse a human skeleton on his knee during his lectures on science. By the 1770s globes, telescopes, microscopes, mathematical instruments, and an electrical machine were as much in use in the Carmarthen academy as were works of divinity. Startled by the unorthodox ways of rationalist Dissenters, local Methodists began to sound alarm bells. In their eyes, the Arminian and Arian faiths were blasphemous, tainted tenets, and the heretics' sphere of influence was dubbed *Y Smotyn Du* (The Black Spot). The hostility was mutual, for Calvinism was a term of abuse in unorthodox circles. Rationalists condemned the pious enthusiasm, moral smugness, and the much-publicized antipathy towards intellectual inquiries which characterized Methodist societies. David Lloyd of Brynllefrith, the brilliantly talented nephew of Jenkin Jones and well-known throughout Cardiganshire as a friend of truth and liberty, declared that Calvinism was simply 'a heap of absurdities'.[31]

After 1714 Welsh Dissenters had loyally supported the Hanoverian succession and had expressed their abhorrence of the exiled Stuarts in no uncertain terms. No group had rejoiced more in the aftermath of the 1745 rebellion when those who were known to be practising papists, or who had uttered disloyal sentiments, were prosecuted in order to satisfy the national sense of outrage. Prior to the accession of George III, however, most Dissenters had eschewed political agitation. They were acutely conscious of the fact that they were seriously compromised in the eyes of the governing authorities by past associations stretching back to the days of Oliver. But as Welsh academies prospered and as liberal, rationalist, and radical ideas began to gain ground within their ranks, many of them began to throw their weight behind parliamentary opposition movements, the campaigns for parliamentary reform, and the repeal of the Test and Corporation Acts. The humiliating religious and civil disabilities which made Dissenters second-class citizens rankled painfully. Many churchmen and Tories were still convinced that Dissenters were wolves in sheep's

---

[31] G. Eyre Evans, *Lloyd Letters (1754–1796)* (Aberystwyth, 1908), p. 29.

clothing. From birth until burial Dissenters were subjected to the oppression of the state in their spiritual and personal affairs. Dissenting ministers who sought to register meeting-houses often found their legal rights denied or frustrated by their enemies. In some communities, clergymen refused to bury the bodies of Dissenters on the grounds that only bona fide members of the established church were entitled to that privilege. By the early 1770s, however, an increasing number of intellectually mature and thoughtful Dissenting ministers had become bold enough to air their grievances in a more effective fashion and to demand a voice in political affairs. In 1772–3, 106 Welsh ministers and 17 students subscribed to the petition which called upon Parliament to reform the Act of Toleration. The rapid advance of liberal and rational ideas, especially in Arian and Baptist circles, led them to revere liberty. David Lloyd of Brynllefrith, Cardiganshire, called his Arian brethren 'hearty friends to liberty',[32] whilst Caleb Evans, a Baptist from Pentre, Glamorgan, who exercised a formative influence on the career of Morgan John Rhees, preached in defence of constitutional liberty in 1774–5 and supported the cause of the American colonists. Radical Dissenters were not disposed to wear their religion comfortably. As they strengthened their campaign to be admitted to equal citizenship, they began to take even greater pride in the heroic labours and achievements of their Cromwellian ancestors. By the 1770s the works of Morgan Llwyd and William Erbery were being read once more. Edmund Jones's extensive library shelves groaned under the weight of seventeenth-century sermons, many of which contained annotations denouncing 'blind malignant royalists'.[33] In 1772, Edward Bagshaw's biography of Vavasor Powell, first published in 1671, was translated into Welsh and published in Carmarthen.

The final and probably the most significant factor which opened up new and potentially exciting possibilities in the field of political reform was the American Revolution. Welshmen had contributed in no small measure to the growth of colonial America and it was natural for Dissenters on this side of the Atlantic to sympathize with the aspirations of kinsmen who dwelt in the colonies on the eastern coast of America. Ever since the heroic days of 'the Great Persecution', many hundreds of Quakers, Baptists, and Anglicans had braved the stormy Atlantic seas and had either established or strengthened churches scattered throughout the thirteen colonies. Some Welsh immigrants had risen to positions of eminence. Five of the signatories to the Declaration of Independence in July 1776 were of Welsh stock.

Among progressive and enlightened minority groups in Britain there were men who believed that the cause espoused by the American colonists

[32] G. Eyre Evans, *Lloyd Letters (1754–1796)*, p. 22.
[33] T. Watts, 'The Edmund Jones Library', *JWBS* 11 (1975–6), pp. 233–43.

was a powerful new force which ought to be accommodated and encouraged. From their ranks Richard Price emerged as the principal standard-bearer of the cause of political liberty and human rights. Born in 1723 in the farmhouse of Tyn-ton in the parish of Llangeinor, Glamorgan, Price became one of the few Welshmen in the eighteenth century to acquire both a European and an American reputation. Not since Morgan Llwyd had Wales produced a thinker of such extraordinary power and originality. Condorcet was convinced that Price possessed one of the genuinely formative minds of the eighteenth century and there is little doubt that in intellect, breadth of vision, and imaginative understanding he towered above most of his contemporaries. Having been reared in a Calvinist home, Price rebelled against his doting but demanding father by acquiring a taste for the unorthodox. It is said that when his father found him reading a volume by the Arian, Samuel Clarke, he seized the book and threw it into the fire. But Price was determined to free himself from Calvinist restraints and, following his education at Samuel Jones's academy at Pen-twyn, Llan-non, Carmarthenshire, he found the Arian religion a powerful and liberating experience. In 1740 he moved to London and soon forged extensive connections with those radical Dissenters, philosophers, and publishers who were the moving spirits behind the growth of Enlightenment thought in England and across the Atlantic. Price combined unusual intellectual talents with conspicuous charm. He was a gentle man, capable of winning genuine affection, forging lasting friendships, and earning the awe and respect of his fellow scholars and radicals. By the 1770s he had acquired an international reputation as a brilliant theologian, mathematician, statistician, and demographer.

Price regularly frequented the 'Club of Honest Whigs', a group of twenty-five Dissenters, philosophers, and scientists that met in the London Coffeehouse in order to discuss ways and means of advancing the interests of liberal and rational thought. He also maintained a lively and extensive correspondence with prominent American radicals, such as Benjamin Franklin, Arthur Lee, Josiah Quincy, jun., and Francis Dana, each of whom was anxious to create an informed opinion on the nature and aspirations of American society. Price was enormously impressed by the vigour and resourcefulness of American society and in particular by the passionate eagerness of the colonists to be free. He studied events in America closely and, having convinced himself of the political maturity of the colonists, he announced in February 1775 that if he were an American he would go barefoot, wear skincloth, and endure 'any inconveniences sooner than give up the vast stake now depending'.[34] In 1776 he published his seminal sermon, *Observations on the Nature of Civil Liberty*, in which

[34] D. O. Thomas, *The Honest Mind* (Oxford, 1977), p. 149.

he declared that liberty was 'a blessing truly sacred and invaluable'.[35] Price believed that all governments should be creatures of the people and he urged the American colonists to raise their horizons of ambition to an intellectual level by affirming the right of every community and every nation to govern itself. His sermon was circulated widely and quoted liberally on both sides of the Atlantic: it was reprinted in Dublin, Edinburgh, Boston, Charleston, New York, and Philadelphia and was translated into Dutch, French, and German. Although Price was convinced that Americans possessed a God-given right to determine their own political future, as a strong loyalist he hoped that the colonists would be allowed to develop their own independent legislature within the Empire. His hopes of reconciliation, however, were thwarted when, following the Declaration of Independence in July 1776, the colonists chose the path of secession. Nevertheless, Price continued to view America as an asylum of liberty and a refuge for the oppressed. Indeed, he hailed the American Revolution as 'a new epoch in the affairs of mankind'.[36]

Richard Price's ideas left an indelible mark on American minds. They also encouraged rational Dissenters in Wales to campaign for greater religious and political freedom. David Williams, one of Price's colleagues in London and a *philosophe* in his own right, was one of the most illustrious heterodox students produced by the Carmarthen academy. Williams was born at Waunwaelod, a remote cotage on Caerphilly mountain, in 1738. By the time of his death in 1816 he had acquired European fame as an educational theorist, a political thinker, and a man of letters. During the 1770s Williams read the works of Helvetius, Rousseau, and Voltaire, turned his back on Calvinism, and became a Deist. His creed was simple: 'I believe in God'. The American cause also influenced him profoundly. He and Benjamin Franklin (who, among others, dubbed him the 'Priest of Nature') formed a Deist club. Following the publication of *A Liturgy on the Universal Principles of Religion and Morality* (1776)—a work which was translated into German and which drew favourable comments from Rousseau, Voltaire, and Frederick II—Williams established the first Deist chapel in Europe in Cavendish Square, London. Williams was a more complex figure than Price, but his commitment to wholesale political reform was genuine. His *Letters on Political Liberty* (1782), written in defence of the American colonists, were translated into French by Brissot and won him considerable esteem in France. In advocating, among other things, universal manhood suffrage, the ballot, payment of MPs, annual Parliaments, and smaller constituencies, David Williams produced what amounted to an early Chartist manifesto.

Although both Price and Williams had distanced themselves from their

[35] Richard Price, *Observations on the Nature of Civil Liberty* (London, 1776), p. 5.
[36] C. Bonwick, *English Radicals and the American Revolution* (Chapel Hill, 1977), p. 157.

native land, their ideas were echoed in intellectual and Dissenting circles in Wales. Among the most prominent pro-Americans in north-east Wales was Jonathan Shipley, bishop of St Asaph. He believed that north America was 'the only nursery of free men left on the face of the earth'.[37] His son-in-law, Sir William Jones, the prodigiously gifted Sanskrit scholar and friend of liberty, launched a scathing attack on the attempts of the British government to hold the American colonists in bondage. His *Principles of Government in a Dialogue between a Scholar and a Peasant* (1782) provoked a storm by advocating the adoption of universal male suffrage and the right of armed resistance to authoritarian monarchs. Captivated by these ideas, William Davies Shipley, dean of St Asaph and Jonathan Shipley's son, facilitated the translation of Jones's pamphlet into Welsh and its publication at Wrexham in 1783. His reforming enthusiasm brought him into disfavour and he was indicted for seditious libel. Following months of delay, the case was finally heard at Shrewsbury in August 1784 when, amid joyous demonstrations of support from his parishioners, Shipley was acquitted.

In several other Welsh counties, too, there were pockets of radical Dissenters who rejoiced in the liberties cherished by Americans. Generally, these were men of independence—craftsmen and farmers—who had been blessed with sharp brains and nimble tongues. They abhorred the 'strange fire' which Methodism emitted, preferring to read and discuss rationalist and liberal ideas. In Cardiganshire there was Ifan Tomos Rhys, an Arminian cobbler of Llannarth, whose workshop was a focus for philosophical and polemical discourse. In Breconshire, Siôn Llywelyn, a poet and Arminian elder at Cefncoedycymer, was a fervent believer in the power of reason and a mouthpiece for the ideas of Voltaire. In Montgomeryshire, William Jones of Llangadfan resembled his hero Voltaire in both physiognomy and doctrines. Domestic constraints obliged Jones to spend virtually the whole of his life on his farm at Dolhywel, near Llangadfan, an 'obscure corner' where he seldom enjoyed 'the pleasure of conversing with men of knowledge'. Jones's unprepossessing appearance and broken English were deceptive. He was, in fact, a voracious reader, an abrasive 'red-hot Welshman' and, in the eyes of his rector, a republican and a Leveller.[38] Similarly, in Glamorgan, John Bradford, a fuller and dyer at Betws Tir Iarll, was a free-thinker and a libertarian who, steeped in the literature of France and England, positively revelled in political and religious debates. Men such as these helped to quicken interest in rational enquiry and the cause of liberty.

The conflict with the American colonists helped to provoke a more vigorous reappraisal of the basis of parliamentary representation. In

[37] A. J. Arberry, *Asiatic Jones* (London, 1946), p. 12.
[38] NLW MS 168C, p. 292; *The Cambrian Register*, 2 (1796), pp. 240–6.

1779–80 Christopher Wyvill and his associates in the North Riding launched a campaign for constitutional reform. Wyvill's Yorkshire Association drew support from disgruntled country gentlemen, many of whom harboured deep suspicions of the executive and were frustrated by growing economic grievances. In his plans specifically for Wales, Wyvill urged that additional Members of Parliament be allocated to the four counties of Carmarthen, Denbigh, Glamorgan, and Monmouth, and called on his supporters to flood Westminster with petitions demanding parliamentary reform. In February 1780 committees were established in Breconshire and Flintshire to organize petitions designed to bring pressure on Parliament to carry out economical and representational reform. Supporters of parliamentary reform at Ruthin, Denbighshire, passed a resolution that 'the unequal representation of the people is a grievance that stands in need of remedy'.[39] Outside north-east Wales, however, Wyvill's scheme failed to elicit widespread sympathy. Support for Wyvillism was poorly organized and no truly sustained campaign of political agitation was launched in Wales. The flurry of reforming enthusiasm had been precipitated largely by opposition to the government's American policy and once hostilities ceased the cause of reform receded into the background.

As British hopes of success on American battlefields dwindled, popular opinion hardened against the colonists and their supporters. Radical Dissenters like Richard Price and David Williams, who had argued so eloquently in favour of liberating the colonists, found themselves shunned and derided as early hopes of victory turned to apprehension and then despair. Pro-Americans became an isolated and often alienated minority. Whatever support there was for the colonists melted away as news arrived of successive military set-backs. Dissatisfaction over the conduct of the war and its ruinous economic consequences was rife. Although the war quickened the pulse of economic life in the iron-producing centres of Merthyr and Wrexham, it placed a crippling strain on British resources. Landowners and merchants were deeply troubled by the disruption of markets and commerce in general. By the end of the 1770s the general consensus was that the war had become a colossal waste of effort and money.

The majority of Welsh people, therefore, were deeply distrustful of the colonists and hostile to the war. Distressed and angered by defeats sustained by British forces, ballad-mongers in north Wales, led by Ellis Roberts, Dafydd Jones, and Huw Jones, vented their feelings in no uncertain terms. Far from championing popular rights and the cause of liberty, their songs vilified the colonists and the conduct of the war. Ellis Roberts, who believed that the war was the work of the Devil, was

[39] D. A. Wager, 'Welsh Politics and Parliamentary Reform 1780–1832', *WHR* 7 (1975), p. 430.

horrified by the thought that savage Indians were cutting down brave British soldiers. William Williams of Llandygái believed that most colonists were either thieves or the sons of thieves, and that their greed for profit and power had led them to enslave black people and treat them like animals. Huw Jones of Llangwm, lamenting over the 'blood of England's sons', set his ballads to the tune of 'God save the King'.[40] Anti-American feeling intensified as the economic effects of war began to bite deeply. Ellis Roberts was troubled more by the soaring price of food, tobacco, and snuff than the merits of the cause of American freedom, whilst Hugh Jones, Maesglasau, complained bitterly in 1782 that taxes had shot up, markets had caved in, and Pharaoh-like landowners were doubling their rents.

Nor did the outbreak of war win sympathy for the cause of liberty and reform within Gwyneddigion circles in London. The notion that members of the Gwyneddigion Society were more radical and egalitarian than their counterparts within the Cymmrodorion is a myth. Not until after the French Revolution of 1789 did the Gwyneddigion Society become a standard-bearer of liberty and sansculottism. Love of metre, music, and mead drew its members together and there is little indication that the libertarian notions publicized by Richard Price and David Williams appealed to them. Indeed, during the American War, the society was the very embodiment of patriotic English xenophobia. The song of the Gwyneddigion, composed by Rhys Jones of Blaenau and sung lustily to the tune *Toriad y Dydd* (Break of Day), contained fulsome expressions of loyalty to the House of Hanover and the British constitution. During celebratory dinners, glasses were raised to 'King and Church' and 'Prince and Principality'. Edward Jones, a fervent royalist and loyalist, was known as 'Bardd y Brenin' (The King's Bard). Owen Jones (Owain Myfyr), the society's founding father and its first chairman, was like some Mafia 'godfather' expecting his fellow members to pander to his whims. As this rotund, dictatorial 'Civic Chief' made his entrance into meetings, members used to stand to attention or rush to supply three chairs, one for him to sit upon and the other two to prop him up. Society meetings were convivial affairs: liquor ran freely, harpers and fiddlers played merrily, and clouds of tobacco smoke hung in the air. But the prevalent interests were Welsh culture and scholarship rather than political reform and the cause of liberty. Although Iolo Morganwg frequented many of their meetings prior to 1789, his correspondence, essays, and verse during that period are noteworthy for the almost total absence of references to radical politics. Indeed, several members of the Gwyneddigion Society were distinctly unreceptive to the ideals of the American colonists. Prior to sailing with Captain Cook on the *Resolution* on 12 July 1776, Dafydd Samwell penned stanzas in support of George III

[40] See, for instance, Huw Jones, *Dwy o Gerddi Newyddion* (Trefriw, 1779).

against the colonists, urging ancient Britons to draw their swords in support of the king. Set-backs on the battlefield deepened his resentments against Americans. When he received news of Cornwallis's surrender in 1781 he bitterly denounced those 'damnable rascals' who cherished the colonists' cause and declared that so much mischief was afoot that 'I shall by and by wish for an arbitrary government'.[41]

Within Wales, too, there were powerful agencies which urged people to fear God, honour the king, and support the 'happy constitution'. The influence of the established church was thrown behind the established order. Church leaders were fiercely hostile to political reform of any kind and clergymen assiduously anaesthetized their flocks by preaching the virtues of subordination to authority. Thousands of adults and children who attended Griffith Jones's circulating schools were taught the value of obedience, morality, and good citizenship. Jones's catechisms, in particular, were widely used to inculcate in young minds the strong sense of duty, strict discipline, and subordination to authority which were believed to be indispensable elements within all prosperous and healthy Protestant nations. The *Welch Piety*, Griffith Jones's annual report, became the mouthpiece of Hanoverian conservatism. Similarly, no people were more prone to view political radicalism with loathing than Welsh Methodists. In order to silence his detractors, Thomas Charles went to some pains in 1799 to affirm the 'unimpeachable loyalty'[42] of Methodists over the previous sixty years. He was right, for Welsh evangelical leaders and their followers had proved almost perversely passive, quietist, and apolitical during that period. Howel Harris and his successive commanders-in-chief, Thomas Charles and John Elias, ruled over the movement as benevolent despots, insisting on total obedience and stifling free thought. Their principal concern was with the condition of souls, with sin and salvation, good works and practical pietism. Society members were ordered to obey the laws of the realm, to exercise discipline in their daily behaviour, and to deem it a Christian privilege to bear each burden, however oppressive or unjust, with faith, patience, and forbearance. Methodist societies thus became a kind of asylum from the outside world; lively radical spirits were either coerced into obedience or expelled from their ranks.

Democratic ideas, therefore, were espoused only by a small and scattered minority, made up largely of literate, articulate, rationalist Dissenters. Within these groups a critical public opinion was emerging. The expansion of road links, the opening up of new commercial enterprises, and the availability of postal services and newspapers helped to create a new awareness of European ideas and transatlantic sentiments.

[41] G. T. Roberts, 'Robin Ddu yr Ail o Fôn', *BBCS* 6 (1932), p. 237.
[42] D. Davies, *The Influence of the French Revolution on Welsh Life and Literature* (Carmarthen, 1926), p. 93.

Clubs, circulating libraries, and reading societies had sprung up. Lively groups of middling sorts, blessed with an impressive range of accomplishments, were emerging as the torchbearers of radicalism as well as the custodians of Welsh culture. Even so, radical ideas moved depressingly slowly over the face of Wales prior to 1789. The problems of disseminating libertarian notions were compounded by geographical divisions, the power of localism, and the hostility of many Welsh presses. From the point of view of political radicalism, David Williams was right to view the Welsh language as 'a perpetual impediment to instruction'.[43] Church leaders, Methodists, and schoolmasters ensured that Welsh people were taught virtually nothing about their political rights. No plans were made to translate and circulate Welsh versions of the works of Richard Price, David Williams, and others. Few Welsh peasants, therefore, heard the early sirens of radical agitation. Moreover, those who lived on the margins of survival found it difficult to enthuse over politics. Common people, trapped in their bleak farms, cottages, and hovels, remained preoccupied with the daily hand-to-mouth struggle for mere survival. The Welsh peasant, according to John Blackwell, 'knows little of political economy; he leaves things that he considers above him to wiser heads'.[44] Habits of deference and submission were still deeply embedded in the minds and hearts of the overwhelming mass of the Welsh people. Most of them continued to live in a condition of dependence on their landowners; they possessed no political rights and had no voice in the shaping of their own destiny. Thus, although Richard Price had struck telling blows against the political structure of the *ancien régime*, what William Cobbett liked to call 'Old Corruption' was still very much alive in Wales before 1789.

Of much greater importance and relevance to the daily lives of the mass of the Welsh people was the administration of local politics and justice. Edmund Burke liked to believe that 'all was harmony within and without'[45] in this period, but there is abundant evidence which reveals that demographic changes, the quickening pace of industrial life, the arbitrary deeds of gentry and stewards, religious antipathies, and legal abuses were increasingly disrupting peace and harmony within local communities. It would be a mistake to believe that stability and quiescence reigned in the counties. Violent spasms of discontent, protest, and riot often convulsed the outward show of deference. For a variety of reasons, there was a growing reservoir of discontent which, when it expressed itself in public demonstrations or deeds of violence, often took local justices of the peace and constables by surprise and rendered them helpless.

[43] David Williams, *History of Monmouthshire*, p. 348.
[44] Prys Morgan, *Eighteenth Century Renaissance*, p. 136.
[45] W. Llewelyn Williams, *The Making of Modern Wales* (London, 1919), p. 8.

Part of the problem stemmed from the fact that justices of the peace were left pretty much to their own devices in this period. Many justices were neglectful of the public good and the system allowed petty and mediocre men to find themselves in positions of unmerited power. In 1731 the property qualification of justices was raised from £20 to £100 in a bid to eliminate or thwart persons of 'mean estate'. The statute, however, had the opposite effect: quite unexpectedly, it opened new doors to ambitious minor squires. All over Wales more and more candidates were admitted to the commission of the peace. Within the two years allowed before the Act was enforced, the number of justices in Merioneth increased from 23 to 42; by 1762 there were 64 justices in the county. In Glamorgan the increase in the size of the commission of the peace, especially after 1760, was dramatic: it rose from 38 in 1730 to 63 in 1760 and to 115 in 1762. In most Welsh counties the bench became composed of a much wider cross-section of society, including lesser squires, stewards, merchants, and lawyers. Nor were spiritual leaders content simply to labour in their ecclesiastical vineyards. The presence of clergymen on the commission of the peace was a growing influence. In Merioneth their numbers increased eightfold during the fifty years after 1726. In Glamorgan clerical justices formed 22 per cent of the commission of the peace in 1774. By 1793 there were 36 clergymen on the Montgomeryshire bench.

Although the commission of the peace grew in size, local government and its administration did not become more efficient. Many justices were non-residents: of 79 country gentlemen added to the Montgomeryshire bench in 1775, 41 were non-residents. Absentees of this kind either served in other Welsh counties or served not at all. Although justices were always gratified to enjoy the prestige of office, a large majority of them were singularly reluctant to shoulder the duties and responsibilities incumbent upon their posts. Left to themselves, and truly grateful for their freedom from outside interference, they either fulfilled the bare minimum of duties or lapsed into torpor. The princely allowance of four shillings a day at Quarter Sessions was scarcely sufficient to persuade them to bestir themselves. In Merioneth only 27 local justices out of a total of 131 attended sessions between 1733 and 1765. The average attendance at Quarter Sessions in Montgomeryshire was around four; in Monmouthshire it was two or three. Most justices were inexperienced amateurs who possessed little or no legal expertise and who exercised their authority only during periods of acute disharmony and crisis. In order to compensate for their lethargy and lack of expertise, semi-professional salaried officials were appointed in several Welsh counties. In 1730 Glamorgan appointed a county treasurer to supervise financial affairs. Merioneth's first county treasurer was paid a pittance of £6 per annum in 1749. Four years later a county surveyor, appointed to survey and organize the repair of highways and bridges, was offered an annual salary of £10. However, his demands on the public purse were judged to be so monstrously high that following his death in 1757 the post was left vacant for some twenty years. The small number of active justices was thus left to deal as best as it could with such wearisome burdens as the repair of roads and bridges, the administration of the county gaol, and the relief of the poor.

Diligent justices, then, were rare. The tedious round of public duties did not appeal to most of them and they earned a reputation as boors and idlers. In 1772 Thomas John of Cilrhedyn, Pembrokeshire, refused to give evidence at Quarter Sessions, declaring loudly that 'he did not value any justice of the peace whatsoever'.[46] As in the case of Members of Parliament, expediency, self-interest, and opportunism triumphed over principle in the conduct of public affairs. The venal used the law to favour or promote the interests of their relatives and friends. Many joined hands with smugglers, tippled with heavy drinkers, or indulged in riotous behaviour. Justices were no strangers to acts of malice or wrathful revenge. They were able to impose unfair parochial and county rates, neglect to provide poor relief, or deny their enemies access to local offices and in particular to the charmed circle of magistracy. Some justices in Cardiganshire in the mid-eighteenth century—as visitors who ventured into the county found to their distress—behaved like gangsters. Sir Herbert Lloyd of Peterwell was a monstrously vain and cruel man whose ruthless exploitation of the law, perfidious deeds, and cavalier indifference to the fate of his inferiors made him the most detested justice in west Wales. Lloyd's lust for fame and power ruined the lives of many citizens and his tyrannical bullying provoked a multitude of protests from wronged suitors, defendants, and witnesses. John Lloyd, a yeoman of Llanddewibrefi, was so infuriated by Lloyd's oppressions that he threatened to run him through with a pitchfork. Although the career of the squire of Peterwell has been exaggerated by legend and tradition, his behaviour demonstrates how unscrupulous and powerful individuals were able to manipulate the law to their own advantage.

Many serious disturbances, which often occurred prior to or during contested elections, were provoked by warring gentry factions. Justices were never in a position to cope when powerful landowners and their stewards determined to flex their muscles in the boroughs. In October 1732 Sir Watkin Williams Wynn raised an army of several hundred tenants, armed them to the teeth with swords, clubs, staves, and pistols, and marched them into Chester to support the Tory Grosvenor family by knocking down every man who declared for King George. At the Pembroke borough election of 1741, supporters of the powerful Orielton

---

[46] D. W. Howell, 'The Landed Gentry of Pembrokeshire in the Eighteenth Century', (unpubl. University of Wales MA thesis, 1965), p. 278.

family, armed with swords and pitchforks, stood on the stairs of the town hall in order to prevent Wiston burgesses from registering their votes. The borough of Carmarthen, riven by internal feuds, often witnessed violence, bloodshed, and riot on its streets. From the 1730s onwards Whigs and Jacobites became involved in a titanic struggle for local supremacy. The factional strife and bitterness which followed adversely affected the administrative efficiency and economic prosperity of the borough. Thwarted in the election of 1741, six years later local Whigs gained the upper hand by enlisting the support of intimidatory mobs in order to win the borough seat. In 1749 further strong-arm tactics were employed to purge the common council of six Tory members and to deprive Sir John Philipps of the recordership. The Tories refused to withdraw and for the next fourteen years both parties acted out a bizarre pageant in the course of which the Tories elected their own officials and transacted formal business side by side with the official council. From time to time underlying tensions bubbled to the surface, with disastrous results. During November and December 1755 the borough of Carmarthen was in chaos. Jacobite mobs, incited by members of the Society of Sea Serjeants and armed with bludgeons, cutlasses, guns, and pistols, poured into the town, attacked the town hall and gaol, killed and wounded several citizens, and threatened to raze the home of prominent Whigs to the ground. When the violence abated, litigation and intrigue continued with such furious passion that the administration of the borough virtually collapsed and there was no alternative but to petition the Crown for a new charter.

Religious animosities also made for instability in Welsh towns. Acts of violence against traditionally unorthodox religious groups were now admittedly fewer in number, especially since the number of Catholics had dwindled and Quakers had become innocuous. Even so, anti-Dissent virulence continued to crop up from time to time. Readers of Theophilus Evans's works cannot fail to discern the rancour and venom which Anglican diehards continued to harbour against Dissent. However, during the middle decades of the eighteenth century, Methodist evangelists were believed to be those most likely to turn the world upside down. In spite of their fierce affirmations of loyalty to king, church, and country, Methodist were viewed by the authorities as a thoroughly suspect and disreputable crew. Enemies of Methodism maintained that tramping evangelists were unfaithful to those principles which they pronounced most sacred and that their true aim was to foment strife. Here, so they argued, was a new generation of mad zealots, arrogant saints, and levelling Roundheads. Dynamic preaching and exhorting, practised in itinerant fashion by Methodists, raised the spectre of Cradockism. Well-established gentry families were convinced that these roving intruders were threatening to unloose local ties and bonds of deference. Wild rumours that Methodists were crypto-papists, bold Jacobites, or servants of Satan gained currency and helped to provoke frequent mobbings. Townsmen in north Wales, in particular, found it hard to fathom or accept the strange accents, curious preaching styles, and spiritual arrogance of Methodists based in the diocese of St Davids. Scenes of great tumult and disorder were seen in Dolgellau, Bala, and Denbigh. Methodist 'intruders' were pelted with stones and turf, tossed into rivers and lakes, captured by press-gangs, driven to prison, and subjected to all kinds of humiliations. Even the leading lights within the movement were forced to endure countless indignities—often at the instigation of gentlemen and clergymen. The duke of Beaufort led the ferocious mob which assaulted Howel Harris for preaching against drunkenness, balls, whoredom, and horse-racing. Local clergymen plied the mobs of Bala with drink when Harris visited the town in 1741. Justices in Merioneth refused to grant preaching licences to 'frantic, moon-struck Methodists',[47] whilst in Anglesey William Prichard was obliged to employ an enormously fierce dog to protect him against mobs armed with clubs, knives, and staves. Indeed, Methodist correspondence and journals are riddled with instances of affluent landowning families and hostile mobs creating terrifying scenes of turmoil and disorder in Welsh towns. Although such tales were often heavily embroidered, itinerant preachers clearly suffered vile treatment at the hands of angry mobs. Since justices and constables were either too weak or not disposed to offer protection or stamp out disturbances, Methodists knew that they risked life and limb by venturing into the towns. Not until the 1760s did Methodists acquire a greater measure of respectability and find themselves more widely acknowledged to be orderly, dutiful, and loyal Protestant subjects.

From time to time local justices were also faced with bursts of destabilizing riots mounted by starving mobs in search of both a square meal and a square deal. Since bread was the principal item in the diet of peasants and industrial workers alike, the price of corn and wheat was of crucial importance. Whenever poor harvests, famine, and soaring prices placed a heavy strain on local resources and deprived people of their basic means of subsistence, social turmoil followed. Storms of anger also burst whenever middlemen, dealers, and farmers abused the values of the old moral economy by forestalling, engrossing, and regrating. People were moved to act violently in order to feed themselves and their families, to avoid the stigma of having to apply for poor relief, and to halt the movement of much-needed grain through Welsh ports. Serious riots occurred in 1740–2, 1752, and 1757–8, when thousands of Welsh families were plunged into misery by famine and death. The most seriously disturbed areas were those towns and ports where grain was regularly moved.

[47] P. R. Roberts, 'The Social History of the Merioneth Gentry', p. 224.

Many parts of Denbighshire and Flintshire were in uproar during May 1740. Following an exceptionally poor harvest, corn prices had soared, and famine and high mortality were widespread. On 21 May around 400 armed colliers from Mostyn and Bychton, accompanied by their wives and children, swept into Rhuddlan, claiming loudly that they would rather hang than starve. Feelings were running high because of the 'illegal' engrossing and shipping of local grain. Two days later, lead-miners, craftsmen, and yeomen from Bagillt, Denbigh, and Mostyn joined the colliers and threatened to burn down the town. The mobs ran riot, seizing wagons, ransacking granaries, and threatening middlemen. Confronted by such furious gales of protest and violence, justices of the peace were forced to call for the assistance of soldiers from Chester to restore order and peace. Elsewhere in Wales, other market towns and ports echoed to the sound of marching colliers voicing their grievances and seeking redress by the use of force. On 23 May 1740 miners attacked a vessel laden with corn at Pembroke and made off with part of the cargo. 1757–8 were also years of famine, steeply rising food prices, and large-scale demonstrations and riots. In many parts of Wales angry crowds besieged storehouses, flour-mills, and ships. Mobs in Anglesey were particularly busy. Storehouses at Holyhead were defended by armed gentlemen against guerrilla attacks launched by the citizens of Beaumaris and Llannerch-y-medd during the winter of 1757–8. Rural incendiarists who raided storehouses in Carmarthen were repulsed by local gentry and burgesses. In 1758 dozens of Cilgwyn quarrymen marched into Caernarfon to ransack corn stores, only to be confronted by armed burgesses. One rioter was shot and a pig-spayer, who had heralded their approach by blowing a horn, was apprehended and lynched by his pursuers.

Those who participated in riots and disturbances were not brutalized, drink-sodden thugs anxious to enjoy themselves or determined to loot and plunder at will. Most of them were lead-miners, colliers, quarrymen, craftsmen, and women. Such elements were more easily and swiftly mobilized than small peasants or farm labourers and were noted for their solidarity. They had no plans to subvert the constitution, demolish the world of private property and privilege, or overthrow the traditional social hierarchy. Their protests were provoked either by sheer hunger or by the additional and unwarranted excesses which the social and economic system had spawned. Campaigning largely for the redress of specific grievances, they presented short-term threats to the maintenance of law and order but no permanent threat to the structure of society. Although their actions gave rise to acute anxiety among members of the bench and a sense of outrage among landed Titans, the conduct of riots was, in fact, remarkably restrained and informed throughout by a sense of justice and fair play. Confronted by the unsympathetic face of growing commercialism, rioters vented their anger on those who had profited by employing methods which offended traditional notions about what was right and proper. Mobs were swift to identify and isolate scapegoats, and the usual targets for their hostility were middlemen, grain factors, large farmers, ships' captains, or any others who created dearth by artificial means in order to swell their own profits or who engrossed valuable corn in order to ship it elsewhere. Rioters at Rhuddlan in May 1740 ransacked the home of George Colley, agent of the Botryddan estate, and threatened that if they caught him 'they would cut his head off and set it upon Diserth finger post and tie his guts about it'.[48] Pembroke was thrown into turmoil in the same month when rioters compelled merchants to abandon plans for the export of grain, forcibly reduced the price of food, and threatened to burn the town unless farmers and magistrates promised to adhere to a just price.

Rioters thus directed their resentment and hostility against those who abandoned the traditional moral precepts which had characterized the paternalistic regulation of the economy. They believed that it was 'lawful' to chastise petty profiteers who, by their 'unnatural' deeds, departed from long-established principles and customs which determined what was and what was not 'a fair price'. Food rioting was a traditional form of protest, steeped in local ceremonies and customs, and legitimized by what participants believed to be their moral obligation to defend concepts about fair and just prices. On the whole, their objectives were limited, their sense of justice admirable, and their behaviour remarkably restrained. Mobs adhered to the rules of the game and justices were well advised to redress specific grievances, especially when they were couched in chilling language. In 1766, tradesmen, colliers, and labourers in Swansea, acting on behalf of starving families, pinned a message addressed to the magistrates and elders of the town to the door of William Davies, portreeve of Swansea. The notice, which voiced furious resentments over the extortionate price of corn and wheat, the dearth of corn, the tolls levied by millers for grinding other people's corn, and the maladministration of forestalling and regrating, clumsily but emphatically reminded their betters of their obligation to abide by well-established rules and conventions:

> Now sirs, we hope that wisdom will teach you
> that have authority to order these things or
> else we cannot perish without—revenge.
> We do intend to meet together on the
> borough [burrow] of Crymlyn on 29 November 1766.[49]

Although the state seldom intervened in local affairs, whenever the

---

[48] K. Lloyd Gruffydd, 'The Vale of Clwyd Corn Riots of 1740', *Flintshire Hist. Soc. Journal* 27 (1975–6), p. 38.
[49] D. Hay and others, *Albion's Fatal Tree* (London, 1981), p. 327.

threat of war loomed, the government was forced to order local governors to supply ready cash and able-bodied men. The demands of military service, especially for the wars against France in 1756-63 and against the American colonists in 1775-83, provided Welsh counties with recurring flash-points and scenes of turbulence. Military service was widely reckoned to be a loathsome burden and there was a good deal of popular hostility to the Militia Act of 1757. Local militia organization had slumped into torpor by the eve of the Seven Years' War, and the Militia Act was designed to revive it by calling on parishes to levy all able-bodied men between the ages of eighteen and fifty, to select a proportion of them by drawing lots, and to equip them for service for a period of three years. Provision was made for the use of substitutes or payment of a fine of £10. Most Welsh counties dragged their feet: by 1761 only seven counties had obeyed the statute. In the counties of mid- and north Wales the militia did not lumber into action until March 1778 when the alliance between France and America precipitated a crisis. Militia units in Wales were generally small, inefficient, ramshackle bands of illiterate, manual workers. Few of them relished the prospect of having to serve outside their own localities and there was a general feeling that they would rather be hanged at home than scalped in America. During periods of war, members of the Flintshire and Glamorgan batallions refused to re-enlist in their regiments unless they were returned to their native counties. Much resentment was aired, too, when the burdens of militia quotas were unevenly distributed and it became apparent that the heaviest financial burdens fell upon poor people. According to Thomas Pennant, those who contributed rates in north Wales to enable poor men to escape service were as penurious as the recipients themselves. Sporadic disturbances broke out in Denbighshire in 1769 and in Merioneth in 1779 as common people displayed their reluctance to serve in the ranks.

Smouldering resentments often exploded into violent deeds, too, whenever the new values of commerce and industry came into conflict with age-old customary relationships based on the ownership and use of land. Intense struggles to gain commercial interests led to bitter and prolonged disputes from the 1740s onwards. As the tempo of industrial change quickened, stewards, acting on behalf of either the Crown or powerful landowners, encroached upon unenclosed common and waste lands. Wherever new mineral deposits were discovered, a rash of disputes over the boundaries of manors, squatting, strays, impounding, and the payment of dues and renders invariably followed. Some justices were personally involved in conflicting claims to mineral rights; other stood aside and allowed mighty men to practise their tyrannies with impunity.

The deeds of pragmatic, hard-headed stewards often lay at the root of conflicts over mineral rights. During the 1750s Cardiganshire was said to be 'in a continual state of war, law, squabbles, wrangling',[50] partly as a result of the appointment of Lewis Morris, the Anglesey-born surveyor, poet, and scholar, as agent and superintendent of the fabulously rich Esgairmwyn mine. In his characteristically forthright and determined way, Morris strove to establish the right of the Crown—of *Y Morthwyl Mawr* (the Sledgehammer), as he called George II—to mine for lead. Local gentlemen and freeholders, who loathed Morris, refused to submit passively to the encroachments of the Crown and eventually took the law into their own hands. In February 1753 Herbert Lloyd of Peterwell and William Powell of Nanteos, both magistrates, led an armed mob of several hundred people to the mines, held a pistol to Morris's head, and invited him to transfer possession of the mine. Shaking with fear, Morris submitted and was incarcerated in Cardigan gaol for six weeks. In Glamorgan, Gabriel Powell, who was christened 'King of Swansea' by his enemies,[51] was a devious, brutal steward whose fidelity to the duke of Beaufort was such that he virtually waged war on gentry and freeholders who sought to deprive his master of economic and industrial rights in the seigniories of Gower and Kilvey. Powell used both legal and illegal means to frustrate the ambitions of rising families, such as the Popkins of Fforest and the Prices of Penlle'r-gaer, by claiming ownership of common land, woods, rivers, and streams. His brief from Beaufort was evidently to eliminate all obstacles which threatened to arrest swift industrial progress in the coal and copper industries. Poor tenants found their rents increased, heriots were claimed with startling promptness, and rights to gather culm and peat were severely restricted. Powell's violent ways begat further violence. Covert intimidation and arson were employed by his enemies against Beaufort's employees and coalworks, and bitter litigation followed in the courts. Nor did stewards, acting on behalf of industrialists, find life rosy in other Welsh counties. As 'immigrant adventurers' swarmed into Anglesey during the 1770s, the island was torn by protracted legal squabbles over the ownership and revenues of the Parys mountain copper mines.

Spirited small gentry and freeholders adopted aggressive tactics in a bid to resist enclosures and protect grazing and mineral rights. On Hirwaun Common and the Royal Oak Common in Carmarthen, mobs declared that, unlike their popish counterparts in France, they would not wear wooden shoes. By burning properties, pulling down fences, and sending threatening letters, they revealed their stubborn determination to protect their 'natural' rights against what they believed to be rapacious tyranny practised by greedy men. 'God damn the corporation and all those that wish it well', cried insurgents in Carmarthen, 'they call us Levellers. We

[50] D. Ll. Thomas, 'Lewis Morris in Cardiganshire', *Y Cymmrodor* 15 (1901), p. 19.
[51] J. Martin, 'Private Enterprise versus Manorial Rights', p. 159.

will level them and their troops of horses that they threaten us with.'[52] Economic tensions clearly sharpened class antagonisms, which, in turn, led to violent protests. A growing number of ballads and interludes voiced the feeling of mistrust between tenants and stewards. Twm o'r Nant used his unique gifts for satire and mockery to expose 'sturdy fellows' who acted as stewards and agents:

> Anger a gentleman, you'll not find him unbending,
> But anger a steward, and the ill's past mending.[53]

When Sir William Jones marshalled arguments against Edmund Burke's plan to abolish the Welsh judicature in 1780, he claimed that if the Courts of Great Sessions were wound up industrious tenants would become 'greater slaves than they are even now to the tyrannical agents and stewards of indolent gentlemen'.[54] The fraudulent and violent behaviour of stewards employed by Sir Watkin Williams Wynn in Montgomeryshire was viewed with profound repugnance by independent freeholders and rationalist Dissenters alike. William Jones of Llangadfan believed that (apart from George Whitefield and John Wesley) Wynnstay agents were the greatest evils let loose on mankind.

Significant increases in the size and number of merchant vessels and in the volume of maritime trade also created greater temptations for smugglers and more opportunities for violent behaviour. As Welsh ports began to hum with activity during this period, smuggling and pillaging became almost a way of life along the coast. Indeed, the mid-eighteenth century was the golden age of Welsh smuggling. Off the coast of north Wales, nippy vessels based on the Isle of Man and Port Rush in north-east Ireland led Revenue cutters a merry chase. Smugglers preyed upon unsuspecting ships or deposited their ill-gotten gains on isolated beaches. In the south, the notorious Thomas Knight, who used Barry Island as an entrepôt, boasted a fleet of nimble ships which enabled him to land goods in remote creeks on both sides of the Bristol Channel. Knight was so powerful and his smuggling gangs so well-organized that customs officials were utterly helpless to prevent the traffic in tobacco, tea, gin, brandy, wine, soap, and salt. So profitable was this illicit trade that prominent smugglers were perfectly prepared to risk a brush with custom officials. They knew that their ships were so swift and strong that they were easily capable of outrunning and outfighting Revenue cutters. In general, customs officials and the ships at their disposal were too few in number and too poorly armed to be able to strike terror into the hearts of armed gangs of smugglers. Customs officials, however conscientious, could not be

---

[52] D. J. V. Jones, *Before Rebecca* (London, 1973), pp. 40–1.
[53] Thomas Parry, *History of Welsh Literature*, p. 270.
[54] Garland Cannon (ed.), *The Letters of Sir William Jones* (2 vols., Oxford, 1970), i. 354.

everywhere at once and the most they could hope for was to keep smuggling within reasonably acceptable bounds.

The task of customs officials was rendered more difficult by the fact that the activities of smugglers were often connived at by the gentry. Exorbitant excise duties had forced many aggrieved gentlemen and merchants to operate outside the law. William Morris, Controller of Customs at Holyhead, wearily confessed to his brother, Richard, that Anglesey had become 'a den of runners, the gentry turned smugglers'.[55] In Swansea, customs officials were summoned by stewards of the Court Leet to serve as jurors in order to permit local smugglers a wider degree of latitude. Often, when smuggling was at its height, justices were nowhere to be found. Some turned a blind eye, while others happily filled their cellars with rum and brandy. The burdens imposed on customs officials were also compounded by the very real possibility of serious injury at the hands of smuggling gangs armed with muskets, pistols, and cutlasses. Diligent and conscientious officials who resolved to harry smugglers with remorseless persistence were often made the target of violent and riotous protests.

Pillaging wrecked ships had also become an extraordinarily lucrative trade. A rich folklore surrounds the subject of 'wrecking' and there are many hair-raising but almost invariably unsubstantiated tales of innocent ships being lured on to rocks by false lights from the shore. Most vessels, in fact, came to grief for other reasons. Treacherous rocks, shifting sands, as well as the normal hazards of rain, high winds, violent storms, and the absence of adequate warning-lights along the shore took their toll of richly laden ships. Local people believed that wrecked ships and their cargo were fair game. In an age of considerable poverty and want, shipwrecks were viewed as a godsend, manna bestowed from heaven by the bounteous Almighty. When disasters occurred, people swarmed in their hundreds along rocks and sands in search of raw materials, household goods, or any luxury items which might supplement their daily requirements. When the *Indian Prince* foundered at Aberthaw during its return journey from Guinea in 1752, local people flocked to the beach and swiftly pillaged its copious cargo of rum, sugar, cotton, ebony, and elephants' teeth with rapacious glee. As soon as the *Phoebe and Peggy* was pounded to pieces close to the entrance of Solfach harbour in January 1773, local mobs stripped over sixty drowned bodies and robbed the body of a wealthy lady of five hundred guineas, cutting rings off her fingers and jewels from her ears. Some gangs of pillagers operated in a highly sophisticated, if sinister, fashion. The Crigyll robbers, near Holyhead, so terrorized the mariners and citizens of the west coast of Anglesey that Lewis Morris, in a celebrated poem, yearned to see them hanged for their misdeeds. Such

[55] *Morris Letters*, ii. 66.

gangs, however, enjoyed a good deal of popular support. Those who inhabited the coastal counties of Wales were convinced that practices such as smuggling and pillaging were entirely legitimate since they were hallowed by custom and tradition. In 1745 pillagers informed an Anglesey customs officer that they had as much right as he to the spoils of the ocean. Whatever the authorities might have thought, common people did not regard emptying wrecked ships of cargo and stripping drowned bodies of possessions and valuables as criminal activity. In their eyes, such actions were morally justified.

Little detailed work has been carried out on crime and punishment in this period, but what evidence exists suggests that the number of prosecutions was falling off. Great Sessions records for Anglesey are riddled with entries such as 'no bills' and 'no business'. In Montgomeryshire, too, the average number of prosecutions declined steadily between 1720 and 1780. Part of the reason lies in the fact that the central government was more concerned than ever before to protect and preserve private property and the lives and liberties of those who held property. To this end, an alarming number of new capital offences was created during this period: thirty-three capital offences during the reign of George II, and a further sixty-three between 1760 and 1810. Indeed, by 1820, the number of statutory capital offences had soared to over 200. From 1736 onwards, pilfering servants were liable to be hanged. Five years later, sheep-stealing became a capital offence. Since many statutes, however, were so savage and oppressive, they were not invoked in practice. In many ways, the severities of the law were blunted. Local justices, especially during periods of acute economic distress, tempered justice with mercy by undervaluing stolen goods. Many of them maintained local harmony by recourse to out-of-court arbitration, mediation, and compounding. By failing to convict or by returning reduced or merciful verdicts, Welsh juries helped to smoothe the rough edges of the law. Many monoglot Welshmen who served on juries were unable to make much sense of the proceedings (both despite and because of the presence of interpreters) and were therefore prone to favour and protect their neighbours. Punishments were often mitigated or waived in order to reveal the humane qualities of the system, maintain its credibility, and avoid any sense of outrage. Only a small proportion of condemned men—mostly murderers—was sent to the gallows. Between 1753 and 1819, only 9 per cent of those sentenced to death by judges in the circuit of Brecknock (comprising the three counties of Brecon, Glamorgan, and Radnor) were actually executed. Those who committed serious crimes were more likely to find themselves transported to America or, later on, to the penal colonies of Australia. Much depended on the character of the accused and the quality of the evidence provided by those of his friends who were prepared to testify to his or her character in court. Judges, who possessed the power to pose as tyrants or merciful men, tended to place a high regard on the evidence of respectable propertied men and to look favourably upon offenders of good character who had committed offences without premeditation and whose subsequent feelings of shame and remorse were plain for all to see.

Although the number of indictments contained in Great Sessions papers is both a fragile and suspect index, it would seem, on balance, that the volume of crime was decreasing and that courts frequently resorted to reprieve and pardon in order to mitigate the harshness of the system. Property offences seem to have proliferated only when economic distress during lean years forced poor craftsmen and labourers to commit felonies in order to feed themselves and their families. In Montgomeryshire, flurries of petty theft invariably occurred during years of poor harvests, high prices, and famine. During the harsh winter of 1742–3, Edward Crow of Montgomery was apprehended slaughtering a neighbour's ewe; in his defence, the hapless Crow maintained that 'he did it for want of meat for his children'.[56] There were many others who felt the pinch of adversity so acutely during years of dearth that they could not resist the temptation to pilfer. When, in May 1763, Margaret Davies of Rhiwaedog, Merioneth, was apprehended stealing a pair of shoes in Bala fair, she tearfully confessed that the shoes were meant for her sick son who was 'very poor and barefoot'.[57]

In spite of efforts by merciful justices to avoid excessive prosecutions and severe punishments, common people were convinced that the legal system had not been designed to protect the interests of the 'swinish multitude'. They were only too aware that, as the number of capital offences increased, property was more keenly protected than humans. William Morris maintained that in Anglesey and Cardiganshire killing a horse or a black steer was judged by the authorities to be a far more heinous deed than killing a human being. Underprivileged people were conscious, too, that the system afforded many opportunities for abuse. There is little doubt that some unscrupulous men of property made use of the law to protect their own interests. Herbert Lloyd—the 'Vulture knight' of Peterwell—ruthlessly exploited the law for his own ends. He took sadistic delight in punishing or incarcerating errant vagrants, hapless women, and insolent labourers. In the famous 'Black Ram' case, the jury which convicted an innocent freeholder 'framed' by Lloyd was chosen by the squire of Peterwell himself. Lloyd's wrath was widely feared and his tyrannical behaviour brought the courts into disrepute. Common people were conscious that justices and prosecutors were in a position to

[56] T. M. Humphreys, 'Rural Society in Eighteenth-Century Montgomeryshire', p. 444.
[57] A Calendar of the Merioneth Quarter Sessions Rolls, ed. K. Williams-Jones (Merioneth County Council, 1965), p. 236.

manipulate and bend the legal machinery and capitalize on the ignorance and misfortune of others. John Evans could not help but sympathize with the 'poor ignorant witness' who found himself confronted with 'a powerful tyrant of his neighbourhood, whose anger expressed or understood he momentarily dreads more than the displeasure of his God'.[58] The unpropertied knew that the dice were heavily loaded against them. 'The bench are a lot of cheaters', declared John Jones of Cadoxton, near Neath, in 1778, 'I look upon them as dividing the spoils, particularly the old cheat and kite Gabriel Powell.'[59]

There was little popular confidence in the impartiality of the law. Since 1536 English had been made the official language of the courts and, though translators were used when necessary, cases were tried in a language which was, for most defendants and witnesses, either hard to understand or totally incomprehensible. Monoglot Welshmen who found themselves before their betters in the Courts of the Great Sessions were confronted by judges bearing unfamiliar names like Anstruther, Jessop, Pocklington, and Shuttleworth, none of whom knew any Welsh or anything of the habits, customs, and culture of Welsh people. William Bulkeley of Llanfechell— admittedly a biased witness—described Rogers Holland, Chief Justice of Anglesey, as having 'not only no law but likewise no common sense' and his colleague, Thomas Martin, as 'a drunken weak man and no lawyer'.[60] Biased and incompetent interpreters did less than justice to the evidence of Welsh witnesses, whilst wily English lawyers indulged in all kinds of trickery in order to bemuse or fleece their clients. Thomas Roberts of Llwynrhudol poured scorn on attorneys who deliberately larded their pleas in court with unintelligible phrases such as 'notwithstanding', 'howbeit', 'judgement by default', 'a subpoena', and 'the hallowed touch of a bum-bailiff'.[61] Ellis Roberts, the Llanddoged cooper and interlude-writer, described lawyers as 'men in black gowns' barking at each other like dogs and 'pouncing savagely like crows upon carcasses'.[62] Their greed, according to Sir William Jones, was proverbial: he observed in 1780 that few of them had 'any public principle or any view but that of exposing to sale in the best market their faculties and their voices'.[63] There was clearly a growing body of criticism of such legal abuses. Welsh patriots and radicals brought many underlying resentments to the surface in the 1790s. In particular, Jac Glan-

[58] John Evans, *Letters Written during a Tour through South Wales in 1803* (London, 1804), pp. 224–5.

[59] T. H. Lewis, 'Documents Illustrating the County Gaol and House of Correction in Wales', *THSC* (1946–7), pp. 243–4.

[60] G. Nesta Evans, *Religion and Politics in Mid-Eighteenth Century Anglesey* (Cardiff, 1953), p. 197.

[61] Thomas Roberts, *Cwyn yn erbyn Gorthrymder*, p. 17.

[62] NLW MS 132C, p. 135.

[63] Garland Cannon, *Oriental Jones* (London, 1964), p. 85.

y-gors's memorable satire, *Hanes y Sesiwn yng Nghymru* (History of the Sessions in Wales) exposed the confusions, contradictions, and limitations of the legal system in Wales.

Although, as we have seen, courts frequently tempered justice with mercy in order to mitigate the acerbities of the law, offenders knew that brutal punishments might be meted out by the authorities. Fear of the consequences of the law moved Nathaniel Morgan of Llanbryn-mair to hang his head and weep when charged with pilfering from his neighbour. Similar dread prompted Lewis Proctor of Pool, who had been apprehended stealing flannel, to sink to his knees before his accuser three times to beg for his release. Court records bear witness to the excruciating punishments and suffering which were inflicted upon offenders. In 1735 an old woman of Llangaffo in Anglesey was burnt in the hand for stealing forty shillings. In 1742 a corn thief from Llandysilio, Anglesey, was 'burnt in earnest, the iron burning half way through his hand'.[64] Countless numbers of vagabonds, rogues, and 'idle persons' were publicly stripped from the waist upward and flogged in the streets until blood flowed from their backs. Hundreds of male and female convicts were transported for having stolen such trifles as a handkerchief, a silver spoon, and a petticoat. Even if all the judges and justices of Wales had been humane and honest men, the courts would still have been a terrifying prospect for common people.

There were, moreover, few compensations for those who were fortunate enough to escape the gallows or transportation. Bleak prospects confronted felons, undischarged debtors, vagabonds, and vagrants who were committed to county gaols or houses of correction. Welsh prisons, according to John Howard, the prison-reform pioneer who visited them in 1774, were in earnest need of refurbishing and reform. The overwhelming majority of them were horrifyingly filthy, insanitary holes, bereft of light and ventilation and a prey to vermin, disease, and the dreaded gaol fever. In Monmouth gaol, felons were housed in a night room which measured twenty-two feet by fifteen feet. Prisoners at Wrexham Bridewell complained of being almost suffocated, while rain poured in upon felons confined in the county gaol of Flint. Many gaols had no water, straw, sewers, or courtyards. Common gaols were often privately owned and tyrannical gaolers seized most opportunities to fill their own pockets by practising extortion and intimidation. Food was meagre and often inedible, and many prisoners were fettered or chained to iron rings fixed into walls in order to restrict their movements.

Historians of late have been at pains to stress that the volume of crime was probably decreasing by the middle of the eighteenth century and that many subterfuges and sanctions were employed by judges, juries, and

---

[64] Hugh Owen, 'The Diary of William Bulkeley', p. 72.

justices to mitigate the harshness of the legal system. Detailed local studies may well confirm this picture. Nevertheless, the fact remains that common people had acquired a less than reverential attitude towards those who practised and enforced the law. Indeed, as the radical literature published in the 1790s bears witness, the abuses, inequalities, and severities of the legal system had become a burning issue.

Demographic changes were also beginning to create troublesome problems for local authorities. As the population began to rise sharply after 1750, justices were forced to turn their minds to the necessity of establishing an efficient system of poor relief. Up until the middle years of the eighteenth century, there had been considerable diversity in the administration of poor relief. Local administrators, left largely to their own devices, had adopted methods which were best suited to prevailing conditions within their own parishes. Most rural parishes in north Wales had not as yet levied poor rates. In the north-west, the poor continued to beg from door to door, and private charities, public collections, and good neighbourliness helped to mitigate suffering. It must be said that the system, such as it was, had worked tolerably well. But as the population began to swell, local authorities were forced to address themselves to the task of coping with rapidly changing social and economic circumstances.

As the needs of small communities became more serious and complex, the first and most pressing requirement was to levy poor rates. Parish authorities, notably in populous urban and industrial parishes, were increasingly compelled after 1750 to levy poor rates in a systematic fashion. The rate, which was assessed and raised by local poor-law officers and imposed upon householders and landowners, brought in funds which enabled local authorities to cushion the defenceless poor from the myriad blows which rained down upon them. These sums of money were used to provide the disabled poor, the aged, and impotent paupers with gifts of clothing (blankets, shifts, and stockings), grants for mending clothes and repairing shoes, grants of food (corn, barley, cheese, butter, bread, and ale) and fuel (coal, peat, and wood). House rents were often paid, the sick received medicines and medical attendance, the pregnant were afforded the services of midwives, and the dead were provided with a shroud, a coffin, candles, and a grave. Chargeable orphans, bastards, and deserted children were placed out as apprentices or were found board and lodging among elderly members of the community. There were many unfortunate souls, like 'Evan the Idiot' of Lampeter,[65] who were found accommodation at local farms and provided with flannel vests, smocks, stockings, coats, breeches, and clogs. In a host of small but vitally important ways, the poor law helped to alleviate the sufferings of impoverished, luckless people.

[65] Bethan Phillips, *Peterwell*, p. 104.

Moreover, a variety of local charities, which enabled parishes to erect almshouses and set up charity schools, continued to mitigate distress caused by poverty and misfortune.

During years of dearth, famine, disease, and unemployment, the number of paupers claiming relief increased sharply: 1741, 1756, and 1766 were particularly bad years. But much greater demands were made upon the time, patience, and stamina of the overseers of the poor from the 1770s onwards. Poor-relief expenditure began to soar alarmingly. Costs rose markedly in every Welsh county as the increase in population, economic depression, and the trials and tribulations of war bred crisis and turmoil. Much to the distress of puzzled local authorities, poor-relief expenditure rose in Wales from £13,407 in 1748–50 to £41,109 in 1775–6 and, most alarming of all, to £70,718 in 1783–5. Some of the most dramatic increases occurred in the counties of Denbigh, Flint, and Montgomery, where the rate rose almost ninefold, eightfold, and sevenfold respectively between 1748–50 and 1783–5. Even in the thinly populated rural counties of north-west Wales, where the problem of pauperism was least pressing, expenditure more than doubled. The real crisis years seem to have been those after 1775, when the demands of the war effort and economic depression produced devastating results. Poor-relief expenditure went through the roof. In Glamorgan, for instance, the total net expenditure rose from £5,301 in 1776 to £8,818 in 1783–5, an increase of 66 per cent. Poor rates levied in both rural and industrial parishes reveal that local authorities were increasingly hard pressed to cope with the problems posed by the swelling ranks of paupers. The rate levied in the hamlet of Coety Higher in Glamorgan rose from 8d. in the pound in 1757 to 2s. in 1780–1; in Llandeilo Gresynni in Monmouthshire it increased from 1s. in the pound in 1729 to 2s. in 1776; in Llanrhystud in Cardiganshire it leapt from 4d. in the pound in 1750 to 4s. in 1800. By the 1770s, therefore, pauperism on a large scale was placing a severe and sometimes intolerable strain on the financial resources of Welsh parishes.

Confronted by such complex, if not incomprehensible, problems, parish officers began to implement the Poor Law Act of 1662 with greater stringency and harshness. Firstly, the number of 'illegal settlers' removed to their native parishes increased strikingly. Since only those who had acquired legal settlement within a parish were entitled to apply for financial aid, more and more parishes strove to shuffle off their responsibilities by rounding up strangers and hounding them back to their native parishes. Overseers of the poor were swift to identify those without a bona fide settlement, and whenever rates began to soar they rallied to the task of driving the poor, the old, the sick, and the pregnant out of their parishes. Often the process of hustling paupers from parish to parish entailed enormous physical and mental suffering. Families were uprooted, mothers and children were separated, and many elderly persons were too ill or incapacitated to embark on long journeys. Some indication of the hardship and distress which landless families suffered as a result of removal is provided by the number of appeals against orders of removal. In Glamorgan there occurred a striking increase in the number of appeals, many of which involved males, widows, spinsters, and pregnant women from populous parishes such as Llangyfelach, Llantrisant, Neath, and Swansea. Appeals heard at Glamorgan Quarter Sessions rose from 40 in the period 1725–50 to 94 in the period 1750–75 and to 209 in the period 1775–1800. Indeed, court records throughout Wales abound with cases of contested settlement and inter-parish litigation. One example of the often lengthy sagas must suffice. In 1779 Cecile Lewis, a widow, and her four children were removed from Llanharan to Penderyn. The authorities at Penderyn appealed against the order and the family was shepherded back to Llanharan only to be dispatched once more—this time to Ystradfellte, whose authorities also successfully reversed the order in 1780. Undeterred, the Llanharan overseers of the poor eventually managed to remove the hapless family to Llantrisant. Removal was an unpleasant, expensive business which also spawned further malpractices. Many overseers of the poor, having spent weeks or even months searching for putative fathers, establishing places of birth, examining pregnant women, and seeking legal advice, were tempted to falsify accounts and to line their own pockets with appropriated expenses. But even though there were heavy burdens, costs, and risks involved in transporting paupers to their native parishes, local authorities were much more disposed to foot the bill than to tolerate the presence of chargeable undesirables.

Secondly, strenuous efforts were made by parish authorities to dissuade penurious people from applying for outdoor relief. In some communities, of course, the social stigma involved was itself a deterrent. Gwallter Mechain believed that many families supported their indigent relations in order to avoid the opprobrium of having to apply for relief. Recipients of relief were increasingly and much more strictly required to wear a red or blue badge, in accordance with the Act of 1697, with a large 'P' marked on it. Badging was more rigorously enforced in order to humiliate individuals and discourage them from seeking relief. Crude attempts were also often made to indemnify the parish by seizing the goods of paupers or preparing inventories of their belongings ready for sale at a later date or on the occasion of their death. Landlords were encouraged by parish officers to avoid letting houses or cottages to impecunious people who were likely to apply for poor relief. The stigma of poverty, moreover, was intensified by the availability of rewards offered to those who were prepared to apprehend rogues, vagabonds, and idle persons. Every possible expedient was used in the ceaseless and ultimately unsuccessful campaign to persuade people not to apply for poor relief.

The third device was to establish workhouses, where recipients of poor relief might earn their keep. The Knatchbull Act of 1723 empowered parishes to buy or lease workhouses, but only a small number were established in Wales. According to the overseers' returns, there were only nineteen workhouses in 1776, eleven of which were in Pembrokeshire, and the total sum expended in rent for workhouses and habitations for the poor was as little as £2,120. Many of these edifices were small, dingy hovels scarcely fit for animals, let alone people. The workhouse erected in Holyhead in 1741, designed chiefly to house incorrigible Irish vagabonds, was described as a pigsty by William Morris. In Swansea, parts of the old castle were fitted up as a poor-house in 1756, while eight years later the parish vestry of St Peter's in Carmarthen turned part of the old Priory into a workhouse. Workhouses enabled parishes to shuffle off their responsibility to provide for the poor. The workhouse which Viscount Windsor provided for the use of the borough of Cardiff was capable of accommodating 200 inmates in 1777. In theory, those who were consigned to workhouses or houses of correction were meant to be taught the virtues of discipline, thrift, and sobriety. But since workhouses were farmed out to contractors whose sense of public duty and paternal obligation was low, few pregnant women, vagrants, and rogues found themselves subjected to short sharp doses of Puritan discipline and piety.

By the 1780s, therefore, a variety of grievances and tensions were present in Welsh communities. Demographic changes, developments in trade and industry, the economic and political powers acquired by absentee landowners, the depredations of stewards and agents, abuses and inequalities within the legal system, and a general hardening of attitude towards the poor had all created mounting resentment. Beneath the veneer of deference and submission—as growing numbers of almanacs, ballads, and interludes testify—there was a good deal of frustration and anger. In print, and sometimes in deeds of law-breaking and violence, people who were often unaffected by radical ideas were provoked to condemn the crude excesses and unwarranted burdens which the economic and political system had created. In venting their resentments against corrupt justices, avaricious merchants, treacherous corn-dealers, meddling excise officers, hard-fisted tax collectors, pettifogging lawyers, and bullying overseers, people were not seeking to subvert the constitution or demolish the world of private property and privilege. They simply sought to protect their 'natural' rights and customs. As a result, the political and economic fabric of the *ancien régime* in Wales remained intact.

CHAPTER 9

THE SPIRIT OF ENTHUSIASM

SOME of the most remarkable gains in eighteenth-century Wales were achieved in the field of religion and education. Although the established church still remained a powerful institution which commanded the respect and affection of most regular worshippers in Wales, it was finding it increasingly difficult to rise above its own administrative shortcomings and to meet the challenge of new rivals. Methodism, led by young men of compelling magnetism, struck genuine roots in Wales from the late 1730s onwards. Its attractive combination of powerful preaching, intimate fellowship, and fervent hymn-singing helped to fulfil the unappeased spiritual cravings of middle sorts. From the outset, the seeds of secession were implicit within Methodism and the trend towards schism was reinforced as the growth of revivalism brought about the reinvigoration of Dissent. These developments were accompanied and sustained by the extraordinary success of the Welsh circulating schools, which, by providing common people with easy access to elementary schooling in the vernacular, led to a striking upsurge in literacy rates. In many ways, the emergence of Methodism, the rejuvenation of Dissent, and the growth of literacy were formative forces in the making of modern Wales. They helped, in the longer term, to generate and satisfy much of the demand for piety, morality, education, and self-improvement which characterized Welsh life in the nineteenth century.

The growing challenge to the monopoly and the authority of the established church was partly provoked by a more acute awareness among its own members of its administrative and spiritual inadequacies. As we have seen, the financial *malaise* of the established church was so deeply rooted that it was powerless to reform itself. Much of its revenue, notably in the southern dioceses, had been siphoned off by lay impropriators and affluent churchmen. Moreover, its administrative structure was so archaic and anomalous that many of its servants were prevented from discharging their duties effectively. Yet, although maldistribution of wealth within the church meant that the quality of religious life varied from see to see and from locality to locality, the influence and popularity of the church remained strong. Throughout this period the majority of worshipping Christians in Wales believed that the Church of England offered the true way of life and belief. The parish church continued to be the focus of the faith of the community and the social life of the parish. Prior to the nineteenth century, there is little evidence of a ground swell of popular resentment towards the established church.

Even so, there were new forces at work which were seriously weakening the capacity of the established church to provide effective spiritual leadership. The appointment of 'foreign' English bishops to Welsh sees increasingly provoked divisive tensions within the church. Between 1727 and 1870 not a single Welsh-speaking prelate was appointed to a bishopric in Wales. Most Welsh bishops in this period were political appointees; they were servants of the state rather than spiritual leaders. Most of them, too, blanched at the prospect of being consigned to a little bishopric in Wales. 'Though I love Wales very much', confessed Thomas Herring, bishop of Bangor, 'I would not choose to be reduced to butter, milk and lean mutton.'[1] Bishops strove manfully to avoid having to make the arduous and expensive journey to their Welsh sees and pressed their masters to provide them with more lucrative preferments. Few of them tarried long: the average tenure of a Welsh bishop in the eighteenth century was six years. Contacts between them and their flocks were few, and Welsh almanackers were obliged to print the names of Welsh bishops annually in order to help the common man recall that his distant shepherd was called Pearce or Newcome or Lisle or Mawson. Grudgingly, bishops made their unwilling way to their dioceses during the summer months to hold annual ordinations or triennial visitations, usually with unseemly haste. As they mumbled their incantations in a tongue foreign to their flocks, their words became 'a mere topic for idle gossip and guesswork'.[2] Many of those being confirmed believed that when English-speaking bishops uttered the words 'more and more', they were referring to the sea (*môr*). Separated from their people by the barrier of language, such bishops were unable to advise, encourage, or reprove their clergy and their flocks. Some of them were, in fact, avowed enemies of the Welsh tongue. Bishop Drummond of St Asaph (1748–61), a Scotsman of harsh prejudices, was so convinced that it was in the interests of the Welsh people 'to unite with the rest of their fellow subjects in language as well as government'[3] that he resolved to drive the Welsh language out of the services held in his see. Many English prelates either turned a blind eye to, or failed to appreciate, the remarkable spiritual and educational movements which were rejuvenating Wales in their absence. Samuel Squire, bishop of St Davids (1761–6), was happy to eat salmon from the Tywi river with his affluent friends in London whereas Methodist evangelists offered a different bait to his flock in Wales.

As the relationship between non-resident English bishops and their

---

[1] Norman Sykes, *Church and State in England*, p. 94.
[2] A. J. Johnes, *An Essay on the Causes which have Produced Dissent from the Established Church* (2nd edn., London, 1832), p. 53.
[3] D. Ambrose Jones, *History of the Church in Wales* (Carmarthen, 1926), p. 225.

flocks became increasingly strained and distant, clamant protests were voiced. The Morrises of Anglesey informed all and sundry that Hanoverian bishops were the most dissolute, feckless, and useless creatures on the face of the earth. Griffith Jones, Llanddowror, was convinced that idle, absentee prelates were robbing the church of its vitality and encouraging scandal, strife, and schism. But the most forthright indictment of careerist *Esgyb-Eingl* (English bishops) was aired by Evan Evans (Ieuan Fardd), a penurious but remarkably cultured curate, who produced a scathing essay in 1764 in which he condemned his superiors for being accessible only to a few, living lives of ease, and speaking a foreign language in a land where Welsh was a sacred tongue. The very sight of well-bred and well-fed English and Scottish bishops arriving during the summer months set Evans's teeth on edge. He yearned for the golden years of Elizabeth's reign, when Welsh bishops of distinction 'fed their flocks on Cambria's plain'. The 'predatory wolves' of the present, he declared, were turning the church into 'a house of merchandise and a den of thieves'.[4]

Even greater resentment was provoked by the practice of English bishops of awarding lucrative ecclesiastical positions to men with extensive connections but few qualifications. Strangers waxed fat in many prize preferments, much to the dismay of conscientious Welsh clergymen. Absentee bishops were unable or not disposed to encourage and appreciate the qualities of eminent Welsh clergymen such as Thomas Ellis, Erasmus Saunders, Griffith Jones, David Havard, Moses Williams, and a myriad others, who gave up all hope of advancement. Forthright critics of church leaders and ardent lovers of the Welsh language always found themselves severely handicapped in the race for better livings. In 1768, John Jones, an Anglesey lawyer, bitterly condemned the 'gay and licentious men of the world' who, 'with a spaniel-like adulation', acquired preferments by fawning and cringing before their patrons.[5] Even the economic sterility of Wales, he complained, was no protection against the rapaciousness of English and Scottish locusts. Those who were prepared to bow and scrape did well, but aspiring Welsh clerics of mean birth and few connections were ignored. Many of them naturally felt hardly done by. Humiliated by his exile to English cures, Goronwy Owen, the celebrated poet, yearned in vain for a comely benefice, a pleasant house, a library, a garden, and a few cows for his wife to tend in his beloved Anglesey. Similarly, Evan Evans, who served in eighteen different cures during his career within the church, chafed miserably under English 'block-heads' whom, he believed, looked upon him 'with an evil eye'.[6] As Lewis Anwyl, vicar of

[4] NLW MS 2009B, *passim*.
[5] John Jones, *Considerations on the Illegality and Impropriety of Preferring Clergymen who are Unacquainted with the Welsh Language* (2nd edn., London, 1768), p. 45.
[6] *Add. Letters*, ii. 620.

Abergele, ruefully remarked in 1762: 'it is a common remark among the clergy that they that labour industriously in the Lord's vineyard are not the luckiest in preferments . . . 'Tis interest, not merit bears the bell.'[7] There was no lack of conscientious clergymen in Wales; many of them strove to supply their flocks with regular sermons, saving literature, and elementary schooling. Nevertheless, few doors were open to them in the upper echelons of the church.

Another growing cause of disaffection was the yawning gulf which separated affluent, non-resident pluralists from impoverished and hard-pressed curates. The eighteenth century witnessed a steady improvement in the value of livings, notably in the more prosperous dioceses of north Wales. In Caernarfonshire in 1778, for instance, the average value of thirty-three benefices was £117 per annum. Some well-to-do clergymen held livings worth more than £200. But there was a wide disparity between the wealth and comforts of the upper and lower clergy. In Glamorgan, the wealthy clergy occupied comfortable livings in the vale, whereas the 'mountain clergy' strove to eke out a miserable living in the poor parishes of the *Blaenau*. As every poor curate knew, privilege and inequality flourished. Hard pressed and underpaid, they lived lives of perpetual insecurity and indigence. Their salaries were so mean and their hopes of advancement so slender that they found it virtually impossible to carry out their pastoral duties effectively. At this level, especially in the penurious dioceses of St Davids and Llandaff, parsons Doolittle and Merryman were numerous. Not surprisingly, therefore, hungry flocks were apt to look elsewhere for spiritual nourishment. According to Evan Evans, whereas north Wales could take pride in 'a decent respectable set of clergy with good salaries', in Cardiganshire 'the clergy were ignorant wretches and, because they were poor, made such a despicable appearance in the eyes of the vulgar that they very soon quitted the established church'.[8] It is significant that both Methodism and Dissent scored their greatest successes in this period in the counties of south Wales, notably within large, remote parishes where parochial administration was least effective. Evan Evans was convinced that the 'poor simple ignorant vulgar suck the very dregs of fanaticism'[9] because of inadequate supervision on the part of impoverished, absentee, or uncaring clergymen.

Powerful protests were also increasingly directed against those clergymen who, encouraged by their bishops, were determined to abandon the time-honoured tradition of conducting public worship within the established church in the Welsh language. In order to appease prelates and patrons alike, clergymen were prone to preach English sermons, much to the consternation of their monoglot flocks. Griffith Jones poured scorn on such

---

[7] NLW MS 2039D, No. 1.   [8] *Add. Letters*, ii. 688-9.
[9] NLW MS 2009B, p. 119.

clergymen for 'heaping words together from a dictionary which could make but an unsavoury discourse in any language', while Evan Evans bitterly resented being passed over in favour of unfit Englishmen who preached 'horrid unintelligible jargon' in Welsh pulpits.[10] In many parishes along the Welsh borders the practice of conducting Welsh and English services on alternate Sundays had become the norm, and absentee bishops were less hesitant than before of appointing non-Welsh-speaking clergymen to plum livings in monoglot Welsh communities. Such presentations were common in the sees of south Wales, but when similar plans were laid for anglicizing the church in the north furious resistance was encountered. The over-whelming majority of clergymen in the dioceses of Bangor and St Asaph were not only Welsh-speaking but also men who set high standards, were diligent in ministering to the needs of their flocks, and generally commanded their respect. Matters came to a head when John Egerton, bishop of Bangor, appointed Dr Thomas Bowles, a non-Welsh-speaking septuagenarian, rector of the parishes of Trefdraeth and Llangwyfan in Anglesey in 1766. Of the 500 parishioners placed under Bowles's care, only five spoke and understood English. Not surprisingly, his appointment provoked a national outcry. The egregious Bowles was ridiculed and ostracized by his flock, and a frenzied campaign, sponsored by local dignitaries and members of the Cymmrodorion Society, was launched to oust him from his living. Their determination to be rid of the Englishman doubled when it became clear that he was not only unfit to minister but also prepared to deceive his parishioners by falsifying evidence in order to protect his stipend.

The prosecution of Thomas Bowles became a *cause célèbre*. The case against him was heard in the Court of Arches in London and Llangefni, where Bowles's attorney voiced the opinion that 'Wales is a conquered country; it is proper to introduce the English language, and it is the duty of the bishops to promote the English, in order to introduce the language'.[11] Since Bowles had been legally inducted, he was permitted to retain his living, but the judge also declared that ignorance of the Welsh language provided sufficient grounds to debar a clergyman from being appointed to a parish where the overwhelming majority of the inhabitants spoke only Welsh. In spite of the verdict, however, absentee bishops continued to discourage the use of Welsh by appointing 'greedy strangers', thrusting Welsh bibles out of pulpits, and opposing the publication of new editions of the Welsh Prayer Book. Evan Evans, who knew that his hopes of a successful career in the church were doomed to disappointment, voiced the opinion of many ardent Welsh churchmen when he denounced 'lordly and

---

[10] Griffith Jones, *Welch Piety* (London, 1740), p. 34; NLW MS 2009B, p. 143.
[11] Geraint H. Jenkins, 'Y Sais Brych', *Taliesin* 52 (1985), p. 58.

tyrannical prelates'[12] who, by appointing unfit shepherds, were driving their flocks into the arms of Methodism.

Although the condition of the established church stirred evangelists to pity and reproach, it would be wrong to judge the Anglican cause in Wales by the yardstick of Methodist ideologies. Early Methodists in Wales, notably William Williams, Pantycelyn, assiduously cultivated the myth that the year 1735 was a critical turning-point in the history of Wales and that pre-revival Wales was characterized by comatose clergymen, arid Dissenters, and immoral peasants. Just as Methodists believed in the power of the Holy Spirit to change the lives of men and women, so they believed in its capacity to transform the history of the nation. As we have seen, however, the notion of slumbering Wales in the pre-Methodist period is a travesty of the truth, and the fact that Howel Harris and Daniel Rowland underwent heart-warming experiences in 1735 did not provoke 'a Great Awakening'. The growth of Methodism was fitful rather than dramatic; it prospered on a local rather than a national level. Outside the counties of south Wales the harvest proved small. Prior to the 1770s only a fraction of the population of north Wales had been touched by Methodism, and no distinctive organization was established there until Thomas Charles, a native of Carmarthenshire, settled in Bala in 1784. In communities distant from the principal headquarters of Llangeitho, Trefeca, Llanddowror, and Llan-gan, Methodism tended to advance and retreat according to the diligence of itinerant preachers, the receptivity of hearers, and the durability of society meetings. Methodism did not spread like wildfire in Wales. From the outset the movement was torn by theological tensions, personal animosities, internal and external rivalries, and heresy hunts. Given these obstacles and frustrations, it is scarcely surprising that the growth of Methodism was piecemeal, painful, and slow.

In many ways, early Methodism defies rigorous analysis, and just as its leaders found difficulty in conveying their enthusiasm in words so, too, have historians laboured to capture its essence. In its initial, formative stages, Methodism was a fluid, amorphous movement, unsure of its identity and confused about its aims. Its leaders had only a muddled grasp of theology and only later did they take up a theological stance which helped the movement to become institutionalized. 'We are all like little children not knowing what to do', said Howel Harris to George Whitefield.[13] Save for their desire to save souls, Methodist evangelists had no concrete objectives. They welcomed to the ranks all those who were 'born of God', were lively in faith, and shared a burning desire to call

---

[12] Evan Evans, *Casgliad o Bregethau*, i. sig. b4b.
[13] Gomer M. Roberts (ed.), *Selected Trevecka Letters (1742–1747)* (Caernarfon, 1956), p. 1.

sinners to repentance. In some ways, Methodism was an attitude of mind. Edmund Jones liked to speak of 'the Methodist way',[14] and among the pilgrims who took the evangelical route there were churchmen and Dissenters, Calvinists and Arminians, ministers and laymen.

Although Methodism was woven from many strands, its principal leaders were members of the church. It is hard to divorce the name of Griffith Jones, Llanddowror, from the story of the growth of early Methodism. His itinerant evangelism earlier in the century and his reputation as an educator and a spiritual adviser meant that youthful evangelists viewed him as a judicious elder statesman. Williams Pantycelyn confessed that the soil in which Methodism was to grow had been tilled in readiness by Griffith Jones's ministry. His enemies significantly referred to him as 'the Methodist Pope'. To Howel Harris he was a patriarchal figure, 'an old and much honoured soldier'.[15] On George Whitefield's arrival in Wales, immediate arrangements were made for him to meet Jones, who, with a characteristic martial metaphor, put him in his place by informing him that he was 'but a young soldier, just entering the field'.[16] Griffith Jones's towering authority enabled him to exercise an enormous influence over the careers, decisions, and preaching styles of young evangelists, and Llanddowror was as much a cradle of Methodism as were Llangeitho and Trefeca. Howel Harris acted briefly as a superintendent of Griffith Jones's circulating schools and regularly visited Llanddowror. Howel Davies—'the Apostle of Pembrokeshire'—served his apprenticeship as curate to Jones. Mali Francis, William Williams's wife, was a friend of Jones's wife and a member of his congregation. At the tender age of 5, Peter Williams was taken by his mother on horseback to Llanddowror to hear Griffith Jones preach, and following his conversion by Whitefield in 1743 Williams was appointed curate at Eglwys Gymyn, next to Jones's parish of Llanddowror. Even more significant is the fact that it was a sermon by Griffith Jones which secured the conversion of Daniel Rowland in 1735.

But although Griffith Jones sustained intimate friendships with young Methodist evangelists, he never gave his heart entirely to the movement. Thus, Howel Harris was able, largely by the sheer force of his personality and his superb gifts as an organizer and a preacher, to exercise a decisive influence on the development of Methodism. Harris was a gauche, restless young man who, following his sensational conversion in 1735, resolved to enter the Anglican ministry. His application for ordination, however, was refused on four separate occasions by Nicholas Claggett, bishop of St Davids, and Harris was forced to devote his considerable energies to the task of exhorting locally. His famous profile, revealing a jutting jaw and a

[14] Edmund Jones, *Some Account of the Life and Death of Evan Williams*, p. 122.
[15] Geraint H. Jenkins, ' "An Old and Much Honoured Soldier" ', pp. 449–68.
[16] Elie Halévy, *The Birth of Methodism in England*, tr. B. Semmel (Chicago, 1971), p. 61.

piercing eye, tells us a good deal about him. Harris was a volatile, abrasive, authoritarian man; Benjamin La Trobe spoke of his 'open and choleric disposition'[17] and others found him massively egotistic. In spite of his modest intellectual gifts and his frail grasp of theology, he was determined to spread the gospel and to become the principal standard-bearer of the Methodist cause. We know more of him than of his colleagues because he was a compulsive writer. In a tiny and barely decipherable hand, Harris wrote copious letters to his friends and acquaintances and filled many journals with meanderingly tedious and rebarbative information. To Harris, life was a mission against Satan and the forces of darkness, a never-ending struggle against sinfulness and evil, and such were his superhuman energy and his regard for precious souls that he was prepared to travel extensively in order to fulfil his ambitions. Although his life was to be engulfed in successive crises and drama, there is no doubt that he possessed an iron constitution and great personal magnetism.

While Harris exhorted in his native Trefeca in Breconshire, Daniel Rowland, a small, dapper man full of nervous energy and burning enthusiasm, was winning souls in Cardiganshire. Preaching was Rowland's forte. He ministered to his flock at Llangeitho for over fifty years and was described by his admirers as 'a second Paul' and 'the greatest preacher in Europe'.[18] Rowland's sermons were delivered with such fervent conviction and compelling urgency that Llangeitho became the Mecca of the movement. It also became a byword for lack of decorum and restraint, for Rowland was endowed with such a rare ability in the pulpit that he was capable of driving hearers into a frenzy. No one knew better than he how to stir the emotions of his hearers to fever-heat. People flocked from far and wide to attend communion on Sundays at Llangeitho and those who experienced the vitality which Rowland radiated were moved to tremble fearfully, leap joyfully, or weep unashamedly. In August 1737 Harris and Rowland met for the first time at Defynnog and resolved to work in harness. What they lacked in learning they made up for in commitment, and even though several years passed before their vague aspirations and sense of common purpose were channelled into a concerted movement, there is no doubt that the late 1730s were exciting and busy years for them. Harris embarked on hectic 'rounds' of exhorting, and pilgrims flocked to Llangeitho. Soon they began to gather round them like-minded young men—Howel Davies, William Williams, and Peter Williams—who, undeterred by episcopal censures and rough treatment at the hands of mobs, were determined to deepen the spiritual lives of Welsh people.

The cockpit of Welsh Methodism was the impoverished and unwieldy

[17] B. La Trobe, *A Brief Account of the Life of Howel Harris* (Trefeca, 1791), sig. A4[r].
[18] Eifion Evans, *Daniel Rowland* (Edinburgh, 1985), p. 1.

diocese of St Davids. Each of the founding fathers was born, bred, and educated within the diocese, and prior to the 1780s the movement prospered best in the counties of south Wales. Methodist leaders were relatively well-born men who had either inherited a comfortable patrimony or subsequently married pious, capable, and well-to-do heiresses. 'Who would be a curate when preachers live so well?', was Lewis Morris's acid comment.[19] Their family connections, the sizeable dowries which fell into their laps upon marriage, and their contacts with affluent gentlemen enabled them to itinerate relatively freely. All of them belonged to the 'twice-born', men who had been restless and dissatisfied until they had undergone that profoundly subjective and spiritual experience of being 'born again', which filled them with an irresistible desire to save 'poor illiterate souls chained in the dens of darkness and infidelity'. They saw themselves as troops who had been given a commission by God to challenge the legions of Satan. Every Methodist preacher required stout legs, a good pair of lungs, and a willingness to travel in fair and foul weather in order to bring the gospel to wretched sinners. Since the world was plainly their parish, they defied bishops by crossing parish boundaries and preaching in churchyards, open fields, fairs, markets, barns, outhouses, and meeting-houses. Speed was of the essence, for these were men with a mission. Neither the style nor the pace of Methodism encouraged its leaders to believe that profound or original thought was necessary; fishers of men's souls were simply too busy to stand back and think. Revelling in austerity, some of them drove themselves to the point of exhaustion: they ate unpalatable meals, contented themselves with a few hours' sleep in flea-ridden beds, and endured a wide range of physical ailments (in Harris's case, toothache, piles, and gout). Insisting on his right to preach Christ 'till to pieces I fall',[20] Harris tramped the roads and rode over hills like a man possessed. 'Great affection for God's people', he wrote in 1737, 'ready to be with them in the mud, or under a hedge, or in a pigsty.'[21] He would often travel 150 miles a week, preach six or seven times each day, and sleep for as little as four hours each night. Little wonder that his body often ached so much that he could scarcely move. His silver-tongued colleagues were no less diligent: William Williams is credited with having travelled around 150,000 miles between 1744 and 1791. Unshackled by the past, driven on by a sense of divine mission, and often dismissive of the labours of older and more seasoned campaigners, Methodist evangelists yearned to save souls.

Below the principal leaders there was an army of subordinate officers,

---

[19] Gomer M. Roberts (ed.), *Y Deffroad Mawr*, p. 432.
[20] Gomer M. Roberts, *Portread o Ddiwygiwr*, p. 31.
[21] Richard Bennett, *The Early Life of Howell Harris*, tr. G. M. Roberts (London, 1962), p. 144.

many of them self-taught and barely educated exhorters and gospel-preachers, who became responsible for carrying out the most enduring field-work on behalf of the movement. These largely unsung heroes took on the prodigious tasks of travelling, preaching, and exhorting, in order to enable the movement to spread widely into the countryside and to win people who were either outside or on the fringes of organized church worship. Public exhorters were permitted to itinerate, whilst private exhorters, who were usually less able and less literate men, exhorted during their leisure hours. Some of them were raw, untutored recruits who were given, for the first time in their lives, an opportunity to reveal their talents. This gave those who were rough in speech and dress a sense of worth, and what they might have lacked in sophistication they compensated for by their enthusiasm and commitment. Although many of them were cruelly treated by constables, mobs, and press-gangs, they 'longed to go more and more'.[22] William Edwards of Solfach in Pembrokeshire was popularly known as the 'cannonball' who was prepared to rend even the devil's heart. When Lewis Evan of Llanllugan in Montgomeryshire died in 1791, he had served the cause of Methodism with selfless devotion for over fifty years.

Although Methodist evangelists were prone to exaggerate wildly in estimating the numbers of their hearers—Harris often claimed to have discoursed before ten or twelve thousand people—they clearly drew large and expectant crowds wherever they preached. Their preaching techniques varied enormously: Griffith Jones's sermons were closely argued and suffused with scriptural references, whilst the homilies of Daniel Rowland and Peter Williams were constructed with scrupulous care and precision. Howel Harris, however, was a master of improvisation: he was capable of preaching impromptu, according to 'where the Book opened',[23] for up to four hours. As he preached, he sweated profusely and sometimes vomited. His imposing presence and thunderous voice were unforgettable: 'never man spake, in my hearing, as this man spake',[24] declared Charles Wesley. At Llangeitho, Daniel Rowland's melodic voice, theatrical gestures, and powerful message transfixed his followers and encouraged many of them to engage in highly emotional public demonstrations. Cries of 'What must I do to be saved?' were commonplace in Methodist gatherings and as those who experienced the 'new birth' felt their hearts strangely warmed, they indulged in wild, convulsive physical movements. Hearers wept aloud, roared in agony, clapped their hands, or fell to the ground. According to Harris, 'some lie there for hours, some praising and admiring Jesus Christ

[22] W. G. Hughes-Edwards, 'The Development and Organization of the Methodist Society in Wales 1735–1750' (unpubl. University of Wales MA thesis, 1966), p. 138.

[23] Gomer M. Roberts (ed.), Y Deffroad Mawr, p. 117.

[24] G. F. Nuttall, Howel Harris 1714–1773: The Last Enthusiast (Cardiff, 1965), p. 54.

and free grace, others wanting words to express their feelings'.[25] Not all Methodists, however, approved of public demonstrations of praise, believing that such emotional outbursts were a violation of good taste and likely to persuade enemies of the movement that the paroxysms which accompanied the 'new birth' were indications of either lunacy or diabolical possession.

Evangelists were capable of provoking scenes of hysteria among their hearers by creating a sense of inadequacy, sinfulness, and shame within them. In their sermons they told and retold hearers of the awfulness of sin and the dire need for repentance and salvation. As they stressed the subjective virtues of inward experience and suffused their message with words such as 'fire', 'life', 'light', and 'power', their hearers experienced enormous psychological crises as they strove to cast off the chains of sin and guilt. By using their best efforts to affect and capture emotions, preachers produced mental and physical stress which found its release in quaking, trembling, leaping, dancing, and singing. The new Jumpers were old Quakers writ large. Clearly, too, many of those who responded to revivalist preaching by crying out, sobbing, and fainting were terrified by fears of the torments of hell and the prospect of eternal damnation. Theophilus Evans vividly revealed how neighbouring Methodists used dramatic gestures to show how unrepentant sinners were 'dropping into hell! into the bottom of hell! the bottom of hell!',[26] while John Owen, chancellor of Bangor, declared that the new evangelists intimidated the timorous by assuring them that their fathers and forefathers were in hell and that the marks of damnation were clearly to be seen on the faces of non-Methodists. With his usual pungency, Lewis Morris likened Methodist members to spaniels: 'the more you threaten them the better they be'.[27] All these, of course, were hostile witnesses, but the morbid fascination of Methodists with mortality, hell, and damnation is well-known. None of their leaders shirked the responsibility of reminding sinners of the horrors of the unquenchable fire. Daniel Rowland used to paint such lurid portraits of hell in his sermons following his conversion that he was known for many years as *y ffeiriad crac* (the angry clergyman), whilst Howel Harris once told Jethro Dafydd Evan of Llanddeusant: 'unless God claims your heart, he will see the devils tearing your body and soul at the hour of death and on the day of judgement'.[28] As the years rolled by, however, Methodist leaders dwelt less often on the terrors of hell, preferring to preach the love of God and the joy and assurance of salvation. As late as May 1769, four

[25] G. M. Roberts (ed.), *Selected Trevecka Letters*, i. 81.

[26] Theophilus Evans, *The History of Modern Enthusiasm*, p. 79.

[27] Hugh Owen, 'The Morrises of Anglesey and the Methodists in the Eighteenth Century', *Trans. Anglesey Antiq. Soc.* (1942), p. 39.

[28] Ioan Thomas, *Rhad Ras*, ed. J. Dyfnallt Owen (Cardiff, 1949), p. 29.

years before his death, Howel Harris was still to be heard declaring loudly to crowds at a public hanging in Haverfordwest: 'Thus did our Lord once hang on the Cross for you and me'.[29]

During the early years, between 1737 and 1742, Methodist leaders—still feeling their way—were anxious to avoid formulating precise dogma lest they alienate both new and potential recruits. But increasing success, greater numbers, and internal tensions forced them to spell out the movement's strategy and organization for the first time. From 1737 onwards a network of close-knit societies, based on the example of Josiah Woodward and Moravian precepts, had been established in many counties in south Wales, and in January 1742 the first Welsh Association (*Sasiwn*), a body designed to exercise supervision over the activities of societies and exhorters, was held at Dugoedydd, near Llandovery. 1743, too, was a critical year in the history of Welsh Methodism since it witnessed the creation of an administrative structure, modes of discipline, and a theological stance. In January, the first meeting of the United Association of Methodist leaders in Wales and England was held at Plas y Watford, near Caerphilly. There, the Welsh decided that the stern Calvinist creed of George Whitefield was not only the true faith but also one which offered the greatest chance of success. While Howel Harris and his colleagues followed the path of Calvinism, John Wesley remained true to his Arminian faith. But, although their theological views were diametrically opposed, a large measure of mutual love and understanding bound Harris and Wesley together, and they were able to arrive at a tacit agreement whereby neither would trespass on the other's fiefdoms. Wesley possessed no knowledge of the Welsh language and the majority of his assistants were similarly handicapped; his right-hand man, Thomas Coke, a native of Brecon, could only summon up enough broken Welsh to announce one verse of the hymn, 'Come, let us join our cheerful songs'. Welsh Wales was thus left almost exclusively to the Calvinists. Indeed, by the time of John Wesley's death in 1791, Arminian Methodists in Wales numbered only 600. As Welsh and English Methodists followed separate paths, the former developed an elaborate federal structure made up of societies, monthly associations, and quarterly associations. At its head stood the General Association—Methodism's Privy Council—which held responsibility for formulating general policies. Public and private exhorters were assigned duties and were placed under the supervision of superintendents. Howel Harris, who had already impressed his colleagues by his swift grasp of complex administrative problems, was appointed chief superintendent of the movement. The immediate future of Calvinistic Methodism in Wales was thus entrusted to an irresistibly attractive, but authoritarian, man.

[29] D. Llwyd Morgan, *Y Diwygiad Mawr* (Llandysul, 1981), p. 92.

Already, however, Methodism was gathering strength, notably in those communities where Dissenters had prepared the ground or where churchmen were infrequent in their ministrations. The tiny cells known as *seiadau* (societies) became the very life-blood of the movement. From the beginning, Methodist leaders had been deeply conscious of the need to create a warm Christian fellowship among their followers in order to ensure that the first stirrings of conversion, usually acquired from hearing sermons, did not fade away. Societies would not only provide an alternative to taverns, recreations, and secular amusements, but also stimulate the exercise of love and faith, together with greater discipline, which would weld Methodism into a cohesive movement. Since only a small number of society houses were built specifically to accommodate meetings, societies were normally held in private homes, chapels of ease, gentry parlours, farmhouses, barns, and stables. Members came together for two or three hours once or twice a week, normally in the evening, to pore over their bibles, chant the catechism, sing hymns, and share their experiences—troubled and joyous. Since Methodism demanded a high degree of commitment, rules of admission to society meetings were strict and the exercise of discipline was awesomely severe. Each applicant was expected to provide evidence of his conversion, his character, his holiness, and his subscription to the Calvinist creed. Every member was taught to abhor not only the sins of the world but also the Devil, the Pope, and the Pretender. As well as moderation and good citizenship, the virtues of moral seriousness, godliness, thrift, and frugality were constantly emphasized and it was these qualities which made Methodists a 'peculiar people' in the eyes of the ungodly.

Although Methodist leaders were conscious of social evils and often deplored them, their principal concern was the salvation of individual souls. In essence, Methodist societies were clinics for the soul, and the corporate identity which the movement achieved during the 1740s stemmed largely from the warm Christian fellowship and the shared spiritual experiences which characterized its meetings. In a sense, Methodism meant popular participation in so far as it offered new opportunities for relatively inarticulate people to discover their own personalities as well as to vent their spiritual troubles. A whole range of emotions and feelings was experienced by individuals as they wrestled with their spiritual and personal problems, and the success of society meetings depended heavily on the ability of stewards and counsellors to channel experiences and to advise wisely. It was their responsibility to persuade members to shed their self-consciousness within class and to unburden themselves of their problems. Some of them exercised a harsh discipline which, by inducing feelings of guilt and mortification, proved counter-productive, but the more gentle and understanding exhorters were sensitive guides who were capable of discovering 'the murky lairs where Satan and sin, the flesh, and lust for the world and its idols, are lurking'.[30]

A powerful aid to recruitment within societies was the hymns of William Williams, Pantycelyn. Although Williams was ordained deacon in 1740, his increasing involvement in the organization of the Methodist movement brought him into bad odour with the authorities and he was refused ordination as priest. He abandoned his curacies in 1744 and dedicated himself to the advancement of the Methodist cause by preaching the gospel and encouraging the more frequent use of hymn-singing. His intuitive grasp of the psychology of conversion and sanctification made him a particularly valuable guide within society meetings, but his most enduring contribution was his hymns. From his flowing pen came some 860 hymns, many of which were memorable for their imagery, intensity, and lyrical quality, and which were sung with great joy and fervour by Methodist brethren. Although there were other proficient hymnologists within the movement, Pantycelyn was the supreme literary artist of his day and it was his influence which ensured that Methodism became strongly committed to the practice of fervent hymn-singing in society meetings and church services.

Although the pattern varied according to local needs, on average Methodist societies numbered between fifteen and twenty-five members. Societies clearly experienced much ebb and flow, since members were prone to drift to Dissenting chapels or return to parish-church services, only to be tempted again in later years by Methodist exhorters. Even so, there is no doubt that Methodism gathered strength during the period from 1737 to 1750. Within five years of the founding of the first permanent society at Y Wernos, a farmhouse in the parish of Llandyfalle, Breconshire, in 1737, the number of societies had increased a hundredfold. By 1750, 428 societies had been established, 346 (81 per cent) of which were situated in the six counties of south Wales. Societies tended to cluster together in local fellowship and prospered best in areas such as Trefeca, Llangeitho-Tregaron, Llanddowror, and the vale of Glamorgan, where guidance and leadership were strong. There were fifty-one societies in Montgomery and Radnor, but in the five counties of north Wales, where there were no outstanding leaders and where the movement relied heavily on subalterns, only thirty-one societies had been founded. Those intrepid evangelists who ventured north often found themselves ploughing lone furrows with little success, and Howel Harris often found cause to bemoan the 'poor silly minds'[31] of the people of Gwynedd. Across Wales as a whole, rural inhabitants were much more receptive to Methodism than townspeople. In

[30] *Gweithiau William Williams Pantycelyn*, ed. G. H. Hughes (vol. ii, Cardiff, 1967), p. 208.
[31] G. M. Roberts (ed.), *Selected Trevecka Letters*, p. 49.

1745, fifty-one members belonged to the society which met in the village of Llansawel, Carmarthenshire, whereas only twelve members came together in the prosperous town of Carmarthen. In most towns Methodism was not made welcome. No societies had been founded in Swansea or Newport and Howel Harris's experiences in the towns of north Wales affected him so deeply that he came to believe that their people lived 'like brutes'.[32]

Nor did Methodism appeal to uneducated labourers, cottagers, and paupers. Few of those poor who seldom or never darkened a parish-church door found themselves eligible to carry a Methodist ticket. For Methodism, like Dissent, was a movement which appealed largely to the middling sorts. Although it is true that support was acquired from affluent benefactors like Marmaduke Gwynne of Garth in Breconshire and Thomas Price, the ironmaster and maltster from Watford in Monmouthshire, as well as from well-bred ladies like Lady Huntingdon and Lady Charlotte Edwin, society members were mostly drawn from among modest middling ranks, notably freeholders, yeomen, tradesmen, craftsmen, and artisans. Many small squires and prosperous freeholders who had suffered economically as a result of the expansion of large estates found solace, status, and respect within the Methodist fraternity. Most superintendents and public exhorters were relatively well-to-do farmers, schoolmasters, and craftsmen, such as carpenters, blacksmiths, weavers, bookbinders, and clock-makers. Private exhorters also tended to be drawn from the same social groups: there were farmers, schoolmasters, blacksmiths, shoemakers, merchants, clothiers, hatters, weavers, carpenters, and coopers among them. In Caernarfonshire, where Methodism prospered best among the yeoman-farmers and craftsmen of Llŷn, the trustees of Brynengan chapel in 1772 included a schoolmaster, a yeoman, a shopkeeper, a joiner, a weaver, a tailor, and a labourer. Ignored or hooted by poor people in urban communities, Methodist leaders directed their crusading zeal largely towards those for whom the message of justification by faith, together with hard work, moderation, thrift, and social respectability, was irresistibly appealing.

The youthfulness of the membership is also striking. The leaders themselves were remarkably young men: Howel Harris was 21 and Daniel Rowland was 24 when they yielded themselves to Christ in 1735. Williams Pantycelyn was 20 when a fiery sermon preached by Harris pierced his heart. Howel Davies was similarly converted in 1737, at the age of 21, while Peter Williams was twenty when he joined the movement. Although young children were not discouraged from attending sermons and meetings, most ordinary members of Methodist societies were in their twenties and thirties. Methodism had the appeal of novelty, especially in areas where the flame of Dissent was burning low or where church-goers

---

[32] R. B. Knox, 'Howell Harris and his Doctrine of the Church', *Journal Hist. Soc. Presbyterian Church in Wales* 49 (1964), p. 67.

had become bored by the blandness of Anglican sermons. Moreover, it drew young unmarried persons in large numbers at a time when the decay of traditional forms of popular culture was helping to sharpen the novelty of the evangelical crusade. In 1743, sixty-seven of the ninety males who were members of the societies at Talyllychau, Llansawel, Llangathen, and Cwm-ann in Carmarthenshire were unmarried. Open-air sermons, emotional prayer-meetings, fervent hymn-singing, watch-night services, and love-feasts were all attractive events for young and unattached males and females.

Young women were particularly attracted to Methodism. The leading evangelists of the movement were young, dynamic, and eye-catching men who were able to appeal to pious, curious, or lonely women. A substantial proportion of society members consisted of young women, for whom Methodism offered greater scope for individual participation than did Anglicanism, as well as opportunities for lasting friendship, warm fellowship, and enhanced prospects of marriage. It also clearly helped to assuage feelings of sexual guilt by enabling them to exchange spiritual and pre-marital experiences within the four walls of a society room. Of 122 Methodists in nine parishes in Llŷn in 1750, 72 were women. In 1743, 129 of the 200 members who belonged to eight societies located in south Cardiganshire and north Pembrokeshire were women, and all but eighteen of them were single. Judging by the evidence of society reports and correspondence, many young women were more susceptible than most to emotional crises and bouts of hysteria whenever intimate gatherings were held. Indeed, the presence of so many vivacious and nubile young women often troubled the minds of Methodist exhorters and placed severe strains on family life. Howel Harris, who always enjoyed the company of attractive women, found himself torn between spiritual and sexual lusts: he dreamt often of young girls and feared on occasions to go to bed 'lest I should sin'.[33] Harris, as we shall see, fell from grace, as did several ordinary members. John Griffith Ellis of Tudweiliog was expelled for adultery, Evan Prichard, a Llangybi miller, confessed to living in sin, and Evan Thomas, also of Caernarfonshire, fell in love with his maidservant at a local society meeting and became so infatuated with her that he murdered his wife by striking her with a shoemaker's hammer and throwing her body into a mill-pool. Although such examples were few, they presented satirists with the opportunity of portraying Methodism as a movement which encouraged secret liaisons, fornication, and ruined marriages. Methodist leaders were depicted as mountebanks who gulled and seduced young and innocent female converts and encouraged them to commit lewd immoral acts. Howel Davies, claimed Lewis Morris, 'hath

[33] T. Beynon (ed.), *Howell Harris's Visits to Pembrokeshire*, p. 76.

turned the hearts of many widows and maids',[34] and a host of ballad-mongers happily brought to light so-called skeletons which rattled in Methodist cupboards. In his devastating satire, *Ffrewyll y Methodistiaid* (Scourge of the Methodists) in 1746, William Roberts declared that by luring brazen young wenches to indulge in 'discreet whoring' in intimate social gatherings held in darkened houses, Methodism was likely to spawn 'a sturdy army of bastards'.[35]

The successes gained by the first generation of Methodists were achieved in the teeth of fierce external challenges and internal conflicts. The emergence of Methodism aroused bitter feelings in many parts of Wales, especially among those who agreed with Bishop Butler that unbridled zeal and enthusiasm were 'a very horrid thing'.[36] Although the persecution of Methodists was spasmodic, it certainly hampered the development of the movement. Preachers and exhorters were derided by noisy poets, assailed by mockers and scoffers, and maltreated by hostile magistrates and mobs. Violent parish 'mobbings', usually carried out by youths but incited by magistrates and clergymen, were designed to humiliate and coerce intruders. Methodist preachers were often met with a stream of obscenities, stripped of their clothes, shouted at, heckled, stoned, pelted with rotten fruit, and thrown into ponds and lakes. Several ingenious stratagems were devised to frustrate visiting evangelists: youths filled bags with stones and rattled them furiously in order to frighten the evangelists' horses; others rang bells, kindled bonfires, or burnt effigies. William Seward was killed by stone-throwing mobs at Hay in 1741. Many of his colleagues were fortunate to escape with their lives during the early 1740s, notably those who visited the towns of north Wales, where resistance to Methodism was much more tenacious and brutal than elsewhere. Howel Harris was fortunate to escape with his life from Bala in January 1741 and, having come so close to death, he came to fear the townspeople of north Wales as much as he feared popery. Many of his colleagues, too, plodded back to the south with bowed heads and bloody noses.

Although Methodist preachers could never feel safe in any urban community, they had particular cause to remember their reception in the towns of north Wales. Methodist gains were small in the north and their members so desperately isolated that it was relatively easy for civil and ecclesiastical authorities to strike terror into the hearts of their ringleaders and to persuade visiting evangelists never to return. In the diocese of Bangor, for instance, the absence of a resident bishop enabled John Owen, chancellor of the diocese, to rule with an iron fist. Dozens of ballads and

[34] Hugh Owen, 'The Morrises and the Methodists', p. 35.
[35] William Roberts, *Ffrewyll y Methodistiaid* (Shrewsbury, 1746), pp. 7, 20, 35, 62.
[36] S. C. Carpenter, *Eighteenth Century Church and People* (London, 1959), p. 204.

interludes were published by zealous churchmen in north Wales, many of whom claimed that Methodists preyed on innocent, credulous people, harboured papists and Jacobites in their ranks, fostered a narrow and humourless morality, and encouraged carnal lusts. The fact that Methodists were often described as 'Cradockites' and 'Roundheads' suggests that the fear of rebellion was still deeply rooted and that memories of past upheavals were still fresh. 'Down with the Rumps', cried a mob as they unloosed their dogs at Llanymawddwy in Merioneth. The arrival of itinerant evangelists invariably evoked fears among landowners of a revival of Levelling doctrines, and every conceivable tactic was employed to frustrate them. Powerful gentlemen were not only able to foment the rabble to perpetrate acts of mischief but also to persuade magistrates to institute legal proceedings against such unwelcome zealots. Between 1741 and 1744, Howel Harris, Daniel Rowland, Howel Davies, and William Williams were all proceeded against in the courts. Some parishes were forced to bow to the will of their governors. 'This parish belongs to the duke of Ancaster', declared John Royle, curate of Trefriw, 'and he can command them to quit the Methodists.'[37] Those who refused to abandon their faith found their homes ransacked and their crops trampled upon or burnt. When Edward Parry of Llansannan was threatened with eviction, he replied with unflinching calm and bravery: 'Your land, sir, is only temporal, while religion is eternal'.[38] Landowners could also count on the support of the clergy, who naturally felt vulnerable and angry when strident strangers burst uninvited into their parishes and preached from 'unhallowed rostrums'.[39] Ordained clergymen were understandably antagonistic towards those 'tinkers, thatchers and weavers' who preached in unconsecrated places and who dubbed them 'carnal priests' or 'dumb dogs'. Nor was it surprising that innkeepers, fiddlers, and harpers should take an instant dislike to those who threatened to ruin their trade, or that common people should choose to make life difficult for intruders who denounced and disrupted their cherished recreations and diversions.

There were also other impediments which prevented Methodists from carrying all before them. Their advances in south Wales had been assisted by the successes achieved by Griffith Jones's circulating schools and this provoked their enemies to suggest that the new charity schools were 'nests of Methodism'. Ever since 1735, Griffith Jones's relationship with his young Methodist protégés had been fraught with tension, and by 1741 matters had come to a head. Jones was a grave, morose man who, in the company of stubborn young men, was capable of bouts of furious temper. Their lack of learning and sheer obduracy vexed him. Determined to

[37] NLW, Records of the Church in Wales, B/QA/5, ff. 104–16.
[38] William Williams, *Welsh Calvinistic Methodism* (London, 1872), p. 66.
[39] R. B. Knox, 'Howell Harris', p. 66.

protect the good name and the decency of the church, Jones strove to curb their wilder excesses and to soften their arrogance. Much to his distress, however, his advice and reproaches were spurned. Howel Davies, whom Jones believed was governed by 'the cry of the crowd',[40] left for Pembrokeshire, whilst Daniel Rowland was roughly treated and subsequently ostracized by Jones. Howel Harris, who neglected to follow Jones's advice to study, read, and prepare himself thoroughly for ordination, lived in dread of his mentor's public and private scoldings. When Harris insisted that he could do more good by exhorting than by reading Jones furiously called him 'a railer, proud and haughty'.[41] To Harris, Jones stood for light without warmth; to Jones, Harris stood for warmth without light. As a result of this dispute, Griffith Jones, even though he remained instinctively in sympathy with every campaign which sought to win souls, distanced himself for several years from the Methodist movement, purged his circulating schools of hot-spirited teachers, and dedicated himself to the promotion of popular education and literacy. For a time at least, Welsh Methodism had been robbed of the services of the most distinguished and respected churchman of the day.

The divisions between Methodist leaders and Griffith Jones were also symptoms of a widening breach between the evangelists and the established church. The early leaders of Methodism were avowed churchmen and their sincere aim was to rejuvenate a church which they cherished deeply. For all their irregularities, they had no wish to take, or be forced to take, the calamitous step of secession. They conformed to the doctrines of the established church, held their meetings outside church hours, and refused to declare themselves Protestant Dissenters in order to avail themselves of the protection afforded by the Toleration Act of 1689. Howel Harris, in particular, constantly bade his followers to stand fast, and it was as a result of his influence that the Dugoedydd Association in January 1742 declared that the movement would not 'go out of the church till turned out'.[42] Not least among their motives was the knowledge that the potential number of converts was much greater for the evangelist who operated within the established church than for the separatist who laboured outside. It was not until 1811 that Thomas Charles plucked up enough courage to sever the Gordian knot which had bound Methodists to the church for three generations. Even so, the seeds of secession were germinating from the inception of the movement. When Welsh bishops closed all doors to its leaders, Methodism was forced to become a 'church within a church' and, as its societies claimed autonomy, it increasingly began to resemble a sect, a trend which was accentuated by the building of meeting-houses and

---

[40] D. Ambrose Jones, *History of the Church*, p. 201.

[41] T. Beynon (ed.), *Howell Harris's Visits*, p. 62.

[42] D. J. Odwyn Jones, *Daniel Rowland Llangeitho* (Llandysul, 1938), p. 47.

chapels. Moreover, schism was implicit within Methodism in so far as it threatened the authority of clergymen, permitted laymen to assume pastoral responsibilities, and loudly expressed its disaffection with the quality of the church's ministrations. Methodist leaders went to their graves defending values which, however admirable they might have seemed to them, were at odds with the views of many rank-and-file members. During the 1740s mounting pressure was applied by exhorters who were anxious to secede from the church in order to acquire the right to administer the sacraments. In March 1745, the exhorters of Groes-wen, Glamorgan, pleaded for the right to ordain their own ministers, and Howel Harris was obliged to use his authority and gifts of persuasion to reveal to them that Methodism was not a sect 'but a people in a Church, called to reform it'.[43] But increasing numbers of Methodists were not disposed to receive the sacrament at the hands of 'carnal' clergymen and were also finding it increasingly hard to remain within a church which persecuted God's servants. With few regrets, many of them severed their links with the church and joined the ranks of Dissent.

The growth of Methodism was also seriously affected by worsening relations between its leaders and prominent Dissenters. Although Methodism was not simply a rejuvenated version of Puritanism, it owed an enormous debt to its Dissenting predecessors. It prospered in those communities which had been thoroughly puritanized and much of its appeal lay in its capacity to 'recharge and articulate existing cells of piety'.[44] Even though Methodist evangelists were in general reluctant to acknowledge their debt to their predecessors, their library shelves were amply stocked with Puritan tomes and their sermons were as redolent of scriptural evidence and imagery as those of their forebears. According to Howel Harris, Daniel Rowland 'did depend much on the old Puritans', and Harris himself admired the works of 'good old' authors such as Baxter, Bunyan, and Llwyd.[45] Harris's diaries are set in the honourable Puritan tradition of self-examination, while Pantycelyn's epic *Bywyd a Marwolaeth Theomemphus* (The Life and Death of Theomemphus, 1764) lies firmly in the same tradition of spiritual autobiography. No book was more widely read in religious circles than the the Welsh version of Bunyan's *Pilgrim's Progress*. Moreover, the ethics and morality preached by Methodists owed much to their Puritan inheritance. It is not surprising, therefore, that in its early stages Methodism gained a good deal from Dissent, notably wherever Dissenting ministers were prepared to encourage and accommodate

[43] G. M. Roberts, 'Calvinistic Methodism in Glamorgan, 1737–1773', in *Glamorgan Co. Hist.* 4 (1974), p. 514.
[44] J. D. Walsh, 'Elie Halévy and the Birth of Methodism', *TRHS* 25 (1975), p. 8.
[45] Eifion Evans, *Daniel Rowland*, p. 264; G. M. Roberts (ed.), *Selected Trevecka Letters*, i. 166.

itinerant evangelists and introduce them to potential converts. Leading Dissenters were strongly attracted to such a prospering enterprise. Henry Davies of Blaen-gwrach invited Harris to 'warm the air'[46] in Glamorgan; Edmund Jones of Pontypool, ever generous and open-handed, accompanied the new evangelists on their journeys through south-east Wales; Lewis Rees of Llanbryn-mair introduced Harris to the citizens of north Wales and propagated the gospel in the manner of his ally; Daniel Rowland's career benefited enormously from the advice of his dear friend, Phylip Pugh, whose pioneering labours among Dissenters between the upper reaches of the rivers Aeron and Teifi in Cardiganshire had won him considerable respect. However, by the early 1740s, the relationship between Methodists and Dissenters had become more subtle and complicated. The early co-operation soon dissolved as the alliance became marked by doctrinal rifts and secessions.

   Both sides were driven apart largely by theological differences and disciplines. Theology had played little part in the development of early Methodism, but as the movement began to crystallize there proved to be no escape from controversial doctrinal issues such as predestination, the sacraments, 'head knowledge', and intellectual values. Increasingly, Dissenters frowned upon the excessive enthusiasm of Methodists, their contempt for intellectual and rational ideas, and their timid reluctance to abandon the church. Methodists, for their part, dubbed their Dissenting colleagues dry-as-dust plodders. The rift deepened as Dissenters disparaged Methodists for permitting unvetted and worldly people to partake of the sacrament and for employing unordained and semi-educated itinerant exhorters. Lewis Rees advised Richard Tibbott to return to his former occupation as a farm labourer, 'since God had not called him' to exhort.[47] As Howel Harris proved a difficult man to live with, many Congregationalists and Baptist ministers urged their members to break away from the Methodist societies. Harris's overpowering egotism and biting tongue were cutting him off from old friends. The imperious tone of his letters and his inability to respect the sensitivities of even the most pious and venerable Dissenters provoked much anger. Harris once informed Christmas Samuel of Pant-teg, author of the first Welsh commentary and a much-loved saint forty years his senior, that his ministry was lukewarm and his congregation dead. It was this insensitive arrogance which prompted David Williams of Caerphilly to pray that God might grant Harris 'a meek and charitable spirit, that you may always treat men as men and Christians as Christians'.[48] After 1744 there was little common ground between Harris and Dissenters and, four years later, the Association formally declared that

   [46] R. L. Brown, *Through Cloud and Sunshine* (Port Talbot, 1982), p. 38.
   [47] R. T. Jenkins, *Yng Nghysgod Trefeca* (Caernarfon, 1968), p. 26.
   [48] Ibid., p. 28.

Methodists were no longer to commune with Dissenters. Relationships had deteriorated badly and angry scenes were witnessed on numerous occasions when opposing groups crossed swords.

Clashes of personality, coupled with deeply rooted doctrinal differences, bade fair to undermine the growth of Methodism after 1740. Personal dislikes prevented Harris and Rowland from working as a team. Whereas Harris was a sombre, humourless man, Rowland possessed a great zest for life and enjoyed occasional bouts of levity. Harris resented Rowland's cheerfulness of manner, whereas Rowland often tired of Harris's earnest moralizing. Such was Harris's anxiety to be acknowledged as the commander-in-chief of Methodism and such his desire to be admired by all and sundry, that he was not prepared to play second fiddle to Rowland. Rowland, for his part, was understandably reluctant to permit an unordained layman to rule the roost. By temperament Harris was a highly autocratic man; Pantycelyn noted his 'desire to be head' and enemies of the movement dubbed him 'the Pope'.[49] Obsessed with his own personal standing within the movement, Harris frequently declared: 'I had the honour of being sent out first to the fields'.[50] There is no doubt that he was jealous of Rowland's gifts and influence and more determined than ever before never to work under him. For their part, Rowland and his colleagues, convinced that Harris's intention was to maximize power in his own hands, became less disposed to pander to his sense of infallibility. Throughout the 1740s, therefore, the relationship between the twin founders of Methodism was punctured by bitter quarrels and tearful reconciliations. Even more serious than these personal differences was Harris's fondness for the heretical doctrine known as Patripassianism. Heavily influenced by Moravian precepts, Harris publicly propagated the view that God had died in Christ and that the blood shed on the Cross was the blood of God. In the pulpit he preached on the theme 'By his stripes we are healed', and suffused his sermons with plaintive cries such as 'the blood of God' and 'the wounds and groans of God'. In many ways, therefore, the 'Father' of the movement had become a serious embarrassment to his peers.

Yet it was not Harris's authoritarianism and his heretical views on the Godhead which raised a storm so much as his public and private behaviour. Harris had always been bewildered by conflicting emotions in the company of women and, following several blundering courtships, had married Anne Williams, the daughter of a well-to-do Radnorshire squire, in 1744. Four years later he met Madam Sidney Griffith, the attractive wife of the squire of Cefnamwlch in Llŷn, and was swept off his feet. His marriage to Anne

[49] T. Beynon (ed.), *Howell Harris, Reformer and Soldier* (Caernarfon, 1958), p. 7; G. M. Roberts, *Y Pêr Ganiedydd* (Aberystwyth, 1949), p. 125.
[50] R. Bennett, *The Early Life of Howell Harris*, p. 179.

Williams had clearly been a mistake: she had failed to bear him a son and had refused to accompany him on his preaching tours. Harris's affection for her was always grudgingly bestowed and he spent an average of six months in London every year between 1746 and 1750. Madam Griffith's unhappy marriage echoed his own—John Wesley likened her drunken and violent husband to one of the ruffians in *Macbeth*—and she so stirred Harris's passions that he became besotted by her. Harris believed that she possessed extraordinary prophetic gifts and he referred to her in his journal as 'my arm', 'my light', and 'my eye'. With callous disregard for his wife's feelings, he invited Madam Griffith to accompany him on his preaching tours and his visits to London. Her presence provoked harsh words of reproach from Harris's colleagues and tongues wagged freely all over Wales as his private life became the subject of popular gossip. His behaviour lent credence to what enemies of Methodism had always suspected: that the movement positively encouraged sexual debauchery. Methodist historians have always strenuously denied allegations of impropriety on Harris's part and some efforts have been made to bowdlerize indelicate passages in Harris's literary remains. But the evidence in his journal leaves no doubt that his relationship with Madam Griffith was adulterous and that by allowing his heart to rule his head he had brought Welsh Methodism into grave disrepute. The whole affair was a nightmare for Rowland and his colleagues. Harris had always shunned the counsel of wiser heads and he was in no mood to heed those who pleaded with him to come to his senses. He was convinced that he was Barak and that his new companion was Deborah. More cynical observers, however, were of the opinion that the relationship of Samson and Delilah was a more appropriate biblical comparison.

Tensions which had long been simmering below the surface were bound to explode eventually, and in 1750 Harris's colleagues decided that enough was enough. Following the Association held at Llanidloes in May, the followers of Harris and those of Rowland went their separate ways, and at Llantrisant in July Harris was formally expelled for heresy. In many ways, the ensuing split was redolent of the breach which had divided Walter Cradock and Vavasor Powell a century earlier. Harris's vanity was deeply wounded by his expulsion; exhausted, sick and resentful, he withdrew to Trefeca. Having spent long and uncomfortable years in the saddle, he gave away his horse in December 1752. Mercifully, perhaps, Madam Griffith died in the same year and, having lost his Bathsheba, Harris set about transforming his small farmhouse at Trefeca into a large castellated monastery which his critics dubbed 'the New Jerusalem'. The settlement was administered on a communitarian basis akin to that of the Moravian community at Herrnhut; the estate encompassed 760 acres and offered employment in sixty different crafts. From 1752 until his death in 1773,

Harris acted as head of the 'Family' and each member was obliged to address him as 'Father'. All who had turned to Christ were made welcome at Trefeca on condition that they forfeited their earthly goods and were prepared to mix freely and on equal terms. Women gathered wool, carded flax, spun, and knitted, whilst men farmed the land and pursued a variety of crafts. Harris threw himself into his labours, seeking consolation from time to time in wistful nostalgia but usually busying himself building walls, laying drains, and cutting timber. When John Wesley visited the community in August 1763, he found the gardens, orchards, and fish-ponds enchanting. By 1759 a printing-press was at work and in 1768 Lady Huntingdon, the pious 'Queen of the Methodists', established a seminary there to train young men. The administration of the scheme owed much to the selfless labours of Harris's right-hand men, Evan Moses, a tailor from Aberdare, and Evan Roberts, a former steward in the lead-mining industry, as well as to the gifts of two successive matrons, Sarah and Hannah Bowen. Harris, meanwhile, imposed an impossibly strict regime on others and ruled his institution like a grenadier. The day's work began at four, the food was plain, and the atmosphere so unremittingly sombre that the number of defections was always high. Harris flogged miscreants, banished suitors, and chastised 'clacking females'. He expected Hannah Bowen to live a life of strident virtue and once, when she failed to live up to his expectations, he turned out her bed and clothes on a rainy night and forced her to sleep in a barn. But in spite of the harshness of the regime, the demands imposed on inmates by the Seven Years' War, and the ravages wrought by smallpox, Howel Harris's 'New Jerusalem' continued to prosper.

While Harris was engaged on his new project, the Methodist movement found itself in turmoil and disarray. Between 1750 and 1762 Methodism lost its impetus and sense of direction. Itinerancy decayed and many societies withered. Indeed, the collapse of some societies was so alarmingly sudden that it seemed to expose the rickety basis of the Methodist framework in some counties. Disenchanted members were lost by the dozens to the Congregationalist cause in the counties of Glamorgan and Monmouth, while defectors flowed swiftly into the ranks of the Baptists and Moravians in Pembrokeshire. In many communities the secessions of the 1750s were never made good. Small wonder, therefore, that several frantic but unsuccessful attempts were made to persuade Harris to return from his self-imposed seclusion. Charles Wesley implored him not to retreat from the battlefield with the fight but half-won. But Harris still believed himself to be more sinned against than sinning and he stubbornly refused to listen to such pleas. Fears for the future of Methodism deepened as new rivals entered the field. By the middle of the eighteenth century a variety of interested parties were just as determined as Methodists to acquire recruits, and the split between 'Harris's people' and 'Rowland's people' enabled a profusion of 'unrespectable', if not heretical sects such as the Moravians, the Muggletonians, the Popkinians, the Rellites, and the Sandemanians to find a niche for themselves in different localities.

During the 1760s, however, Methodism began to recover lost ground and to strike out in new directions. Much of the initial impetus stemmed from an extraordinary local revival at Llangeitho in 1762, where pentecostal scenes were inspired partly by Daniel Rowland's ministry and partly by the influence of an anthology of hymns by Pantycelyn, *Caniadau (y rhai sydd ar y Môr o Wydr)* (The Songs of Those who are on the Sea of Glass), 1,200 copies of which were sold within a few months of its publication in 1762. Much to the disgust of local Arians, who frowned on the 'wild pranks'[51] of 'Welsh Jumpers', Llangeitho became the focus of joyous singing, leaping, and dancing, the like of which even seasoned Methodists had never seen before. Many complaints were addressed to the bishop of St Davids in the wake of the revival of 1762 and Daniel Rowland was turned out of his cure. His flock, however, continued to follow him and chose to worship and take the sacrament at the New Chapel, Gwynfil. Once more, people flocked from all parts of Wales to Llangeitho. Peter Jones of Caerwys, Flintshire, completed the round journey of over two hundred miles on eleven separate occasions. He was only one among many who preferred the joyous fellowship of meetings at Llangeitho to Harris's spartan institution at Trefeca. The regular public demonstrations of praise at Llangeitho filled Williams Pantycelyn with new hope and optimism: 'Blessed summer's day!', he cried, 'It is come! It is come!'[52] The movement's renewal coincided with the emergence of Pantycelyn himself as the mouthpiece of Welsh Methodism. The splendid collections of poetry and prose which he published during the 1760s and 1770s not only captured the enthusiasm which fired Welsh Methodism but also created a new language of praise and worship.

Piqued by Rowland's success in reanimating Methodism, Howel Harris rejoined the cause in 1763 only to find that he had lost his youthful vigour and, more crucially, his former authority. In many quarters the behaviour of the prodigal son had been neither forgotten nor forgiven. Harris's expulsion had undermined confidence in his judgement and, in his absence, greater responsibility had devolved upon Rowland. Many leading Methodists remained bitterly critical of Harris's grandiose 'monastery' at Trefeca, his relationship with Rowland was still strained, and many young exhorters were neither amenable to his dictatorial ways nor disposed to seek his opinion on the future development of the movement. Indeed, they

[51] G. Eyre Evans, *Lloyd Letters*, p. 52.
[52] R. Geraint Gruffydd, 'Diwygiad 1762 a William Williams o Bantycelyn', *Journal Hist. Soc. Presbyterian Church in Wales* 55 (1970), p. 13.

were determined that he should no longer be sovereign, particularly since Rowland had shouldered most burdens during his absence and had built up a reputation as a leader. Exhorters who had laboured to sustain the movement during the split were also irritated by Harris's implacable opposition to the notion of separation, for they were anxious to acquire the authority to minister the sacraments to members of their societies and to begin the process of severing their links with the church. Moreover, Harris's links with the Moravians continued to be a bone of contention. His attempts to carry the revivalist banner were not conspicuously successful: crowds hooted derisively in Montgomeryshire as he travelled regally in his chaise (on which the words 'God is my peace' had been painted) and other cynical observers dubbed him the Welsh Zinzendorf.

Part of the reason why Harris was so coldly received on his return lies in the fact that Methodism was in the hands of a new generation of forward-looking men who had lost faith in the ideals of the founder of their movement. A number of elder statesmen, who had always been reluctant to countenance change, had died: Griffith Jones in 1761, Howel Davies and George Whitefield in 1770. In July 1773, Howel Harris died at the age of fifty-nine; his passing occasioned widespread mourning and his burial was accompanied by obsequies fit for a king. Shortly before his death, Edmund Jones of Pontypool paid fitting tribute to his contribution to the profound changes which had taken place in Welsh life: 'Everywhere, where the gospel is preached, there is no want of people to hear: and you sir, through the favour of God's providence have been at the bottom of all this'.[53] Harris's death opened a new phase in the history of Welsh Methodism. New faces were emerging—Thomas Charles of Llanfihangel Abercywyn, David Jones of Llan-gan, and William Davies of Neath—and this was clearly a time for fresh energies. Young clergymen and exhorters were now charged with the task of recruiting new members, refurbishing or building chapels, and extending missionary efforts to north Wales. And although the decision to abandon the established church lay in the future, the trend was overwhelmingly towards separation.

It is important not to exaggerate the influence of Methodism on Welsh life in the period before 1780. Much of north Wales was still *terra incognita* to the evangelists, and Congregationalists and Baptists were holding their own in several counties in south Wales and were probably stronger than the Methodists in Glamorgan and Monmouthshire. There were many people, particularly among the rich and the poor, who resisted all attempts to persuade them to change their ways. When John Wesley warned drunkards in Cardiff that 'you abide in death, you choose death and hell', a young man cheerfully replied, 'I am one, and thither I am going'.[54] The

[53] G. M. Roberts, *Portread o Ddiwygiwr*, p. 147.
[54] A. H. Williams (ed.), *John Wesley in Wales*, p. 9.

poor were hardly likely to view Calvinistic Methodism as an opiate for wretchedness. Many of them preferred to place their faith in the influence of superstition and magic by wearing charms and amulets; consulting wizards, cunning men, and almanacs; visiting shrines and healing wells; and placating witches. Belief in the occult and witchcraft had penetrated the warp and weft of peasant life so deeply that not even the most fearsome Methodist sermons could exorcize it. Indeed, in some ways, the emergence of Methodism served to enhance belief in supernatural forces. Howel Harris and John Wesley believed in witches. Griffith Jones was acutely conscious of the corporeal existence of the Devil. 'Methodist books', claimed Robert Roberts, 'swarmed with marvels, supernatural appearances, warnings, singing in the air, sudden judgments on rulers and persecutors . . . and for people who read the Old Testament histories so much, what more natural than to expect miracles everywhere.'[55] As late as 1800, fraught Methodist chieftains were still having to urge their brethren to desist from dabbling in magic and witchcraft.

The effect of Methodism on pious middling sorts, however, was striking. It introduced enthusiasm into their spiritual lives, taught them to worship publicly and privately, set new standards of piety and devotion, and implanted certain moral values which became an inseparable part of their way of life. By bringing souls to Christ, Methodism brought enormous spiritual joy to thousands of people. Although its impact on Welsh society as a whole was marginal in this period, it nevertheless developed its own standards of personal conduct and social morality which would eventually characterize the lives of most practising Christians in the nineteenth century. Most Methodist evangelists and exhorters were fastidiously devout men who abhorred the pleasures of Vanity Fair. Tears came more easily than laughter to most of them. Howel Harris, for instance, despised innocent mirth and always found it hard to smile. 'Had a temptation to laughter tonight',[56] he wrote self-reprovingly in his diary on 30 November 1741. Griffith Jones detested any form of flippancy and Thomas Charles simply could not remain in the same room as a harpist. Stewards exercised an unsleeping watchfulness over society members and periodic purges were carried out against 'disorderly walkers'. Since Methodists condemned cock-fighting, bull-baiting, balls, wakes, interludes, ballads, drunkenness, smuggling, snuff-taking, vanity, sloth, avarice, Sabbath-breaking, and evil-speaking, it is not surprising that their appeal was almost exclusively confined to pious middling sorts who placed a heavy premium on spiritual conviction and strict morality. Most other people found the scrupulous and censorious ways of Methodism hard to live with.

Although Methodist leaders, with the signal exception of Williams

[55] J. H. Davies (ed.), *The Life and Opinions of Robert Roberts* (Cardiff, 1923), p. 49.
[56] T. Beynon (ed.), *Howell Harris's Visits*, p. 65.

Pantycelyn, did not consciously cultivate the Welsh language, the movement did produce a splendid corpus of Welsh religious literature. Sermons, tracts, epics, hymns, and elegies multiplied in striking profusion, especially from 1760 onwards, and helped to strengthen the Welsh language and its culture. Calvinistic Methodism was also a pillar of the social and political order. Although its enemies deplored its excessive zeal, in political terms Methodism was unrepentantly quietist and other-worldly. Authority, its leaders insisted, derived from God alone. By calling for passivity and resignation, evangelists encouraged meek and quiet spirits to join the fold and bred within them a profound respect for the king and the constitution. Howel Harris never required a second bidding to drink the king's health and in 1759 he expressed his loyalty to the Crown and his burning xenophobia by joining the Brecknockshire Militia and becoming a red-coat gospeller. Methodism offered few means for its poorer members to aspire above their station, and those who suffered more than most were urged to bear every cross with joyful contentment. Later political radicals were to discover, to their cost, that not least among the achievements of Methodists was their success in teaching the duty of obedience to their flocks.

Methodism also succeeded, to some degree, in influencing the habits of churchmen and Dissenters. Its emphasis on morality, pietism, and enthusiasm left its mark on many clergymen. Thomas Ellis, vicar of Holyhead, risked his own popularity by reforming local wakes and insisting on stricter observance of the Sabbath. Richard Nanney, vicar of Clynnog and rector of Llanaelhaearn, was an avid promoter of the circulating schools and a fervent evangelical preacher who drew large and appreciative congregations. As we shall see, Methodism also helped to reanimate Dissent by persuading Congregationalists and Baptists to recover the sense of mission which had impelled their Puritan forefathers. By adopting more flexible and dynamic techniques of winning souls, Dissent became a popular evangelical movement and, by the nineteenth century, a triumphantly successful religion in both rural and industrial areas.

Finally, it must also be said that there was a dark side to Methodism. Its morbid preoccupation with the state of souls, with mortality, and the afterlife produced a people who were relentlessly solemn. Only the unspotted were made welcome and converts who attended society meetings became more austere and smiled less readily than before. By elevating emotional experiences above all others, Methodism also precipitated psychological stresses which, in turn, often bred feelings of guilt and confusion. The reforming missions which helped to undermine or eliminate popular customs and recreations alienated potential friends in high places and earned the contempt of the poor. Above all, many old hands among churchmen and Dissenters despised the self-righteousness of the reborn evangelist. Theophilus Evans was appalled by their conviction that they were privileged people bound for heaven. William Morris found them hard-faced and uncharitable, and Joshua Thomas singled out their penchant for bitterly criticizing all but themselves. Methodism might have saved many souls in the eighteenth century but its exacting and sometimes tyrannical discipline did not endear it to everyone.

In many parts of Wales the growth of Methodism coincided directly with the setting up of Griffith Jones's highly successful network of circulating schools. This remarkable educational scheme, first launched in 1731, is one of the major success stories of the eighteenth century. Griffith Jones was forty-seven when he began to organize itinerant schools, and in some ways it is strange that a middle-aged, asthmatic, and often neurotic man should have embarked on such a challenging and time-consuming venture. But, like so many notable eighteenth-century Welshmen, Jones was a man of inexhaustible energy and determination. Although he gave the impression that the burdens of the world rested upon him and liked to prophesy that his own death was at hand, he was in fact a born survivor. Ever since his conversion, saving souls had been the ruling passion of his life, but his concern for the spiritual welfare of 'the vulgar sorts' became even more acute when much of Wales, especially the counties in the south-west, were devastated by a typhus epidemic between 1727 and 1731. Hundreds of people died, many of them, Jones feared, without ever having truly known Christ. Deeply aware of the desperate plight of the unfortunate lower orders, Jones dedicated himself to the task of improving the spiritual and material condition of sick, undernourished, and ignorant people. He constantly fretted whether the people of Llanddowror and neighbouring parishes had enough bread to eat, clothes to wear, and medicines for their myriad ailments. By offering doles of bread to the impoverished he coaxed them to attend church. He clothed the needy and strove to protect them from the cruelty of others. Something of a hypochondriac himself, Jones cared for the sick by providing them with local herbal remedies and distributing pills, drugs, ointments, and life-enhancing cordials which he regularly ordered from London. We have seen how Methodist evangelists regarded Griffith Jones as their mentor and father confessor, but it is also important to stress that he possessed the inestimable gift of being able to win the affection of underprivileged and poor people. When John Thomas of Rhayader, who became a servant in Jones's household, first met him, he likened the experience to gazing at 'an angel of God'.[57] Many others, too, fell under his spell as his circulating schools began to spread.

Hitherto, as we have seen, educational opportunities among peasants

[57] Ioan Thomas, *Rhad Ras*, p. 46.

and their children had been largely dictated by economic constraints, the size and wealth of families, and the widespread aversion within farming communities to schooling. Unlike Sweden and Finland, where revolutionary success had been achieved by charging parents with the responsibility of instructing their children in the catechism, the Scriptures, and scriptural verses known as the *Hustavla*, charitable societies in Wales had chosen to provide education by means of charity schools which were not geared to the peculiar needs of peasant people. As a result, by the late 1720s, most of the schools sponsored by the SPCK had either collapsed or were in decline. By contrast, Griffith Jones's scheme was economical, flexible, and efficient. He knew that people's lives were governed by the rhythms of their agricultural environment and by the demands of the farming calendar. His own experience as a schoolmaster in SPCK schools had shown him that attendance numbers always collapsed during the summer months and that poor children seldom came. He therefore implemented a peripatetic system of intensive schooling. The notion of ambulatory schools was not new, for Griffith Jones, whatever else he might have been, was not an original thinker. The SPCK had encouraged a similar scheme in the northern counties of Scotland and in 1719 Sir Humphrey Mackworth had advocated the use of itinerant schoolmasters. In some ways, too, the use of itinerant teachers was the logical extension of the use of itinerant preachers. But the crucial point is that Griffith Jones was the first educationalist to launch and administer such an enterprise in Wales.

Since Griffith Jones's schools were held in parish churches, barns, farmhouses, cottages, and almshouses, they were easily accessible. No pupil was obliged to travel far, for the schools went directly to the poor, generally for a period of three or four months on the invitation of the incumbent of the parish. Since the spring and summer months had to be devoted to pressing agricultural tasks in the fields, most schools were held during the relatively slack autumn and winter months when both adults and children were able to attend regularly. Whereas most children attended day-schools, two-thirds of the total number of scholars were adults, and it is remarkable that so many of them were sufficiently single-minded to sacrifice hours of leisure in order to acquire the ability to read at night schools. In some parishes, servants hired labourers to deputize for them whilst they gained a few hours' schooling at night. Individuals mastered their letters swiftly, with the phonetic characteristics of the Welsh orthography enabling the brightest pupils to learn to read within six or seven weeks. Once a schoolmaster was convinced that his pupils were able to read and had been solidly grounded in Christian principles, he moved on to his next assignment, usually in the neighbouring parish. Often, however, he would return later on in order to refresh memories and consolidate gains.

Much of Griffith Jones's success stemmed directly from his decision to trim severely the curriculum adopted by his predecessors. Part of the price to be paid for instant success was the abandonment of writing and arithmetic, accomplishments which Jones believed were unnecessary and overdemanding in rural communities. He instructed his schoolmasters to offer a rudimentary but practical education by teaching pupils to read the Scriptures, thereby providing them with the means to salvation. Catechizing, too, was a central plank in his scheme. Over the years he had become increasingly aware of the fitful and ephemeral effects of preaching and of the need to catechize the lower orders more effectively. Children and adults were catechized twice daily and Jones himself provided schools with translations of popular English catechisms and other useful latimers. Pupils were also taught to sing psalms, to pray, to learn portions from Welsh versions of *The Whole Duty of Man*, and to memorize the crude but popular verses in Rees Prichard's *Canwyll y Cymry*. Much of the teaching may have been mechanical and unimaginative, but in enabling scholars to master the basic principles of the Christian faith and to familiarize themselves with biblical stories, parables, and songs, it served its purpose. Griffith Jones strongly believed that the ability to read and understand was a pre-condition of profitable religious endeavour and his overriding concern was always to save the souls of his fellow countrymen. He never considered literacy as a tool for acquiring radical opinions or as a vehicle for social change. Haunted by the spectre of the upward mobility of the labouring classes, he prayed fervently that those who toiled in the fields would not be tempted to learn English, desert their calling, and seek greater prosperity either in England or across the seas. Fear of popery and its attendant evils preyed heavily on his mind, especially during years of political crisis such as 1745 and 1756, and whenever opponents of his scheme pointed out the perils of mass education Jones reminded them of the propensity of the common enemy to flourish wherever ignorance and ungodliness reigned. His schoolmasters were instructed to instil or fortify the fear of Catholicism in the minds and hearts of their pupils in order to encourage deference and obedience to authority. In many of his own sermons and tracts, he warned the heedless that 'a suffering day cannot be far off'.[58] Fervently pro-Hanover, Griffith Jones opposed every Jesuit, Catholic, Jacobite, or Dissenter who threatened to storm Protestant citadels and weaken the establishment.

The vital key to Griffith Jones's success, however, was his steadfast determination to instruct Welsh children in the vernacular. Schoolmasters were permitted to conduct their schools through the medium of English in long-established Englishries such as south Pembrokeshire, Gower, east

---

[58] Griffith Jones, *Welch Piety* (London, 1750–1), p. 26.

Monmouthshire, and other border counties, but the principal medium of instruction in the overwhelming majority of schools was the Welsh language. Learning English texts by rote had been a central feature of the schools run by Jones's predecessors and this had led to widespread popular hostility towards schooling among monoglot Welsh communities. Thomas Ellis of Holyhead referred contemptuously to the 'useless smattering of English'[59] which children in Anglesey had acquired in SPCK schools, and there is no doubt that, prior to the launching of the itinerant Welsh schools, much of the teaching had been lifeless and unimaginative. Griffith Jones himself had often personally witnessed the enormous difficulties with which Welsh children had to contend as they grappled with material in a foreign tongue. However, many English philanthropists had serious misgivings about Welsh-medium schools and Griffith Jones was obliged to persuade them of the merits of the Welsh tongue and to impress upon them the force of opinion in Wales in favour of his policy. He showed how teachers were able to capitalize on the phonetic advantages of the Welsh orthography to produce literate pupils within a maximum period of three months. The Welsh language acted as a solid barrier against the evils of libertinism and vice, protecting innocent peasants from 'atheism, deism, infidelity, Arianism, popery, lewd plays, immodest romances and love intrigues'. Moreover, Jones insisted, there was no practical alternative. 'Welsh is still the vulgar tongue and not English', he informed doubting Thomases and any Welsh bishop who might choose to listen, 'shall we be more concerned for the propagation of the English language than the salvation of our people?' He believed that setting up English charity schools in Wales was as absurd as planting French charity schools in England. Speed was essential, for he feared that, as a result of his predecessors' attempts to instruct pupils in an alien tongue, hundreds of innocent and ignorant souls had been allowed to fall into 'the dreadful abyss of eternity'.[60]

The secret of Griffith Jones's success also lay partly in his ability to recruit able schoolmasters and secure the enthusiastic co-operation of clergymen. He assembled a band of willing teachers who were paid a miserable pittance of around £5 per annum but who were prepared to make material sacrifices in order to sustain his venture. Among the most gifted of them were Jenkin Morgan, Morgan Rhys, John Thomas, and Richard Tibbott. As principal director of the scheme, Griffith Jones provided his recruits with precise information and a detailed plan of action. He took on the responsibility of instructing them at a seminary known as *Yr Hen Goleg* (The Old College) at Llanddowror and impressed upon them the need to catechize regularly, eradicate ignorance, and arrest the

[59] *Welch Piety* (1755), p. 39.   [60] *Welch Piety* (1740), pp. 32–49.

drift to immorality. Each volunteer was carefully vetted, trained, and supervised before being sent out to the countryside to spread the habit of reading and enforce obedience to the moral and social code. A critical role was played by the parish clergy, many of whom shared Griffith Jones's ideals and were prepared to throw themselves whole-heartedly behind the scheme. Without their readiness to act as teachers, to offer administrative assistance, and to promote popular education in general, the schools could never have flourished.

In order to employ teachers, subsidize pupils, order bibles, catechisms and devotional books, and to hire schoolrooms, Jones depended heavily on the financial support of wealthy benefactors and well-disposed parishioners. Although Jones was a man of few intimates, his career and plans were furthered by a number of pious and enthusiastic philanthropists. The death in 1737 of Sir John Philipps, his most committed benefactor, was a loss which he felt deeply, but it served to bring him closer than ever before to Madam Bridget Bevan of Laugharne. Madam Bevan was the heiress of John Vaughan of Derllys and the wife of Arthur Bevan, sometime MP for Carmarthen boroughs. She was a lady of considerable beauty, charm, and piety, and when Howel Harris, as a young man without *savoir-faire* or experience of affluent women, first met her he found it 'a taste of heaven'[61] to be in her company. Griffith Jones, too, was enchanted by this pious lady who was thirteen years younger than he and twenty-two years younger than his wife. Jones's wife, Margaret, was a solitary and often sick woman, and Madam Bevan, both as spiritual confidante and a financial adviser, helped to meet his frustrated emotional and spiritual needs. An active and selfless philanthropist, she was, in Jones's view, 'the greatest mistress of contrivance and of directing affairs that I know'.[62]

Since virtually no support was forthcoming from Welsh bishops, deans, or archdeacons, Madam Bevan's financial support and extensive social connections were of crucial importance. It was she who enabled Griffith Jones to enter the charmed circle of polite life in the towns of south Wales and to meet men and women who counted in Bath. Jones was not above using his considerable social charm and persuasive tongue to beguile funds from wealthy peers and members of the moneyed professional middle-class in England. Eminent bankers, physicians, and scientists were made acutely aware of the sufferings of the poor in Wales and of the need to sustain humane and enlightened educational schemes. 'Every soul you help to save', Jones informed them, 'may be as so many shining pearls to your never-fading crowns of glory.'[63] According to John Evans of Eglwys

[61] R. Bennett, *The Early Life of Howell Harris*, p. 60.

[62] Jac L. Williams and G. R. Hughes (eds.), *The History of Education in Wales* (Swansea, 1978), p. 68.

[63] W. Moses Williams (ed.), *Selections from The Welch Piety* (Cardiff, 1938), p. 36.

Gymyn, Jones shamelessly flattered the piously disposed: 'he strokes their heads, calls them his fine boys; flatters, coaxes them; gives them sugar plums'.[64] This was probably true, but it should also be borne in mind that Griffith Jones was equally adept in pricking the consciences of miserly men by reminding them that charity was a prudent investment and that 'terrible judgements' were hanging over their heads. By pandering to and berating the rich, he ensured a regular flow of funds which helped to swell the more modest contributions which regularly came to hand from church collections. The munificence of the SPCK also proved invaluable to the scheme. Although its educational plans had withered, the SPCK continued to supply thousands of bibles, prayer books, catechisms, psalters, and manuals of devotion, many of which were distributed free of charge among deserving scholars by local clergymen, schoolmasters, and agents. Over a period of fifty years, around 70,000 Welsh bibles were provided by the SPCK and were distributed, via horses, wagons, and ships, among common people in every county in Wales. This largely unsung work not only helped Griffith Jones to conserve much-needed cash but also exercised a powerful influence on the growth of literacy in general.

Griffith Jones administered his scheme with strict efficiency. He was a devoted fund raiser, kept his books in good order, and did not waste a single penny. Virtually all the funds raised were used to pay schoolmasters and to buy religious texts. According to his calculations, it was possible to educate pupils at a cost of some two or three shillings a head. It was a matter of pride to him that the scheme was 'husbanded in the most frugal and saving manner'.[65] To his considerable business acumen Jones also added a fierce determination to succeed. He may have been a neurotic, thin-skinned, and sickly man, but he was also highly resourceful, energetic, and single-minded. Like the Methodists, he was an early riser (if not an insomniac) who felt it was his duty to carry out his daily pastoral routine, and to provide his countrymen with the means by which they could acquire the gift of reading and the salvation of their souls. So complete was his absorption in his work that no obstacle was formidable enough to deter him.

From the beginning the schools flourished, and spread especially rapidly in Cardiganshire, Carmarthenshire, Glamorgan, and Pembrokeshire. By 1740, 150 schools had been established, with 8,767 scholars in attendance. During the early 1740s, however, Griffith Jones was forced to fight for survival. His employment of Methodist exhorters as teachers brought his movement into grave disrepute. Leading churchmen, mindful of Jones's intimate links with Methodist leaders, argued that his schools were a covert means of spreading evangelical religion and perilous schism. Schoolmasters,

---

[64] John Evans, *Some Account of the Welsh Charity-Schools* (London, 1752), p. 59.

[65] Griffith Jones, *Welch Piety* (London, 1750–1), p. 13.

especially in north Wales, were cruelly harassed and maltreated: some were prosecuted in the courts, others pressed into the armed forces. As a result, only 74 schools were maintained during 1743–4. During the crisis, Jones wisely distanced himself from his Methodist friends and removed committed enthusiasts from his army of schoolmasters. He also cleverly disarmed his enemies by inviting the clergy to inspect his schools, assess the qualifications and behaviour of schoolmasters, and prepare reports on the quality of their teaching. Having rid his schools of the taint of Methodism, Jones extended his network of schools into many parts of north Wales. By 1751–2, 130 schools were offering education to 5,724 pupils, and as

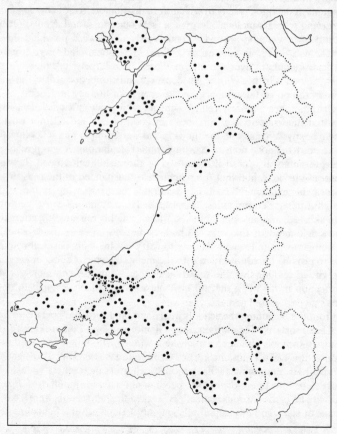

MAP 2. The Location of Griffith Jones's Circulating Schools, 1756–7

Methodism fell away during the 'Great Split' of the 1750s the circulating schools prospered as never before. It is true that John Evans of Eglwys Gymyn, Jones's inveterate foe, continued to assemble trumped-up charges against his enemy in hostile pamphlets, but few were now disposed to heed his poisonous comments. 'Should the traveller be disturbed', wrote Griffith Jones disdainfully, 'by the little animals that bark at him on his way, or stop to correct their rudeness?'[66] It mattered not to William Morris 'who pushes the good work on, whether he be Turk, brindled Jew, Pagan or Methodist'.[67] There were 218 schools in 1758, with nearly 10,000 scholars, over a third of whom hailed from Carmarthenshire. Save for Flintshire and Montgomeryshire, where the number of schools was small, attendances were buoyant everywhere; over a thousand pupils were receiving education in each of the counties of Anglesey, Caernarfon, and Cardigan. The number of pupils who attended individual schools varied from parish to parish. Classes of between thirty and forty pupils were the norm, although in some populous parishes membership, especially at night, soared to eighty or a hundred. Parishes vied with each other for schoolmasters and sought to emulate each other's number of pupils.

When his wife died in 1755, Griffith Jones settled in Madam Bevan's house in Laugharne. There, hard-pressed servants refused to revere the asthmatic and cantankerous old patriarch and dubbed him 'Old Peevish'. Those who knew him best, however, were aware of his staggering achievements. By his death in 1761, aged 77, Griffith Jones had been responsible for establishing 3,325 schools in nearly 1,600 different places in Wales. The total number of pupils—both adults and children—who were taught to read fluently in his schools may well have numbered 250,000, an extraordinary achievement, given the fact that the population of Wales was around 490,000 at the time. With enormous passion and perseverance, Griffith Jones had launched and sustained a national system of schools and turned it into a truly Welsh institution. Even after his death, the schools continued to flourish under Madam Bevan's benevolent and watchful eye. Between 1761 and 1777, 3,325 schools were established, offering education to 153,835 pupils. The peak year was 1773, when 242 schools were set up and 13,205 scholars received instruction. However, most of the gains achieved under Madam Bevan's supervision were made in anglicized communities, notably in the towns of Monmouthshire and Pembrokeshire where pupils were taught through the medium of English. When Madam Bevan herself died in 1779 and was buried alongside Griffith Jones in accordance with her wishes, she bequeathed her estate of £10,000 to the scheme in order to ensure the perpetuation of the circulating schools. However, two of her trustees challenged the will and the money became

[66] Thomas Kelly, *Griffith Jones, Pioneer in Adult Education* (Cardiff, 1950), p. 36.
[67] *Morris Letters*, i. 197.

tied up in the Court of Chancery for thirty-one years. From this set-back there was to be no recovery. Deprived of essential financial aid, the circulating school system withered and died.

Conscious of the need for good public relations, ever since 1737 Griffith Jones had published an annual report, *Welch Piety*. These reports invariably included dozens of letters from appreciative clergymen and laymen who gratefully spoke of the beneficial effects of regular schooling within their localities. An army of common people and children had been created who were able to read the Bible, understand the catechism, and give a decent account of their faith. Once the harvest had been safely gathered in, parish churches echoed to the sounds of infant and adult voices chanting the alphabet aloud, spelling words, repeating the catechism, and reading passages from the Scriptures. Many 'poor and ignorant' young children braved cold mornings in order to acquire reading skills. Some of them went barefoot and dressed in rags. George Parry, curate of Gelli-gaer, was impressed by the diligence of 'poor harmless babes in their mean rags', whilst hearing the poor children of Llangernyw at prayer moved John Kenrick to tears: 'they seemed even beautiful in their rags, while they thus learnt to put on Christ Jesus'.[68] Some pupils were prodigiously gifted: at Y Ferwig in Cardiganshire a three-year-old child could spell even the most difficult Welsh words, while at Cynwyl Elfed in Carmarthenshire a child of seven learnt to read fluently in three weeks. At Llwyngwril in Merioneth a thirteen-year-old boy learnt to read the relevant text relating to the visitation of the sick as fluently as his own clergyman. Often the progress made by children during the day shamed their parents and even their grandparents into seeking the same proficiency at night schools. At Tre-lech, Carmarthenshire, a seventy-one year-old-man, with spectacles on his nose, a catechism in his hand, and five other penurious and aged adults at his side, strove to acquire a basic understanding of letters, syllables, words, phrases, and sentences. Married couples, usually farmers, cottagers, servants, and labourers, brought their own candles and fuel to night schools, which often remained open until nine or ten. At Llan-ddew in Breconshire, day-labourers attended night school twice a week, whilst the colliers of Llangyfelach in Glamorgan sacrificed precious leisure hours following arduous twelve-hour shifts in order to master their letters.

Griffith Jones's major triumph, therefore, was to provide large numbers of tenants, labourers, and servants, together with their sons and daughters, with the opportunity to learn to read. Many factors contributed to the dramatic upsurge of literacy in Wales after 1730—the benevolence of affluent gentlemen and their wives, the role of Methodism and revivified Dissent, the influence of pious and active middling sorts, and the growth of

[68] Griffith Jones, *Welch Piety* (London, 1753), p. 53; *Welch Piety* (1750), p. 52.

flourishing printing-presses—but none of these played such a decisive role in the dissemination of reading habits as the circulating schools. For the first time in the history of Wales most rural inhabitants had access to elementary schooling in the vernacular. 'Reading among the lower class of people', wrote Thomas Llewelyn in 1769, 'is become much more common and general . . . than formerly.'[69] Much of the credit for this lay with the itinerant schools, for Griffith Jones had successfully geared his scheme to the economic and religious needs of hewers of wood and drawers of water. And although his experiment produced a restricted kind of literacy, in the sense that it involved exclusively the ability to read, it was nevertheless a vital element in the modernization of Wales. Indeed, Jones's scheme was such a seminal influence that, in 1764, Catherine II of Russia instructed a commissioner to investigate the circulating schools in action and to prepare a detailed report on their practicality and merits.

The effects of the circulating schools also ramified in all directions in Wales. 'Great were the blessings which followed',[70] claimed Robert Jones, Rhos-lan, who had himself mastered his letters after six weeks' tuition at a circulating school in Llanystumdwy and who subsequently made the long journey to Laugharne on two occasions in order to persuade Madam Bevan to maintain a network of schools in Caernarfonshire. The fact that so many clergymen, laymen, and Methodist exhorters pleaded with Griffith Jones and Madam Bevan to extend the period of tuition or promise them a fresh teacher in their respective parishes reveals that they were acutely aware of the direct and indirect benefits which regular schooling implied. Many overworked and underpaid clergymen testified that the itinerant schools had served to rejuvenate the church in their localities. The demand for Welsh bibles was seemingly insatiable: when limited supplies of the 1748 edition of the Welsh Bible reached Anglesey, poor people nearly scratched out the eyes of Thomas Ellis, vicar of Holyhead, as they surged forward and fought to acquire a copy; similarly, there was such an extraordinary demand for the Scriptures among the parishioners of the vale of Conwy that poor people borrowed money in order to buy copies. All the evidence suggests, too, that by the 1750s and 1760s parishioners were worshipping more regularly and reverently, that monthly rather than quarterly communion had become common, and that standards of personal morality had improved. Itinerant schools had not only instilled reading habits into untutored masses but had also promoted family prayers on the hearth and the practice of reading aloud in knitting-groups and workshops. Indeed, had not the circulating schools helped to renew church life, Dissent would have grown much more rapidly than it did.

[69] Thomas Llewelyn, *Historical and Critical Remarks on the British Tongue* (London, 1769), p. 2.
[70] Robert Jones, *Drych yr Amseroedd*, p. 104.

Methodism, too, reaped the benefits of the circulating school movement. Robert Jones of Rhos-lan believed that the origins of Methodism were at least partly attributable to the itinerant schools which 'like the crow of the cockerel signified the appearance of a new dawn'.[71] Certainly, wherever circulating schools were well attended, there, too, Methodism prospered. Although Methodist leaders never revered learning for its own sake, they did encourage their members to learn to read. In many areas, the growth of literacy and the development of Methodism tended to advance hand in hand. Methodist chapels of ease and meeting-houses, as well as private farmhouses, were made available to the circulating schools, and it is not hard to appreciate why clergymen, especially in the 1740s, believed that the schools were Methodist seminaries. At least a third of the farmhouses in Carmarthenshire where Methodist society meetings were held were also placed at the disposal of itinerant schoolmasters. It is doubtful, therefore, whether Welsh Methodism would have borne so splendid a harvest had not Griffith Jones sown such valuable seeds.

Although it would be an exaggeration to claim that Griffith Jones's scheme saved the Welsh language from extinction, it is certainly true that the circulating schools were the chief means by which the native tongue was strengthened and preserved during the eighteenth century. Many historians have claimed that Griffith Jones abandoned the linguistic policies pursued by the SPCK for practical and utilitarian reasons. But he was not insensible of the purity and antiquity of the Welsh language and, unlike his superiors within the church, he was always prepared to do battle with those who disparaged his mother tongue. For over fifty years he preached and taught in the language of his flocks in the Tâf valley in Carmarthenshire, insisting always that the vulgar sorts received no more benefits from an English service than did their ancestors from the Latin Mass. Moreover, his schools encouraged the use of Welsh as a spoken and written language and thus enhanced the prestige-value of the language. By 1780 the Welsh language was in a much stronger position to withstand the pressures of anglicization than it had been fifty years earlier. Even in communities where grammar schools had traditionally been foci for anglicization, much ground was recovered. Iolo Morganwg argued that the Welsh language was 'greatly increasing' in Glamorgan by the 1780s 'and this in great part through the Welsh schools being more numerous in our county than in almost any county in Wales'.[72] Griffith Jones's arguments in favour of the more widespread use of the Welsh language also went a long way towards making the vernacular a respectable tongue in Wales. He shared the growing appreciation of eighteenth-century scholars of the

[71] Robert Jones, *Drych yr Amseroedd*, p. 29.
[72] B. Ll. James, 'The Welsh Language in the Vale of Glamorgan', *Morgannwg* 16 (1972), p. 24.

beauties of the language and its potential role in the field of poetry, literature, and academic study. Furthermore, he sincerely believed that the survival of Welsh had been providential and that those who sought to hasten its demise were flying in the face of 'the decrees of heaven'.[73] Not only did Griffith Jones increase literacy levels dramatically, but he also infused new life into an old and honourable tongue.

Dissent, meanwhile, was also growing in Wales. The Toleration Act of 1689 had seriously damaged the coercive powers of the church, the profaneness of sottish curates had provoked many defections, and increasing numbers of pious middling sorts found the sober and dignified worship of the chapel and the meeting-house more to their taste. However, not all dissenters had survived the heroic years of persecution. Although wealthy families in south-east Wales continued to offer succour to the followers of Rome, Catholicism as a movement had virtually withered to nothing by the middle of the eighteenth century. The Jesuit mission at Powis Castle had perished in the 1740s, while those who had steadfastly refused to forsake the old faith bore the brunt of anti-popish passions during years of political crisis. Not until after 1790, when large-scale industrialization and Irish immigration occurred, did the number of Catholics in Wales begin to increase sharply. The disciples of George Fox were also numerically small and without influence. The Quakers had become a people of curiously limited ambitions who clung to their witness in small, isolated groups scattered around Wales but who made no concerted or serious effort to communicate their faith in the Welsh language or to proselytize in anglicized market towns. Friends did not help their cause by adopting clannish marriage customs, failing to establish schools, academies, or a distinctive headquarters, and by segregating themselves from the world. In most communities they had become the objects of curiosity rather than of hostility.

By contrast, Congregationalists and Baptists had not experienced the same loss of momentum. Modest gains were made after 1730, and by 1742, according to Edmund Jones's estimate, there were 106 Congregationalist or Baptist churches in Wales, 88 of which were located in the six counties of south Wales. Dissent had yet to penetrate Anglesey and Flintshire. Membership of their churches continued to be spread over extensive areas and ministers were obliged to travel widely in order to minister to the needs of their flocks. Although Dissenters had lost much of their old evangelical fervour, their influence in the fields of religion, culture, popular education, business, and industry was far greater than their numbers might suggest. Most of them were serious-minded, pious men and

[73] Griffith Jones, *Welch Piety* (London, 1740), pp. 47-9.

women who were capable of giving a full and reasoned account of their faith and convictions. In the towns they won support from the merchant community, while in rural areas they appealed mostly to small farmers, craftsmen, and artisans. They met in small, sober, sparsely furnished but dignified meeting-houses and were ministered to by academy-trained and generally well-to-do pastors, who preached carefully prepared sermons designed to appeal both to the intellect and the heart. Dissenters practised domestic devotions with scrupulous care, encouraged the growth of literacy and charitable work, and insisted upon strict discipline and morality. Like Methodists, Dissenters were eager to bring Satan's kingdom tumbling down and they heartily condemned those who drank excessively, sold beer without a licence, danced at weddings, swore and blasphemed, or plundered wrecked ships. Membership was a hard-earned privilege: each candidate was carefully 'examined and received' and backsliders and delinquents were swiftly expelled. Dissenting congregations were highly disciplined and knowledgeable cadres, and surviving records are replete with references to members who possessed 'a good stock of knowledge' or who were of 'a serious and good character'.[74] Instinctively, many of them deplored the lack of intellectual muscle and the curious naïvety which characterized the worship of their Methodist neighbours.

Since few Dissenting ministers prior to the 1740s believed that the world was their parish, recruits dribbled rather than flowed into their congregations. Yet there existed in many communities, especially in south Wales, a considerable and largely unappeased religious craving which prompted disaffected church-goers to throw in their lot with either Methodists or Dissenters. In large parishes, low standards of pastoral care and infrequent preaching persuaded many to turn their back on the church. Griffith Jones, Llanddowror, who was a better judge than most, believed that secessions to Dissent were provoked by the want of 'plain, practical, pressing and zealous preaching in a language and dialect they understand; and freedom of friendly access to advise about their spiritual state'.[75] The evil of appropriated pews was also a growing cause of resentment. Since the most affluent parishioners occupied the most prestigious seats in church, freeholders found themselves thrust out to the galleries normally reserved for the poor. The stigma involved was such that independently minded people, with some stake in property and pride in their calling, preferred to turn to Dissent. Furthermore, there were growing numbers of Methodists who were not prepared to receive communion from unworthy clerics and who, despairing of ever being able to eradicate flagrant abuses within the established church, joined the cause of Dissent.

Prior to the coming of Methodism, however, Dissent was hamstrung by

[74] E. D. Jones, 'Llyfr Eglwys Mynydd Bach', *Y Cofiadur* 17 (1947), *passim*.
[75] Griffith Jones, *Welch Piety* (London, 1742), p. 13.

its introversion and its hostility to enthusiasm. Although it did not lack lively preachers, able scholars, and thoughtful members, its relatively modest numbers and steady progress did not suggest that it was likely to take Wales by storm. From the 1740s onwards, however, and increasingly after 1760, Dissent caught the revivalist enthusiasm. There is no doubt that it drew 'an enormous blood-transfusion from the veins of the Evangelical Revival'[76] and that this enabled its leaders to set about their work with greater commitment, energy, and sense of purpose. As its preachers became filled with conversionist zeal, Dissent became more flexible and more able to expand in terms of numbers and influence. Not all Congregationalists, of course, welcomed the new revivalist spirit: Philip David of Pen-maen in Monmouthshire was appalled to hear Methodist preachers 'screaming with some hideous noises and unbecoming gestures', actions which he judged to be 'no part of the religion of Jesus'.[77] And there were others who despised public demonstrations of grief, yearning, or pain. Dissenting worship could often be formal and dignified, but under the highly charged evangelical ministry of men like Lewis Rees and Edmund Jones it could also be animated, warm, and fervent. Lewis Rees, a native of Glamorgan who built a Congregational chapel at Llanbryn-mair in Montgomeryshire in 1739, brought new life and vitality to the religion practised by the knitters and weavers of mid-Wales. Rees 'descended like lightning on the quiet congregations'[78] of rural mid- and north Wales, propagated the gospel in the manner of the Methodists, and served in the ministry for sixty-five years. Edmund Jones, a native of Aberystruth in Monmouthshire, was the eighteenth-century equivalent of Ben Jonson's 'Zeal-of-the-land Busy'. A remarkably active and evangelical minister at Pontypool, Jones gained a reputation for being more Calvinist than Calvin himself. Although his salary was only £10 per annum (most of which he gave to needy parishioners), he assembled a huge personal library comprising mostly seventeenth-century tracts and sermons, took leading Methodist preachers under his wing, and embarked on annual preaching tours of mind-boggling length. Jones lived through almost every year of the eighteenth century, served the Congregationalist cause for sixty-nine years, and on his death claimed proudly that he had been 'for a long time a soldier against the spirit of error in this country'.[79]

Many other prominent Dissenters, like John Griffiths of Glandŵr, Thomas Davies of Pant-teg, and John Thomas of Rhayader, were deeply affected by the balmy breezes of revivalism. The theatrical preaching styles

[76] R. Davies and G. Rupp (eds.), *A History of the Methodist Church in Great Britain* (vol. i, London, 1965), p. 293.

[77] R. Tudur Jones, *Congregationalism in England 1662–1962* (London, 1962), p. 161.

[78] R. T. Jenkins, *Hanes Cynulleidfa Hen Gapel Llanuwchllyn* (Bala, 1937), p. 54.

[79] G. F. Nuttall, 'Cyflwr Crefydd yn Nhrefddyn, Sir Fynwy, 1793, gan Edmund Jones', *Y Cofiadur* 46 (1981), p. 27.

of Methodist itinerants were imitated and tearful sermons melted the hearts of congregations. At Cae-bach, Radnorshire, in 1769, John Thomas found men and women groaning, crying, and weeping in frenzied joy. Crug-y-bar church in Carmarthenshire became noted for the remarkably fiery sermons of its minister, Isaac Price, and the fervent singing and praying led by Nansi Jones (Nansi Crug-y-bar). One of Crug-y-bar's most illustrious members was Dafydd Jones, the Caeo drover and hymnologist who translated Isaac Watts's psalms and hymns, composed some 800 hymns of his own, and persuaded his fellow Congregationalists to sing them with as much gusto as did neighbouring Methodists. Similarly, Morgan Rhys of Cil-y-cwm and Dafydd William of Llandeilo-fach composed lyrical hymns of great beauty and appeal. Baptists, too, were jolted into more vigorous activity by Methodist advances: a full-scale Baptist mission, led by Dafydd Evans and Morgan Evans, was launched in north Wales between 1776 and 1779 and their powerful, awakening preaching won new converts. Indeed, the Baptist movement entered a period of considerable expansion: its membership rose from 1,600 in 1760 to 3,257 in 1780 and 5,786 in 1790. Such heartening successes were achieved largely because Dissent had become a more popular and attractive religion. It was capable of wooing disgruntled churchmen and unhappy Methodists, as well as the mercers, printers, doctors, and schoolmasters who peopled the growing commercial and industrial communities. And when, at the turn of the century, Methodists came to accept that the formation of a new denomination was inevitable, Dissent stood poised to rob the Church of England of its primacy in Wales.

Rationalist Dissenters, on the other hand, were by nature and doctrine hostile to the 'tyranny' of Methodism. Just as evangelists abhorred liberal principles, so did rationalists deplore the blind faith of Methodists in the power of the spirit. From the 1720s onwards, the bracing winds of rationalism and anti-trinitarianism had been blowing with increasing vigour from the direction of the Carmarthen academy. During Thomas Perrot's tenure, men of considerable learning and strength of mind were openly advocating unorthodox theological views. The cause of Arminianism was championed by Jenkin Jones, a blacksmith's son, who influenced the minds of a new generation of intellectuals and ministers. These sharp and alert Arminians possessed a fund of ideas and arguments which they deployed with such fluency in oral and written debates that Calvinist congregations in north Carmarthenshire and south Cardiganshire were thrown into turmoil. The contours of 'the Black Spot' were already apparent by the 1750s as anti-Calvinist doctrines spread. There were splits and secessions at Cefnarthen in Carmarthenshire and at Cwm-y-glo and Ynys-gau in Glamorgan. Much to the chagrin of Phylip Pugh, the 'new invention'[80] of

<hr />

[80] T. O. Williams, *Undodiaeth a Rhyddid Meddwl* (Llandysul, 1962), p. 121.

Arminianism spread among his carefully nurtured flock in mid-Cardiganshire and Howel Harris often refused to canvass Methodist views in those communities where flinty, learned Dissenters were likely to prove more than a match for him.

By offering an increasingly liberal and broadly based scheme of study, the Carmarthen academy acquired a reputation for unorthodox theology and intellectual rigour. The inclination of Samuel Thomas, one of its most progressive tutors, towards Arianism did not endear him to the Congregational Board which withdrew its financial support and, cheered on by the likes of Edmund Jones, set up a new Calvinist academy at Abergavenny in 1757. Undeterred, Samuel Thomas and Jenkin Jenkins continued to rear students who were receptive to liberal principles but hostile to fire-eating gospellers. Arianism swiftly took root. When Dafydd Dafis, Castellhywel, was ordained under an old oak tree at Llwynrhydowen in 1773, most of the sixteen ministers present were Arians. These were dogged and pugnacious men, determined to recover their radical roots and renew the struggle for religious and civic equality. Convinced that Calvinism offered no more than a reward hereafter, they openly despised the political inertia implicit in Methodism and its leaders' hostility to the cherished ideals of liberty and toleration. When David Lloyd of Brynllefrith died in 1779, there were many enthusiastic 'friends to liberty' among the 800 members of his church. Such people would become, in due course, the most vigorous and determined champions of the cause of political radicalism in Wales.

CHAPTER 10

CULTURAL REVIVAL AND INVENTION

ONE of the most striking features of this period was the emergence of men and women who, blessed with a multitude of overlapping talents, were determined to enrich the cultural life of Wales. Changing cultural tastes were not only the result of wider educational opportunities but were also closely related to the contours of social and economic change. Those who concentrated their intellect and energy in bolstering Welsh culture were chiefly drawn from the increasingly affluent middling sorts, comprising civil servants, clergymen and ministers, prosperous farmers, skilled craftsmen, and artisans. As the dominant ruling landed classes severed themselves from native Welsh culture, these newer men became the most conspicuous and influential patrons and animators in the world of Welsh letters. It was a source of considerable vexation to them that the gentry were no longer sensitive to the plight of the Welsh language and were only too willing to lose the valuable culture bequeathed to them by their ancestors. But since they were not dependent on the financial support or social approval of the landed classes, they were able to stake a claim to determine the nature and quality of Welsh culture. Deeply conscious of their obligations to their cultural inheritance, they sought to create a framework which would enable popular societies and printing-presses to revive celebrated traditions and canvass new ideas. In so doing, they gave Welsh culture a new lease of life.

A number of social and economic changes opened the way for middling sorts of differing social backgrounds to play a larger and more significant role in cultural matters. The growth of an energetic urban middle class in Welsh towns released new talents. Welsh Dissenting academies produced a stream of brilliant alumni. Moreover, as the century advanced, the reading public expanded swiftly, with the result that more and more people were reading a wide range of books, discovering new ideas, and voicing their opinions. In the absence of capital resources, rich endowments, and representative institutions, men of letters were compulsively driven to rediscover their cultural inheritance, embrace it with fierce pride and enrich it by creating new myths and traditions. Where customs were decaying, new ones were either deliberately invented or grafted on to the old and presented as indigenous, original, and attractive Welsh characteristics. As a result, Welsh scholars not only recovered genuine literary treasures from the past but also created new heroes and cults, ceremonies and rituals, which, in the long run, helped to create a distinctive national identity.

These initiatives owed much to the drive and talents of gifted all-rounders as capable of mastering a variety of crafts as differing literary genres. In many ways, this was the age of the virtuoso, the dilettante, the many-sided amateur of eclectic interests. The range of the skills and interests of these self-styled ancient Britons was formidable. Even autodidacts in their midst became as dazzlingly versatile as the men of the Renaissance. No man of letters was more distinguished and many-sided in this period than Richard Price, a native of Tyn-ton in the parish of Llangeinor in Glamorgan. An extraordinarily learned man, Price became a philosopher, mathematician, theologian, and libertarian of truly international stature. Lewis Morris, the most celebrated of the Morris brothers of Anglesey, was a remarkable polymath. His encyclopaedic knowledge made him appear capable of discussing anything. His wide-ranging interests included surveying, mining, farming, carpentry, mechanical inventions, literature, philology, antiquarianism, and music. Morris could make watches and harps, compose *penillion* (stanzas) and set them to music, build a boat and sail it. His tireless energy, however, was not always well directed and he might well have been too versatile for his own good. He had so many irons in the fire and was so insatiably curious that he never truly fulfilled his potential as a scholar. Equally protean and learned, but less scrupulous, was Edward Williams, self-styled Iolo Morganwg, a marble-mason from Pennon in the parish of Llancarfan in Glamorgan. The most erudite, yet mysterious, of men, Iolo became Wales's most celebrated literary forger. In spite of his eccentric and often violent behaviour, he was an extraordinarily versatile scholar, poet, musician, hymnologist, folklorist, theologian, botanist, geologist, and horticulturist. The depth of his wisdom, the sharpness of his intelligence, and his personal magnetism made him a uniquely influential figure in the shaping of Welsh national consciousness from the 1770s onwards.

There were also many other less celebrated but equally many-sided scholars who, without significant formal training, contributed handsomely to the development of cultural awareness in eighteenth-century Wales. Lewis Hopkin of Llandyfodwg in Glamorgan was an erudite man with a practical bent to his mind. He was a carpenter, stone-cutter, wire-worker, glazier, builder, surveyor, shopkeeper, and farmer, as well as a highly regarded poet, scholar, and antiquarian. Widely esteemed as a wise, pious sage, Hopkin exercised a decisive influence on the careers of many poets and authors in his native county. In the fastnesses of Montgomeryshire, William Jones of Llangadfan, a self-taught farmer who spent the whole of his life in the parish of Llangadfan, developed an expertise in the fields of classical studies, poetry, genealogy, folksongs, traditional dances, astronomy, and medicine. An avowed enemy of Saxon bishops, an outspoken critic of anglicized gentlemen, and a fervent admirer of Voltaire, William Jones was a force to be reckoned with in the cultural and political life of late eighteenth-century Wales. The growth of the press in Welsh towns also enabled humble but protean men to gain confidence, win modest incomes, and reveal their blossoming talents. One of the most imaginative and successful was John Robert Lewis of Holyhead, the founder of the celebrated *Almanac Caergybi* (The Holyhead Almanac): he was an author, bookseller, astrologer, schoolmaster, bookbinder, watch-maker, mathematician, lexicographer, poet, and hymnologist. Women, too, were far less anonymous than ever before, especially within the Dissenting fraternity. Some were notably cultured and versatile. Margaret Evans of Penllyn in Merioneth, who lived through every single year of the eighteenth century, became a legend in her own time: she was a carpenter, joiner, blacksmith, shoemaker, boat-builder, hunter, shooter, and fowler. She could fashion and play a fiddle and a harp and, according to Thomas Pennant, 'all the neighbouring bards paid their addresses to Margaret, and celebrated her exploits in pure British verse'.[1] Bound together by a thirst for knowledge and a reverence for learning, a rich variety of aptitudes and skills, and a determination to use periods of leisure profitably, men and women such as these became pace-setters in the cultural affairs of Wales.

Some of the most novel and dramatic developments in the field of Welsh culture were focused on London in this period. Wales was still a relatively poor, geographically diffuse, and underdeveloped country of less than half a million inhabitants. It remained primarily a nation of small farmers. It lacked flourishing commercial centres and people with money to invest in culture. Intellectual currents which ran swiftly elsewhere were slow to penetrate Wales and only in Dissenting academies was a stimulating education available. Shielded in their native land from contact with contemporary fashions and tastes in European culture, many of Wales's most talented sons were drawn to English universities, cities, and towns. The long-distance flow of migrants tended to run in an easterly direction, for there was little contact between the inhabitants of north and south Wales. Indeed, Iolo Morganwg went so far as to claim, with typically colourful exaggeration, that north and south Wales had 'no more intercourse with each other than they have with the man in the moon'.[2] Moreover, the lack of major cities and towns inhibited the ambitions of the gifted and prompted them to look elsewhere for intellectual stimulus, colour, and excitement. Wales possessed few clubs, salons, societies, or

[1] Thomas Pennant, *Tours*, ii. 158–9.
[2] G. J. Williams, 'Bywyd Cymreig Llundain yng nghyfnod Owain Myfyr', *Y Llenor* 18 (1939), p. 74.

coffee houses which might act as foci for the development of the arts. Although a small number of societies sprang up in various parts of Wales after 1750, few were able to thrive. Most were flimsy or esoteric affairs. In rural Merioneth, local gentlemen and poets established *Y Gymdeithas Loerig* (The Lunar Society) in the 1760s, a literary society which met monthly at the time of the full moon at Drws-y-nant, near Dolgellau. According to Rhys Jones of Blaenau, members were called upon to exchange doggerel, praise Bacchus, gulp like fish, howl like wolves, and toast Hymen and Sir John Barleycorn. More genteel habits were evident at the weekly gatherings in Cardiff of the Sociable Society of Ladies, which discussed the world of letters over tea and coffee in the 1750s. Fostering literature was rather less prominent among the aims of the Druidic Society of Anglesey, founded in Beaumaris in 1772: this was a private benevolent organization designed to encourage good works, stimulate agricultural improvements, and provide life-saving facilities at sea.

In contrast, the city of London could boast a rich variety of societies, clubs, meetings, and associations, as well as a host of attractive salons, coffee houses, chocolate houses, theatres, concert halls, taverns, and whore-houses. It was well known to Welshmen as a fount of pleasure and a sink of impiety. Indeed, by the mid-eighteenth century, the annual flow of gentlemen and masterless men to the capital was increasingly swollen by professional men, merchants, and craftsmen. London was by far the largest urban complex in England and Wales and growing numbers of middling sorts were attracted by the glitter of its lights. Isolated and often frustrated by the lack of economic opportunities in Wales, they ventured to London in search of new and exciting challenges. Welsh bards assured them that it was a dynamic, cosmopolitan city which offered resourceful and diligent settlers seemingly limitless opportunities for making their fortunes. Those who grasped the widening economic opportunities generally inhabited the densely populated regions around St Paul's or settled in the new and prosperous residential areas of the city. Not all ambitious Welshmen, however, were either impressed by the glamour of London or able to make their fortunes. To Lewis Morris, London was 'a bush of thorns',[3] a devilish world of scribblers, cheats, drunkards, prostitutes, and pickpockets. Those who failed to profit financially were either obliged to master evil habits, live on their wits, or return to their native land. During his sojourn in 'Folly's hateful sphere',[4] Iolo Morganwg yearned for his native Glamorgan more than words could tell. He was able to return to 'the Garden of Wales', but those who were trapped in poverty never escaped from their misery. Robert Lewis of Plas Llanfihangel in Anglesey, who had set

[3] Hugh Owen, *The Life and Works of Lewis Morris*, p. 262.
[4] R. Garlick and R. Mathias (eds.), *Anglo-Welsh Poetry 1480–1980* (Bridgend, 1984), p. 103.

himself up as a coach-builder in London, died deaf, deranged, and penniless in a workhouse.

Yet London proved to be, in many ways, a major focal point in the campaign to bolster and enrich Welsh culture. It was natural for London Welshmen to seek ways of maintaining their links with their native land and expressing their patriotic zeal. The Society of Antient Britons had done little to encourage Welsh letters but, thanks largely to the initiative of the Morris brothers of Anglesey, a new and forward-looking society, christened the Cymmrodorion (Aborigines), was founded in 1751. The Cymmrodorion Society, under the patronage of the Prince of Wales, met on the first Wednesday of each month, normally in the Half Moon tavern in Cheapside. Welshmen in exile, mostly gentlemen, lawyers, doctors, merchants, goldsmiths, glovers, brewers, apothecaries, printers, grocers, and craftsmen, gathered together at these meetings to eat, drink, and be merry. Society meetings, which were open to Welshmen by birth or extraction, were often extravagantly noisy and high-spirited. Most members were loyal, upright citizens, who drank effusive toasts to the Hanoverian dynasty and the established church and vowed to help promote the cause of Welsh learning. There were inevitably numerous hangers-on, few of whom nursed pretensions to literary taste but were attracted by the snob value of the Society. Lewis Morris, who always set great store by social niceties, would have liked to attract a stronger aristocratic element to the ranks of the Cymmrodorion and he unashamedly urged his brother, Richard, to disguise the obscure origins of the lowliest members. 'Let their titles be disguised as much as possible', he observed, 'that every English fool may not have room to laugh in his sleeve and say "such a society, indeed".'[5]

Richard Morris, the acknowledged father of the Cymmrodorion, bore the brunt of organizing the Society as its president from 1751 until his death in 1779. The aims of the Society, enshrined in the exotically framed manifesto, *Gosodedigaethau* (Constitutions) in 1755, were strikingly ambitious. The Society pledged itself to succour Welsh poets and authors, collect valuable ancient manuscripts, promote research into the study of Welsh history, stimulate scientific research, encourage economic developments, and publish learned material. This blueprint, though redolent of Moses Williams's dreams published as early as 1718, bears the unmistakable stamp of Lewis Morris's agile and fertile mind. Yet, few of these fine-sounding aims and noble promises were realized. It is true that the Cymmrodorion offered much-needed financial support to penurious poets and printers like Dafydd Jones and Huw Jones; it also sponsored campaigns against the appointment of non-Welsh-speaking incumbents to Welsh livings; and it awarded medals and bounties to acknowledge

---

[5] *Morris Letters*, ii. 386.

improvements in agriculture, forestry, and commerce. But in spite of much huffing and puffing, the Cymmrodorion Society failed not only to publish any scarce or valuable collection of Welsh manuscripts between 1751 and 1787, but also to maximize the considerable literary potential available to it. Indeed, only Thomas Pennant's *British Zoology* (1766) and the Welsh Prayer Book of 1770 bear the official imprint of the Society.

The Society's members turned out to be a huge disappointment to Richard and Lewis Morris. In spite of the shining example set by the 'Chief President', William Vaughan of Corsygedol, a colourful patron, poet, and bon viveur, few members either understood or cared about Welsh scholarship. They might style themselves 'ancient Britons' and develop a liking for ritual and pomp, but a wealth of good intentions, nostalgia, and empty patriotic gestures was simply not enough. Lewis Morris was appalled by the lethargy and ignorance of members. When Hugh Hughes's *Cywydd yr Ardd* (The Cywydd to the Garden) was read aloud during a meeting in 1757 the members unanimously called for an immediate English translation and exegesis. Most members attended meetings simply in order to drink and be merry into the small hours, and they were not prepared to open their purse-strings sufficiently widely to enable the Society to fulfil its aspirations. Both Richard and Lewis Morris plied members with a number of fertile projects, but few positive signs of encouragement were received and every attempt to create a 'learned' society bore little fruit. Owing to the shortage of ready cash, Richard Morris constantly found himself mollifying exasperated authors or stalling critics. As a result, many promising schemes died of inanition. Moreover, death robbed the Society of some of its most faithful supporters in the 1760s: William Wynn died in 1760, William Morris in 1763, and Lewis Morris in 1765. Even so, its membership grew from 168 in 1759 to 228 in 1778. The most significant downturn in its fortunes came following the death of Richard Morris in 1779. By 1787, the year in which the Society became defunct, membership had plummeted to seventy.

Hard upon the heels of the Cymmrodorion came the Gwyneddigion (Men of Gwynedd), a society founded in 1770 especially for the benefit of exiles from north Wales. Following Richard Morris's death, Owen Jones (Owain Myfyr), a prosperous currier from Llanfihangel Glyn Myfyr in Denbighshire, became the most enthusiastic promoter of Welsh causes in London. He and Robert Hughes (Robin Ddu yr Ail o Fôn), a solicitor and assistant secretary and librarian of the Cymmrodorion, resolved to turn the Gwyneddigion into the show-piece of Welsh culture by providing a popular forum for stimulating and wide-ranging discussions. The Society's doors were opened to all London-based Welshmen, provided they were fluent Welsh-speakers and fond of singing. Unlike the Cymmrodorion, it attracted people from more modest backgrounds, usually teachers, printers, solicitors, merchants, craftsmen, and taverners. Meetings were crowded with talented, lively, even mischievous, young men who put a high premium on warm sociability and jollification. Huddling together each month in intimate groups in taverns such as the 'Goose and Gridiron' in St Paul's Churchyard and the 'George and Vulture' in Lombard Street, they were all animated by a burning desire to be of service to their native land. Members were more optimistic and democratic, less pretentious and less eager to get on in the world than the Cymmrodorion, and they found the study of the current cultural and political predicament of Wales at least as invigorating as the study of the past. If Gwyneddigion meetings always reverberated to the sound of the harp they also often, especially after the French Revolution, echoed to the noise of passionate political debate. By the 1790s the Gwyneddigion had become not only the promoters of Welsh history and literature but also the power-house of early Welsh radicalism.

Owing to the parsimony of its members, the Cymmrodorion Society yielded a disappointingly thin crop of literary fruit. Most of the worthwhile literary ventures of the mid-eighteenth century were thus sustained either by individual initiatives or by the Morris Circle. The Morris Circle was an exclusive circle of savants, critics, poets, and scholars, all of whom were men of considerable distinction and talent. The hub of the circle was Lewis Morris, a man who had a great talent for gathering like-minded spirits about him and firing them with his own enthusiasms. In a sense, Morris headed a disparate group, but each member was in fact sustained by shared intellectual aspirations and by the frequent interchange of copious letters. Lewis Morris was a surveyor, a steward, and a Crown agent, who pursued his literary interests during hard-earned moments of leisure. He was a capable poet, a perceptive literary critic, and a writer of considerable skill and vitality. But, above all else, he loved to manœuvre and manipulate people. An inveterate social climber, he hungered for public acclaim and loved to hob-nob with men of superior rank and wealth; in an age of sycophants, Lewis Morris was among the most extravagant of flatterers. Nothing gave him greater pleasure than to receive an invitation to a spacious country or town house where he might coax a nobleman to heap lavish praise on his projects. He basked in the favour of the earl of Powis, plying him with ornate pedigrees and collections of specimens as a mark of his gratitude. A volatile, egotistical man, he established contacts with the best minds of day. 'His knowledge', declared James Phillips sarcastically, 'is only equalled by his modesty.'[6] By all accounts, he was a singularly unpleasant man and certainly a difficult one to live with. John Owen, his nephew, took no pains to hide his contempt for his self-seeking, boastful, and libidinous uncle. Londoners referred to him as 'the proud hot

[6] *Add. Letters*, ii. 496.

Welshman', while Iolo Morganwg, who resented Morris's reputation as a literary critic and his habit of disparaging south Walians, called him 'a damned scoundrel'.[7] Yet he was the presiding genius of the Morris Circle. An enormously busy and influential man, he supervised and counselled young poets and authors, and genuinely sought to advance their careers. His door or post-bag was always open to receive requests for guidance, and those who deigned to shun his attentions were never forgiven. Like so many of his contemporaries, he was slow to forget a wrong and he often allowed personal grudges to cloud his critical faculty. During his blackest moods, Morris seldom disguised his hatreds and many of his protégés came to resent and fear his sarcasm. Yet for all his fickle ways, his loathing for hack-poets, his contempt for philistine gentlemen, and his abomination of Methodism, he was impossible to ignore. Indeed, Lewis Morris was convinced that the responsibility for recovering, maintaining, and enriching Welsh letters and antiquities had fallen upon him and his brothers.

Whereas Lewis Morris provided the dynamic ideas and scholarly authority which governed the activities of the Morris Circle, his brother, Richard, was saddled with the administrative burdens of linking members and advertising the official activities of the Cymmrodorion. Richard Morris had arrived in London from Anglesey around 1722, had fallen in love with the city, and spent the next fifty-seven years of his life attending to his duties as a clerk in the Navy Office, where, according to his own testimony, he was almost constantly submerged under administrative chores. Like his brother Lewis, Richard's capacity for hard work was proverbial. But unlike Lewis, Richard was incorruptible: tumbling with prostitutes was not to his taste. And whenever he found himself at odds with others, he took great pains to pour oil on troubled waters. Credulous, soft-hearted, and almost naïvely open-handed, he was forever worrying over or cossetting lame ducks and it is not surprising that unscrupulous people often took advantage of his solicitude. His other brother, William, was an excise officer at Holyhead and a man who clung solidly to his Anglesey roots. William was a scholar, a sage, an amateur physician, and an expert horticulturist, whose botanical collections and gardens were a wonder to behold. He was a gentle, modest, solemn man who liked to ponder life's adversities and little ironies with an air of melancholy, and sometimes cynical, resignation.

The Morris brothers saw themselves as not only the heirs of Edward Lhuyd but also as the guardians of Welsh letters. They, in effect, were the new patrons of the Welsh literary heritage and their enthusiastic labours did much to compensate for the hostility of anglicized gentlemen and the lethargy of the rank and file of the Cymmrodorion. They established

[7] *Morris Letters*, i. 346; B. F. Roberts, 'Ymagweddau at Brut y Brenhinedd', p. 138.

contact with a number of scholars and poets who were beginning to rise to maturity and who, like themselves, were prepared to devote a substantial part of their leisure hours to the task of recovering and preserving 'old writings on vellum'.[8] Those who came under the wing of the Morrises were men of diverse talents, style, and attainments, but they all shared a warm enthusiasm for their native land, a keen awareness of the civilizing influence of classical Greece and Rome, and a deep affection for the literary and poetic treasures of the past.

Among the most prominent members of the Morrises' charmed circle was Goronwy Owen. Born in a small cottage in Llanfair Mathafarn Eithaf in Anglesey in 1723, Owen acquired a classical education, attended Jesus College, Oxford, was ordained a deacon at the age of 22, and seemed destined not only to win high preferment within the church but also to achieve greatness as a poet and a classical scholar. But Owen was a highly strung and insufferably self-centred man who was almost constantly at odds with himself and the rest of the world. He served successively as schoolmaster and curate in places as far apart as Oswestry, Uppington, Donnington, Walton, and Northolt, and pined for his native county—'the serene and beautiful Mother of Wales'.[9] His life was characterized by fecklessness, drink, and despair, and, as his disaffection grew, the petulance and boorishness which had been evident since his excessively spoilt childhood found increasingly ready expression. His self-destructive failings prevented him from climbing the ladder of preferment within the church and he found friendships hard to cultivate and even harder to sustain. Often, only drink could assuage his bouts of depression. Lewis Morris used his best endeavours to map out his life for him and to persuade fellow poets and scholars that Owen was 'the greatest genius of his age'.[10] But relations between them soon deteriorated as Morris received reports of his protégé's bibulous ways. 'What beggar, tinker or sowgelder ever groped more in the dirt?', Morris thundered, 'he drinks gin or beer till he cannot see his way home . . . and yet when he is sober his good angel returns and he writes verses sweeter than honey and stronger than wine.'[11] Such criticisms caught Owen on the raw and he composed a satirical cywydd—Cywydd i'r Diafol (The Cywydd to the Devil)—in which he averred that there was more evil in Lewis Morris than in the Devil himself. Owen continued to lurch from crisis to crisis, his spurts of creative writing became fewer and fewer, and in 1757 he emigrated to the colony of Virginia in search of settled employment. His life in America, however,

---

[8] Add. Letters, ii. 790–1.
[9] J. Gwilym Jones, Goronwy Owen's Virginian Adventure (Williamsburg, Virginia, 1969), p. 23.
[10] Add. Letters, i. 232.
[11] Morris Letters, i. 489.

was also beset with misfortune and, according to one of his pupils, a surfeit of rum proved his ultimate destruction.

Another scholar who joined the Morris Circle and whom Lewis Morris showered with sonorous aphorisms and practical advice was Evan Evans. Born in Lledrod, Cardiganshire, in 1731 and educated at Merton College, Oxford, Evans developed into a prodigiously learned scholar. A ruddy, vigorous, athletic man, Evans was known as 'Ieuan Brydydd Hir' (Ieuan the Tall Poet). He possessed all the attributes of the true scholar—learning, dedication, honesty, and perseverance—but he, like Goronwy Owen, was a maddening man with whom to deal. Save for an aberrant four-day sojourn in the 34th Regiment of Foot, Evans devoted his life to seeking a church preferment commensurate with his abilities, to serving the cause of Welsh scholarship, and imbibing prodigious quantities of alcohol. In spite of his undoubted learning and passionate attachment to the Anglican cause, avenues of advancement within the church remained closed to him. For Evans, like Moses Williams and Griffith Jones, was an outspoken critic of the system of clerical promotion, the miserable stipends paid to curates, and standards of pastoral efficiency. Moreover, he was an avowed enemy of Saxon bishops, leaping Methodists, and tithe-grabbing landowners. His biting tongue, vanity, and heavy dependence on alcohol did not endear him to the men who counted in Welsh society. Lewis Morris regularly chided him for 'running into all manner of vices'[12] and begged him to abandon his dissipated and foolish habits. Evans, however, continued to flit from Wales to England and back again, from curacy to curacy, and from tavern to alehouse. He remained edgy, bitter, and unfulfilled, and his principal consolation came from his scholarly labours. He had an enormous appetite for study, and his books and voluminous transcripts were so bulky that two men and horses were required to move his library in 1767. He plodded or rode around Wales, visiting private libraries, gathering and copying manuscripts, and selling books. At times he was virtually forced to beg in order to keep body and soul together. For seven years he enjoyed the patronage of Sir Watkin Williams Wynn, but the last ten years of his life after 1778 were spent in abject and utterly disorganized penury. Even his friends and acquaintances tired of his financial importunities and he died penniless, in 1788, in the lonely farmhouse where he had been born.

The Morris brothers possessed a happy knack of coaxing scholars who were addicted to solitude to write creatively: one of them was Edward Richard of Ystradmeurig, Cardiganshire. A tailor's son, Richard was a burly, bookish bachelor who buried himself in rural Cardiganshire and devoted six years of his life to the arduous task of mastering the classics,

<hr>

[12] Ibid., i. 356.

divinity, and mathematics. From 1746 onwards, young classical scholars flocked to his school from all parts of Wales. Richard steeped himself in the works of Spenser, Milton, Dryden, Swift, and Pope, gained a working knowledge of French, and devoted his talent and energy to building up the reputation of his school. A modest, self-effacing man who enjoyed good food and wine, Richard would have shut himself away from the pressing needs of Welsh culture had not Lewis Morris and Evan Evans persuaded him to nurture his blossoming gifts as a poet and to establish links, by letter, with other leading scholars within the Circle. 'You do me a great deal of honour', he wrote to Lewis Morris in 1762, 'and yourself a little credit in taking me by the hand, and by forcing me to turn out with you into the field of criticism.'[13] William Wynn, successively vicar of Llanbryn-mair and Llangynhafal, was also a fastidious scholar who, in his own words, dwelt in an 'obscure corner' of Wales. Wynn was a melancholy, fretful soul who, until he began to correspond with other Welsh scholars and benefit from their infectious enthusiasm, feared that life promised nothing more for him than 'scribbling Welsh sermons'.[14] Spurred on by the Morrises, however, he collected and copied an enormous corpus of manuscript material, composed a smattering of verse, and even plucked up enough confidence to lecture Robert Hay Drummond, bishop of St Asaph, for anathematizing the Welsh language.

An erudite scholar like Thomas Pennant of Downing in Flintshire was also attracted by the buzz of cultural activity animated by the Morris Circle. Pennant was an agreeably civilized, if vain, Oxford-trained man, who took great pride in his Welshness and in his extensive learning in the fields of ornithology, geology, and antiquity. At first, Lewis Morris found him a soft, innocuous 'namby-pamby sort of man',[15] but Pennant's literary and scientific interests soon won over the Morrises. Evan Evans, too, was impressed by his erudition and versatility. Equipped with an enviable breadth of travel and experience in Europe—he once visited Voltaire, who revealed to him his whole repertoire of English curses—Pennant astonished even himself by the multiplicity of his works. He wrote a mass of important and unimportant literature, ranging from *British Zoology* (1766) and the *History of Quadrupeds* (1771) to essays on the improper behaviour of married ladies towards men.

Many other poets, scholars, and historians found themselves almost irresistibly drawn into the Morris Circle, even if only by means of sporadic correspondence. Among them were Hugh Hughes, *Y Bardd Coch* (the Red Poet), of Anglesey, an accomplished bard noted for his asperities; Robert Thomas, a gifted autodidact and sexton of Llanfair Talhaearn in

---

[13] *Add. Letters*, ii. 554.
[14] R. G. Hughes, 'William Wynn, Llangynhafal', *Llên Cymru* I (1950-1), p. 24.
[15] *Morris Letters*, i. 337.

Denbighshire; and John Bradford, an extraordinarily well-read Deist from Glamorgan. Although members of the Morris Circle dwelt in different parts of Wales (and England), they wrote copious and frequent letters to each other. The Morrises themselves urged them to keep in constant contact, bestowed upon them large helpings of advice, and bade them fill their correspondence with details of their researches and compositions. In this way, patriotic sentiment was fostered; so, too, was the interchange of information, the development of critical comment, and the emergence of new ideas. Until he died, grossly overweight and apoplectic, in 1765, Lewis Morris was the major driving-force of the Circle. Every spare moment in his busy life, so it seemed, was spent promoting literary and antiquarian projects, advising, criticizing, and scolding poets, transcribing manuscripts, and reading proofs. His life provided clear testimony of the triumph of the will and spirit over the weakness of the body. Moreover, he succeeded in kindling in others a burning passion for knowledge. His fellow scholars laboured without stint to collect, collate, and copy old Welsh manuscripts, and their letters rarely failed to convey the intellectual excitement and sheer delight which they experienced whenever priceless literary treasures were uncovered in worm-eaten chests or dusty vaults. 'What do you think I have at my elbow, as happy as ever Alexander thought himself after a conquest?', wrote Lewis Morris smugly to Edward Richard in 1758, 'we have found an epic poem in the British called Gododdin, equal at least to the Iliad, Aeneid or Paradise Lost.'[16] They scoured book catalogues avidly, eyed private collections with pent-up frustration, pestered gentlemen for access to their libraries, and treasured their own collections with jealous pride. Goronwy Owen once informed Evan Evans that he would sooner part with his own wife than entrust him with his manuscripts.

It is not easy to measure precisely the influence of the labours of the Morris Circle upon the Welsh language, its poetry, literature, and history. There is no doubt that its members worried profoundly about the condition of the Welsh language and its capacity to withstand the gradual encroachment of the English tongue. Although Welsh continued to be the predominant language of the overwhelming majority of the people of Wales, and although only a few relatively small areas could be said to be totally anglicized, Saxon incursions were a matter of some concern to scholars. Along the Welsh borders, in particular, the advance of the English language was presenting a growing challenge to the strength of the native tongue. Jonathan Hughes, the Llangollen poet, claimed in 1757 that the English language was flowing irresistibly into eastern Wales and drowning monoglot communities. In fact, by the latter half of the eighteenth century, a relatively clearly identifiable bilingual zone stretched

[16] *Add. Letters*, i. 349.

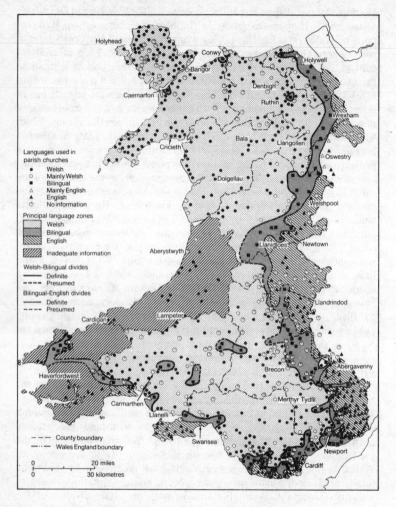

MAP 3. The Principal Language Zones in Wales, *c.* 1750

from north-east Flintshire, through east Montgomeryshire and east Breconshire into the lowlands of east Monmouthshire, and thence along the coast into the vale of Glamorgan. Small, but significant, shifts in the linguistic patterns of church worship were occurring in the eastern counties of Wales, especially in communities where English incumbents had settled or where Welsh clergymen were too pusillanimous to resist the demands of insistent immigrants or local landowners. The English language was clearly gaining rapid ground at the expense of Welsh, notably in the Marcher towns. In 1770 Joseph Cradock observed that the citizens of the towns of coastal Flintshire were so much more anglicized than their country cousins in the uplands that 'they could be taken as natives of different countries'.[17] The town of Wrexham was said to be 'perfectly Englished',[18] whilst migrant workers were swiftly establishing commercial footholds in the lead-mines and coalfields of the north-east. Further south, the Welsh language had receded westwards so rapidly in Radnorshire that it had vanished from the lips of all but the most aged inhabitants of the county. It is not surprising that an English evangelist like John Wesley had no difficulty in making himself understood in these parts. Similarly, the decay of Welsh in eastern Gwent was well under way by the latter half of the eighteenth century and gathered pace as new industrial developments were established.

Members of the Morris Circle could do little to stem the flow. But they lost few opportunities to berate Welsh landowners who, having been groomed at English public schools, the universities, and the inns of court to take up their place in society, were no longer willing to speak the Welsh language or to shoulder the responsibility and expense of supporting Welsh culture. In 1766 Richard Morris observed, more in sorrow than in anger, that many of the Welsh gentry bore malice in their hearts towards the Welsh language. Many of the leading gentry, conscious of the social disadvantages of their mother tongue, believed that the Welsh language was a handicap to learning and a barrier to economic prosperity and social acceptance. Powerful social and economic changes had led them to adopt English habits of speech, thought, and behaviour, and few of them were now prepared to succour the poets, the traditional guardians of the Welsh tongue. In his most celebrated poem, Evan Evans caught the mood of the age as he mourned the passing of old shrines of patronage:

> The Court of Ivor the Generous! How pitiful the sight,
> It lies a tumbled heap among the alders.

---

[17] Joseph Cradock, *Letters from Snowdon* (London, 1770), p. 106.
[18] W. T. R. Pryce, 'Approaches to the Linguistic Geography of Northeast Wales, 1750–1846', *NLWJ* 17 (1972), p. 354.

> Thorns and thistles have inhabited there,
> And bramble where once was splendour.[19]

Evans firmly believed that those who abandoned their native language for that of their conquerors publicly wore the badge of their vassalage. He bitterly assailed Anglo-Welsh bishops who decried the Welsh language and hastened its demise by appointing English incumbents to serve in parishes where the Welsh language was predominant. The Morris correspondence is riddled with satirical cameos of pompous non-Welsh-speaking bishops and gentlemen, and this reflected their determination not only to sustain the Welsh language but also to vent long-buried resentments against the English. Those scholars who settled briefly in England nourished anglophobia by airing their prejudices. Goronwy Owen—not the most balanced witness—chafed miserably in English cures, finding the people of Donnington surly, hard-faced, and intolerant. The good people of Walton, he insisted, were no better than Hottentots. Within Wales, too, patriotic scholars and truculent peasants were equally hostile to the English. 'A Scot or a Saxon is above correction',[20] claimed Lewis Morris, whilst Hugh Hughes, 'the Red Bard', seldom concealed his scorn and contempt for *plant Alis* (the children of Alice). A growing awareness of the country's historic past and of the plight of the Welsh language fostered a new sense of patriotism which English travellers were swift to note. The Honourable John Byng, fifth Viscount Torrington and the most dyspeptic and insular of Little Englanders, was horrified to find Welshmen who spoke of England as a foreign country: 'this idea', he fumed, 'their language has kept up'.[21] *Sais yw ef syn* (He is a Saxon, beware) was a common sentiment among peasants, and Joseph Cradock was much irked by the opprobrious epithets which Welshmen attached to the words 'English' and 'Saxons'.

The Morris Circle not only bolstered the Welsh language by fostering patriotic sentiments; they also strove to standardize its orthography and purify its vocabulary. They believed that whereas the English language was an impoverished mongrel language, pieced and patched from the tongues of other nations, the Welsh language was copious, felicitous, elegant, and virile. It was, according to Goronwy Owen, 'adequate to the highest strains of panegyric and abundantly fitted by copiousness and significance to express the sublimest thoughts'.[22] Staunch efforts were made to enrich the Welsh vocabulary in order to invest it with even greater flexibility and esteem. Thomas Richards of Coychurch in Glamorgan, a cultured cleric who believed that the Welsh language was the ancient language of the 'aborigines' of Britain, received handsome financial support and advice

---

[19] Saunders Lewis, *A School of Welsh Augustans* (Wrexham, 1924), p. 143.
[20] *Add. Letters*, ii. 623.   [21] John Byng, *Torrington Diaries*, i. 293.
[22] J. H. Davies (ed.), *The Letters of Goronwy Owen*, p. 38.

from the Morris brothers as he strove to publish a Welsh–English dictionary in 1753. His *Thesaurus Antiquae Linguae Britannicae* enabled authors and poets who possessed no Latin to study the pioneering dictionary of Dr John Davies, Mallwyd, published in 1632. Similarly, John Walters's *tour de force*, a massive English–Welsh dictionary published in parts between 1770 and 1794, contained new words, such as *geiriadur* for 'lexicon' and *tanysgrifio* for 'subscribe', deliberately invented in order to meet current demands. Fervent Welsh scholars remained convinced that Welsh was a primeval language, and their claims were fortified by Bullet's sweeping assertion in *Mémoires sur la langue celtique* (1754–60) that Celtic was 'a dialect of the original language communicated by the Creator to the first parents of mankind'.[23] Some extraordinarily bizarre notions were peddled. Rowland Jones, a Welsh-born barrister in London who liked to count himself among the friends and acquaintances of the Morrises, published five books between 1764 and 1771 in which he argued the case for recognizing the Welsh language as the first universal and philosophical language of mankind. Small wonder that Lewis Morris believed Jones to be 'touched in the head'.[24] However, even those who did not subscribe to such romantic notions were convinced that the Welsh language was a gift from God and that its survival had been nothing less than providential. Griffith Jones of Llanddowror, whose admiration for the Welsh language is writ large in his correspondence, believed that divine wisdom had decreed that a variety of tongues should flourish in different parts of the world and that God had vouchsafed his favours to the Welsh language. No self-respecting Welsh scholar would have disagreed with Rhys Jones of Blaenau when he maintained that 'the most High has given us strength and resilience to withstand all the incursions of our enemies'.[25] Nor would he have gainsaid a word of Richard Rolt's encomium:

> A language fit for angels; graceful, rich,
> Gay, copious and sublime; transcending far
> The voice of nature spoke in other climes.[26]

The Morris Circle was also deeply interested in Welsh poetry, notably the heroic poetry of medieval times. Following the example set by Edward Lhuyd and Moses Williams, Lewis Morris strove to publish anthologies of Welsh medieval poetry. As early as 1732, he publicized his hopes of establishing in his native Anglesey a Welsh press, a free school, a bookshop, a national library, and a museum. Three years later he published *Tlysau yr Hen Oesoedd* (Jewels of Ancient Times), a popular

---

[23] C. W. Lewis, 'The Literary History of Glamorgan', in *Glamorgan Co. Hist.* 4 (1974), p. 634.
[24] *Add. Letters*, ii. 616.
[25] Rhys Jones (ed.), *Gorchestion Beirdd Cymru* (Shrewsbury, 1773), sig. B1ᵛ.
[26] Richard Rolt, *Cambria: A Poem* (London, 1749), p. 26.

selection of Welsh classical poetry. However, penny-pinching gentlemen refused to support his ambitious ventures and Morris proceeded to turn to advantage his own undoubted abilities as a poet. His free stanzas, notably *Caniad y Gog i Feirionnydd* (Song of the Cuckoo to Merioneth)—a *laudatio* to the fair maidens of Merioneth—and *Lladron Grigyll* (The Robbers of Grigyll)—a vivid portrait of notorious smugglers—were accomplished pieces of craftsmanship. Moreover, he set himself the task of collecting literary treasures and visiting as many major libraries as possible. Not even the parsimony of noblemen nor the indifference of bishops could stifle his driving ambition to revive the Welsh tradition of heroic poetry. He and his brothers found the duty of supporting and encouraging promising young poets irresistible. 'Pwy na lithia feirdd fel hyn?' (Who would not nurture poets like these?) was a constant refrain in the Morris correspondence.

Goronwy Owen was probably their most brilliant and promising pupil. In more ways than one, Owen was a rum bird. A cultivated but feckless man, his capacity for exuding self-assurance and self-pity at the same time often tested the patience of his patrons. Essentially a cerebral poet and a conscious stylist, Owen's poetry, more than that of any other Welsh contemporary, reflected the style and manners of the Augustan mode. His reverence for Homer, Virgil, and Horace was unbounded and his best poems reflected the canons of measured eloquence, politeness, and clarity which his classical masters had perfected. He also steeped himself in the muse of the English Augustans and in the metrical devices of traditional Welsh poets. No one brooded longer than he over the possibilities and frailties of the Welsh poetic tradition and he nursed a much-publicized, but unfulfilled, ambition to compose a definitive Miltonic epic in Welsh. The quality of his poetry has always been the subject of debate and in recent years the pendulum has swung in his favour and probably rightly so. His *cywyddau*, notably *Cywydd y Farn Fawr* (The Cywydd to the Day of Judgement)—which Lewis Morris confessed was 'the best thing I ever read in Welsh'[27]—were dignified, eloquent pieces of work which exercised a profound influence on future generations of poets. As a poet, however, he shone brightly for a brief period only; he found more solace in alcohol than the pen and his promising career ended in drunken obscurity in the fastnesses of Virginia in 1769.

Like Goronwy Owen, Edward Richard also wrote sparsely and his major contribution to Welsh letters was the pastoral poems which, composed in classical style, were published in 1770. Richard was devoted to the classics and it was at his feet that Evan Evans acquired his reverence for Greek and Latin texts. Evans feverishly devoted long hours to the task of discovering,

[27] Glenda Carr, 'Goronwy Owen (1723–1769)', *Trans. Anglesey Antiq. Soc.* (1969–70), pp. 114–15.

collecting, and transcribing Welsh poetic treasures, and by the mid-1760s he had acquired a reputation as the outstanding authority on early Welsh poetry and literature. He was determined to place Welsh scholarship on a sound and enduring foundation and it is in him that tensions between patriotic enthusiasm and intelligent scepticism come into sharpest focus. English poets and antiquarians such as Gray, Carte, Percy, and Pegge had developed a consuming interest in Welsh poetry and legends and swiftly established close contacts with Evans. Thomas Gray's celebrated poem *The Bard* (1757) related how the last Welsh bard to survive the bitter persecution of Edward I hurled a curse at the conquering invading armies before leaping into Conwy's foaming flood. Shades of romanticism were clearly lengthening over the study of Welsh poetry, and Evans, though he welcomed the growing interest in the heroic poetry of his native land, was reluctant to be caught up in these enthusiasms. For his principal aim was to set standards of scholarly rigour and professionalism. He viewed the romantic notions of ill-informed Celtic scholars with unqualified mistrust and strenuously urged the need for painstaking and reliable scholarship. He was particularly contemptuous of the poems attributed to Ossian. In 1760 James Macpherson, a Scottish scholar, published a translation of what purported to be ancient Gaelic poems composed by Ossian, a Caledonian bard reputed to have lived in the third century. In Europe, Ossian's works were hailed as extraordinary discoveries. English scholars, too, greeted them with such great applause that they swiftly became the talk of coffee houses and drawing-rooms. Evan Evans, however, pronounced them patently spurious and sourly censured contemporary scholars for their naïvety.

Determined to assert Wales's own cultural identity and to publicize its glorious poetic tradition, in 1764 Evan Evans published his major work, *Some Specimens of the Poetry of the Antient Welsh Bards*. This volume was a real landmark in the history of Welsh letters, for it revealed the emergence of an acknowledged master of the intellectual past. The *Specimens* contained three sections: translations of ten Welsh poems into English; a Latin treatise entitled *De Bardis Dissertatio*; and a collection of original Welsh poems. Although it was mauled by several ill-informed English scholars, Evans's volume was a truly pioneering work which offered scholars the first serious study of the development of Welsh poetry from the sixth to the fifteenth century. Uncluttered by fabrication or artifice, it was a solid and enduring testimony to the genius of the greatest Welsh scholar since Edward Lhuyd. Few works exercised a more decisive influence on Welsh scholarship prior to the twentieth century.

The Morris Circle also revived interest in the Welsh poetic tradition by encouraging less celebrated but equally dedicated poets to publish collections of verse and making them available to humbler sections of the

Welsh reading public. Lewis Morris's attitude towards 'hack-poets' was ambivalent: he was happy to consult them, but he did not recognize them publicly among his circle of friends and acquaintances. He admired the florid verses of Huw Morys, Wales's leading poet in Stuart times, but the amateur poets of his own day he regarded as blockheads and idiots. Janus-like, he scorned and yet supported the labours of printers, poets, and booksellers. Conscious of Lewis Morris's pride and his notions of status and social niceties, cultured peasants such as Huw Jones of Llangwm and Dafydd Jones of Trefriw pressed him with mischievous glee to assist them. By filling his *Dewisol Ganiadau yr Oes hon* (Select Poems of this Age, 1759) with selections of the poetry of Evan Evans, Goronwy Owen, and William Wynn, Huw Jones secured dozens of subscriptions from Lewis Morris's well-heeled friends in London. Indeed, *Diddanwch Teuluaidd* (Family Entertainment, 1763), an anthology of poems composed by several Anglesey poets (including Lewis Morris himself), was edited and prepared for the press by Lewis and Richard Morris on behalf of Huw Jones. Members of the Morris Circle always viewed themselves as a more than ample substitute for waning aristocratic patronage and strove to cater for current tastes in Wales. Their most popular and handsome publication emerged in 1773: *Gorchestion Beirdd Cymru* (The Masterpieces of the Welsh Poets), edited by Rhys Jones, a freeholder and poet of Blaenau in Merioneth, was a collection of extracts drawn from the works of the bards of the Welsh princes and gentry. Over six hundred subscribers were prepared to pay for the privilege of reading the 'oldest and most splendid' poetry of Aneirin, Taliesin, Dafydd ap Gwilym, Iolo Goch, Dafydd Nanmor, Tudur Aled, and Wiliam Llŷn. One of the most impressive achievements of the Morris Circle, therefore, was not only to cajole, encourage, and bully poets to bestir themselves but also to cater for the needs of the scholarly middle class and bookish peasants. In so doing, they ensured the survival of the Welsh poetic tradition, protected its integrity, and evoked a new sense of pride and confidence. Rhys Jones of Blaenau rejoiced to find 'the Muse bursting forth from the graves of the skilled bards in unalloyed splendour'.[28]

Conversely, the Morris Circle was less successful in fostering Welsh prose. Although many of its members were well-versed in the works of Milton, Dryden, Pope, and Swift, and regularly subscribed to English periodicals and journals, they were not inspired to fill the considerable gap which existed in the field of the essay, the novel, and *belles-lettres*. Lewis Morris was probably the only Welsh scholar of his day to believe that the literate middling sorts should be given the opportunity to exercise their minds on something other than sermons, devotional books, classical prose,

[28] Rhys Jones (ed.), *Gorchestion Beirdd Cymru*, sig. B2ᵛ–B4ʳ.

and poetry. By pillaging the works of Boileau, l'Estrange, Pope, and Swift and turning their ideas and material into lively and humorous Welsh prose, he produced essays, lampoons, and epigrams which were enormously entertaining. His satires, such as *Doctor y Bendro* (Doctor Staggers) and *Llythyr Mari Benwen* (Mary Whitehead's Letter), were brilliantly inventive and witty. Many of his unpublished manuscripts are remarkable for their cutting edge and swift, penetrating insights. Indeed, Lewis Morris's prose works merit far more respectful attention than they have hitherto received.

However, it is the correspondence of the Morris Circle which provides the most admirable and enduring proof of the skills of these scholars as writers of prose. The eighteenth century was the golden age of letter-writing, and the most agreeable and informative body of Welsh correspondence in this period is the celebrated 'Morris Letters'. Over eleven hundred letters have survived and they clearly reveal that members of the Morris Circle did for Wales what Horace Walpole achieved for letter-writing in England: they turned it into a form of art. Each member, but more particularly the Morris brothers themselves, was endowed with 'an itch for scribbling'.[29] 'While we are in this world', declared Lewis Morris, 'it is a good thing to keep up the old custom of doing as the horses do, to rub against one another.'[30] Correspondents viewed letter-writing as the continuation of conversation by other means, and, as a result, they often wrote as they spoke, writing at great speed and interspersing their sentences with spontaneous cries of *Wawch*! or *Wala hai*! Many letters, written in exuberant and irrepressible vein, were riddled with sentences which spilled over into parentheses, digressions, ejaculations, and subordinate clauses. Since their 'epistles', as they often called them, were a natural extension of conversation, much of their appeal lies in their spontaneity. In such a garrulous age, short letters were frowned upon, and to neglect to reply to a letter was an unforgivable sin. Indeed, one suspects that many letters were couched in deliberately provocative tones in order to encourage swift replies. Letters were filled with vivid flesh-and-blood portraits of contemporaries, scandalous gossip, venomous anecdotes, bursts of spleen, and frivolous asides. Correspondents often leapt disconcertingly from subject to subject, moving with ease and assurance from matters of local gossip to scholarly debates. Whole paragraphs were devoted to the symptoms and effects of coughs, colds, sneezes, and other more dire ailments. Deeply sensitive to each other's cries of pain, they were also acute observers of other men. Lewis Morris's letters, in particular, are crammed with wonderfully witty, malicious, and indelicate comments about his contemporaries. His letters to or about Goronwy Owen, for instance, are a mixture of admiration and adjuration, affection

[29] *Morris Letters*, i. 342.   [30] *Add. Letters*, ii. 603.

and abuse, compassion and calumny. Impelled by a burning desire to inform and entertain recipients, Lewis Morris and his fellow scholars produced a corpus of correspondence which vividly conveys what it was like to live in mid-eighteenth-century Wales. Almost every page of these fascinating letters yields information of unusual interest and animation.

The importance of the Morris Letters, however, lies not only in their considerable originality and freshness. What also raises them far above other collections of correspondence prior to the twentieth century is their extraordinary literary merit. The fact that the vast bulk of the letters were couched in Welsh is in itself significant. Among the gentry, English was the language of private correspondence and members of the Morris Circle were the first to respond enthusiastically to persistent calls made by Moses Williams, John Rhydderch, and Dafydd Jones to enhance the prestige of the Welsh language by using it as their medium of correspondence. Although their letters were written in Welsh and English, sometimes both, Welsh was their first love. They were deeply interested in words—both old and new—and took mischievous delight in parodying dialects and modes of speech. Indeed, much of the appeal of the letters lies in the allusive subtlety of their written prose, their curious juxtaposition of words, and their unusual application of local and metropolitan dialects. As befitted men who enjoyed the cut and thrust of literary debates, they plied each other with ancient proverbs, wise sayings, snatches of poetry, and intriguing intellectual problems. Only industrious and intelligent scholars who were conscious of the literary potential of the letter could have produced such a readable and informative source of reference.

The study of the history of Wales was also a cause close to the hearts of members of the Morris Circle. No group of scholars did more than they in the eighteenth century to rescue their native history from 'the dirt that is thrown upon it'.[31] They were so acutely aware of the injustices of the past that, to them, Welsh history was a tale of repeated injuries, usurpations, and conquests. In order to foster a renewed sense of patriotism and to protect the good name of their nation, they strove to shore up rickety Welsh legends and fables. Although Theophilus Evans had once more revealed his gift for making history come alive by publishing a new and amended version of his highly popular *Drych y Prif Oesoedd* in 1740, Geoffrey of Monmouth's fabulous tale had lost much of its lustre and credibility by the mid-eighteenth century. Sceptical English scholars poured scorn on the 'British history' and scholars reared in the new rationalism of the Welsh academies were equally contemptuous of old medieval tales. But Lewis Morris and his disciples were convinced that their ancestors were being 'shamefully abused in their graves by our

[31] Ibid., ii. 447.

modern wits'.[32] Morris himself was insatiably curious about the past and was determined to rehabilitate the 'British history' and pursue research in the fields pioneered by Edward Lhuyd. He spent thousands of leisure hours during a period of forty years compiling his 'Celtic Remains, or the Ancient Celtic empire described in the English tongue', two bulky manuscript volumes which he feared would eventually be used for wrapping tobacco but which, in fact, were published in part in 1878. Morris also sent new blood coursing through the veins of pallid Welsh legends. He was convinced of the authenticity of Geoffrey of Monmouth's work and went to some pains to traduce those Welshmen—both dead and living—who had the temerity to deny the substance of the myth of glorious origins. By definition, he insisted, those who poured scorn on Geoffrey were traitors. Thus, William Lloyd, former bishop of St Asaph, was reviled as 'the despiser of his country', a shameless coward who had 'shit in his nest'.[33] Following prolonged and fruitful correspondence with Thomas Carte, a highly regarded English antiquary, Lewis Morris became convinced that the original author of *Brut y Brenhinedd* was Tysilio, son of Brochwel Ysgithrog, a seventh-century saint, and that Geoffrey of Monmouth had simply amended and embellished this early version. He became obsessed with this theory, and although other commitments prevented him from venturing into print he continued to bore his friends and acquaintances with tedious recitals of his discoveries until his death.

Evan Evans was also deeply conscious of the need to render accessible to the Welsh reading public valuable historical treasures, which had for too long been locked away in the dust-covered vaults and libraries of the gentry. He regularly importuned the Cymmrodorion Society, the Society of Antiquaries, and prosperous noblemen to publish historical manuscripts lest they be made 'liable to a thousand accidents'.[34] Renewed interest in Welsh antiquarian studies led to the publication of Lord Herbert of Cherbury's *Life* in 1764, an edition of Sir John Wynn's celebrated *History of the Gwydir Family* in 1770, and a new *History of Anglesey* by the learned Welsh scholar, John Thomas of Beaumaris, in 1775. Evan Evans's patriotism was invariably supported by an appeal to history. He urged men of learning to beware of Saxon historians, notably 'despicable scribblers'[35] such as Lord Lyttelton and Joseph Cradock, who had looked askance at the valiant deeds of Welsh princes. He strove to rehabilitate 'brave Llywelyn' and 'valiant Glyndŵr' in the eyes of his countrymen, and sang their praises in fulsome verse:

[32] W. J. Hughes, *Wales and the Welsh in English Literature* (Wrexham, 1924), p. 155.
[33] *Add. Letters*, ii. 623, 631.
[34] Aneirin Lewis (ed.), *The Correspondence of Thomas Percy and Evan Evans* (Louisiana State UP, 1957), p. xxxi.
[35] D. Silvan Evans (ed.), *Gwaith y Parchedig Evan Evans* (Caernarfon, 1876), p. 131.

> The great Glyndŵr no longer could contain,
> But, like a furious lion, burst the chain,
> None could resist his force: like timorous deer
> The coward English fled, aghast with fear.[36]

Not least among the many achievements of the Morris Circle was their success in bringing into the limelight faded Welsh heroes whose valorous exploits had lain in obscurity.

Although the unstinting efforts of the polymathic members of the Morris Circle exercised a decisive influence upon Welsh literary and historical studies, they did not impose a rigid, father-like rule on Welsh culture and scholarship. The group itself was too loosely knit to be able to bring together conflicting convictions and philosophies. In many ways, in fact, they divorced themselves, sometimes unconsciously but often deliberately, from some of the most creative and dynamic forces at work within Wales. The literature of inward experience, as expressed by Methodist evangelists and hymnologists, was foreign to them. Methodism, in their eyes, was an odious religion peddled by Jesuits, goblins, thieves, and counterfeits— 'vermin [who] creep into all corners through the least crevices'.[37] Their contempt for tub-thumping preachers was prompted largely by their fear that Methodism represented seventeenth-century fanaticism in a new but more sinister form. The natural reflex of the Morris brothers, in particular, was to view change with suspicion, and although they sought to focus on what was distinctive about Welsh culture, they did not always reflect the changing world in which they lived. Those looking for perceptive comments on the quality of Methodist literature and the blossoming artistry of Pantycelyn will find the Morris letters a sad disappointment. Part of the explanation for their neglect of Methodism lies in their contempt for the language, dialect, and literature of south Wales. John Bradford believed that the men of Gwynedd found the 'hodge podge' of his Glamorgan neighbours as distasteful as it was unintelligible. Iolo Morganwg, too, deeply resented the disparaging comments of arrogant northerners, and it is as well perhaps that Lewis Morris had died before Iolo truly began to dip his pen in vitriol. To Goronwy Owen, the vocabulary of Glamorgan was 'Gibberish, Hottentotice',[38] and it was against this background of abuse and contempt that Evan Evans deliberately baited Robert Hughes by insisting that none had done more to sustain the Welsh language than the scholars of south Wales.

Even though members of the Morris Circle were intensely inquisitive men they did not chronicle every salient movement in the cultural life of Wales. They either disparaged or ignored peasant culture. The Morris

---

[36] Ibid., pp. 141–2.
[37] Add. Letters, ii. 394.
[38] J. H. Davies (ed.), The Letters of Goronwy Owen, p. 69.

brothers believed that the works of 'hack-poets', rhymesters, scribblers, interlude-writers, and almanackers were contemptible and worse than useless. Huw Jones of Llangwm, an incorrigible plagiarist and rogue, was variously described by the Morrises as a 'sneak', a 'cur', and a 'foolish owl',[39] whilst Dafydd Jones of Trefriw was bitterly assailed for 'murdering' *Blodeu-gerdd Cymry* (Welsh Anthology, 1759) by including in it 'the works of the greatest blockheads in the Creation'.[40] Lewis Morris constantly bemoaned the fact that there were 'more geese than swans' in Wales, while Goronwy Owen, whose scorn for peasant poets was as great as that of Pope for the hacks of Grub Street, despised what he liked to call 'gibberish à la mode'.[41] Owen advised Ellis Roberts, the cooper-poet, to buy string to measure his sorry verse, a saw to cut it into lengths, and a plane with which to trim it. 'All sorry stuff', observed William Morris of Welsh almanacs, 'it wouldn't pay to pick them up off the ground.'[42]

However articulate, well-informed, and influential members of the Morris Circle might have been, there were other kinds of culture in Wales which were fuelled by an increasingly thriving printing and bookselling trade. The volume of printed material grew considerably in this period and much of it was cheap, accessible, and tailored to suit popular demand. Between 1731 and 1760 as many as 452 Welsh books were published. During the two decades from 1761 to 1780, however, the number of published works increased swiftly to 746. The average publication of Welsh books rose from ten a year in the 1730s to forty a year by the 1770s. As Welsh towns grew, so did the number of printing-presses. The success of the circulating schools and the flowering of Methodism and Dissent in general helped to advance educational standards and broaden the reading public. Literate peasants were eager for a regular fare of devotional books, doctrinal works, printed sermons, religious verse, elegies, chap-books, interludes, almanacs, ballads, and anthologies of poetry.

As a result, the book trade in Wales flourished as never before. Sensing a growing market and the probability of reasonably worthwhile profits, printers and booksellers began to proliferate in number. Along the Welsh border, printing-presses at Shrewsbury, Wrexham, and Chester continued to supply the needs of the reading public in mid- and north Wales. Lack of gentry support thwarted Lewis Morris's plans for establishing a permanent printing-press at Holyhead in 1735, but his Anglesey colleagues were sufficiently resourceful to make full use of presses in Dublin. Following

---

[39] Tom Parry, *Baledi'r Ddeunawfed Ganrif* (Cardiff, 1935), p. 4.

[40] *Add. Letters*, ii. 432.

[41] G. J. Williams (ed.), 'Llythyrau at Ddafydd Jones o Drefriw', p. 8; J. H. Davies, *Letters of Goronwy Owen*, p. 140.

[42] *Morris Letters*, i. 81.

years of dogged industry as a publisher and bookseller, Dafydd Jones set up his own press at Trefriw in Caernarfonshire in 1776. In south Wales the Gwent market was tapped by the Farley family of Bristol, which, sponsored by local Baptists, established a short-lived press in Pontypool in 1740. The Trefeca press, established in Howel Harris's commune in Breconshire in 1759, helped to promote the cause of Methodism, whilst Rhys Thomas proved a pleasingly accomplished and skilful printer at Carmarthen (1760-4), Llandovery (1764-71), and Cowbridge (1771-90). From the 1760s onwards, Carmarthen probably supplanted London and Shrewsbury as the most vigorous and prolific centre of Welsh publishing. John Ross, a Scotsman who served his apprenticeship as a printer in London and who became a fine craftsman and an experienced businessman, settled in Carmarthen in 1763. He swiftly revealed an unusual capacity for maximizing profits and pleasing the reading public, and over a period of forty years he published hundreds of books, pamphlets, sermons, and bibles. By 1780 further printing-presses had been established at Brecon, Swansea, and Haverfordwest.

Not all Welsh printers, by any means, were proud craftsmen. In his books Dafydd Jones of Trefriw regularly included suitably contrite explanations for printing errors, even on one occasion blaming his infelicities on a dearth of the letter 'y'. Books published by John Rowland at Bodedern and Bala were appallingly shoddy and riddled with misprints. The texts published by Shrewsbury printers were also, according to William Morris, littered with intolerable typographical errors. Yet, small printers who were endowed with a peasant shrewdness and a nose for business managed to earn a precarious living. None of them expected to make a fortune, but those who were prepared to work hard, assemble an efficient team of booksellers and agents, and offer a variety of small, cheap, and attractive books were rewarded. By selling a thousand copies of *Blodeu-gerdd Cymry* (1759) at 2s. 6d. a copy, Dafydd Jones made a profit of some £63. Authors and publishers either stumped the countryside themselves as salesmen, or employed pedlars and carriers to collect subscriptions and distribute books. Jonathan Hughes of Pengwern, Llangollen, travelled from county to county in a bid to increase sales of his anthology, *Bardd a Byrddau* (Poet and Tables, 1778) while Richard Roberts, a schoolmaster, took 500 copies of *Y Credadyn Buchedol* (The Virtuous Believer, 1768) to distribute among subscribers at Chester fair. Not all booksellers and agents, however, were trustworthy. Indeed, many of them were feckless, mischievous men, given to hard drinking and cunning deceit. Evan Thomas (Ieuan Fardd Ddu) of Llanfair Caereinion, an almanacker, printer, and bookseller, was reputed to drink beer as an ox drinks water and, predictably perhaps, died in a Shrewsbury workhouse in 1814. Huw Jones of Llangwm pocketed all the profits accruing from the sale of *Dewisol Ganiadau* (1759) without sending as much as a penny to the printer, William Roberts of London, who subsequently ended his days in a workhouse. Evan James, one of Evan Evans's assistants, made a habit of scratching out the names of subscribers from his account book with his penknife and making off with his employer's hard-earned profits.

Yet subscription ventures were indispensable in so far as they offered publishers the comfort of security. Such schemes might attract up to 1,500 buyers, and those who subscribed for multiple copies received favourable terms. As a result, attractively packaged anthologies of Welsh poetry were particularly well received. Huw Jones's *Dewisol Ganiadau* (1759) included twenty-six pages of subscribers, totalling 1,045 individual names, made up largely of tanners, corvisors, smiths, miners, weavers, curriers, glaziers, tailors, glovers, millers, joiners, farmers, gardeners, bookbinders, harpers, and poets. Similarly, Dafydd Jones's popular anthology of the works of Welsh poets both old and new—*Blodeu-gerdd Cymry* (1759)—attracted 738 subscribers. The circulation of books such as these was, of course, considerably greater than the number of subscribers. Books, especially those which contained poems or religious verse, were passed from hand to hand and from home to home. They were evidently listened to either on the hearth or at informal reading groups. This meant that the products of the press were made more easily available to a widening cross-section of society.

Such schemes demonstrate clearly that the common man's zest for poetry had never been greater. By this period a new class of Welsh poets, many of them humble farmers and craftsmen, had emerged. In Denbighshire, a small but gifted coterie of lively poets, led by Jonathan Hughes of Llangollen, John Thomas of Pentrefoelas, and John Edwards (*Siôn y Potiau*) of Glyn Ceiriog assembled regularly to practise their craft and discuss ways and means of advancing the cause of popular poetry. Similarly in Glamorgan, a highly versatile band of poets and grammarians (mostly Dissenters)—Rhys Morgan of Pencraig-nedd, Lewis Hopkin of Llandyfodwg, John Bradford of Betws Tir Iarll, Dafydd Nicolas of Aberpergwm, and Edward Evans of Aberdare—were steeped in medieval and modern poetry and laboured diligently to stimulate wider interest in strict-metre poetry, the vocabulary of the bards, dialectology, and lexicography. Old masters, well-versed in the ancient metres, continued to shape the values of young poets. Cultured greybeards like Rowland Huw of Y Greienyn, near Bala, or Siencyn Thomas of Cwm-du, Cardiganshire, ensured that the bardic tradition lived on as an oral art in their communities. Siôn Dafydd, a humble but cultivated clogmaker and labourer who spent the whole of his life in the upland village of Pentrefoelas, Denbighshire, proved an inspiring tutor to many budding poets. It was he who nurtured the careers of Huw Jones, Dafydd Jones, Ellis Roberts, and Jonathan Hughes, and who taught Twm o'r Nant the principal elements of the poetic art. Furthermore, by assiduously copying and assembling an astonishingly wide variety of poetry in manuscript form, antiquarians like Benjamin Simon of Abergwili, Margaret Davies of Coedcae Du, Trawsfynydd, and Dafydd Jones of Trefriw rescued invaluable material from oblivion. Local *eisteddfodau*, too, helped to foster competitive standards as well as preserve old traditions. Even so, it was the printing-press which increasingly revivified Welsh poetry. John Rhydderch's grammar book, published in 1728, was heavily thumbed by Glamorgan poets throughout the eighteenth century. Goronwy Owen first learnt the essentials of the poetic craft from printed books. 'Oatmeal poets'[43] such as Huw Jones and Dafydd Jones earned their pennies by editing and selling popular and entertaining collections of poetry.

If the press was vital to the purposes of Welsh poetry, so it was too for Welsh music. As we have seen, the nature and quality of indigenous Welsh music were shrouded in obscurity. As the gentry acquired a taste for flutes, harpsichords, and violins, the *pibgorn* and *crwth* vanished. The triple harp was now counted the principal national instrument of Wales, much to the distaste of Margaret Davies of Coedcae Du, who believed that the new Italian styles were as incomprehensible as they were sophisticated. Harp music remained close to the hearts of common people, and in Caernarfon-shire and Merioneth—'the singing countries',[44] as Lewis Morris called them—*canu gyda'r tannau* (singing to the harp) flourished mightily. Posses of wandering harpists, minstrels, and gypsies (the last-named led by the legendary Abraham Wood and his family) roamed the countryside, entertaining the peasantry with their fiddles and harps and searching for temporary employment in gentry mansions or taverns. Elizabeth Baker, the Dolgellau diarist, found harp music alarmingly durable in her locality during the 1770s. During his tour of north Wales in 1784 John Byng, fifth Viscount Torrington, was entertained for two hours by a Welsh harper, who played melodies such as 'Sweet Richard', 'Sir Watkin's Delight', and 'Morfa Rhuddlan', airs which Byng believed might in bygone days have gladdened the breast of Llywelyn ap Gruffudd and stiffened the resolve of Owain Glyndŵr.

Seminal works in the sadly neglected field of Welsh music were also emerging. In spite of his blindness, John Parry, the most celebrated Welsh harpist of Georgian times, began to study native Welsh music from refreshingly new perspectives. A native of Nefyn in Caernarfonshire, Parry was a highly accomplished musician who, under the patronage of the Wynns of Wynnstay, shone among the galaxy of talent which filled the concert halls and salons of London. By the 1740s he was lionized by

[43] G. J. Williams (ed.), 'Llythyrau at Ddafydd Jones o Drefriw', p. viii.
[44] *Add. Letters*, ii. 583.

aristocrats and composers alike. His recitals of the music of Corelli, Geminiani, Handel, and Vivaldi were played with vivid distinction. Indeed, it was Parry's skill as a harpist which inspired the poet Thomas Gray to complete his ode, *The Bard*. Aided by his amanuensis, Evan William, Parry sifted painstakingly through a mass of manuscripts, the fruits of which were published in *Antient British Music* (1742) and *British Harmony* (1781), both invaluable and handsomely printed collections of ancient Welsh airs. Further detailed research by Edward Jones of Henblas, Llandderfel—'the King's Bard'—brought to light many haunting but long-forgotten airs, stanzas, and *penillion* which helped to 'save from oblivion the remains of the bards'.[45] Jones's *Musical and Poetical Relicks of the Welsh Bards* (1784) was another major landmark in the campaign to recover and sustain the musical treasures of Wales.

There were also other profitable veins to be worked. Increasingly, during this period, popular Welsh music was being influenced by the songs and arias sung in English ballad-operas in the theatres, taverns, and streets of London. Welsh ballad-mongers and harpists tailored this material to suit the needs of humble social groups, notably small farmers, craftsmen, and labourers, who were availing themselves of the opportunity to attend schools and acquire reading skills. Although, like most ephemera, only a small proportion of Welsh ballads has survived, they clearly enjoyed a wide and ever-growing circulation. Sold by pedlars, hawkers, and ballad-mongers in packs of two or three, at a penny or two a time, ballads had no pretensions to literary merit. Printed on poor paper and sometimes illustrated with crude woodcuts, they were simply designed to appeal to peasants who were anxious to be instructed and entertained. Their strength lay in their novelty and variety. Many of the extraordinary topics which scandalized Methodists—romantic courtships, monstrous births, strange visions, and gruesome murders—were grist to the ballad-mongers' mill. Such themes never staled with repetition.

Indeed, the demand for ephemera was seemingly insatiable. Thousands of Welsh almanacs were sold annually, on the one hand providing publishers with their principal source of income and on the other supplying humble people with edifying and entertaining reading material. Although the almanacs compiled and peddled by Evan Davies, John Prys, and Gwilym Howel lacked the freshness, wit, and variety which had characterized the work of the earliest pioneers like Thomas Jones and John Rhydderch, they sold in greater numbers. They remained cheap, popular, and accessible. Intrepid almanackers were scarcely deterred by heavy stamp-duties, judging by the enormous sales of pirated and unstamped almanacs. In order to circumvent taxes, the most enterprising pirates published

---

[45] T. Ellis, 'Edward Jones, "The King's Bard" (1752–1824)', *Journal Merioneth Hist. and Record Soc.* 4 (1961–4), p. 127.

mongrel almanacs in Dublin, christened them *Cyfaill* (Companion), and
from 1761 onwards flooded the Welsh market with up to 20,000 annual
copies. Indeed, 1761 is something of a landmark in the history of Welsh
almanacs, for it was in that year that John Robert Lewis established the
Holyhead dynasty, which published remarkably popular annual almanacs
until 1954.

The growth of the Welsh reading public also impelled poetasters,
printers, and publishers to search for fresh and entertaining material which
would create new tastes. The popular but sadly short-lived periodical,
Trysorfa Gwybodaeth, neu Eurgrawn Cymraeg (Treasury of Knowledge,
or Welsh Magazine, 1770) offered a rich variety of interesting and
entertaining tit-bits, including collections of poetry, domestic and foreign
news, medicinal advice, and short essays on such subjects as the merits of
tobacco and 'Shall we know each other in heaven?'. The most effective
publicist of new popular tastes was Dafydd Jones, the versatile and
colourful sexton of Trefriw. Jones, a firm believer in the maxim that no
good ever came from idleness, was an inveterate collector of oddities and
ephemera. Animated by a burning desire to provide common readers with
entertaining literature, he published a regular flow of small and often
crudely illustrated chap-books, filled with love stories, adventures, horrors
and wonders, prophecies and visions. Tales of Judas Iscariot, Dr Faustus,
and 'A Pennyworth of Wit' were presented in a Welsh garb and quickly
found favour with humble readers. Variety was the keynote: Jones's
enormously popular *Cydymaith Diddan* (Lively Companion 1766), for
instance, included allegories, dialogues, religious verses, satirical portraits,
conversation pieces, snippets from old essays and letters, extracts from
medieval literature, and extempore sermons. Subscription lists clearly
reveal that a large and appreciative audience derived great pleasure from
such works.

As the eighteenth century advanced, the need to create and sustain a
theatrical tradition in Wales was also recognized. Here, more than in any
other field perhaps, the absence of Welsh institutions, large cities, and
ready capital had proved inimical to the development of artistic talent. But
as Welsh towns began to grow and the literate public acquired new tastes
and a greater sense of confidence, amateur playwrights began to fashion
popular satirical interludes to meet the needs of the new society. Nothing
appealed more to rustic audiences in north Wales than the coarse humour
and biting satire of these plays. Most of them were composed by farmers,
craftsmen, and artisans who dwelt in the vales of Conwy, Clwyd,
Edeirnion, and Llangollen: Jonathan Hughes of Llangollen was a farmer
and a sexton; Huw Jones of Llangwm was a farmer-cum-bookseller; and
Ellis Roberts (*Elis y Cowper*) of Llanddoged was a cooper. The prince of

Welsh interlude-writers, however, was Thomas Edwards (*Twm o'r Nant*). Born in 1739 in the parish of Llanefydd, Denbighshire, Edwards is a splendid example of a child who inherited few advantages but was determined to exploit his capacities to the full. He was brought up in harsh circumstances; his father, who was illiterate, sought to thwart his literary ambitions by beating him furiously. Save for a brief period of schooling, Edwards was more or less self-taught. As a young child, his main pleasure was 'to read and trace a poem',[46] and so eager was he to learn that he made ink from elderberries and practised his letters on scorched sheets of paper rescued from a fire at the village shop. An old cooper of Nantglyn and Twm Tai-yn-Rhos, an illiterate local poet, offered him tuition in the art of poetry, whilst Siôn Dafydd of Pentrefoelas, introduced him to the secrets of the ancient bards and to the world of books in general. Edwards read everything he could lay his hands on and soon blossomed into a gifted poet, dramatist, and humorist. For most of his life, however, he remained down on his luck, and in order to eke out a living he was obliged in turn to be a labourer, timber haulier, tollgate-keeper, publican, and stone-mason. A born survivor, he weathered a number of traumatic experiences which would have flattened lesser men. Whenever personal problems and debts weighed unduly heavily upon him, he composed and sold interludes in order to earn a few extra pounds. These rough-hewn plays were a blend of comic fun, biting satire, and brooding irony. So popular were they that Edwards was saluted in exaggerated fashion as 'the Cambrian Shakespeare'[47] by his contemporaries.

Anterliwtiau (Interludes) commanded widespread affection among the peasantry. Companies of amateur actors advertised their arrival either by sounding trumpets or by informing the parish sexton, who announced details of forthcoming performances to his congregation during church services. An admission fee of a penny often attracted two or three hundred people each night in Welsh market towns, especially during wakes and festivals held between May and September. A handful of male actors provided some two hours of entertainment on makeshift stages outside taverns, in streets, or on barn-floors in farmyards. The interludes themselves were essentially loosely strung dialogues and snatches of song. Few of them were formally or deliberately divided into specific acts and scenes. They were informal, often slapdash, compositions turned out at great haste; Elis y Cowper was reputed to be able to compose an interlude within three days. Twm o'r Nant's compositions, by his own admission, were like magpies—pied and patchy. Like all peddlers of ephemera, interlude-writers were none too scrupulous about appropriating the labours of others without acknowledgment. Themes and plots were culled

[46] O. M. Edwards (ed.), *Gwaith Twm o'r Nant* (Llanuwchllyn, 1909), pp. 108–9.
[47] Prys Morgan, *Eighteenth Century Renaissance*, p. 46.

from the Scriptures, old Welsh legends and fables, and English chap-
books.

The stock characters in a Welsh interlude, generally presented as types
or 'humours', usually included an innkeeper, a miserly landlord, a bullying
steward, a persistent tax-collector, and a hard-pressed husbandman. The
principal characters were invariably the Fool and the Miser. The Fool
normally wore a colourful waistcoat, peruke, mask, tail, and bells, and
carried a phallus. His role was to sing, dance, interrupt other actors, and
offer snatches of pithy advice or ribald hints to the audience. Conversely,
the Miser, who usually dressed in an old tattered cloak, cap, and mask, cast
a misanthropic gloom over the proceedings and was duly mocked for his
avarice and dishonesty. Although printed interludes appear to be crude
and unpolished, as a form of oral communication they were often so
brilliantly clever that they held audiences in thrall. Much of their appeal lay
in their preoccupation with exposing gross injustices and petty deeds of
tyranny within society. They deliberately championed the cause of the
underdog and the oppressed. To that extent they provide an invaluable
looking-glass into the values and prejudices of the peasantry. Twm o'r
Nant took particular delight in unbuttoning the pretensions of humanity.
His most celebrated and frequently performed interludes—*Tri Chryfion
Byd* (The Three Strong Men of the World), *Pleser a Gofid* (Pleasure and
Sorrow), and *Cybydd-dod ac Oferedd* (Avarice and Vanity)—were littered
with satiric portraits, colourful expressions, and canny home truths. Nothing
gave him greater pleasure than exposing the hypocrisy, covetousness, and
sloth of the rich and the privileged, and his cameos of characters, such as
Sir Tom Tell Truth, Reginald Money-bags, and John Eye-of-the-Penny,
were especially artfully sketched. Dissolute clergymen, self-righteous
evangelists, and parasitic lawyers were also mercilessly lampooned.
Nevertheless, the use of obscene gestures and lewd expressions on stage,
however much they were relished by the participants and hearers, was
despised by those who affected more delicate sensibilities. In the eyes of
Elizabeth Baker, the well-bred diarist of Dolgellau, no Welsh interlude
was free from the taint of obscenity. William Bulkeley, of Bryn-ddu in
Anglesey, judged interlude-playing an 'abominable custom',[48] whilst Evan
Evans believed that such frivolous pursuits were fit only for 'clowns and
rustics'.[49] The truth is, however, that Thomas Edwards was a master of
irony and ridicule. He was a poet who has not received the recognition and
acclaim he deserves. Theatrical experiences through the medium of Welsh
were few and precious to common people, and it is significant that many of
his verses embedded themselves in the popular memory until the late

[48] Hugh Owen, 'The Diary of William Bulkeley', p. 58.
[49] T. J. R. Jones, 'Welsh Interlude Players of the Eighteenth Century', *Theatre Notebook*
2, No. 4 (1948), p. 62.

Victorian period. Indeed, there is much still to admire in his works, rich as they are in aphorisms, insights, and flashes of genius.

The development of the urban economy of Wales also stimulated the interest of the gentry and the middling sorts in the popular English theatre. Welsh towns, especially in the south and along the borders, were seldom unable to offer some means of popular entertainment. Strolling players, entertainers with bears, puppets, or dancing dogs, conjurers, clowns, mountebanks, jig-makers, and actors showed off their talents in fairs and market-places. Some of the more gifted professional actors travelled in bands to prosperous market towns, seaside resorts, and fashionable watering-places. Their numbers increased markedly after 1737 when the Theatre Licensing Act, which curtailed the number of accredited playhouses in London, drove many talented actors out into the provinces. Travelling actors were often able to secure the support of affluent and enthusiastic patrons. Sir Watkin Williams Wynn of Wynnstay established, in a converted kitchen at his mansion, a playhouse where four plays were performed by local and visiting actors during an annual festival held between 1773 and 1787. Leading families in north-east Wales thus availed themselves of the rare opportunity of seeing performances of the plays of Shakespeare and Farquhar.

Many companies from Ireland, too, stopped off to perform in the towns of north Wales on their way to English theatres. In 1766 a Company of Comedians from the Theatre Royal, Dublin, performed plays such as *King Richard III* and *The Beggar's Opera* before large and appreciative audiences in Wrexham, Denbigh, and Oswestry—much to the envy and chagrin of Twm o'r Nant, who bitterly censured the upper classes for patronizing English comedy while never gracing his own performances. Travelling English companies helped to widen the range of culture available to polite audiences in country towns such as Brecon, Llandrindod, Monmouth, Swansea, Carmarthen, and Haverfordwest. In these towns people of cultivated tastes welcomed companies of touring players with enormous enthusiasm. At regular intervals after 1755, John and Sarah Ward's company of strolling players toured the Welsh borders, performing some of Farquhar's plays. During their first visit on 5 July 1755 to 'The Shoulder of Mutton' in Brecon, their daughter Sarah gave birth to a girl, Sarah Siddons, who later became a remarkably successful actress. Ward's son-in-law, John Kemble, also brought the wit, style, and sophistication of metropolitan life to Welsh provincial towns. During the 1770s he took his cast to towns as far apart as Brecon, Monmouth, and Carmarthen to perform works such as *She Stoops to Conquer* and *The Country Wit or Humours of Sir Mannerly Shallowbrains*.

Increasingly during this period the upper classes, especially along the

Welsh borders and in Glamorgan and Monmouthshire, immersed themselves in metropolitan culture and were delighted to acquire the intellectual gifts and polite virtues which city life conferred upon them. Frequenting London not only enabled them to familiarize themselves with the new cultural tastes which were freely discussed in smoke-filled clubs, taverns, and coffee houses, but also helped them to distance themselves from their native heritage. Wales suffered much more than either Ireland or Scotland from England's ability to attract men of talent. To many affluent landowners and sophisticated intellectuals, the Welsh language was an embarrassment and its attendant culture tedious and uncultivated. More and more emphasis was being placed on the English tongue as the language of polite taste and advancement. The presence of academies, petty schools, dame schools, and grammar schools within provincial towns in Wales ensured that a high proportion of gentlemen, merchants, tradesmen, lawyers, and doctors were bilingual. English prose and poetry clearly enjoyed a wide circulation among the educated and leisured citizens who frequented coffee houses in polite centres such as Denbigh, Wrexham, Chester, and Shrewsbury. Lively minds kept abreast of current affairs by subscribing to weekly or monthly journals, such as the *Spectator*, *Tatler*, or *Gentleman's Magazine*, which were dispatched to the provinces in increasing numbers. Wood's *Shrewsbury Chronicle* and Adams' *Weekly Courant* from Chester were widely read in the Marcher counties and many bilingual readers in south-east Wales subscribed to the *Hereford Journal* and the *Gloucester Journal*. By 1780 John Potter, printer, binder, and stationer at Haverfordwest, was selling London newspapers to local gentlemen.

The elegance and brilliance of upper class society in London exercised a powerful influence on the major landowners of Wales. Their links with city life were made easier, too, as the emergence of the turnpike trust system during the latter half of the eighteenth century helped to improve the quality of major Welsh highways and thereby facilitated the speedy dispatch of newspapers, journals, and books. Lord Mansell of Margam bought copies of *Joseph Andrews* and *Clarissa Harlowe* shortly after their publication. Book clubs and subscription libraries also supplied gentlemen and clergymen with a wide range of political literature, current periodicals, philosophical works, and travel memoirs. Members of the Pembroke Literary Society, founded in 1741, were able to borrow the works of Adam Smith and Montesquieu as well as those of Leland and Camden. Individuals could also help to broaden the horizons of their friends and acquaintances. Elizabeth Baker, who settled in Merioneth in 1771, took the Shrewsbury papers regularly, read the works of Shakespeare, Swift, and Pope, and circulated them among her friends. During the 1770s John Griffith, curate of Llandysilio in Carmarthenshire and the proud possessor of over eight hundred books, cheerfully permitted his friends to borrow such works as Erskine's *Sermons*, *Robinson Crusoe*, and *The Life of Mahomet the Impostor*.

There is no doubt, too, that knowledge of the English tongue was spread through the academies. Not only did they promote oral and written communication through the medium of English, but they also emerged as forums for the intellectual ideals of the Enlightenment and radical thought. Most of those who exercised a considerable influence on international culture were products of academies. Richard Price established such a formidable expertise in the fields of theology, insurance, public finance, philosophy, and politics that eminent men such as Benjamin Franklin, Thomas Jefferson, David Hume, and Joseph Priestley corresponded regularly with him. David Williams of Caerphilly, a man of rare intellectual gifts who founded the Royal Literary Fund and was known as the 'Priest of Nature',[50] was deeply versed in the educational thought of Helvetius and Rousseau as well as the libertarian ideas of Voltaire and Franklin.

Nor should it be forgotten that members of the Morris Circle were genuinely interested in English letters. They corresponded regularly with English savants, antiquaries, and poets. Urban modes of poetry made a profound impression on Goronwy Owen, while Evan Evans was strongly influenced by the historical studies of Percy, Carte, and Macpherson. Edward Richard spent heavily on English and classical books in order to fill the shelves of his splendid library at Ystradmeurig school. The Cowbridge Book Society furnished Glamorgan scholars with a wide range of historical, literary, and topographical works. John Bradford and Lewis Hopkin were steeped in English and French literature. Lewis Morris pillaged the works of Dryden, Pope, and Swift for ideas, and some of his most vivid epigrams and lampoons carry the unmistakable imprint of burlesque 'Cockney' writers like Brown, D'Urfey, and Ward. Both William Williams, Pantycelyn, and Peter Williams published collections of hymns in English. They, like Evan Evans, composed English verse 'in order that men of learning in both languages may understand it'.[51] However, their principal literary medium was Welsh.

This was not the case among writers who pursued their literary careers outside Wales. Sir William Jones, son of the Anglesey mathematician of the same name, won international fame as a philologist and an expert on Hindu law. Wales and its language, however, were of little interest to him. He was once introduced to the French king as 'a man who knew every language except his own'.[52] Poets and writers who settled permanently in

[50] David Williams, *Incidents in My Own Life*, ed. P. France (University of Sussex, 1980), p. 2. [51] D. Silvan Evans, *Gwaith y Parchedig Evan Evans*, p. 132.
[52] Lord Teignmouth (ed.), *Memoirs of the Life, Writings and Correspondence of Sir Willliam Jones* (London, 1807), pp. 465–78.

London normally wrote in English. The diplomat, Charles Hanbury Williams (1708–59), a native of Pontypool, was a writer of such wit and elegance that Horace Walpole called him the greatest poet of his generation. Zachariah Williams, a madcap inventor from Rosemarket in Pembrokeshire, took his daughter Anna with him to London in 1727 and there, in spite of failing eyesight, she composed and translated poetry, essays, and plays, and established literary contacts with Garrick, Goldsmith, Johnson, and others. In 1766, through the good offices of Samuel Johnson, she published *Miscellanies in Prose and Verse*, a collection of elegant but superficial odes, elegies, fairy-tales, and short plays which is, perhaps, best left to rest in obscurity. Far more accomplished was the work of Evan Lloyd, a native of Bala who, from 1763 onwards, was the absentee vicar of Llanfair Dyffryn Clwyd. Lloyd was a talented letter-writer and a comic, satirical poet with a great zest for life. His contemporary reputation was built largely on the publication of four long poems between 1766 and 1768 —*The Powers of the Pen*, *The Curate*, *The Methodist*, and *Conversation*— which were hailed as remarkably witty and almost libellous attacks on vice and folly. In David Garrick's judgement, Lloyd was 'a man of genius'.[53]

Anglo-Welsh literature, however, was of small consequence when compared with the remarkable outpouring of sermons, hymns, elegies, prose classics, devotional books, and doctrinal works to which Welsh Methodism gave rise. The middle years of the eighteenth century witnessed an extraordinary awakening of interest in the language of enthusiasm which, in a sense, reflected the emerging mood of romanticism. By creating a pressing demand for a more intense, personal religion, Methodism not only helped to bring hope, confidence, and happiness into the hearts of many seekers but also produced a unique and indigenous culture of its own. Welsh Methodism was a 'heart-religion' and its most fervent adherents were both unshakably convinced of their own spiritual rectitude and hostile to what they believed to be the highbrow modishness of middle-class littérateurs and the arid intellectualism of Dissenters. Not all Methodists were bigots and obscurantists but most of them were not, by their very nature, deeply concerned with matters of scholarship. Indeed, they distrusted the intellect, shrank from rational discourse, and abhorred liberal ideas, thus inviting gibes that their religion was a compound of empty rhetoric and foolish paroxysms.

Yet the emotionalism which fuelled the fervour of the Methodist cause also produced a rich body of verse and prose. No one appreciated more than the leaders of Welsh Methodism the crucial role which hymnology could play among simple, unsophisticated people. Prior to the emergence

[53] C. J. L. Price, '*A Man of Genius, and a Welch Man*' (University College of Swansea, 1963), p. 3.

of Methodism, worshippers in the established church sang Edmund Prys's celebrated metrical psalms. Early Welsh Dissenters were anxious to ensure that hymns should evoke and express spiritual experiences, but the pioneering hymns of modestly talented men such as Thomas Baddy and James Owen were mostly based on scriptural teaching and were limited in the range of their imagery. But the 'vital religion' of Methodism gave birth to passionate and powerful hymns which not only expressed the essence of the movement but also helped to liberate and spread the evangelical message. In particular, the hymns of William Williams, Pantycelyn, became the major vehicle for disseminating the profound spiritual convictions which lay at the root of Welsh Methodism. The son of a Carmarthenshire farmer, Williams was born in 1717 and, like his fellow evangelists Harris and Rowland, was educated at Llwyn-llwyd academy. An exceptionally intelligent, discerning, and erudite man, he was trained as a doctor and he steeped himself in science, geography, and anthropology. Although he shared the same profound spiritual convictions as his Methodist colleagues, Williams was much more open-minded than they and much more receptive to different ideas and theories.

No Welsh hymn-writer has ever aspired to, or reached, greater heights than William Williams. Although his contemporaries, Dafydd Jones, Morgan Rhys, and Dafydd William, were fluent and accomplished hymnists, Williams Pantycelyn had much the greater reputation in his day. He is incomparably the greatest Welsh poet of the eighteenth century. He was also remarkably prolific. His first three publications—*Aleluia* (1744–7), *Hosanna i Fab Dafydd* (Hosanna to the Son of David, 1751–4), and *Rhai Hymnau Newyddion* (Some New Hymns, 1757)—were the work of an apprentice yet to achieve maturity. When Methodism recovered its vitality after 1760, however, Williams composed a series of works—notably *Caniadau (y rhai sydd ar y Môr o Wydr)* (1762), *Ffarwel Weledig* (Farewell Visible, 1763, 1766, 1769), and *Gloria in Excelsis* (1771, 1772)—which was immeasurably richer in content and expression. Always alive to the need to command the widest possible audience, Williams deliberately utilized the sway which music exercised over the sentiments of Welsh people. He was a fervent admirer of Vicar Prichard's catchy verses and he was also prepared to experiment with popular new measures in order to couch the Methodist message in intelligible and attractive forms. Some of his most celebrated hymns—*Iesu, Iesu, 'rwyt Ti'n ddigon* (Jesus, Jesus, Thou sufficest) and *Pererin wyf mewn anial dir* (A Pilgrim I in desert land)—are deeply rooted in scripture and replete with striking images. Williams became Wales's *Pêr Ganiedydd* (The Sweet Singer) and his hymns have been treasured by countless generations of worshippers to this day.

By fusing both oral and literary traditions, Williams articulated the great popular enthusiasm created by Methodism in vibrant hymns and sonorous prose. Given his education at a Dissenting academy and his experience as preacher, exhorter, and spiritual counsellor, he was uniquely equipped to convey in his literature the emotion, pain, longing, and eroticism which characterized the experience of so many converts. In his scriptural epics, for instance, he sought to capture the enormous passion and dynamic of evangelicalism. Where Goronwy Owen had failed, Williams succeeded: he composed two magisterial epics. The first, *Golwg ar Deyrnas Crist* (A View of Christ's Kingdom, 1756), the fruit of his compulsive curiosity, was designed to unfold the mysteries of the creation and the secrets of science but was effectively a hymn of praise to Christ. The second, *Bywyd a Marwolaeth Theomemphus* (The Life and Death of Theomemphus, 1764), the adventures of a pilgrim in search of salvation, was the work of a man reared on the Puritan notion that life was a pilgrimage from the cradle to a heavenly goal. In effect, it is a dramatic, stirring account of his own spiritual odyssey. The period after the Llangeitho revival of 1762 also yielded a fertile crop of remarkably penetrating prose works. Williams was ever conscious that the world was full of satanic temptations and his gifts as an amateur psychologist helped him to vent the daily spiritual problems of ordinary society members in *Templum Experientiae Apertum, neu Drws y Society Profiad* (The Door of the Experience Society, 1777) and sexual and marital relationships in *Ductor Nuptiarum, neu, Gyfarwyddwr Priodas* (A Guide to Marriage, 1777). Indeed, between 1744 and his death in 1791, Williams published at least ninety-two volumes, booklets, pamphlets, essays, and sermons. His lucid and dignified use of finely wrought images and rhythms of great lyrical beauty sets him apart as a literary craftsman of the highest order. It is true that a good deal of his work is uneven, colloquial, repetitive, and sometimes unduly coarse, but only the most myopic critic would deny his greatness as a writer. In his readiness to experiment and create material which was boldly innovative and yet wide in its appeal, he produced works of extraordinary imaginative power. It is his writings, more than any others, which best capture the ethos and dynamic of Methodism.

The discovery of Wales during the second half of the eighteenth century was also a vital element in the development of romantic sensibilities and the cult of the picturesque. Hitherto, the inaccessibility of Wales and its forbidding terrain, together with deeply ingrained prejudices against the Welsh, had deterred many travellers and painters from visiting Wales and recording the beauties of the landscape. But attitudes were now changing. Far from being a tedious and possibly perilous journey, a visit to Wales was now an adventure holding the prospect of aesthetic pleasures and rewarding experiences. Less daunted than their predecessors by hazardous roads, inclement weather, and what Wyndham called the 'heavy glutinous ale'[54] served in inns and taverns, travellers and tourists took their expeditions more seriously and, on balance, commented more favourably on what they saw. During the 1770s Joseph Cradock, William Gilpin, and Lord Lyttelton were all impressed by the natural beauty and diversity of Wales and spoke in admiring tones of jagged peaks, fertile valleys, sylvan meadows, and imposing ruins. But the most valuable and vivid account of Wales on the eve of the Industrial Revolution was provided by Thomas Pennant, the cultivated scholar, naturalist, and antiquary of Downing, Flintshire. On horseback, Pennant undertook three leisurely Welsh tours in 1773–6 and subsequently published his perceptions and discoveries. Inquisitive and indefatigable, he had a sharp eye for the unusual and a remarkable sense of time, place, and character. His evocative descriptions of country houses, churches, abbeys, castles, towns, tombs, artifices, flora, and fauna were interspersed with potted histories, pleasant anecdotes, and beguiling asides. His discoveries, moreover, were captured and enlivened by the felicitous drawings of his assistant, Moses Griffith, a labourer's son from Bryncroes, Caernarfonshire, who, as an 'untaught genius',[55] had entered Pennant's service in 1769 and accompanied him on his tours. Griffith produced watercolours of exceptional elegance and delicacy which evoked admiring comments from his master and other topographical artists.

The emergence of an indigenous artistic tradition in the field of painting also helped to project Wales as a land of romantic beauty. In the early 1740s the brothers Samuel and Nathaniel Buck became the first artists to depict the antiquities of Wales on a large scale. Inspired by a passionate desire to record the historic buildings of Wales, they produced attractive and valuable illustrations of an assortment of abbeys, castles, churches, mansions, and towns. Their labours and discoveries whetted the appetites of others. Beauty, mystery, and wonder were elements which were awakening profound emotions by the middle of the eighteenth century, and it was during this period that Richard Wilson, the founder of the British school of landscape, acquired his reputation as an artist of European distinction. A native of Penegoes in Montgomeryshire, Wilson was a coarse, irascible, ugly man who, sponsored by Sir George Wynne of Leeswood, served an apprenticeship as a portrait painter in London from 1729 onwards. In 1750 he left for Italy, the home of the Renaissance, and profited immensely from his studies in Venice and Rome. Six years later, he returned to Wales steeped in the classical tradition and committed to the cause of landscape painting. Although Wilson was indebted to the work of artists such as Poussin, Cuyp, and Ruysdael, there is no doubt that the most powerful influence upon him was Italian classicism. To Wilson,

[54] H. P. Wyndham, *A Gentleman's Tour*, p. 133.
[55] Thomas Pennant, i, p. iv.

Wales was a land of primitive simplicity, solitude, and tranquillity. But although his depictions of the peaks of Snowdon and Cadair Idris, the lakes of Llyn Cau and Llyn Peris, all captured the wildness and mystery of the native landscape, they still remain paintings of vistas through Italian eyes. Nevertheless, Wilson's capacity for expressing romantic emotion within a classical framework earned him undisputed supremacy in the world of the visual artist in Georgian Wales.

Widening interest in Druidic cults also epitomized the growing romanticism of the age. As historians, both reputable and otherwise, delved feverishly into the lore of the past, the study of Druidism acquired an even more seductive fascination than ever before. The search for druidic survivals intensified as new interest was generated, largely by middle-brow intellectuals, in native bardic traditions and the history of the Celts. Those who recoiled from the cool rationalism of Enlightenment thought were particularly susceptible to romantic, and sometimes bizarre, interpretations of the past. In cultured and debonair circles, there was no stigma attached to Druidism. The symbol of an ancient Druid appeared on the arms of the banner of the Cymmrodorion Society in 1751. In 1770 the Society's 'Chief President', Sir Watkin Williams Wynn of Wynnstay appeared in a London masquerade dressed in the costume of a Druid. John Parry, the harpist, believed that the Welsh musical tradition stretched back to the days of the ancient Druids, while Edward Jones's collections of traditional Welsh airs included 'A Druidical Song' and 'Y Derwydd—the Druid'. New editions of popular works stirred old nostalgias. A new and revised edition of *Mona Antiqua Restaurata* in 1766 enabled Henry Rowlands to cast a posthumous spell over learned opinion. Puzzled by the content of early Welsh poems and not too proud to admit his bemusement, Evan Evans hesitantly ventured the opinion that Taliesin's poetry might have contained 'Druidical Cabbala'. Some crazy individuals burst on the scene: in his *Philosophy of Words* (1769), a farrago of wishful thinking, Rowland Jones went so far as to dub Japhet a Druid, while John Cleland, author of *Fanny Hill*, offered the view that the Mass derived its provenance not from the words *missa est* but from the Druid's mistletoe!

No one was more obsessed by Druidism than Iolo Morganwg and it is fitting that this chapter should close with him, for he embodied most of the elements which loomed large in the lives of Welsh scholars—burning patriotism, a passionate commitment to Welsh poetry and literature, an acute awareness of the glorious origins of the Welsh, and a compulsive romanticism. Iolo Morganwg ranks among the most curious, wayward, imaginative, and wonderfully gifted scholars ever seen in Wales. He was born in 1747 and by the time of his death in 1826 his reputation for learning and virtuosity was legendary. As a child, he was frail and consumptive. He never attended school and he learned the alphabet by watching his father inscribe epitaphs on gravestones. His mother, a cultured but possessive woman who harboured great ambitions for him, taught him to read, write, and recite poems. She enveloped him in warm affection, encouraged his literary gifts, introduced him to the works of Milton, Pope, and Steele, and plied him with copies of the *Spectator*, *Tatler*, and *Guardian*. During his late teens he began to blossom as a poet. Like many other Glamorgan scholars, he was reared in a milieu of considerable intellectual activity. He profited by joining a circle of patriotic poets, antiquarians, and scholars and incurred a particular debt to Thomas Richards of Coychurch and John Walters of Llandough, who revealed to him the literary treasures of the past and awakened his interest in lexicography and dialectology. In 1770 Iolo was devastated by his mother's death and, rather than suffer the miseries of solitude, he packed his bags and left for London. However, he never acquired a taste for the 'tinsel glare' of the capital and around 1776 he returned to the clovered pastures of 'Davona's Vale' in his beloved Glamorgan.[56] During his colourful life he earned a precarious living as a mason, farmer, journalist, and grocer. He never settled or succeeded in any trade and he lived almost permanently on the edge of self-destruction.

From the early 1770s until the end of his long life, Iolo took daily doses of laudanum, a powerful drug which helped to ease the asthma which plagued him as much as, if not more than it afflicted Griffith Jones and Lewis Morris. Laudanum, however, clearly affected his mental balance. It heightened his imaginative flights of fancy, encouraged him to dream dreams, and to create a fictitious past. He buried himself under ever-growing piles of manuscripts, books, notebooks, marginalia, and journals in his tiny cottage in Flemingston and dedicated himself to the task of becoming the most learned and knowledgeable Welsh scholar of his day. He became a familiar and easily recognized figure on the roads of south Wales: a diminutive, rather ugly man, in a tall black hat, with spectacles on the end of his nose, and a canvas satchel slung over his back. Thrusting his stout, muscular legs forward, he rambled from library to library 'in quest of knowledge'.[57]

Iolo's addiction to laudanum fuelled his extraordinary powers of imagination. All kinds of bizarre and seductive notions began to ferment in his head. He became enraptured with the history of Glamorgan. Inspired by the 'gentleness' of Glamorgan, its magic and illusion, he came to believe that the ancient order of the Druids had—against all the odds—miraculously survived in his native county. Furthermore, he was convinced that he and Edward Evans of Aberdare were the sole remaining descendants of the Druidic bards. There was no doubt in his mind that Glamorgan, not

[56] Edward Williams, *Poems, Lyric and Pastoral* (2 vols., London, 1794), i. 212.
[57] G. J. Williams, *Iolo Morganwg*, p. 190.

Stonehenge or Avebury, certainly not Anglesey, was the headquarters of Druidism in Britain. Gazing back to this hypothetical golden age, Iolo rejoiced in the fact that the Welsh language was the only druidic language in the world and that he was the heir of a truly honourable tradition of lore and wisdom.

As he wandered through the secluded glades of Glamorgan, Iolo composed a number of strikingly beautiful lyrical poems. But, mesmerized by opium, he also used his remarkable inventive powers to fabricate chronicles, triads, and proverbs. In particular, he began composing medieval poems after the manner of Dafydd ap Gwilym. Not until the twentieth century did Welsh scholars learn the extent of his subterfuges and begin to penetrate the obscurities of his mythology. His heavy dependence on drugs drove him into a world of fantasies wherein he was unable to distinguish fact from fiction and myth from reality. Iolo's fabrications were neither fashioned out of wilful deceit nor deliberate dissimulation—like Luther, he simply could not take any other course. Nor should we forget that he was a genius: only a man steeped in the history and literature of Wales could have created such a profound and impressive body of material. By dint of his extensive knowledge, immense learning, and critical acumen, Iolo Morganwg exercised a decisive influence on the course of Welsh scholarship. In a period which nurtured men of great talent, he was the only scholar who possessed the gifts necessary for reinterpreting the past, investing it with colour and vividness, and making it relevant to the needs of the nation.

BIBLIOGRAPHY

The object of this bibliography is to provide the serious student and the interested layman with a guide to the location and nature of the principal manuscript and printed sources, as well as an indication of the range of secondary material available in the form of books, articles, and theses. I have resisted the temptation to include a list of Welsh and English books printed during the period under study, partly in order to avoid swelling the bibliography unnecessarily but mainly because a major bibliography by Eiluned Rees, *Libri Walliae: A Catalogue of Welsh Books and Books Printed in Wales, 1546–1820* (The National Library of Wales, Aberystwyth, 1987) provides a comprehensive catalogue.

Most British bibliographies are characterized by a marked anglocentric bias, and those which cover this period are no exception. There are short and generally inadequate sections on Wales in: *Bibliography of British History: Stuart Period, 1603–1714*, ed. Godfrey Davies, revised by Mary Frear Keeler (2nd edn., Oxford, 1970); *Bibliography of British History: The Eighteenth Century, 1714–1789*, eds. Stanley Pargellis and D. J. Medley (Oxford, 1951); *A Bibliography of British and Irish Municipal History*, eds. G. H. Martin and Sylvia McIntyre (vol. 1, Leicester, 1972).

Until very recently, the chief bibliographical aid was *The Bibliography of the History of Wales* (2nd edn., Cardiff, 1962), together with supplements published in the *Bulletin of the Board of Celtic Studies* 20 (May) 1963, 22 (November) 1966, 23 (November) 1969, and 25 (November) 1972. However, this has now been superseded by a splendid comprehensive bibliography commissioned by the History and Law Committee of the University of Wales Board of Celtic Studies. Edited by Philip Henry Jones, *A Bibliography of the History of Wales* (3rd edn., University of Wales Press, Cardiff, 1989) contains around 22,000 citations in microfiche form. The reader may also consult copious lists of new works in *Bibliotheca Celtica: A Register of Publications relating to Wales and the Celtic Peoples and Languages* (1909–   ). Recent publications in article form are printed annually in the December issue of *The Welsh History Review*. An extremely valuable publication, especially for those interested in exploring this period in detail, is Alun Eurig Davies (ed.). *Welsh Language and Welsh Dissertations accepted by British, American and German Universities, 1887–1971* (Cardiff, 1973), together with supplements in *Studia Celtica* 10–27 (1975–92). Up-to-date checklists of recently completed theses have also been published by David Lewis Jones in *The Welsh History Review* 6 (June) 1971, 7 (June) 1974, 9 (June) 1978, 11 (December) 1982, 13 (June) 1986, 14 (June) 1989.

The standard bibliography of secondary material on Welsh language and literature is Thomas Parry and Merfyn Morgan (eds.), *Llyfryddiaeth Llenyddiaeth Gymraeg* (Cardiff, 1976). There is a supplement to this edition, compiled by Gareth O. Watts, in the *Bulletin of the Board of Celtic Studies* 30 (November) 1983.

Y Bywgraffiadur Cymreig (1953) and *The Dictionary of Welsh Biography* (1959) are invaluable works of reference, while *The Oxford Companion to the Literature of Wales*, ed. Meic Stephens (Oxford, 1986) and its Welsh counterpart *Cydymaith i Lenyddiaeth Cymru* (Cardiff, 1986) not only include an immense amount of fascinating information but also guides to further reading under most individual entries.

A. MANUSCRIPTS

1. The Bodleian Library, Oxford

Ashmole
Aubrey
Carte
Rawlinson
Tanner
Willis

2. The British Library, London

Additional MSS
Egerton
Harleian
Lansdowne
Stowe

3. Cardiff Central Library

Cardiff MSS

4. Clwyd Record Office

i. *Ruthin Branch*
   Erddig
   Quarter Sessions Records
   Trevor of Bryncunallt
   Wynnstay

ii. *Hawarden Branch*
   Fitzhugh of Plas Power
   Gwysaney
   Mostyn
   Mostyn of Talacre
   Nerquis Hall
   Plas Teg
   Quarter Sessions Records

5. Dr Williams's Library, London

Dr John Evans's List of Dissenting Congregations in England and Wales, 1715–18

6. Dyfed Archives Service

i. *Carmarthenshire Area Record Office, Carmarthen*
 Cawdor/Campbell
 Cawdor/Lort
 Cwmgwili
 Derwydd (Stepney-Gulston)
 Dynevor
 Golden Grove
 Quarter Sessions Order Books

ii. *Pembrokeshire Area Record Office, Haverfordwest*
 Haverfordwest Borough Records
 Quarter Sessions Records

7. Friends House Library, London

Diary and Manuscripts of John Kelsall
Great Book of Sufferings
Lloyds of Dolobran MSS

8. Glamorgan Record Office, Cardiff

Aubrey
Bute
Carne of Nash
Carne and Turberville of Ewenny
Fonmon Castle
Kemeys-Tynte
Margam
Quarter Sessions Records
Rice (Dynevor) Glamorgan estates
Society of Friends

9. Gwent County Record Office, Cwmbrân

Hanbury-Williams
John Capel Hanbury
Kemeys-Tynte

10. Gwynedd Archives Service

i. *Caernarfonshire Area Record Office, Caernarfon*
Bodfel
Caernarfon Borough Records
Glynllifon
Poole
Rug
Quarter Sessions Records

ii. *Merioneth Area Record Office, Dolgellau*
Quarter Sessions Records

11. Lambeth Palace Library, London

Commonwealth Records (Augmentation Books)
Court of Arches Records

12. The National Library of Wales, Aberystwyth

Aston Hall
Bachymbyd
Badminton
Bettisfield
Bodewryd
British Records Association
Brogyntyn
Bronwydd
Broom Hall
Bute
Canon Trevor Owen
Carreglwyd
Castle Hill
Chirk Castle
Coed Coch
Coedymaen (Group 1)
Coleman
Crosse of Shaw Hill
Crosswood
Cwrt Mawr Deeds
Cwrt Mawr MSS
Diocesan Records of the Church in Wales
Dolaucothi
Dynevor
Eaton, Evans and Williams
Edwinsford
Esgair and Pantperthog
Glansevern
Glansevin
Glynllifon
Glynne of Hawarden
Gogerddan
Griffith of Garn
Harpton
Hawarden
Iolo Morganwg Letters
Kemeys-Tynte
Kinmel
Leeswood
Llanfair and Brynodol
Llangibby Castle
Llansteffan
Mayberry
Milborne
Mostyn
Muddlescomb
Nanhoron
Nanteos
NLW General Collection
Noyadd Trefawr
Ottley
Panton
Peniarth Deeds and Documents

Peniarth MSS
Penlle'r-gaer
Penpont
Penrice and Margam
Picton Castle
Pitchford Hall
Plasgwyn (Vivian)
Plas Power
Plas yn Cefn
Plymouth
Powis Castle
Records of the Courts of Great
   Sessions

Records of the Courts of Quarter
   Sessions in Powys
Rhual
Sir John Williams Add. MSS
Slebech
Sotheby
Talbot of Hensol
Tredegar Park
Wigfair
Wynn (of Gwydir)
Wynnstay

13. The Public Record Office, London

Chancery Records
Exchequer Records
Home Office Papers
State Papers Domestic, Charles I
State Papers Domestic, Interregnum (1649–1660)
State Papers Domestic, Charles II to George III
Treasury Papers

14. University College of North Wales, Bangor

Baron Hill
Bodorgan
Cefnamwlch
Garthewin
General Collection
Henblas
Kinmel
Mostyn
Nannau
Penrhos
Penrhyn
Plas Coch
Plas Newydd
Porth-yr-aur
Tynygongl

15. University College of Swansea

Mackworth
Morris
Swansea Corporation Records

16. William Salt Library, Stafford

Bishop Compton's ecclesiastical census returns, 1676.

B. PRINTED SOURCES AND CALENDARS

(London is the place of publication, unless stated otherwise)

Acts and Ordinances of the Interregnum, 1642–1660, eds. C. H. Firth and R. S. Rait (3 vols., 1911)

Acts of Parliament concerning Wales, 1714–1901, ed. T. I. Jeffreys Jones (Cardiff, 1959)

Calendar of Home Office Papers of the Reign of George III, 1760 to 1775 (4 vols., 1878–99)

Calendar of Letters relating to North Wales 1533–c. 1700, ed. B. E. Howells (Cardiff, 1967)

Calendar of Proceedings of the Committee for the Advance of Money 1642–1656 (3 vols., 1888)

Calendar of Proceedings of the Committee for Compounding with Delinquents 1643–50 (5 vols., 1889–92)

Calendar of Salusbury Correspondence 1553–circa 1700, ed. W. J. Smith (Cardiff, 1954)

Calendar of State Papers (Domestic) of the Commonwealth (13 vols., 1875–86)

Calendar of State Papers (Domestic) of the Reign of Anne, 1702–1704 (2 vols., 1916–24)

Calendar of State Papers (Domestic) of the Reign of Charles I (23 vols., 1858–97)

Calendar of State Papers (Domestic) of the Reign of Charles II, 1660–1685 (28 vols., 1860–1947)

Calendar of State Papers (Domestic) of the Reign of James II, 1685 (1 vol., 1960)

Calendar of State Papers (Domestic) of the Reign of William and Mary, 1689–1702 (11 vols., 1895–1937)

A Calendar of the Merioneth Quarter Sessions Rolls 1733–65, ed. Keith Williams-Jones (Merioneth County Council, 1965)

Calendar of the Records of the Borough of Haverfordwest 1539–1660, ed. B. G. Charles (Cardiff, 1967)

Calendar of Treasury Books (vols. i–xxxii, 1660–1718)

Calendar of Treasury Books and Papers (5 vols., 1729–45)

Calendar of Treasury Papers (6 vols., 1556–1728)

Calendar of Wynn (of Gwydir) Papers, 1515–1690, ed. J. Ballinger (Cardiff, 1926)

Correspondence and Minutes of the S.P.C.K. relating to Wales 1699–1740, ed. Mary Clement (Cardiff, 1952)

Correspondence and Records of the S.P.G. relating to Wales 1701–1750, ed. Mary Clement (Cardiff, 1973)

Digest of Welsh Historical Statistics, ed. John Williams (2 vols., The Welsh Office, 1985)

Herbert Correspondence: The Sixteenth and Seventeenth Century Letters of the Herberts of Chirbury, Powis Castle and Dolguog, ed. W. J. Smith (Cardiff, 1963)

Historical Manuscripts Commissioners Reports (several hundreds of volumes, some
   of which include valuable Welsh material)
Journals of the House of Commons 1642–1780 (vols. ii–xxxvii)
Journals of the House of Lords 1642–1783 (vols. v–xxxvii)
Manuscripts Commission Reports on Manuscripts in the Welsh Language, ed.
   J. Gwenogvryn Evans (2 vols., 1898–1910)
Seventeenth Century Economic Documents, eds. J. Thirsk and J. P. Cooper (1973)
The Statutes of Wales, ed. Ivor Bowen (1908)

C. WORKS OF REFERENCE

(London is the place of publication, unless stated otherwise)
A Bibliography of Welsh Ballads printed in the Eighteenth Century, ed. J. H. Davies
   (1911)
*British Museum Catalogue of the Pamphlets, Books, Newspapers, and Manuscripts
   relating to the Civil War, the Commonwealth, and Restoration collected by George
   Thomason, 1640–1661*, ed. G. K. Fortescue (2 vols., 1908)
Y Bywgraffiadur Cymreig hyd 1940 (1953)
Catalogue of Printed Literature in the Welsh Department of the Cardiff Free Library,
   eds. J. Ballinger and J. Ifano Jones (Cardiff, 1898).
A Catalogue of the Manuscripts relating to Wales in the British Museum, ed. Edward
   Owen (1900–22)
*Catalogue of Tracts of the Civil War and Commonwealth Period relating to Wales
   and the Borders* (Aberystwyth, 1911)
Cydymaith i Lenyddiaeth Cymru, ed. Meic Stephens (Cardiff, 1986)
The Dictionary of National Biography (and Supplements)
The Dictionary of Welsh Biography down to 1940 (1959)
*A Gallery of Ghosts: Books published between 1641–1700 not found in the Short-
   Title Catalogue*, ed. Donald Wing (New York, 1967)
Handbook of British Chronology, eds. E. B. Fryde and others (3rd edn., 1986)
Llyfryddiaeth Llenyddiaeth Gymraeg, eds. Thomas Parry and Merfyn Morgan
   (Cardiff, 1976)
The Oxford Companion to the Literature of Wales, ed. Meic Stephens (Oxford,
   1986)
Pedigrees of Anglesey and Caernarfonshire Families, ed. J. E. Griffith (Horncastle,
   1914)
Rowlands, William, *Llyfryddiaeth y Cymry*, ed. D. Silvan Evans (Llanidloes, 1869)
*Short-Title Catalogue of Books printed in England, Scotland, Ireland, Wales and
   British America and of English Books printed in other countries 1641–1700*, ed.
   D. G. Wing (3 vols., New York, 1945–51)
*Traethodau Ymchwil Cymraeg a Chymreig 1887–1971: Welsh Language and Welsh
   Dissertations 1887–1971*, ed. A. Eurig Davies (Cardiff, 1973)

D. SECONDARY WORKS

The reader should understand that the division of works into sections is intended simply as a general guide. For the sake of brevity individual items are not mentioned in more than one section. Entries are confined largely to material on Welsh history, although some works on English history which throw light on Welsh matters have also been included wherever appropriate. (London is the place of publication, unless stated otherwise).

1. General Works

Bowen, E. G. (ed.), *Wales: A Physical, Historical and Regional Geography* (1957)
Davies, L. T. and A. Edwards, *Welsh Life in the Eighteenth Century* (1939)
Davies, R. R. and others (eds.), *Welsh Society and Nationhood* (Cardiff, 1984)
Dodd, A. H., *A History of Caernarvonshire 1284–1900* (Caernarfonshire Hist. Soc., 1968)
—— *Life in Wales* (1972)
—— *Studies in Stuart Wales* (2nd edn., Cardiff, 1971)
—— 'Nationalism in Wales: A Historical Assessment', *THSC* (1970)
Dodgshon, R. A. and R. A. Butler (eds.), *An Historical Geography of England and Wales* (1978)
Emery, F. V., *The World's Landscapes, 2: Wales* (1969)
Evans, E. D., *A History of Wales 1660–1815* (Cardiff, 1976)
Evans, Gwynfor, *Aros Mae* (Swansea, 1971)
Evans, J. J., *Cymry Enwog y Ddeunawfed Ganrif* (Aberystwyth, 1937)
Hechter, Michael, *Internal Colonialism: The Celtic Fringe in British National Development, 1536–1966* (1975)
Humphreys, Emyr, *The Taliesin Tradition* (1983)
James, J. W., *A Church History of Wales* (Ilfracombe, 1945)
Jenkins, Geraint H. (ed.), *Cof Cenedl: Ysgrifau ar Hanes Cymru* (Llandysul, 1986)
—— *Hanes Cymru yn y Cyfnod Modern Cynnar, 1530–1760* (Cardiff, 1983)
Jenkins, R. T., *Yr Apêl at Hanes ac Ysgrifau Eraill* (Wrexham, 1930)
—— *Hanes Cymru yn y Ddeunawfed Ganrif* (Cardiff, 1928).
John, A. H. and Glanmor Williams (eds.), *Glamorgan County History, vol. v: Industrial Glamorgan from 1700 to 1970* (Cardiff, 1980)
Jones, D. Ambrose, *A history of the Church in Wales* (Carmarthen, 1926)
Jones, Gareth E., *Modern Wales: A Concise History c. 1485–1979* (Cambridge, 1984)
Jones, R. Brinley (ed.), *Anatomy of Wales* (Peterston-super-Ely, 1972)
Lloyd, D. M. (ed.), *The Historical Foundations of Welsh Nationalism* (Cardiff, 1950)
Lloyd, J. E. (ed.), *A History of Carmarthenshire* (2 vols., Cardiff, 1939)
Moore, Donald (ed.), *Wales in the Eighteenth Century* (Swansea, 1976)
Morgan, Prys and David Thomas, *Wales: The Shaping of a Nation* (Newton Abbot, 1984)
Morrice, J. C., *A Manual of Welsh Literature* (Bangor, 1909)
Parry, Thomas, *A History of Welsh Literature*, tr. H. Idris Bell (Oxford, 1955)

Rees, J. F., *Studies in Welsh History* (Cardiff, 1965)

Rees, William, *An Historical Atlas of Wales from Early to Modern Times* (new edn., 1972)

Roberts, Glyn, *Aspects of Welsh History* (Cardiff, 1969)

Roderick, A. J. (ed.), *Wales through the Ages* (vol. ii, Llandybïe, 1960)

Thomas, David (ed.), *Wales: A New Study* (Newton Abbot, 1977)

Thomas, Hugh, *A History of Wales 1485–1660* (Cardiff, 1972)

Walker, David (ed.), *A History of the Church in Wales* (Penarth, 1976)

Williams, David and Ieuan Gwynedd Jones, *A History of Modern Wales* (2nd edn., 1977)

Williams, Glanmor (ed.), *Glamorgan County History, vol. iv: Early Modern Glamorgan* (Cardiff, 1974)

—— *Grym Tafodau Tân* (Llandysul, 1984)

—— *Religion, Language and Nationality in Wales* (Cardiff, 1979)

—— *Welsh Reformation Essays* (Cardiff, 1967)

Williams, Gwyn, *An Introduction to Welsh Literature* (Cardiff, 1978)

Williams, Gwyn A., 'Twf Hanesyddol y Syniad o Genedl yng Nghymru', *Efrydiau Athronyddol* 24 (1961)

—— *The Welsh in their History* (1982)

—— *When was Wales?* (1985)

Williams, J. E. Caerwyn (ed.), *Literature in Celtic Countries* (Cardiff, 1971)

Williams, M. I., *The South Wales Landscape* (1975)

Williams, W. Llewelyn, *The Making of Modern Wales* (1919)

2. Population and Social Life

Ashton, O. S., 'Eighteenth Century Radnorshire: A Population Survey', *Trans. Radnorshire Hist. Soc.* 40 (1970)

Butterworth, G., 'The Anglesey Druidical Society, 1772–1844', *Trans. Anglesey Antiq. Soc.* (1980)

Byng, John, *The Torrington Diaries*, ed. C. B. Andrews (4 vols., 1934–8)

Carr, A. D., 'An Introduction to the Endowed Charities of Anglesey', *Trans. Anglesey Antiq. Soc.* (1966)

Davies, A. Eurig, 'Wages, Prices and Social Improvements in Cardiganshire, 1750–1850', *Ceredigion* 10 (1984)

Davies, J. H. (ed.), *The Letters of Lewis, Richard, William and John Morris of Anglesey (Morrisiaid Môn) 1728–1765* (2 vols., Aberystwyth, 1907–9)

—— *Rhai o Hen Ddewiniaid Cymru* (1901)

Davies, L. T. and H. J. Lloyd-Johnes, *Welsh Furniture* (Cardiff, 1950)

Defoe, Daniel, *A Tour through the Whole Island of Great Britain*, eds. G. D. H. Cole and D. C. Browning (2 vols., 1962)

Denning, Roy, 'William Thomas of Michaelston-Super-Ely', *Glamorgan Historian* 9 (1975)

Dineley, Thomas, *The Account of the Official Progress of the First Duke of Beaufort through Wales, 1684*, ed. R. W. Banks (1888)

Emery, F. V., 'Edward Lhuyd and Some of His Correspondents: A View of Gower in the 1690s', *THSC* (1965)

Emery, F. V., 'Edward Lhuyd and Some of his Glamorgan Correspondents', *THSC* (1965)

—— 'A New Reply to Lhuyd's *Queries* (1696): Llanboidy, Carmarthenshire', *Arch. Camb.* 124 (1975)

Etheridge, K., *Welsh Costume in the Eighteenth and Nineteenth Century* (Swansea, 1977)

Evans, G. Nesta, *Social Life in Mid-Eighteenth Century Anglesey* (Cardiff, 1936)

Evans, Hugh, *The Gorse Glen*, tr. E. M. Humphreys (Liverpool, 1948)

Flinn, M. W., *British Population Growth 1700–1850* (1970)

Foulkes, E. J., 'Glimpses of Hanoverian Flintshire', *Journal Flintshire Hist. Soc.* 24 (1969–70)

Gruffydd, Eirlys, *Gwrachod Cymru* (Caernarfon, 1980)

Hall, E. Hyde, *A Description of Caernarvonshire (1809–1811)*, ed. E. Gwynne Jones (Caernarfon, 1952)

Haslam, Richard, *The Buildings of Wales: Powys* (Penguin, 1979)

Hilling, J. B., *The Historic Architecture of Wales* (Cardiff, 1976)

Howells, Brian E., 'The Historical Demography of Wales: Some Notes on Sources', *The Local Historian* 10 (1973)

Howells, Brian E. and John, 'Peasant Houses in Stuart Pembrokeshire', *NLWJ* 21 (1979–80)

Howells, Brian E. and K. A. (eds.), *Pembrokeshire Life: 1572–1843* (Pembrokeshire Record Society, 1972)

Howells, John, 'Haverfordwest and the Plague, 1652', *WHR* 12 (1984–5)

Hubbard, Edward, *The Buildings of Wales: Clwyd* (Penguin, 1986)

Jackson, J., 'Letters from and relating to North Wales', *Journal Merioneth Hist. and Record Soc.* 3 (1960)

Jarman, Eldra and A. O. H., *Y Sipsiwn Cymreig* (Cardiff, 1979)

Jenkins, David, 'The Population, Society and Economy of late Stuart Montgomeryshire c. 1660–1720' (unpubl. University of Wales Ph.D. thesis, 1985)

Jenkins, Geraint H., *Geni Plentyn ym 1701: Profiad 'rhyfeddol' Dassy Harry* (Cardiff, 1981)

—— 'Popular Beliefs in Wales from the Restoration to Methodism', *BBCS* 27 (1977)

Jones, B. W., 'The Population of Eighteenth Century West Glamorgan', *Glamorgan Historian*, 12 (1981)

Jones, E. D., 'The Brogyntyn Welsh Manuscripts', *NLWJ* 5–6 (1948–50), 8 (1953)

—— 'Llyfrau Cofion a Chyfrifon Owen Thomas 1729–1775', *NLWJ* 16 (1969–70)

Jones, Emyr Gwynne, 'Correspondence of the Owens of Penrhos, 1712–1742', *Trans. Anglesey Antiq. Soc.* (1954)

Jones, G. Penrhyn, 'Folk Medicine in Eighteenth Century Wales', *Folk Life* 8 (1969)

—— 'A History of Medicine in Wales in the Eighteenth Century' (unpubl. University of Liverpool MA thesis, 1957)

—— *Newyn a Haint yng Nghymru* (Caernarfon, 1963)

Jones, R. W., *Bywyd Cymdeithasol Cymru yn y Ddeunawfed Ganrif* (Cardiff, 1931)

Jones, Tegwyn, *Y Llew a'i Deulu* (Tal-y-bont, 1982)

Jones, T. Gwynn, *Welsh Folklore and Folk-Custom* (new edn., Cambridge, 1979)

Lewis, F. R., 'Lewis Morris and the Parish of Llanbadarn Fawr, Cardiganshire, in 1755', *Arch. Camb.* 93 (1938)

Lhuyd, Edward, 'Parochialia', ed. R. H. Morris, *Arch. Camb. Supplement* (1909–11)

Lloyd, T. Alwyn, 'The Georgian Period in Welsh Building', *Arch. Camb.* 106 (1957)

Lowe, Jeremy, *Welsh Country Workers Housing 1775–1875* (Cardiff, 1985)

—— *Welsh Industrial Workers Housing 1775–1875* (Cardiff, 1977)

Luxton, B. C., 'William Jenkin, the Wizard of Cadoxton-juxta-Barry', *Morgannwg* 24 (1980)

MacDonald, R. W., 'The Parish Registers of Wales', *NLWJ* 19 (1975–6)

Morris, C. (ed.), *The Illustrated Journeys of Celia Fiennes 1685–c. 1712* (1982)

Myddelton, W. M. (ed.), *Chirk Castle Accounts, 1666–1753* (Manchester, 1931)

Owen, Hugh (ed.), *Additional Letters of the Morrises of Anglesey (1735–1786)* (Parts 1–2, 1947–9)

—— 'The Diary of William Bulkeley of Brynddu, Anglesey', *Trans. Anglesey Antiq. Soc.* (1931)

Owen, Leonard, 'The Growth of Population in Anglesey, 1563–1801', *Trans. Anglesey Antiq. Soc.* (1960)

—— 'The Letters of an Anglesey Parson, 1712–1732', *THSC* (1961)

—— 'The Population of Wales in the Sixteenth and Seventeenth Centuries', *THSC* (1959)

—— 'A Seventeenth-Century Commonplace Book', *THSC* (1962)

Owen, T. M., *Welsh Folk Customs* (2nd edn., Cardiff, 1968)

Parry, J. Glyn, 'Autobiography of a Smuggler', *NLWJ* 24 (1985)

Parry, Owen (ed.), 'The Hearth Tax of 1662 in Merioneth', *Journal Merioneth Hist. and Record Soc.* 2 (1953–6)

Peate, I. C., *Diwylliant Gwerin Cymru* (2nd edn., Denbigh, 1975)

—— *Tradition and Folk Life* (1972)

—— *The Welsh House* (3rd edn., Liverpool, 1946)

'Pembrokeshire Hearths in 1670', *West Wales Historical Records*, 9–11 (1920–6)

Pennant, Thomas, *A Tour in Wales* (2 vols., 1778–83)

Pope, Dudley, *Harry Morgan's Way* (1977)

Pryce, W. T. R., 'Parish Registers and Visitation Returns as Primary Sources for the Population Geography of the Eighteenth Century', *THSC* (1971)

Roberts, B. Dew, *Mr. Bulkeley and the Pirate* (1941)

Roberts, Carys, 'Piracy in Caernarvonshire and Anglesey', *Trans. Caernarfonshire Hist. Soc.* 21 (1960)

Roberts, Stanley, *Black Bart* (Llandybïe, 1966)

Smith, Peter, *Houses of the Welsh Countryside* (1975)

Stevens, Catrin, *Arferion Caru* (Llandysul, 1977)

Suggett, R. F., 'Some Aspects of Village Life in Eighteenth Century Glamorgan' (unpubl. University of Oxford B.Litt. thesis, 1976)

Teale, Adrian, 'The Economy and Society of North Flintshire, c. 1660–1714' (unpubl. University of Wales MA thesis, 1979)

Thomas, Ben Bowen, *The Old Order* (Cardiff, 1945)

Thomas, Keith, *Religion and the Decline of Magic* (1971)

Waddington, H. M., 'Games and Athletics in Bygone Wales', *THSC* (1954)

Wiliam, Eurwyn, *The Historic Farm Buildings of Wales* (Edinburgh, 1986)

—— 'A Pair of Eighteenth-Century Labourers' Cottages at Banc Tai Newydd, Pontyberem, Carmarthenshire', *The Carmarthenshire Antiquary* 11 (1975)

—— 'Peasant Architecture in Caernarfonshire', *Trans. Caernarfonshire Hist. Soc.* 43 (1982)

—— *Traditional Farm Buildings in North-East Wales 1550–1900* (Cardiff, 1982)

—— 'The Vernacular Architecture of a Welsh Rural Community, 1700–1900: The Houses of Mynytho', *Trans. Caernarfonshire Hist. Soc.* 36 (1975)

Williams, David, 'A Note on the Population of Wales, 1536–1801', *BBCS* 8 (1935–7)

Williams, G. H., 'Caernarfonshire House Interiors 1660–90', *Trans. Caernarfonshire Hist. Soc.* 38 (1977)

Williams, G. J., 'Dyddiadur William Thomas o Lanfihangel ar Elái', *Morgannwg* 1 (1957)

—— 'Glamorgan Customs in the Eighteenth Century', *Gwerin* 1 (1957)

—— 'Wil Hopcyn and the Maid of Cefn Ydfa', *Glamorgan Historian* 6 (1969)

Williams, J. Gwynn, 'Rhai Agweddau ar y Gymdeithas Gymreig yn yr ail ganrif ar bymtheg', *Efrydiau Athronyddol* 30 (1968)

—— 'Witchcraft in Seventeenth-Century Flintshire', *Journal Flintshire Hist. Soc.* 27 (1975–6)

Williams, M. I., 'Life in Seventeenth Century Carmarthenshire', *The Carmarthenshire Historian* (1977)

Williams, William, 'A Survey of the Ancient and Present State of the County of Caernarvon', *Trans. Caernarfonshire Hist. Soc.* 33–4 (1972–3)

Williams, W. Gilbert, *Anesmwythyd yn Arfon yn y Ddeunawfed Ganrif* (Caernarfon, 1930)

Williams, W. Ll., 'Sir Henry Morgan, the Buccaneer', *THSC* (1903–4)

Wrigley, E. A. and R. S. Schofield, *The Population History of England, 1541–1871* (1981)

3. Landed Estates and the Gentry

Apted, M. R., 'Social Conditions at Tredegar House, Newport, in the Seventeenth and Eighteenth Centuries', *The Monmouthshire Antiquary* 3 (1972–3)

Beckett, J. V., 'The Pattern of Landownership in England and Wales, 1660–1880', *Economic History Review* 37 (1984)

Cust, A. L. (ed.), *Chronicles of Erthig on the Dyke* (2 vols., 1914)

Davies, D. L., 'Miss Myddelton of Croesnewydd and the Plas Power Papers', *Trans. Denbighshire Hist. Soc.* 22 (1973)

Davies, John, *Cardiff and the Marquesses of Bute* (Cardiff, 1981)

Gresham, C. A., *Eifionydd: A Study in Landownership from the Medieval Period to the Present Day* (Cardiff, 1973)

Howell, David W., 'The Economy of the Landed Estates of Pembrokeshire c. 1680–1830', *WHR* 3 (1966–7)

—— 'The Landed Gentry of Pembrokeshire in the Eighteenth Century' (unpubl. University of Wales MA thesis, 1965)

—— 'Landed Society in Pembrokeshire, c. 1680–1830', *The Pembrokeshire Historian* 3 (1971)

—— *Patriarchs and Parasites: The Gentry of South-West Wales in the Eighteenth Century* (Cardiff, 1986)

—— 'Pembrokeshire Gentry in the Eighteenth Century', in *Carmarthenshire Studies*, eds. T. Barnes and N. Yates (Carmarthen, 1974)

Howells, J. M., 'The Crosswood Estate, 1547–1947', *Ceredigion* 3 (1956)

—— 'The Crosswood Estate: Its Growth and Economic Development, 1683–1899' (unpubl. University of Wales MA thesis, 1956)

Hughes, Glyn T. and others (eds.), *Gregynog* (Cardiff, 1977)

Humphreys, T. Melvin, 'Rural Society in Eighteenth Century Montgomeryshire' (unpubl. University of Wales Ph.D. thesis, 1982)

Jenkins, David, 'The Pryse Family of Gogerddan', *NLWJ* 8 (1953–4)

Jenkins, Philip, 'The Creation of an "Ancient Gentry": Glamorgan, 1760–1840', *WHR* 12 (1984)

—— 'The Demographic Decline of the Landed Gentry in the Eighteenth Century: A South Wales Study', *WHR* 11 (1982)

—— *The Making of a Ruling Class: The Glamorgan Gentry 1640–1790* (Cambridge, 1983)

—— 'Mary Wharton and the Rise of the "New Woman"', *NLWJ* 22 (1981)

—— 'A Social and Political History of the Glamorgan Gentry c. 1650–1770' (unpubl. University of Cambridge Ph.D. thesis, 1978)

Jones, Francis, 'The Affair of Cefnarthen', *Brycheiniog* 15 (1971)

—— 'Owen of Orielton', *The Pembrokeshire Historian*, 5 (1974)

—— 'The Vaughans of Golden Grove', *THSC* (1964)

Jones, J. Gwynfor, 'The Wynn Family and Estate of Gwydir' (unpubl. University of Wales Ph.D. thesis, 1974)

Martin, Joanna, 'Estate Stewards and their Work in Glamorgan, 1660–1760', *Morgannwg* 23 (1979)

—— 'The Landed Estate in Glamorgan, circa 1660–1760' (unpubl. University of Cambridge Ph.D. thesis, 1978)

—— 'Landed Estates in Glamorgan, c. 1660–1760', *Glamorgan Historian* 12 (1981)

Mingay, G. E., *The Gentry* (1976)

Mostyn, Lord and T. A. Glenn, *History of the Family of Mostyn of Mostyn* (1925)

Parry, J. Glyn, 'Stability and Change in Mid-Eighteenth Century Caernarfonshire' (unpubl. University of Wales MA thesis, 1978)

Phillips, Bethan, *Peterwell* (Llandysul, 1983)

Phillips, J. Roland, *Memoirs of the Ancient Family of Owen of Orielton* (1886)

Pritchard, T. W., 'Sir Watkin Williams Wynn, Fourth Baronet (1749–1789)', *Trans. Denbighshire Hist. Soc.* 27–8 (1978–9)

Roberts, Askew, *Wynnstay and the Wynns* (Oswestry, 1876)

Roberts, P. R., 'The Decline of the Welsh Squires in the Eighteenth Century', *NLWJ* 13 (1963–4)

—— 'The Gentry and the Land in Eighteenth Century Merioneth', *Journal Merioneth Hist. and Record Soc.* 4 (1961–4)

Roberts, P. R., 'The Social History of the Merioneth Gentry, c. 1660–1840', *Journal Merioneth Hist. and Record Soc.* 4 (1961–4)

Thomas, D. Ll., 'Iscennen and Golden Grove', *THSC* (1940)

Usher, Gwilym A., *Gwysaney and Owston* (Denbigh, 1964)

Vaughan, H. M., *The South Wales Squires* (1926)

Waterson, M., *The Servants' Hall* (1980)

Williams, A. H., 'The Gwynnes of Garth, c. 1712–1809', *Brycheiniog* 14 (1970)

Williams, G. H., 'Estate management in Dyffryn Conwy, c. 1685', *THSC* (1979)

Wynne, R. O. F., 'The Wynne Family of Melai and Garthewin', *Trans. Denbighshire Hist. Soc.* 5 (1956)

4. Agriculture and Crafts

Bowen, I., *The Great Enclosures of Common Lands in Wales* (1914)

Colyer, R. J., 'Aspects of the Pastoral Economy in Pre-Industrial Wales', *Journal Royal Agricultural Society* 144 (1983)

—— 'Crop Husbandry in Wales before the Onset of Mechanization', *Folk Life* 21 (1983)

—— 'Early Agricultural Societies in South Wales', *WHR* 12 (1985)

—— 'Limitations to Agrarian Development in Nineteenth-Century Wales', *BBCS* 27 (1976–8)

—— 'The Size of Farms in Late Eighteenth and Early Nineteenth Century Cardiganshire', *BBCS* 27 (1976–8)

—— *The Welsh Cattle Drovers* (Cardiff, 1976)

Davies, A. Eurig, 'Enclosures in Cardiganshire, 1750–1850', *Ceredigion* 8 (1976)

Davies, Walter, *General View of the Agriculture and Domestic Economy of North Wales* (1810)

Dodd, A. H., 'The Enclosure Movement in North Wales', *BBCS* 3 (1926–7)

Edmunds, H., 'History of the Brecknockshire Agricultural Society, 1755–1955', *Brycheiniog* 2–3 (1956–7)

Edwards, Ifor, *Y Brodyr Davies: Gofaint Gatiau* (Cardiff, 1977)

Emery, F. V., 'The Mechanics of Innovation: Clover Cultivation in Wales before 1750', *Journal of Historical Geography* 2 (1976)

Evans, B. M., 'Settlement and Agriculture in North Wales, 1536–1670' (unpubl. University of Cambridge Ph.D. thesis, 1966)

Howells, Brian E., 'Social and Agrarian Change in Early Modern Cardiganshire', *Ceredigion* 7 (1974–5)

Jenkins, David, 'Harvest Failure and Crisis Mortality: The Example of Montgomeryshire 1699–1708', *Papers in Modern Welsh History* 1 (1983)

Jenkins, J. Geraint, *Life and Tradition in Rural Wales* (1976)

—— *Traditional Country Craftsmen* (1965)

—— *Welsh Crafts and Craftsmen* (Llandysul, 1975)

Jones, E. W., 'The First Carmarthenshire Agricultural Society', *The Carmarthen Antiquary* 3 (1961)

Jones, Francis, 'A Squire in Anglesey: Edward Wynne of Bodewryd', *Trans. Anglesey Antiq. Soc.* (1940)

Linnard, W., *Welsh Woods and Forests* (Cardiff, 1982)

Oliver, J., 'The Weather and Farming in the Mid-Eighteenth Century in Anglesey', *NLWJ* 10 (1957–8)

Osborne, B., 'Glamorgan Agriculture in the Seventeenth and Eighteenth Centuries', *NLWJ* 20 (1977–8)

Payne, Ffransis G., *Yr Aradr Gymreig* (Cardiff, 1954)

Peate, I. C., *Clock and Watch Makers in Wales* (3rd edn. Cardiff, 1975)

Pryce, W. T. R. and T. A. Davies, *Samuel Roberts Clock Maker* (Cardiff, 1985)

Skeel, C. J., 'Social and Economic Conditions in Wales and the Marches in the Early Seventeenth Century', *THSC* (1916–17)

Thirsk, Joan (ed.), *The Agrarian History of England and Wales, vol. v: 1640–1750* (Parts 1–2, Cambridge, 1984–5)

Thomas, David, 'Arthur Young on Wales', *BBCS* 20 (1964)

Tibbott, S. M., 'Knitting Stockings in Wales—A Domestic Craft', *Folk Life* 16 (1978)

Williams, G. H., 'Farming in Stuart Caernarfonshire', *Trans. Caernarfonshire Hist. Soc.* 42 (1981)

—— 'A Study of Caernarfonshire Probate Material 1603–1690' (unpubl. University of Wales MA thesis, 1972)

Williams-Davies, J., '"Merched y Gerddi": A Seasonal Migration of Female Labour from Rural Wales', *Folk Life* 15 (1977)

5. Industry

Addis, J. P., *The Crawshay Dynasty* (Cardiff, 1957)

Ashton, T. S., *Iron and Steel in the Industrial Revolution* (3rd edn., Manchester, 1963)

Ashton, T. S. and J. Sykes, *The Coal Industry of the Eighteenth Century* (2nd edn., Manchester, 1964)

Bevan-Evans, M., *Gadlys and Flintshire Lead-Mining in the Eighteenth Century* (Hawarden, 1963)

Beynon, O., 'The Lead Mining Industry in Cardiganshire from 1700 to 1830' (unpubl. University of Wales MA thesis, 1937)

Burt, R., 'Lead Production in England and Wales, 1700–1770', *Economic History Review* 22 (1969)

Chaloner, W. H., 'John Wilkinson, Ironmaster', *History Today* May (1951)

Davies, Alun Eurig, 'Paper-mills and Paper-makers in Wales 1700–1900', *NLWJ* 15 (1967–8)

Davies, Clifford, 'The Evolution of Industries and Settlements between Merthyr Tydfil and Abergavenny from 1740 to 1840' (unpubl. University of Wales MA thesis, 1949)

Davies, D. J., *The Economic History of South Wales Prior to 1800* (Cardiff, 1933)

Deane, P. and W. A. Cole, *British Economic Growth 1688–1959* (Cambridge, 1964)

Dodd, A. H., *The Industrial Revolution in North Wales* (3rd edn., Cardiff, 1971)

England, J., 'The Dowlais Iron Works, 1759–93', *Morgannwg* 3 (1959)

Evans, M. C. S., 'The Pioneers of the Carmarthenshire Iron Industry', *The Carmarthenshire Historian* 4 (1967)

Flinn, M. W., *The History of the British Coal Industry* (vol. ii, Oxford, 1984)

Gruffydd, K. Lloyd, 'The Development of the Coal Industry in Flintshire to 1740' (unpubl. University of Wales MA thesis, 1981)

Harris, J. R., *The Copper King* (Liverpool, 1964)

Jenkins, J. Geraint, *The Welsh Woollen Industry* (Cardiff, 1969)

John, A. H., *The Industrial Development of South Wales* (Cardiff, 1950)

Lerry, G. G., 'The Industries of Denbighshire', *Trans. Denbighshire Hist. Soc.* 7–8 (1958–9)

Lewis, W. J., *Lead Mining in Wales* (Cardiff, 1967)

Linnard, W., 'A Swedish Visitor to Flintshire in 1760', *Journal Flintshire Hist. Soc.* 30 (1981–2)

Lloyd, Humphrey, *The Quaker Lloyds in the Industrial Revolution* (1975)

Lloyd, John, *The Early History of the Old South Wales Iron Works (1760 to 1840)* (1906)

Lindsay, J., *A History of the North Wales Slate Industry* (Newton Abbot, 1974)

Martin, Joanna, 'Private Enterprise versus Manorial Rights: Mineral Property Disputes in Mid-Eighteenth Century Glamorgan', *WHR* 9 (1978)

Mathias, P., *The First Industrial Nation: An Economic History of Britain 1700–1914* (2nd edn., 1983)

Mendenhall, T. C., *The Shrewsbury Drapers and the Welsh Wool Trade in the Sixteenth and Seventeenth Centuries* (Oxford, 1953)

Minchinton, W. E., *The British Tinplate Industry* (Oxford, 1957)

—— (ed.), *Industrial South Wales 1750–1914* (1969)

Morgan, Prys, 'The Glais Boundary Dispute, 1756', *Glamorgan Historian* 9 (n.d.)

Palmer, Marilyn, *The Richest in all Wales: The Welsh Potosi or Esgair Hir and Esgair Fraith Lead and Copper Mines of Cardiganshire* (Sheffield, 1983)

Rees, D. M., *Mines, Mills and Furnaces* (1969)

Rees, William, *Industry before the Industrial Revolution* (2 vols., Cardiff, 1968)

Rhodes, J. N., 'The London Lead Company in North Wales, 1693–1792' (unpubl. University of Leicester Ph.D. thesis, 1970)

—— 'The London (Quaker) Company and the Prestatyn Mines Scandal', *Journal Flintshire Hist. Soc.* 23–4 (1967–70)

Richards, H. P., *William Edwards* (Cowbridge, 1983)

Roberts, R. O., 'The Development and Decline of the Non-Ferrous Metal Smelting Industries in South Wales', *THSC* (1956)

—— 'Enterprise and Capital for Non-ferrous Smelting in Glamorgan, 1694–1924', *Morgannwg* 23 (1979)

Rowlands, John, *Copper Mountain* (Llangefni, 1966)

Skeel, C. A. J., 'The Welsh Woollen Industry in the Eighteenth and Nineteenth Centuries', *Arch. Camb.* 79 (1924)

Trott, C. D. J., 'Coal-Mining in the Borough of Neath in the Seventeenth and Early Eighteenth Centuries', *Morgannwg* 13 (1969)

Williams, L. J., 'The Welsh Tinplate Trade in the Mid-Eighteenth Century', *Economic History Review* 13 (1960–1)

6. Urban Life, Transport, and Trade

Archer, M. S., *The Welsh Post Towns before 1840* (Chichester, 1970)

Boon, G. C. (ed.), *Welsh Tokens of the Seventeenth Century* (Cardiff, 1973)

Carter, Harold, *The Towns of Wales* (Cardiff, 1966)

Chappell, E. L., *History of the Port of Cardiff* (Cardiff, 1939)

Colyer, R. J., *Roads and Trackways of Wales* (Ashbourne, 1984)

Davies, H. R. (ed.), *A Review of the Records of the Conway and the Menai Ferries* (Cardiff, 1942)

Dawson, J. W., *Commerce and Customs: A History of the Ports of Newport and Caerleon* (Newport, 1932)

Dodd, A. H. (ed.), *A History of Wrexham* (Wrexham, 1957)

—— 'The Roads of North Wales, 1750–1850', *Arch. Camb.* 5 (1925)

Eames, Aled, *Ships and Seamen of Anglesey 1558–1918* (Anglesey Antiq. Soc., 1973)

Evans, D. Gareth, 'The Market Towns of Denbighshire 1640–1690' (unpubl. University of Wales MA thesis, 1978)

Evans, Kenrick, 'Eighteenth Century Caernarvon', *Trans. Caernarfonshire Hist. Soc.* 7–11 (1946–50)

Goddard, T., *Pembrokeshire Shipwrecks* (Swansea, 1983)

Hawkes, G. I., 'Illicit Trading in Wales in the Eighteenth Century', *Maritime Wales* 10 (1986)

Jenkins, David, *The Maritime Heritage of Dyfed* (Cardiff, 1982)

Jenkins, Elis (ed.), *Neath and District* (Neath, 1974)

Jenkins, J. Geraint, *Agricultural Transport in Wales* (Cardiff, 1962)

—— *Maritime Heritage: The Ships and Seamen of Southern Ceredigion* (Llandysul, 1982)

Jenkins, R. T., *Y Ffordd yng Nghymru* (Wrexham, 1933)

Jones, Emrys, 'The Welsh in London in the Seventeenth and Eighteenth Centuries', *WHR* 10 (1981)

Jones, Ieuan Gwynedd (ed.), *Aberystwyth 1277–1977* (Aberystwyth, 1977)

Jones, I. Wynne, *Shipwrecks of North Wales* (Newton Abbot, 1973)

Lewis, A. H. T., 'The Early Effects of Carmarthenshire's Turnpike Trusts, 1760–1800', *The Carmarthenshire Historian* 4 (1967)

Lewis, W. J., *Born on a Perilous Rock* (2nd edn., Aberystwyth, 1980)

Kissack, K., *Monmouth: The Making of a County Town* (1975)

Lloyd, L. W., *Maritime Merioneth: The Town and Port of Barmouth (1565–1973)* (Harlech, n.d.)

Matthews, J. H. (ed.), *Records of the County Borough of Cardiff* (6 vols., Cardiff, 1898–1911)

Moore, Donald (ed.), *Barry: The Centenary Book* (Barry, 1984)

—— 'Early Views of Towns in Wales and the Border', *THSC* (1981)

Owen, David J., *The Origin and Development of the Ports of the United Kingdom* (2nd edn., 1948)

Parry, E. G., 'Brecon: Occupations and Society, 1500–1800', *Brycheiniog* 19 (1980–1)

Pawson, E., *Transport and Economy: The Turnpike Roads of Britain* (1977)

Pritchard, R. T., 'The Caernarvonshire Turnpike Trust', *Trans. Caernarfonshire Hist. Soc.* 17 (1956)

—— 'Denbighshire Roads and Turnpike Trusts', *Trans. Denbighshire Hist. Soc.* 12 (1963)

—— 'The Post Road in Caernarvonshire', *Trans. Caernarfonshire Hist. Soc.* 13 (1952)

Rees, William, *Cardiff: A History of the City* (2nd edn., Cardiff, 1969)

Riden, Philip, *Cowbridge Trades and Tradesmen 1660–1750* (Cardiff, 1981)

Sanderson, P. E., 'The Importance of External Factors in the Development of the Port of Holyhead', *Trans. Anglesey Antiq. Soc.* (1963)

Thomas, David, *Hen Longau Sir Gaernarfon* (Caernarfon, 1952)

Thomas, W. S. K., 'The History of Swansea from the Accession of the Tudors to the Restoration Settlement' (unpubl. University of Wales Ph.D. thesis, 1958)

Tucker, Norman, 'The Councell Booke of Ruthin, 1642–95', *Trans. Denbighshire Hist. Soc.* 9–11 (1960–2)

Walker, E., 'The Development of Communications in Glamorgan, With Special Reference to the Growth of Industry, between 1760 and 1840' (unpubl. University of Wales MA thesis, 1947)

Willan, T. S., *The English Coasting Trade 1600–1750* (Manchester, 1967)

Williams, D. T., *The Economic Development of Swansea* (University College of Swansea, 1940)

—— 'The Port Books of Swansea and Neath, 1709–19', *Arch. Camb.* 95 (1940)

Williams, G. H., 'Masnach Forwrol Arfon', *Maritime Wales* 3 (1978)

Williams, M. I., 'Cardiff—its People and its Trade, 1660–1720', *Morgannwg* 7 (1963)

—— 'Carmarthenshire's Maritime Trade in the Sixteenth and Seventeenth Centuries', *The Carmarthenshire Antiquary* 14 (1978)

7. The Civil Wars and the Interregnum

Berry, J., *A Cromwellian Major General: The Career of Colonel James Berry* (Oxford, 1938)

Brown, Eluned, ' "Learned Friend and Loyal Fellow-Prisoner": Thomas Powell and Welsh Royalists', *NLWJ* 18 (1973–4)

Davies, David, *Ardudwy a'i Gwron* (Blaenau Ffestiniog, 1914)

Davies, J. H. (ed.), *Hen Gerddi Gwleidyddol: 1588–1660* (Cardiff, 1901)

Dodd, A. H., 'Anglesey in the Civil War', *Trans. Anglesey Antiq. Soc.* (1952)

—— 'The Civil War in East Denbighshire', *Trans. Denbighshire Hist. Soc.* 3 (1954)

—— 'The Pattern of Politics in Stuart Wales', *THSC* (1948)

Dore, R. N., 'Sir Thomas Myddelton's Attempted Conquest of Powys, 1644–5', *Montgomeryshire Collections* 57 (1961–2)

Eames, Aled, 'Sea Power and Caernarvonshire, 1642–1660', *Trans. Caernarfonshire Hist. Soc.* 16 (1955)

Fletcher, Anthony, *The Outbreak of the English Civil War* (Paperback edn., 1985)

Hill, Christopher, 'Arise Evans: Welshman in London', in *Change and Continuity in Seventeenth-Century England* (1974)

—— *The World Turned Upside Down* (Penguin, 1975)

Howells, Brian E., 'The Kidnapping of Griffith Jones of Castellmarch', *Trivium* 15 (1980)

Hutton, Ronald, *The Royalist War Effort 1642–1646* (1982)

Jenkins, Geraint H., 'Dau broffwyd rhyfedd: Arise Evans a Thomas Jones', *Journal Merioneth Hist. and Record Soc.* 9 (1982)

Johnson, A. M., 'Bussy Mansell (1623–1699): Political Survivalist', *Morgannwg* 20 (1976)
—— 'Wales during the Commonwealth and Protectorate', in D. Pennington and K. Thomas (eds.), *Puritans and Revolutionaries* (Oxford, 1978).

Jones, E. D., 'The Gentry of South West Wales in the Civil War', *NLWJ* 11 (1959)

Leach, A. L., *The History of the Civil War (1642–1649) in Pembrokeshire and on its Borders* (1937)

Lewis, D. G., 'Sir Thomas Morgan, 1604–79, "Soldier of Fortune"' (unpubl. University of Wales MA thesis, 1930)

Lewis, Thomas T. (ed.), *Letters of the Lady Brilliana Harley* (Camden Society, 1853)

Lindley, J. K., 'The Impact of the 1641 Rebellion upon England and Wales, 1641–5', *Irish Historical Studies* 18 (1972)

Lloyd, J., 'Colonel John Jones, Maesygarnedd', *Journal Merioneth Hist. and Record Soc.* 2 (1953–6)

Mackenzie, N. H., 'Sir Thomas Herbert of Tintern: A Parliamentary Royalist', *Bulletin of the Institute of Historical Research*, 29 (1956)

Morrill, J. S., *The Revolt of the Provinces: Conservatives and Radicals in the English Civil War* (Paperback edn., 1980)

Owen, Geraint D., 'The Conspiracy of Christopher Love', *THSC* (1966)

Phillips, James, 'Haverfordwest in the Civil War', *Arch. Camb.* 15 (1915)

Phillips, J. Roland, *Memoirs of the Civil War in Wales and the Marches 1642–1649* (2 vols., 1874)

Rees, J. F., 'Breconshire during the Civil War', *Brycheiniog* 18 (1962)

Raymond, S. A., 'The Glamorgan Arraymen, 1642–45', *Morgannwg* 24 (1980)

Roberts, B. Dew, 'Cheadles against Bulkeleys', *Trans. Anglesey Antiq. Soc.* (1945)
—— *Mitre and Musket: John Williams Lord Keeper, Archbishop of York 1582–1650* (1938)

Roots, Ivan, *The Great Rebellion 1642–1660* (1966)

Thomas, C. M., 'The First Civil War in Glamorgan 1642–46' (unpubl. University of Wales MA thesis, 1963)

Thomas, G. R., 'Sir Thomas Myddelton 1586–1666' (unpubl. University of Wales MA thesis, 1968)

Thomas, J. D. H., 'James Howell, Historiographer Royal', *Brycheiniog* 9 (1963)
—— 'Judge David Jenkins, 1582–1663', *Morgannwg* 8 (1964)

Tilney, A. C., 'The Battle of St. Fagan's', *Glamorgan Historian* 8 (1972)

Tucker, Norman, 'Breconshire's Maimed Soldiers', *NLWJ* 14 (1965–6)
—— *Denbighshire Officers in the Civil War* (Denbigh, n.d.)
—— *North Wales in the Civil War* (Denbigh, 1958)
—— *Royalist Major-General Sir John Owen* (Denbigh, 1963)
—— 'Rupert's Letters to Anglesey and other Civil War Correspondence', *Trans. Anglesey Antiq. Soc.* (1958)

Veysey, A. G., 'Colonel Philip Jones, 1618–74', *THSC* (1966)

Williams, W. Gilbert, 'Dau Gywydd o Waith John Gruffydd, Llanddyfnan', *Trans. Anglesey Antiq. Soc.* (1938)

Woolrych, Austin, *Commonwealth to Protectorate* (Oxford, 1982)

Worden, Blair, *The Rump Parliament 1648–1653* (Cambridge, 1974)

8. Propagating the Gospel, 1642–60

Bassett, T. M., *The Welsh Baptists* (Swansea, 1977)

Bevan, Hugh, *Morgan Llwyd y Llenor* (Cardiff, 1954)

Braithwaite, W. C., *The Beginnings of Quakerism* (2nd edn., Cambridge, 1961)

Capp, B. S., *The Fifth Monarchy Men* (1972)

Davies, W. T. Pennar, 'Baledi Gwleidyddol yng nghyfnod y Chwyldro Piwritanaidd', *Y Cofiadur* 25 (1955)

Dodd, A. H., 'The Church in Wales during the Reformation Period', *Welsh Church Congress Handbook* (1953)

—— 'New England Influences in Early Welsh Puritanism', *BBCS* 16 (1954)

—— 'A Remonstrance from Wales, 1655', *BBCS* 17 (1958)

Evans, E. Lewis, *Morgan Llwyd* (Liverpool, 1931)

—— 'Morgan Llwyd and the Early Friends', *Friends' Quarterly* 8 (1954)

Gibbard, Noel, *Elusen i'r Enaid: Arweiniad i Weithiau'r Piwritaniaid Cymreig, 1630–1689* (Bridgend, 1979)

Gruffydd, R. Geraint, *'In that Gentile Country': The Beginnings of Puritan Nonconformity in Wales* (Bridgend, 1976)

Hill, Christopher, 'Propagating the Gospel', in H. E. Bell and R. L. Ollard (eds.), *Historical Essays 1600–1750* (1963)

—— 'Puritans and the "Dark Corners of the Land"', *TRHS* 13 (1963)

Huntley, F. L., *Jeremy Taylor and the Great Rebellion* (Michigan, 1970)

Jenkins, Geraint H., 'The Early Peace Testimony in Wales', *Llafur* 4 (1985)

John, Mansel (ed.), *Welsh Baptist Studies* (Llandysul, 1976)

Jones, Francis, 'Disaffection and Dissent in Pembrokeshire', *THSC* (1946–7)

Jones, J. M., 'Walter Cradock a'i Gyfoeswyr', *Y Cofiadur* 15 (1938)

Jones, Richard, *Crynwyr Bore Cymru 1653–1699* (Barmouth, 1931)

Jones, R. Tudur, *Hanes Annibynwyr Cymru* (Swansea, 1966)

—— 'The Healing Herb and the Rose of Love: The Piety of Two Welsh Puritans', in *Reformation, Conformity and Dissent*, ed. R. Buick Knox (1977)

—— 'The Life, Work, and Thought of Vavasor Powell (1617–70)' (unpubl. University of Oxford D. Phil. thesis, 1947)

—— 'Puritan Llanvaches', *Presenting Monmouthshire* 15 (1963)

—— *Vavasor Powell* (Swansea, 1971)

—— 'Vavasor Powell and the Protectorate', *Trans. Congregational Hist. Soc.* 17 (1953)

Llwyd, Morgan, *Gweithiau Morgan Llwyd o Wynedd*, eds. J. H. Davies and T. E. Ellis (2 vols., Bangor, 1899; London, 1908)

Morgan, Merfyn (ed.), *Gweithiau Oliver Thomas ac Evan Roberts* (Cardiff, 1981)

Morton, A. L., *The World of the Ranters* (1970)

Nickalls, J. L. (ed.), *The Journal of George Fox* (Cambridge, 1952)

Norris, W. G., *John ap John and Early Records of Friends in Wales* (1907)

Nuttall, G. F., *The Puritan Spirit* (1967)

—— *The Welsh Saints 1640–1660* (Cardiff, 1957)

Owen, G. W., 'Astudiaeth hanesyddol a beirniadol o weithiau Morgan Llwyd o Wynedd (1619–1659)' (unpubl. University of Wales Ph.D. thesis, 1982)

Rees, T. Mardy, *A History of the Quakers in Wales* (Carmarthen, 1925)

Richards, Thomas, 'Eglwys Llanfaches', *THSC* (1941)

—— 'Flintshire and the Puritan Movement', *Journal Flintshire Hist. Soc.* 12–14 (1951–4)

—— *A History of the Puritan Movement in Wales, 1639–53* (1920)

—— 'Meirionnydd: Piwritaniaeth Gynnar', *Journal Merioneth Hist. and Record Soc.* 2 (1953–6)

—— 'The Puritan Movement in Anglesey: A Reassessment', *Trans. Anglesey Antiq. Soc.* (1954)

—— *Religious Developments in Wales 1654–1662* (1923)

Stearns, R. P., *The Strenuous Puritan: Hugh Peter (1598–1660)* (Urbana, 1954)

Thomas, Joshua (ed.), *Hanes y Bedyddwyr* (Carmarthen, 1778)

Toon, Peter, *God's Statesman: The Life and Work of John Owen* (Exeter, 1971)

White, B. R., 'William Erbery (1604–1654) and the Baptists', *The Baptist Quarterly* 23 (1969)

Whiting, E. S. and others, *The Background of Quakerism in Wales and the Border* (1952)

Williams, G. J., 'Cerddi i Biwritaniaid Gwent a Morgannwg', *Llên Cymru* 3 (1954–5)

Williams, M. Fay, 'Glamorgan Quakers 1654–1900', *Morgannwg* 5 (1961)

—— 'The Society of Friends in Glamorgan, 1654–1900' (unpubl. University of Wales MA thesis, 1950)

9. Politics, 1660–1714

Adams, D. R. Ll., 'The Parliamentary Representation of Radnorshire 1536–1832' (unpubl. University of Wales MA thesis, 1970)

Davies, E. T., 'The "Popish Plot" in Monmouthshire', *Journal Hist. Soc. Church in Wales* 25 (1976)

Dodd, A. H., 'Caernarvonshire and the Restoration: Four Letters', *Trans. Caernarfonshire Hist. Soc.* 2 (1950)

—— 'Flintshire Politics in the Seventeenth Century', *Journal Flintshire Hist. Soc.* 14 (1953–4)

—— 'Tuning the Welsh Bench, 1680', *NLWJ* 6 (1950)

Downie, J. A., 'The Attack on Robert Harley M.P.', *NLWJ* 20 (1977)

Elis-Williams, D. M., 'The Activities of Welsh Members of Parliament 1660 to 1688' (unpubl. University of Wales MA thesis, 1952)

Evans, J. R., 'The Popish Plot', *NLWJ* 6 (1949–50)

Grant, R., *The Parliamentary History of Glamorgan 1542–1976* (Swansea, 1978)

Griffiths, G. M., 'Chirk Castle Election Activities 1600–1750', *NLWJ* 10 (1957)

Havill, E. E., 'The Parliamentary Representation of Monmouthshire and the Monmouth Boroughs 1536–1832' (unpubl. University of Wales MA thesis, 1949)

Henning, B. D. (ed.), *The History of Parliament: The House of Commons 1660–1690* (3 vols., 1983)

Holmes, Geoffrey, *British Politics in the Age of Anne* (1967)

—— *The Trial of Doctor Sacheverell* (1973)

Howse, W. H., 'A Family Feud at New Radnor', *Trans. Radnorshire Hist. Soc.* 28 (1958)

Hutton, Ronald, *The Restoration: A Political and Religious History of England and Wales 1658–1667* (Oxford, 1985)

Jenkins, Philip, 'Anti-Popery on the Welsh Marches in the Seventeenth Century', *The Historical Journal* 23 (1980)

—— 'Francis Gwyn and the birth of the Tory Party', *WHR* 2 (1983)

—— '"The Old Leaven": The Welsh Roundheads after 1660', *The Historical Journal* 24 (1981)

—— 'Two Poems on the Glamorgan Gentry Community in the reign of James II', *NLWJ* 21 (1979–80)

John, Ll. B., 'The Parliamentary Representation of Glamorgan, 1536–1832' (unpubl. University of Wales MA thesis, 1934)

Jones, Francis, *The Princes and Principality of Wales* (Cardiff, 1969)

Jones, M. E., 'The Parliamentary Representation of Pembrokeshire, the Pembroke Boroughs and Haverfordwest, 1536–1761' (unpubl. University of Wales thesis, 1958)

Keeton, G. W., 'George Jeffreys: His Family and Friends', *THSC* (1967)

—— 'Judge Jeffreys: Towards a Reappraisal', *WHR* 1 (1962)

—— *Lord Chancellor Jeffreys and the Stuart Cause* (1965)

Kenyon, J. P., *The Popish Plot* (1972)

Lloyd, R. J., 'Welsh Masters of the Bench of the Inner Temple', *THSC* (1933–5)

Mathew, David, 'The Welsh Influence among the Legal Advisers of James II', *THSC* (1938)

O'Keeffe, M. M. C., 'The Popish Plot in South Wales and the Marches of Hereford and Gloucester' (unpubl. University of Galway MA thesis, 1969)

Porritt, E. and A. G., *The Unreformed House of Commons* (2 vols., Cambridge, 1909)

Ransome, M., 'The Parliamentary Career of Sir Humphrey Mackworth', *University of Birmingham Historical Journal* 1 (1947–8)

Richards, Thomas, 'The Anglesey Election of 1708', *Trans. Anglesey Antiq. Soc.* (1943)

—— 'Declarasiwn 1687', *Trafodion Cymdeithas Hanes Bedyddwyr Cymru* (1924)

—— 'The Glamorgan Loyalists of 1696', *BBCS* 3 (1926)

—— *Piwritaniaeth a Pholitics (1689–1719)* (Wrexham, 1927)

—— 'Richard Edwards of Nanhoron: A Restoration Study', *Trans. Caernarfonshire Hist. Soc.* 8 (1947)

Taylor, D. F., 'Sir Leoline Jenkins' (unpubl. University of Liverpool M.Phil thesis, 1974)

Taylor, H., 'Flint Boroughs Election, 1697', *Journal Flintshire Hist. Soc.* 2 (1925)

Thomas, P. D. G., 'Anglesey Politics, 1689–1727', *Trans. Anglesey Antiq. Soc.* (1962)

—— 'The Montgomery Borough Constituency, 1660–1728', *BBCS* 20 (1963)

—— 'Parliamentary Elections in Brecknockshire, 1689–1832', *Brycheiniog* 6 (1960)

Tucker, Norman, 'Civil War Aftermath in Caernarvonshire', *NLWJ* 13 (1963–4)

Williams, J. Gwynn, 'Sir John Vaughan of Trawsgoed, 1603–1674', *NLWJ* 8 (1953–4)

Williams, W. R., *Parliamentary History of Wales, 1541–1895* (Brecknock, 1895)

10. Politics, 1714–80

Colley, Linda, *In Defiance of Oligarchy: The Tory Party 1714–60* (Cambridge, 1982)

Cronin, J. M., 'Local Jacobites, 1715–1745', *St. Peter's Magazine* 5 (1925)

Cruickshanks, E., *Political Untouchables* (1979)

Evans, G. Nesta, *Religion and Politics in Mid-Eighteenth Century Anglesey* (Cardiff, 1953)

Fortescue, Sir John (ed.), *The Correspondence of King George the Third from 1760 to December 1783* (6 vols., 1927–8)

Goyder, A. G., 'David Morgan and the Welsh Jacobites', *The Stewarts* 10 (1955–8)

—— 'Welsh Jacobite Societies', *The Stewarts* 11 (1960)

Jenkins, Philip, 'Jacobites and Freemasons in Eighteenth-Century Wales', *WHR* 9 (1979)

—— 'Tory Industrialism and Town Politics: Swansea in the Eighteenth Century', *The Historical Journal* 28 (1985)

—— 'The Tory Tradition in Eighteenth-Century Cardiff', *WHR* 12 (1984–5)

Jones, E. A., 'The Society or Garrison of Fort Williamsburg', *Y Cymmrodor* 44 (1935)

—— 'Two Welsh Correspondents of John Wilkes', *Y Cymmrodor* 29 (1919)

Jones, Francis, 'The Society of Sea Serjeants', *THSC* (1967)

Jones, W., 'Robert Morris, The Swansea Friend of John Wilkes', *Glamorgan Historian* 11 (1975)

Lenman, Bruce, *The Jacobite Risings in Britain 1689–1746* (1980)

Llewellin, W., 'David Morgan, the Welsh Jacobite', *Trans. Liverpool Welsh National Society* (1894–5)

Lloyd-Johnes, H. J., 'The Cardigan Boroughs Election of 1774', *Ceredigion* 7 (1972–5)

Morgan, Walter T., 'Correspondence relating mainly to Monmouthshire Elections 1720–82', *NLWJ* 12 (1962)

—— 'County Elections in Monmouthshire, 1705–1847', *NLWJ* 10 (1957–8)

Namier, Sir Lewis and John Brooke, (eds.), *The History of Parliament: The House of Commons 1754–1790* (3 vols., 1964)

Nicholas, D., 'The Welsh Jacobites', *THSC* (1948)

Owen, R. H., 'Jacobitism and the Church in Wales', *Journal Historical Soc. Church in Wales* 2 (1953)

Price, J. A., 'Sidelights on Welsh Jacobitism', *Y Cymmrodor* 14 (1901)

Richards, H. P., *David Williams (1738–1816)* (Cowbridge, 1980)

Roberts, Glyn, 'The County Representation of Anglesey in the Eighteenth Century', *Trans. Anglesey Antiq. Soc.* (1930)

Roberts, Glyn, 'The Glynnes and the Wynns of Glynllifon', *Trans. Caernarfonshire Hist. Soc.* 9 (1948)

Ross, J. E. (ed.), *Radical Adventurer: The Diaries of Robert Morris 1772–1774* (Bath, 1971)

Sedgwick, Romney (ed.), *The History of Parliament: The House of Commons 1715–1754* (2 vols., 1970)

Taylor, H., 'Sir George Wynne, Baronet, M.P.', *Journal Flintshire Hist. Soc.* 9 (1921–2)

Thomas, D. O., *The Honest Mind* (Oxford, 1977)

—— *Richard Price 1723–1791* (Cardiff, 1976)

—— *Richard Price and America (1723–91)* (Aberystwyth, 1975)

Thomas, P. D. G., 'The Cardigan Boroughs Election of 1741', *Ceredigion* 6 (1968)

—— 'County Elections in Eighteenth Century Carmarthenshire', *The Carmarthenshire Antiquary* 4 (1962–3)

—— 'Eighteenth-Century Elections in the Cardigan Boroughs Constituency', *Ceredigion* 6 (1968)

—— 'Glamorgan Politics 1700–1750', *Morgannwg* 6 (1962)

—— 'Jacobitism in Wales', *WHR* 1 (1962)

—— 'The Montgomeryshire Election of 1774', *Montgomeryshire Collections* 59 (1965–6)

—— 'The Parliamentary Representation of Caernarvonshire in the Eighteenth Century', *Trans. Caernarfonshire Hist. Soc.* 19 (1959)

—— 'The Parliamentary Representation of Merioneth during the Eighteenth Century', *Journal Merioneth Hist. and Record Soc.* 3 (1958)

—— 'The Parliamentary Representation of North Wales, 1715–84' (unpubl. University of Wales MA thesis, 1953)

—— 'Sir George Wynne and the Flint Borough Elections of 1727–1741', *Journal Flintshire Hist. Soc.* 20 (1962)

—— 'Wynnstay versus Chirk Castle: Parliamentary elections in Denbighshire 1716–1741', *NLWJ* 11 (1959)

Vaughan, H. M., 'Welsh Jacobitism', *THSC* (1920–1)

Wager, D. A., 'Welsh Politics and Parliamentary Reform, 1780–1832', *WHR* 7 (1975)

—— 'Welsh Politics and Parliamentary Reform, 1780–1835' (unpubl. University of Wales Ph.D. thesis, 1972)

Williams, David, *Incidents in My Own Life*, ed. P. France (University of Sussex, 1980)

Williams, David, 'Cardiganshire Politics in the Mid-Eighteenth Century', *Ceredigion* 3 (1959)

Williams, Gwyn A., *The Search for Beulah Land* (1980)

11. Local Government and Administration

Allin, W. E., 'Poor Law Administration in Glamorganshire before the Poor Law Amendment Act of 1834' (unpubl. University of Wales MA thesis, 1936)

Bassett, T. M., 'A Study of Local Government in Wales under the Commonwealth with Special Reference to its Relations with the Central Government Authority' (unpubl. University of Wales MA thesis, 1941)

Bowen, Ivor, 'Grand Juries, Justices of the Peace, and Quarter Sessions in Wales', *THSC* (1933–5)

Davies, A. Eurig, 'Some Aspects of the Operation of the Old Poor Law in Cardiganshire, 1750–1834', *Ceredigion* 6 (1968)

Dodd, A. H., 'The Old Poor Law in North Wales', *Arch. Camb.* 6 (1926)

Evans, G. Eyre, *Aberystwyth and its Court Leet* (Aberystwyth, 1902)

—— 'Murders, Crimes, Executions at Carmarthen: 1559–1769', *Trans. Carmarthenshire Antiq. Soc.* 6 (1910–11)

Glassey, L. K. J., *Politics and the Appointment of Justices of the Peace 1675–1720* (Oxford, 1979)

Griffiths, G. M., 'Glimpses of Cardiganshire in Sessions Records', *Ceredigion* 5 (1966)

—— 'Glimpses of Denbighshire in the Records of the Court of Great Sessions', *Trans. Denbighshire Hist. Soc.* 22 (1973)

Gruffydd, K. Lloyd, 'The Vale of Clwyd Corn Riots of 1740', *Journal Flintshire Hist. Soc.* 27 (1975–6)

Hay, D. and others, *Albion's Fatal Tree* (1975)

Howell, B., 'Local Administration as Exemplified in Monmouthshire 1536–1835' (unpubl. University of Wales MA thesis, 1951)

Hughes, E., 'The Letters of Chief Justice Spencer Cowper from the North Wales Circuit, 1717–19', *THSC* (1956)

Jones, B. P., 'An Administrative History of the Borough of Newport 1623–1850' (unpubl. University of Wales MA thesis, 1955)

Jones, D. J. V., *Before Rebecca* (1973)

—— 'Life and Death in Eighteenth-Century Wales: A Note', *WHR* 10 (1981)

Jones, E. D., 'Gleanings from Radnorshire Files of Great Sessions Papers, 1691–1699', *Trans. Radnorshire Hist. Soc.* 13 (1943)

Jones, J. Gwynfor, 'Aspects of Local Government in Pre-Restoration Caernarvonshire', *Trans. Caernarfonshire Hist. Soc.* 33 (1972)

—— 'Caernarvonshire Administration: The Activities of the Justices of the Peace, 1603–1660', *WHR* 5 (1970–1)

—— 'The Caernarvonshire Justices of the Peace and Their Duties during the Seventeenth Century' (unpubl. University of Wales MA thesis, 1967)

Jones, T. I. J., 'The Court Leet Presentments of the Town, Borough, and Liberty of St. Clears, 1719–1889', *BBCS* 13 (1948)

Landau, Norma, *The Justices of the Peace, 1679–1760* (1984)

Lewis, E. A., 'Leet Proceedings of the Borough of Newtown, 1665–1683', *Montgomeryshire Collections* 48 (1943–4)

—— 'The Proceedings of the Leet Courts of North Radnorshire in 1688', *Trans. Radnorshire Hist. Soc.* (1934)

Lewis, T. H., 'The Administration of Justice in the Welsh County', *THSC* (1945)

—— 'Attendance of Justices and Grand Jurors at the Courts of Quarter Sessions in Wales', *THSC* (1942)

—— 'Documents Illustrating the County Gaol and House of Correction in Wales', *THSC* (1946–7)

Lewis, T. H., 'The Justice of the Peace in Wales', *THSC* (1943–4)
—— 'Local Government in Wales from the Sixteenth to the Eighteenth Century'
   (unpubl. University of Liverpool Ph.D. thesis, 1941)
Owen, G. D., 'The Poor Law System in Carmarthenshire during the Eighteenth
   and Early Nineteenth Centuries', *THSC* (1941)
Owen, Hugh, 'Corporation of Beaumaris Minute Book 1694–1723', *Trans.
   Anglesey Antiq. Soc.* (1972)
Owen, H. J., 'The Common Gaols of Merioneth during the Eighteenth and
   Nineteenth Centuries', *Journal Merioneth Hist. and Record Soc.* 3 (1957–60)
Oxley, G. W., *Poor Relief in England and Wales 1601–1834* (Newton Abbot, 1974)
Parry, J. Glyn, 'Terfysgoedd Ŷd yng Ngogledd Cymru 1740–58', *Trans. Caernar-
   fonshire Hist. Soc.* 39 (1978)
Phillips, J. R. S. (ed.), *The Justices of the Peace in Wales and Monmouthshire 1541
   to 1689* (Cardiff, 1975)
Roberts, Peter R., 'The Merioneth Gentry and Local Government circa
   1650–1838', *Journal Merioneth Hist. and Record Soc.* 5 (1965–8)
Skinner, K. E. M., 'Poor Law Administration in Glamorgan 1750–1850' (unpubl.
   University of Wales MA thesis, 1956)
Thomas, B. B., 'The Old Poor Law in Ardudwy Uwch-Artro', *BBCS* 7 (1934)
Till, R. D., 'Local Government in the Borough of Neath: A Study in Urban
   Administration, 1694–1884' (unpubl. University of Wales MA thesis, 1970)
—— 'Proprietary Politics in Glamorgan: The Mackworth Family and the Borough
   of Neath, 1696–1794', *Morgannwg* 16 (1972)
Webb, Sidney and Beatrice, *English Local Government* (9 vols., 1906–29)
Williams, W. R., *The History of the Great Sessions in Wales 1542–1830*
   (Brecknock, 1899)

12. The Established Church and Methodism

Bennett, G. V. and J. D. Walsh (eds.), *Essays in Modern English Church History*
   (1966)
Bennett, Richard, *The Early Life of Howell Harris*, tr. G. M. Roberts (1962)
Beynon, Tom (ed.), *Howell Harris, Reformer and Soldier* (Caernarfon, 1958)
—— *Howell Harris's Visits to Pembrokeshire* (Aberystwyth, 1966)
Bowen, Geraint, 'Yr Halsingod', *THSC* (1945)
Carpenter, S. C., *Eighteenth Century Church and People* (1959)
Davies, J. E. Wynne (ed.), *Gwanwyn Duw* (Caernarfon, 1982)
Davies, J. V., 'The Diocese of St David's during the First Half of the Eighteenth
   Century' (unpubl. University of Wales MA thesis, 1936)
Davies, R. and G. Rupp (eds.), *A History of the Methodist Church in Great Britain*
   (3 vols., 1965–83)
Evans, Eifion, *Daniel Rowland* (Edinburgh, 1985)
—— *Howel Harris Evangelist* (Cardiff, 1974)
Evans, Heber A. (ed.), *Y Gwyrthiau Gynt* (Lampeter, 1962)
Evans, R. W., 'The Eighteenth-Century Welsh Awakening, with its Relationships
   to the Contemporary English Evangelical Revival' (unpubl. University of
   Edinburgh Ph.D. thesis, 1956)

Griffith, William, *Methodistiaeth Fore Môn 1740–1751* (Caernarfon, 1955)

Griffiths, G. M. (ed.), 'John Wynne, a Report on the Deanery of Penllyn and Edeirnion, 1730', *The Merioneth Miscellany* 1 (1955)

—— 'A Visitation of the Archdeaconry of Carmarthen, 1710', *NLWJ* 18–19 (1974–6)

—— 'Ymweliad Deon Gwlad Rhos â'i Ddeoniaeth yn 1729', *Trans. Denbighshire Hist. Soc.* 13 (1964)

Gruffydd, R. Geraint, 'Diwygiad 1762 a William Williams o Bantycelyn', *Journal Historical Soc. Presbyterian Church in Wales* 44–5 (1969–70)

Guy, J. R., 'An Investigation into the Pattern and Nature of Patronage, Plurality and Non-residence in the Old Diocese of Llandaff between 1660 and the Beginning of the Nineteenth Century' (unpubl. University of Wales Ph.D. thesis, 1984)

Hart, A. Tindal, *William Lloyd 1627–1717* (1952)

Havard, W. T., 'The Eighteenth Century Background of Church Life in Wales', *Journal Hist. Soc. Church in Wales* (1955)

Higham, R. B., 'The Life and Work of the Rev. David Jones of Llangan, 1736–1810', (unpubl. University of Wales M.Th. thesis, 1981)

Hobley, W., *Hanes Methodistiaeth Arfon* (6 vols., Caernarfon, 1910–24)

Hodges, H. A., 'Over the Distant Hills: Thoughts on Williams Pantycelyn', *Brycheiniog* 17 (1976–7)

Hughes, Glyn Tegai, *Williams Pantycelyn* (Cardiff, 1983)

Hughes-Edwards, W. G., 'The Development and Organization of the Methodist Society in Wales 1735–1750' (unpubl. University of Wales MA thesis, 1966)

James, L. J. Hopkin, *The Soul of a Cathedral* (Cardiff, 1930)

Jenkins, D. E., *The Life of the Rev. Thomas Charles of Bala* (3 vols., Denbigh, 1908)

Jenkins, Geraint H., 'Y Sais Brych', *Taliesin* 52 (1985)

Jenkins, R. T., *The Moravian Brethren in North Wales* (1938)

—— *Yng Nghysgod Trefeca* (Caernarfon, 1968)

Jones, D. J. Odwyn, *Daniel Rowland Llangeitho* (Llandysul, 1938)

Jones, E. D., 'Some Aspects of the History of the Church in North Cardiganshire in the Eighteenth Century', *Journal Hist. Soc. Church in Wales* 3 (1953)

Jones, E. P., *Methodistiaeth Galfinaidd Dinbych 1735–1909* (Denbigh, 1936)

Jones, J. Morgan, *Y Tadau Methodistaidd* (2 vols., Swansea, 1895–7)

Jones, M. H., 'Howell Harris, Citizen and Patriot', *THSC* (1908–9)

—— *The Trevecka Letters* (Caernarfon, 1932)

Jones, O. W., 'The Case against Bishop Jones of St Asaph', *Journal Hist. Soc. Church in Wales* 14 (1964)

Jones, Robert, *Drych yr Amseroedd*, ed. G. M. Ashton (Cardiff, 1958)

Jones, R. Tudur, 'Eglwys Loegr a'r Saint, 1660–1688', *Diwinyddiaeth* 14 (1963)

Knox, R. Buick, 'Howell Harris and his Doctrine of the Church', *Journal Historical Soc. Presbyterian Church in Wales* (1964)

La Trobe, B., *A Brief Account of the Life of Howell Harris* (Trefeca, 1791)

Lane, M., 'The Queen of the Methodists', *Brycheiniog* 15 (1971)

Lewis, Saunders, *Williams Pantycelyn* (1927)

Morgan, D. Llwyd, *Y Diwygiad Mawr* (Llandysul, 1981)

Morgan, D. Llwyd, *Williams Pantycelyn* (Caernarfon, 1983)

Morgan, Walter T., 'The Consistory Courts in the Diocese of St David's', *Journal Hist. Soc. Church in Wales* 6 (1957)

—— 'The Consistory Courts of the Diocese of St David's, 1660–1858' (unpubl. University of Wales MA thesis, 1962)

Nuttall, G. F., *Howel Harris 1714–1773: The Last Enthusiast* (Cardiff, 1965)

Owen, A. W., 'Howell Harris and the Trevecka "Family" ', *Journal Historical Soc. Presbyterian Church in Wales* 44 (1959)

—— 'A Study of Howell Harris and the Trevecka Family (1752–1760)' (unpubl. University of Wales MA thesis, 1957)

Owen, G. P., *Methodistiaeth Llŷn ac Eifionydd* (Swansea, 1978)

Owen, Hugh, 'The Morrises and the Methodists of Anglesey in the Eighteenth Century', *Trans. Anglesey Antiq. Soc.* (1942)

Pryce, A. I., *The Diocese of Bangor during Three Centuries* (Cardiff, 1929)

Richards, Gwynfryn, 'The Diocese of Bangor during the Rise of Welsh Methodism', *NLWJ* 21 (1979–80)

—— 'Royal Briefs for the Restoration of Churches in Wales', *Journal Hist. Soc. Church in Wales* 5–7 (1956–7)

Roberts, Gomer M., *Bywyd a Gwaith Peter Williams* (Cardiff, 1943)

—— *Dafydd Jones o Gaeo* (Aberystwyth, 1948)

—— (ed.), *Hanes Methodistiaeth Galfinaidd Cymru, cyf. 1, Y Deffroad Mawr; cyf. 2. Cynnydd y Corff* (2 vols., Caernarfon, 1973, 1978)

—— *Y Pêr Ganiedydd* (2 vols., Aberystwyth, 1949, 1958)

—— *Portread o Ddiwygiwr* (Caernarfon, 1969)

—— (ed.), *Selected Trevecka Letters (1742–1747)* (Caernarfon, 1956)

—— (ed.), *Selected Trevecka Letters (1747–1794)* (Caernarfon, 1962)

Roberts, Gomer M. and G. H. Hughes (eds.), *Gweithiau William Williams Pantycelyn* (2 vols., Cardiff, 1964–7)

Roberts, G. T., *Dadleuon Methodistiaeth Gynnar* (Swansea, 1970)

—— *Howell Harris* (1951)

Roberts, John, *The Calvinistic Methodism of Wales* (Caernarfon, 1934)

Saunders, Erasmus, *A View of the State of Religion in the Diocese of St. David's 1721* (repr., Cardiff, 1949)

Sweet-Escott, B., 'William Beaw: A Cavalier Bishop', *WHR* 1 (1963)

Sykes, Norman, *Church and State in England in the Eighteenth Century* (Cambridge, 1934)

Thomas, D. R., *History of the Diocese of St. Asaph* (3 vols., Oswestry, 1908–11)

Thomas, S. R., 'The Diocese of St. David's in the Eighteenth Century: The Working of the Diocese in a Period of Criticism' (unpubl. University of Wales MA thesis, 1983)

Tudur, Geraint, 'Gwir Ffrewyll y Methodistiaid', *Y Cofiadur* 46 (1981)

Vickers, J. A., *Thomas Coke: Apostle of Methodism* (1969)

Walsh, J. D., 'Elie Halévy and the Birth of Methodism', *TRHS* 25 (1975)

Williams, A. H. (ed.), *John Wesley in Wales 1739–1790* (Cardiff, 1971)

—— 'The Leaders of English and Welsh Methodism 1738–91', *Bathafarn* 16–17 (1961–2), 22–24 (1967–9)

Williams, William, *Welsh Calvinistic Methodism* (1872)

Wright, E. G., 'Dean John Jones 1650–1727', *Trans. Anglesey Antiq. Soc.* (1952)
—— 'Humphrey Humphreys, Bishop of Bangor and Hereford', *Journal Hist. Soc. Church in Wales* 2 (1950)

13. Religious Dissent, 1660–1780

Attwater, D., *The Catholic Church in Modern Wales* (1935)
Besse, Joseph (ed.), *A Collection of the Sufferings of the People Called Quakers* (2 vols., 1753)
Bowen, E. G., 'The Teifi Valley as a Religious Frontier', *Ceredigion* 7 (1972)
Browning, C. H., *The Welsh Settlement of Pennsylvania* (Philadelphia, 1912)
Calamy, Edmund, *An Account of the Ministers . . . Ejected after the Restoration in 1660* (2 vols., 1713)
Cleary, Martin, 'The Catholic Resistance in Wales: 1568–1678', *Blackfriars* 38 (1957)
Davies, D. E. J., *Y Smotiau Duon* (Llandysul, 1981)
Davies, T. Eurig, 'Philip Pugh a'i Ragflaenwyr yng nghanolbarth Sir Aberteifi', *Y Cofiadur* 14 (1937)
Davies, W. T. Pennar, 'Episodes in the History of Brecknockshire Dissent', *Brycheiniog* 3 (1957)
Dodd, A. H., 'The Background of the Welsh Quaker Migration to Pennsylvania', *Journal Merioneth Hist. and Record Soc.* 3 (1958)
—— *The Character of Early Welsh Emigration to the United States* (Cardiff, 1953)
Ellis, T. P., *The Catholic Martyrs of Wales 1535–1680* (1933)
Evans, E. Lewis, *Capel Isaac* (Llandysul, 1950)
Evans, G. Eyre (ed.), *Lloyd Letters (1754–1796)* (Aberystwyth, 1908)
Glenn, T. A., *Welsh Founders of Pennsylvania* (2 vols., Oxford, 1911–13)
Guy, J. R., 'The Anglican Patronage of Monmouthshire Recusants', *Recusant History* 15 (1981)
—— 'Eighteenth-Century Gwent Catholics', *Recusant History* 16 (1982–3)
Hartmann, E. G., *Americans from Wales* (Boston, 1967)
James, Wyn (ed.), *Cwmwl o Dystion* (Swansea, 1977)
Jenkins, Geraint H., 'From Ysgeifiog to Pennsylvania: The Rise of Thomas Wynne, Quaker Barber-Surgeon', *Journal Flintshire Hist. Soc.* 28 (1977–8)
—— ' "Goleuni gwedi torri allan Ynghymru": Her y Bedyddwyr yn y 1690au', *Trafodion Cymdeithas Hanes y Bedyddwyr* (1981)
—— 'James Owen versus Benjamin Keach: A Controversy over Infant Baptism', *NLWJ* 19 (1975)
—— 'Llythyr Olaf Thomas Wynne o Gaerwys', *BBCS* 29 (1980)
—— 'Quaker and anti-Quaker Literature in Welsh from the Restoration to Methodism', *WHR* 7 (1975)
Jenkins, Philip, ' "A Welsh Lancashire"? Monmouthshire Catholics in the Eighteenth Century', *Recusant History* 15 (1980)
Jenkins, R. T., *Hanes Cynulleidfa Hen Gapel Llanuwchllyn* (Bala, 1937)
Johnes, A. J., *An Essay on the Causes which have Produced Dissent from the Established Church in the Principality of Wales* (3rd edn., 1835)
Jones, Anthony E., *Welsh Chapels* (Cardiff, 1984)

Jones, E. D., 'Llyfr Eglwys Mynydd Bach', *Y Cofiadur*, 17 (1947)

—— 'Nonconformity in Merioneth', *NLWJ* 8 (1953–4)

—— 'Phylip Pugh', *Diwinyddiaeth* 15 (1964)

Jones, R. Tudur, 'Religion in Post-Restoration Brecknockshire 1660–1688', *Brycheiniog* 8 (1962)

Jones, R. Tudur and B. G. Owens, 'Anghydffurfwyr Cymru 1660–1662', *Y Cofiadur* 32 (1962)

Lee, M. H. (ed.), *Diaries and Letters of Philip Henry* (1882)

Lewis, D. M., 'Morgan Rhys a'i Gyfnod', *Y Cofiadur* 10–11 (1934)

Lynch, G. J. J., 'The Revival of Roman Catholicism in South Wales in the Late Eighteenth and Early Nineteenth Centuries' (unpubl. University of Wales MA thesis, 1941)

Martin, Aubrey J., *Hanes Llwynrhydowen* (Llandysul, 1977)

Matthews, A. G. (ed.), *Calamy Revised* (1959)

Morgan, Walter T., 'The Prosecution of Nonconformists in the Consistory Courts of St. David's, 1661–88', *Journal Hist. Soc. Church in Wales* 12 (1962)

Mullins, D. J., 'Catholicism in Wales in the Eighteenth Century', *Journal Welsh Ecclesiastical History*, 2 (1985)

O'Keeffe, M. M. C., 'Three Catholic Martyrs of Breconshire', *Brycheiniog* 17 (1976–7)

Owen, Jeremy, *Golwg ar y Beiau*, ed. R. T. Jenkins (Cardiff, 1950)

Owen, W. T., 'Wales and the Congregational Fund Board', *THSC* (1978)

Palmer, A. N., *A History of the Older Nonconformity of Wrexham* (Wrexham, 1888)

Peate, I. C. (ed.), *Hen Gapel Llanbryn-mair 1739–1939* (Llandysul, 1939)

Phillips, Edgar, *Edmund Jones 'The Old Prophet'* (1959)

Rees, Thomas, *History of Protestant Nonconformity in Wales* (2nd edn., 1883)

Rees, Thomas and John Thomas (eds.), *Hanes Eglwysi Annibynol Cymru* (4 vols., Liverpool, 1871–5)

Richards, Thomas, 'Henry Maurice: Piwritan ac Annibynnwr', *Y Cofiadur* 5–6 (1928)

—— 'The Religious Census of 1676', *THSC* Supplement (1925–6)

—— *Wales under the Indulgence 1672–1675* (1928)

—— *Wales under the Penal Code 1662–1687* (1925)

Underhill, E. B. (ed.), *The Records of a Church of Christ Meeting at Broadmead, Bristol* (1847)

Watts, Michael R., *The Dissenters* (Oxford, 1978)

Williams, J. Gwynn, 'The Quakers in Merioneth during the Seventeenth Century', *Journal Merioneth Hist. and Record Soc.* 8 (1978–9)

Williams, T. O., *Undodiaeth a Rhyddid Meddwl* (Llandysul, 1962)

14. Printing, Publishing, and Education

Ballinger, J. and J. Ifano Jones, *The Bible in Wales* (1906)

Cavanagh, F. E., *The Life and Work of Griffith Jones of Llanddowror* (Cardiff, 1930)

Clement, Mary, 'A Calendar of Welsh Letters to the S.P.C.K. 1745–1783', *NLWJ* 10 (1957)

—— *The S.P.C.K. and Wales 1699–1740* (1954)

Davies, D. Eurig, *Hoff Ddysgedig Nyth* (Swansea, 1976)

Davies, Gwyn, *Griffith Jones, Llanddowror: Athro Cenedl* (Bridgend, 1984)

Davies, Iolo, '*A Certaine Schoole': A History of Cowbridge Grammar School* (Cowbridge, 1967)

Evans, Leslie W., *Education in Industrial Wales 1700–1900* (Cardiff, 1971)

Gittins, C. E. (ed.), *Pioneers of Welsh Education* (Swansea, n.d.)

Griffiths, G. M., 'Education in the Diocese of St. Asaph 1729–30', *NLWJ* 6 (1949–50)

Jenkins, David, 'The Part Played by Craftsmen in the Religious History of Modern Wales', *The Welsh Anvil* 6 (1954)

Jenkins, Geraint H., 'Bywiogrwydd Crefyddol a Llenyddol Dyffryn Teifi, 1689–1740', *Ceredigion* 8 (1979)

—— *Hen Filwr dros Grist: Griffith Jones, Llanddowror* (Llandysul, 1983)

—— *Literature, Religion and Society in Wales 1660–1730* (Cardiff, 1978)

—— 'Llenyddiaeth, Crefydd a'r Gymdeithas yng Nghymru, 1660–1730', *Efrydiau Athronyddol* 41 (1978)

—— '"An Old and Much Honoured Soldier": Griffith Jones, Llanddowror', *WHR* 11 (1983)

—— *Thomas Jones yr Almanaciwr* (Cardiff, 1980)

Jenkins, R. T., 'A Conspectus of Griffith Jones's Schools, 1738–1761', *BBCS* 5 (1929–31)

—— *Gruffydd Jones, Llanddowror* (Cardiff, 1930)

Jones, Brynmor, 'Argraffwyr Cymreig y Gororau', *JWBS* 10 (1970)

Jones, D. Ambrose, *Griffith Jones, Llanddowror* (Wrexham, 1923)

Jones, D. Gwenallt, *Y Ficer Prichard a 'Canwyll y Cymry'* (Caernarfon, 1946)

Jones, Griffith and Bevan, Bridget, *The Welch Piety* (1737–76)

Jones, H. Pierce, 'An S.P.C.K. Activity in Eighteenth Century Anglesey', *Trans. Anglesey Antiq. Soc.* (1963)

Jones, J. Ifano, *A History of Printing and Printers in Wales* (Cardiff, 1925)

Jones, M. G., *The Charity School Movement* (Cambridge, 1938)

—— (ed.), 'Two Accounts of the Welsh Trust, 1675 and 1678', *BBCS* 9 (1937)

Kelly, Thomas, *Griffith Jones Llanddowror: Pioneer in Adult Education* (Cardiff, 1950)

Lewis, Aneirin, 'Llyfrau Cymraeg a'u Darllenwyr 1696–1740', *Efrydiau Athronyddol* 34 (1971)

Lewis, E., 'The Cowbridge Diocesan Library, 1711–1848', *Journal Hist. Soc. Church in Wales* 4 (1954), 7 (1957)

Nuttall, D., *A History of Printing in Chester* (Chester, 1969)

Nuttall, G. F., 'The Correspondence of John Lewis, Glasgrug, with Richard Baxter and with Dr. John Ellis, Dolgellau', *Journal Merioneth Hist. and Record Soc.* 2 (1953–6)

—— 'The Students of Trevecca College 1768–1791', *THSC* (1967)

Owen, Geraint D., 'James Owen a'i Academi', *Y Cofiadur* 22 (1952)

—— *Ysgolion a Cholegau'r Annibynwyr* (Llandysul, 1939)

Pretty, D. A., *Two Centuries of Anglesey Schools 1700–1902* (Anglesey Antiquarian Soc., 1977)

Rees, Eiluned, 'Bookbinding in Eighteenth Century Wales', *JWBS* 12 (1983–4)

—— 'Developments in the Book Trade in Eighteenth Century Wales', *The Library* 24 (1969)

—— 'An Introductory Survey of Eighteenth Century Welsh Libraries', *JWBS* 10 (1971)

—— 'Pre-1820 Welsh Subscription Lists', *JWBS* 9 (1973–4)

—— 'Welsh Publishing before 1717', in *Essays in Honour of Victor Scholderer*, ed. D. E. Rhodes (Mainz, 1970)

Rees, Eiluned and G. Morgan, 'Welsh Almanacks, 1680–1835', *The Library* 1 (1979)

Richards, G. M., 'Yr Awdur a'i Gyhoedd yn y Ddeunawfed Ganrif', *JWBS* 10 (1966)

Roberts, H. P., 'Nonconformist Academies in Wales (1662–1862)', *THSC* (1928–9)

Shankland, Thomas, 'Sir John Philipps, the S.P.C.K. and the Charity-School Movement in Wales, 1699–1737', *THSC* (1904–5)

—— 'Stephen Hughes', *Y Beirniad* 2 (1912)

Vincent, W. A. L., *The State and School Education, 1640–60, in England and Wales* (1950)

Watts, T., 'The Edmund Jones Library', *JWBS* 11 (1975–6)

Wiliam, Urien, 'Education in Glamorgan, 1650–1800' (unpubl. University of Wales MA thesis, 1956)

Williams, G. J., 'Stephen Hughes a'i Gyfnod', *Y Cofiadur* 4 (1926)

Williams, Jac L. (ed.), *Ysgrifau ar Addysg* (vol. iv. Cardiff, 1966)

Williams, Jac L. and G. R. Hughes (eds.), *The History of Education in Wales* (Swansea, 1978)

Williams, W. Moses, *The Friends of Griffith Jones* (1939)

—— (ed.), *Selections from The Welch Piety* (Cardiff, 1938)

15. The Welsh Language

Bradney, J., *A Memorandum . . . of the Decay of the Welsh Language in the Eastern Part of the County of Monmouth* (Abergavenny, 1926)

Dodd, A. H., 'Welsh and English in East Denbighshire: A Historical Retrospect', *THSC* (1940)

Durkacz, V. E., *The Decline of the Celtic Languages* (Edinburgh, 1983)

Humphreys, H. L., *La Langue galloise* (2 vols., Université de Bretagne Occidentale, 1979–80)

James, B. Ll., 'The Welsh Language in the Vale of Glamorgan', *Morgannwg* 16 (1972)

Jones, E., 'The Changing Distribution of the Celtic Languages in the British Isles', *THSC* (1967)

Lewis, G. J., 'The Geography of Cultural Transition: The Welsh Borderland 1750–1850', *NLWJ* 21 (1979–80)

Morgan, T. J. and Prys Morgan, *Welsh Surnames* (Cardiff, 1985)

Owen, L. H., 'A History of the Welsh Language in Radnorshire since 1536' (unpubl. University of Liverpool MA thesis, 1954)

Price, Glanville, *The Languages of Britain* (1984)

Pryce, W. T. R., 'Approaches to the Linguistic Geography of Northeast Wales, 1750–1846', *NLWJ* 17 (1972)

—— 'Wales as a Culture Region: Patterns of Change 1750–1971', *THSC* (1978)

—— 'Welsh and English in Wales, 1750–1971', *BBCS* 28 (1978)

Rees, W. H., 'The Vicissitudes of the Welsh Language in the Marches of Wales' (unpubl. University of Wales Ph.D. thesis, 1947)

Richards, G. Melville, 'The Population of the Welsh Border', *THSC* (1971)

Southall, J. E., *Wales and her Language* (1892)

Stephens, Meic, *Linguistic Minorities in Western Europe* (Llandysul, 1976)

—— (ed.), *The Welsh Language Today* (Llandysul, 1973)

Thomas, R. M., 'The Linguistic Geography of Carmarthenshire, Glamorgan and Pembrokeshire from 1750 to the Present Time' (unpubl. University of Wales MA thesis, 1967)

Williams, D. T., 'Linguistic Divides in North Wales: A Study in Historical Geography', *Arch. Camb.* 91 (1936)

—— 'Linguistic Divides in South Wales: A Historico-Geographical study', *Arch. Camb.* 90 (1935)

Williams, Michael, 'The Linguistic and Cultural Frontier in Gower', *Arch. Camb.* 121 (1972)

16. Welsh Poetry, Literature, and Scholarship

Ashton, Charles, *Hanes Llenyddiaeth Gymreig o 1651 hyd 1850* (Liverpool, 1893)

Bell, H. Idris, *The Development of Welsh Poetry* (Oxford, 1936)

Bowen, E. G., *David Samwell 1751–1798* (Cardiff, 1974)

Bowen, Geraint (ed.), *Y Traddodiad Rhyddiaith* (Llandysul, 1970)

Carr, A. D., 'John Morgan, Matching, 1688–1733', *Journal Merioneth Hist. and Record Soc.* 5 (1966)

Carr, Glenda, 'Goronwy Owen (1723–1769)', *Trans. Anglesey Antiq. Soc.* (1969–70)

—— *William Owen Pughe* (Cardiff, 1983)

Carter, P. W., 'Edward Lhuyd the Scientist', *THSC* (1962)

Charles, R. A., 'Teulu Mostyn fel Noddwyr y Beirdd', *Llên Cymru* 9 (1966)

Davies, G. Alban, 'The Morris Letters', *Yorkshire Celtic Studies* 6 (1953–8)

Davies, John, *Bywyd a Gwaith Moses Williams 1685–1742* (Cardiff, 1937)

Davies, J. H. (ed.), *The Letters of Goronwy Owen (1723–1769)* (Cardiff, 1924)

Davies, W. Ll., 'Phylipiaid Ardudwy', *Y Cymmrodor* 42 (1931)

Donovan, P. J. (ed.), *Cerddi Rhydd Iolo Morganwg* (Cardiff, 1980)

Edwards, Charles, *Y Ffydd Ddi-ffuant*, ed. G. J. Williams (Cardiff, 1936)

Edwards, Hywel T., *Yr Eisteddfod* (Llandysul, 1976)

Ellis, Tecwyn, *Edward Jones, Bardd y Brenin* (Cardiff, 1957)

—— 'Edward Jones, "the King's Bard" (1752–1824)', *Journal Merioneth Hist. and Record Soc* 4 (1961–4)

—— 'William Jones, Llangadfan', *Llên Cymru* 1 (1951)

Emery, F. V., '"The Best Naturalist now in Europe": Edward Lhuyd, F.R.S. (1660–1709)', *THSC* (1969)

—— *Edward Lhuyd F.R.S. 1660–1709* (Cardiff, 1971)

Evans, A. O., 'Dafydd Jones, Trefriw, 1708–1785', *JWBS* 5 (1937)

Evans, D. Silvan (ed.), *Gwaith y Parchedig Evan Evans* (Caernarfon, 1876)

Gruffydd, W. J., *The Morris Brothers* (Cardiff, 1939)

Gunther, R. T., *Early Science in Oxford, vol. xiv: Life and Letters of Edward Lhuyd* (Oxford, 1945)

Hughes, G. H., 'Cefndir Meddwl yr Ail Ganrif ar Bymtheg', *Efrydiau Athronyddol* 18 (1955)

—— 'Dafydd Manuel', *Llên Cymru* 6 (1960)

—— *Iaco ab Dewi 1648–1722* (Cardiff, 1953)

—— (ed.), *Rhagymadroddion 1547–1660* (Cardiff, 1951)

Hughes, R. G. 'William Wynn, Llangynhafal', *Llên Cymru* 1 (1950–1)

Humphreys, E. M., 'Morysiaid Môn', *THSC* (1953)

Jarman, A. O. H., 'Llythyrau'r Morrisiaid', *Y Llenor* 27 (1948)

Jarvis, Branwen, *Goronwy Owen* (Cardiff, 1986)

Jenkins, David, 'Bywyd a Gwaith Huw Morys (Pont-y-Meibion) (1622–1709)' (unpubl. University of Wales MA thesis, 1948)

—— 'Rhai o Lawysgrifau Huw Morys', *NLWJ* 7 (1951)

—— 'Rhys Jones o'r Blaenau (1713–1801)', *NLWJ* 1 (1949–51)

Jenkins, Geraint H., '"Dyn Glew Iawn": Dafydd Jones o Drefriw, 1703–1785', *Trans. Caernarfonshire Hist. Soc.* 47 (1986)

Jenkins, R. T., 'Bardd a'i Gefndir (Edward Ifan o'r Ton Coch)', *THSC* (1946–7)

Jenkins, R. T. and H. M. Ramage, *A History of the Honourable Society of Cymmrodorion 1751–1951* (1951)

Johnston, C., 'Evan Evans: Dissertatio de Bardis', *NLWJ* 22 (1981)

Jones, Bedwyr Lewis, 'Goronwy Owen, 1723–69', *THSC* (1971)

Jones, E. D., 'Thomas Lloyd y Geiriadurwr', *NLWJ* 9 (1955–6)

Jones, Emyr Gwynne, 'Llythyrau Lewis Morris at William Vaughan, Corsygedol', *Llên Cymru* 10 (1968)

Jones, Gwenllian, 'Bywyd a Gwaith Edward Morris, Perthi Llwydion' (unpubl. University of Wales MA thesis, 1941)

Jones, H. P., 'The Conway and the Elwy Valleys: Some Literary Men of the Eighteenth Century', *Trans. Denbighshire Hist. Soc.* 4–5 (1955–6)

Jones, John Gwilym, *Goronwy Owen's Virginian Adventure* (Williamsburg, Va., 1969)

Lewis, Aneirin (ed.), *The Correspondence of Thomas Percy and Evan Evans* (Louisiana State UP, 1957)

—— 'Evan Evans ('Ieuan Fardd') 1731–1788: Hanes ei fywyd a'i gysylltiadau llenyddol' (unpubl. University of Wales MA thesis, 1950)

—— 'Ieuan Fardd a'r Gwaith o Gyhoeddi Hen Lenyddiaeth Cymru', *JWBS* 8 (1956)

—— 'Ieuan Fardd a'r Llenorion Saesneg', *Llên Cymru* 7 (1962–3)

—— 'Llythyrau Evan Evans (Ieuan Fardd) at Ddafydd Jones o Drefriw', *Llên Cymru* 1 (1950–1)

Lewis, Henry (ed.), *Hen Gyflwyniadau* (Cardiff, 1948)

Lewis, Saunders, *Meistri'r Canrifoedd*, ed. R. G. Gruffydd (Cardiff, 1973)
—— *A School of Welsh Augustans* (Wrexham, 1924)
Lloyd, Nesta, 'Welsh Scholarship in the Seventeenth Century, with Special Reference to the Writings of John Jones, Gellilyfdy' (unpubl. University of Oxford D.Phil. thesis, 1970)
Morgan, D. Llwyd, 'A Critical Study of the Works of Charles Edwards (1628–1691?)' (unpubl. University of Oxford D.Phil. thesis, 1967)
Morgan, Prys, *The Eighteenth Century Renaissance* (Llandybïe, 1981)
—— *Iolo Morganwg* (Cardiff, 1975)
Morgan, T. J., 'Geiriadurwyr y Ddeunawfed Ganrif', *Llên Cymru* 9 (1966)
Nicholas, W. Rhys, *The Folk Poets* (Cardiff, 1978)
Osborne-Jones, D. G., *Edward Richard of Ystradmeurig* (Carmarthen, 1934)
Owen, Hugh, *The Life and Works of Lewis Morris 1701–1765* (Anglesey Antiq. Soc., 1951)
Parry, Thomas, *Baledi'r Ddeunawfed Ganrif* (rev. edn., Cardiff, 1986)
—— *The Oxford Book of Welsh Verse* (Oxford, 1962)
Ramage, H., 'Anrhydeddus Gymdeithas y Cymmrodorion', *Llên Cymru* 1 (1950–1)
Roberts, Brynley F., *Edward Lhuyd: The Making of a Scientist* (Cardiff, 1980)
—— 'Edward Lhuyd y Cymro', *NLWJ* 24 (1985)
—— 'Llythyrau John Lloyd at Edward Lhuyd', *NLWJ* 17 (1971)
Thomas, Gwyn, *Y Bardd Cwsg a'i Gefndir* (Cardiff, 1971)
—— 'Y Portread o Uchelwr ym Marddoniaeth Gaeth yr Ail Ganrif ar Bymtheg', *Ysgrifau Beirniadol* 8 (1974)
—— 'A Study of the Changes in the Tradition of Welsh Poetry in North Wales in the Seventeenth Century' (unpubl. University of Oxford D.Phil. thesis, 1966)
Roberts, G. T., 'Robin Ddu yr Ail o Fôn', *BBCS* 6 (1932)
Waring, Elijah, *Recollections and Anecdotes of Edward Williams* (1850)
Watkin-Jones, A., 'The Popular Literature of Wales in the Eighteenth Century', *BBCS* 3 (1926)
Williams, Daniel, *Beirdd y Gofeb* (Denbigh, 1951)
Williams, G. J., *Agweddau ar Hanes Dysg Gymraeg*, ed. Aneirin Lewis (Cardiff, 1969)
—— 'Bywyd Cymreig Llundain yng nghyfnod Owain Myfyr', *Y Llenor* 18 (1939)
—— 'The History of Welsh Scholarship', *Studia Celtica* 8–9 (1973–4)
—— *Iolo Morganwg* (Cardiff, 1956)
—— (ed.), 'Llythyrau at Ddafydd Jones o Drefriw', *NLWJ* Supplement, 3 (1943)
—— *Traddodiad Llenyddol Morgannwg* (Cardiff, 1948)
—— 'The Welsh Literary Tradition of the Vale of Glamorgan', *Glamorgan Historian* 3 (1966)
Williams, O. Gaianydd, *Dafydd Jones o Drefriw* (Caernarfon, 1907)
Williams, W. D., *Goronwy Owen* (Cardiff, 1951)
Wynne, Ellis, *Visions of the Sleeping Bard*, tr. T. Gwynn Jones (Gregynog, 1940)

17. Anglo-Welsh Literature

Bartley, J. O., *Teague, Shenkin and Sawney* (Cork, 1954)

Conran, A., *The Penguin Book of Welsh Verse* (Penguin, 1967)

Delany, P., *British Autobiography in the Seventeenth Century* (1969)

Garlick, Raymond, *An Introduction to Anglo-Welsh Literature* (Cardiff, 1970)

Garlick, Raymond and Roland Mathias (eds.), *Anglo-Welsh Poetry 1480–1800* (Poetry Wales Press, 1984)

Hook, D., 'John Davies of Kidwelly', *The Carmarthenshire Antiquary* 9 (1975)

Hughes, W. J., *Wales and the Welsh in English Literature* (Wrexham, 1924)

Humfrey, Belinda, *John Dyer* (Cardiff, 1980)

Hutchinson, F. E., *Henry Vaughan: A Life and Interpretation* (corrected repr., Oxford, 1971)

Jones, Gwyn (ed.), *The Oxford Book of Welsh Verse in English* (Oxford, 1977)

Martin, L. C. (ed.), *The Works of Henry Vaughan* (2nd edn., Oxford, 1957)

Morgan, Gerald, *The Dragon's Tongue* (Cardiff, 1966)

Post, Jonathan F. S., *Henry Vaughan: The Unfolding Vision* (Princeton, 1982)

Price, C. J. L., *'A Man of Genius, and a Welch Man'* (University College of Swansea, 1963)

—— 'Polite Life in Eighteenth-Century Wales', *The Welsh Anvil* 5 (1953)

—— 'The Unpublished Letters of Evan Lloyd', *NLWJ* 8 (1953–4)

Rudrum, Alan, *Henry Vaughan* (Cardiff, 1981)

—— (ed.), *Henry Vaughan: The Complete Poems* (Penguin, 1976)

—— (ed.), *The Works of Thomas Vaughan* (Oxford, 1984)

Snyder, E. D., *The Celtic Revival in English Literature* (Cambridge, 1923)

Thomas, R. G., 'Myles Davies of Tre' Rabbat: A Candidate for Pope's Dunciad', *THSC* (1963)

Walters, G., 'The Eighteenth-Century "Pembroke Society" ', *WHR* 3 (1967)

Watkyns, Rowland, *Flamma Sine Fumo, 1662*, ed. P. C. Davies (Cardiff, 1968)

Williams, Ralph M., *Poet, Painter and Parson: The Life of John Dyer* (New York, 1956)

18. History, Genealogy, and Antiquarianism

Boon, G. C. and J. M. Lewis (eds.), *Welsh Antiquity* (Cardiff, 1976)

Davies, P. W., 'Astudiaeth o ysgolheictod hynafiaethol Lewis Morris (1701–1765)' (unpubl. University of Wales MA thesis, 1982)

Evans, D. Ellis, 'Theophilus Evans ar Hanes Cynnar Prydain', *Y Traethodydd* 128 (1973)

Evans, Theophilus, *Drych y Prif Oesoedd 1716*, ed. G. H. Hughes (Cardiff, 1961)

Greene, D., *Makers and Forgers* (Cardiff, 1975)

Griffiths, G. M., 'John Lewis of Llynwene's Defence of Geoffrey of Monmouth's "Historia" ', *NLWJ* 7 (1952)

Hobsbawm, E. and T. Ranger (eds.), *The Invention of Tradition* (Cambridge, 1983)

Jarman, A. O. H., 'Y Ddadl ynghylch Sieffre o Fynwy', *Llên Cymru* 2 (1952)

—— 'Lewis Morris a Brut Tysilio', *Llên Cymru* 2 (1952)

Jenkins, Philip, 'From Edward Lhuyd to Iolo Morganwg: The Death and Rebirth of Glamorgan Antiquarianism in the Eighteenth Century', *Morgannwg* 23 (1979)

Jenkins, R. T., 'William Wynne and the History of Wales', *BBCS* 6 (1931–3)

Jones, Francis, 'An Approach to Welsh Genealogy', *THSC* (1948)

—— 'Hugh Thomas, Deputy-Herald', *THSC* (1961)

Kendrick, T. D., *British Antiquity* (1950)

—— *The Druids* (1927)

Morgan, D. Llwyd, 'Ffynonellau Hanes Charles Edwards', *Trans. Denbighshire Hist. Soc.* 18 (1969)

Morgan, Prys, 'The Abbé Pezron and the Celts', *THSC* (1965)

Morgan, R., 'Robert Vaughan of Hengwrt (1592–1667)', *Journal Merioneth Hist. and Record Soc.* 8 (1977–80)

Owen, A. L., *The Famous Druids* (Oxford, 1962)

Parry, T. E., 'Llythyrau Robert Vaughan, Hengwrt (1592–1667)' (unpubl. University of Wales MA thesis, 1961)

Percival, A., 'William Baxter (1649–1723)', *THSC* (1958)

Piggott, Stuart, *The Druids* (1968)

—— *Ruins in a Landscape* (Edinburgh, 1976)

Roberts, Brynley F., *Brut y Brenhinedd* (Dublin, 1971)

—— 'Cyfieithiad Samuel Williams o De Excidio Brittaniae Gildas', *NLWJ* 13 (1963–4)

—— 'Ymagweddau at Brut y Brenhinedd hyd 1890', *BBCS* 24 (1971)

Thomas, J. G., 'Henry Rowlands, the Welsh Stukeley', *Trans. Anglesey Antiq. Soc.* (1958)

Watkins, D., 'A Study of Seventeenth Century Historiographical Literature relating to Wales' (unpubl. University of Wales MA thesis, 1955)

Williams, Gwyn A., *Madoc: The Making of a Myth* (1979)

19. Music, Drama, and Painting

Ashton, G. M. (ed.), *Hunangofiant a Llythyrau Twm o'r Nant* (Cardiff, 1948)

Bell, David, *The Artist in Wales* (1957)

Blake, Lois, *Welsh Folk Dance and Costume* (2nd edn., Llangollen, 1954)

Brinkley, Richard, 'Welsh Topographical Literature c. 1770 to 1870', *The Local Historian* 2 (1974–5)

Crossley-Holland, P. (ed.), *Music in Wales* (1948)

Edwards, Thomas, *Tri Chryfion Byd*, ed. N. Isaac (Llandysul, 1975)

Ellis, Osian, *The Story of the Harp in Wales* (Cardiff, 1980)

—— 'Welsh Music: History and Fancy', *THSC* (1972–3)

Evans, G. G., 'Yr Anterliwt Gymraeg', *Llên Cymru* 1 (1950)

—— 'Yr Anterliwd Gymraeg' (unpubl. University of Wales MA thesis, 1938)

—— 'Henaint a Thranc yr Anterliwt', *Taliesin* 54 (1985)

Gowing, L., *The Originality of Thomas Jones* (1985)

Griffith, Wyn, *Twm o'r Nant (Thomas Edwards) 1739–1810* (Cardiff, 1953)

Jenkins, A. D. Fraser, 'The Romantic Traveller in Wales', *Amgueddfa* 6 (1970)

Jones, Elis Gwyn, *Richard Wilson 1713–1782* (Cardiff, 1983)

Jones, Emyr Wyn (ed.), *Yr Anterliwt Goll* (Aberystwyth, 1984)

—— 'Twm o'r Nant and Siôn Dafydd Berson', *Trans. Denbighshire Hist. Soc.* 30 (1981)

Jones, T. J. Rhys, 'Yr Anterliwt Gymraeg' (unpubl. University of Wales MA thesis, 1939)

Jones, T. J. Rhys, 'Welsh Interlude Players of the Eighteenth Century', *Theatre Notebook* 2 (1948)

Lewis, Mostyn, *Stained Glass in North Wales up to 1850* (Altrincham, 1970)

Moir, Esther, *The Discovery of Britain* (1964)

Moore, Donald, *Moses Griffith 1747–1819* (Welsh Arts Council, 1979)

Morgan, Prys, 'Thomas Jones of Pencerrig', *THSC* (1984)

Parris, Leslie, *Landscape in Britain c. 1750–1850* (1973)

Parry-Williams, T. H. (ed.), *Llawysgrif Richard Morris o Gerddi* (Cardiff, 1931)

Price, C. J. L., *The English Theatre in Wales* (Cardiff, 1948)

—— *The Professional Theatre in Wales* (University College of Swansea, 1984)

Rhys, E., 'A Welsh Interlude Writer and the Village Drama', *The Vineyard* 1 (1911)

Rosser, Ann, *Telyn a Thelynor: Hanes y Delyn yng Nghymru 1700–1900* (Cardiff, 1981)

Rowan, Eric (ed.), *Art in Wales 2000 B.C.–A.D. 1850: An Illustrated History* (Cardiff, 1978)

Solkin, D. H., *Richard Wilson: The Landscape of Reaction* (1982)

Steegman, John, *A Survey of Portraits in Welsh Houses* (2 vols., Cardiff, 1957–62)

Thomas, Wyn, *Cerddoriaeth Draddodiadol yng Nghymru: Llyfryddiaeth* (Cardiff, 1982)

Watkin-Jones, A., 'The Interludes of Wales in the Eighteenth Century', *BBCS* 4 (1928)

Williams, I. A., 'Notes on Paul Sandby and his Predecessors in Wales', *THSC* (1961–2)

Williams, J. Lloyd, *Y Tri Thelynor* (1945)

Williams, W. S. Gwynn, *Welsh National Music and Dance* (4th edn., Llangollen, 1971)

INDEX

INDEX 487

OXFORD

MORE OXFORD PAPERBACKS

This book is just one of nearly 1000 Oxford Paperbacks currently in print. If you would like details of other Oxford Paperbacks, including titles in the World's Classics, Oxford Reference, Oxford Books, OPUS, Past Masters, Oxford Authors, and Oxford Shakespeare series, please write to:

UK and Europe: Oxford Paperbacks Publicity Manager, Arts and Reference Publicity Department, Oxford University Press, Walton Street, Oxford OX2 6DP.

Customers in UK and Europe will find Oxford Paperbacks available in all good bookshops. But in case of difficulty please send orders to the Cash-with-Order Department, Oxford University Press Distribution Services, Saxon Way West, Corby, Northants NN18 9ES. Tel: 0536 741519; Fax: 0536 746337. Please send a cheque for the total cost of the books, plus £1.75 postage and packing for orders under £20; £2.75 for orders over £20. Customers outside the UK should add 10% of the cost of the books for postage and packing.

USA: Oxford Paperbacks Marketing Manager, Oxford University Press, Inc., 200 Madison Avenue, New York, N.Y. 10016.

Canada: Trade Department, Oxford University Press, 70 Wynford Drive, Don Mills, Ontario M3C 1J9.

Australia: Trade Marketing Manager, Oxford University Press, G.P.O. Box 2784Y, Melbourne 3001, Victoria.

South Africa: Oxford University Press, P.O. Box 1141, Cape Town 8000.

HISTORY IN OXFORD PAPERBACKS

Oxford Paperbacks offers a comprehensive list of books on British history, ranging from Frank Stenton's *Anglo-Saxon England* to John Guy's *Tudor England*, and from Christopher Hill's *A Turbulent, Seditious, and Factious People* to Kenneth O. Morgan's *Labour in Power: 1945–1951*.

TUDOR ENGLAND
John Guy

Tudor England is a compelling account of political and religious developments from the advent of the Tudors in the 1460s to the death of Elizabeth I in 1603.

Following Henry VII's capture of the Crown at Bosworth in 1485, Tudor England witnessed far-reaching changes in government and the Reformation of the Church under Henry VIII, Edward VI, Mary, and Elizabeth; that story is enriched here with character studies of the monarchs and politicians that bring to life their personalities as well as their policies.

Authoritative, clearly argued, and crisply written, this comprehensive book will be indispensable to anyone interested in the Tudor Age.

'lucid, scholarly, remarkably accomplished . . . an excellent overview' *Sunday Times*

'the first comprehensive history of Tudor England for more than thirty years' Patrick Collinson, *Observer*

Also in Oxford Paperbacks:

John Calvin   William J. Bouwsma
Early Modern France 1515–1715   Robin Briggs
The Spanish Armada   Felipe Fernández-Armesto
Time in History   G. J. Whitrow

OPUS

General Editors: Walter Bodmer, Christopher Butler, Robert Evans, John Skorupski

OPUS is a series of accessible introductions to a wide range of studies in the sciences and humanities.

METROPOLIS

Emrys Jones

Past civilizations have always expressed themselves in great cities, immense in size, wealth, and in their contribution to human progress. We are still enthralled by ancient cities like Babylon, Rome, and Constantinople. Today, giant cities abound, but some are pre-eminent. As always, they represent the greatest achievements of different cultures. But increasingly, they have also been drawn into a world economic system as communications have improved.

Metropolis explores the idea of a class of supercities in the past and in the present, and in the western and developing worlds. It analyses the characteristics they share as well as those that make them unique; the effect of technology on their form and function; and the problems that come with size—congestion, poverty and inequality, squalor—that are sobering contrasts to the inherent glamour and attraction of great cities throughout time.

Also available in OPUS:

The Medieval Expansion of Europe   J. R. S. Phillips
Metaphysics: The Logical Approach   José A. Benardete
The Voice of the Past 2/e   Paul Thompson
Thinking About Peace and War   Martin Ceadel

PAST MASTERS

General Editor: Keith Thomas

The people whose ideas have made history . . .

'One begins to wonder whether any intelligent person can afford not to possess the whole series.' *Expository Times*

JESUS

Humphrey Carpenter

Jesus wrote no books, but the influence of his life and teaching has been immeasurable. Humphrey Carpenter's account of Jesus is written from the standpoint of an historian coming fresh to the subject without religious preconceptions. And no previous knowledge of Jesus or the Bible on the reader's part is assumed.

How reliable are the Christian 'Gospels' as an account of what Jesus did or said? How different were his ideas from those of his contemporaries? What did Jesus think of himself? Humphrey Carpenter begins his answer to these questions with a survey and evaluation of the evidence on which our knowledge of Jesus is based. He then examines his teaching in some detail, and reveals the perhaps unexpected way in which his message can be said to be original. In conclusion he asks to what extent Jesus's teaching has been followed by the Christian Churches that have claimed to represent him since his death.

'Carpenter's *Jesus* is about as objective as possible, while giving every justifiable emphasis to the real and persistent forcefulness of the moral teaching of this charismatic personality.' Kathleen Nott, *The Times*

'an excellent, straightforward presentation of up-to-date scholarship' David L. Edwards, *Church Times*

Also available in Past Masters:

Muhammad Michael Cook
Aquinas Anthony Kenny
Cervantes P. E. Russell
Clausewitz Michael Howard

OXFORD LIVES

Biography at its best—this acclaimed series offers authoritative accounts of the lives of men and women from the arts, sciences, politics, and many other walks of life.

STANLEY

Volume I: The Making of an African Explorer
Volume II: Sorceror's Apprentice

Frank McLynn

Sir Henry Morton Stanley was one of the most fascinating late-Victorian adventurers. His historic meeting with Livingstone at Ujiji in 1871 was the journalistic scoop of the century. Yet behind the public man lay the complex and deeply disturbed personality who is the subject of Frank McLynn's masterly study.

In his later years, Stanley's achievements exacted a high human cost, both for the man himself and for those who came into contact with him. His foundation of the Congo Free State on behalf of Leopold II of Belgium, and the Emin Pasha Relief Expedition were both dubious enterprises which tarnished his reputation. They also revealed the complex—and often troubling—relationship that Stanley has with Africa.

'excellent . . . entertaining, well researched and scrupulously annotated' *Spectator*

'another biography of Stanley will not only be unnecessary, but almost impossible, for years to come' *Sunday Telegraph*

Also available:

A Prince of Our Disorder: The Life of T. E. Lawrence
John Mack
Carpet Sahib: A Life of Jim Corbett   Martin Booth
Bonnie Prince Charlie: Charles Edward Stuart   Frank McLynn

OXFORD LETTERS AND MEMOIRS

Letters, memoirs, and journals offer a special insight into the private lives of public figures and vividly recreate the times in which they lived. This popular series makes available the best and most entertaining of these documents, bringing the past to life in a fresh and personal way.

RICHARD HOGGART

A Local Habitation
Life and Times: 1918–1940

With characteristic candour and compassion, Richard Hoggart evokes the Leeds of his boyhood, where as an orphan, he grew up with his grandmother, two aunts, an uncle, and a cousin in a small terraced back-to-back.

'brilliant . . . a joy as well as an education' Roy Hattersley

'a model of scrupulous autobiography' Edward Blishen, *Listener*

A Sort of Clowning
Life and Times: 1940–1950

Opening with his wartime exploits in North Africa and Italy, this sequel to *A Local Habitation* recalls his teaching career in North-East England, and charts his rise in the literary world following the publication of *The Uses of Literacy*.

'one of the classic autobiographies of our time' Anthony Howard, *Independent on Sunday*

'Hoggart [is] the ideal autobiographer' Beryl Bainbridge, *New Statesman and Society*

Also in Oxford Letters and Memoirs:

My Sister and Myself: The Diaries of J. R. Ackerley
The Letters of T. E. Lawrence
A London Family 1870–1900   Molly Hughes

ART AND ARCHITECTURE IN
OXFORD PAPERBACKS

Oxford Paperbacks offers a growing list of art and architecture books, ranging from Michael Baxandall on Renaissance Italy to George Melly on pop art and from Anthony Blunt on art theory to Bram Dijkstra on fin-de-siècle 'erotic' art.

ENGLISH PARISH CHURCHES AS
WORKS OF ART
Alec Clifton-Taylor

In the course of his life Alec Clifton-Taylor visited thousands of churches and recorded his observations and opinions on their merits. The result, in this book, is not a dry analysis of the chronological evolution of churches and their styles, but a revealing tour of the parish church with the greatest emphasis on aesthetic value.

As all those who got to know him through his television appearances will agree, Alec Clifton-Taylor was the ideal guide to architecture—deeply knowledgeable and enthusiastic in his responses. His first book, *The Pattern of English Building*, is regarded as a classic and his popular BBC television series, *Six English Towns*, and its sequels, claimed a wide audience.

'"What a church!" writes Alec Clifton-Taylor of Walpole St Peter in Norfolk . . . "an unforgettable experience" . . . [Mr Clifton-Taylor] was one of the most individual, civilized, and lovable historians I have ever met.' Patrick Nuttgens, *Times Higher Educational Supplement*

Also in Oxford Paperbacks:

Painting and Experience in 15th-century Italy
Michael Baxandall
American Buildings and their Architects: The Colonial and Neo-Classical Styles   William H. Pierson
Vision and Design   Roger Fry
Revolt into Style   George Melly

HISTORY IN OXFORD PAPERBACKS

Oxford Paperbacks' superb history list offers books on a wide range of topics from ancient to modern times, whether general period studies or assessments of particular events, movements, or personalities.

THE STRUGGLE FOR
THE MASTERY OF EUROPE 1848–1918
A. J. P. Taylor

The fall of Metternich in the revolutions of 1848 heralded an era of unprecedented nationalism in Europe, culminating in the collapse of the Hapsburg, Romanov, and Hohenzollern dynasties at the end of the First World War. In the intervening seventy years the boundaries of Europe changed dramatically from those established at Vienna in 1815. Cavour championed the cause of *Risorgimento* in Italy; Bismarck's three wars brought about the unification of Germany; Serbia and Bulgaria gained their independence courtesy of the decline of Turkey—'the sick man of Europe'; while the great powers scrambled for places in the sun in Africa. However, with America's entry into the war and President Wilson's adherence to idealistic internationalist principles, Europe ceased to be the centre of the world, although its problems, still primarily revolving around nationalist aspirations, were to smash the Treaty of Versailles and plunge the world into war once more.

A. J. P. Taylor has drawn the material for his account of this turbulent period from the many volumes of diplomatic documents which have been published in the five major European languages. By using vivid language and forceful characterization, he has produced a book that is as much a work of literature as a contribution to scientific history.

'One of the glories of twentieth-century writing.' *Observer*

Also in Oxford Paperbacks:

Portrait of an Age: Victorian England   G. M. Young
Germany 1866–1945   Gorden A. Craig
The Russian Revolution 1917–1932   Sheila Fitzpatrick
France 1848–1945   Theodore Zeldin